SARTRE

SARTRE

ANNIE COHEN-SOLAL

A LIFE

TRANSLATED BY ANNA CANCOGNI

EDITED BY NORMAN MACAFEE

PANTHEON BOOKS

NEW YORK

LIBRARY OF CONGRESS CATALOGING-IN-PUBLICATION DATA

Cohen-Solal, Annie, 1948–
Sartre : a life.

Bibliography: p.
Includes index.
1. Sartre, Jean Paul, 1905–1980 —Biography.
2. Philosophers—France—Biography.
French—20th century—Biography.   I. Title.
B2430.S34C5413   1987   848ʹ.91409   [B]   86–42615
ISBN 0–394–52525–6

I am ill at ease except in freedom,
escaping objects, escaping myself . . .
I am a true nothing, drunk with pride, translucid . . .
Therefore it is the world that I wish to possess.
                                        —THE WAR DIARIES

CONTENTS

viii

RESEARCH for this book was made possible by the assistance of: Lionel Abel, René Achéen, Arieh Aharoni, Rachel Aharoni, René Aillet, Jean-Pierre Alacchi, Jeanne Allard, Noël Arnaud, Raymond Aron, Aaron Ascher, Louis Audibert, Colette Audry, Louis Autin, Armand Bachelier, Jean Baillou, Jean Balladur, Doctor Baron, William Barrett, Karel Bartosek, Marc Beigbeder, Armand Bérard, Mauricette Berne, Mlle Billoux, Tom Bishop, Carl-Gustav Bjurström, Louis Blanc, Gaston Blanchard, Gérard Blanchet, Francis Bobée, Thierry Bodin, Jean-Marie Borzeix, Claire Bost, Jacques-Laurent Bost, Jean-Marcel Bouguereau, Marcel Bouisset, Jacques Boutineau, Dominique Braut-Klar, Marie-Sophie Brianceau, Menahem Brinker, Victor Brombert, Jean Bruhat, Jean Bruller-Vercors, Pierre Brument, Henri Brunschwig, Jean-Pierre Busson, Jean-Pierre Callot, Georges Canguilhem, Michel Cantal-Dupart, Mlle Carpentier, Christian Casadesus, Jean Cau, Claude Chartrel, Jerome Charyn, François Châtelet, Admiral Chatelle, Jean-René Chauvin, Georges Chazelas, Jean Chouleur, Stéphane Courtois, Robert Cruège, Jean Daniel, Simone Debout, Régis Debray, Jacques Debû-Bridel, Maurice Deixonne, Maurice Delarue, Émile Delavenay, Jean-Pierre Delilez, Alex Derczansky, Dominique Desanti, Jean-Toussaint Desanti, Mme Roland Dorgelès, Michel Drouin, Bertrand Dufourcq, Roland Dumas, Doctor Durieux, Hector Elisabeth, André Encrevé, François Erval, Patrick Esclafer de la Rode, Etiemble, Pierre Fanlac, Denise Fargeot, Beatrice Farwell, Claude Faux, the whole group from the FBI—John R. Burke, Louis P. Goelz, James K. Hall, Russell A. Powell, Robert M. Smalley, Darnall C. Stewart, and John H. Wright, Marianne de Fleury, Roger Fleury, Renée-Claire Fox, Paul Fraisse, Nino Frank, René Frédet, Anne Frejer, Amalia Furstenberg, Fiska Furstenberg, Étienne Fuzellier, the patriarch, and the whole Fuzellier tribe—Isabelle, Ljiljana, Raymond, and Vladimir, Maurice de Gandillac, Jean Gatel, Philippe Gavi, Alain Geismar, Jacques Ghinsberg, Valéry Giscard d'Estaing, Jean Giustiniani, Erving Goffman, Michel Gordey, Maître Grangé, Jean-yves Guérin, Henri Guillemin, Norbert Guterman, Guillaume Hanoteau, Charles Hernu, Pierre Hervé, Stanley Hoffmann, Irving

Howe, Ilios Iannakakis, Joris Ivens, Roger Jaccou, Vladimir Jan-kélévitch, Jean-Noël Jeanneney, Henri Jourdan, Jean-Daniel Jurgensen, Mme Pierre Kaan, Dani Karavan, Lucien Karhausen, Jean Karoubi, Hughes de Kerett, Brigitte de Kergorlay, Edith Kurzweil, Olivier Lacombe, Claude Lanzmann, Georges Lefranc, Éric Lemaresquier, Jean Lescure, Jacques Levavasseur, Harry Levine, Laurent Lévi-Strauss, Benny Lévy, Raoul Lévy, Haviva Limon, Youzek Limon, Daniel Lindenberg, Gérard Loiseaux, Marceline Loridan, Robert Lucot, Canon Raymond de Puiffe de Magondeaux, Mlle Martin, Gilles Martinet, Dionys Mascolo, Suzanne Merleau-Ponty, Alain Meyer, Arthur Miller, Robert Misrahi, Selim Mohor, André Monchoux, Alberto Moravia, Jean-Paul Mougin, Maurice Nadeau, Louis Nagel, Marie Nimier, Nadine Nimier, Henriette Nizan, Mme de Nomazy, Marcel Paquot, Geneviève Pastier, Jacqueline Paulhan, General Pauly, François Périer, Marc Perrin de Brichambaut, M. Petitmengin, Henri Peyre, Claude-Jean Philippe, William Phillips, Jean Pierre, Pierre Piganiol, Bernard Pingaud, Vincent Placoly, J.-B. Pontalis, Jean Pouillon, Vladimir Pozner, Jean Rabaut, Jacques-René Rabier, Alain D. Ranwez, Yehoshua Rash, Mme Raynaud, Jeannine Richet, Louis Robert, Denis de Rougemont, David Rousset, Susan Rubin-Suleiman, Michel Rybalka, Edward Said, Olga de Saint-Affrique, François-Marie Samuelson, Alain Savary, Judith Schlanger, Michèle Schmitt-Joannou, Louis Schweitzer, Édouard Selzer, Nathan Shaham, Jean-François Sirinelli, Raphaël Sorin, Michel Suchod, Roland Suvélor, Paul Tabet, Paule Thévenin, André Tiercet, Guy Toublanc, Maurice Vaïsse, Dolorès V. Michelle Vian, P.C.V., Monique Vignal, Pierre Vilar, Jeanne Virmouneix, André Vogel, Robert-Léon Wagner, Georges Werler, Jean-Didier Wolfromm, Philippe Bernert, Charles Courtney.

I also wish to thank Simone de Beauvoir and Arlette Elkaïm-Sartre for the warmth and the unfailing support with which they followed my research. Not only did they let me consult their personal archives, but they also made themselves available to discuss and elaborate different points, as the need arose.

For the analysis, the premises, and the revision of each chapter I am infinitely grateful to my friend Christian Bachmann: with him I shared my questions, my doubts, and my discoveries, so much so that it would be impossible for me now to say which ideas were his and which my own.

ROOM NUMBER 1 in the Nouveau Drouot is carpeted in red; the ceiling's neon tracks cast a brutal, almost unbearable light onto the spectators. Paris, June 12, 1984, three o'clock on a muggy afternoon. "Welcome, ladies and gentlemen. Shall we commence? What am I bid? The gentleman in the corner . . . The lady on my left bids 16 . . . Come now, ladies and gentlemen . . . Do I hear higher?" Room Number 1 is a passageway: tourists come and go through the open door; girls in shorts or jeans stop by for a peek. It's like a bus station, where the bidders—proxies, junior clerks in gray suits—do their strange dance, raising a hand, making barely perceptible signs, emotionless, like robots.

That day, I was attending the auction of Montherlant's love letters, some scraps by Gérard de Nerval, a note from Proust to his mother, an autographed book by Romain Rolland. Then Sartre. "And now, lot 115," the auctioneer announces. "Several manuscripts by Jean-Paul Sartre." The first is a six-page, quarto rough draft of *What Is Literature?* Starting price, 3,000 francs; sold for 4,800. The second is the entire manuscript of *Troubled Sleep*: 544 pages, snapped up for 85,000 francs. A 274-page notebook, his *Cahiers pour une morale*: 75,000 francs. The auctioneer, impatient, swallows a Valda drop. Is Sartre's value declining? "Here we have two pages of *Dirty Hands*" . . . 1,800 francs. The rest follows fairly quickly: 3,500 francs for seven pages of *The Devil and the Good Lord*; 6,000 for six pages of *The Words*; 12,000 for a 29-page, unpublished manuscript on the Bertrand Russell Vietnam War Crimes Tribunal.

Sartre's been dead four years. Some of his friends are in the room; they nod to each other. The Bibliothèque Nationale has exercised its right of pre-emption over the manuscripts of *Troubled Sleep* and *Cahiers pour une morale*. It look like the remaining buyers are all foreigners, probably Americans. At the end, people greet each other and drift back into the furnace of the street. When he was alive, Sartre scattered his manuscripts all over the world, giving some away, losing others.

Of the Sartre manuscripts, some hadn't even been published yet. And now that they were all gone, would they ever resurface? Since Sartre's death, in April 1980, his work had been going through a period of uncertainty, a strange malaise of which this auction was probably the least painful symptom. And yet, this mysterious dance of the manuscripts—appearance, disappearance, chance of imminent reappearance—suggested a constant movement around Sartre's oeuvre, a perpetual mobility, an afterlife.

*T*HE YEARS immediately following a writer's death are generally problematic; and the biographer who undertakes an inquiry into that particular period is inevitably exposed to all sort of storms and contrary winds. Just when you think you have seen and know everything, some unexpected event forces you to start all over again. At other times, it is a missing piece of the mosaic that haunts you until it is found. For example, I had heard quite a lot about the novel "Une Défaite" [A Defeat], which Sartre had written when he was twenty. His former classmates considered it partly responsible for the myth that surrounded him at the Ecole Normale. I had sought out the text, full of anticipation, and at first I was disappointed: what I had awaited so long seemed so imperfect, so much the first novel, neither polished nor a slapdash rough draft, developing through juxtaposed chapters of varying quality, like ill-fitting pieces of a puzzle. But, in the middle of this mess, I found some twenty pages, titled "A Fairy Tale," which shone like a gem. The hero of the novel, Frédéric, a tutor in a bourgeois family, invents a fairy tale for his two young pupils, Jenny and Louise, and their mother, whom he is trying to seduce. Like all fairy tales, Frédéric's begins "Once upon a time . . ." What follows is the story of a Prince, "wondrously intelligent, exquisitely handsome" but also impassive and cold, who does not believe in the human soul. And so he lives as though surrounded by robots. His subjects call him "the tyrant." One day, he goes off on a long ride through the forest.

"The Prince whipped his horse and took off at a gallop. Then, he had a frightening thought. 'Does everything have a soul?' He was galloping through a field of long, shivering green grass. 'Does every-thing . . . ?' What shiver was passing through the grass like a soul? What obscure life moved within it? The idea filled him with an immense disgust. He spurred his horse, which, suddenly skittish, shot off like a dart. Trees disheveled by speed raced toward him, then vanished like trick cards. . . . And everything seemed alive with a dark, angry life—which made him feel sick—a life reaching out to meet his own. He felt as if he were in the midst of an immense world, which was observing him. He was being watched by the brooks and the puddles on his path. Everything was alive, and filled with thought. And suddenly he looked at his horse: it too was living, thinking. You, Jenny, you're so afraid of spiders, imagine yourself on a horse, fleeing an army of spiders when suddenly you realize your horse is an immense spider. I'm telling you this to give you a clearer idea of the Prince's terror and disgust. Barely able to hold onto his saddle, the Prince kept staring at the trees, these dark, huge beings, which he had thought he knew so well and now seemed to him monstrous apparitions. He started screaming. But a low branch hit him on the forehead, knocking him off his saddle. In his disordered imagination, the Prince saw his excursion through the forest as an infernal ride that would end in his annihilation, and he fell to the ground, unconscious."

I discovered the Prince's ride soon after the ceremony at the auction house, and I sensed that it meant a great deal. For, at the end of it, the heretofore isolated Prince discovers the world, a world much too full of life, which brings him the evidence of both his freedom and the existence of others. At the end of his ride, the Prince is politically transformed. "He recovered," Sartre writes, "and as time went by he grew accustomed to being surrounded by souls. He became a man like all the others, except that he was now a little better than they. He couldn't bear the thought that a soul could suffer. He fired all his ministers and began to govern by himself, with justice." And then, the Prince discovered love; he fell in love with a shepherdess, who became his wife and adviser. The Prince's ride turned out to be a labyrinth where all the themes and motifs of the Sartrean oeuvre intersect, where all future issues are already implied. The ride, the words of a twenty-year-old student, prefigured the major themes of his works to come: *Nausea* and *Being and Nothingness*. Indeed, it reads like a children's version of *Nausea,* an allegory of Sartre's own life.

*A*N AUCTION, an unpublished text: five years after Sartre's death, his work was still alive with a rhythm all its own, unpredictable, headstrong. Sartre had generously given away many of his manuscripts and nonchalantly mislaid others. These two gestures, today, mean there are still thousands of his pages scattered around the world, preserving his work open, alive, and, for the foreseeable future, incomplete. As if, before leaving, he had deliberately neglected to close his file cabinet and switch off the light.

I

TOWARD GENIUS
1905–1939

SPOTLIGHT ON JEAN-BAPTISTE

> *My father had been so gallant as to die in the wrong*
> *. . . in slipping away, Jean-Baptiste had refused me*
> *the pleasure of making his acquaintance. Even now*
> *I am surprised at how little I know about him.*
> *. . . But no one in my family was able to make me*
> *curious about that man.*
>
> —THE WORDS

"MY DEAR little sister, I'm keeping my promise to tell you about Saturday's ball. It was wonderful, splendidly organized. It took place in the drawing rooms of the Hotel Continental, huge rooms, luxuriously appointed. There were at least three thousand people, but quite a select group. The women's dresses were beautiful, a delight to the eye. Of course, there were also lots of uniforms, handsome ones, such as those worn by high-ranking officers and naval engineers. Cavaignac and Guieysse, two ministers, old alumni, were also present. At eleven, M. Faure was announced. As he entered the room, the ushers of the ball (of which I was one) lined up and presented him their swords. The president looked very pleased, and he later demonstrated his pleasure by giving us all Monday off." Paris, January 22, 1896. Every week, a young student at the Polytechnic School wrote a letter to his sister Hélène, back home in Thiviers (Dordogne), to tell her all about his new life. At twenty-one, Jean-Baptiste Sartre had matriculated forty-sixth out of 223 candidates, class of '95. Son of a doctor in the Southwest of France, Jean-Baptiste was a small, thin, dark, sullen young man; there was no spark in his eyes, only the seriousness, weariness, intensity of the ageless, too mature at twenty, too old at thirty. Eleven years later, he will be dead, having sired a son, Jean-Paul, whom he will never get to know. In his beautiful uniform, with his gigantic mustache, he looked like a child in costume, a little toy soldier. And, indeed, he probably would have passed unnoticed had it not been for that extraordinarily disproportionate mustache: aggressive, authoritative, dark, fiery, an absolute provocation.

Jean-Paul Sartre spoke of his father, Jean-Baptiste Sartre, only in passing and never devoted more than a page to him. He never

4

mentioned that he had been a Polytechnicien, nor did he ever dis-
close the few things that he certainly knew about him: namely, that
his father, a brilliant pupil, twice recipient of a *baccalauréat*, thrice
a laureate in the *concours général* (the competitive examinations for
secondary-school children), and the son of a well-to-do family had,
early in life, decided to pull up stakes, break free, look for adventure
far from the small Périgordian town of his birth. Yet, Jean-Baptiste
and Jean-Paul had a lot in common. Physically, they were almost
doubles: the father was five feet two inches tall, the son five feet two
and a half. Despite their excellent family background, their natural
talents, their privileged social standing, and the promising futures
that awaited them, both men were outsiders by temperament. Once
he was established as a writer, Jean-Paul Sartre chose to cover his
tracks, confuse his biographers, mislead his followers. Officially de-
ciding that his father never existed, he saw himself as the son of
nobody. In fact, he never really knew his father, since he was only
fifteen months old when Jean-Baptiste died. Asked about him later,
he would answer indifferently, "My father? He was only a photo in
my mother's bedroom." Then, with that flat, curt voice that immedi-
tely severed all contact with the interrogator, he would conclude,
"I've never had a father," and the whole matter was shelved.

And yet, in 1960, the fifty-five-year-old writer Jean-Paul Sartre
was working on an autobiography—in some ways his best book—
The Words, published three years later. Suddenly, one day, he
boarded a train at the Gare d'Austerlitz and got off at Périgueux. He
vaguely remembered that his father had a sister there, Aunt Hélène
Lannes, who used to live on the Rue Saint-Front, which ran perpen-
dicular to the cathedral. Seven, Rue Saint-Front was a bourgeois
home facing the old, now dilapidated building that had once been
the center of freemasonry in Périgueux. Jean-Paul Sartre rang the
bell. No answer. He rang again. Still no answer. Then he went down
to the antique dealer who lived on the ground floor and inquired
about Madame Lannes. "She died a while ago, I think, three
months." It was over thirty years since he had lost all contact with
this aunt whom he did not love, his last surviving relative on his
father's side. She had spent her last years an "aging beauty," as her
neighbors put it, a droll old lady with a weakness for lipstick and
rouge, who strolled through Périgueux summer and winter wearing
a black suit, her neck wrapped in a mousy silver-fox stole on which
she had pinned a red rose.

On the day of Sartre's visit, the only thing left behind that closed door was a trunk full of letters, photographs, and other souvenirs, which would later be recovered by the landlord. So, despite this one brief burst of curiosity, the writer had nothing truly exciting to say about Jean-Baptiste, and the little he knew he chose to forget when he came to write *The Words*. Jean-Baptiste's trunk, letters, and souvenirs re-emerged in 1984 amidst a labyrinth of research. As a prelude to the biography of this fatherless child, here is a story within a story, Jean-Baptiste's, and some of the information that Jean-Paul Sartre, the writer, had gone to look for that day in Périgueux.

SIX IN the morning: up at reveille. From six to six-thirty: study. From six-thirty to eight-thirty: class in the amphitheater. Eight-thirty: breakfast of either a cup of milk or a chunk of cheese (Gournay or Roquefort). Did Jean-Baptiste appreciate this inflexible military ritual as much as his prestigious uniform? Overcoat with hood and cape, vest, two pairs of dress trousers, riding breeches, two tunics, a dress kepi with its box. A few months later he asked his parents for a small allowance: "It is absolutely imperative that I buy something to wear this summer. I will not be able to use my old uniform because by then I'll be an officer. I have found where I can buy inexpensive but elegant clothes. If my father could send me eighty or a hundred francs I'll be able to outfit myself from head to toe. It will be the beginning of my new wardrobe. If my father prefers, he could loan me the money. By next year, I'll be able to start reimbursing him."[1]

During the last three years of study in Paris at the Lycée Henri IV he had been writing home regularly, sharing with his family the social observations and political gossip to which the capital gave him access. He knew that his older brother, Joseph, was still buying pigs at the Excideuil Fair and, game-bag on his shoulder, still went off collecting eggs, ducks, and capons from the small farms that belonged to their family. He knew that, at home, with the help of his mother's talents, his sister Hélène was learning to cook truffle-skin omelettes, can tomato preserves, and bake cherry pies. He knew that his mother, as pious as she was conventional, only went out to go to Mass, and that, every Friday, she entertained the two Demoiselles de Magondeaux along with the mayor's wife and the notary's daughter. He knew that his father still screamed "Hue, dia" from the seat of his cart to speed his horse to the bedside of a woman in labor or a farmer with tetanus. And, finally, he knew that his Grandmother

Theulier, seated in the drawing room of the old family house on the Rue du Thon, still accompanied her knitting with a running commentary about the comings and goings of the people who lived in the two buildings she could see from her window: the church and the pharmacy. Jean-Baptiste, the young provincial in Paris, spoke to them all when he wrote about a ball the president of the republic had attended or the public celebrations of the new Franco-Russian alliance. Just as it was all of them he addressed on the day when, having waited in vain for his brother and sister, who were supposed to arrive by the two-thirty train, he wrote a scathing letter: "It was surely the horror of spending seven cents for a telegram," he added near the end, "that prevented you from informing me of this change of plans."

With his move to Paris, Jean-Baptiste had started to burn the bridges that connected him to his family. Now, his success at the Ecole Polytechnique allowed him to widen the gap further. Proud of his new experiences in the capital, he felt free to lecture his sister Hélène: "Your tendency to be dazzled by commotion and parties worries me," he wrote her on November 12, 1893. "Just think about it and you'll see how shallow and empty it all is. . . . If you could spend some time alone in the indifferent crowd . . . Think of all the young girls your age who come to Paris every day. Their parents can no longer support them in the provinces and so they plunge into the capital, with only a few francs in their pockets. After a few months of misery, they find a job in some store and begin to earn 35 francs, or even 45 francs, here, in Paris!!!!" He even tried to raise his sister's political consciousness: "If you have suffered from the cold these past few days," he wrote in January 1894, "you must begin to feel more compassion for the misery of the poor. I see so many here, covered with rags, shivering in the cold! Last Thursday, in a urinal, I saw a man trying to warm his hands by spitting on them. And when they look up, they see beautiful carriages driven by coachmen in furs. I understand their outrage, exasperation, anarchism. And faith is no longer there to turn them into martyrs. Be generous with them, and consider yourself lucky. Even if you don't have everything you want, at least you're comfortable." Jean-Baptiste had landed in Paris almost a quarter century after the Commune, when, to the observant traveler, the city's streets showed the dazzling signs of an industrial cycle at its peak. He had come to the center of the nation at a particularly turbulent time in its history: the carryover effects of the Second Empire, the first stirrings of the radical era, the humiliating memories of the war of 1870, which had crippled the nation. Difficult years for a country groping for an identity. Years marked by the assassination of the president of the republic, Sadi-Carnot, then the condemnation of Captain Dreyfus.

Jean-Baptiste wasn't particularly affected by the jolts of history. He wanted to succeed, as he told his sister; he wanted to get into the Ecole Polytechnique. For over a century, this prestigious military school had provided the country not only its best engineers but also philosophers like Auguste Comte and Georges Sorel, politicians like Sadi-Carnot, and seamen—whose uniforms Jean-Baptiste so admired—like the Admirals Rigault de Genouilly and Courbet, central figures in the French colonial wars in Indochina. For a century, France had supplied the Ecole Polytechnique with its math whizzes after screening them via competitive examinations. And for a century, the Ecole Polytechnique had returned the favor by producing students who, after two years of military school and intensive studies, would become the ruling elite of the country. There, Jean-Baptiste studied astronomy, stereotomy, mechanics, architectural design, and literature, and, from the very first, his performance confirmed the promise he had displayed in his entrance exam. He lived the privileged, studious life of the class of '95, voraciously attending all the season's balls (at Saint-Cyr and the Hôtel de Ville), and indulging his fondness for the theater and interminable poker games with friends.

After two years of study, Jean-Baptiste graduated twenty-seventh out of 223 students,[2] but he almost immediately decided that he preferred not to profit from his enviable situation and instead joined the navy. A sailor from landlocked Périgord was rare indeed. Jean-Baptiste fashioned his own dreams and plans around a fleet of battleships, destroyers, cutters, and gunboats, the new naval craft that had come to replace the old frigates and other high-boarding vessels. After Paris and the Ecole Polytechnique, his enrollment in the navy was his sharpest break of all with Thiviers. He knew that his new career would take him all over the world, far from his country for three, four, even five years, and so, before embarking, on October 1, 1897, on the frigate *La Melpomène,* anchored in the port of Brest, Jean-Baptiste went back to Thiviers for one last look.

He revisited the narrow steep streets that lead from the station to the church, and the beautiful medieval houses of old Thiviers, with their cob walls and wood beams. He revisited the plane trees of the main square, and, directly behind it, the square-steepled church, his friend Magondeaux's chateau, and the adjacent pharmacy that his great-grandfather had bought in 1821 and had then bequeathed to his son, Jean-Baptiste Chavoix, respected pharmacist. Finally, he found himself again before the large family house on the Rue du Thon, which his grandfather had bought in 1892 from Joseph Faure for 11,000 francs and where Jean-Baptiste himself had been born and grew up. It was a sturdy, sizable house, a large cube of polished white stones, three stories high, conveniently situated in the center of town, less than ten yards from the church and five from the pharmacy. With its twenty rooms and large garden, it constituted, along with their estate at La Brégère with its farms and fifteen acres, the most substantial portion of the family fortune. All these acquisitions had been made by his mother's family, which, thanks to the joint advantages of a prosperous pharmacy and a flair for dowries, over two decades had managed to accumulate, in and around Thiviers, a small but solid real estate fortune. Moreover, when she married Doctor Eymard Sartre, Jean-Baptiste's mother had been granted a dowry of 20,000 francs, "12,000 of which in cash." She was the direct heiress of the accumulated fortunes of the Theulier, Chavoix, Poumeau-Delille, Barailler-Laplante, and Fuehle-Sablière families, who had come from Tourtoirac, Excideuil, Bordeaux, and Juillac, in the Corrèze region, and had settled in Thiviers to profit from the commercial activity of this lively little town. So, in the summer of 1897, Jean-Baptiste revisited this part of green Périgord, where his mother's family had left so many traces. In fact, since the Revolution of 1789, both the Theuliers and the Chavoix had provided France with countless mayors, subprefects, county councilors, and deputies representing Dordogne and Périgord at the national superior court. If Jean-Baptiste had forgotten all this, the voices of the past in the street signs and graveyards would surely have served to remind him.

First of all, they would have brought to mind his most remote ancestor, Léonard Barailler, sieur de Laplante, surgeon in the navy of Louis XV in 1740; and Jean-Baptiste Chavoix (1738–1818), a lawyer from Juillac, in Corrèze, who had attended the Constituent Assembly of 1789 as a deputy of the Third Estate to the Estates-General for the jurisdiction of Limoges; and yet another Jean-Baptiste, Jean-Baptiste Chavoix (1805–1881), a doctor from Excideuil, who had represented his region at both the Constituent and the Legislative Assemblies in 1848–49, before being elected democratic-radical deputy from 1849 to 1881 and before his well-known electoral race against the local "rightwinger," Maréchal Bugeaud. And finally, they would tell him of Jean Theulier, first mayor of Thiviers in 1792, and his descendants, Jacques, Jules, Albert, pharmacists and local politicians who eventually sold their mansion and magnificent park to the municipality. Besides all these figures from the past, there were those still alive and active, such as Albert Theulier, a doctor and a republican deputy since 1881, who, during his electoral campaign in 1889, had asked to levy a tax on capital; and Henri Chavoix, a notary who had also entered the Assembly in 1881 as a republican deputy. And now, Jean-Baptiste was going to reject this long heritage of leading citizens so central to the history of the French Southwest, to build his professional life in an area that had always been alien to both the Chavoix and the Theuliers. It was immaterial to him that, in the historical memory of the Southwest, his ancestors had for so long been the symbols of the radical left, possibly even freemasons, "violently anti-clerical, happily sectarian." He was also rejecting the more peasant background of his father's side of the family, leaving the responsibility for that tradition entirely to his brother Joseph. He could still remember how, as a child, he loved to accompany his father, the doctor, on his visits in his horse-drawn cart. It took one hour to go from Thiviers to Corgnac-sur-l'Ile, and then twenty more minutes to climb from Corgnac, along the narrow, winding road that goes by Coulonges, all the way to Puifeybert, a small cluster of lights, barely a hamlet.

At the end of the path, past the farmyards, chicken houses, cow sheds, and stables, sat the central farm of the Sartre property. Long, low, stretched out according to a rather haphazard architectural arrangement that wedded corner millstones to brick walls, it had been built in 1805 by Jean-Baptiste's great-grandfather. During the Restoration, a bread oven and a large cistern with a capacity of 240 barrels had been added to the garden. Its proportions made it the perfect Sartre farm: no single door-frame was higher than five feet six inches. In addition, it offered a superb view, which, at a glance, encompassed the entire career of the Sartre family, history and sociology integrated. If one stood by the entrance wall, a little to the left of the door, one could see, on the same axis and separated only by several feet, first the slate towers of the Château de Laxion and then, higher against the horizon, the square steeple of the church of Thiviers. The history of the family was inscribed in these three buildings: the first Sartre ancestor was a peasant. After the French Revolution, in 1805, he erected the first groups of buildings on his farm. Then, his son Pierre, born in 1806, developed the family property until it extended sixty or seventy acres; and finally, Pierre's son, Eymard, born in 1836, left the hamlet of Puifeybert to continue his studies first at Thiviers, then at Périgueux, and finally at the prestigious medical school of Montpellier, where, three centuries after Rabelais, he graduated as a doctor of medicine with a thesis on lipomas. After this, he moved to Thiviers, where, for a while, he was the only doctor in town. There, he married one of the area's richest heiresses, the pharmacist's daughter, and, with her, moved to the house on the Rue du Thon, next to the church. From the Château de Laxion to the steeple of Thiviers, through the farm of Puifeybert, it had taken three generations of Sartres to accomplish this arduous social climb: a peasant begets a tenant farmer who, in turn, begets a country doctor ... Jean-Baptiste was going to push this success yet further: he would go to Paris, then to the Ecole Polytechnique. And yet, for the country folks, there is hardly a name that's more peasant than Sartre: "Lou sartrou," they say, rolling the "r's" and stressing the last syllables, "but everybody knows it comes from 'sartor,' which means 'tailor' in Périgord dialect!"

In the affectionate regional speech that greeted his father every time he visited Puifeybert, Jean-Baptiste could hear just how far he had come. Doctor Eymard was the hamlet's favorite son: till his death, in 1913, he returned regularly, once a month, to treat the people from there and the neighboring villages. He saw his patients in a little room of the family farm. "If you could pay, you paid," the neighbors still recall, "and if you couldn't, he took care of you anyway: the ideal doctor for the poor."[3]

For all his dedication and charity, however, the country doctor remained a rather taciturn man within the family, known for his radical atheism, his hearty appetite, and his caution in money matters. That summer of 1897, Jean-Baptiste once again witnessed the long silent dinners, the pent-up tensions, the sterile, undeclared war always brewing between his parents. Religion, money, and social origin were still the three major bones of contention. Jean-Baptiste's parents came from different worlds, and their marriage had not helped bridge the gap. Between Doctor Eymard and his wife, Elodie, née Chavoix, there was only silence and an indifference that lasted forty-six years. Fortunately, the house in Thiviers was large enough for everyone to withdraw into their private shells.

During the fifteen years he had lived with his family, Jean-Baptiste had always been aware of how his mother threw herself into extraordinarily rigorous religious or gastronomical programs that would consume most of her day. There were times when she would play the butcher or the preserve maker, turning the kitchen into a food-processing factory. After all, she lived at the heart of the finest gastronomical region of France and was herself the sole repository of a few recipes that could be bequeathed only from mother to daughter. Truffled foie gras, *confits* of duck, sausages with chestnuts, stews, guinea-hen salmis, omelettes with boletes, quince jam, plum brandy, these were some of her specialties. In the summer of '97, for her Jean, her J.B., as she called him, she outdid herself with maternal care and gastronomic devotion. She was very proud of his success at the Ecole Polytechnique, and if she now grieved for his imminent departure, it was mostly because she did not know when she would see him again. Of course, her two older children, Joseph and Hélène, would stay with her in Thiviers, but somehow it wasn't the same. Indeed, the couple Eymard Sartre–Elodie Chavoix had produced a rather odd litter. The first, Joseph, would be thirty that summer— then, Hélène, twenty-seven, and finally Jean-Baptiste, who would be twenty-four on August 5.

Hélène was not very pretty—she looked like her mother, with her broad, moon-shaped face, tiny eyes and a sad, large mouth that drooped at the corners. Hélène remained unmarried until she was thirty-three; till then she stayed home helping her mother in the kitchen, disconsolately daydreaming, and nearly dying of admiration for her heroic, younger brother, the only adventurer in the family: J.B. As for Joseph, to this day, in Thiviers, he is remembered as a "simpleton," a "happy idiot," "the one you asked to carry a candle to the altar, just to give him something to do"; but was he really as dim-witted as they made him out? True, he didn't have much schooling, and spoke with difficulty and a heavy stammer, but he was kind and very obliging. He never had a woman and seldom held a job, though he may have worked briefly as an "insurance agent." Soon a kind of complicity was established between "Madame Eymard" and Joseph, the son bringing to the mother the sort of devotion his father failed to give her. He went to the post office, mowed the lawn, reprimanded the servants, rushed to help the lady next door; he was at once errand boy and butler, probably unaware of the contempt his mother, sister, and brother felt for him, of the contortions they would go through in order to forestall any possible blunder on his part whenever they went visiting.

That summer, Jean-Baptiste came back to Thiviers, though nothing tied him to his hometown, just as nothing, at that point, could keep him from going to Brest and embarking on his new career as a sailor, neither his mother's gastronomic zeal, nor the trips to Puifeybert, nor his handsome room on the Rue du Thon. Not even those wild bike rides, around the château, that he and his two childhood friends Magondeaux and Durieux took before going for a swim in the Laveau, surrounded by magnolias, hazels, and bulrushes. Jean-Baptiste had no difficulty tearing himself away from Thiviers; he hated the stifling atmosphere of provincial life, its gossip, its Masses, its peasants, and most of all the poisonous atmosphere of his home.

O N OCTOBER 1, 1897, in the port of Brest, Sartre M.J.B.E.—Marie Jean-Baptiste Eymard: this would be his name from now on— was inducted into the navy. On October 20, he shipped out on the frigate *Melpomène*, where, under Commanding Officer Testard, captain of the ship, he would learn to be a seaman. "Serves with great zeal and dispatch, and shows much appreciation for the work of a seaman," Commanding Officer Testard noted of Jean-Baptiste after only six months of service, probably already sensing in him the making of a future admiral.[4]

After his introduction to navy life, in the Western Mediterranean and Middle Eastern fleet, things suddenly became more serious. At Cherbourg, he boarded the *Bruix* bound for Manila and then the Bay of Kuangchou-Van, where the *Descartes,* the ship to which he had been assigned, lay anchored. This second-class cruiser, only four years old, had fourteen cannons and 5,500 horsepower. It belonged to the Far Eastern and Western Pacific fleet. The *Descartes,* under Captain Philibert and Commander Serpette de Bersaucourt, would be an important element in the strategic role of the fleet. It was to cruise for two years from the Bay of Along, past Haitou, Hong Kong, Woosung, Nagasaki, Pagoda, Nanking, and Manila, to the splendid bays, islands, and ricefields around Kuangchou-Van, near China, Indochina, Japan, and the Philippines. Jean-Baptiste had barely time to learn the rudiments of his new post before he was called upon to play a crucial part in the battle for the Gulf of Tonkin. His mathematical knowledge was immediately put to use in his capacity as navigator and helmsman. He mastered the rigorous punctuality demanded of any officer of the watch, learned to calculate sight-lines, to sail by dead reckoning, to operate sextants, to keep a logbook, to listen carefully to the topman shout out the soundings.

But his apprenticeship did not last long; there was a war going on.

Jean-Baptiste entered the navy at a time when France, Germany, Great Britain, Spain, and America all held precious territories in the Far East. It was a time when Vice-Admiral de Beaumont, commander-in-chief of the Middle Eastern squadron, was pressing Admiral Besnard, secretary of the navy, and Secretary Hanoteaux, at the Quai d'Orsay, to give him more troops and more modern ships to facilitate his schemes of annexation. "From a commercial standpoint," de Beaumont wrote, "the acquisition of Kuangchou-Van is most desirable. The country is rich, populous, well-cultivated; it produces various crops and is irrigated with numerous fluvial and maritime arteries. The working population has looked on our arrival with benevolent indifference, being mostly concerned with how they might profit from us. Of course, things have been quite different with the mandarins and the more literate citizens, who are well aware of the dangers of our closeness and the inevitability of future expansion."[5] The acquisition of the Bay of Kuangchou-Van was the first campaign in which Jean-Baptiste—in charge of both navigation and artillery—participated on board the *Descartes*. The admiral had been sending men into the area for a number of years to draw maps, demarcate territories, and generally familiarize himself with this crucial area, which would allow him to increase his sphere of influence. And indeed, it was enough to look at Kuangchou-Van's location— northeast of the Gulf of Tonkin, north of the Isle of Hainan, right above the southeastern coast of China, between Hong Kong and the delta of the Red River—to understand its strategic importance. Jean-Baptiste spent May and June under Captain Philibert, who directed the entire operation from the *Descartes*. Jean-Baptiste served "with zeal and courage" though not really identifying with the general attitude of his superiors.

"Captain Philibert is hard and restless," he wrote his father a year later, when, seizing the first opportunity, he left the *Descartes*. He simply obeyed when Captain Philibert showed him his plans: the captain had met Colonel Tcheng, commissioner of the Bay of Kuangchou-Van, and had listed all his grievances against the people of the nearby village, a "restless populace" given to thefts and armed attacks; he had also met with the subprefect of Sui-Kai, who was "upset and annoyed," Captain Philibert told his men; "he had just been poorly received by the inhabitants of the village of Hoiteou, whom he found stupid, stubborn, sectarian, and absolutely opposed to any conversation with the French."

13

The inevitable confrontation occurred between July 12 and July 15, 1898, and the admiral took pleasure in relating its most minute details to the secretary of the navy. "On July 12, at 3:50 p.m.," he wrote, "near Haitou, bands of Chinese marauders, consisting of 500 to 600 men armed with guns, knives, lances, and shields, suddenly poured out of a ravine. At the same time, another group of at least 300 men rushed out of a village to the south; the orders seemed to come from one man in this group; he was carrying a red flag; a bright fire was coming toward us. Once in port, Captain Philibert signaled his ship to fire on the crowd and on Haitou-Can and the neighboring villages; we counted about ten dead and several wounded among the Chinese. At 4:45, the shooting was over." There followed a period of support strikes, military patrols, squads of sailors sent ashore "to make sure that no band was hiding in the numerous bushes and ditches of the field," and intimidation—for example, on July 15, the "slow artillery bombardment of the nearby abandoned villages executed at various hours by the 100-millimeter guns of the *Descartes* and the 65-millimeter guns of the fort changing range at every shot, so as to prevent the inhabitants from returning home and resuming their everyday activities, and to keep them constantly on the alert." It is understandable that this ruthless imperialist campaign would disgust Jean-Baptiste. "Tonkin Campaign," his superiors proudly wrote on his dossier, but the war had had a profound impact on him. On May 1, 1898, in the Manila rout, he had witnessed one of the most spectacular episodes of the Spanish-American War, the annihilation of the Spanish fleet in a few hours under the heavy, constant fire of U.S. Admiral George Dewey.

After the colonial campaigns, foul weather; the summer of '98 was a disaster: squalls, stormy seas, typhoons, serious military problems. Then came new campaigns of repression: "The recent annexations of territory by the Europeans," the vice-admiral writes to the secretary of the navy, "have caused great unrest in China." Once again, Jean-Baptiste is assigned to keep order among the populations of the Middle Empire, but disgusted by the bellicose Captain Philibert, Jean-Baptiste leaves the *Descartes* for the *Jean-Bart.* "The service, here, is far less strenuous," he explains to his family, "and the administration much friendlier. It seemed a much easier way to complete my tour." Then, he goes on to describe the events awaiting him. "We are to leave the bay of Along. The *Entrecasteaux,* the *Descartes,* and the *Jean-Bart* will steam toward Kuangchou-Van . . . where we must engage in a show-of-force to back up our territorial claims. I have no idea how long we will stay there: a month, two months, or only a few days. And then? I know even less. All this is not very interesting: I'd have preferred a trip to Japan. . . . The Far Eastern campaign is a mess, completely uninteresting: our governors have such a horror of any conflict with England that they block all the French ships in Indochina to make sure that no one will see us. So, all I do is await my return, which is getting closer every day."

Jean-Baptiste has lost his greatest illusions and become a bitter, disappointed man. The only thing missing from this long list of disappointments is disease, and that comes in August 1899. He is not a victim of the epidemics of dengue or typhoid fever; he has been struck by an enterocolitis from Cochin China, which necessitates his immediate repatriation to France.

It is a long, tiring journey for Ensign First Class Sartre, who finally arrives at the Fifth Depot for returnees in Marseilles. Ironically, while Jean-Baptiste, sick in bed, is brought back to France, Captain Philibert can boast of yet another triumph. Since August 24, "the French flag has been flying above the bay of Kuangchou-Van, on the island of Nachau" and Philibert wants to go back to Tonkin by land. His wish is soon granted, and he undertakes the forty-mile journey accompanied by Colonel Tcheng and "a hundred soldiers, well-armed and equipped with flags, trumpets, tam-tams, parasols, sedan chairs, coolies for luggage. . . . [the journey] lasted over three days and passed through astounded native populations who had never even seen a European before. Their attitude was neither enthusiastic nor aggressive but rather one of curiosity mixed with the peculiar awe of the unruly Chinese toward Europe. The impression we produced was strong, and more than one serious face told us that some of those people clearly sensed that my passage through these populations marked a turning point in their history, and that a new era was opening up for them."

*A*s for Jean-Baptiste, he returned to France worn out by both campaigns and illness. In more than one way, his career as a navy officer was already over, at least in his head, though his shipboard existence went on till November 1905. He was often tired or ailing, often assigned to posts for which he had neither competence nor interest, and often found himself in impossible situations. As a result, his advancement was slow. Jean-Baptiste's life, then, reduced

itself to a few dates, a few relocations: December 1, 1899, at the depot
in Marseille; from December 13 to March 13, 1900, at the Toulon
hospital; from March to June 1900, at Thiviers, on convalescent
leave. Then, ten months of service at sea, aboard the *Linois*, in the
Mediterranean, and four months of hospital care in Plombières followed by a year of service on the *Loiret*, on the Cherbourg routes.
Then, he embarked again, on the *Calédonien*, the *Couronne*, the
Dupuy de Lôme, and the *Bouvines*. In 1903, he was appointed assistant
to the training officer and made responsible for the gunnery schools.
For a while, it looked as if he had regained his stride. During the next
two years, all his superiors remarked on the excellent state of his
health. Then, one day, he was given a furlough and found himself
in Cherbourg. He knew that one of his fellow students of the class
of '95, Georges Schweitzer, had found a position there as naval
engineer. He paid him a visit. A few days later, Schweitzer introduced Jean-Baptiste to his sister Anne-Marie, then only twenty-one.
After only a few weeks, Jean-Baptiste had written two marriage
proposals: the first addressed to Anne-Marie's father, Charles
Schweitzer, a professor in Paris, and the other, according to custom,
to his naval commander.

Jean-Baptiste Sartre and Anne-Marie Schweitzer married on May
5, 1904, in Paris. Only his mother came from Thiviers to attend the
wedding ceremony. "Mademoiselle, in the cultured milieu where
you have lived, you received the education of a modern woman,"
Abbé Dibildos remarked without the slightest hint of irony, during
the address he delivered in the Passy church. "You have learned to
love works of pure and classic beauty, you have been initiated into
scientific methodology. You are, therefore, quite ready to become
the mate of a man nurtured on mathematics. . . . Let him be your
teacher, Mademoiselle: read the books he tells you to read and pay
close attention to his comments; follow him in his own studies. Give
your intelligence that solidity and breadth that we are fatuous
enough to call virile."[6] At a time when the division of roles between
man and woman—his, the mind; hers, the heart—was still quite
rigid, this speech did not shock the audience: Anne-Marie had the
stuff to become the perfect bride of a French navy admiral. The
pretty woman who stood a head taller than her uniformed officer
husband was certainly not marrying for money: the statutory inquiry held by the police verified that the young woman's dowry
would compensate for the slimness of his navy salary. Anne-Marie

had received a dowry of forty thousand francs from her father, and that was enough for them.

Three months after his marriage, Jean-Baptiste rejoined his battle-ship, the *Bouvines,* in the Brest routes; and he immediately expressed his desire to obtain a six-month leave, without pay, in Paris, for personal reasons: "I want to leave the navy," he explained, "and this leave would allow me to look for another position." The leave was granted, from November 15, 1904 to May 15, 1905, so that, for six months, Jean-Baptiste shared his wife's life on the Rue de Siam, in the sixteenth arrondissement of Paris. For Christmas, the young couple went to Thiviers. On December 24, 1904, a Thursday, Jean-Baptiste and Anne-Marie arrived at the Thiviers station on the six-o'clock train, accompanied by Joseph, who had cut short his visit with some cousins at Croisset in order to take the same train. In her long, black taffeta skirt, black astrakhan jacket, and light blue-gray felt hat trimmed with a bouquet of white violets to hide the combs, "You" (as Anne-Marie was called by her family, and later by the Sartres as well) made quite an impression. "She was dressed simply, but tastefully," her mother-in-law, who had feared some eccentricity on the part of this Parisian, noted with relief. "You" had brought along a large, fine, black wool scarf for Grandmother Theulier, two bags of candies for her father-in-law, and, a small, yellow satin cushion trimmed with Richelieu lace, which she had sewn herself, for her mother-in-law. There were several gastronomically memorable family dinners. The only missing person was Hélène, who, having recently married Captain Frédéric Lannes, stationed in Montpellier, had not been able to come. For three days the weather was wonderful, and the Sartre family, particularly Doctor Sartre, seemed to appreciate the new member, whom they found pretty, well-bred, reserved. Three days later the pair left on the two o'clock train. Then, in Thiviers, the rumors started: J.B. did not look well, he had lost weight, and everybody worried about the recurrence of his migraines. "You," on the other hand, was radiant.

"She is carrying her child beautifully," Mme Sartre Senior wrote to her daughter Hélène, "her belly is not terribly strong, but her hips are. Her face has not changed much; she still has a lovely complexion: in other words, it looks as if she will have an excellent pregnancy. She is already halfway through her term, and the happy event should be in the first days of June."

The pregnancy delighted the Thivieriens and allayed some of their fears concerning Jean-Baptiste's failing health. "They look very happy together," Doctor Sartre's wife had concluded. "You" wrote them to say that the trip had not tired her at all, quite the contrary, that her father-in-law had been "an absolute dear," that their "dear mamma" had gone out of her way to spoil them, and, finally, that everybody had "welcomed them in the most charming fashion"— mostly the usual empty chit-chat, as suited the canons of bourgeois propriety.

The child she was carrying would become Jean-Paul Sartre. And he will not say much about his father's town: just a few allusions, very discreet and almost impossible to decode, as in his first book, *Nausea.* But he will never talk explicitly of either Thiviers or Périgord. One day, in a restaurant, he is approached by a young woman named Sartre, also from the Southwest, who introduces herself as a distant cousin. Sartre answers her questions with great civility, but as soon as he can, he lets the conversation drop and resumes eating. Yet, as a unique homage, perhaps ironic, to Jean-Baptiste's home, the only foie gras that Jean-Paul would ever eat for Christmas had to come from Périgord and had to be cooked as it was in Thiviers and Puifeybert, in an earthenware pot. As for the few books he inherited from Jean-Baptiste—a work by Le Dantec about the future of science, and Weber's *Toward Positivism, via Absolute Idealism*— he leafs through them absent-mindedly, then quickly sells them.

THE SORROWS OF ANNE-MARIE

> *I am shown a young giantess, I am told she is my mother. I myself would take her rather for an elder sister. . . . She tells me her troubles, and I listen compassionately. Later, I'll marry her to protect her. I promise . . .*
>
> —THE WORDS

*L*A COQUILLE . . . Bussière-Galant . . . Lafarge . . . Nexon . . . Limoges . . . Anne-Marie sat, in her elegant astrakhan jacket, staring at the names of unknown towns and villages through the window of the train taking her back home.

She had grown up in forlorn idleness, without any precise plan for the future. "The Schweitzers are born musicians," her father had decreed. So she learned to play Beethoven's most difficult sonatas, and to sing Schubert's and Brahms's lieder, accompanying herself on her parents' piano. She also learned to sew and draw, quietly submitting to the role of the proper young lady who demands nothing, and absorbs the blows of fate with the dignity befitting a woman of her class. Like all the Schweitzers, she was tall, thin, well educated. Her beauty was neither devastating nor aggressive: she had large blue eyes, a sensuous mouth, thick hair, and the tranquil look of a wise, resigned girl who has been rather oppressed by men.

Charles Schweitzer, Anne-Marie's father, and Philippe-Chrétien, her grandfather, were both known for their strong character. In the little town of Pfaffenhofen, in the northeastern triangle of France, just the mention of the name Schweitzer is enough to bring back memories, and Philippe's opulent home remains the wealthiest on the main street: sturdy, clean, full of flowers. Since Jean-Nicolas Schweitzer, the son of a boatman from Frankfurt, had arrived in Strasbourg in 1660 and become a minister, all the men in the family had chosen to devote themselves to teaching. Like a dynasty, from the minister's son all the way to Anne-Marie's grandfather, seven generations of Schweitzers had succeeded one another in the schools of the small Alsatian towns of Boofzheim, Eckwersheim, and even Pfaffenhofen. Then, prompted by new historical circumstances, Anne-Marie's grandfather decided to break with tradition and terminate the long chain of teachers from which he had descended. At the reestablishment of the empire, he openly vented his leftist views, refused to pledge allegiance to Napoleon III, lost his civil service status, and became a grocer. In love with politics, an ardent republican, he later became mayor of Pfaffenhofen from 1875 to 1886. Conscientiously, he kept a trilingual journal of most of the political events of the period—alternating French with German and his native Alsatian dialect: "In the name of freedom and order, the country demands that I vote 'No,' " he angrily scribbled at the moment of the referendum of May 8, 1870.[1] And yet Philippe-Chrétien was too old by the time, at the advent of the Third Republic, his pedagogical and political ideas finally became a reality. After the French defeat in 1870, he had chosen to reside on German soil; and, at the beginning of the period that some will later define as the "golden age of Protestantism," when Jules Ferry surrounded himself with Protestant teachers and liberal Protestants, he had already reached the age of retirement. The *Dictionnaire pédagogique,* the bible of primary education, reiterated most of the ideas that the liberal Protestants upheld and transmitted: faith in the free will of the child, in reason, history, and nature, with the goal of shaping autonomous individuals with sharp critical minds. "It was the privilege of the Third Republic," Ferdinand Buisson proclaimed, "to resume the educational program of the Revolution." These enlightened pedagogues set forth a clear, ambitious ideal: to rescue France from the sclerotic teaching of countless Catholic congregations and to educate people while reinforcing their sense of individual responsibility. All the Schweitzers had belonged to this strong, proud minority so sure of its faith, to this pure, militantly republican minority, to this minority within a minority, the liberal Protestants.

Philippe-Chrétien Schweitzer had five children, of which three were boys: Auguste, "the wealthiest," who, in Paris, started a commercial venture with Peru; Louis, "the most pious," a minister first in Kaysersberg and then in Gunsbach, the father of the famous Albert; and then Charles, "the most intelligent," as he himself maintained, Anne-Marie's father. Charles was the first of the five children, "a child prodigy," according to his mother, who would have liked to see him become a minister. Reckless strong-minded Charles had been expelled from the Protestant seminary where he was a student because of his involvement with a woman. He nevertheless passed with ease his *agrégation* in German, qualifying him to teach in the *lycées*. On May 1, 1872, after the Franco-Prussian war, he chose French citizenship, and then in Macon, where he was teaching, he married a young woman, Louise Guillemin. From this couple came three children: Georges, who became a Polytechnicien, class of '95; Emile, a future professor of German, like his father; and Anne-Marie. "Of the three, Georges is my favorite child," Anne-Marie's mother would often note, adding, with absolute seriousness, "He is the least noisy." Louise Guillemin did not seem to be much of a mother; on the other hand, she did not seem to be much of a wife either. In another age, this strong, assertive, intelligent, and witty woman might have lived a free, autonomous life; instead, she locked herself in a weird chronic illness to resist her rather oppressive husband. When he was transferred to the Lycée Janson de Sailly, she refused to follow him to Paris, enrolled her three children in boarding schools—the two boys with the Dominicans (Louise was Catholic), the girl with the nuns—and abandoned herself to her illness. She went on like this for years—on strike against life—leaving her bed in the nursing home of Arcachon only for the one in her parents' country house, near Saint-Albain, or for the one that she occasionally occupied, in a separate room, under Charles Schweitzer's roof. For this proud, cynical, tolerant woman who loved to quote from Voltaire, Diderot, and the *Encyclopédie*, this was just another way, however self-destructive, of asserting her own identity. She did not live *with* but rather *next to* Charles, oppressed but undefeated by his overconfidence, his spite, his histrionics, and the interminable jokes in Alsatian dialect he loved to exchange with his brothers over family dinners.

*T*HOSE IMAGES were certainly among the ones that passed through Anne-Marie's head during the bumpy train trip between Périgueux and Paris. Of course, there was also a foggy sense of the considerable cultural disparities between the Schweitzers and the Sartres, which would very probably increase with time. But, above all, there was the deep conviction that the life of a couple was not a given: with her parents she had seen the turmoils of a failed though colorful relationship; Jean-Baptiste's parents, on the other hand, had found themselves mired in a much more conventional kind of marriage, one made of constant conflicts, which, indifferent, disillusioned, they shared every day, under the same roof. Nevertheless, everything suggests that the months right after their marriage were very happy: Jean-Baptiste took good care of Anne-Marie, like an older brother and protector, just as he had once taken care of his sister Hélène; and Anne-Marie finally found someone who would talk to her, advise her on what to read, and appreciate her talents. Soon it would be 1905, and only a few months later Anne-Marie would give birth to "a little Annie" or "a little Paul," as she would say, showing some preference for the former. Soon it would be 1905, and, for the sake of Anne-Marie and their child, the navy officer gave up the trip to Japan he had dreamed about for so long. Now Jean-Baptiste wanted only to live out his life on land.

Little Annie or little Paul would be born the first days of June, maybe, or, with a little luck, the last days of May: so hoped Jean-Baptiste, whose unpaid leave would be over on May 15. It was a real struggle to find a job before that fatal May 15, all the while hoping the child might be born a little premature. But "You" and Jean-Baptiste soon realized the vanity of their hopes; the navy administration was rigid, and it looked as if they had miscalculated the birth by at least a month. On May 14, 1905, reluctantly, Jean-Baptiste left Paris for Toulon. On May 29, he had to report as first officer on the destroyer *La Tourmente,* bound for Sicily and Crete, with layovers in Messina, Palermo, and Canea. He called his wife from every port, expecting to hear about his child's birth. "I am going to ship out from Toulon," he wrote to Thiviers, "very sad about leaving 'You' so close to labor, and dreadfully sorry not to be able to hug my child." Then, in Crete, Thiviers, and Paris, the wait began. The Schweitzers had rented a large house in the region around Macon for the month of July, and the miscalculation was disrupting their plans; the later the child was born, the smaller the chance that it would be allowed to leave Paris. "Still no news about our young sailor," wrote the future Grandmother Sartre from Thiviers on June 21, but a few hours later, two cables were dispatched by Grandfather Schweitzer, one to Crete and the other to Thiviers, both announcing the birth of a boy.[2]

Jean-Paul Sartre was born at the time that a number of important political events were taking place: 1905 was the year of the first Russian Revolution, of the Russo-Japanese war, and, closer to home, of the law of separation between church and state—very close to home because, while his family was awaiting his birth, the streets of Thiviers saw demonstrations and riots between opponents and partisans of the law. All Périgord had been astir since 1901 when a law was passed to take teaching out of the hands of religious institutions; the issue was particularly burning because the Lord Bishop of Périgueux had publicly opposed the president's counselor on religious matters. On February 22, 1904, a group of 300 women gathered in front of the church of Thiviers and solemnly promised "to give the kingdom of God back to France." "I am marching to protest against religious and congregational omnipotence and for secular society," the general counselor replied. "Down with Jews and Freemasons," was the women's response. "Down with clerical bigotry! Long live reason, light, and secular education!" chanted their enemies. From her window on the Rue du Thon, Dr. Sartre's wife had an excellent view of the struggle among her fellow citizens.

On August 21, 1905, she wrote her daughter Hélène: "Little Marie Jousseix has just received a teaching appointment here. I spoke with her mother after church. I feel so sorry for her," she went on, "knowing how some people here think. Poor girl, she will be watched all the time. She is already scared but is determined not to change her religious practice." The law separating church and state was voted on December 9, 1905; the heir of the Sartres and the Schweitzers was not yet six months old.

22

For those two families, the real event of the year was the birth of Jean-Paul. Charles Schweitzer, a photography buff, had snapped his grandson, with and without mother, from every possible angle. Some of these shots were immediately sent to the destroyer *La Tourmente,* now outside Crete; some went to Thiviers. The photos were received ecstatically; they were shown to all the visitors to the Rue du Thon, and even sent to Hélène, in Montpellier. Then, in Thiviers, they began making preparations to give the heir a proper reception. "I have spent part of the afternoon," the new Grandmother Sartre wrote, "assembling my cradle, or rather, your cradle. I had it repainted, and have bleached the netting and the fringe. I lined this with some cretonne I found that looks exactly like the lining of the curtains, and then I am going to make new curtains out of some old muslin bed curtains. In short, with very little money this will be a gorgeous cradle. It is ready to receive J. P. whenever you want to bring him to me." The child had already acquired a number of nicknames, all aimed at integrating him into the family.

Meanwhile, Jean-Baptiste, on his destroyer, was bored. "My life here isn't nearly as comfortable as yours at home," he answered his sister Hélène; "it is not so easy to find time to write a letter. Do you know what a destroyer is? I have been living on one for four months: I eat here, I sleep here, I never leave it. . . . Just try to imagine it a bit, the rough seas around Crete, the hot summer down here, and you might begin to understand." And then, overwhelmed: "I foresee my return. I think it will be the definitive one. It is possible that in October I may be able to leave the navy for good. . . . I won't be happy till I start living a normal life again. You have received some news of my wife and little Paul. At least I am lucky enough to know they are in good health. It seems Paul is beautiful. You don't know how I long to meet him and to be again with his mommy." Despite his efforts and hopes, Jean-Baptiste found no opportunity to leave the navy. On June 2, he put in a request for shore duty; on July 18, he received the desired recommendation from the secretary of commerce; on August 23, his name was added to the list of applicants for the position of news editor, and on September 10 he asked for a one-year leave, without pay, to regain his health: all in vain. August, September, October: His "little Paul" was two months old, then three, then four, and Jean-Baptiste languished, helpless, in the waters off Crete.

Finally, illness brought him back to his son: on November 5, he was repatriated to Toulon, exactly five years after his first return

from the Bay of Along. A week later he was home on the Rue de
Siam, with "You," whom he found in wonderful health, and their
son.

24

First meeting between father and son. "We trod the same earth
for a while, that is all," the son later wrote. As for Jean-Baptiste, "My
little Paul is lovely," he wrote his parents. "He seems to enjoy
everything, he is forever moving, forever excited, he screams at the
top of his lungs, roars with laughter, never cries. His eyes are curious, intelligent, and very sweet. . . . Next to me in his chair by the
window, he looks at the street and plays with a rosary, which I have
to pick up off the floor every minute. . . . He is very precocious. I
know nothing about children, but I find him very beautiful." Jean-
Baptiste was in a state of ecstasy over his child, but his health kept
deteriorating: "These six months of summer have been very hard on
me, from every point of view. Now I need rest and good care, but,
mostly, I need to be home." That Christmas of 1905, the three celebrated at their home; the child loved the tree, the candles. Jean-
Baptiste was pleased by the package sent from Thiviers. He felt
"better, but still not strong." It was time to think about the christen-
ing of little Paul: should it take place in Paris or Thiviers?

Despite Jean-Baptiste's hopes, neither rest nor care nor family life
healed him. Those summer months in Crete had provoked a relapse
in his enterocolitis while revealing a bronchial condition, tuberculosis, or "pulmonary hardening of the right lobe." From that moment
on, J.B.'s life fell into the sinister pattern of frequent visits to the
Navy Health Council and endless administrative letters requesting
that the sick leave with half pay be changed to sick leave with full
pay, since the treatment of his two illnesses was long and expensive.
He was granted sick leave of three months, starting on November
12, which was then extended for three more months, starting on
February 12, and then three more, starting on May 12, and the same
again on August 4. In the meantime, Grandmother Theulier, already
well over eighty, died in the house on the Rue du Thon. In her will,
she left most of her property to the three Sartre grandchildren.
Jean-Baptiste would share the estate of La Brégère with his brother
Joseph. On May 11, 1906, Jean-Baptiste wrote his mother, on black-
bordered stationery, to give her an odd piece of news: "There has
been a change. We are going to move to Thiviers with all our
furniture. . . . I have already found movers who will take care of the
whole thing. . . . "You" and Minet [Jean-Paul] are very happy,
indeed, delighted, to go back to Thiviers, and, to tell you the truth,

so am I. Its fresh air will do me good. . . . A big hug to his grandmother from Minet." So, on May 15, 1906, the three Sartres and all
their belongings returned to Thiviers. It was a difficult, strained
return, but, all in all, a sensible one, since J.B. needed a convalescence
in the country, had no great fortune, and had just inherited a large
estate five minutes from Thiviers. J.B. and "You" quickly settled in
at La Brégère, but, for practical reasons, the child remained in Thiviers. The doctor, Grandmother Sartre, and Joseph spent a great deal
of their time and energy going back and forth between the two
houses.

In July, Grandfather Schweitzer came to pay a visit to his son-in-
law, at La Brégère, and to lend some moral support to Anne-Marie,
who was getting increasingly worried. "Poor dear," Doctor Sartre's
wife noted, "she is so unhappy; let's hope her father's presence
provides her the balm she needs. Jean is also glad to see him. M.
Schweitzer has found him aged, and quite changed, and though he
still likes to entertain some hope, I think he has begun to realize the
sad truth." During those three summer months Jean-Baptiste's
health kept deteriorating; he looked "miserable," then "a little better," then, again, "prostrated by sudden attacks of fever," and later
"desperate." He was under the simultaneous care of two doctors: his
father, and a childhood friend, Jean-Louis Durieux, who came to see
him every day. But Jean-Baptiste's enterocolitis kept weakening
him, and his tuberculosis worsened. As for the child, he was also
doing poorly, perhaps because he was seeing so little of his mother.
Grandmother Sartre began talking about her "two patients": "Poulou," she writes her daughter, "immediately recognized his Grandfather Schweitzer, and showed he was very happy to see him. But the
poor baby is tormented by his teething," and, at the end of the letter,
she adds, "I am old, very old, and yet, despite all my troubles, I have
to be young and sing to keep Poulou happy and to put him to sleep."
So, everybody was summoned to entertain Poulou, who, being now
over a year old, must certainly have felt that something was the
matter. Joseph spent a lot of time with him, as did a young maid,
Juliette.

On September 16, 1906, at the end of this terrible summer, Mme
Sartre again wrote her daughter, "I've had to go to La Brégère. Jean
had a very bad day due to the sudden cooling of the air after a heat
wave. We have decided that they're going to move back here, with
us, tomorrow. Your father will go and fetch Jean, taking all necessary precautions. As for the poor baby, Joseph will care for him; he

is as sickly as he was beautiful in the photo. . . . He wants a little lamb and smiled when I told him: 'I'm going to write Aunt Hélène and ask her to send one to her little Poulou.' " As agreed, on September 17, Doctor Sartre went to La Brégère to escort J.B. and "You" back to Thiviers. Jean-Baptiste coughed all the way. His father helped him in and out of the carriage, and got him settled on the second floor of their home. They brought him his "little Paul," who cried a lot, because he was teething. A few minutes later, at about six in the evening, Jean-Baptiste died in the bedroom of his childhood.

*T*HE THIVIERS cemetery, Wednesday, September 21, 1906, eleven in the morning: a huge crowd awaits the arrival of the funeral procession at the Place du Docteur-Jules-Theulier. J.B.'s childhood friends are his pallbearers; his fellow students from the Ecole Polytechnique, who have come as a delegation, hold the funerary cloth. Jean-Baptiste's sword and insignia lie on his coffin. Flowers, wreaths, and bouquets are spread everywhere. Durieux, Jean-Baptiste's childhood friend and last doctor, gives a eulogy in which he recalls the stages of the career and illness of a young man who had done everything to succeed in life, and had failed, who had set up his pawns but had been unable to play them: "If the only things needed to obtain the miracle of renewed health were enlightened care, loving attention, innumerable nights spent by the bedside, and stifled sobs, this miracle would have been realized by someone who showed herself to be a true angel of the hearth. And how much gratitude did she receive from her dear patient! During the final struggle, the dying man was still able to find, between gasps, the superhuman strength to smile a few last times at the woman he was leaving . . . like the waving of the hand with which, a long time ago, he used to greet the people he was leaving behind on his receding ship, these last smiles seemed to me not an *adieu* but an *au revoir.* This is why, joining his widow, his child, his unhappy parents, and his numerous friends in mourning, I now wave our lost loved one a good-bye that is full of hope."

The local weekly, *L'Indépendant du Périgord,* in an article about the event, reminded its readers that Jean-Baptiste died facing "a brilliant future that would have brought glory to the town of Thiviers." Anne-Marie was twenty-four years old, her son fifteen months. She wore long black dresses, with long, black crepe veils attached to her hair by means of a white headband. She dressed her young boy in those sailor suits children love to wear, with a large collar striped in white and blue. And this was all that was left of Jean-Baptiste, except a rather solemn portrait of the ensign in uniform, which hung over his son's bed till 1917, when it suddenly disappeared.

*F*OR ANNE-MARIE, the interlude at Thiviers had lasted only till Jean-Baptiste's death. She had thought it would be much longer and had feared it might end up tying her down more than she wished. But now she was going back to her parents, too devastated to settle a number of questions concerning her inheritance with the notary of Thiviers. On the Rue du Thon, she was leaving two aged parents-in-law torn between a feeling of guilt for their son's early departure and a feeling of discomfort in front of this young woman. They had witnessed two deaths in the family at just a few months' distance, but the wheel kept turning. In a few days, Hélène and her husband would be visiting them in Thiviers. That's where the new baby of the family would be born. Everybody hoped it would be a little girl, a playmate for Poulou.

Limoges . . . Nexon . . . Lafarge . . . Bussière-Galant . . . La Coquille . . . Anne-Marie was once again staring at the names of the stations on the way to Paris. Her little boy, sitting by the window, watched rivers, woods, and horses go by. It was a strange return. She had left Thiviers immediately after the funeral: without J.B. there was no reason for her to stay on. Thiviers and La Brégère now could only remind her of J.B.'s agony.

THE PRIVATE BESTIARY
OF A CHILD-KING

A spoiled child isn't sad; he's bored, like a king. Like a dog.

—THE WORDS

*T*HE BLOND child in a sailor suit and the tall young woman in black got into the red carriage that shuttled between Thiviers and Limoges, and then into the train from Limoges to Paris. From his birth, he had been the only man who could claim any closeness to Anne-Marie, then Jean-Baptiste had come back and, for a rather unfortunate spell before disappearing again, had dethroned Poulou. Now, the child resumed full possession of her and was taking her away for good. The next ten years were the best ones for these two desperate lovers, these hapless shipwrecks, mother and son. They were also ten Schweitzer years, Anne-Marie having chosen, wisely, to return to live with her parents. Her marriage had come to nothing, but her son was "very advanced for his age." "Families, to be sure, prefer widows to unmarried mothers, but just barely," as her child will later write.[1]

1907–1917: later, Sartre will tell of those years, and only those, in his autobiographical novel, *The Words.* He will write, erase, search, rewrite, with the fierce perfectionism of a jeweler grinding out, cutting, chiseling a precious stone. But, for understandable reasons, he will "bracket" the two periods that frame these happy years: immediately before them, there was Jean-Baptiste; immediately after them there will be Joseph Mancy, his mother's second, and more hated, husband. Indeed it is almost indecent for an obstinate biographer to try to break through the ore of these "Schweitzer years," so carefully recast, almost fifty years later, by the writer of *The Words.* It is a powerful, seductive book that seizes the reader with contrasting strategies, excites him, ravishes him, and then, finally, abandons him, traumatized, defenseless, in a state of shock. This book, published in 1963, will be read for a long time as Sartre's own narrative of his childhood, but, in fact, it is much more and much less. First of all, it is a novel of apprenticeship, written in adulthood, highly interpretive, subjective, and lyrical, a powerful divagation around childhood, which deliberately forgets a few important themes, such as Jean-Baptiste, and all of Thiviers. It is a self-analysis, happily ironic, in which the author generously mistreats himself. It is a way of getting even. It is an ode to his mother. It is a beautiful work of art. It is, in other words, more than a biography.

We will glimpse the places where the child-king lived surrounded by all those figures he would later describe: the grandfather, haughty and omnipotent, "a man of the nineteenth century who took himself for Victor Hugo . . . a handsome man with a flowing beard who was always waiting for the next opportunity to show off, as the alcoholic is always waiting for the next drink."[2] Charles Schweitzer, sixty-two ("Karl" to his grandson) despite his break with the theological training that would have led him into the ministry, "retained the Divine," according to Jean-Paul, "and

invested it in Culture.["]3 Among the achievements of this grandfather, we find a series of serious, well-argued books, as befits his
cultural roots: a thesis on Hans Sachs, sixteenth-century musician,
singer, and poet; a thesis in Latin on Guillaume d'Aquitaine; the
Deutsches Lesebuch, a new approach to the teaching of German by
the direct method; and finally a book on Johann Sebastian Bach,
composed with two closely related minister-musicians: his brother
Louis and his nephew Albert. Next to Charles Schweitzer, insolent
and proud, was Grandmother "Mamie," Louise Schweitzer, fifty-
eight, "a lively and shrewd but cold woman [who] thought straight
but inaccurately, because her husband thought accurately but
amiss. . . . Surrounded by virtuous play-actors, she conceived an
aversion for play-acting and virtue."4 And then, of course, there
was Anne-Marie, twenty-four, the sister-mother whose room he
shares, his incestuous mistress: "Even now—1963," he will mod-
estly note in *The Words,* incest "is the only family relationship
which moves me."5 In the middle of this peculiar trio sits a two-
year-old child with curly blond hair, beautiful, adored, Poulou the
child-king. The nicknames he was given in Thiviers have been
forgotten, no more "J.P.," no more "Minet," no more "little Paul":
now it is "Poulou," the name given him by Anne-Marie, that pre-
vails. Whether in the large house of Meudon, or in their Paris
apartment high above the Rue Le Goff, or at Saint-Albain, with
Mamie's family, or with Uncle Georges, at Guérigny, in the
Nièvre, or at Arcachon, for the summer holidays, or at Gunsbach,
or at Pfaffenhofen, in occupied Alsace, the four Schweitzers from
then on live an intense and colorful family life.

"It was Paradise," *The Words* claims.6 "Every morning I woke up
dazed with joy, astounded at the unheard-of luck of having been
born into the most united family in the finest country in the world."
It was the middle of the Belle Epoque, the apogee of bourgeois
serenity, bathed in the happy illusion of progress and science, the
miraculous era when cinema, radio, the telephone, the automobile,
and the airplane were born. The earth seemed nearly conquered by
the joint efforts of Western imperialism and technological promise.
It was an era of social balance, of world order, which gratified all the
members of the bourgeoisie, including the Schweitzers. And yet,
under the presidency of Armand Fallières, that falsely complacent
balance was suddenly and brutally upset by a number of social
upheavals, riots, demonstrations, strikes. The revolt of the beggars

in Languedoc shook up the peasant world; the farmers' unions convened in increasingly violent congresses; the largest crowds of demonstrators that had ever gathered together under the Third Republic stampeded through Perpignan, Nîmes, and Montpellier; the mayor of Narbonne hoisted a black flag over the city hall, and Prime Minister Georges Clémenceau received the peasant delegates in person. In Paris, in a corner building between the Panthéon and the Luxembourg Gardens, behind the curtains of a high-ceilinged apartment on the sixth floor overlooking the street, the Schweitzer quartet kept abreast of daily events through the newspapers *Le Temps* and *Le Matin,* which Grandfather would then only rarely discuss. "That staunch supporter of Dreyfus never spoke of Dreyfus to me," the grandson would later say regretfully. But, despite this silence, despite the extreme restraint that Charles exercised in all matters— including politics—reserved to men and forbidden to women and children, the excluded trio was able to guess that on January 17, 1912, citizen Schweitzer had voted for the radical Poincaré over the future secretary of agriculture, Pams, "a tobacconist." Women would not get the vote until 1944. With their chin-high tulle chemisettes, their long flounced skirts, their waists squeezed into corsets, their lace bodices, their shirred sleeves, and their sunbonnets, tilted to the side and overtrimmed with veils and flowers, Louise and Anne-Marie— "my women," as Charles liked to call them—maintained, in this first decade of the twentieth century, the behavior and manners that the best families still transmitted from mother to daughter. On July 3, 1907, the first law for the protection of women workers had been passed by the Chamber of Deputies. For Charles Schweitzer's two women, helped in their domestic chores by a young Alsatian maid, the realities of the workers' riots that ended the left coalition had little meaning.

It took the outbreak of World War I to upset the beautiful serenity of the Schweitzer family. The restitution of Alsace and Lorraine to France was suddenly more than a remote possibility; the country was swept by a nationalist delirium that assumed a variety of forms —such as the "patriotic play with ten characters" that Charles Schweitzer wrote and staged to amuse his grandson and his friends, a play in which Poulou took the role of a young Alsatian who, "his father having chosen France," decided "to sneak across the border to join him. I had a number of bravura speeches: I would put out my right arm, bow my head and murmur, hiding my prelate-like cheek in the hollow of my shoulder: 'Farewell, farewell, our dear Alsace.' "[7] The child had already read and reread Uncle Hansi's large albums, with their colored drawings of charming Alsatian villages whose inevitable steeples were inevitably crowned by inevitable storks. "For forty years," he would read, "under Prussian occupation, nothing has changed in our country. Two peoples, two races coexist without ever mixing. On one side, there is the Alsatian, proud of his legacy and his suffering; on the other, the noisy, arrogant invader trying to impose his Kultur under the pretext of Germanization."[8] For a century, all the children of Alsace-Lorraine were artificially nurtured on French culture with the help of those drawings, those caricatures, and a history of France that had been especially written for them. During the first year of the war, Charles Schweitzer confided his worries and his fears in this letter to a friend: "Will my dear country still be breathing next year? We need great tact. The worst blunder would be to blanket the country with mandarins who don't understand a word of the language, and know nothing about the Alsatian soul. . . . [My] anxiety . . . has somewhat relaxed its hold since I received the assurance, from a relative of President Poincaré, that they will send over only Alsatian administrators who already know the country. Unfortunately, all this will be decided in Parliament, and you know as well as I what sort of Parliament we have." The child did his best to play along with the old man; though he had always lived in Paris, he would later avenge his Alsatian grandfather: "I would take the royal road: in my person, martyred Alsace would enter the Ecole Normale Supérieure."[9]

For Poulou, World War I marked the discovery of a new form of hero, the collective hero. Up to now the child prodigy had been initiated only into the deeds and actions of the various individual heroes he had encountered in the books in his grandfather's library. He himself was one, thanks to Karl's attentions: young Poulou, star of an interminable opera replayed every day in the Schweitzer household. This, at least, according to *The Words*: taken in hand by his grandfather, the curly-haired baby in a sailor suit had been turned into an odious little monster, somewhere between a pretentious adult and a lapdog. Charles Schweitzer's letters give us a different version: "I have become," he explains to a friend in January 1915, "my grandson's private tutor. I'm trying to teach him, and myself, some knowledge of history and geography. There is nothing quite as exquisite as seeding and cultivating young intelligence." Eight generations of Schweitzer instructors, all the way back to the very first year of the Alsatian eighteenth century, will come together and bend over the books, the destiny, the mind, and the culture of their five-year-old descendant, Poulou. This new role as universal mentor of a young man filled the old teacher with such pride and delight that he invested it with all the talents he had wasted during his career as a model teacher, to offer them, in an act of virtuosity, to his gifted pupil, his special, private, unique student.

"My grandfather taught me the history of our country. France had been poorly ruled by kings for a long time till 1793. Then, in the nineteenth century, it was governed by emperors who had to be closely watched because the electoral law, which had established universal suffrage, by then exercised great power over the government, and the majority always got its way. This is how I learned about democracy, and how I learned to love it, provided it was headed by particularly courageous and talented individuals. So, I was able to reconcile anarchy and democracy, which, ultimately amounted to having men dominated by personalities, heroes. Of course, none of this was my invention; it was the spirit of the times."[10]

Charles Schweitzer's two sons had been educated not by him but by Dominican friars. Charles undertook the education of his grandson with passion, devotion, and exuberance. He left his retirement to go back to work and did not hesitate to give up the books he could have read or written after such a full professional life to do what he considered his duty. For his Poulou, he rediscovered youth, and for this Charles was infinitely grateful. This was his last card, and it redeemed his life.

"My young pupil—please, forgive a doting grandfather—is naturally and prodigiously intelligent in everything. . . . I don't think he will be a mathematician, though he is the son of a Polytechnicien. . . . It is clear that he has a particular aptitude for language—on his father's side he comes from the country of Bertran de Born—and dreams only of adventures and poetry, both useless interests in this twentieth century. He is eloquent and combative; I'm afraid that, at best, he could be a lawyer or a deputy! In the meantime, he is well, has the happiest disposition, and sings all day long." The comparison with Bertran de Born was peculiarly apt. The troubador was both writer and soldier. According to legend, Richard the Lion-hearted died beside him. In the English Aquitaine where Thiviers was a frontier town, Bertrand wrote his most beautiful poem, in the language of the South, *langue d'oc,* before he went blind and retired to an abbey in the valley of La Vézère, to spend his remaining years in meditation.

Aside from one brief experience, Poulou received no form of public education till the age of ten (when he entered the Lycée Henri IV). Bach's music, the eighteenth-century *philosophes,* a deep nostalgia for Alsace, salvation via ethics and art—these were the ideas and influences with which, almost three generations behind the times, Poulou was initiated into life. "Between the first Russian Revolution and the First World War," Sartre writes, "a man of the nineteenth century was foisting upon his grandson ideas that had been current under Louis-Philippe. . . . I started off with a handicap of eighty years."[11]

Charles Schweitzer's library contained over a thousand volumes. This is where Poulou learned to live. "Books were my birds and my nests," he writes later, "my pets, my stable and my open fields; the library was the world in a mirror." And Jean-Paul, the son of Jean-Baptiste the adventurer, threw himself into reading the way his father had at first thrown himself into the life of the navy.

It was an adult library, mostly French and German classics: the child could roam through it at leisure while his grandfather was away. Stretched out on the rug, his head propped on his elbows, Poulou would spend hours leafing through dictionaries and such compilations for adults as *The Lives of Illustrious Men,* which his Uncle Georges had received as the second prize in arithmetic twenty years earlier. *Les Misérables, La Légende des siècles, Madame Bovary,* all the classics of French literature, all the books of Greek history passed through his hands. Here, in this reading room, the child first learned about great men, and in a very particular fashion, which would remain Sartre's all his life: he read them, recognized them, kept their company, and addressed them naturally, as a friend, with the ease of those who aren't put off by obstacles, feeling on equal footing with geniuses: Hugo, Voltaire, Corneille, Racine, La Fontaine.

According to *The Words,* the child reader soon became a boastful, ridiculous child writer. But was this really, as he maintains, the direct result of his grandfather's ambitions? If Charles had pushed Poulou to write, it wasn't only to prepare him for a writer's career. In fact, there is no evidence that it was he who excited the immoderate ambitions of the child, luring Poulou to the paths of immortality. Quite the contrary. When Poulou, inspired by his precocious genius, wrote his first texts—"Pour un papillon" (For a Butterfly) and

34

"Le Marchand de bananes" (The Banana Merchant)—Charles merely shrugged his shoulders, grumbled, and slipped off. It was the others who applauded the little monster and loaded him with compliments. It was Anne-Marie who, ecstatic, read, reread, and copied her son's texts for all her acquaintances. It was Anne-Marie's brother, Uncle Emile, who immediately contributed a typewriter. It was Poulou's grandmother who warmly encouraged him to go on. And, finally, it was Mme Picard, a friend of the family, who brought a globe of the earth to inspire the child.

Sartre got very angry the day when—he must have been almost fifty then—a letter he had written, as a child, to Georges Courteline was published. It was a funny letter, but did it really reveal the monster described in *The Words*? Could it be that Sartre got so furious precisely because this letter belied the system of interpretation he had adopted in *The Words*? Here is the letter, unadorned by any commentary:

> *1, rue Le Goff, January 26, 1912*
>
> *Dear Mr. Courteline,*
>   *Grandfather told me you have been given a great decoration. It pleases me cause I laugh when I read Théodore and Panthéon Courcelle which pass right in front of our house. I have also tried to translate Théodore with my German maid but my poor nina could not understand the sence of the joke.*
>   *Your future friend*
>   *(happy new year)*
>   *Jean-Paul Sartre, 6 and 1/2 years old*

The Words is a chaste, often masked, ode to Anne-Marie. Its underlying themes remind us of the Sartrean biography: incest, creativity, immortality, the rival, seduction. Only the interpretation of the writer will later cover the tracks, mask the actors.

Politics? Men's business. History? Men's business. Poetry? Also men's business. But, thanks to Anne-Marie, Poulou also had access to amusements more suited to a child his age and which she shared with him. This is how he became acquainted with American comic books and discovered the movies. This is how they would spend long hours, the mother at the piano, the child at his games, sharing dreams and distractions.

"Lacrosse is one of the worst criminals in the United States. He beat me this time, but I won't rest till I've made him pay for it. I'm going to see him hang, that rat." Nick turned toward Chick and Patsy, and said, "I've got just enough time to catch the train for New York; see you!"

Nick Carter, "America's Greatest Detective," made his Paris debut on March 22, 1907 and was an immediate runaway success. For seven years, every Wednesday, the French public eagerly paid 25 centimes for the magazine in which the famous detective disposed of crooks, gangsters, and thugs. And all this thanks to his intuition, grit, and charm—which allowed him to win over policemen, cabbies, nurses—and his general mistrust of "stupid craven niggers." Swooping down on some Manhattan opium den, changing identities and disguises like a magician, uncovering spy rings, crisscrossing America by kayak, trolley, train, car, or horse, with a simple "My name's Nick Carter," the detective would elicit respect, admiration, and cooperation. It didn't matter if his world was Manichean, racist, and egocentric, and if his investigative techniques were intuitive, and without method; Nick Carter could sustain the suspense week after week, in "Coyote Walk," "Gold Thieves of Grubstake Mine," and "Smugglers of Detroit, Michigan." Nineteenth-century America with its sinister vacant lots, the rooftops of New York, the Bowery, Harlem, became, to the mind of the child-king, the privileged site of exoticism and adventure.

He collected the magazines, dragging his mother along through the *bouquinistes* of the Quai des Grands Augustins, who sold old issues at reduced prices. Soon, with the help of Anne-Marie, he had amassed a complete Nick Carter collection. Then, he discovered other heroes. Colonel W. F. Cody, alias Buffalo Bill, spiriting away beautiful heroines on his steed and protecting convoys against the "attacks of Indians always lusting after blood and loot," soon became, with Nick, the child's new idol. And so did Texas Jack, "scourge of the Indians," in constant pursuit of outlaws, bandits, and desperados, and so did the brave and noble Sitting Bull.[12]

The Knight of Pardaillan and his epic adventures, as told by the novelist Michel Zevaco, similarly inflamed the young reader's imagination. From America, the child passed to Spain, where the fiery, solitary knight, proud and free, in revolt against all authority, is forever confronting his sworn enemy, Princess Fausta. "Pardaillan was my master," Sartre was to write. "Firmly planted on my spindly legs, I slapped Henry III and Louis XIII."[13] More or less at the same time, Poulou makes the intoxicating discovery of a new art, film. With Anne-Marie, he experiences the joy of matinees, in the dark of a former legitimate theater, where a pianist improvises accompaniments to the adventures on the screen, supporting Pardaillan, in Seville, pursuing Nick Carter in New York, or intensifying the fear of the Parisian shadow, Fantomas, implacable enemy of society.

"The war years were the happiest of my childhood. My mother and I were the same age and were always together. She called me her knight attendant, her little man. I told her everything."[14] With their intimacies, linguistic rituals, adolescent complicities, they are a perfectly harmonious couple: "One day, on the quays, I came upon twelve numbers of Buffalo Bill that I did not yet have. She was about to pay for them when a man approached. He was stout and pale. . . . He stared at my mother. . . . 'They're spoiling you, kid, they're spoiling you. . . .' I noticed the maniacal look on his face, and Anne-Marie and I were suddenly a single, frightened girl who stepped away."[15] Picture the mother, ecstatic before her child, still with his baby curls, snapping photos, retouching them, learning to draw to heighten the haughtiness of his cheekbones, the sensuality of his mouth, the pride in his expression, the gold of his hair, his sophistication, his delicacy.

Grandfather Schweitzer encouraged a kind of polygamy in the boy that remained with him ever after. Whenever Poulou played with a girl his own age, in Vichy or Arcachon, Charles would boast about his grandson's new "fiancée." At Thiviers, the honor fell to his first cousin, Annie Lannes, Aunt Hélène's daughter. They were similar in age, personality, culture, curiosity. Every time Poulou wrote his Thiviers grandmother, he would tell her how much he missed Annie, and that he would certainly visit her the following summer. Between the two cousins there was real affection, a childhood love affair of sorts. Eighteen months older, Poulou took care of Annie like a protective older brother, a gallant companion. The two children spent their vacations together and the rest of the year exchanged letters and presents. He gave her dolls, she gave him books, and often he would venture an opinion as to his cousin's choice of toys: "I have such a horrible memory of Ninie's lumpy doll that I am sending her another one on condition that she tosses out her beloved baby," he wrote to his grandmother. These childish games continue throughout adolescence. Later, in 1938, "Anny" will be the heroine of Sartre's first book, *Nausea*, the most positive female character in his entire oeuvre.

. . .

The Schweitzer women successfully introduced Poulou to
and until the age of twelve, he was a believer. His faith was fos
by the Abbé Dibildos—who had married his parents—and Po
was assigned long reports on the life of Christ. The subject of religion was somewhat delicate as it was represented, on one side, by
a Protestant grandfather violently allergic to popes and priests, on
another by a grandmother who was, almost despite herself, more
freethinker than Catholic, and, on a third side, by a mother who was
moved whenever she heard an organ recital or a Bach cantata in
Notre-Dame, though she did not know whether it was because of
her love of God or of music. During Poulou's vacations with the
Magondeaux in Thiviers, she would write him "not to offend anyone, and to conform to Catholic practices." And yet, on August 15,
during a ceremony to the Virgin Mary, the child forgot the words
of the act of contrition he was supposed to recite to his confessor,
and at school a few years later, in 1920, he miraculously lost his faith.

On the whole, Poulou was forced to perform a difficult balancing
act between the protective, generous young man Charles wanted to
form in his image, and the androgynous child whose hair the women
loved to curl. One day, in 1912 or 1913, Charles decided to assert his
power, decided his grandson would no longer look like a little girl,
a sissy: without informing anybody, he had Poulou's hair cut. Suddenly Anne-Marie lost her soft, golden creature. "I looked like a
toad," the object of these conflicts later noted.

M EANWHILE, ANNE-MARIE had other battles to fight. Jean-Baptiste's estate had not yet been settled. His brother, Joseph, kept
avoiding the necessary administrative steps, including signing documents, authorizing proceedings, and conferring powers-of-attorney.
Anne-Marie tried to assert her rights with kindness, at first, then
more and more firmly. This long bureaucratic-legal struggle may
explain, at least partly, why Anne-Marie's maternal love soon became so passionate and possessive. Poulou, in turn, was divided
between two Schweitzers who invested in him all that life had taken
from them. Deprived of his sons, Charles found the ideal pupil in
Poulou. Deprived of her husband, her rights of custody in limbo,
Anne-Marie was left alone with her son, who became the only man
in her life. So, whether by pedagogical overinvestment or emotional
excess, two strong, aggressive adult wills ended up grappling over

the head of the child. Grandmother Schweitzer, Louise, was often moody or irritable because of Anne-Marie's increasing control over her home. Poulou managed as best he could: he became his grandfather's double and his mother's husband. At five, he was at once sixty-two and thirty years old.

"Dear Mother," Anne-Marie wrote to her mother-in-law, "Poulou has bronchitis, which is keeping him in bed. The doctor will certainly allow him to get up by tomorrow, but he won't be able to go back to the lycée, at least not this winter; even if schoolwork is like a game for Poulou, he must not be exposed to those murderous drafts." "At the moment he is doing well," Grandfather Schweitzer wrote, "and we are relieved after seeing him so weak for so long." He was a sickly child, skinny, frail, often ill with the flu, bronchitis, ear inflammations. Difficult to pierce the language of illness in a child, to deduce its possible causes and consequences, to determine the real meaning of his weaknesses. This state of unstable health did not last, but following a bout with the flu, he developed a sty in the right eye; he was only four years old, and he would never again use that eye.

While Poulou was probably finding an antidote to madness in pride and illness, Anne-Marie was involved in a tiresome correspondence with Thiviers. At Jean-Baptiste's death, a few oversights had occurred in the settlement of the will, and Anne-Marie had been unable to recover some of the assets from her dowry. To receive the 100 francs resulting from the maturation of her Indochinese bonds, she had to obtain power-of-attorney from both her father-in-law and her brother-in-law. At first, her letters were polite and confident: "You can be sure that I will never do you the slightest wrong"; then they became a little more apprehensive: "Your silence surprises me"; then progressively more annoyed and wounded: "You accuse me of having sent a letter to your notary without first informing you"; and finally quite combative: "If it had not been very *urgent* for me to establish my situation as guardian, I never would have brought up any of these questions." The relations between Paris and Thiviers deteriorated so rapidly that they soon continued only through intermediaries, M. Hellier, a friend of the Sartres, and Doctor Durieux, Jean-Baptiste's best friend. "For everybody's good, this rupture should be healed as soon as possible," both declared without forgetting to add that Mme Sartre's "only wish is to solve this whole matter" and that she had "no other desire but that of bringing up her child."

In October 1913, at the age of sixty-eight, Doctor Eymard Sartre died, and an extraordinary number of people came to Thiviers to attend his funeral. He was buried in the family vault, a white marble mausoleum adorned with a huge cross, next to the families Theuliers and Chavoix and to his son, "Jean-Baptiste Sartre, Navy Ensign." From all over the Southwest of France, more than two hundred letters of condolence arrived, confirming the extraordinary popularity of the "good doctor," "whose entire life had been devoted to the service of humanity." All the illustrious people of the region, mayors, prefects, subprefects, deputies, senators, general counselors, justices of the peace, lawyers, barristers, notaries, as well as the entire local aristocracy and the parish priests, abbés, canons, vicars, mother superiors, doctors, assistant doctors, military doctors, pharmacists, bank directors, and professors, all sent letters. It was like a long procession of people come to mourn and tell the widow, over and over again, how this third loss in so short a time—her mother, her younger son, her husband—was cruel, but that there were compensations: after all, Doctor Sartre had died a Christian. Strangely enough, however, while several letter writers mentioned little Annie, none thought of Jean-Baptiste's son, the only descendant still bearing the name of Sartre, even though he came to the funeral with Anne-Marie.

With Doctor Sartre's death, Poulou's surrogate guardian also disappeared. So, on September 22, 1913, the justice of the peace of Thiviers decided that the vacant role would now be filled by Jean-Baptiste's brother, Joseph Sartre: Poulou was then seven, Uncle Joseph was forty-four, and for the next four years, the presumed family idiot became, along with Anne-Marie, the legal guardian of the child prodigy. "The weather has been disastrous," Joseph wrote sometime in 1910. "If it gets better the harvest won't be bad, but, at this stage, we need a lot of heat and absolutely no rain to reinforce the soil; and the wheat is already yellowing. Mme Comet should really not play such nasty tricks on us. We saw her last night." Between the solar eclipse of August 30, 1905, which he watched, like an astronomer, from the balcony of his bedroom, and the comet of June 1910, between a harvest and a rain, a vintage and a regional market, Joseph continued to lead the life of a country man, assisting his mother, writing to his sister, tending the family farms. The breach between Anne-Marie–Poulou and Élodie-Joseph actually occurred much faster, and much more naturally than one would have expected. "It's been a long time," Grandmother Sartre writes, "since I have had any news from 'You' and Poulou. Of course, I could always write her, but what can I tell her?" At times she exhibits bitterness: " 'You' travels everywhere, everywhere, that is, except to Thiviers." And Joseph writes: "She has just returned from Vichy and is already thinking of spending September with her parents by Lake Lucerne: I guess this will help teach Poulou geography!" "I don't know whether I'll be able to visit Thiviers this year," the offender writes her sister-in-law Hélène. "I would like to receive some news from 'maman'; I don't exactly spoil them with my correspondence, but they are even more silent than I!"

On April 14, 1917, Anne-Marie requested a meeting of the board of guardians to solve the problem of the custody of Jean-Paul Sartre, then eleven. The decision somewhat reassured her: "In response to Madame Sartre's concern for her child, the board of guardians has decided that, given the respectability of M. Mancy, former general manager of the navy and current president of the Delaunay-Belleville plant in La Rochelle, Mme Sartre can now assume full custody of her son, with the assistance of the above-mentioned M. Mancy, to whom we hereby confer the title of co-guardian."

Anne-Marie was remarrying, another Polytechnicien, a fellow graduate of her brother Georges. Joseph Mancy was the son of a railway employee on the Paris–Lyon–Marseilles line. The pension of military widow that she had been able to extract from the Council of State was not very generous. Now Anne-Marie would be fully supported in her maternal struggles, backed by a solid income. It took six months of wrangling between the Department of the Navy, the Council of State, and the Superior Council of Health to answer the question of whether Ensign Sartre succumbed to a relapse of his first illness or whether, definitely recovered from his tropical enterocolitis, he had died of tuberculosis. The debate hinged on whether Anne-Marie Schweitzer had deliberately married a man she knew would die in order to inherit his pension. On July 13, 1907, her request was granted: she would receive 833 francs a year for herself and her son. In 1917, with her second marriage, all her financial problems suddenly disappeared. Now rid of Thiviers, she removed Jean-Baptiste's portrait from her bedroom and, again, left the Schweitzers' household. She thought that, by so doing, she would finally possess her child for good. In fact, she was losing him.

Thus ended the Schweitzer era, which had, unexpectedly, lasted almost ten years. In his fifties, Sartre will write about those years in *The Words* and Anne-Marie, hurt, will reply, "Poulou didn't understand a thing about his childhood." Sartre was not nostalgic about his mother's family, so little so that one day, when one of his cousins sent him a Schweitzer family tree, he tossed it into the waste basket without so much as a look. After the sale of Jean-Baptiste's books, he created a fictional combat in which he pitted Schweitzer versus Sartre, the two families from which he had sprung and of which he, alone, had survived unharmed.

SCENES FROM LA ROCHELLE

> *At La Rochelle I discovered something that was going to mark the rest of my life: the most profound relationships between men are based on violence.*
> —"MATERIAUX AUTOBIOGRAPHIQUES"

THE STIFF twelve-year-old who entered the fourth grade at the public school in La Rochelle just in time for the beginning of classes in 1917, would a few years later recall the town whose magic light in early autumn attracted artists by the dozen: "La Rochelle is a five-to-six-o'clock town, an autumnal twilight town. The old port at sunset is softened by the livid evening grayness of the final rays. . . . The sky's colors encroach on the old guard towers on the Anse. . . . In the port, dense water, coated white, lies drowsing, like the black swamps of oil that automobiles drop on the pavement. The sailboats float silently, supernaturally back."[1]

For Sartre, though, life in La Rochelle was a calvary from start to finish. So much so, he never after referred to it willingly. La Rochelle was a turning point in his life, the beginning of a series of trials that took him by surprise, almost treacherously. His narcissism was rudely tested, and Poulou was suddenly rocked from the Schweitzer paradise—where nothing was too good for the cherished child—to the real world of cruel and violent teenagers who felt only contempt for this pompous little monster with his stuffy speeches, stale wit, absurd appearance, and Parisian manners.

Joseph Mancy's entrance onto the scene broke up the Schweitzer nucleus and provided Anne-Marie with financial autonomy, psychological and social support, and legal assistance in the management of her child's custody. Thus, he saved her from the ambiguous economic status of the young widow dependent on her parents. Suddenly, at thirty-four, she was married, had a house of her own, a maid, a new social life, a father for her child. In short, she had fallen into the lot common to all those women who derive their own sense of worth from the status of their husbands.

"One thing is certain, my mother did not marry my stepfather for love. Besides he was not very pleasant. He was a tall, thin man, with a black mustache, a very uneven complexion, a very large nose, rather handsome eyes, black hair. He must have been about forty."[2] Her new husband had been a schoolmate of Jean-Baptiste at the Polytechnique, but the day Mancy entered Anne-Marie's life, the photo of the unfortunate sailor in his handsome uniform disappeared from her bedroom forever. And Joseph Mancy managed to defeat Jean-Baptiste on more than one front. The latter had been able to offer only the charm of his adventures in the navy, reigning as master because of his absence. Joseph Mancy started ten years later, but he made up for lost time. Whether or not the iron master Sartre portrayed, Mancy played the role he had inherited from J.B. with a firmness his predecessor had never been able to muster. In the two opulent houses that the trio successively occupied in La Rochelle, each member had difficulty getting used to the other two: a twelve-year-old child versus the forty-three-year-old man who had taken his mother away, and a woman who was desperately trying to handle both. Joseph Mancy, the intruder, would also try to inherit Charles Schweitzer's educational role. It was an abrupt change: every evening, first in the large living room in the house on the Avenue Carnot, then in the one on the Rue Saint-Louis, Joseph Mancy felt obligated to drag his stepson into interminable sessions on geometry and algebra, which often ended in a slap.

Along with the education of his pupil, Mancy also tried to deal more effectively than Anne-Marie with Grandmother Sartre's will. She had died in 1919, leaving three heirs: Jean-Paul, his Uncle Joseph, and his Aunt Hélène. The division immediately assumed sordid dimensions: the aunt was shrewd, the uncle greedy, and Poulou had to content himself with leftovers: six towels, six teaspoons . . . And, when Anne-Marie asked her brother-in-law to reserve a few rooms at La Brégère—Joseph's part of the inheritance, which he was now going to inhabit by himself—for her and her son's vacations, Joseph refused. Mancy, acting for his wife, worked hard to reclaim his stepson's rights as well as the money for the boy's studies and even the furniture for his room. And yet, Poulou never showed him any gratitude. Jean-Paul soon realized that this authoritarian man, this strike-busting boss, this conventional bourgeois, lived in a world diametrically opposed to his own. When, fifteen years later, Sartre mentioned Simone de Beauvoir to his stepfather, Mancy refused to meet her because they were neither married nor engaged. But for the moment, Poulou, the child-king, was dethroned by Joseph Mancy, who took his queen away and relegated him to the role of usurped prince.

"Moral rigidity, the work ethic, apostolic rigor: La Rochelle is the capital of French Calvinism," the biography of a local painter states. In this ravishing provincial town, protected from the rest of the world by its towers and harbor, proud of all the chapters in all the books of French history that show it staunchly resisting the many attacks to which its Protestant faith was subjected, the best society, reserved, refined, sluggish, meets at dinners that no outsider ever attends. Ladies serve tea with the famous little pastries baked by Langlade; and every Sunday the most respectable families take long walks on the promenade, along the gardens of the casino, the exclusive club where they play bowls. La Rochelle is the epitome of the French provincial bourgeoisie: egotistically complacent, smugly secure in its pre-eminence. Behind their money, their rituals, their linguistic conventions, and their lace curtains, the locals, diffident and fastidious, are oblivious to newcomers.

At the beginning of the First World War, an American base was installed in the port of La Pallice, at the edge of town. It received 800,000 tons of weapons and 175,000 horses and mules to fight the Germans, while, at sea, German submarines were torpedoing ocean liners and fishing boats. The public school donated some space for an infirmary, which received prisoners of war, who were immediately transferred to the fortress of the Ile de Ré; the port welcomed shiploads of refugees from Belgium and the French Northeast. "What can one say about this awful war?" Charles Schweitzer raged with typical Alsatian pride: "Those abominable filthy Germans . . ." At La Rochelle, Jean-Paul Sartre first detected the traces of History in the world. There he heard about the Russian Revolution of 1917, and realized that World War I had forever eroded the nineteenth century and the legacies of his two grandfathers.

The France of Eymard Sartre and Charles Schweitzer, that fragmented, jigsaw country with no cultural unity and strong regional boundaries, had, by the end of the Great War, assumed its more modern shape, hexagonal, unified. Between the middle of the nineteenth century and Sartre's adolescence at La Rochelle, the country had undergone a period of profound and upsetting social restructuring. Sartre's grandparents were witnesses of an archaic, closed world, whose fading light would soon be completely extinguished. Its last bastions were already too weak to resist the impact of World War I. To the privilege of being fatherless, Sartre could add that of reaching maturity at the very moment when the world of his grandfathers was in its death throes. He was a child with no ties, issued from a dissolved family in a period of intense social upheaval: all these factors converged to produce in him a feeling of almost ethereal freedom, to hand him the liberating role of "nobody's child" that he would play with such relish. His only legacy was rupture.

At the La Rochelle public school, partly requisitioned by the military, Sartre was immediately noticed because of the way he dressed. Within the bourgeoisie of the town, boys wore their fathers' retailored clothes. Sartre's Parisian elegance quickly suggested the kind of difference that is seldom forgiven in a child. "Skimmed at the top" by the Collège Fénelon—where the local Catholic aristocracy sent its offspring—and deprived, at the bottom, of all those children who had to quit school in order to work, the classes of the boys' high school were still a fairly heterogeneous mix of children of the Protestant high bourgeoisie, children from the countryside (boarders, for the most part) and those of the oyster farmers and fishermen from the neighboring villages.

"A violent class," Sartre would later write. And, indeed, among the kids his age, who, having lost their fathers to the eastern front, hang out on the town's streets, the public school group is like a buffer-zone caught between two extremes: the "covacs," the students of the Fathers' school, more conventional, wiser, and in uniform, and the "hooligans," who have left school to work. These rival bands fight for their turf through the streets of the town, and Sartre, like all the other public school students, sides with the covacs. Their confrontations are brutal, real class conflicts, as might be expected in this town where one's door opens only to people of the same social class. The conflicts are even more severe in the case of the new boy, who, from the beginning, is made to feel ridiculous and out of place. To top it all, he is not growing much and so spends his time telling "tall stories."

Children are never kind, but in this intensified situation, poor Sartre got a particularly rough deal. He became the misfit, the outsider, the scapegoat—not very different from the role he had played in Thiviers; he did not like croquet, did not like playing ball or any other game, and so he was not exactly popular among the boys of the French Southwest. He was very self-conscious, unable to have fun. The only thing that attracted this little intellectual and flattered his narcissism was the discovery of the new cameras with photographic plates. It seems that Sartre loved to be photographed. "Be sure to reproduce the exact expression on my face!" he would say.[3] His reputation for being an "awful brat" followed him all the way to Périgueux, and even his favorite cousin Annie suffered from a number of Poulou's stupid tricks, during their vacations together.

"He was an irascible, cantankerous, quarrelsome boy, most unpleasant toward his peers," remembers Guy Toublanc, the youngest student in his class, still intrigued by Sartre's "belief that he was better than anybody else . . . a strange boy, often absent,"[4] who astonished the other students by publicly correcting his professor of French for having awkwardly transposed some verse into prose. At his age, he was already part of the mythology, which, as is the case more or less everywhere, always seized on the more unusual individuals. Father Loosdregt, the professor of French, a rather ridiculous man, was one of the main targets. His large, violet nose had earned him the nickname "Bluebeak"—later, he will inspire one of Sartre's first short stories, "Jesus the Owl, Small-Town Schoolteacher."

"He was an extraordinary young man," admits Gontrand Lavoissiere, one of Sartre's classmates, "a very intelligent person, who worked well and effortlessly . . . an excellent classmate, but very reserved."[5] At La Rochelle, everybody would remember him, for his character, his knowledge, and his odd manners, but everybody would forget that he was also the class fibber and scapegoat. Fantasizing about the women of the red-light district and the houses on the Rue des Voiliers, Sartre invented an intricate sex life that could hold its own against the verbal exploits of his classmates. "I told them that there was this woman with whom I went to the hotel, that I met her in the afternoon, and that we did what they said they did with their whores. . . . I even asked my mother's maid to write me a letter: 'Dearest Jean-Paul . . .' they guessed my trick. . . . I confessed . . . and became the laughingstock of the class." The struggle of the drowning man, the blunders of jealousy, the failures of a grotesque child: thinking he was defending himself, he sank ever deeper, thinking he was smarter than they, he made a fool of himself. "I still see myself, walking up and down the promenade," he continues,

"watching my classmates . . . waiting for them to call me over, to
invite me into their group. And, in the end, they would, but I'm sure
they liked to wait as long as possible."⁶ La Rochelle, the town of bad
luck. Hating the "Boches" who had taken their fathers away, the
youth of La Rochelle felt the pent-up collective violence common
to adolescents in periods of war. A violence so ready to pour out that
it might have transformed anyone into a scapegoat, particularly a
victim who had put himself at a disadvantage, as had young Sartre.

"My schoolmates at La Rochelle were much rougher and far less
cultivated than those in Paris," Sartre will note later. "They often
beat me up. Most lived alone with their mothers while their fathers
were away at the front. Their family life was very much upset by
the father's absence. . . . One classmate, the son of the drawing
teacher, went so far as to threaten his mother with a knife for having
served him potatoes at both lunch and dinner."⁷ It is at La Rochelle
that Sartre first learned about violence, and that he first looked at
the world with political awareness; it is here that he discovered
anticolonialism: "It happened spontaneously," he will explain later,
"maybe looking at the blacks, Arabs, and Chinese who were dragged
away from their countries into our factories."

In this class of nervous adolescents, in this town at war, where
nothing could relax the tensions and the conflicts—neither society
nor history nor age—the sufferings of young Sartre were genuine,
though not as bad, for example, as those of Deschênes, a scholarship
student whose mother worked as a cleaning lady in a hospital and
who nonetheless managed to take first prize in math every year. This
might help explain why, at the end of the war, Sartre suddenly
changed sides. If, in 1917, he was still siding with the rich, by 1919 he
had passed over to the other side, that of the marginals. In France,
World War I erased any traces of the aristocracy that the Revolution
had failed to bury: the child, cherished by his grandparents but
weighed down by their heavy history, also chose to start again from
zero. Having decided to erase his origins, to break with his grandfathers, he launched into a rather exaggerated battle; the battle of a
fifteen-year-old, desperate, lucid, fiercely proud, in revolt against his
stepfather, society, his own roots. World War I changed him profoundly. He had already experienced some of the worst tensions
within the society of La Rochelle. His uncle, Captain Lannes, his
cousin Annie's father, was killed in 1917 and was buried in Thiviers,
near Jean-Baptiste. The adolescent emerged out of the war years

fatherless, classless, a bastard of sorts, and an avant-gardist—in short, well-prepared to face the coming era.[8]

Between twelve and fifteen years of age, having been attacked on all fronts and having borne so many stigmas, Jean-Paul Sartre angrily poured the foundations for his new social personality. He had to summon up an extraordinary amount of energy to tear himself away from the role of the little adult, from the fragility of the spoiled child, the only child, the hothouse flower that Anne-Marie had so lovingly created and nurtured. He became lucid, painfully so, and that may well have been his salvation. "I'm a genius," he kept repeating to himself. Hate, violence, and clumsiness are the reflexes of the hunted animal: the adored prince woke up a toad; the child-king became a pitiful braggart, stumbling through a morass of failures, rejection, lies, and self-hatred. The key to all this was the usual one of incipient puberty: rivalries of boys looking for girls. Seduction was the ultimate means of saving face in provocation, competition, arm wrestling.

In 1919, he is fourteen, he is walking with his group of friends along the promenade, close by the harbor. He is waiting for Lisette Joirisse, "a ship chandler's daughter. . . . I thought her very beautiful." Sartre unwittingly confides his desire to meet Lisette. His friends promise to help, but, behind his back they warn the girl. "She set off on her bicycle along the alleys and I followed. Nothing came of it, but the next day, as I approached her, she turned toward me and, in front of my friends, said, 'Old fool, with his spectacles and his big hat.' " His friends jeer: "Looks like you're too ugly for her."[9]

The lover will also be the final role he plays at La Rochelle in his search for one last chance. A return to childhood mother-love is impossible; and the public disaster with the chandler's daughter is probably more than he can handle. His classmates are all he has left, and so he has a brilliant idea: he will seduce them with presents, and since they have a sweet tooth, his presents will be sweet, but not the banal chocolate breads from the school bakery. He will buy them babas at Langlade, on the Rue du Palais. But there is only one way to achieve his goal—by stealing money from Anne-Marie's purse. For a few weeks, the child is again king, grandiosely generous, despite a sense of guilt, until Anne-Marie discovers a large sum of money in his breast pocket: seventy francs. He tells her he stole it from a friend, as a joke. In the end, he is found out, loses face in front of his mother, his schoolmates, himself, and, to his great dismay, Grandfather Schweitzer, who refuses all explanation and even insults him by sneering at the child's zeal in picking up a coin from the floor.

Thus, stumbling from ridicule to farce, miserably unmasked after each attempt at disguise and falsification, publicly scorned in his role as seducer, what was left him but to sink back into his books? He abandoned himself to his reading, became a member of every library and reading room in town, and, steeped in adventures by Ponson du Terrail and novels by Claude Farrère, he opened himself up to new influences. Of course, he went on writing, since, by doing so, he protected himself against both his schoolmates and Joseph Mancy. "The fact of writing put me above him. . . . He thought that you shouldn't decide to take to literature at the age of fourteen. To him that made no sense. . . . So, he was always the person I wrote against. All my life."[10]

By the time he arrived at La Rochelle, the child was already a budding writer. War, violence, solitude, persecution, jealousy, failure, these instigated several autobiographical texts. His first novel, "The History of Private Perrin," told the story of a courageous soldier, who "sneaks into the German camp where the Kaiser is staying during a visit to the front. He captures him and carries him, bound and gagged, to the French camp. There, he unties him and challenges him to a boxing match. The Kaiser accepts the challenge, which will decide the outcome of the war, and proceeds to be knocked out by the valiant soldier, an excellent boxer. . . . I never finished that novel, but I was as proud of it as if I myself had won the war."[11] The second novel, "Goetz von Berlichingen," a cloak-and-dagger tale he wrote between the ages of thirteen and fourteen, served the triple function of refuge, reflection, and revenge. The title character, from the German Middle Ages, was a terrible tyrant who believed the good of his subjects depended on the constant use of the whip, a fact that will finally earn him a horrible death: his head stuck through the steeple clock in a hole at the Roman numeral XII, he will be excruciatingly aware of each passing second that brings him closer to decapitation at the stroke of noon.

Coincidentally, a few months after beheading Goetz von Berlichingen, toward the end of the summer of '21, during his last vacation at La Rochelle, Sartre himself suffered from a serious head condition. "Poulou must have caught a bad cold while swimming in the sea," a worried Anne-Marie explains to her brother-in-law, Joseph. "The abscess in his ear got worse and we had to resort to an operation—he had to be trepanned—to avoid meningitis. . . . Poulou is again walking proudly through the streets alert and strong as ever, if it weren't for his head, all bandaged up."[12] As a provocation, the sixteen-year-old leaves La Rochelle and puts himself back under Charles Schweitzer's thumb, in Paris. The child writer leaves La Rochelle "macrocephalus," a man with a bandaged brain. Another act is ended. Childhood is over. Curtain. "Besides, by now the reader should have understood that I hate my childhood and all that survived it," the author of *The Words* will write.

A THOUSAND SOCRATES

> *I distinguish three periods in my life as a young man and as a man. The first goes from 1921 to 1929 and is a period of optimism, the time when I was "a thousand Socrates."*
>
> —THE WAR DIARIES

*B*ACK IN Paris, the rebellious adolescent fibber immediately re-enrolled at the Lycée Henry IV, where he had studied for two years before moving to La Rochelle. But this time, supreme punishment, he went as a boarder: so much for girls. He was allowed to visit his grandparents only once a week, on Sunday, after singing in the morning Mass, and slept in a large dormitory with other boys from the provinces. Among the bourgeois offspring of the Latin Quarter, he found some of his classmates from three years before: Bercot, Gruber, Nizan, Frédet. Now suddenly he could measure La Rochelle's full impact by how far behind them he was in his readings. When he saw that Claude Farrère and Ponson du Terrail would never be very popular with his peers he began devouring the books they were reading: Morand, Proust, Valéry, Giraudoux. . . . In a few weeks, he had caught up with his classmates.

For this outsider, this only child, the outstanding feature of those years was his friendship with another only child, another young writer, Paul Nizan. Nizan had the advantage over Sartre of being prolific. He had already written several poems and short stories, and, in the next four years, he would publish, in school magazines and avant-garde journals, three more short stories, two poems, and four pieces of literary criticism, in which he saluted Proust, imitated

Laforgue and Giraudoux, tried his hand at dadaism, consulted Jean-Richard Bloch, and commemorated Maurice Barrès. Self-assured, precocious, mature, Nizan would enter the literary world of Paris without delay or obstacle, paving the way for Sartre.

They are sixteen, seventeen, eighteen years old, are boarders at the Lycée Henry IV, and share certain characteristics: childhoods marked by death, a precocious love of reading, and the longing for a literary career. They will naturally join forces and together invent a united front, a common manner, a common personality. From now on, for six or seven years, they will be Nitre and Sarzan, Sartre and Nizan, Nizan and Sartre. "I cannot speak of Sartre without also speaking of Nizan," Raymond Aron—who met them later—confessed when asked for a statement after Sartre's death. From now on, they will walk hand in hand, two associates, two accomplices. Sartre later says, "I could easily have drawn his portrait: medium height, black hair. He too suffered from strabismus, but whereas he was agreeably cross-eyed, I was wall-eyed, which made my face look like fallow land. He always appeared maliciously absent, even when he was paying the closest attention."[1]

Although Nizan was the grandchild, on his father's side, of submissive, illiterate Breton peasants, what he brought Sartre was the ardor, eagerness, cultural voraciousness that had become his means to success. What Sartre had received passively, Nizan had had to struggle for, amid deprivation and chaos. With the support of his hard-working father, Nizan had also benefitted from the miracles of public education under the Third Republic. Both Sartre and Nizan had been brought up in the cult of secular, republican education, but whereas for the former it was a natural right, for the latter it was a miracle. For Nizan, the social mobility he had been able to achieve through culture was his father's most precious gift. Because of this, he possessed that most exciting and irrepressible eagerness, the passion to know. Sartre was old wealth, Nizan a parvenu. All things considered, Sartre would be much more passive than Nizan.

Nizan is of average height, Sartre way below it. Nizan, delicate, refined, reserved, and elegant, strikes one with his taste in clothes. Sartre looks more like a salacious, slovenly rascal. The friendship between the two boys soon becomes brotherhood: with proper ceremony, Sartre introduces Nizan to his favorite cousin, Annie Lannes, who is living alone with her mother in Périgueux, where Nizan had spent much of his childhood. "My classmate Nizan," Sartre writes to his cousin, "has become the director of the anti-alcohol league, and would like to found a chapter in Périgueux. . . . Would it interest you?" By and by, Nizan approaches the young Annie: "I have heard," he states with complete self-assurance, "that you're most interested in the work and plans of the National League Against Alcoholism, of which I am the vice-president. . . . For the time being, the League exists only in Paris but we intend to extend to the provinces. I would be delighted if I could number you among my most gracious assistants." Between Paris and Périgueux, between the girls of the private school where Annie studies and our two Parisian boarding students, between adolescents who hardly ever meet but constantly idealize each other, a correspondence begins. One day, "John-Paul" writes "Anny" to give him a call because, as he mysteriously explains in English: "I want to talk with you about something —that, perhaps, you'll not be sorry to do." Then he launches into an account of his boarding years. He recalls "the miserable period leading up to the baccalauréat, and afterwards, disaster." He evokes "the usual inane little chores (philosophy [!] and physics), indispensable if you want to end up mouldering away in some academic post." He exults at success: "big sigh of relief after that useless, boring exam." He describes his evenings out: "I finally managed to catch *Dédé,* that operetta you once danced in, Anny . . . as they sang the couplet 'Je m'donne . . .' I thought of Thiviers and Easter holidays there." He is still the advice-dispensing big brother: "I'm sending you only one of the two papers I promised you; the other struck me as totally idiotic. . . . I kiss you, like a brother, on the forehead." And, finally, he prepares for Annie's arrival in Paris: "I hope you'll come visit me at the Normale, hospitable old hostel, where I'll be quite free. I send a tender embrace." Sartre-Nizan-Anny: interesting trio. Nizan will eventually become Annie Lanne's friend, but it is Poulou, "the good-looking cousin," who more often visits the young girls of Périgueux in their dreams.[2]

S UPPORTED BY the complicity, camaraderie, and friendship of Nizan, Sartre lands on his feet and, in just a few months, again creates an impressive persona for himself. To the members of this chosen class—Greek and Latin—in one of the best lycées of France, Sartre will soon be the "O.S."—Official Satyr. "I had long wished I were, or at least looked, dangerous," he later explains. With his irony and Gallic scorn, Sartre excels at quipping, teasing, wisecracking. And Nizan is there to back him up and inspire him. Galvanized by his own success, Sartre embarks on a long period of seductions and celebrity. His academic career is proceeding exceptionally well: he receives the Prix d'Excellence, given at the end of the year to the best student in each high school class, plus the two *baccalauréats,* as well as numerous prizes in French composition, Latin translation, and philosophy (which he shares with Nizan). According to M. Georgin, the professor of French who sees Nizan as "truly destined for literature," Sartre possesses "enormous talent and originality." Both are advised to acquire some method, to secure their grammatical background, in short, to strengthen their knowledge. Our explosive duo will soon be well known enough to desert the courses of "Cucu-philo" (M. Chabrier, their philosophy professor) and plunge into interminable discussions with the *khâgneux* (the high school students preparing for the college-level Ecole Normale Supérieure) of the famous Professor Alain. Indeed, they even manage to get invited to his courses. "Sartre and Nizan," Georges Canguilhem, one of Alain's students, remembers, "used to walk very rapidly around the schoolyard and talk, talk, talk, incessantly; and though we, Alain's *khâgneux,* were two, three, even four years older, we considered them our peers."[3] Thus discussing philosophy and literature, evoking the loves of Swann and Charlus as if they had known them personally, the two friends walk next door to the Lycée Louis-Le-Grand where they are preparing for their exams to enter "L'Ecole." Final image of their high school years: Nitre and Sarzan, drunk, joyous at their *baccalauréat,* vomit, either to win a bet or because they are carried away by the general excitement, on the feet of the principal of the Lycee Henry IV—this, at least, according to legend. Regenerated, excited, and happy, Sartre spends his summer vacation between Guérigny and La Brégère. He feels strangely optimistic and full of ideas: he is a thousand Socrates.

The *khâgneux* were never known for their propriety, but, at the Lycée Louis-le-Grand, their slovenliness is the result of a cultivated snobbery, in which, as would be expected, Sartre finds himself perfectly at home. Hands sunk in the pockets of their long sloppy gray smocks, the boarders uphold the tradition of "pure spirit" to the point of undressing as seldom as possible. Moving from the study hall to their dormitory beds involves simply removing the smock; when they get to class in the morning, they are still wearing bedroom slippers and nightshirt, with a sweater stuffed into a pair of baggy pants, and, of course, the eternal smock on top of it all. They shower once a week, and never while writing a paper. This is how boarders, semi-boarders, and day students used to spend two years in the best cases, four or five in the worst, in groups of over a hundred, on the tiers of a large amphitheater where the professors of the five disciplines that constituted the entrance examination— philosophy, French, Latin, Greek or modern languages, and history —lectured every weekday. All those students recently judged by the director of the Ecole Normale Supérieure to be "the crack regiments of the nation"—all the *prix d'excellence,* the valedictorians, those who had passed their Bac with highest honors, all the prizewinners at the *concours général*— having been selected by teachers and principals from all over the country, poured into the classes of *hypokhâgne* and *khâgne* of the Lycée Louis-le-Grand. They would thus enter the Ecole Normale Supérieure under optimal conditions and perpetuate an educational system based on both elitism and intense cramming. A true cultural lab, the *khâgne* of Louis-le-Grand deserved its reputation: every year, half the class would make it through the narrow gate of the *concours.* The several hundred yards separating Louis-le-Grand, at the corner of the Rue Saint-Jacques and the Place du Panthéon, from the Ecole Normale Supérieure, tantalizingly increased the thirst for success.

Among the provincials were several children of teachers, professors, and principals, as if the culture of the twenties had decided to continue, via spontaneous generation and as long as humanly possible, the so-called Republic of Professors that had been in force since 1878. Parisians and provincials, boarders and semi-boarders, the children of the upper middle class, faculty brats, *talas* (a term used at the school to signify most churchgoers as well as militant Catholics, "[ceux qui von]t à la [messe]") and atheists—all these people with different origins, accents, and ambitions came to sit together, first in the fall of 1922, for *hypokhâgne,* and then, in the fall of 1923 for *khâgne.* For two or three years, these boys of sixteen to nineteen would read thousands of pages, write a few hundred themselves, and listen to hundreds of hours of lectures, take notes, write essays, take exams, give oral reports, discourse on immanence and transcendence in Plato and Kant, explicate a text by Flaubert, translate Shakespeare, Homer, and Virgil, retrace the origins of the French Revolution or the Paris Commune, mired, sunk in questions from which they couldn't be pulled out by any of the techniques—exposition, discourse, explication—that they were trying to master. A greenhouse for rare plants, a well-tended nursery, a solid fortress on which the events and politics of the outside world have absolutely no impact, where nothing can threaten the tyranny of Latin prose and Greek translation. Still, the students manage to relax, as much as their pride and diligence allow, inventing farces, grouping and regrouping according to social conventions, or even because of real affinity.[4]

"Nous allons en Hypokhâgne/Travailler comme des cochons/ Cependant que—sans un pagne—/Les copains sont au boxon (bis)/ Nous faisons bien de l'Histoire/Tandis qu'ils p'lot'nt des putains/Le calice est long à boire/Et de merde il est tout plein (bis)/A la plac' des seins de femme/Nous caressons des Bailly/Quand on a Dieu dans l'âme/On cuve ça sans un cri."* (We're going to *hypokhagne* to work like pigs while our penniless buddies go to the whorehouse. We learn history while they ride the whores. Our cup's a bottomless pit chock-full of shit. Instead of tits we caress our classical dic's. When God's in your soul, you put up with a lot.) This poem, cosigned Sartre-Nizan, indicates the kinds of sacrifices and temporary privations endured during their self-imposed exile from the world. It also indicates the two students' status at the school: during their first two years, Nitre and Sarzan had become the mascot of their class, entertaining the public whenever the professors disappeared into their lounge on the first floor. There is the mock phonograph: Sartre, standing in front of a table covered with black cloth, turns an imaginary lever while Nizan, hidden under the table, imitates the nasal sound of a song by Bruand. . . . And they involve the whole class in a linguistic game they have invented by unexpectedly mixing the solemn tone of the Comtesse de Ségur with bawdy Gallic jokes. This new concoction of theirs soon becomes the *ne plus ultra* of sophistication, a sign of recognition among the most literary Normaliens, a mark of their superiority over all those students they consider too dismally scholarly. "The Lycée was like a large barracks of pale brick," Nizan remembered, "with gold-numbered sundials, where nineteen-year-olds lived too intensely among the ancient Greeks, the Romans, idealist philosophers, and the Doctrinaires of the July Monarchy."[6]

"It was a Vosgian plateau with hirsute slopes": during these years, Sartre tries his hand at his first serious literary compositions. Spurred by Nizan, he publishes two short stories in an ephemeral literary review, *La Revue sans titre*. Both are sinister accounts of teachers'

*Cf. Jules Laforgue.[5]

lives in the provinces, detailed pessimistic portraits in which he gives free rein to his biting irony, his ability to detect and reveal meanness, his disgust at the cowardice of conventional lives. "Louis Gaillard," he writes, "had the terrible idea of reading some of his verse to his students, typical Alsatian brutes: he was booed, hit on the head by several inkpots. He became bitter and sad; during the summer vacations, he would pamper his melancholy in the serene fresh silence of the Vosges." Alsace, La Rochelle, in these writings we can retrace Sartre's own displacements, and discomforts. "Her daughter," he writes, "seemed to have inherited from her that desperate desire to be noticed. One could already sense how time, thinning her lips, yellowing and uncovering her teeth, wrinkling her cheeks, would soon turn her into a bitch just like her mother."[7] There is pleasure in this joint provocation of bourgeois, provincials, and teachers: the time has come to settle old scores. Has his reading of Bergson already had an impact? In "Jesus the Owl, Small-Town Schoolteacher," Sartre uses first-person narration to tackle once again autobiographical aspects of the La Rochelle years. Self-analysis and writing: Sartre, at age eighteen, was already experimenting with the techniques that, during his long life, would be his path to salvation.

While Sartre was writing these two stories, delving into recent history, exploring the darker areas of his young inner life, Nizan was laying the foundations for his own oeuvre with a series of more complex and ambitious short stories titled "Lament of the Medic Who Dissected His Girlfriend While Smoking Two Packs of Marylands." Whereas Nizan seemed to be asserting himself with his early writing, Sartre, mired in autobiographical narratives, resorted to hiding behind the borrowed maiden name of his maternal grandmother (the pseudonym of Jacques Guillemin).

Then one day, by chance and much to his dismay, reading an article by Nizan, Sartre comes across a reference to an idea he communicated to his friend a short time earlier. "That beast," he complains to his friend Frédet, "he's really gone too far!" There are already two definite styles, two personalities, two distinct literary profiles: Sartre, bogged down in his personal discoveries, completely devoted to self-decoding, writing texts that are egocentric through lack of distance; Nizan, more elegant and daring, perhaps even more precocious, moved by an urgency Sartre seems not to feel.

During the time of their actual quarrel, Sartre writes "The Seed and the Aqualung," in which he tells, quite overtly, the story of their friendship. "It was more tempestuous than a love affair. I was tough, jealous, inconsiderate, like a maniacal lover. Lucelles, independent and sly, seized every opportunity to cheat on me, and often invented pretexts to disappear. He went so far as to invent some friends for himself. He had a brief crush on an Algerian Jew and then on a guy from Marseilles. On those occasions, for days he would try to avoid me. I couldn't stand it. Then, tired of strangers, he'd come crawling back. He would again find me aggressive and irritable, even though, inwardly, I was choking on the tenderness I couldn't express."[8]

In this typical adolescent friendship, possessive and exclusive, who could have guessed, looking at the odd couple, Gaul and dandy, that it was Nizan, independent and sly, who had hurt Sartre? Who would have thought that Sartre, with his verbal ease and his mocking aggressiveness, experienced the pain of rejection? In a complete reversal of roles, Sartre pulls out all the stops, while Nizan buries himself in his books, deriving all the verbal aggressiveness, the laughter, the scorn, and the cynical power he formerly lacked, seduced by Sartre's new and provoking brutality. One is silent, the other one vociferous, one elegant, the other slovenly, one calm, the other violent, and so it will go until 1927. Nizan relishes Sartre's taking on the whole world, playing the role of the Grand Inquisitor. They take interminable walks through Paris. They encounter Rastignac in Montmartre, or Proust at the Rondpoint des Champs-Elysées, experiencing, as if they were characters in novels, the Quai d'Orsay, Sainte-Chapelle, the avenues of the Bois de Boulogne. "We would walk through Paris," Sartre recalled, "like two supermen taking advantage of their adolescence to perfect their myths and theories. At times, a third superman would join us, some friend or other: Nizan and I knew he didn't have a trace of the superman, but out of kindness we let him think he did. . . . Actually, we loved humanity. . . . Paradoxically, the notion of the superman had fostered in us the idea of equality. We hadn't yet become average men, I thought, like those vast crowds we, at times, joined. They remained inferior to us, but we were profoundly equal to each other, and to all the other supermen of the world, whom we did not know, and who did not know us, but who must surely have existed in the provinces, or somewhere. So we were members of a club of equals of which we knew only two members, ourselves. In a way, these ideas were the result of both a slightly Nietzschean aristocratism and the vaguely egalitarian notion of a society that did not exist."[9]

"SAY, THIS is really fine; write it down in your notebook . . . if only to have a good laugh at it later." Amused and ceremonious, Sartre returns the little notebook in which, every day, his friend Frédet records citations and thoughts inspired by his readings, his discoveries, his passions. There, Montherlant, Proust, Hâfiz coexist with Saint-John Perse, Giraudoux, the Hebrew alphabet, cuneiform characters, and hieroglyphs. In the euphoria of discovery and eclecticism, Sartre will become an avid devotee of this notebook, which he will read, reread, and copy, using it as a source for new ideas. With Frédet, a surgeon's son, who shares with him the cultural ease of the Paris bourgeoisie, Sartre seeks out the period's most avant-garde texts.[10]

This intense eclecticism, this relentless dilettantism continue till Colonna d'Istria, their unforgettable professor of philosophy—"a cripple terribly shrunken, much smaller than I"—suggests reading *Time and Free Will* as background material for a dissertation on duration. Sartre will never become completely Bergsonian, and yet, during these years of intellectual gestation, Bergson will indisputably play a crucial, intense, revelatory role: "In Bergson, I immediately found a description of my own psychic life." After this discovery of an instrument far more powerful and useful than any he has yet encountered, Sartre will become a philosopher almost by necessity. He will attribute extreme omnipotence to what he calls philosophy, even though his definition of the term is strictly and exclusively personal, as he will later admit: "What I at that time called 'philosophy' was actually 'psychology.' "[11] The reading of Bergson meant the discovery of a center. Philosophy would become his supreme tool, and an ideal assistant allowing him simultaneous access to two privileged fields of interest: the psychic life of the budding writer, and the fictional world he was going to create. Secure in his possession of this magic key, Sartre began to prepare for his entrance examination to the Ecole Normale Supérieure.

M. Colonna d'Istria had good reason to be proud: of the twenty-eight candidates accepted by the ENS, half had passed through his hands in the *khâgne* of Louis-le-Grand. "I am delighted to have this opportunity to express my warmest congratulations to you," he writes to Nizan on August 28, 1924. "The results of the *concours* have pleased me enormously. . . . At the Ecole, you will belong to a group of new philosophers whom I will delight in following through all the success that awaits you."[12] As for success, he was absolutely certain his wishes would come true. What he could not know was that our two brilliant *khâgneux* would share their future laurels with several other philosophers in the same class, Raymond Aron and Daniel Lagache, both students at the Lycée Condorcet.

*T*HEIR FIRST contact with the Ecole Normale Supérieure was something of a shock: "The conditions of life at the Ecole violate the most elementary hygienic norms. The dormitory is practically never aired or swept. Dust grows under the beds, impregnates our clothes, saturates the air we breathe. Our morning ablutions take place in the most primitive conditions: lucky are those who manage to keep a small wash bowl on their windowsill! Otherwise, one has to manage with a tiny faucet dripping into a filthy sink in the same closet where we brush our shoes and keep our brooms and garbage cans. The food is acceptable, but the service isn't: the plates and forks are poorly washed and caked with dark sediment—a marvelous vehicle for germs."[13] In 1924, this exclusive nursery, the object of years of work, is even dirtier and more dilapidated than Louis-le-Grand. The students hurriedly spoon their breakfast out of soup bowls, and drinks are available during meals only to those who have brought their own tumblers. Behind the iron gate at 45, Rue d'Ulm, there is a tall square building with endless hallways, ninety-degree angles that muffle all echoes, and a glassed-in inner court that fills up with roses every spring and in whose celebrated pool ancient goldfish dart beneath a jet of water. Within this enclosed bowl, young Normaliens, these disembodied minds, pure spirits, journey through the lengthy corridors every time they leave their living spaces for class. In 1924, the Ecole Normale Supérieure is one of the most prestigious institutions in the country, flag-bearer of a typically French tradition probably unique in all the world: that of the Great Schools. Due to the puritanical snobbism of intellectuals or perhaps the budgetary restrictions of the postwar period, all complaints of material hardship soon dim as the new system of studies, relationships, and readings, of networks, codes, and rituals is established, creating the friendships and enmities of the next four years.

" 'Tu es un conquistador!' 'Dis plutôt un con qui t'adore!' " (You're a contender! You mean, a tender cunt!) Disguised as Gustave Lanson—the principal of the Ecole Normale Supérieure—with white beard, pith helmet, and spats, Sartre was a hit during his very first months at the Ecole. "On Saturday, March 28, 1925, the Theater of the Folies Normaliennes presents the spectacular show: 'La Revue des Deux Mondes, ou le Désastre de Lan-son.' " The audience of parents, professors, and marriageable faculty daughters is most amused by these jokes, puns, raillery: everything is allowed to Normaliens.

Second Act: his eyes amorously glued on those of Daniel Lagache, who—with a French twist, a flowered blouse, and a long gypsy skirt —impersonates Dona Ferentes,[14] Sartre sings a song about "the streetwalkers in their boas,"[15] with all its double entendres. Together with Canguilhem and Lagache, Sartre and Nizan made the rounds of all the secondhand stores, from the Marais to Place Pigalle, to find costumes and exotic accessories. Everything is designed to poke fun at the new Normalien mania: the pursuit of careers in large international organizations like the League of Nations, a vogue that the scene involving Lanson's seduction by Dona Ferentes, a wealthy, plump, alluring Brazilian, is supposed, gently and metaphorically, to mock. The music is professional, with Sartre at the piano—"The Schweitzers are born musicians!": Charles Schweitzer—the costumes are suggestive, the lines full of literary allusions and Gallic license. The families of the professors laugh softly; now and then, their daughters, in their Sunday best, delicately blush. Lagache, in drag and outrageous makeup, is at least three heads taller than the bearded Sartre, who is now flinching under the attack of the Brazilian bombshell. The seduction scene is about over when the door at the back of the room opens and their excellencies M. Edouard Herriot, the prime minister, M. Paul Painlevé, chairman of the Chamber of Deputies, and M. François Albert, secretary of public education, enter and take seats in the front row. All three are former students ("archicubes," in Normalien), respectively the products of the classes of 1891, 1883, and 1898. With their three-piece suits and chain watches, these dignified members of the Coalition of the Left smilingly applaud the jokes of an unknown, twenty-year-old Jean-Paul Sartre. What else can one say about this elitist complicity that, for the length of a social evening, brings together such different people, with opposing convictions, simply because of a ridiculous yet powerful tie, the address: 45 Rue d'Ulm?

On this occasion, Normalien spirit plays a crucial role for a man like Edouard Herriot, because today he is only a prime minister on a reprieve. Since the accession of the left to power, on May 24, the financial crisis and a number of managerial mistakes have accelerated the political decline that will result in Poincaré forcing him to resign, on April 10 of the following year. "What a surprise," Georges Canguilhem kept repeating to himself in the wings while jotting down a short text to greet the illustrious guests. In a few minutes, he scribbled a few lines of verse, variations on the theme of "The Little Wooden Soldier," which charmed the professors, enchanted their daughters, and delighted Herriot—all in all, a great success. Then the desks were moved and drinks were poured. Only when Herriot climbed onto a table and started speaking did some begin to feel they had solved the mystery of his visit. Up there, surrounded by parents, professors, and actors, he sang a song he had sung the day of his graduation. But this song was not a gratuitous gesture, in the spirit of a young, irreverent Normalien. Rather, it expressed his desire—unconscious or deliberate—to reassert his ties with his alma mater, and maybe also gain its political support.[16]

D URING THE following years, Sartre delighted in displaying his talents as actor, singer, and pianist. He had found a perfect way to put his inadequate height to good use, since all he needed was a beard and the Legion of Honor to become a perfect double of Gustave Lanson. In 1926, he even received the recognition of the press after appearing in a revue with a Proustian title: "A l'Ombre des jeunes billes en fleurs" (something like "In the Shade of Billiard Balls in Bloom"). The March 22 issue of *l'Oeuvre* read, "A student by the name of Sartre brilliantly essayed the role of M. Lanson," and featured a photo of the young actor. On the other hand, the Revue of 1927 went down in the school's annals as the nastiest, most violent, most scandalous ever. Sartre was very likely involved in it. Rifts had appeared in the close-knit Normalien milieu, first of all on the issue of religion—between the "talas," and their non-Catholic and atheist counterparts, the "patalas"—and then politics. Socialists, communists, valoisians, there were enough groups to suit any taste. Sartre joined the patalas and the pacifists, a minority group essentially consisting of Alain's former students, all quite fervent when the subject turned to the army and World War I. Their vehemence reached extreme proportions in 1927 when they revolted against the Paul Boncour law, which proposed to "reorient the nation's intellectual resources toward the national defense." They drew up a petition for which they managed to collect fifty-four signatures representing nearly all the classes and disciplines of the school. Finally, they focused the entire Revue of 1927 on the Ecole's resistance to "militarization." That year, the main actors were Sartre, of course, and a few other known Alainiens: Canguilhem, Peron, Lebail, Lucot, and Broussaudier.

To the tune of *La Marseillaise*— scandal!—a student disguised as an army captain expresses his pride in a very particular form of bellicose cynicism: "Je suis entré dans la carrière/Quand le métier avait du bon/On pouvait espérer la guerre/Et gagner pas mal de galons . . ." (I joined the army. It offered several perks. You could always hope for war while earning a couple of stripes.) The point is driven home even harder to the tune of *Le Temps des cerises:* "Mais quand reviendra la guerre bénie/Lieut'nants, colonels, députés, séna-teurs/Seront tous en fê-ê-te."[17] (But when we get back our lovely war, then, lieutenants, colonels, deputies, and senators will all be justly jubilant.) The first rehearsal is greeted by a few hisses, but the first public performance causes a real uproar: the hall is filled with violent protest against this band of "tyrannical blackguards who enjoy harassing people under the pretext of pacifism." Some students boo, others get up and leave. A real scandal. A few days later, the press gets hold of the matter and Gustave Hervé, a journalist of *La Victoire,* pulls no punches in attacking these arrogant members of the French intellectual elite who besmirch the French flag and vilify the French army with impunity. Gustave Lanson lost his only son in World War I and has since lapsed into a depression that, it is ru-mored, has caused him to lose all interest in mundane matters. But the scandal caused by the Revue of 1927 hits him directly: court of inquiry, disciplinary counsel, the students are blamed, the press is suspected, the reputation of the school is threatened. The gentle mockeries of 1925 and 1926 have been replaced by an act of subver-sion. The traditional folklore of respectable Normaliens has ex-ploded, without any tact, in this bomb, this gob of spit in the face of the principal. "Party propaganda and social hatred," notes the military report, which labels the perpetrators "R P," Revolutionary Party.

During his first years at the Ecole, Sartre was the fearsome instiga-tor of all the revues, all the jokes, all the scandals.[18] On one occasion, he sent a letter to the police accusing a fellow student of having murdered a woman, the wife of a diplomat, whose body had recently been found in the neighborhood. Some time later, with the help of Maurice Larroutis, Jean Baillou, Louis Herland, and Nizan, he spread the news that the famous Charles Lindbergh had been named an honorary student at the ENS. The press is summoned, the event announced in all the papers. In no time, that part of the Rue d'Ulm that goes from the Rue Rataud to the Rue Claude-Bernard is jammed with journalists, photographers, spectators. "We asked Bérard, who looked a bit like Lindbergh, to climb out his window, slide down a lamppost onto the Rue Rataud, and come back to the school a quarter hour later, by cab. As soon as he arrived, we gave him a terrific ovation, grabbed him by the shoulders, and carried him around in triumph. The public followed us; an old gentleman kissed 'Lindbergh's' hands. Meanwhile, a piano and two violins struck up *La Marseillaise* and the public joined in. Little by little, the crowd dispersed and when Bérard left to get to one of his classes, the only people remaining were three policemen, who tailed him the rest of the morning."[19] An investigation is immediately started, the evening papers toss "a few barbs in the direction of Lanson," and the principal of the Ecole Normale resigns.

How directly was Sartre responsible for Lanson's departure and the damage to the school's image? Did Sartre really try to provoke Lanson as a personal challenge, from the moment he entered the Ecole, or did he merely follow a general movement, initiated by others? For Sartre, to attack Lanson was not merely to attack a banal expression of authority; it meant casting into doubt the summit, the reference point, the very "patron of the French language," to use Charles Péguy's terms. Since the beginning of the century, Lanson had accumulated power, first as the author of a scholastic manual that revolutionized the methods, techniques, and subjects of all high school courses in French literature; then as the founder of an historical approach to literary research, and finally as an influential critic. He had addressed all sorts of audiences, from the most erudite to the most popular, mastering all forms of expression, from journalism to scholarship via biography and hermeneutics. Lanson had readers everywhere. Sartre's own professors had been formed by him; the books on French literature Sartre studied had been written by him. Lanson had abolished the teaching of rhetoric from all university and high school programs in favor of literary history. He had dealt the death blow to the tradition of subjective analysis. He had scrapped the authors of the seventeenth century, such as La Bruyère and Fénelon, in favor of those of the Enlightenment, such as Voltaire and Diderot. Indeed, what Sartre attacks, through Lanson, is that very tradition to which he will remain one of the most talented, as well as the most violently rebellious, heirs. Let's not forget this image of Sartre mocking Lanson in front of the prime minister: it is the Republic of Professors against the Republic of Letters, the old guard witnessing the jokes of the new generation. This image of a provoking, disrespectful, subversive Sartre recurs again and again, like a leitmotif, throughout his life. Nor should we forget that behind the pedagogical attributes Sartre ridiculed in his caricature of Lanson loomed Charles Schweitzer's haughty profile.

What hid behind that clowning façade? What quest underlay the cruelty of that short, hirsute, clumsy man? What depths lay within that broad-backed swaggerer, who had developed formidable muscles in the school gym so he could box and wrestle, the most brutal and aggressive sports?[20] What else hid behind his reputation, his prestige, and a renown that others must have, perhaps secretly, envied him? Was it his mythic novel that people spoke of with shining eyes?[21] Was it that superb, strong voice of his, or his improvisational talents at the piano—which he taught in the music room—the combined talents of the born musician, actor, writer, scenarist, and instigator? Sartre had presence; his entrance into the dining hall was inevitably greeted by a resounding "Sartre!" followed, after a few seconds of suspense, by a new outburst: "et Nizan!" Conversely, this community of young men provided him with friends and a public, which made him happy. After two years of intense cramming and competition—first in *hypokhâgne* and then in *khâgne*—the Ecole Normale brought him a feeling of freedom, and euphoric lightness that might be sufficient explanation for everything that happened there.

During these years of uncertainty, in a country that will celebrate the anniversary of the Great War with a long roll of the drums, and where Poincaré is again hailed as the strong man, the man sent by Providence, Normaliens read and explore, trying to find, in the instability of the French government, footholds from which to build a political identity. The "Jean Jaurès circle" brings together socialist students, organizes meetings, discussions, and debates, often with famous political personalities. The school's gate admits, one after the other, Léon Blum, Marcel Cachin, and Marc Sangnier—an ex-Polytechnicien who, by alphabetical chance, appeared next to Jean-Baptiste Sartre in the 1895 graduation photo. On November 25, 1924, the group of socialist students will attend a demonstration during the conveyance of Jaurès's ashes to the Panthéon: Herriot delivers the address and then introduces some Normaliens to several political figures, including Léon Blum. The mastermind behind all these events is Lucien Herr, the school librarian who, although he retires in June 1925, will leave a very strong mark on the members of the circle as both a socialist and a "Dreyfusard." Some of the socialist students of those times, such as Georges Lefranc or Raymond Aron, later support the Coalition of the Left, independent of their ties with the French Socialist Party. Later, at the National Assembly, Aron witnesses as a spectator the budgetary debates between Herriot and Poincaré throughout 1926. "Wild with joy" at the victory of the coalition, Aron enjoys demonstrating through the streets of Paris, particularly when it is against the students from the right-wing Action Française. Aron reads *L'Oeuvre, Le Quotidien, Le Temps,* papers that contribute to his political identity, and he dreams of an eventual Franco-German reconciliation.[22] As for Sartre, he shares neither the rebellious romanticism of Nizan nor the realistic reflections of Aron. Spontaneously anarchic, Sartre feels no interest either in institutional political parties or in parliamentary debates. He does not participate in demonstrations or read the papers, does not get all fired up by causes, and can lose no illusions, having none to start with. Among his pacifist friends, he finds a verbal violence and an ironic distance that well suit his character. He takes advantage of these four years at the Ecole Normale—which he will later remember as "four years of happiness"—by engaging in a long self-analytical exploration.

While, in 1926, Jean-Paul Sartre, disguised as Lanson, uses revues, songs, and pranks to get back at authority, active pedagogy, his grandfather's generation, the French army, and a few other private bêtes noires, and while, excited by his reading of Cocteau, the dadaists, and the surrealists, he starts inventing a higher form of esthetic violence, Paul Nizan leaves for a long trip: England, Egypt, Ethiopia, and, finally, Aden, where he finds work as a tutor in a French family. It will be a cathartic journey, a rupture: on his return, he is different. On Bastille Day, 1926, after an evening with his friends, Nizan writes to a girlfriend: "It was our national holiday: my friends have dragged me along through the streets—Sartre, Péron, Larroutis, Cattan, and I. But the era of this group is over. It was no longer five friends walking together but rather Sartre and Péron and Nizan, each being with the others only for lack of anything better to do. By midnight, Larroutis and Sartre were drunk, and so was Cattan. Péron and I did not find it funny. We left and went back home."[23] Nizan is twenty-one. Soon he will get married, have children, join the Communist Party, and pursue his career as a journalist and a writer. But first, he violently repudiates the years spent at the Ecole Normale, the systems of a school "presumed normal and so-called superior," its professors, its students, its premises. "If anyone wants to know why I remained there, it was out of laziness, uncertainty, and ignorance of any trade, and because the state fed me, housed me, lent me free books, and gave me an allowance of a hundred francs a month."[24]

In 1924, when they chose to stay together in the "hole" they shared with a few others, they were still Nitre and Sarzan. Just as they were still Nitre and Sarzan in the pranks they played on the rest of the world and in their reading, which fused them into a superior impenetrable couple, or when, as an act of provocation, they pinned Mussolini's portrait on a wall of their room,[25] and even when, a little too high and a little too merry, they provoked each other into a heated discussion, at La Baronne's—a rather banal café on the Rue Guy-Lussac, where they plotted most of their pranks by phone and which they cherished because it afforded them the luxury of answering, whenever questioned as to where they had been spending their time: "But where else, La Baronne!"

The Nitre-Sarzan cell will split without drama or hatred, but rather with the languor of a slow drifting apart, as often happens with certain couples, when silence builds up and each turns naturally toward his own interests and away from the other with both determination and fondness. Sartre developed other friendships and, during Nizan's trip to Aden, lived with Aron and Pierre Guille. With Aron, he shared the status of not being on a scholarship, four students in their class having been judged, given the financial resources of their families, as too well-off to receive the modest stipend of 100 francs a month that their classmates used as pocket money. Lecoeur, Bérard, and the other two received only free room and board. But, like the others, they also went "tapir chasing," a favorite sport of most Normaliens, looking for private tutees to help them make ends meet by teaching Latin, English, or literature. That's how Nizan ended up among royalists in a Vendée castle, and then in the family of a rich trader on their way to Aden. Guille "tapirized" a young Parisian, Albert Morel, and then proceeded to fall in love with the boy's mother. And when he brought Sartre along, Sartre fell in love as well.

"The little man is playing possum again," Pierre Guille tells Raymond Aron. They have concocted a strategy to figure out what Sartre really thinks of their work. "One of Sartre's peculiarities," Raymond Aron remembers, "was that he could not stand any direct confrontation, so that, in order to know what he really thought of my papers, I had to ask Guille, who would then collect the information and convey it to me. . . . And yet, I don't think it would have bothered me," he adds, "if he had told me that an essay of mine was no good. Once he liked something I had written on Rousseau, another time he did not care for the way I had broached a question of psychology. He was perfectly right in both cases; still, I wish he had told me himself!" So, these sensitive young men develop a code whereby "the little man" is either "playing possum" or "in the mood for compliments," depending on whether his confidences to the third member are negative or positive. There is absolutely no constraint, however, in their philosophical exchanges, the interminable duels that Guille, a man of letters, often witnesses between his two philosopher friends. According to Aron, "He had a new theory every week, every month. . . . He would present it to me, and I would discuss it. He was the one who developed ideas, and I was the one who discussed them. On the other hand, if I never presented him with any theory it was simply because I had none. So, he would try an idea on me, and if it did not work, he would pass on to the next one. When he felt cornered he would get angry, as when I failed to appreciate his version of a Nietzschean opposition between the absurd inertia of things and consciousness, or being-for-itself. I just couldn't see how the shadow in front of us could be meaningless matter."[26]

Those years of lofty philosophical games fostered an extraordinary complicity and complementarity between Jean-Paul Sartre and Raymond Aron. Sartre was the mad inventor, daring in his eagerness to master, know, and conquer. Aron, much more methodical, rational, and prudent, explored the universe of philosophy with the extreme keenness of his scrupulous and attentive mind. Sartre was more involved in deciphering himself, Aron deciphering the world. Sartre was more rigid, more obscure, Aron was much suppler and more willing to compromise. Sartre was the master of peremptory assertion, Aron that of refined speculation. Where Sartre liked to construct impressive visions of the world, Aron developed stronger theoretical tools. Where Sartre expounded definitive projects, Aron remained vague, merely suggesting different readings, gentleness, and prudence. What went on between the two of them during the years in which they shared the same room, the same books, and the same courses was a real match, an endless philosophical ballet. Of course, they had their quarrels, their breakups, their insults, but when, toward the end of their lives, they unexpectedly met again on the steps of a large public building, and Aron, approaching a nearly blind Sartre, addressed him as "mon petit camarade," the tenderness of their years at the Ecole, their philosophical intimacy, their friendly jousting, as well as their differences over Saint Anselmus's ontological argument—so harshly criticized by Aron in Léon Brunschvicg's class—and the notion of freedom in Kant, all these memories came flooding back into Aron's mind and erased the rest.

Behind Sartre-the-reveler, who likes parties and bawdy jokes, there is Sartre-the-worker, devouring some three hundred books a year, Plato, Schopenhauer, Kant and Spinoza, Chrétien de Troyes and Mallarmé, Nerval and Cervantes, Aristotle, Bergson, Shakespeare and Tolstoy, Maine de Biran, Erasmus and Giraudoux, Seneca, Lucretius, Saint Augustine, Casanova, Ramuz, Stendhal, and Cicero.[27] He was "a thousand Socrates," insatiable, productive, scandalous. In 1926 alone he wrote, in white heat, songs, poems, short stories, novels—including a mythological one about Ganymede and his sister Hebe, with an account of the Titans attacking Mount Olympus—and literary and philosophical essays. He even developed a "complicated theory about the role of the imagination in the artist," the prelude to a complete esthetics. And, finally, he discovered the concept of contingency.

To prepare for his exams, he studiously adopted a technique of textual assimilation popular at the time: he copied down everything. In his hurried scrawl, letters overlapped, mingling notes from his readings of Kant, Plato, Descartes, or thoughts on freedom. In 1928, he obtained certificates in Psychology and in the History of Philosophy, and the next year in General Philosophy, Logic, Ethics, and Sociology. He attended his courses without much enthusiasm, failed to recognize himself in Brunschvicg's tradition of idealist rationalism, found himself totally immune to positivist scientism, and continued the exploration of the author who had first attracted him to philosophy: Henri Bergson. He tried to find a third way for himself, somewhere between spiritualism and positivism, groping toward ideas on creativity and becoming, and he invented piecemeal a philosophy based on the notion of a totally secular freedom. Following the intuition of his own intellectual needs, he associated with great works just as, when a child, he had associated with great men. Finding his professors lacking in breadth, he addressed his questions directly to Descartes, Kant, and Spinoza, borrowing from this one or that, gathering here and there the concepts and categories necessary to invent his own composite, but coherent, system of thought. "Nizan, Aron, and myself were most unfair to those poor people [the professors], who actually had the *feeling* for philosophy but simply lacked the tools." To counter those "elegant soft thoughts," the three place themselves "under the sign of Descartes" and of his "revolutionary thought," which "cuts and slashes," and suddenly no other philosopher seems to be as beneficial as this "explosive thinker."[28]

One day, asked by the magazine *Les Nouvelles Littéraires* to participate in a survey on "today's students," Sartre contributes a short, extremely dense text. "It is the paradox of the mind," he writes, "that man, whose business it is to create what's necessary to him, should be so unable to raise himself to the level of being, like those soothsayers who can predict the future of others but not their own. This is why I see sadness and boredom in the depths of man as well as nature. . . . We are as free as you want, but impotent. . . . Otherwise, the will to power, action, life, are all vain ideologies. . . . Everything is too weak; too mortal. Adventure is a decoy; I am referring to the belief in necessary connections that would really exist. The adventurer is a rational determinist who thinks he is free. . . . We are probably unhappier, but much nicer."[29] Sartre is only twenty-four, but, in this little text, one can detect the future themes of both *Nausea* and *Being and Nothingness.* Can one turn one's life into an esthetic creation? This is the choice of the adventurer, the only man who lives his life like a novel. Bergson helps Sartre anchor his philosophy in his own inner experience; Descartes ensures the rational dimension of this subjectivism; and Plato contributes its esthetic aspects. Sartre is creating his own system, a form of psychological realism: at once the conceptualization of his inner experience and the basis for his esthetic plan. For him, philosophy is a sort of preparation for psychology and fiction. In his reading of Karl Jaspers's *General Psychopathology,* in his visits to the patients of the Sainte-Anne Hospital—where he goes every Sunday morning with Nizan, Aron, and Lagache—and in his advanced studies, which he will prepare with Henri Delacroix, Sartre is mostly involved in the field of psychology. His essay "The Image in Psychological Life: Its Role and Nature" receives a grade of "very good." Nizan, already a follower of Spinoza, finds reassurance in communism, while for Sartre, philosophy will always be a convenient, privileged tool and a means of access to fiction. He borrows his instruments from the great philosophers, but without recognizing himself in any of them, unable to sympathize. He has no master, no mentor: "I want to be the man who knows the most about everything," Sartre exclaims to Daniel Lagache, who is dumbfounded by so much self-assurance and pride.[30] As philosopher, he studies human behavior, develops a passion for psychology and psychopathology, writes his first novel. The philosopher falls in love with new art forms, sees the latest Murnau and Griffith, writes an enthusiastic article, "An Apology for Cinema: Defense and Illustration of an International Art." "Cinema is the emblem of our era," it concludes. "Thus, those who were twenty in 1895 blame it for the inevitable gap between our way of thinking and theirs. They accuse it, as they once did Socrates, of corrupting the morals of youth. . . . But cinema speaks to everyone. . . . This should please that government minister who used to look at his watch and say; 'At this very hour, throughout France, all our students are doing the same homework. Now, at 10 P.M., in Saint-Denis, at the Barbès, on the Boulevards, at the Marivaux, at the Gaumont, people from every social background sit together in a dark room as if in the nave of a cathedral, craning their necks toward a screen that joins them in the same anguish or the same joy, depending on whether they see the crazy face of André Nox or Chaplin's grin. The people have abandoned themselves to this new art form."[31]

ON DECEMBER 24, 1927, Nizan married a young woman he had met at the first dance given by the Ecole. The civil ceremony took place in the municipal hall of the fifth arrondissement, and the best men were Aron and Sartre. Traditionally, those Normaliens who do not opt for a career in the diplomatic service or in finance tend to marry either their female counterparts, the students of the Ecole Normale Supérieure for women at Sèvres, or the candidates for *agrégation,* or faculty daughters. In general, the choice of a mate is indicative of the kind of future contemplated. Sartre, in love as elsewhere, seemed to prefer trying different options.

His first real relationship started in a rather morbid way, near Thiviers, in 1925. The Sartre house on the Rue du Thon had been sold at auction in 1910, and since then, Joseph Sartre had been desolately following its various transformations by its new owners. Since Joseph had refused to let Poulou have a room at La Brégère for his vacations, relations between the two had been cool. But if Jean-Paul did not particularly relish going to Thiviers, he would soon have to: his cousin Annie, whom he had chaperoned through Paris during the few months she had spent studying there, had fallen ill with tuberculosis, and died in 1925, at the age of nineteen, while Sartre was finishing his first year at the Ecole Normale. She was the only interesting young person he had ever known in Thiviers, and, according to one of her schoolmates, she had become a sort of "female double of her cousin."[32] Provocative, brilliant, and arrogant, she was feared and admired by her professors. Sartre never spoke of Annie, but he gave her name to the female character in *Nausea,* and to the friend he uses as an example in *Being and Nothingness.*

After attending the funerals of his father in 1906, Doctor Eymard Sartre in 1913, Captain Lannes in 1917, and Grandmother Sartre in 1919, once again death called him to Thiviers. He no longer knew many people there, but he saw his Aunt Hélène, his Uncle Joseph, and, of course, Madame Mancy, who had also come to join them for that sad occasion. And he met one of Annie's cousins, on her father's side. She was the daughter of Joseph Jollivet, a pharmacist in Toulouse, and of one of Frédéric Lannes's sisters. She had just turned twenty-one that year. Sartre immediately noticed her in the middle of all those unknown adults: "We followed the funeral lightheartedly. Then my aunt invited some fifteen people for dinner. All those Thiviers personalities, doctors, notaries, what bores! I couldn't understand them. I kept trying to talk to this young woman, who also seemed to want to talk to me, but we were constantly interrupted by the questions of some doctor or notary. So, as soon as we had finished our coffee, we went out for a walk through the fields. That's how our relationship started. It would last several years."[33] Openly courting literary personalities, Simone Jollivet led, in Toulouse, the kind of licentious, exhibitionistic life that other women of the 1920s led in the cafés of Montparnasse. In those years, Nancy Cunard met Louis Aragon, and Colette Peignot ran into Crevel, Picasso, and Buñuel. Simone Jollivet, alias "Miyette," "Camille," and "Toulouse," introduced scandal and excitement into Sartre's and Nizan's lives. Once she offered them a lampshade made from a pair of her panties—according to Henriette Nizan, "a small pair of panties, in purple cotton, trimmed with ocher machine-made lace." At a dance given by the Ecole, she appeared wearing a rather extravagant and, according to some, fairly daring dress, on the arm of an elegant Sartre in spats. The relationship between the enamored Sartre and this tall young woman with long blond hair, hard blue eyes, and flashy elegance, was fairly troubled and painful: to satisfy his mistress's whims, Sartre had to spend several sleepless nights on park benches under the stars listening to accounts of her adventures with rich men, better able to entertain her.

"We should really try to reach some agreement. Do you want to see me—yes or no? I can no longer accept being treated like some guy kept happy with a letter every fifteen days, and the charity of three days of intimacy a year."[34] But, despite these rebuffs, their on-again-off-again affair lasts almost three years, in Thiviers, Toulouse, and Paris, resulting in an extensive correspondence. Continuing the role he had played with Annie, Sartre suggests books to read, asks her opinions, reveals his secret projects, speaks of his works in progress. "My love," he writes later on, "I don't like to hear you say that you love me 'passionately, like La Marietta,' who, after all, was only a slut with a crush on Fabrice. . . . I'd rather your love for me were like that of Sanseverina for Fabrice."[35] At times he lapses into the confessional mode: "The man with that famous 'power to work' has to make an extraordinary effort to work more than fifteen minutes a day."[36] Or else: "Till last year I was often melancholy because I thought I was ugly, and that hurt me. But now I have rid myself of that feeling, because I realize it is a weakness."[37]

Sartre wrote his first novel, "A Defeat" for Simone Jollivet, his little "China doll," as he liked to call her. "A Defeat" was inspired by the relationship between Richard and Cosima Wagner and Friedrich Nietzsche, and Sartre's own recent experiences as a tutor at the Morels and in his affair with Simone Jollivet. There are three main characters: Richard Organte, the older artist, a writer and composer; Cosima, his young wife; and Frédéric, the tutor of their three daughters, at once a great admirer of Richard and madly in love with his wife. The perfect triangle had obvious parallels in Sartre's own life: J.B., Anne-Marie, and Poulou; Charles Schweitzer, Anne-Marie, and Poulou; Joseph Mancy, Anne-Marie, and Poulou. For research, he reread Schopenhauer, Nietzsche, histories of music, and the biographies of Wagner and several other musicians. He also reread E. T. A. Hoffmann and Nietzsche's *Ecce Homo,* and, through the library of the Ecole Normale Supérieure, he ordered the score of *Götterdämmerung.* Did he remember that his mother's cousin, Albert Schweitzer, often visited Cosima in Bayreuth, when she was quite old, and had an interesting correspondence with her? If "A Defeat" is a perfect outline of all the future themes of Sartre's oeuvre—the esthetic of creativity; incest; the triangle; the strong man against the weak man and the young against the mature; the other; social and metaphysical freedom; social fixity and the advent of the *salaud* (the swine); bad faith—as well as a love story, and an unhappy one at that, it is also a *Bildungsroman.* As the title indicates it is also a novel of a failed experience—a double failure, intellectual and emotional —which, however, leads to a certain optimism. "All in all, his defeat was a victory," as the author writes at the end of one chapter.

Reading the book, one has the impression of Sartre projecting himself into both Richard and Frédéric. Their relationship, their dialogue have a strange resonance, as if, in fact, they were taking place between a twenty-year-old Sartre and his seventy-year-old counterpart—as if, together, they constituted a slow intellectual progress involving the minds of two people, the incessant feedback between master and pupil. "Frédéric was not Organte's friend since he did not feel like his peer. He had an affection for him that has no name. . . . What he loved most about him was the strength Richard lent him. When Frédéric thought of him, he could not see his face. He would clench his fists as his mind was crisscrossed by the image of a torrent or a cavalry charge. Now and then, he would whisper words such as 'a torrent' or 'the Strength,' and he would immediately feel some inner Presence, without ever knowing whether he was registering Richard's Strength or his own. . . . He loved the big body of that stooping athlete. The sight of it made him shiver with ecstasy at the prospect of their future combats. The body was always there: he would have liked to rub against it as if it were a wall, but, particularly, he would have liked to fight with it, to clasp it with all his might and try to throw it down."[38]

The Normaliens who read this manuscript[39] recognized in it something of the boxer who went to the gym regularly, the powerful cruel prankster, creator of a theory a day. "His muscles, the muscles of a wrestler, felt a relentless need to fight, to crush. The joys and sufferings of his huge organism were in a constant, extraordinary state of frenzy. While writing, he would grip his penholder so hard it would almost crack. There isn't a single sentence in his books, a single melody in his operas that did not bear the full weight of his abandon."[40] And the similarities were not lost on others: Madame Morel was fond of taunting Sartre, "See, you're just like that awful Frédéric!"

Sartre's relationship with Simone Jollivet ended on the same tone that had always colored it: that of an episodic passion. The two lovers would remain friends for the rest of their lives. She will realize one of her plans: to be the actor-manager Charles Dullin's mistress. She will also be an actress, a playwright, a woman of letters.

After Simone Jollivet's extravagance, Sartre moves toward convention and becomes engaged to the cousin of one of his fellow graduates, Alfred Péron, whom he meets at Usson-en-Forez, where he has been invited to spend his summer vacation. "I think she needed a passion, and I managed to make her magnify what she felt for me." Later, he will reconstruct this episode, which stretched over nearly a year, in an extremely cynical and fantastic fashion. Both Aron and Guille sent letters of congratulations to the new "fiancé," who complained about their epistolary mediocrity. The young woman lived in Lyon, so they did not see much of each other. "Since her parents wanted to know more about me, they hired a private detective to tail me, and he told them that, at the Ecole, somebody had heard me say a few unpleasant, even vulgar, things about my 'fiancée.' "[41] The relationship ended by itself at the time of Sartre's first exam for the *agrégation*. Much to everybody's surprise—as the principal of the school noted, while Aron, who got first place, was jumping up and down with delight—Sartre flunked his written exam. His future parents-in-law immediately refused to give their daughter's hand in marriage to a student who, though a Normalien, had failed to pass the supreme test. This constituted a double failure for both Sartre and his mother and stepfather, who found themselves scorned when they came to present their official request to the Pérons. "I took a bottle and went off into a field, alone, and there I drank, and even wept. Maybe I wept because I was drunk . . . still, it felt good. I don't mean I was doing it on purpose, still I was quite glad to pay my debt with a few tears. I felt relieved."[42] Later, he will only seldom allude to this "fiancée," and then only as a "philistine's daughter."

*T*HE AGRÉGATION put an end to the years of apprenticeship, the *Bildungsjahren*, as our Germanophile philosopher would have called it. If Sartre became part of Normalien folklore, he did not do it like so many others, who end up depending on 45 Rue d'Ulm all their lives, who become members of the Alumni Association, attend the revues of the younger students and their own class reunions. Sartre never set foot again in the Ecole Normale Supérieure and never drifted into the cult of the Rue d'Ulm. Indeed, he was such a renegade that, when he died, the question of whether to publish an obituary notice caused heated debate: "He never joined the Alumni Association, so he has no right to a notice," maintained the hard-liners. "Still he was the most famous Normalien in the world," the liberals retorted. Insofar as I know, the Alumni Association never rendered this last homage to him who had spent, in his own words, "four years of happiness" at their school.

Sartre took his second exam for the *agrégation* in June 1929. Out of seventy-six candidates competing for the *agrégation* in Philoso-

74

phy, he placed first: "He shows a keen, rigorous, and well-rounded, if not always dependable, intelligence," noted M. Parodi and M. Wahl, two members of the jury. Sartre had outscored the first runner-up probably thanks to Raymond Aron, who had advised him to rely more on good sense and safe answers, than on originality. So, Sartre avoided all slips of genius in both his written dissertations, "Freedom and Contingence" and "The Role of Induction in Deductive Sciences." For his famous oral lesson, "Psychology and Logic," he abandoned himself more to his own ideas. It was remarkable, according to Maurice de Gandillac, who still remembers it today: "He spoke of everything he knew about phenomenology with extraordinary poise; the entire jury, particularly the president, Lalande, were captivated."[43] The first runner-up in the philosophy exam for the 1929 *agrégation* was one Mademoiselle Simone Bertrand de Beauvoir. "She was rigorous, demanding, precise, very technical," Gandillac remembers. "She was also the youngest student in her class, only twenty-one, three years younger than Sartre; but she was motivated enough to skip a whole year and prepare for both her Diploma of Advanced Studies and her *agrégation* at the same time. As two members of the jury, Davy and Wahl, told me later, it had not been easy to decide whether to give the first place to Sartre or to her. If Sartre already showed great intelligence and a solid, if at times inexact, culture, everybody agreed that, of the two, she was the real philosopher."

Sartre had spent the second year of exam preparation at the *cité universitaire* on the Boulevard Jourdan, since, after his first failure, he no longer had a right to the room on the Rue d'Ulm. It was an exciting year spent between courses at the Sorbonne and preparation for the exams with Nizan, Maheu, and Gandillac. All the candidates of that year, 1928–29, had spotted the imposing trio of the Normaliens, Sartre-Nizan-Maheu; especially Sartre, who was supposed to be the most formidable of the three—whether as thinker or drinker. Among the young women whom Maheu met daily at the Bibliothèque Nationale and Sorbonne, Sartre had already commented on one philosophy candidate, tall, serious, with blue eyes: "Charming, pretty, dresses horribly." Now begins Sartre's relationship with Simone de Beauvoir—whom Maheu nicknamed "le castor" "because 'Beaver' is English for *Castor* . . . and a beaver is a symbol of hard work and energy." The relationship lasted fifty-one years.

This mythic meeting will later become the central episode of the first volume of Simone de Beauvoir's work, *Memoirs of a Dutiful Daughter*. Maurice de Gandillac, one of their closest friends during that year, gives us a rather different version of those first moments: "It was nothing like 'At last Sartre arrived,' as she makes it sound in her *Memoirs.* There was a whole group of people, contemporaries, who knew each other fairly well and saw each other quite often. Among these were Sartre, Nizan, Maheu, Merleau-Ponty, Simone de Beauvoir, and myself. I met Simone through Merleau-Ponty, she met Maheu through me, and finally got closer to Sartre and Nizan via Maheu." According to Gandillac, it was not "love at first sight," as Beauvoir puts it, but something slower, more rational, and, maybe, more banal than one would like to think.

They met over the texts they had to prepare for the program. Their first real time together was during the last tense days before the orals. Sartre had invited the young woman to cram with him in the room he shared in the Cité Universitaire: "There were books all over the place, cigarette butts in all the corners, and the air was thick with tobacco smoke. Sartre greeted me in a wordly manner; he was smoking a pipe. Nizan, who said nothing, had a cigarette stuck in the corner of his one-sided smile and was quizzing me through his thick lenses, with an air of thinking more than he cared to say. All day long, petrified with fear, I commented on the 'metaphysical treatise.' "[44] She might have been a bad dresser, but, intellectually, they all agreed, she was one of them. Sartre, Nizan, and Maheu included the young woman in their working trio. "To tell the truth, it was always he [Sartre] who knew most about all the authors and all the aspects of our syllabus," she remembers. "He used to do his utmost to help us benefit from his knowledge. 'He is a marvelous trainer of intellects,' I noted. I was staggered by his generosity, for these sessions didn't teach him anything, and he would give of himself for hours without counting the cost. . . . When he had done the lion's share of the work for the day, he would put on a record."[45] Entertaining, accessible, generous, funny, stimulating, Sartre became boyfriend and adviser of Simone de Beauvoir, who, three years younger, was in the process of breaking with her past as a proper young lady, educated in a private Catholic institution, surrounded by family conventions she could no longer respect. "From now on, I'm going to take you under my wing," Sartre informed her, almost as a challenge.

Their meetings became more and more frequent as did their intellectual jousts, since, despite the exhaustion that followed the exams, these two thinking machines never failed to get excited by new ideas. "Day after day and all day long I set myself up against Sartre, and in our discussions I was simply not in his class. One morning in the

Luxembourg . . . I outlined for him that pluralist morality which I had cooked up . . . : he soon demolished it."[46] When, after three months, she started speaking of him as the "double" of her adolescent dreams, when their correspondence became a daily matter, when leisure allowed them to invent a life free of any constraint, and, finally, when Sartre became aware of the imminence of military service, and of the kinds of freedom he would have to relinquish, they started to think about their future. Sartre wasted no time in stating his credo: travel, polygamy, transparency. He had no intention of giving up any of his interests. To avoid the boredom of a teaching career in the provinces, he had requested a position as an assistant lecturer in Japan for the year immediately following his release from military service. He wanted to make this journey (ironically, since his father had desperately wanted but failed to take it), and nobody was going to stop him. Similarly, he had always enjoyed the company of women, and he was not going to do without it. In order to sustain this impossible situation without risking either the loss of his new friend or the surrender of his basic principles, he invented the concepts of "necessary love," "contingent love," as well as the "two-year lease." Simone de Beauvoir would thus remain his privileged but not his only female companion. He meant to see her as often as possible during the two years of military service before his departure for Japan. "I dreamed above all of asserting this freedom against women," he later writes, remembering his pre-Beauvoir years. "It was all the more comical since women certainly weren't chasing me; indeed it was I who was chasing them. . . . The Beaver accepted this freedom, and kept it."[47]

Military life elicited from this new member of the meteorological corps what he described as "an extreme modesty." First at the fort of Saint-Cyr, and then in the barracks of Saint-Symphorien, near Tours, Sartre was taught how to handle balloons, theodolites, sextants, octants, and compasses. He had some difficulty enduring boredom, the "situation common to all the condemned."[48] To protect himself, he wrote, producing three "intermediary" texts during those three years of wavering between the Rue d'Ulm and teaching. The first was "La Légende de la vérité" (The Legend of Truth), a tale in three parts concerning respectively the legend of certainty, the legend of probability, and the legend of man alone with himself. Only part of this work would eventually be published. Two plays, "Epiméthée" (Epimetheus) and "J'aurai un bel enterrement" (I'll Have a Lovely Burial) end up at the bottom of some drawer. Both continue the theme of the artist, here opposed to the technician, as man facing his own death, alone.

Simone de Beauvoir was the first reader of these texts, their first critic. She had decided to postpone the day she would start to teach, so that, for as long as Sartre was in the service, she could live in Paris, not too far from him. "I wanted to relax a bit, to sink back into happiness, into Sartre's love. . . . And he was the person who said, 'But Castor, why have you stopped thinking, why aren't you working? I thought you wanted to write! You don't want to become a housewife, do you . . . ?' "[49] And he pushed her, both to preserve her autonomy and to write, to remain in a state of relentless creative activity, of permanent critical research. As a result, she decided to begin a novel. But circumstances suddenly changed their plans: the young soldier learned that he had not gotten the job as assistant lecturer in Tokyo, and that, instead, on March 1, 1931, he would have to start teaching in a high school in Le Havre, in the Northwest, substituting for a teacher who had had a nervous breakdown. The two-year lease was over, the journey would not take place; they had to rewrite their agreement. To make matters worse, on October 31, at the beginning of the academic year, she was assigned to Marseilles, in the Southeast! Strait is the gate out of youth. While a soldier, he was still a thousand Socrates. He boarded the train for Le Havre. "Just enough time to read a detective novel," he joked after his first trip.

JUST ONE SOCRATES

> For, all of a sudden, I was becoming just one Socrates. Until then I'd been preparing to live. . . . And then, all at once, I was acting in the play; everything I did from now on was done with my life.
>
> —THE WAR DIARIES

*I*RREVOCABLY, THE curtain rose on March 31, and Sartre found himself in the provinces playing the dreaded role of high-school teacher. He would remain there until 1936. The French army, the French provinces, the life of a high-school teacher: he fell with both feet into the real world, into work and routine, the life of schedules, salaries, and fixed, hierarchical, social relations, in short, into that place for which his studies had prepared him—a well-defined, well-centered place, ready to receive him, integrate him, program him, keep him on one track, the right one, the rest of his life. He had a specific task, specific obligations, specific rituals, and a specific status: he had become a civil servant, a state employee. Until the age of retirement, he would be taken care of, receiving a salary even during school vacations and sick leaves. All he had to do was cross the threshold and then the courtyard of the Lycée François Ier, climb up to "the principal's office," which always smelled of soap and wax behind its heavy black-leather door, enter the long, high corridors, visit the chapel and the main courtyard in which no student was ever allowed, and listen to the heavy, static silence of all the places reserved for the teachers, to feel immediately caught up in the timeless reassuring world of the French provinces, with its silence, propriety, and boredom. He was captured. Suddenly, he was just one Socrates. Suddenly, everything had collapsed.

On July 12, 1931, four months after he had begun his high-school career, he made his first public appearance in the city of Le Havre. The occasion was the ritual Prize Day ceremony, attended every year by all the principals of France. It is a fixed ceremony, with the patina of years of repetition and tradition, a social familial ceremony, that invites outsiders, such as famous guests and the parents of the students, into the closed universe of the high school, which suddenly razes the classroom walls to view the honors lists. It is an unjust, cruel ceremony, which pushes to the extreme an educational system whose key words are selection and competition: the "best" are picked, all others forgotten; laurel crowns and piles of gilt-edged books are bestowed, prize lists are read out, top students are introduced. At one end of the room is a large platform decorated with garlands of boxwood and flowers and connected to the courtyard by means of a long red carpet. In the center of the room sit the spectators. To the sides, the students occupy the stands.

"My dear friends, as Sainte-Beuve, whom I am now quoting by heart, used to say, each country has its own peculiar national celebrations. Belgium has its cockfights, Spain its corridas; we have our prize-days." Jean-Paul Sartre proceeded to stun his audience in a spare and grating tone of voice such as they had never heard before. In July 1931, Sartre is barely twenty-six years old, and tradition demands that the introductory address be delivered by the youngest teacher. The parents and other citizens are finally going to meet him, the brilliant one, a Normalien, the first of his class at the exam of the *agrégation* in Philosophy. In a black gown with ruffles and a yellow cloak trimmed with three rows of white ermine, the gown much too long for him, Sartre finds himself in front of the distinguished audience of a provincial subprefecture, fully responsible for the inauguration of a ceremony surely not very much to his taste. So, he decides to address the students, and the students alone, hurling his speech like a grenade at the rest of the audience. Omitting the prerequisite "His Excellency the County Councilor" or even a "Ladies and Gentlemen," he belts out his speech at an extraordinary speed, absolutely disdainful of the murmurs he is provoking.

"Prize Day," he goes on, "is generally preceded by an expiatory sacrifice. The youngest professor assumes all the sins of the year and does penance for them in public: this is what we call the customary address. When he utters the last word, his purification is complete: thus, each fall, all the high schools of France can start the new academic year in a state of grace. On the other hand, this punishment is often less difficult for the scapegoat than for those who have to listen to him: at least he can choose his subject; nor does this subject have to be absolutely pertinent to the ceremony. And so I am going to take advantage of my rights and talk to you about movies." The students react with smiles and laughter, the parents with consternation, discomfort, and silence. Invoking Anatole France, Aesop, and Pirandello, Sartre shows this cold, affected town and its frozen, haughty bourgeois that cinema is "really an art." And he is happier than ever at his final thrust. "Your parents," the orator goes on without actually addressing the elders but rather provoking them through their children, "your parents may rest assured; the motion picture is not a bad school. It is an art which . . . reflects civilization in our time. Who will teach you about the beauty of the world you live in, the poetry of speed, machines, and the inhuman and splendid inevitability of industry? Who, if not your art, the motion picture . . ." And, catching his breath, he adds: "Go to the movies often. But do it preferably during bad weather; first, enjoy your vacation."[1]

The aristocracy of Le Havre were not appreciative. These respectable citizens dreaded the nefarious, pernicious influence he might have over their children. They mistrusted him, they sensed him as a danger, they found him outrageous, offensive. Behind the veils of their hats, the ladies of the coast, their gloved hands nervously clasped in their laps, had difficulty repressing sighs of dismay and outrage at such a display of bad taste. And, on Prize Day the follow-

ing year, the same devil, supported on right and left by two colleagues, advanced haltingly along the red carpet and, after being
hoisted onto the platform, disappeared hastily through an emergency exit. Later, they learned with distress, and repeated in horror, that he had been drunk; he had spent the previous evening celebrating the success of a few graduates, in a . . . in a . . . you know . . . with certain ladies.

*F*OR FIVE years, Sartre and Le Havre engage in a wrestling match. No other town in the French provinces displays such a brutally clear topographical representation of its class structure: down below, around the port, not far from the railway station, is the red-light district, the slums, the docks. Higher up, above the cliffs, dominating the whole city, are Sainte-Adresse and the Côte Felix-Faure, with their bourgeois villas, their splendid views over the sea, their English gardens, their nannies, and their model children. Every year, Sartre's classes brought together the children of shipbuilders and those of dockers. In the 1930s, the upper middle class of Le Havre still consisted of the offspring of all the Protestants who had moved there from Alsace or Switzerland in the nineteenth century. Drawn by the industrial development of great ports, they had successfully thrown themselves into the sugar, coffee, cotton, and spice trades, and had grown rich. They owned three- or four-story houses, employed up to six servants, and "went down" to the railway station by carriage or coach. Given this division, Sartre had no problem selecting his turf: the slums and the children of dockers. And he chose the dirty, seedy, sinister Hotel Printania to live in.

First, however, he had tried to rent a room on the Rue François Ier, in the house of a lady who had been recommended to him by a friend: "I found myself in front of a bourgeois home. I entered a bourgeois vestibule steeped in bourgeois penumbra. . . . Mme Dufaux, the widow, appeared. . . . To me, she looked like the epitome of widowhood and human abjection. The very idea of living in her house made me run away."[2] And so, to the princely Printania. In a desolate, windswept triangle between the Rue Charles-Laffite—more a blind alley than a street—and another narrow street with no name, between the railway station and the docks, the Hotel Printania was mostly frequented by traveling tradesmen and other transients who had arrived with the last trains. Sartre's "shady room in a shady house"—as described by one of his students—looked out onto the railroad yard with its lively glass roof, and onto the power station. Green and gray circuit breakers and transformers frayed the tall brick walls with their tangle of wires and steel, their relentless buzzing pervading the room night and day. "A hellish din," according to another student, but that's exactly what Sartre wanted: to sit in his room as if it were a watchtower and hear the howls of sirens and the whistle of trains passing below. From this place, open to both sea and land travels, he would listen to the city of Le Havre, as if he were himself a clandestine traveler, on constant alert, ready to jump from a moving train. "I can hear everything men do at night," he writes, "the entire street passes through my room and washes over me."[3]

It was the early 1930s, and this district was the worst hit by the economic crisis. Sartre loved the lost populations who found shelter in the cafés and bars near the docks. On damp winter evenings, he walked along the docks, which smelled of fish, fuel, tar, and brine; dust and cinders whirled in the air, cargo careened and dockers gathered, hooks in hand, waiting for the call to work. He came to know the greasy paving stones, the harsh light of early morning, the magic lights of night skimming the water, the ballet of crates being unloaded, the weird animation of cranes, the hooking of bales of cotton, the dance of the port, the violent, rhythmic male movements of machines, tugboats, lock gates, cargo boats, and moorings orchestrating commerce, the trade of one country with the rest of the world. It was the universe of mysterious pirates wearing earrings and trying to sell their parrots, tattooed sailors, drunk seamen, fights and brothels already dealt with in the novels of Francis Carco, the poems of Pierre Mac Orlan, and the photos of Brassaï. Sartre loved the Rue des Galions and the whorehouses with names like The Purple Star, The Red Lantern, The Java. He loved the coarse voices of Damia and Fréhel's songs: "Dans les bas-quartiers de la ville/Il est une rue sans nom" (In the slums of the city there's a street with no name), Damia sang. "Dans la tristesse et la nuit qui revient/Je reste seule isolée sans soutien" (As sadness and night return, I'm helpless, lonely, all alone), Fréhel answered. Here, in this city of Le Havre, Sartre acquired daily habits he would never relinquish: he became involved with public places, and turned his patronage of cafés and hotels into a moral necessity. At noon he would have a *choucroute* at the Guillaume Tell, with its large, worn, red velvet seats, gold moldings, and green plants. Sitting in the Café de la Grande Poste, in front of a tall glass of beer, with his pipe, his pen, and a distracted look on his face, he would work for hours and hours.

*L*IKE THEIR parents, the students of Le Havre had not remained indifferent to Sartre's speech, his apology for cinema, particularly since for quite some time the daily *Le Havre Libre* had been fighting for the protection of youth against such dangers as the movies. "The parents couldn't believe their ears," Jean Giustiniani remembers, "but I immediately fell in love with what he was saying. . . . When Sartre first entered our classroom, the following October, we knew who he was: 'That's the anarchist, he's OK.' " During his entire stay at the high school, Sartre used only one classroom on the second floor, in the farthest corner of the left wing. It was a large room with stepped rows of seats and, in back, a huge coal stove, and large bright windows that looked out over the trees and the pavilions of the empty street. "We would watch this little man enter the room, hands in his pockets and no hat on, very rare for our school. He smoked a pipe—also quite unusual. He immediately started talking, off the top of his head, without notes, sitting on his desk—we had never seen anything like it."[4] Between Sartre and the first generation of his students there is a difference of only eight or nine years: they immediately become accomplices. The same thing happens at the beginning of the academic year in October 1935. "The first time he entered our class, he was wearing a sports jacket, and a black shirt without a tie; we immediately understood that he was not going to be a teacher like all the others. . . . He was friendly, a nonconformist," Robert Marchandeau adds. "In fact, he did not really 'profess' anything; he was just speaking with some friends."[5]

Sartre taught them individual responsibility; he literally woke them up. Every week, a student would take the floor and deliver an oral report—at the time, a totally new approach. Sartre's pedagogy was based on the respect of the students, and the systematic demolition of all the artificial barriers of hierarchy and authority. "The other teachers used to talk to us as if we were 'little brats.' Sartre spoke to us as if we were men, his peers," Jean Giustiniani remembers. "He forced us to think and to analyze ourselves, he encouraged us to approach the world with a critical mind, to question constantly every acquired notion . . . he wanted us to develop an exemplary intellectual honesty." According to Pierre Guitard, Sartre's concept of class discipline was like "a premature May '68 . . . We could smoke in class and, in summer, we took off our jackets and ties."[6]

Logic and psychology were the two fields of study to which Sartre devoted most of his courses, delighted as he was to have the opportunity to sort out his latest readings in pathological psychology in front of these eager youths just beginning to discover philosophy. He would tell them about his visits to Sainte-Anne, a few years earlier, and, during breaks, about his years at the Ecole Normale. On the other hand, when it came to ethics and metaphysics, two fields for which they had to prepare for the exams, he sent them back to the textbooks.

The relationship between Sartre and his students was not limited to the classroom. They often met at the Guillaume Tell or at La Grande Poste for a shandy or a small glass of beer before a game of ping-pong or poker, and endless discussions. Sartre would ask them about their tastes, their lives; he would tease them and tell them about himself. Giustiniani and several other students invited Sartre and two other teachers to join their picnics on the beach as soon as the weather permitted, in May and June: "First of all, we went swimming. Sartre could swim for quite a long time; he had great endurance. Then we ate and drank and sang. Sartre sang bawdy songs, arias from an operetta, and a few things he had written himself. We would be together till about midnight." "Traîne tes couilles par terre/Prend ta pine à la main mon copain/Nous partons en guerre/A la chasse aux putains" (Drag your balls on the ground, take your cock in your hand, my friend. We are marching off to war, we are looking for a whore), Sartre sang with all his heart.[7] And then, of course, there were the movies, at the Kursaal Theater, on the Rue de Paris. During the first years of the talkies, the audience used to scream and shout, to participate in the action any way they could. One day, three of Sartre's most nonconformist colleagues—Isoré (English), Rasquin (physical education), and Bonnafé (French)—asked him to go with them to the Charles Porta gym where they boxed. Soon it became a habit. Le Person, from Le Havre, was the bantamweight champion of France and the idol of many a young man. Sartre soon brought his students along to the gym, where he taught them the left uppercut and the right hook, training them with punching bag and jumping rope, soon producing several worthy sparring partners.

But Sartre found not only fans in his high school. The principal and vice-principal were frankly perplexed at the increasing size and leftist tendencies of his class, which they saw as a revolutionary meeting ground where all the rules, laws, and traditions of the school were cast aside. Sartre used no discipline, no punitive sanctions, no attendance rosters, no grades, no exams; he discouraged competition, note taking, and rote learning; and yet, at the *baccalauréat,* his students were as successful as those of his colleagues. As if by magic, he had also managed to erase the legendary line of demarcation between teachers and students, between school and daily life, between learning philosophy and learning to live. In the 1930s, such a pedagogical approach turned him into a pioneer . . . and a scandal.

Jacques-Laurent Bost—the youngest child of the minister Charles Bost, who was for several years the chaplain of the school—was among Sartre's new students in 1935, before becoming a friend and a faithful companion of Sartre for the rest of his life. "When I was with the boy scouts I first noticed the difference between the Protestants of the upper middle class and the others; between the people of the coast, with their houses, their servants, and their carriages and my family, for instance, the family of a poor minister. In the scouts I also met a few young men who had quit after elementary school."[8] In Sartre's courses there was a high percentage of bourgeois students; some of them told their parents about the general atmosphere of their classes and the style of their philosophy teacher. Some parents, outraged, came to complain to the principal. Some students, annoyed by his system, went out of their way to be provocative: one would arrive ten minutes late every Monday morning, remove his felt hat, and interrupt the course with a "Good morning, Monsieur Sartre." "Fascist idiot!" notes Bost.

The most vehement expression of this inevitable antagonism was probably the intense dislike that another teacher, a M. Troude from Rouen, felt for Sartre, a dislike that wouldn't have bothered anybody if Troude hadn't decided to take it out on Sartre's students during the final exams for the *baccalauréat*. Sartre tried to thwart Troude's plans by preparing his students himself for the exam in metaphysics —a subject in which Troude intended to rake them over the coals —and by intervening personally in defense of his "flock." "Sartre's keen intelligence," Georges Le Sidaner remembers, "and determination really got on the nerves of poor Monsieur Troude, who was never able to forgive him for being such an outstanding teacher."[9] On the other hand, the school inspectors immediately recognized Sartre's "fluent speech," "valuable pedagogical approach," "excellent presentations, solid and well informed on current scholarship," "firm, personal way of thinking which the students seem to appreciate," "uncommon zeal, originality and intellectual vigor, remarkable talent, outstanding performance, all promising a brilliant future."[10] Sartre always retained a fond memory of his Le Havre students, his first graduating classes. After all, that's where he first felt this complicity with adolescence, its energy, its rebellious anger. As he explained later, "I preferred those who had ideas to those at the very top."[11] The first homage that Le Havre rendered Sartre after his death was to rename the Rue Ancelot, which passes right below the windows of his old classroom, the Rue Jean-Paul Sartre. But, according to the principal, the street sign has been regularly vandalized ever since.[12]

*T*O HIS students, Simone de Beauvoir was mysterious and intriguing. Sartre told them she taught at Marseilles, and then at Rouen; and all the students knew that every Wednesday, after class, their teacher had to make a dash to the station so as not to miss the last train to Rouen. It was probably not coincidental that some of them chose a Wednesday to insert a lock between two buttonholes of his overcoat; since the key was nowhere to be found, Sartre had to rush off wearing only his jacket in the middle of winter. The students also knew a few other names of the people that formed the little circle of friends around Sartre and Beauvoir: Fernando and Stépha Gherassi, Maheu and his wife, Albert Morel and his sister, Pierre Guille's wife, Marc Zuorro, Hélène de Beauvoir, Paul and Henriette Nizan. Simone de Beauvoir was immediately welcomed into the Morel tribe, and, with Sartre, she was invited to their apartment on the Boulevard Raspail, to their house at La Pouëze, on the banks of the Loire, and to the house at Juan-les-Pins, on the Mediterranean. A few of Sartre's student friends will also join some of the more or less intimate circles of this network.

"We found a name for our relationship before we had decided just what that relationship was going to be. 'It is a morganatic marriage,' we said. As a couple, we possessed a dual identity. In the ordinary way we were Monsieur and Madame M. Organatique, unambitious, easily satisfied, not very well off, the husband a civil servant. But sometimes . . . we would go to a cinema on the Champs Elysées, or dancing at La Coupole, and then we were an American millionaire and his wife, Mr. and Mrs. Morgan Hattick."[13] In the volume of her memoirs *The Prime of Life*, Simone de Beauvoir gives us an account of her and Sartre's experiences in the period between the two wars, retracing the details of their journeys, their readings, their meetings under a "we" that confuses the two individuals into two indistinguishable Siamese twins. The prosaic contract imposed by Sartre at the beginning, his "two-year lease," now sounds like a joke. For several generations, this couple would become a model to emulate, a dream of lasting complicity, an extraordinary success since, apparently, it managed to reconcile the irreconcilable: the two partners remained free, equal, and honest with each other. By accepting Sartre's contract and developing her own autonomy while respecting his, Simone de Beauvoir beat him at his own game. Together, they developed similar likes and dislikes, and gradually invented a true counterculture based on frequenting certain public places, the notion of transparency, provocation, and the hatred of clichés, conventions, and the *salauds* (swine). "Vous me faites regret" (You give me regret), "Ça me fait tout poétique" (It makes me all poetic), "Ça m'a rarement fait si gratuit et si nécessaire" (It has seldom made me so gratuitous and so necessary), Sartre would write his "little flower," his "charming, little Beaver," developing a private language that would soon become the most impenetrable and whimsical sign of their complicity. Together, they hunted down news items and worshiped transparency: "My least feelings and thoughts were public from birth," he wrote in 1939. "Until the present war I *lived publicly.* "[14] Together, they discovered Céline, Faulkner, and Kafka, visited Naples and Barcelona, London and Athens, Hamburg and Rabat, stalked the latest jazz clubs in Paris and emptied their glasses, in one gulp, till they were drunk. If, as a couple, they are physically mismatched—she tall, he small (just like Anne-Marie and Jean-Baptiste before them); she strikingly beautiful, he rather ugly—they will nevertheless be inseparable in their rhetoric and friendship. He will play the role of the big brother and staunch supporter, as he did while they were preparing the oral exams for the *agrégation,* and she will listen and advise. They will share books, plans, friends, money —spending, on one trip for two, all he inherited from his paternal grandmother. Two intellectuals in revolt against society and the provinces, they will invent, in defiance of the society in which they refuse to participate, a set of customs, norms, codes, and new models that later will earn them a tremendous following. But, for the moment, they are only two teachers of philosophy who hate the French provinces, dislike their colleagues, live in hotels and cafés, and oddly enough, address each other with the formal *vous.*

Meanwhile, Sartre kept on writing, In cafés or in the public library. In 1930, Nizan proposed the manuscript of "The Legend of Truth" to Jacques Robertfrance, publisher of Rieder, who rejected it. Around the same time, "A Defeat" was proposed by Malraux, via Nizan, to the publisher Gallimard. It was also rejected. An excerpt of "The Legend of Truth" appeared in an issue of the literary review

Bifur, under the sponsorship of Nizan, but its argument was severely compromised by the editors. During his military service, Sartre returned to these reflections, pursued his research, and, elaborating the ideas he had already sketched in 1928, during an interview with *Nouvelles Littéraires,* he started a long work on contingency. Immediately polemical, he chose a form, at once didactic and serious, that he borrowed from the seventeenth and eighteenth centuries, the "factum." Following the tradition of Voltaire, Beaumarchais, and Furetière, he had gotten into the habit, shared by Nizan, of calling factum any kind of aggressive analysis.

"I picture glory," he once wrote to Simone Jollivet, "as a large ballroom filled with gentlemen in tails and ladies in low-cut gowns raising their champagne glasses in my honor. [This image] has haunted me since my childhood. [It] doesn't tempt me, but glory does."[15] He was only twenty-one then, and basked in the certainty that he would soon be a famous writer. "Whoever is not famous at twenty-eight must give up all thought of glory forever," he had later jotted down in his notebook. It was a quotation from Rodolphe Töpfer, which he had then easily appropriated, far as he was from imagining that he would not be famous at twenty-eight, or thirty, or thirty-two, but that he would be over thirty-three when his first literary work would finally be published. As for fame and glory, he will have to wait till he is already forty.

*W*HILE SARTRE was at Le Havre, his friends Aron and Nizan were making real breakthroughs. Aron was in Germany, and on his return, he published his thesis and his first two books. Nizan had joined the Communist Party and was going to turn into a radical, intransigent militant. He published his first two pamphlets in 1931 and 1932, and his first novel in 1933. Next to these two brilliant careers, Sartre's is mediocre. While Aron teaches French philosophy at the University of Cologne and Nizan is running for office in Bourg-en-Bresse, Sartre is going through a very hard time in Le Havre, feeling totally cut off from the rest of the world. The little Schweitzer monster, the rowdy, greedy Normalien had anticipated everything but failure. What Sartre had not foreseen was that the house of cards he had built with his life would pitifully collapse with the rejection of his first works by a few publishers, a rejection that he took as a death sentence. As a child, he had never doubted that to write and be famous were one and the same thing. Anne-Marie had always made copies of everything he had written, she had always applauded everything; later, his own friends had appreciated what he had done and had often smiled approvingly. At twenty-five, he had still believed in this extraordinary contract between himself and fame with writing as intermediary. Now he realized he had misled himself. He shelved his rejected manuscripts and went back to work, to his research, with determination. In those years, his "factum on contingency" followed him wherever he went: three successive complete versions of the manuscript, three different titles, several readers, innumerable cuts, and, on the way, many influences, trips, encounters; all were vested in the manuscript that emerged, in the spring of 1938, as *Nausea*.

According to Raymond Aron, Sartre had first started to develop his idea of contingency in 1926, while he was studying Nietzsche in Léon Brunschvicg's course.[16] Then, almost for fun, he had illustrated this idea in his article on the movies. Later, he began reflecting on the notion of "man alone" and had written texts on the subject, including "The Legend of Truth," where he settled his scores, first with his grandfather (in his treatment of idealist philosophy), then his stepfather (in his treatment of scientific knowledge). His experience in Le Havre had validated his choices as a "man alone": from that moment on, his reflections on contingency would develop in a new experimental context. The first version of the manuscript that will later become *Nausea* is already written in the first person, in the form of a journal, the journal of Antoine Roquentin, who lives alone in Bouville, where he is pursuing his research on an eighteenth-century scholar, Adhémar, the marquis de Rollebon.

"I live alone, absolutely alone. I never speak to anyone, never; I get nothing, I give nothing. The Self-Taught Man doesn't count. There is Françoise, who runs the Railwaymen's Rendezvous."[17] Of all his manuscripts *Nausea* was the one that caused Sartre the worst labor pains. The desolate, sluggish people of Bouville, its Sunday promenades, the nocturnal noises of kitchen maids through the thin partitions of a sordid hotel room—like Sartre, Roquentin lives in a small town where his life just drags on. He is a stranger and a voyeur; he likes to look behind the scenes to discover what lies under the most masked of all societies, the society of the provinces. As his days slug along, he passes from "a sort of sweetish sickness," a sort of "nausea," to a gradual detachment from both objects and people. He wants purity and freedom, seeks them in heightened lucidity, drunkenness, vertiginous loneliness, hatred—"For a moment I wondered if I were not going to love humanity. But, after all, it was their Sunday, not mine . . . for me there is neither Monday nor Sunday." He goes from insomnia, in his own hotel room, to a dismal, pointless affair with the owner of the café; from a dreary afternoon in the public library to an ontological experience on a park bench: "I have nothing to lose: no wife, no children, no special mission in this world. I am not a leader, nor a representative, nor any other kind of asshole."[18]

The first version of the "factum on contingency" employed all the themes that would later be developed and strengthened in the second and third versions: the notion of "verisimilitude," the epitome of bourgeois thought and refuge of all the *salauds,* a criticism of human- ism, the reduction of memory to true fiction, the illusion of adven- ture, and the perception of existence and of contingency, in a liminal experience, just before the onslaught of hyperlucidity and madness. From Simone de Beauvoir we know about her crucial role in the progressive elaboration of this manuscript: she sensed the affectation of a nineteenth-century style in the first version, sneered at its flat account of contingency, suggested the adoption of a dramatic pro- gression. She also commented on the secondary characters, Roquen- tin's companions—Ogier P., the Self-Taught Man, and Anny—and on the role they play in Roquentin's lunar universe. Sartre's love affair with Simone Jollivet was transformed into the frustrating, stifling dialogue between Roquentin and Anny, with its tirades on "privileged moments." The character of Anny, the only important female character in his first novel, was Sartre's gift to Simone Jol- livet. It was a double gift, because he was also giving her the name of his cousin Annie Lannes, at whose funeral they had first met.

In the same manuscript, knowledge and adventure emerge as two privileged ways of appropriating the world. "Every single one of my theories was an act of conquest and possession," he wrote in 1939. "I thought that, one day, with the help of them all, I'd conquer the world. For Jean-Paul, the philosopher, son of Jean-Baptiste, the adventurer, discovery, conquest, and the appropriation of the world all depend on knowledge. It is no coincidence that, after the *agréga- tion,* he so wished to get a post abroad. He hoped he would be sent to Japan and confided his dreams and desires to Beauvoir. "In Con- stantinople," she writes, "he would fraternize with the dockworkers; he would get blind drunk with pimps . . . he would go right around the world, and neither the pariahs of India nor the popes of Mount Athos nor the fishermen of Newfoundland would have any secrets for him."[19] But instead he was sent to Le Havre. The following year, he applied for a post in Morocco but did not get it. So, he remained at Le Havre. Sartre and Simone de Beauvoir traveled during every academic holiday, like most teachers: for Christmas, for Easter, and during the three summer months. But they never went beyond the reasonable boundaries of Europe—Spain, Italy, Great Britain, Norway, Belgium, Greece—except for one trip to Morocco. And wherever he went, he always brought along his own obsessions, his own notebooks, now and then jotting down an atmosphere, an idea, a bit of reading whenever his absolute despondency would let him perceive a link, a wink, some sort of complicity, scraps of experience that he haphazardly gleaned from different sources and then, maybe, would use in his factum.

"The idea of traveling, or, rather, of adventure became an obsession," Antoine Roquentin writes in a passage of his journals cut from the definitive version of *Nausea*. "At times, I'd stop in my tracks and count, on my fingers, all the cities and countries I'd visited: it was not enough, never enough. And then I would take off again. . . . I went to Japan. . . . I spent a year in Tokyo and Osaka. I saved some money, then took a trip through Java, Shanghai, Indochina. My last ties with France were broken: I learned of Vélines's death in Tokyo, on my way back from a quick trip to Korea. I was really alone now. Of all my family, there must have been only one cousin left in Périgord, a certain Roquantin, with an 'a.' "[20] Traces of Thiviers, traces of Jean-Baptiste, whose son would send his first hero, his adventurous counterpart, on all those trips he would never undertake. Along with Jean-Baptiste and Annie, Thiviers lurks everywhere throughout *Nausea,* and particularly when, giving vent to his hatred, Roquentin screams: "You, Ducoton, M. Prefect, and you Impétraz, inspector of schools, and you, Bourgadié, roads inspector . . . so powerful in your virtue, the respect of upright citizens, and your received ideas, your bank accounts and good manners; and you, minor geniuses with your names on street signs . . . town counselors, doctors, economists . . . and you too, all the warlocks who rule Bouville: you won't get me, I'm not afraid of your hexes!"[21]

*A*PRICOT COCKTAIL or mug of beer? Simone de Beauvoir maintains that, on the day when Aron, passing through Paris, met Sartre and Beauvoir and told them about his most recent philosophical discoveries, they drank apricot cocktails. Aron, on the other hand, writes it was just beer. As far as I know, Sartre never gave his version. At the café, Sartre spoke of his factum on contingency, and Aron of his latest readings and of German philosophy. The miracle occurred when Aron understood Sartre's intentions and sketched an approach to phenomenology: this glass, this table . . . phenomenologists spoke of them philosophically. That was all Sartre needed to hear: he immediately felt a strong sense of kinship with them. He bought a recent book by Emmanuel Levinas, *Théorie de l'intuition dans la phénoménologie de Husserl,* eagerly leafed through it, constantly recognizing his own thoughts in its pages: the concept of contingency was obviously very familiar to Husserl. Thus Sartre discovered the German philosopher, the only philosopher he will read for the next six years, exploring *Cartesian Meditations* and *Ideas: General Introduction to Pure Phenomenology.* In order to deepen his knowledge of Husserl, he asks to replace Raymond Aron at the French Institute of Berlin for a year of research: to study "the relationship between the psychic and the physiological," as he explained in his application. It was an interesting proposal; he would keep his teacher's salary and Aron would replace him at the high school in Le Havre.

Sartre's sudden fascination with Husserl was partly due to Descartes, the Descartes of the *Meditations* who had fascinated Husserl as the "hero who had decided to aim for absolute knowledge in total solipsism and who, in order to do so, had to begin by doubting everything, methodically and hyperbolically . . . making a tabula rasa of all previous beliefs and all accepted sciences."[22] At the Ecole Normale Sartre's disdain for his professors of philosophy went hand in glove with his attraction for the great men of his readings, such as Kant, but particularly Descartes, the "explosive thinker" whose "revolutionary thought"—which he opposed to "elegant soft thoughts"—sought knowledge with a "shining sword."[23] These were only the first steps toward a Cartesian purification, an ontological austerity, the demand for an extreme rigor that implied, at once, the rejection of speculative philosophy and the affirmation of a new fundamental philosophical project that would "establish its foundation in its very articulation."[24] What Sartre discovered in Husserl's phenomenology was an intellectual process whose every stage and every theme referred him back to his own. Surprisingly enough, Sartre had not attended the lectures Husserl had given at the Sorbonne in 1929. Similarly, he had paid very little attention to Heidegger's essay "What Is Metaphysics?" which had appeared in the issue of *Bifur* that carried an excerpt from his own "The Legend of Truth." Only after he has meditated on contingency, experienced it in his life, and illustrated it in the first version of his factum, will Sartre meet Husserl, this "genius," his "master."[25] In him, this "twentieth-century Descartes," Sartre discovers his most revolutionary, urgent, and essential philosophical perspective: phenomenology. It will remain *the* encounter of his life. He will never abandon it.

"Husserl had gripped me," he writes later. "I saw everything through the perspectives of his philosophy.... I was 'Husserlian' and longed to remain so. At the same time, the effort I'd made to *understand*— in other words, to break my personal prejudices and grasp Husserl's ideas on the basis of his own principles rather than mine—had exhausted me philosophically for that particular year. ... It took me four years to exhaust Husserl."[26] Sartre's days in Berlin will indeed be exhausting; the schedule he has devised for himself is draconian. In the morning he reads Husserl, in the afternoon he revises the factum with a passion and an intensity that consume all his energy and all his attention. He is already busy on a critique of Husserl's refutation of solipsism as put forth in both *Formal and Transcendental Logic* and *Cartesian Meditations*: "The conception of the Ego which we propose," Sartre writes, "seems to us to effect the liberation of the Transcendental Field, and at the same time its purification. The Transcendental Field purified of all egological structure, recovers its primary transparency."[27] These are abstract debates, essential debates in which Sartre the philosopher takes his stance vis-à-vis the question of the ego: "For most philosophers, the Ego is an 'inhabitant' of consciousness.... We should like to show here that the Ego is neither formally nor materially *in* consciousness: it is outside, *in the world*. It is a being of the world, like the Ego of another."[28] Are these purely formal debates? Sartre insists on this punctilious refutation of Husserl, which, according to him, rids phenomenology of all idealism and belies all those who justly see it as a "doctrine-refuge." "It seems to us that this reproach no longer has any justification if one makes the *me* an existent strictly contemporaneous with the world," he concludes, "whose existence has the same essential characteristics as the world."[29] And to drive the point home, he declares: "Nothing is more unjust than to call the phenomenologists 'idealists.' On the contrary, for centuries we have not felt in philosophy so realistic a current. The phenomenologists have plunged man back into the world; they have given full measure to man's agonies and sufferings, and also to his rebellions. ... No more is needed in the way of a philosophical formulation for an ethics and a politics which are absolutely positive."[30]

In 1936, Sartre published an article, "The Transcendence of the Ego: A Sketch for a Phenomenological Description," in *Recherches philosophiques*. Thus, Sartre's philosophical research began inscribing itself in the French phenomenological current along with Jean Wahl's preface to *Vers le concret*, with the translations of a few articles by Heidegger, Conrad-Martius, Oskar Becker, and Karl Löwith, with Gabriel Marcel's essays on "La Phénoménologie de l'avoir" (The Phenomenology of Having), and with Hermann Minkowski's "Esquisses phénoménologiques" (Phenomenological Sketches). Over the next fifty years, Sartre's critique of Husserl will provoke internecine and intercontinental debates among phenomenologists in Latin America, Portugal, Sweden, Israel, Germany, England, and the United States, as to whether or not the transcendence of the ego established by Sartre in answer to Husserl is "profoundly erroneous."[31]

93

Back from Germany and still under the influence of Husserl, Sartre continued his philosophical research. In 1935 and 1936, he wrote *Imagination* and *The Psychology of Imagination;* in 1937, he "sought . . . to elucidate . . . [his] ideas by beginning a big book *La Psyché,*"[32] which he abandoned shortly thereafter keeping only *L'Esquisse d'une théorie des émotions (Emotions: Outline of a Theory).* The 1930s is a crucial period that will lead to the elaboration of the central Sartre, the philosopher. During those productive years, he matures, he tries out the intellectual instruments that will be his later on, he develops concepts, categories, and arguments that will later become the very foundations of his world view. This dimension, probably unique among the novelists of his time, should not be underestimated: the plan for an intimate union between philosophy and literature, which Sartre had already started formulating at the Ecole Normale, is beginning to take shape, though not according to the chronology he had expected. The philosopher will emerge before the novelist; the creator of concepts will precede the creator of fictions. But the plan will be respected, the two careers will walk abreast. "Today's writers are way behind yesterday's philosophers," he writes to Jean Paulhan, in 1939, speaking of Faulkner. "His notion of time is the novelistic counterpart of theories already found in Descartes and Hume. I think it would be more interesting to try and make a novel of Heidegger's time, which is precisely what I want to do."[33] This philosophical-literary dialogue will be difficult; conflicts, tensions, emergencies, will often force him to choose between one and the other, as happened in 1937, when he found himself steeped in philosophy: "I enthusiastically wrote four hundred pages of [*La Psyché*] in three months, then stopped because I wanted to finish my book of short stories. But I was still so steeped in my researches that, for more than two months, my literary work seemed entirely pointless."[34] Ultimately, Sartre will be a philosopher before he is a novelist.

In Le Havre, he pursues his discovery of contemporary writers and his interpretation of their techniques, his meticulous analysis of all the mechanisms at work in the fiction of his time. Every month, in the hall of the Lyre Havraise, he delivers a lecture on literature. Lovers of literature of all kinds attend this long evening series that precedes, by six or seven years, the articles of literary criticism he publishes in the *NRF (Nouvelle Revue Française)*, and which, in 1938 and 1939, consolidate his reputation. Faulkner, Dos Passos, Virginia Woolf, Joyce, Huxley, and the technique of stream of consciousness are all presented, introduced, taken apart, with the utmost culture, seriousness, and rigor, in a provincial city where, in 1931 and 1932, both these novelists and these kinds of remarks were still unknown. During one of his first "chats," as Sartre himself calls them, he shows the evolution of stream of consciousness, which, according to him, appeared for the first time in 1887, in Edouard Dujardin's novel *We'll to the Woods No More*. "Why in 1887?" he wonders. "Why not in 1870 or 1900?" This question finally leads him to connect the appearance of this technique to the height of the symbolist movement, with its "cult of the inner life" and its discovery of the unconscious—"this great wave of which consciousness is only the foam," he notes. He emphasizes the influence of Richard Wagner on the "total work of art," to show how "this procedure, the product of an idealist trend, passes into the hands of the English neorealists, where it gets richer, more stylized, and, no longer limited to the revelation of a consciousness, ends up encompassing the entire universe . . . in the service of an absolute realism."

The unpublished manuscript of these lectures, consisting of small sheets full of underlinings and corrections, indicates extensive academic preparation as well as suggesting a novelist in the making. Joining philosophy and literary criticism, they become the conceptual instrument, the reflective and theoretical side of a still unrecognized writer, his personal research. In mentioning the names of Dos Passos, Faulkner, Schnitzler at the beginning of the 1930s, Sartre is playing a new role, the pioneer, the innovator.[35]

*M*EANWHILE, Sartre had moved to Berlin. For nine months, he abandoned the cafés of Le Havre in favor of the enormous variety of dark beers he could consume in the irresistible Berliner Kneipen. He continued his philosophical research, though now in the context of the Französische Akademikerhaus, Landhausstrasse 14, district of Wilmersdorf, Berlin. The new geographical context was to dictate a new historical context as well. The students of Le Havre had watched him scribble away, for hours, at the café, in the public library, between classes; his colleagues in Berlin now watch with great astonishment as he buries himself in his research at bars and in his first-floor bedroom, oblivious to the book burnings of 1933 and von Papen's speeches in front of Humboldt University.

Goethe, Schiller, Heine, and Novalis—in these postwar years, the German cultural tradition fascinated European intellectuals. For Sartre and Aron, as well as for all the generations that had preceded them, a cultural sojourn beyond the Rhine was an essential pilgrimage toward the foundation of European thought, toward the origin of their own influences and passions. If we recall the Alsatian roots of the Schweitzer family, the composition of the grandfather's library, and the themes that Jean-Paul Sartre chose for his novel when he was still at the Ecole Normale, then, for him even more than for Aron, the trip to Germany was a necessity.

Berlin's Maison Académique Française on Landhausstrasse shared in this cultural tradition. For the two years it had been open, it brought highly qualified young researchers, all of them *agrégés* and most of them Normaliens, to Germany. A German counterpart in Paris had been planned, but Nazi politics buried the project. When, encouraged by Aron, Sartre filed an application for the year 1933–34, he was immediately accepted and in the fall of 1933 was warmly welcomed to the Wilmersdorf villa. He had a large bedroom on the first floor, with ancient wood panels and a balcony overlooking the garden.[36] There, he met a rather peculiar community, which vaguely reminded him of his years at the Ecole Normale: a group of young professors more or less his age who had come there to continue their researches in literature or science, all under the direction of Henri Jourdan. At the Maison, Sartre met Eugène Susini, a Germanist from the ENS, two years his senior. He was a very learned, warm, open, young man of Corsican origin, a practicing Catholic, stocky, short, with jet-black curly hair. One day, Sartre tells him: "Husserl to me has been the greatest revelation in German Philosophy after Kant!"[37] He also met a certain Klee, a huge Alsatian—almost six feet four inches tall—*agrégé* in German, arrogant and openly racist, who clearly preferred the company of Germans. Jean Erhard, a schoolmate of the class of '24, was also there, but Sartre did not seem too pleased to encounter him again. Then there was Jean André Ville, an old Normalien *agrégé* in mathematics, and his wife, whom Sartre dubbed "the two moons"; and Henri Brunschwig, *agrégé* in history from the University of Strasbourg, who was a little intimidated in the presence of all those Normaliens. Brunschwig is not thrilled with his stay in Germany, does not like the Germans, and is particularly sensitive to the anti-Semitism already hovering over the Weimar Republic; nevertheless, he will remain in Berlin for four years. Finally, there is Pascal Copeau, son of Jacques—one of the founders of the *NRF* —a recent graduate in political science and now the Berlin correspondent for *Le Petit Journal* and *Les Nouvelles Littéraires.* He also lived at the Maison before finding a place in the city. Given his work, he will be by far the member of the group most receptive to the local political situation.

"An out-and-out failure," "The spell is broken," "The force of attraction is exhausted," wrote André François-Poncet, the French ambassador in Berlin, after the general election of 1932. A former journalist and *agrégé* in German, who remained in his post from 1931 to 1938, François-Poncet was still trying to analyze the German crisis optimistically. He was not the only French observer who committed this diagnostic error. "We can already predict Hitler's imminent disappearance from the political scene," *Le Populaire* wrote. "Hitler's influence is declining . . . he will not achieve supreme power": *L'Echo de Paris.* These were only some of the enlightened predictions of presumably well-informed political correspondents on the eve of the elections of January 30, 1933, when Hitler became, officially and legally, the new chancellor of the Third Reich. *Mein Kampf,* which had been published in 1925 and which François-Poncet had read in the original, should have worried a person as knowledgeable as he was, but it didn't. Even François-Poncet, respected Germanist, "scholar of the eternal Germany," whose witticisms were on everybody's lips, was not really worried.[38]

"For all those of us not used to massive street demonstrations, the spectacle was both solemn and powerful. At the sign of an adolescent drum major, a band of fifes and drums struck up a military march. White and red standards bearing swastikas rose above the bare heads of the crowd. A black band was tied around the poles of the flags whose wards had received casualties during the riots. There were several of them. At the end of Goebbels's speech, the crowd let out three short shouts. . . . Those populations who have a taste and a need for some sort of mysticism often display the most monstrous aspects of collectivity."[39] Pierre Mac Orlan, sent by *Paris-Soir* to cover Hitler's rise, kept dispatching dark descriptions of the Berlin streets back to Paris, but at no point did he take it upon himself to sound the alarm. The most sinister faces of the city seemed to hold a great charm for Mac Orlan: "One is aware of the full destitution of Berlin on first contact," he wrote; "it is there, lurking behind every corner like a beast, but one does not see it right off. . . . Mülackstrasse, just next to Alexanderplatz, basks in misery, like a popular song. It is announced by a bunch of dismal whores, waiting for clients. . . . This is where we can see the true colors of a criminal German romanticism."[40] Sartre, who arrived in Berlin in the fall of 1933, nine months after Hitler's election, was not particularly sensitive to those colors either.

Christopher Isherwood, there at the same time, penetrated into the sordid and sinister guest houses on Wassertorstrasse; was a frequent visitor at Bernhard Landauer's opulent apartment near the Tiergarten and at his country estate on the Wannsee; discussed literature with Natalia Landauer and philosophy with her cousin Bernhard; was intimate with several Jewish bourgeois families at the summit of European cultural sophistication; read, along with them, the threatening letters they received every day; witnessed the expropriations, the insults, and all the other pressures to which they were submitted. But Sartre, hungering after Husserl, remained alone. As during the good times on the Rue d'Ulm, he found himself again taken care of, in an organized group, with a regular salary, guaranteed housing, regular mealtimes in the dining room, a good library, and nearby, an avant-garde cinema, a student club, the Humboldthaus, the theaters around the Kurfürstendamm, and sailing on the Wannsee. One should also not forget that he was Raymond Aron's successor, and that nobody on the Landhausstrasse could avoid contrasting the two personalities: Aron's German was fluent; Sartre's was a struggle. Aron bore himself with an air of superiority, Sartre with humility. Aron, sensitive to what happened in the outside world, enjoyed visiting the eighteenth-century hotels around the Tiergarten or on Unter den Linden, and liked to engage in conversations with the students he met in trolleys. Sartre, almost exclusively obsessed with his reading, his research, and his writing, disliked meeting people—

probably because of the language barrier. Besides, how could Aron have been other than sensitive to the anti-Semitism of the Nazi regime? The director of the Humboldthaus, who had asked Henri Jourdan, the director of the Maison Française, to choose one of Jourdan's protégés to sit in on the German Student Committee meetings, had successively rejected the candidacy of both Aron and Brunschwig: "It would be a little . . . problematic . . . you understand?" he explained.[41]

At the heart of this little French colony, Sartre continued his struggle with Husserl, thrashing about in the middle of the master's most abstract concepts, while at the same time rewriting the second version of his factum, and sketching his first refutations of Husserl's solipsism. Late at night, he would often accompany Brunschwig up to Susini's room, which, given its lofty station, they had nicknamed "the dovecote." At times, he would even let Copeau drag him along to his latest discovery, some new homosexual *Kneipe* in a working-class district of old Berlin, near the Canal. Every morning, he would put on a number of sweaters and then, after pushing the window wide open, would do calisthenics, hoping to lose some of the weight he had gained from too many beers and *Würsten*. Or he would convince Brunschwig to go with him to the supermodern Neue Welle swimming pool, where they would swim till they were breathless in an extraordinary setting which even included mechanically produced waves. In his friendship with Brunschwig, he would soon find moments of great affinity. Sartre explains his "theory" of the *salaud*, Brunschwig talks to him about his perceptions of anti-Semitism. Brunschwig mentions an article on Chateaubriand he has just finished writing. Sartre asks to see it and launches into a page-by-page critical commentary. Together, they share some odious examples of triumphant fascism, as on the day a band of excited SS and SA snatched Susini's felt hat from him, or the day Copeau, beside himself, told them about the book burnings he had witnessed and about Goebbels's radio speeches.[42] Or the day when, in a group, they went to the Tempelhof to attend, in this large *Halle* of the working-class districts of North Berlin, those immense parties that only Germans can produce. Floods of beer, the relative nudity and scrumptiousness of plump little women, and all defenses down: people sing, stagger, dance, touch each other, kick up their heels, join hands in the happy merry-go-round of group pleasure.

*T*HE LITTLE French contingent existed as a disconnected microcosm, an islet lost in the middle of the sea and yet quite impermeable to its surroundings. It was not contemporary Germany that drew them there, but some writer of the *Sturm und Drang* or some nineteenth-century philosopher.[43] Speaking French, working, reading, exchanging French jokes at meals, singing French songs, they met Germany only by accident.

One day, before Easter, Sartre told Brunschwig that Simone de Beauvoir was coming to visit, and they discussed the problem of lodging: Brunschwig immediately offered him the room he had rented in town, more practical for two people. Of course, the landlady might object to an unmarried couple, so to avoid all hassles and provide a fitting welcome to Beauvoir, they went into the first jewelry shop they could find and bought two wedding rings.

"I've been surrounded by women for years, and I still want to meet new ones. . . . I prefer to talk to a woman about the tiniest things than about philosophy to Aron. . . . I'm not so sure I didn't seek out women's company, at one time, in order to get rid of the burden of my ugliness. . . . I certainly had an appetite for beauty, which wasn't really sensual, but more magical."[44] With Beauvoir, Sartre had found both beauty and dialogue. With her he would form a double couple, a male-female couple, which allowed him the pleasure of identifying with her beauty; and a couple of friendship, which permitted him to pursue, as he had done before with Nizan, Guille, and Aron, his meditations, his theories, his projects. She, solid, active, organized, realistic, had soon become his best counselor, his support, his first and foremost admirer. Then, he had moved to Berlin: "I'd set off determined to experience the love of German women, but soon I realized I did not know enough German to converse. Stripped thus of my weapon, I was left feeling quite idiotic and dared attempt nothing—I had to fall back on a French woman."[45]

Once Beauvoir was welcomed to Berlin with the wedding ring, Sartre told her of a "lunar woman," whom he seemed to like a great deal. From their very first meeting, Marie Ville, who as the wife of one of the boarders shared her meals with the group, had fascinated Sartre with her silence, her nonchalance, her passive beauty. Brunschwig remembers, "She interested him because she was amorphous, and he was determined to hear her express herself, to draw her out of her cocoon." Later, Sartre will wonder about this phenomenon, this "most essential structure," this "kind of lonely greed . . . to understand all 'natures,' suffering, pleasure, the being-in-the-world." "That's the source," he will later write, "of the magical attraction dark, drowning women have on me."[46]

First crisis in Sartre and Beauvoir's emotional relationship, first appearance of contingent love next to necessary love. Beauvoir went to Berlin under very difficult conditions and stayed way beyond the vacation time allowed her. According to some, before her arrival, Sartre had hoped to remain for another year, but after her departure, he never said another word about it and returned to Le Havre as scheduled. That particular year, he had not only been "philosophically exhausted by Husserl," he had also tried to tackle Heidegger, but in vain: "I did begin Heidegger and read fifty pages of him, but the difficulty of his vocabulary put me off. . . . My mistake had been to believe that one can *learn* successively two philosophers of that importance, as one learns one after another the foreign trade patterns of two European countries."[47] In June 1934, at the moment of his departure from Berlin, this twenty-nine-year-old, saturated with Husserl and fattened by alien gastronomic excesses, is no longer just one Socrates, he is a philosopher in the making, a laborious writer about to confront a personal crisis, a rite of passage: he is going to turn thirty.

He leaves a few friends—Brunschwig, for instance—and several memorable images, such as the one recalled by Ambassador François-Poncet: Sartre sitting silently throughout an entire dinner at the embassy, not deigning to say a word to his neighbors.[48] Or the enthusiastic impression that the literary critic Albert Béguin, then an assistant professor at Halle, brought back from his visit to Berlin. He returned, his wife remembers, "quite stunned by the intelligence of a young philosopher by the name of Jean-Paul Sartre. . . . He spoke of him for several days, as though still staggering from the impact."[49] Oddly enough, though Sartre was an ardent explorer and lover of cities—Paris and Le Havre, and, later, Naples, Rome, and New York—he has not left a single trace of any such attachment to Berlin. Nowhere does he refer to his walks through the town nor does he mention any of the charms of this city that, more than any other at that time, could have fired his imagination.

DARK MOOD, MADNESS,
OTHER JOURNEYS . . .

> *We needed immoderation, having for too long been*
> *moderate. All this culminated in that strange black*
> *mood which turned to madness around March of that*
> *year.*
>
> —THE WAR DIARIES

*B*ACK FROM his "vacation in Berlin," as he later called it, Sartre is recaptured by Le Havre, his life as a teacher, the ironic greetings of his colleagues, his trips to Rouen—obligations that seem even more unbearable after the interlude at Wilmersdorf. "The Beaver and I, sitting in a café called Les Mouettes on the ocean front at Le Havre, were bemoaning the fact that nothing new could happen to us." He is seized by nostalgia for a "life of disorder" and authenticity; he feels disillusioned, weary, sad, caught in the claws of a "doughy, abortive existence . . . so very far from the 'great man's life' " he had dreamed of. Then there was the shock of turning thirty. It all started in front of the mirror when he realized he was going bald. "It was a symbolic disaster for me . . . and for ages I used to massage my head in front of mirrors: balding became the tangible sign for me of growing old."[1] With the loss of the first few hairs, the gorgeous child is finally dead; the memory of the first golden locks sacrificed to his grandfather and the agonies of the shorn toad he had then experienced, are now blurred, pathetic wounds. By the fall of 1934, at Le Havre, Sartre is only a small, fat, aging provincial teacher. His certainties of grandeur and his dreams of glory are over. He has a physique like a stuffed tobacco pouch, a gruesome little Buddha. Guille teases him by grasping handfuls of his paunch through his sweater, to squeeze out some fat.

A gloomy period followed Sartre's return from Germany, hard dry years marked by social marginality and the exploration of liminal situations. It was a period of depression, so that "on several occasions," he "contemplated death with indifference"; and yet, he continued his work as an observer, more than ever bent on deciphering the world. During his years at Louis-le-Grand, he had decided that philosophy was going to be his supreme weapon. First of all, he explored various psychological tendencies so that he could start by deciphering himself; then, with the same obstinacy and determination, he began investigating the world. So, when Delacroix, his old professor at the ENS, asked him to write something for the collection of philosophical studies that he directed for the publisher Alcan, Sartre proposed a book on imagination, which would allow him to assimilate his reading of Husserl and pursue his reflections on the image. It would also permit him to explore the nature of the image in hallucinating subjects: the idea of experimenting with a hallucinogen tempted the researcher, fascinated the explorer, excited the philosopher.

He paid a visit to his friend Daniel Lagache, now a doctor at the Sainte-Anne Hospital, where, ten years earlier, they had both been introduced to psychopathology. Lagache himself had just finished a book, *Verbal Hallucinations and Speech,* for Delacroix's collection. The visual hallucinations that interested Sartre seemed to occur mostly with mescaline, derived from peyote, "the plant that fills the eyes with wonder." The drug wears off after from four to twelve hours and is not addictive, but it can cause more or less agreeable flashbacks up to a year after the experience. In January 1935, at the Sainte-Anne Hospital, Lagache injected Sartre with mescaline. Sartre had a short hallucination. As he later wrote in *The Psychology of Imagination*: "Someone was singing in the room nearby and as I tried to listen—stopping completely to look in front of me—three small parallel clouds appeared before me. The phenomenon naturally disappeared as soon as I tried to get a hold of it. . . . It could exist only *by stealth* and as a matter of fact it occurred as such; there was, in the way in which these three small clouds appeared in my memory, right after they had disappeared, something at once inconsistent and mysterious, which, it seemed to me, only translated the existence of these freed spontaneities *on the margins* of consciousness."[2] In fact, Sartre had a very bad trip and never repeated the experience. According to Beauvoir, "The objects he looked at changed their appearance in the most horrifying manner: umbrellas became vultures, shoes turned into skeletons, and faces acquired monstrous characteristics, while behind him, just past the corner of his eye, swarmed crabs and polyps and grimacing Things."[3] Sartre's hallucinations were neither oneiric nor esthetic, but rather cosmic and fantastic, with the usual dislocations of both time and space. His trip later caused a few painful "flashbacks" and, given the period of doubt and fatigue he was then going through, probably contributed to rendering him more vulnerable to psychological shocks than he had been before. Thanks to this experience, however, he was now part of a large family of French artists, including Baudelaire, Artaud, Michaux, and the surrealists, and more recently René Daumal, who had turned drugs into a vehicle to achieve a state of transcendence, hyperlucidity, and clairvoyance without which the poetic activity seemed to lose its capacity to decipher the world. His decision to explore his inner limitations during the theoretical and conceptualized development of his philosophical researches had no mystical, poetic, or purely formal intentions. In the esthetics of life that he developed in the 1930s he discovered a few basic points of agreement with the surrealists. Sartre's esthetics of marginality, so opposed to the communist ethics of the new man and of a socialist structure, will eventually contribute to classify him—in the eyes of the French Communist Party (PCF)—as a degenerate, decadent product of capitalism, the last cockroach of a system in a state of advanced decomposition.

Among his failures in those gloomy years, an unhappy love, which for lack of a better title could be called "Olga's story," forced Sartre and Beauvoir to reevaluate their plans and habits. Simone de Beauvoir wrote a novel about this affair, *She Came to Stay*—published in 1943—and then mentioned it again in her various memoirs, thus providing the public with a great deal of information about Sartre's private life. Olga Kosakiewicz had been a student of Simone de Beauvoir's in Rouen, but the professor had not noticed this original young woman, who went by the name of "the little Russian," until the end of the year. Olga, Simone de Beauvoir remembered,[4] was very intelligent and proud, "with a great deal of elegance and refinement. There was an incredible strength in her that she had acquired when she was a little girl and had been able to keep. She had received a very systematic, odd education, which had marked her profoundly, like her habit of walking barefoot in the grass, early in the morning, in summer as well as in winter. . . . Her mother was French. She had gone to Russia alone, to become a governess in a family of rich aristocrats. The son had fallen in love with this pretty woman and had married her." They had two daughters, Olga and Wanda. Olga, who was born in Moscow before her parents fled the Revolution in 1917, retained the "disdain of an exiled aristocrat," which, "fitted in very well with our own antibourgeois anarchism."[5]

Olga was mysterious and capricious. Her blond hair straying over a long, triangular face, her pale skin, her large wide-set eyes, her sudden crazes, her dance steps in the middle of the street, her wild whims, her innate honesty, her spontaneity, all these traits drew a ring of fire around the disenchanted professor. In 1934, against a background of music, literature, chess games, stiff drinks, and heady strolls through Rouen, Olga had become Beauvoir's best friend. It was only later, during his mescaline "flashbacks," that she got close to Sartre. As he went through his difficult crises, thinking he was followed by lobsters, the young woman listened to him, cheered him up, shared his hallucinations with laughter, dragged him along on long walks, journeys, rigorous verbal exchanges— privileged moments when they believed themselves masters of space. And suddenly, Sartre was seized by an all-consuming passion that possessed him for two years: "I was nervy and restless, each day I used to wait for the moment of seeing her again—and beyond that moment for some kind of impossible reconciliation. The future of all those moments . . . was that impossible love."[6] Two years of unhappy, tortured love; two years filled with morbid, exacerbated jealousy, obsessions, and giddiness. Olga won't give in, but won't push him away either; thus, he is suspended in the turbid and unbearable limbo of uncertain love, in a state of fever and despair, waiting for a sign, an overture, a change; he tries to seduce with his wit, intelligence, generosity, and imagination. "As for O.," he writes, "my passion for her burned away my workaday impurities like a Bunsen-flame. I grew thin as a rake and distraught."[7] It was a period of crises, terrors, dangerous games. She could not stand the "tyranny" of his jealousy; he was going mad at her incessant whims; they had countless scenes in which Beauvoir was often involved as a witness. "Passion and madness" are the words he will later use to describe those years.

That wayward, charming young woman rattled the structure that had been intellectually elaborated five years earlier. Sartre had wished to keep a door open to new loves; and suddenly, indeed quite brutally, the opportunity was there, shattering, with its mere presence, the notions of "necessary love" and "contingent love," uprooting, in a whirlwind of jealousy, madness, and despair, all the frameworks that had been so carefully constructed by intelligence alone, according to a disembodied procedure that as yet knew no deep wound. "For the first time in my life," he again writes, "I felt myself humble and disarmed before someone, felt that I wanted to learn."[8] All his dreams and certainties collapsed before the dainty, delicate rejections of the eighteen-year-old Olga. No more biographical delusions, no more "great man" on the horizon, just a man who did not know how to be liked, and who felt all at once "old, fallen, finished." The fall of the angel left no hope: a young woman had refused him the world. All his life, Sartre will eagerly turn to the young, looking for some appreciation for his research, his thoughts, his texts. He will put his famous factum and his first short stories into Olga's hands, begging her for approval, recognition; a word from her is so much more important than any publisher's. Youth owns strength, arrogance, provocation, laughter, self-confidence, power, a fierce critical mind, elegance, nonchalance, the present: this is an axiom Sartre will never renounce. "Much more than honest," Olga noted after her first reading of the manuscript that will later become *Nausea.*

"Without putting my feelings into conscious terms," Simone de Beauvoir confesses, "I was vexed with Sartre for having created this situation, and with Olga for taking advantage of it. There was something innately shameful about this obscure resentment on my part, and I consequently found it harder to endure than I was prepared to admit."[9] In the story with Olga, Sartre and Beauvoir will be rivals —potentially a return to the old order of possessiveness, exclusion, jealousy, to conventional notions and the brutal denial of any possibility for free union and transparency. "From now on we would be a trio rather than a couple," notes Beauvoir, who, with her writing, was able to acquire a new perspective and some control over a painful situation. "The three of us would share a balanced life, where no one would be sacrificed: it involved a big risk, but it was worth trying."[10] This idea of the "trio," this attempt to "annex" Olga onto the couple, was this also the way Sartre saw things? Or was this mostly an *a posteriori* reconstruction by a very capable, very unhappy woman? According to Beauvoir, at the very beginning of their relationship, she and Sartre had entertained the idea of "adopting" a young woman they had met in a bar. And she provides us with a ruthless analysis of the different stages of this phenomenon of fascination, of this attempt at annexation, of youth versus experience: "We . . . pursued the cult of youth," she writes. "This was why we loaded her [Olga] with values and symbols. She became Rimbaud, Antigone, every *enfant terrible* that ever lived, a dark angel judging us from her diamond-bright heaven."[11] It is difficult to reconstruct the duel that must have taken place between Sartre and Beauvoir under the circumstances. What is sure, however, is that her strength, self-control, and determination met their greatest challenge: "I therefore determined," she writes, "not to allow Olga too important a place in my life, since I could not cope with the disorder she would have sown there. . . . I set about reducing her to what she had always been for me. . . . Nor had I any intention of yielding up to her the sovereign position that I had always occupied, in the very center of the universe."[12]

"Olga was strange and sweet [with] the affected tenderness of a crushed flower." Some time after his "madness for Olga," Sartre describes to Beauvoir one of his lunches with the young woman whose unhappiness, on that particular occasion, assumes the aspect of "slightly unctuous moistness."[13] Indisputably, Olga remains one of the two or three passions of Sartre's life. He seldom spoke of her directly, except for the few times when the conversation turned to the subject of jealousy. "I am not jealous," he would assert, in a different tone of voice. On the other hand, if somebody really pushed him, he would admit: "Yes, maybe, about Olga . . . once I even broke a window pane." In his trilogy of novels, *The Roads to Freedom*, which he started in 1939 and published in 1945, the character of Ivich has many of the disquieting refinements of Olga, particularly in those chaotic scenes with Mathieu, Sartre's fictional double. Perhaps the most poignant passage is the café scene between Mathieu and Ivich, sitting in front of a glass of mint water she has just ordered —and which she later admits she detests, but nevertheless refuses to cancel the order since she is not really thirsty, anyway. "She looked at the glass and Mathieu looked at her. A violent and undefined desire had taken possession of him: a desire to *be* for an instant that distracted consciousness so pervaded by its own odor, to feel those long slender arms from within . . . to be Ivich and not cease to be himself."[14] A few lines from the *War Diaries* echo these scenes: "I certainly had an appetite for beauty, which wasn't really sensual, but more magical. I should have liked to eat beauty and incorporate it. I suppose, in a certain way, I used to suffer from an identification complex with respect to all those good-looking women."[15]

Six years later, Olga married Jacques-Laurent Bost, one of Sartre's favorite students at Le Havre. She never left the "little family," was often financially supported by the couple, and took a lead role in Sartre's first play, but she never earned her own autonomy within the circle of friends, intimates, and admirers. Nor did she ever break up with Sartre; in fact, by marrying one of his friends, she doubled her ties with him. A few years later, her sister Wanda would also become Sartre's mistress. Slowly, the family takes shape: Lionel de Roulet, another student of Sartre's, will marry Hélène de Beauvoir, Simone's sister.

Olga's story cast some light on the whole myth of transparency. Its different treatments in the oeuvres of both Sartre and Beauvoir are in themselves fairly eloquent. *She Came to Stay* tells the story of an impossible trio and ends in a murder, that of the young woman, Xavière, who had been the possible third member of the couple. There is nothing similar in Sartre's novel, no idea of a "trio," only the story of an unhappy love. Did Sartre and Beauvoir really share the myth of transparency? For her it is a sort of protective weapon, the means to a truthful narrative. More discreetly, for him it is an esthetic of life.

*T*HE LAST stage in the fall of Pardaillan's narcissism took place when Gallimard rejected Sartre's factum on contingency, still titled "Melancholia." Back from Berlin, he had worked on a third version, integrating philosophy with narrative tension. Paul Nizan then proposed the work to Gallimard. After a few weeks, Sartre received a short note informing him that the work had been rejected. "It hit me. I had put all I had into this book and a great deal of time; by rejecting it, they were rejecting me as well as my experience."[16] Disappointed, Sartre continues to write, both because and in spite of the bind he is in, to occupy his time as intensely as possible between his courses, his affairs, his train trips, his inevitable dinners with M. and Mme. Mancy. All the texts he wrote then bear the deep mark of those gloomy years: violently anarchical and intolerant of all rejection, he searches the world, the margins of society, the slums, wallowing in their most morbid, obscene, and repulsive aspects. In the meantime, his taste for trivial and criminal events gets him deeply involved in the Violette Nozières affair. Eighteen-year-old Violette was accused of having poisoned both her father and her mother. Her trial started in October 1934, causing much ink to flow and shocking petit-bourgeois French morality—the young woman had also accused her father of having maintained an incestuous relationship with her since her early adolescence. The surrealists—André Breton, Paul Eluard, Mesens, Benjamin Péret—took great interest in Violette and the scandal she had provoked, and particularly admired the way she had managed to rumple family respectability. We find the same reaction in the Sartre-Beauvoir couple, who also shared with the surrealists a fundamental anarchism, a rejection of social hypocrisy, and the radicalism of their demands.

During these gloomy years, Sartre wrote with the eyes of a scrupulous, if not quite maniacal, observer, something of a voyeur, taking inventory of the flaws, monstrosities, obscenities of life, with no desire to correct them. This atmosphere can be sensed in the letters he wrote at the time, in his short stories, his travelogues, his encounters with new cities. "Neapolitans," he writes Olga in a thirty-two-page letter from Naples in the summer of 1936, "are probably the only Europeans a foreigner can talk about . . . because they are the only ones whose lives can be witnessed from beginning to end. . . . Children everywhere, shaking their bare bottoms and their little quavering sexes all over the place. . . . This swarming of dirty buttocks and bare sexes is terribly animal." The absolute indecency of Neapolitan street life fascinates him: "It is in this intermediary world that Neapolitans perform the most important actions of their lives. So much so that there is no longer an inside and an outside, and the street is merely an extension of their bedroom: they fill it with their most intimate smells and their furniture." The secret of Naples's magical attraction for Sartre is that, shameless and transparent, it has no secret, that its inhabitants do outside "what the French do only in hiding."[17]

The moods that permeate this correspondence occur again, as obsessively but in an infinitely more scabrous manner, in the short stories he wrote around the same time: in "Soleil de Minuit" (Midnight Sun), "Erostrate" (Erostratus), "Dépaysement" (Disorientation), "La Chambre" (The Room), and "Intimité" (Intimacy), literary concentrates such as he will never again write in his life, the results of this intense gaze fixed on morbidity, madness, and sexual aberration, he reveals the most sensitive part of his self. A character like Paul Hilbert, for instance, who suddenly starts firing his machine gun into the crowd at the corner of the Rue Delambre and the Boulevard Edgar-Quinet, in the Sartrean perimeter of Montparnasse, is almost surely a double of the writer, but a double who is irrevocably plummeting toward madness. All these texts are explorations by Sartre, who, himself increasingly confused, is becoming more and more interested in understanding the pathological expressions of daily life from the inside. And perhaps this is why he feels such an attraction for liminal places, the lairs of madness, insane asylums: he, Beauvoir, Bost, and Olga spend an unforgettable day at the psychiatric hospital of Rouen.

. . .

The crisis of maturing, which announces itself with the loss of some charm, capacity, or talent, hit Sartre at an early age. The spectators, admirers, readers with whom, out of necessity and with utmost confidence, he had peopled the dreams of his childhood and youth, suddenly disappeared. And Anne-Marie's admiration, the steel frame that had so long and singlehandedly supported all that structure of self-love and self-assurance, suddenly became a useless bauble. Everything collapsed around him and inside him; and the identity he had shaped so early out of such a hard alloy suddenly started assuming a monstrous form. It was a radical, fatal wound to his narcissism. Without warning he was brutally forced to face himself and the world in a harsh, naked, blinding light. But he stood his ground and turned the fall into salvation. He was propelled into the "how" of things, on that tenuous edge that few dare approach and only when in a state of psychosis or extreme drunkenness. If his life failed to follow the outline he had drawn for it so long ago, then his hero would have to die unless he could undergo a radical change. This sudden breakdown killed the child prodigy and his potential genius but did not dismantle the resources of a man who, seven years later, was able to re-emerge, the mechanism fixed, the engine still running. In the meantime, he had gone through the experiences of a drunken boat, at the margins of society, to the absolute limits. From a distance, from his favorite post as watchman of society, he had followed the movements of men in cafés and hotels. During his insomnious nights in the French provinces, he had listened, he had waited, he had welcomed all the noises, all the movements, all the jolts of life as if they were coming from a different world. "I hear everything men do at night . . . the entire street comes through my room and flows over me . . . I'm just passing by . . . a mere visitor . . . free."[18]

THE 1930s, for so many the golden years of French literature, became for him years of despair, doubt, isolation. France bloomed with writers, publishers, reviews: André Malraux, André Gide, Henri Barbusse, Romain Rolland, Roger Martin du Gard, Paul Nizan, Paul Morand, Louis Aragon, Drieu La Rochelle, Jean Guéhenno, André Chamson, André Maurois, Georges Duhamel, Jean-Richard Bloch, the surrealists, George Batailles. They wrote, published, traveled, and, together, wove the history of their times, while Sartre, mired in a life and career he despised, was slowly slipping back, losing his footing, his eyes straining away from the line of a horizon that had yielded only mirages. The 1930s will be both his demise and his apotheosis, the cruelest and luckiest years of his life, the most marginal and the most exciting, the most asocial and the most fertile. While he worked, observed, recorded, and fought, everything else disappeared: history, politics, the Spanish Civil War, demonstrations, strikes, the rise of fascism in Germany, the leagues of the extreme right, great popular waves, vast collective aspirations, the new belief in an internationalism based on justice and equality, revolutionary songs, flags, raised fists, the certainty of final victory, the hatred of exploiters, the drunkenness of the exploited, the myth of the Soviet Union, paradise of all social justice, intellectuals holding hands with workers in innumerable associations, committees, conventions to fight fascism, to sing about better days to come, to celebrate the absolute ideal of the world's health about to be reawakened, to get drunk on this imminent triumph, to be militant, to convince, to denounce, to enunciate the only true revolutionary line.

One of the most painful years for Sartre, 1935 was also a year of literary solidarity, of celebration of the united left, just before the Popular Front—the alliance of the left—and the antifascist congresses of European artists. On June 23, 1935, on the platform of the Mutualité in Paris, Gide, Malraux, Aragon, and Nizan, side by side, raising their right fists, welcomed the first bars of the "Internationale" before an enthusiastic audience; this international congress of writers for the defense of culture brought together, for five days, Aldous Huxley, E. M. Forster, Boris Pasternak, Isaac Babel, and numerous French writers. Even the centrist Roger Martin du Gard agreed to participate, and, just two months before his death, old Henri Barbusse read Gorki's message to the public in a solemn voice. There were guests from every side of the political spectrum, with the exception of Henry de Montherlant, who, reputedly too rightist, had not been invited. Aragon said a few words in memory of René Crevel, who had just committed suicide. André Breton tried in vain to rouse the crowd in favor of Victor Serge, imprisoned in the USSR. Later, he took his revenge in a violent article, in which he maintained that the congress occurred "under the sign of systematic suppression . . . of real cultural problems"; and he accused the communists of extreme conformism, sycophancy, and infantilism.[19] Given the sharp ethical divergence between surrealists and communists, the only thing that could bring two men such as Breton and

Bataille together in the movement called Counter-Attack was the wish to fight fascism without having to merge into one political structure, one single party.

In 1935, Sartre was involved in a political discussion with Nizan, who, having spent a year in the USSR, liked to speak of his Soviet experience during his political tours in the provinces. The two men met in Rouen. After Nizan's speech, they had dinner with Beauvoir and Colette Audry, her friend and colleague, who, being also a militant of the communist teachers union, had already had a number of political discussions with them and had repeatedly tried to convince them to join the Teachers Union. Sartre and Beauvoir had nicknamed her "the communist," though they did not quite understand her critical yet sympathetic attitude toward the PCF: "Either you belong to the PC or you don't," Sartre used to say; he firmly believed that for a worker there was really no other choice. That evening, Nizan gave a speech about the Soviet Union; Audry found the speech "very revolutionary." After a dogmatic, sectarian period, Nizan was now going through a phase of open-mindedness with respect to the Party. Aside from his defense of the Soviet Union, he was also in charge of implementing a friendly approach toward the Catholics. A permanent member of the Communist Party for over three years, Nizan had got a few stripes out of the year he had spent in Moscow and in the Soviet republics of Asia and the Caucasus. He was also an important figure on the French literary scene; his first book had been a candidate for the Prix Goncourt, he was in correspondence with both Gide and the novelist Drieu La Rochelle, he had guided Malraux through the USSR. "If you seized power, what would you do with André Malraux?" Sartre abruptly asked him. "We'll lock him up in a room and keep an eye on him while he writes," Nizan calmly answered.[20]

A few months later, Gallimard published Nizan's fourth book, a novel, *The Trojan Horse,* his most dogmatic work. One of its characters, a certain Lange, is a provincial high-school teacher, a particularly desperate, pessimistic, anarchical fellow who acts as foil for a group of positive heroes, all communist militants. "Lange had come out of the Ecole Normale," Nizan writes, "which was in itself enough of a reason for his colleagues to hate him. . . . He had reached the extreme limit where culture merges with exhaustion in the no man's land of solitude and death. . . . Lange smiled: 'I don't like Marxists. I don't like psychoanalysts either. . . . You are asking me a senseless question. The only thing that matters is the relationship between the individual and Being. . . . My indifference is more radical than yours.' "[21] Gradually, this radical pessimism becomes one of the dynamics of the book; during a mass demonstration Lange veers toward unbridled terrorism and joins the most detestable enemies of the working class. Surely, Nizan meant no harm to his "petit camarade," and, in fact, the two men will continue to be friends till Nizan's death in 1940. On the other hand, when, during and after World War II, Sartre tries to reestablish contact with the PCF, this image of Lange, fleshed out with Sartre's own texts, will prevent all dialogue. "It was the first time in Lange's life," Nizan also writes, "that he was introduced to the proceedings of a group: it was a complete failure. Not a chance."[22] And indeed Sartre could not conform to the ideology of this passionate novel, nourished as it was with the militant experiences and the definitive convictions of the friend of his adolescence. Nor could he adhere to the idealist stances that announced "the explosion of History," victory over death, the birth of a new world, and the ineluctable power of the international proletariat that would reverse the order of things. With its collectivist ethics and "propagandist tone," as a critic had noted, *The Trojan Horse* had little chance of gaining Sartre's endorsement. He told Nizan that he could recognize himself in the character of Lange. Beauvoir: "Nizan declared, nonchalantly but firmly, that his actual model had been Brice Parain. Sartre said cheerfully that he didn't believe a word of it."[23]

*I*N THE spring of 1936, Gallimard had sent "Melancholia" back to Sartre. A few months later, a second attempt was launched by Pierre Bost—the older brother of Sartre's student-friend, a novelist, playwright, and reader at Gallimard—and Charles Dullin, who was then living with Simone Jollivet and had undertaken to present the book to Jean Paulhan. On April 30, 1937, a Friday, Sartre was finally able to tell Simone de Beauvoir that "Melancholia" was practically taken, and that Paulhan wanted to place one of his short stories in the *NRF*, and another one in *Mesures*. Then he added a modest, sober sentence, an apt conclusion to those years of doubt and black moods: "If I could, I would also like to tell you how strange and yet pleased I feel inside, but the little time at my disposal prevents me from launching into a detailed description of my mood."[24]

INTERLUDE: TWO YEARS OF HAPPINESS

> *Everything began to smile on me. . . . All of a sudden*
> *I felt full of a tremendous, intense youthfulness; I*
> *was happy and found my life beautiful. Not that it*
> *had anything of the "great man's life," but it was*
> *my life.*
>
> —THE WAR DIARIES

H OWEVER UNOFFICIAL, the fact that "Melancholia" was "practically taken" had a magical effect on Sartre's frayed life. And two more successes prolonged his joys. First he was told that for the next academic year, beginning October 1937, he would teach in Paris, at the Lycée Pasteur, in Neuilly. Secondly, the young women he had been courting suddenly started accepting his attentions. Alas, this lucky period would soon end with the beginning of World War II, but in the meantime, Sartre would have a few months, little more than a year, to make his entrance on the French literary scene. And it will be quite an entrance despite a series of new delays caused by his factum.

The relationship between Sartre and Gallimard began ominously. The writer who one day, according to the figures of December 31, 1978, would rate as one of the ten most profitable products of the publishing house was rejected twice before a few friendly nudges from private sources facilitated his acceptance. Some of his titles have sold nearly two million copies each in French alone. Before his death, Sartre signed a contract with Gallimard giving it exclusive rights, without restrictions, to all his unpublished manuscripts: a magnanimous gesture, proof that his memory of the first two rejections—"The Legend of Truth" in 1930 and "Melancholia" in 1936 —was not too painful after all. "A superior mind, to grab without hesitation," the philosopher of the publishing house, Bernard Groethuysen, had written on his card. "Sartre is a remarkable fellow we can't afford to lose," Brice Parain had concurred, partly convinced by Nizan and partly by Normalien rumblings. "A brilliant, remarkable, extraordinary book, which may be the only work of this writer," Jean Paulhan had written on the last card, the one that had sealed a definitive acceptance.[1] Later he gave Sartre an explanation that, whatever its worth, had the merit of protecting their respective positions: there had been a misunderstanding, Paulhan explained. Initially, the manuscript of "Melancholia" had been directed to the *NRF* to be serialized, a proposition that, of course, was rather untenable. Only when the manuscript was submitted a second time, by Dullin and Bost, were things straightened out; it was to be published as a book.

"I entered proudly. Seven guys were sitting in the hallway, waiting for Brice Parain, Hirsch, and Seeligmann. I refused to give my name and told the receptionist I was there to see Paulhan. She announced me. I was told to wait five minutes, so I sat down in a corner, on a small kitchen chair. I saw Brice Parain go by, but he didn't seem to recognize me. Then a dashing little gentleman walked in. Dazzling shirt, tie pin, black jacket, striped pants, spats, bowler hat pushed back. His face was reddish, with a long sharp nose and hard eyes. It was Jules Romains."[2] These are the first impressions, the first notes, of his first visit to his future publisher. Sartre's initial steps at Gallimard must have been a little like Roquentin's in a public park: no wonder, no admiration, no specific mood, just a stark perception of the world. His trials with Olga and others had extinguished his enthusiasm, his frenzies, his old impatient pride. During his first journey through Gallimard, Sartre remained consistently ironic and distant, indeed almost superficial. Paulhan? "A big, swarthy guy . . . graying mustache . . . a bit fat."[3] Brice Parain? "I dislike his air of being the young older child."[4] On the other hand, hadn't the whole thing started almost like a joke when, a few months earlier, he had had to answer Paulhan's letter? Jacques-Laurent Bost had dictated the text, stamped, and posted the envelope: the student leading the professor into an upside-down world. It was Bost's appeal to his brother that had gotten Sartre an answer and an appointment with the editor. Despite his renown, Nizan's two efforts had been in vain. It had taken the insistence of Dullin and of this "twenty-year-old kid," Sartre's student during his last year at the high school, to get anywhere.

"Little Bost" was a handsome young man, the youngest child of a liberal minister in Le Havre: light blue eyes, smooth complexion, princely profile, innate charm, his ease checked by that slight reserve proper to Protestants, which often makes them bend their head to the side, or cross their arms, or display, with awkward gestures, a minute discomfort that renders them all the more seductive. Back from Berlin, Sartre had noticed this interesting young man who was repeating his class and whose relationship with Raymond Aron, the previous year, had not been the warmest. "Then," the young Bost remembers, "I was a die-hard leftist." Bost's friendship with Sartre, sparked perhaps by the complicity of two Protestants in rupture with their tradition, by the recognition of two similarly radical temperaments, or simply by mutual admiration, will last till Sartre's death. Friends and allies, they will become practically inseparable, and Bost will play two key roles at particularly crucial moments in the life of the writer, acting as intermediary with his brother and the Gallimards, and also, without knowing it, serving as model for and instigator of Sartre's short story "The Wall," the first of Sartre's texts to be published. Often traveling to Paris to participate in the huge demonstrations that, in 1935 and 1936, paved the way for the Popular Front's walk to power, Bost would ask Sartre to come along. "No, it doesn't interest me. I don't like parades," Sartre would invariably answer. Then, one day, Bost asked Sartre for help in joining the revolutionary troops in the Spanish Civil War. "Halfheartedly," Sartre sent him to Nizan who sent him to Malraux who asked him two questions—"Have you done your military service? Can you use a machine gun?"—with negative answers.[5] Bost's trip to Spain stopped at Malraux's desk, but Sartre drew inspiration from this anecdote for "The Wall," which he apparently wrote during the first months of 1937, and which was immediately accepted by Paulhan, to whom Sartre had submitted it during his first interview.

On April 30, 1937, the day of Sartre's first admission to the inner sanctum and his meeting with Paulhan, two of his works began their parallel lives inside Gallimard: the short stories Sartre brought with him and the factum. For the former, everything is quick and simple: they are published in their entirety and hailed only two months later. The factum, on the other hand, takes twelve months to publish. Brice Parain has the task of "making the author work"; he is the one who has to negotiate the cuts of the roughest pages, those most "open to prosecution": this means six weeks of work that Sartre submits to halfheartedly, knowing it is necessary for final acceptance of the manuscript. "My dear Parain, there isn't a single crude word left in the text," he writes, exhausted, at the beginning of June. "I hope everybody will be happy. Anyway, this is all I can do."[6] Suppressed under the joint pressure of Parain and Maurice Garçon, Gallimard's legal consultant, were all those passages that, as Sartre put it, were "a little too . . . free." To begin with, he allowed them to excise some forty pages, without balking. "Garçon would like a few more corrections, fewer crudities," Parain persisted brutally, and, to drive the point home, he added, "Gaston Gallimard is of the same opinion."[7] Sartre had no choice. These cuts, even if retrospectively justified, were the condition *sine qua non* of publication.

"Dear Sir, please find enclosed a contract for your work titled *Melancholia.* We would appreciate it if you could change the title, unsuited to the promotion of the work. Could you please think about it?" Gaston Gallimard himself wrote to Sartre[8] about the title, chosen—apparently at Simone Jollivet's suggestion—as a reference to Dürer's engraving "Melencolia," and, more generally, to the tradition of melancholy in classical thought.[9] Sartre's awkward reply read: "Since you don't like the title *Melancholia,* what do you think of something like *The Extraordinary Adventures of Antoine Roquentin*? Then, in a blurb one could explain: 'There are no adventures,' or something like that. . . . I hope this title will suit you because I can't come up with anything else." Brice Parain's brief answer intimated that "such a blurb could be appropriate only if they wanted to scare the public off."[10]

"I'm walking in the streets like an author": as with any book, the credibility of "Melancholia" is confirmed by numerous readings, by the way the manuscript survives group criticism, which legitimizes it, transforms it, and anticipates the response of readers and reviewers. Before its final acceptance, "Melancholia" was examined by all the readers at Gallimard: first Paulhan, then Groethuysen, then Parain, and finally the boss himself, Gaston Gallimard. Subsequently, it was read and commented on in the corridors, along staircases, in private meetings. Soon a rumor spread throughout the house: "Sartre has made it."

"Gaston Gallimard has proposed an excellent title for your book," Parain writes on October 12, 1937, "a title that is all the more admirable as nobody here seems to resent its forbidding implications. What do you think of *Nausea*?"[11] The fetal existence of the manuscript, successively titled "Factum on Contingency," "Essay: On the Loneliness of the Mind," "Melancholia," "The Extraordinary Adventures of Antoine Roquentin," ended with Gaston Gallimard's superb idea: *Nausea* saw the light in April 1938, more than eight years after its beginnings.

*W*HILE NEGOTIATIONS went on, Sartre had gone back to his writing, his private correspondence, stories, articles, and notes on Heidegger, whom he had just begun to discover. He was also establishing himself in a new context, that of the students at the Lycée Pasteur. His classes were socially mixed since the high school was shared by both Neuilly, a middle and upper-middle-class neighborhood, and Levallois, a much more modest suburb. The confrontations inside the classroom were fairly tame, but they were much more violent outside, and particularly on those days when fascist students of Action Française and the Camelots du Roi hawked their respective papers. As Raoul Lévy recalls, "Sartre arrived wearing a worn, rumpled suit and with a huge red pimple on his nose. With his hands in his pockets, he started delivering a totally incomprehensible lecture. . . . Despair! Then, suddenly, everything cleared up. . . . Sartre started speaking about madness, deviations, psychopathology . . . with an interest and an enthusiasm we had never witnessed before."[12] Lévy later graduated with honors and a first prize in philosophy. Teacher and student remained friends.

The mechanism is the same we encountered at Le Havre. Pasteur is also polarized by Sartre, in very much the same way: some people like him, others don't, some are bewitched by him, others repelled. The administration remains perplexed by this new professor who always arrives at the last minute, by cab, and literally dives into his class where he immediately starts his lectures. In the evening, during family dinners, nice middle-class students suddenly declare, "Madmen aren't mad unless everybody is mad in which case nobody is"; and, to their parents' outrage, they insist, "Anger is the last resort of the weak . . . or of the *salaud.*" Half digested fragments of sentences, outbursts of adolescent provocation: this is the first time these bright young men have taken a hard look at their social background. Sartre only encouraged a critical attitude proper to their age. "Thanks to Sartre," Gérard Blanchet remembers, "I changed generation."[13] What happened in Le Havre happens again in Neuilly; the parents complain, speak of "contamination," worry about the final exam for two whole years. In Neuilly as at Le Havre, people notice the holes in the socks, the old shoes, the weird coat of synthetic brown fur he wears in winter: "He looked like the little king in the comics of those years," Blanchet notes. They also notice the pipe, the Boyard cigarettes, and the way he alternates a black turtleneck sweater—a most peculiar item for a professor at the time —with a white shirt. "Did you leave the shirt at the laundry?" a

117

student asks him one day when he is wearing his turtleneck. "Yes, that's it, exactly," the professor answers before launching into the topic of the day.

But, the most authentic part of Sartre's relationship with his students was enacted at the Sabot Bleu, the café where the boys of the Lycée Pasteur met the girls of the high school across the street. It was a sacred place, a privileged meeting ground at a time when the hierarchy of professors and students and the separation of boys and girls made life very difficult. The Sabot Bleu restored some balance and allowed a degree of freedom, the kind of breathing space forbidden in classrooms. That's where the idea of the paper *Le Trait d'union* was first conceived; Serge Dumartin brought the project to fruition. He gathered a few others around him, including Chris Marker (later a filmmaker) as editor-in-chief, and the ravishing Simone Kaminker, later Signoret, who conquered the hearts of all the male students, who fought to see who would accompany her to the printer.[14] Sartre, of course, was the perfect companion at the Sabot Bleu; he offered drinks and cigarettes, teasing, prodding, questioning these adolescents, among whom he felt so much at ease. "But sir, how can you spend so much time with us when you have so much work to do?" they would ask him, at once delighted and amazed at this unusual situation. "One can always learn, even from idiots,"[15] Sartre would answer before telling them about René Clair's latest movie or Hemingway's latest novel, or before getting deeply involved, at someone else's instigation, in a discussion about the existence of God. "Why do you need to confess?" he would ask. "You enter a little wood box, and then? Please explain it to me, I want to understand," he egged them on, perversely. He even agreed to give them an article for *Le Trait d'union*, and, between two glasses of beer, he wrote it—a piece on the American novel. In the meantime, *Nausea* had been published and the professor had become a star. His students asked him to write dedications in their copies. "To Raoul Lévy, for his personal library," Sartre had written before signing.

Sartre's class gathered quite a few worthy recruits: Lévy, Jean Kanapa, Bernard Lamblin, Jacques Besse, Guy Joffroy, Jean-Pierre Huberson, Timoutchine Adjibeyli-Bey. Besse and Lamblin, two jazz experts, had their reservations about Sartre's use of the song "Some of These Days" in his novel; the professor was a little out of step in his musical knowledge, he loved jazz the way Cocteau did, they surmised, more because it was in the air than because he really liked it. These two students end up studying philosophy at the Sorbonne, where they become some of Sartre's fiercest defenders, disdaining the rest of their fellow students in the name of their intimacy with the great literary and philosophical genius. Later, they manage to achieve a healthy distance. But in 1939, the students at the Sorbonne thought them odd animals and called them "the little Sartres."

Of course, from an intellectual standpoint, Sartre has a double hold on his students: he is at once an extraordinary professor and a novelist of genius. Besides, he gives them the example of a life, his own, that is totally opposed to the models upheld by their families: "I don't have anything, I don't own anything," the professor tells them referring to his hotel room on the Rue Delambre. He even invites them over: bed, sink, table, chair, gray suit, some books, that's all. According to Alfred Tomatis, "A young woman, an actress, often came looking for him after class. And we would think: That's odd, that a man his age isn't married; he doesn't look like a homosexual; he has several mistresses." Sartre scored his greatest victory over reticence the day Heidegger, with whom he larded all his courses, was included in the exams of the *baccalauréat*. Thanks to him, his students acquired keen critical minds, a strong sense of responsibility, clear perceptions of class struggle and of racism, and an acceptance of otherness; they had demystified madness and other taboos, as well as marriage, private property, and the other symbols of bourgeois life. In short, they had truly confronted otherness to the detriment of all fictitious hierarchies, all useless conventions. "There are good Jews and bad Jews," one student told Sartre in 1938. "You're talking like a barbarian," Sartre answered him with exasperation. "Do you need a scapegoat that badly?" It was in those days, while he was nonchalantly observing the students of the extreme right, that he wrote "The Childhood of a Leader." Among his students there are also the inevitable detractors, like Alfred Tomatis, who, while appreciating the "brio of his improvisations, the vitality and brilliance of his intelligence," later noted how "that part of the class who took everything he said seriously sank into despair and went looking for a solution to their anguish in drugs and, in certain extreme cases, even in suicide."[16]

On March 14, 1939, the school inspector, already sensitive to the stature of the writer-professor, wrote a half-humorous, rather ambiguous report, hardly justified in that the Lycée Pasteur already employed a number of other writer-professors. "Whoever is familiar with the *NRF*, and has read *Nausea* and *The Wall*, could not walk into M. Sartre's class without expecting to find a great deal of skill.

And, indeed, M. Sartre has undeniable talent for expression, and his language is remarkably sound, proper, and refined. His hold on his students is obvious; but then again, given their ages and their status as students of a great Parisian high school, they could not but be favorably disposed toward a professor who, though he is quickly becoming a name in the world of letters, is nevertheless still able to remain a friend to them and to walk among them, speaking with ease, without notes. On the other hand, this only enhances the contrast between his attitude and the absolutism and dogmatism that I heard in his lecture on emotion. Even those students who are fairly familiar with a phenomenological point of view must have some difficulty following a lesson whose digestibility the professor never seems to consider, just as he does not seem to question to what extent emotion really 'denies the world,' and 'destructures reality,' or 'simplifies behavior.' One often has the impression of listening to ready-made formulas that are being presented as definitive truths regardless of whether they adequately and exhaustively explain the truth of emotion."[17] An interesting report which already reveals all the contradictions of a philosopher whose awareness of contemporary German thought goes way over the head of even the worthiest inspector. A philosopher-theoretician who teaches beginners, a novelist who earns his livelihood as a professor: these are the facts that complicate the narrow contingencies of preparation for the *baccalauréat*. From that time, Sartre begins to feel very restricted in the role of a professor, a role that is deteriorating under the increasing pressure of his other activities.[18]

"*W*HO IS this new Jean-Paul?" André Gide asks Paulhan immediately after reading "The Wall" in the *NRF*. "I think we can expect a great deal from him," he continues. "As for his short story, it's a masterpiece."[19] This first discovery becomes the subject of literary conversations: "You have no idea how I prefer this to Malraux's *Days of Wrath*," Jean Schlumberger tells his friend Gide, who answers: "I do too. Besides, although what Malraux writes is often very interesting, he has no sense of language."[20] Everything is primed for success. Now it is the turn of the critics, and seldom has their applause been so sustained. The publication of *Nausea* and *The Wall* a few months apart assures Jean-Paul Sartre's acceptance into the world of letters and gives the public the opportunity to experience all at once the terrible universe of Sartre.

Nausea: "One of the most striking literary débuts of our times"; "He brings together various tendencies of contemporary literature . . . Kafka, Joyce, Rabelais, Dostoevsky, Flaubert, Céline, Proust, Nietzsche"; "A magnificent design . . . a disturbing experience . . . to exist without being . . . in a contract not with things, but with their existence"—Maurice Blanchot. "An original mind"; "A true poet"; "One of the purest artists"; "A ruthlessly rigorous critical mind, . . . a brilliant future"—Jean Cassou; "The first novel of a writer from whom we can expect everything . . . a singular and vigorous mind . . . we impatiently await his future works and lessons"—Albert Camus; "A real philosophical novel . . . has been able to lend objects the maximum of their existence"; "Sartre has undertaken to annex new territory to the sensibility of the twentieth century"—Claude-Edmonde Magny.[21] Only Céline, a few years earlier, had been able to provoke such a storm of interest with his first work, *Journey to the End of Night*.

The Wall: "A masterpiece . . . time will break its teeth on it"; "What wonderful gifts! What an easy authoritative way of plunging us into the troubled waters to the point of choking or vomiting. . . . Nobody has been able to express the horror of living better than Sartre"; "One can already refer to an oeuvre when speaking of a writer who, in two books, has been able to go straight to the essential problem"—Albert Camus; "A ferocious analytical gift, a strikingly sharp eye, an excellent, clean, fluid, flawless style characterize his undeniable talent"; "*Nausea* had been last year's revelation; *The Wall* is far from disappointing us as to the rare talent of its author . . ."; "the language is pure, naked and full. . . . With his meditation on existence, Sartre brings a new theme into our literature"—Gaëtan Picon; "*The Wall* can be compared to the best moments of *The Human Condition*"—Gabriel Marcel.[22]

In the meantime, though perhaps prematurely, his name has already been mentioned for the Prix Goncourt: "Public opinion brings titles to the Goncourts," the *Paris-Midi* critic writes. "Have they read M. J.-P. Sartre's *Nausea?* They must read it even if they don't feel like it. Several critics, and some of the best, have and have thought it tasted like a masterpiece. It is written about in all the papers, it makes its way by word of mouth. . . . In short, it is an 'odds-on favorite,' so to speak, since publishers have 'stables' and prizes are 'races.' "[23] The Parisian whirlwind is in full swing, and, even if Sartre does not win the Prix Goncourt, this *vox populi*, so quick, so precocious, so instantaneous, seems already a guarantee of his success as a writer. Besides, since November 1938, Paulhan has signed him at the *NRF* for a regular monthly column and a fixed salary of 400 or 500 francs a month, while leaving him complete freedom as to the subjects he will write about. And, in the wake of his short stories, he has already started a new novel: "I have suddenly found the subject of my novel, its proportions and its title," he writes to Beauvoir, "its subject is freedom. Here is the title (the second volume will be called *Le Serment* [The Oath])."[24]

So much praise, so many yesses—but nobody seemed to notice that among five stories comprising *The Wall*, two revealed for the first time Sartre's increasing interest in the historical problems of his day: "The Wall" and "The Childhood of a Leader." No contemporary text presents a sharper analysis of the French fascist movements in the period between the two wars than "The Childhood of a Leader." In the account of Lucien Fleurier's life from birth to maturity Sartre displays an extraordinary understanding of the various moments in the adolescence of a young French bourgeois—and particularly so when showing us Lucien's first steps in the group of young fascists. At first, Lucien must be seduced, flattered, agitated against the Jews, and then, one day he will himself take the initiative and murder a good French citizen. "It's done, I am with you," he will proudly announce the following day. "The real Lucien—he knew now—" Sartre writes, "had to be sought in the eyes of others, in the frightened obedience of Pierrette and Guigard, the hopeful waiting of all those beings who grew and ripened for him, these young apprentice girls who would become *his* workers."[25] Wavering between fear, spite, power, cowardice, in the course of seventy-five pages Lucien Fleurier becomes a symbol; once his metamorphosis is accomplished, he looks in a mirror: "I'll grow a mustache," he decides.[26]

Jean Paulhan's press campaign is paying off; he addresses all his friends in the world of letters: to Jules Supervielle, "Have you read Sartre?";[27] to André Gide, "Have you read Sartre's *The Wall*? He is going to become somebody";[28] to Roger Martin du Gard, "I'm trying to push Sartre toward a 'novelistic campaign.' I don't know a single young writer who'd be better at it than he";[29] to Giuseppe Ungaretti, "Have you seen *Mesures*? I think Sartre is a great writer. His feet are still stuck in the mud of postwar literature, but he is already moving beyond."[30]

*E*NCOURAGED BY his new champion and the assurance of future publication, Sartre spends the first half of 1938 in a creative frenzy. Among his new projects is an article on François Mauriac for the *NRF*. Finally freed of all contingency and all urgency, in the act of writing he finds the identity that his excessive fears had earlier prevented him from expressing. His prewar image rests primarily on these two texts: feisty, aggressive, hard, uncompromising. In them, without the slightest hesitation, he demarcates his territory, surrounds it with barbed wire, and denounces his enemies: on the one hand, the fascist extreme right, which, under the intellectual influence of Charles Maurras, blooms in the students of the Action Française, and, on the other hand, the moralistic, Catholic, slightly academic literature represented by François Mauriac. Paulhan sniffs the air and, with his publisher's intuition, decides this is the moment for Sartre to attack.

"Dear Sir, I quite agree with you as to the cuts you suggest. On the other hand, I'd like to retain the notion that the Action Française is a conspiracy. . . . We both know that Maurras once wrote: 'We are not a party, we are a conspiracy! . . . I have already added a page to the bottom of the first page of the proofs of my article on Mauriac. . . . Should I say something else?"[31] This is a perfect example of the correspondence between Sartre and Paulhan during the first years of their relationship: Sartre, deferential, courteous, grateful, accepts the cuts, the toning down that Paulhan proposes. But this won't last; later the "great Sartre" will seldom be brought to agree to any compromise. A steady correspondence between the two men of letters begins, concerning questions of cuts, other suggestions, and invitations to fashionable gatherings. "My dear sir and friend, I have just finished reading your letter on the power of Words," Sartre writes in a shaky hand from the ship taking him to Casablanca for a vacation, "and I agree with you entirely. . . . Your own words seemed to imply a challenge: show me somebody who, at the very moment he is speaking, can say 'I am sensitive to the power of words.' At this point you are no longer dealing with the question sociologically . . . but rather psychologically: you are appealing to introspection. And if this is the case, I can certainly answer that I am that rara avis (not so rare after all). I am sensitive to something in words that is not their conceptual sense but rather what I would call their magical sense."[32] And here he abandons himself to a brilliant dissertation on the magical power of words, forcing Paulhan to soar beyond himself. After "The Childhood of a Leader," Sartre writes, back to back, a note on Husserl and articles on Nizan and Faulkner, and then, in the wake of his last short story, he decides to begin a novel to be titled *Lucifer*; this is the first in a long series of uncompleted projects.

On and on he pursues his interests, his obsessions. After his article on Faulkner's notion of novelistic time, he announces that "this is just a sketch for other studies on the phenomenon of the dissolution of time in contemporary literature."[33] His first articles are a continuation and elaboration of the lectures he had delivered in Le Havre: Dos Passos and Faulkner play equally important roles in the theory of the novel that is gradually evolving out of this series of articles. His premises are invariably the same: "A novel is a mirror. . . . A novel does not show us things but signs. . . . With due distance, good novels are very similar to natural phenomena."[34] He is going to clear the way, slash, massacre, praise to the skies. On the one hand, he'll claim that "Dos Passos is the greatest writer of our time," and on the other, that "God is not an artist, nor is M. Mauriac." His words have the violence of a left uppercut in mid-match, and the literary world staggers! His reputation as a critic will be built entirely on his article "Monsieur Mauriac and Freedom," published by the *NRF* in February 1939. Hammering away at *Thérèse Desqueyroux* and its author, he takes up arms against a writer twenty years his senior, a member of the Académie Française since 1932, widely respected. In discrediting Mauriac, a regional writer of the French Southwest, he was perhaps exorcising a bit of Thiviers as well. It took Mauriac a good while to recover from this rampage.

His second immediate enemy in the Paris literary world is Robert Brasillach, who, provoked by "The Childhood of a Leader," uses *L'Action française* to rail against this "boring" author who writes so "poorly about a rather dirty type of eroticism." While conceding Sartre an "ingenious, subtle mind not without a certain hate-filled intelligence," Brasillach virtuously attacks the general atmosphere of his short stories, "because, really, my dear Sartre, it must not be much fun spending all day surrounded by bad smells, repulsive habits, dirty laundry, unhealthy rooms, and people who have never heard of showers and toothpaste."[35] His criticism is echoed by that of Jean-Pierre Maxence in *Gringoire*, who is revolted by a "universe, at once powerful and horrible, a universe teeming with larvae, traversed by malignant fevers, weighed down by a leaden sky; a universe so radically pessimistic that, compared to it, M. Louis-Ferdinand Céline's is quite cheerful."[36]

"M. Jean-Paul Sartre, who is, I think, a professor of philosophy, has just made a brilliant debut in the novel"—This is the teasing manner, the complicitous wink, with which Paul Nizan greets his little comrade, publicly recognizing a "French Kafka," a "first-class novelist-philosopher," as well as "the fierce humor and violent significance of his social caricatures."[37] This is Sartre's official welcome by the paper *Ce Soir,* of which Nizan has become one of the managing editors (with Aragon and Jean-Richard Bloch). The Spanish Civil War, the meetings of the League of Nations, the Munich Pact, the movements of French officials in Eastern Europe, nothing eludes the foreign affairs column of this Marxist reporter, now pursuing a parallel career in the novel: in 1938, Nizan was among the candidates for the Prix Goncourt with his *Conspiration,* which was published by Gallimard the same year as *Nausea* and received the Prix Interallié, for writer-journalists. A grateful Sartre will use the *NRF* to raise his hat to "Nizan's bitter and somber personality," to this man "who cannot forgive his youth," and to his "beautiful style, dry and intelligent, his long Cartesian sentences, which sag in the middle, as if they lacked the strength to keep going, then spring up again to soar into space."[38] How they must have dreamed of such a play of mirrors in their adolescence! At last, a year before the war, it is all theirs. But in 1940 Nizan dies, and with him the winks of complicity, the lineage of Captain Sartres that Nizan used to sneak into his books, and the Gendarme Nizans with which Sartre reciprocated.

And yet, their complicity was entirely literary and distant, since the two friends were no longer seeing each other as much. Later, Sartre explains that it was enough for him to know that his friend was daily writing an editorial on foreign policy for *Ce Soir,* to feel "superficially" relieved from having to play any active role in politics, and to believe that Nizan's journalistic functions automatically turned him into a big shot within the hierarchy of the French Communist Party. A series of events soon proved the contrary. In the meantime, however, welcomed, accepted, legitimized, Sartre started looking at the world as if he were an actor in it. He became personally concerned about the signing of the Munich Pact in September 1938, and, gradually, began feeling more vulnerable to the twists and turns of politics and European history. Sartre spent the prewar years slowly emerging from his "dogmatic sleep."[39]

"Starting in 1930," he later wrote, "a series of events—the advent of Nazism, incidents in China, the Spanish Civil War, the world crisis—came to wake us up; we felt as if the rug was pulled out from under our feet and, suddenly, we found ourselves caught in a big lie. Suddenly, we realized that the first years of this great World Peace were in fact only the last years between two wars."[40] Sartre was more sensitive than most to the mood that preceded the Munich Pact, to the "misleading calm" and "cowardly relief" that celebrated Daladier's return. A few months later, he will use the days of September 1938 as the historical background for *The Reprieve*, the second novel of his trilogy, *The Roads to Freedom*. As war gets closer, he becomes more and more concerned. It may seem ironic that his recent readings are more concerned with cinema—Fritz Lang, Charlie Chaplin, Max Ophüls, Ernst Lubitsch, G. W. Pabst, Marcel Carné, Jean Renoir, and René Clair—than with politics; nonetheless, he will become the supreme witness of these difficult hours. "Is it even remotely conceivable that we could sit back and watch the crushing of a nation whose integrity we have guaranteed?" he writes to Simone de Beauvoir, after the Munich Pact and the abandonment of Czechoslovakia; "the democrats have lost all hope of pushing Hitler back," a fact that marks "a real victory for fascism, not just on the level of international politics but also within different nations."[41]

"*A*RE YOU happy here, Poulou?"
      "Yes Maman."
   "Are you sure?"
   "Yes Maman, I am."
   "Anyway, it's good for you . . . healthy."[42]
   During the first weeks of the summer of 1939, a thirty-four-year-old Poulou, seated between mother and stepfather, submits to the ritual of family vacations. In the Yonne, near the writer Colette's house, they walk, read, have lunch with the Emerys, play bridge: the eternal boredom of the French countryside, of summer socializing, of perfunctory talk with his stepfather, his routine asthma attacks in the middle of the night. In these years he is also involved in a complex, almost acrobatic system of vacations with Beauvoir et al. Polygamy has become the rule: Wanda, Olga's younger sister, "Lucile," and "Martine Bourdin," both students of Dullin, and "Louise Védrine," one of Simone de Beauvoir's students, all come, one by one, to share Sartre's nights in his Montparnasse hotel. His vacations are apportioned equally between his mother, near Auxerre, Beauvoir, in Marseilles and Juan-les-Pins, "Louise V." at La Clusaz, and

Wanda in Marseilles. And, every day, he writes to those who are not there, and tells them everything, from his sexual encounters to his meals and his readings. Thus, aided by his pen and his dexterity, he entertains his harem, sending money, giving presents and promises, cultivating each relationship for fear of losing even one.

By now, he and Beauvoir have established a balance that all the "peripherals" are supposed to respect. Despite his new love for Wanda or for "Louise V.," it is with Beauvoir that Sartre will spend two weeks of his vacation at Mme Morel's house by the sea, swimming, writing, reading, with his friends. Nothing can deprive Simone de Beauvoir of this priority. She is also the one who receives the greatest amount of information from Sartre and shares the most confidences with him. Since Olga, there haven't been any serious risks, and if Sartre has, at times, fallen in love with his new women, he has never again felt a similarly exclusive, devouring, suicidal passion. With all that Sartre tells her, she has really no reason to complain. "We played with each other without saying a word," he tells her about one of his nights with "Martine Bourdin." "Except for fucking her, I did *everything*. . . . She's quite a lover. . . . this is the first time I've slept with a brunette . . . full of smells, oddly hairy, with some black fur in the small of her back and a white body . . . a tongue like a kazoo, endlessly uncurling, reaching all the way down to my tonsils."[43] Extreme transparency, voyeurism, and polygamy: the students at the Lycée Pasteur had been stunned by the freedom they sensed; had they only known!

The last weeks of August 1939, the port of Marseilles: fortuitous meeting with the Nizans, before they leave for Corsica, followed by a group lunch and the exchange of war news. This is the last time Sartre and Nizan meet. "Do you understand, my love," he writes "Louise Védrine" at the end of August. "Even if there is a war there will be a time after it for all three of us, I'm sure. Our lives will go on. Besides, I don't really believe in the war."[44] Did he wish to reassure an eighteen-year-old woman or was he really unconscionably calm? Even after the pact between Germany and the Soviet Union, and Nizan's clamorous resignation from the PCF, which he publicly announced in the paper *L'Oeuvre,* Sartre still remains unmoved: "Hitler can't possibly think of starting a war with the current mood in Germany," he writes to the young woman. "He must be bluffing."[45] The following day he was mobilized.

Forced to abandon his mother, Simone de Beauvoir, and his mistresses, his student-friends, his career as literary critic and journalist, the manuscript of his novel, and his Heidegger, he was ordered to report to Essey-lès-Nancy and to wear the uniform of a second-class soldier meteorologist. "He looks barely thirty, slight build, pale hair, eyes drowned in spectacles, and lips that seem to stare at you with subtle sinuosity." This is the portrait of the recent literary sensation as sketched by Claudine Chonez for a women's magazine. "He looks like a pure philosopher, a being in whom flesh and blood have been sucked inside to nourish the mind."[46] This pale, frail novelist, this pure philosopher, this prisoner of books, had to leave his familiar grounds, so recently conquered, for the war that was swallowing all Europe, a war from which, whether he knew it or not, nobody would come back unscarred.

II

THE
METAMORPHOSIS
OF WAR
1939–1945

*At times I feel as if I were about to "find myself,"
as biographers would put it around page 150 . . .*
—LETTER TO SIMONE DE BEAUVOIR,
January 6, 1940

*W*AS THIS little soldier clad in navy blue, wearing knickerbock-ers, knee socks, and thick boots, jacket with gold buttons, beret tilted to the side, large leather belt strapping him round like a packet, really "about to find himself"? The only visible physical attributes that still connect him to his past are a meerschaum pipe and a pair of round, horn-rimmed glasses.

"The war really divided my life in two,"[1] he will later say. The Sartre of 1945 is no longer the Sartre of 1939. The war is the great mutation, the great metamorphosis of his life. On his way into the tunnel, he is a high-school philosophy teacher with two published books, an isolated person, an individualist hardly involved in the affairs of this world, totally apolitical. On his way out, he is a writer who spreads his talents over different genres, politically active, and intentionally so: a writer who, in the space of a few months, will be an international celebrity.

For the time being, the grand maneuvers between Stalin and Hitler, international strategies, and the thoughts of generals in uni-forms and other mustached chiefs of state have very little impact on the lead actor in our play, our second-class soldier, a rank reserved to men over thirty-two. But now he is about to acquire a new identity, to undergo the ritual leveling of the army. He has become Private Sartre, regimental number 1991, assigned to the meteorologi-cal section attached to an artillery headquarters, in sector 108, under the orders of General François, Colonel Larminat, and Corporal Pierre.

A WAR À LA KAFKA

> *Since my mobilization I have often thought about Kafka; he would have liked this war; it would have been a good subject for him. He would have shown a man, named Gregory K., stubbornly looking for war everywhere, feeling its threat everywhere, and yet never finding it. A suspended war, like some of the sentences in* The Trial.
>
> —LETTER TO JEAN PAULHAN,
> December 13, 1939

THE PHONY war of 1939–40 is no war at all. From their fathers, grandfathers, and uncles, from the old soldiers, from all the veterans of World War I, they had come to expect trenches, visible enemies, real confrontations, heroic soldiers. For over nine months they will just wait, interminably and absurdly, among other French soldiers waiting for the Germans to attack. It is a period of unexpected holidays fraying away aimlessly, statically, in a somber climate of disarray, boredom, and dull passivity. They will play cards, read, talk of their wives or mistresses, without understanding what is happening either around or to them. "Here I am, in practice, a soldier," Sartre writes. "But not a warrior. I launch balloons. I let them go as if they were doves, near the batteries of the artillery, and then I follow them with a pair of binoculars to determine the direction of the winds. . . . I have all the time I want to continue my novel and hope I'll be done by the end of winter. I am also thinking, to keep abreast of current news, of some 'Reflections on Death,' which I could give to the *NRF*."[2]

On September 2, 1939, the day of the general mobilization, in the Essey-lès-Nancy barracks, on the eastern front, Private Sartre receives his military outfit. He must disguise himself. When Corporal Pierre, who directs the section of meteorological testing for the 70th infantry division, comes into the barracks room looking for some soldiers on his list, he finds, much to his amazement, a soldier sitting on his bed, busily writing. For nine months, four soldiers, ill-assorted individuals, will share everything in a hectic absurd daily life. These are Piederkowski, a big Parisian wholesale dealer in women's clothes; Müller, a telephone company employee from the provinces; Pierre, the corporal, a math teacher at the lycée of Bar-le-Duc; and Sartre, who immediately strikes the others as someone who does not like to mix and hates confidences. All they know about him is that he teaches philosophy in Paris.

Thirty-five years later, when he tells Simone de Beauvoir about his very first impressions as a mobilized soldier, Sartre will still remember the absurdity of the situation. "So, there I was, in military clothes that fitted me badly, surrounded by other men who wore the same clothes as myself. We were connected by a bond that was neither of family nor friendship but that was nevertheless very important. We had parts to play, and these parts were given to us from outside. I launched balloons and watched them with binoculars. . . . It called for some mental effort to see the connection between launching a red balloon into the sky and the whole of this invisible war that surrounded us. . . . I had been taught this at a time when I never thought I should make use of it, during my military service. And there I was, engaged in this occupation, among other men I did not know who were following the same pursuit, men who helped me to do so and whom I helped, and we watched my balloons vanish in the clouds. All this was a few miles from the German army in which there were people like us busily doing the same thing; and there were other men who were preparing an attack. There one had an absolutely historical occurrence. All at once I found myself part of a mass of men in which I had been given an exact and stupid part to play, a part I was playing . . . opposite other men, dressed as I was in military clothes, whose part was to thwart what we were doing and finally to attack."[3]

He was used to being in control over ideas and words. At different stages in his life, he had basked in the sweet life of the elite: family, bourgeois society, Ecole Normale, *agrégation*, lycée, exclusive places, cocoons that had allowed him to avoid all sociopolitical turmoil. Early on, he had planned out his career as a writer and measured the strange elusive megalomania of words. Then, suddenly, this phony war had come to break the spell. It was like a rape: ridiculous clothes, perfunctory actions, unpleasant roommates. In short, he had to go through a number of trials radically unlike anything up till then.

Sartre, Pierre, Piederkowski, Müller: the group will travel from Nancy to Ceintrey, from Ceintrey to Marmoutier, from Marmoutier to Brumath, from Brumath to Morsbronn-les-Bains, to discover the beauties of the Alsatian and Lorrainean countryside, with its neat little villages, its white half-timbered houses, its schools filled with flowers, its inviting cafés and bars, its smell of German culture. At the end of the winter, they spend a few weeks at Bouxvilliers, then return to Morsbronn in May 1940. Their first orders are to report to the Ceintrey barracks, where they will put together the staff headquarters of the 70th infantry division. They are sent to the Blaudan barracks to get a hold of a truck, "but, if we were able to get the truck, we could not get a single drop of gas because it was against regulations." All their pleas remain unheeded. Finally, Sartre finds a way out of the bind. "He had the idea," his corporal explains, "of writing an order for the requisition of fuel on a sheet of paper with 'République française' on it, and that's how we got five gallons of gas."[4] But then, back at headquarters, Colonel de Larminat hasn't yet received any paper concerning their mission and so refuses to see them. Hence, the four unemployed musketeers are sent back to a month of endless, idiotic waiting in the beautiful Lorraine countryside, at the beginning of autumn.

"Seventeen of us [are] in an evacuated hotel whose clients, in peace time, were poor rheumatic patients," Sartre writes to Jean Paulhan. "There are still a few high beds and wardrobes with mirrors. Installed in these small rooms with flowery wallpaper, military socialism looks more idyllic and phalansterian, like a Fourierist experiment about to sour, when the members of the expedition begin to hate one another. It's quite poetic and interesting."[5] Their stop at Brumath lasts a few months. This little town, typical of the Lorraine, is the perfect counterpart, on the French side of the border, to Baden-Baden. They lodge in private homes but eat their meals in town restaurants with picturesque names: La Taverne du Cerf (The Deer's Inn), Le Boeuf Noir (The Black Ox), Le Lion d'Or (The Golden Lion), a border bestiary. And they launch balloons. "Afterwards," Sartre explains, "I phone the battery artillery officers and tell them the wind direction: what they do with this information is their affair. The young ones make some use of the intelligence reports; the old school just shove them straight into the wastepaper basket. Since there isn't any shooting, either course is equally effective. This extraordinarily peaceful job (only pigeon fanciers, if they still exist in the army, could have as poetic and sweet a task) leaves me a great deal of free time."[6]

Soon, the Soviet Union attacked Finland, France and Great Britain agreed not to sign a separate peace, and Denmark and Norway were invaded by troops of the Third Reich. Of the incredible details that Sartre jotted down, few involve an analysis of political events. This return to the land of the Schweitzers, however, provoked a few unexpected reflections in this proud man, generally so disdainful of roots. On September 2, 1939, it was decided that a large number of people residing in Alsace-Lorraine should be massively transplanted into the French Southwest, in order to prevent any possible reunion between them and their German neighbors. The newspaper *L'Oeuvre* dubbed the operation "Strasbourg/Dordogne," so as to convey the fantastic nature of the project: the merging of two radically different populations, the Alsatians and the Périgordians. For Sartre, there was nothing surprising about this transfer of populations: it was the Schweitzers visiting the Sartres, Anne-Marie transplanted in Thiviers, Grandfather Schweitzer discovering the oddities of Grandfather Sartre, the brutal encounter between Pfaffenhoffen and Puifeybert. "One of the oddest phenomena of this technical war," he writes, "will turn out to have been the methodical transplantation of the Alsatians. . . . They were packed off to the yokels of Limoges, lowest of the low, backward, slow-witted, grasping, and poverty stricken. Those Alsatians, still quite bedazzled by the memory of their ordered, well-tended fields and their fine houses, have landed up in that countryside of those dirty towns, among suspicious, ugly, and for the most part dirty people. . . . Their standards of cleanliness must have been outraged by little towns like Thiviers, where only twelve years ago household refuse and excrement was still being emptied into open ditches. At any rate, the result is clear: every Alsatian who writes home describes the Limousins as *savages*. The word recurs in every letter, it is really a collective description: 'We are among savages.' The Limousins, for their part, react by calling the Alsatians 'Boches.' "[7]

Once again, Sartre prefers to think of himself as a Schweitzer and an Alsatian, identifying with those proud Alsatians who despise the "primitive agricultural tools of those savages," express their disgust at the sight of certain Périgordian dishes, resent the mistrust of the locals, and are profoundly disappointed that they cannot tell the Périgordian peasant how to work. Then, as if spurred by such an incongruous, disorienting situation, Sartre decides to make a "pilgrimage" to Pfaffenhoffen, "cradle of my mother's family if I remember rightly," he notes, with detachment.

"I felt myself obliged to make a pilgrimage there. Why?" he wonders. "Basically I had some vague hope that this sudden contact with a town where I'd lived would cause a cloud of memories abruptly to crystallize. And then it struck me as poetic—that little city buried at the back of my memory, like the town of Ys at the bottom of the sea." The summer holidays of 1913 had been spent at the house of his aunt Caroline Biedermann—Charles Schweitzer's sister—in the little town of Pfaffenhoffen, where the child wrote one of his first texts, an adventure novel, "For a Butterfly." Twenty-six years later, Private Sartre goes back with his rifle and helmet, "not the classic pilgrim's accessories." On December 22, 1939, at dawn, Sartre leaves on a truck driven by a big mustached Alsatian: Sartre is sitting next to him, in the front seat; his friend Grener sits in the back. . . . Eberback . . . Schweighausen . . . Niedermodern. It is very cold: 13 degrees Fahrenheit. The three soldiers don't see anything much on the small country road, except for a few plough horses, several other soldiers, some peasants. A sad, pale sun filters through a cloudy sky. It is seven in the morning. A round of Schnapps, a round of rum, just to warm the blood, then they arrive at Pfaffen-hoffen. Sartre feels no romantic nostalgia. "I . . . wandered round that solid market town, prosperous but rather dismal, which held no message for me," he writes. "All that particular past is well and truly buried—nothing can resurrect it. . . . Round a bend in the road, I found myself in front of a big ocher construction very ugly, with slate roofs, turrets and gables: it was the Biedermann emporium. There, too, my memory remained mute."[8] The pilgrim-soldier returned to Brumath with only a few cynical words about the village of his origins. And yet, for nearly a month, he had been writing and pondering a few fragments from his past. Perhaps this unexpected proximity to his roots had had something to do with it.

His days are mostly wasted on the inevitable problems of daily cohabitation, and endless hassles with his superior, Corporal Pierre, "a thin, nervous individual, with iron-rimmed glasses, a professor of mathematics." Does the corporal remind him of his algebra lessons with Joseph Mancy? "Was it because Pierre was a professor of mathematics," Sartre continues, "that he could not live without points of reference? During the winter, he took his bearings every day, and would often walk ten miles in the snow to listen to the news in the radio truck. . . . During that whole rotten war, he always knew the exact distance between himself and his wife, the amount of time he would have to spend in that sector, and his number on the list of soldiers waiting for their leave."[9] Sartre is sure that Corporal Pierre cannot stand him: "We were both teachers," he will later remember.

"He vaguely felt that that ought to have been a bond between us; I didn't. As far as I was concerned, the bond did not exist, so he wasn't pleased."[10] The corporal is compulsive, totally respectful of order and hierarchy, perfectly integrated into the army, pathologically in control of reality. Sartre is marginal, solitary, atypical, awkward with his tools, contemptuous of order and army. "This afternoon you would have seen me looking sad and grinding my teeth," Sartre writes to Beauvoir, "so much so that Pierre, who's always looking for a sign of weakness in me, asked me, with condescending irony, whether I was feeling homesick or had bad news from home. I told him to mind his own business."[11] Later, Pierre will also recall Sartre's weird moods as a sign of his instability. During a maneuver, he writes, "he refused to listen to my advice as to where to place a theodolite, and he showed me his displeasure by saying, 'I'm not one of your students.' "[12]

In the army, Sartre violently rejects the authoritarian hierarchy. All of Pierre's comments reinforce the sense of Sartre as a marginal figure, who neither is interested in the army nor has any esteem for it, who likes to behave like an anarchist and an eccentric. Pierre constantly alludes to Sartre's casualness, his sloppiness, his awkwardness. "From the very start," he points out, "we had the feeling that he couldn't be of any use to us at a military level."[13]

Indeed, Sartre cannot play the game. He cannot stand his secondary role, those forced friendships among males, those situations of unexpected intimacy, uncalled-for confidences. "The emotional bond created by his looking upon me as the person who knew about his life and with whom he talked about things that I was to remember afterward seemed to me unbearable," he writes about another soldier, possibly Müller. "It shifts the relationship. . . . You are caught; you have to give advice. The other relies on you, refers to you, has a kind of respect for the person who receives his confidences. In the end I was becoming what I don't want to be, the master with his disciples, and I didn't like being confided in."[14] Feeling neither superior nor inferior, Sartre can't stand paternalism or admiration. So, he withdraws into a seemingly obsessional attitude. He bends over his specific occupations so as to be forgotten, respected, left alone. Soldier-typist, this will be his privileged, reserved role. And he will receive the respect of officers, colonels, or captains, as soon as they become aware of his joint activities. "A captain comes— dashing, war school, dines with the general—and says to me: 'And what about the soldier who looks so depressed, what does he do?' I didn't look depressed at all, I simply looked the way I always do when I'm working. 'Something personal, captain.' 'And what would that be?' 'Some writing.' 'A novel?' 'Yes, captain.' 'What about?' 'It's difficult to explain.' 'Unfaithful wives and cuckold husbands?' 'Of course.' 'That's wonderful! You're lucky you've got time to work.' After which, he tells his secretary, not without some melancholy: 'Writers, you know . . . better keep your distance.' "[15]

According to the corporal, other army bigshots soon became aware of this uncommon soldier: "At Morsbronn-les-Bains," he remembers, "Colonel Larminat showed great interest in him. He had heard that he was a writer but had never read any of his works. He saw Sartre's beard, seldom shaved, as the ornament of the division. Sartre used to go around with a sign that read, on one side, 'You may bug me,' and on the other 'You may not bug me.' The colonel happened to stop by on a day when the sign was showing its friendly face and was delighted by this happy coincidence."[16] Indeed, within this little group, the soldier-writer is a very interesting phenomenon: whether he provokes mistrust or admiration, no one remains indifferent. He certainly stands out. He is famous for his "pestilential room," for the weeks he spends "without taking a bath when all he had to do was cross the street and pay ten sous to have exclusive use of a bathroom in the heated building," and for his nickname in the barracks, "the man with the black gloves," because his hands "were black with dirt up to his elbows."[17] We also have a number of anecdotes, such as this one, provided by the corporal: "Once I had a real fight with him while trying to stop him from burning the furniture of the house we lived in: he didn't want to waste time chopping wood when he could read or write instead."[18] During these nine months, Sartre manages to spend an average of twelve hours a day writing: in classrooms, while other people talk, on his knees, when he is working outside, during his watches, in between supply duties. "I asked Pierre to let me stand guard in his stead this evening," he writes to Beauvoir, "so I could write a little more."[19] He writes all the time, whenever he is not launching balloons; he writes as others breathe.

IN ORDER to survive, he keeps a diary. The notebook will become his lifebuoy, his daily savior. And yet this kind of writing is completely different from everything he has engaged in till now. Just a few months earlier, when Paulhan had asked him to contribute a piece for a "Homage to André Gide," planned by the *NRF*, Sartre had expressed clear misgivings about this sort of genre. This was in August 1939. Paulhan must have been quite baffled when that December he received the following letter from Sartre: "I've finally made up my mind: I've been keeping a journal for two months now despite the disgust that this sort of practice has always inspired in me. It's a question of personal hygiene: I pour into it all the feelings provoked in me by the war and my condition as soldier; this way, I pay my debt to the present and am free to write a peaceful novel that takes place in 1938."[20] Accomplice, muse, old friend, the notebook soon transcends its status as finite object and becomes magical. "I have a lot of ideas at this moment," he writes to Beauvoir, "and I'm glad I have this little notebook because it produces them. It has given me another, secret life above and beyond the actual one, a life with its own joys, its own problems, its own remorse, none of which I would have known without this little black leather object."[21] One day, between two duties, Sartre will cover eighty pages of his notebook with writing. Some time later, it will be some thirty pages of a "beautiful night-blue notebook" given him by Simone de Beauvoir.[22] "I have never felt such freedom of thought," he confides. "And it is not just because of the war and all it has thrown into question, but because of this little notebook: its free, fragmentary style liberates me from the slavery of previous ideas. I write on the spur of the moment, leaving any conclusions for later."[23] The form of the notebook brings Sartre to the discovery of a new hedonism of writing.

Between September 23, 1939 and June 21, 1940, Sartre survives the phony war thanks to the beneficent intimacy of more than fifteen little notebooks, all beautiful, whether bound in black leather, gray moleskin, or night-blue canvas. More than fifteen, all densely covered with a handwriting that runs all over the place, from left to right and from top to bottom, and then all around the margins. More than fifteen, of which only five are now left, the five survivors of what could easily have been a complete literary oeuvre. They will be published several years after Sartre's death, thanks to his adopted daughter, as *The War Diaries.* In them, Sartre writes about everything—his readings, his barracks companions, his experiences at Le Havre, Laon, Berlin, his schoolmates at the Ecole Normale, his friendships with women, his unhappy loves, his relationship with politics—vignettes filtered through the eyes of the soldier. Thus, these useless absurd nine months will ultimately have served to force

the writer to turn inward and produce this first work of "decipher-
ment," as he calls it. The notebooks already contain the first sketches,
the first traces of what will later, toward the middle of the 1950s,
become the initial manuscript of his autobiography, which will be
published in 1964 as *The Words*.

Jumping from one subject to the next, mixing everything, philosophy, literary criticism, political analysis, observations about his
grandfather and his relationship with money, with candor and often
naïveté, he tells himself his own life, both to explore and understand
it, in an indescribable, brilliant confusion, which brings together
Husserl and Heidegger, Flaubert and Guillaume II, Aron, Guille,
and Nizan, Simone de Beauvoir, Olga and his stepfather, Faulkner,
Bost, and Hemingway. But *The War Diaries* also prefigure works
then in progress, *Being and Nothingness* and *The Age of Reason*, and
future works, suggested or only sensed, such as *The Words* or
Flaubert. They illuminate his character traits: pride, intelligence,
lucidity, megalomania, generosity. "I need to spend," he writes, "not
in order to *buy* anything, but in order to blow up that monetary
energy: get rid of it in some way and dispatch it far away from myself
like a hand-grenade. There is a certain kind of perishability that I like
about money: I like to see it flow from my fingers and vanish.
. . . It must disappear on insubstantial fireworks—for example, on
an *evening out*."[24]

Why in 1939 did he feel he had to analyze his life? "I think I'm
respecting the truth," he writes one day, "if I distinguish three
periods in my life as a young man and as a man. The first goes from
1921 to 1929."[25] What do all these memories, flashing back as in the
brain of a dying man, and all these awkward efforts to classify,
analyze, objectivize, tell us about this peculiar soldier, but that a
metamorphosis is at hand, that he is facing a precipice and that he
writes to exorcise his fear.

Realizations, decipherings, obsessive analyses: "[my novel] is
clearly Husserlian, which I find rather distressing considering that
I am now a partisan of Heidegger."[26] Self-doubt succeeds exaltation, retrospective self-analysis is never totally without snags, never
complacent. This might well be a permanent trait of Sartre's personality: his harsh, implacable, retrospective self-criticism, always
accompanied by the certainty of radical change. The belief that a
brutal rupture guarantees a new identity, the conviction that life
can stem only from discontinuity. Thus, on January 6, 1940, he
writes: "Since I've broken my inferiority complex toward the far

142

left, I've experienced an unprecedented freedom of thought. This is also true of my relationship with the phenomenologists."[27] The notebooks contribute to the birth of a new individual, virginal, coherent, and reassuring even to Sartre himself. "I have reread my five notebooks, and they don't please me nearly as much as I had expected. I find them a little vague, too discreet, even the clearest ideas are little more than rehashings of Heidegger's: in the end, all I have done since September, all these things about 'my' war etc., is only a long re-elaboration of the ten pages he devoted to the question of historicity."[28] This is the kind of severity and precision he shows every time he considers, models, destroys, or re-centers himself. "To know where I am has meaning only in regard to where I was." The *Diaries* are a long meditation on the road he has already covered and on the man he is becoming. His new obsession with the concept of historicity is another token of change. On October 26, he devotes ten pages of his notebooks to the subject. That same day, already vaguely sensing his growing discontent with his prewar apoliticism, without however going so far as to analyze it, he begins to realize that if he had experienced and considered "the imminent war as the historical possibility of his age," he might have then "seized [its] historicity."[29] Much of this he owes to Heidegger, but also to a new, still quite tentative, sense of himself in relation to the world.

NEXT TO the *Diaries* and daily introspection, philosophical practice also plays an important role in this period of Sartre's life. It protects him "against the melancholy, moroseness, and sadness of war."[30] He adds: "I'm not trying to protect my life, *a posteriori*, with my philosophy, which would be pretty bad, nor am I trying to make my life conform to my philosophy, which would be pedantic: in fact, I don't have to do either because, actually, my life and my philosophy are one and the same."[31] At the beginning of December, he writes Simone de Beauvoir: "I have *seen* this *morale*, which I have been practicing for three months now without my making it a theory yet, just the opposite of what I usually do. . . . Everything seems to revolve quite naturally around the ideas of freedom, life, and authenticity."[32] Less than a week later, he will gloriously proclaim: "I have completed my *morale*." He discovers Heidegger, an existential approach to reality, history. It is the hard work of patient research but also cathartic. "We find ourselves in a condition that implies a great deal of irrationality," he writes then, "and it is not by masking it that we will suppress it. All masks involve an attitude of inauthenticity. We have already enumerated a few (birth, generation, social class, etc.), but there is also war . . . I must have masked it."[33] In the end, he progressively discovers his own truth via this exercise in clairvoyancy. "I no longer think along the lines prescribed by my past (Husserl, the left) but in complete freedom and gratuitousness, with curiosity and disinterestedness, accepting from the very start that I may well end up a fascist if the reasoning that leads me there is correct."[34] His novel, which will eventually become *The Age of Reason,* the first volume of *The Roads to Freedom,* is intimately mixed up with this research and these changes. In July 1938 he had written to Simone de Beauvoir: "I have suddenly found the subject of my novel, its dimensions and its title . . . : the subject is freedom."[35]

On October 22, 1939, he completes the ninetieth page of this novel on freedom. He is happy and sure he'll finish the book. On December 31, at once proud and surprised, he exults: "You know, I have *finished* the novel. I have actually affixed the word 'end' at the bottom of a page."[36] And he immediately starts a sequel, which he wants to call *September.* Then he returns to the original text and starts revising it, into the spring of 1941. And yet, Sartre's initial intention was to see it published as soon as possible, and that's why he had studied the best means to get it to his publisher with the least delay. He even typed the text himself to save time. On May 1, 1940, he is fairly sure his novel will be serialized in the *NRF* starting in July. The phony war is like a long stay away from the capital to take advantage of the calm and to work at his leisure. "You know," he writes one day, "this novel is a real stage in my life. I was so afraid I'd never finish it."[37]

This is when the period of endless corrections begins. He has doubts—"I'm afraid the text as a whole may not be existential at all"[38]—questions—"Maybe I don't have enough novelistic imagination"[39]—certainties— "Now I know it will be finished. But I don't have the slightest idea when it will be published" (October 22, 1939). He even indulges in some critical distance: "This morning, waking up, I had a clear glimpse of the way in which I compose a novel . . . no, decidedly, I am not a novelist."[40] Up to a few days before the German attack and the beginning of the rout, he keeps on repeating with both conviction and determination: "The book should come out in October."[41] Nor does his notoriety leave him indifferent. In April 1940, he received a prize for *The Wall* and spent much of his time searching for any mention of it. Finally, he got a hold of *Paris-Midi,* which announced the prize under the headline "An Uncommon Laureate."

"I'm dying to write a play,"[42] he says one day. Then, a little later: "It's all over, I have just torn up the first six pages. . . . I was ashamed of them. . . . I felt like a fallen Valkyrie."[43] Soon, he gets another idea, "a little volume of literary criticism,"[44] which he will never mention again. And, on yet another occasion of unabashed inspiration, he confesses, contemplating the amount of paper he has covered with writing: "I have always considered quantity a virtue."[45]

Then there is his epistolary output. Just as the diaries, philosophy, and the novel managed to pull him out of the world and protect him against his comrades, the daily presence of his women helped restore his emotional balance. "He wrote three or four long letters every day," Corporal Pierre remembers. "To Mademoiselle Simone de Beauvoir and to a few other women. Two of them did not know each other, the other ones were fully aware of this complex correspondence but tolerated it. . . . Once, while he was on leave, he put us in charge of sending a daily letter to one of his correspondents. He left us fifteen letters, already written, addressed, and duly numbered. Toward the middle of his leave we were also to send a telegram."[46] In this group of frustrated males, who, at best, have a wife or a fiancée and, at worst, nobody at all, this marginal, aggressive, irritable fellow with his typewriter and his women is scandalous! On the other hand, Sartre's polygamy fits the phony war to a tee. What his companions do not know is that among his correspondents is a certain Mme Mancy, the writer's mother.

However, only one of these correspondents benefits from his rare leaves: Simone de Beauvoir. On October 31, 1939, she takes the initiative and travels to Alsace. There, from the Taverne du Cerf, she informs him of her arrival and waits for him. "Down the street," she writes, "I recognize him at once from his walk and his pipe and his size, though he has grown a horrible scrubby beard, which makes him look simply awful. . . . He comes back . . . clean-shaven." They spend four days together at Brumath, from November 1 to November 5, after eluding the crassest controls, which, in times of war, tend to hinder unmarried couples. Finding a hotel that will rent a room with a double bed without provoking a scandal is even more difficult than it was in Berlin. The Taverne du Cerf, the lounge of the Boeuf Noir, and the Café de l'Ecrevisse are the public places frequented by this unusual couple, who have so much to talk about after eight weeks of separation. The atmosphere is like a waiting room in a train station or a visitors' room in a prison: incessant bustle, insolent gazes, a permanent buzz, and a most unusual population. "Sartre . . . thinks that there won't be any real fighting," she notes in her journal, "this will be a modern war, without slaughter, just as modern painting has no subject, modern music no melody, and modern physics no solid matter."[47] They drink horrible Alsatian coffee, huge glasses of beer, and long glassfuls of rum, eat choucroutes and black puddings, and talk for hours and hours. Beauvoir has brought along a large supply of notebooks, ink, and books, and while, during the day, Sartre fulfills his military duties, she reads the notebooks he has been filling for the past two months. Sartre writes her just a few hours after her departure, "I've been deeply and quietly happy. . . . Today feels like the day after a holiday."[48] In another letter, he tries to justify himself: "There are moments when I feel funny knowing that, as I write, there are people dying like flies up North, and that the destiny of Europe is at stake. But, what can I do about it? This is *my* destiny, my own private destiny, and no collective terror can make me renounce it. . . . My novel must be finished by June 15. That's all there is to it. Then, it will no longer depend on me. . . . Still, I can only see my writing as a symbolic gesture *against* the fall of democracy and freedom and against the defeat of the Allies."[49]

His writing, along with his extraordinary correspondence, will soon amount to something like two thousand pages in the course of the phony war. He wrote uninterruptedly, several letters each day, several pages each, for almost a year. At least part of his impulse to write seems to stem from a desire to control all that happens in Paris during his absence. "Tell me everything in detail," he asks Simone de Beauvoir. "It is incredible how much it all interests me." From the eastern front, he still tries to get as much information as he can, while, at the same time, expressing opinions about the life of his friends and students, and entertaining, particularly with Simone de Beauvoir, an unbroken daily relationship exactly as if there were nothing out of the ordinary. He helps her solve administrative problems, asks her to lend him 1,000 francs for his own personal use, advises her to borrow some money from his mother, to lend some to Camille or to the Kanapas. He exchanges notes with her about their respective readings, requests such and such a book, recommends another, speaks of his future projects . . . as if daily life and literary life still went on: "After the war, I'll buy myself a typewriter so I can type my own articles like Nizan."[50] Simone de Beauvoir, now alone at the head of a scattered "family," tries to keep track of all their protégés. Wanda is at Laigle. Bost is at Morzine. Olga is still in Paris. Camille is in the country. Kanapa has moved to the South. She records their whereabouts, their letters, their occasional encounters, their conversations at the Café de Flore: in short, her journal is like the other face of Sartre's. "You know," he admits, "it's hard to write three letters, five pages of a novel, and four pages of my journal day in and day out: I've never written as much in my whole life."[51]

*T*HEN ONE morning in May 1940, at Morsbronn-les-Bains, after seven months of the phony war, during which they all thought they'd just go on playing soldiers till the end, they receive news of the German attack. Suddenly, everything speeds up and the war begins to exist. Suddenly, Sartre has to wake up. He has always considered the war with optimism and humor, without sparing jokes and witticisms. Suddenly, he is shaken, stunned by the urgency, the proximity and presence of the enemy. The French retreat will bring him and his companions to Haguenau, to Breschwillers—near Donnon—all the way to Padoux, where they will be taken prisoners on June 21.

Sartre is still keeping his diaries, the ones he is soon going to lose. But when, in 1942, he agrees to write a piece for Jean Lescure's review *Messages,* he will write a beautiful text in the form of a journal about the days of June 10 and 11, 1940, starting with the arrival at Haguenau, at the farthest limits of northeastern France. "The town has been entirely evacuated for a month."[52] The small group of soldiers files slowly into the dead town: the city hall, the school, a classroom. "On the rostrum, there are two piles of pink notebooks; I leaf through them. French composition. All the entries stop on May 10, 1940: 'Your mother is ironing. Describe her.' "[53]

Soon, new information comes in; it is chaotic, of doubtful accuracy, but already quite harrowing: "Where are the Germans? Near Paris? In Paris? Are they already fighting in Paris? We have been without papers or letters for five days now. I am haunted by an image: I see a café I sometimes frequented on the Place Saint-Germain-des-Prés. It's packed with people, lots of Germans. I don't see the Germans—since the beginning of the war I have never been able even to *imagine* a single German—but I know they are there."[54]

Group scenes with stunned French soldiers. Eruption onto an

opera stage. The discovery of a spectral reality, a skeletal town. The sudden awareness of chaos and war. "We look around, somewhat disoriented when, suddenly, it is Sunday. A Sunday afternoon, in the provinces, in midsummer, truer than nature. . . . I shake myself, and try to tell myself: 'It's Wednesday, a Wednesday morning; and behind those curtains there are only abandoned rooms, dark and empty.' But nothing changes. Sunday is still there. At Haguenau it's always the same day, all week long, always the same hour, all day long."[55]

This writer, novelist, philosopher, second-class soldier enters the war through the door of the fantastic. It's a discovery. The reality of the war is a pink notebook halted in the middle of a student's life, a false Sunday, so insistent, so obvious, reality in Machiavellian disguise, truth as lie. Later, speaking to Simone de Beauvoir, he will emphasize precisely these first instants, the ones through which the war revealed itself, "occurrences that were trifling in themselves and that wouldn't appear in any textbook or any history of the war. One little village was being shelled; another, which was going to be taken in its turn, was waiting. . . . I went out and I remember the strange feeling I had of a film, the feeling that I was acting in a scene in a film and that it was not true."[56]

These days of June 1940 have such an impact on the writer that he will later turn them into the subject of one of his books. This is June 16, a Sunday, in *Troubled Sleep*: "Mathieu opened his eyes and stared at the sky. It looked pearl gray, cloudless, bottomless, merely a negative presence. Another morning was slowly gathering like a drop of light, which would fall on the earth and drench it with gold. The Germans are in Paris and we have lost the war. Another morning, another beginning. . . . In Paris the Germans were looking at the sky, reading in it the signs of victory and of many morrows. I've got no future."[57] Two days later, Tuesday, June 18: "The motorcyclists made the round of the square, their exhausts roaring. Some sparrows flew off, but otherwise nothing stirred. . . . Mathieu, fascinated, thought: 'They are Germans'. . . . He was not afraid of death, he was afraid of hatred."[58] This is June 21, described à la Kafka for Simone de Beauvoir: "We marched, and we didn't know what they were going to do with us. There were some who hoped they would set us free in a week or two. It was actually June 21, my birthday and also the day of the armistice. We were marched to a gendarmerie barracks, and there again I learned what historical truth really was. I learned that I was someone who lived in a nation exposed to various dangers, and that this someone was himself exposed to these dangers. There was a kind of unity among the men who were there."[59]

148

Such are the rhythms of a life: fantastic, whimsical, unpredictable. Just a few hours, a few days can mark a whole life and extend their influence over it. They can often last much longer than many years of waiting and drowsiness. Such are the cycles of a life. Sartre has given those days a form and an image, has lent them evidence, relevance. The debacle of May–June 1940 will remain a watershed, wedged between the peculiar vacation of a writer at the front and eight months of captivity. It will be the first real meeting between the anarchical writer and social history, the first real rupture: "All I had learned and written during the years before seemed to me no longer valid nor even as having any content."[60] This is the first line of fracture: clear, straight, as sharp as a knife. No bad faith, no compromise: a new man is born. "During our retreat," Corporal Pierre writes, "we learned that we were surrounded. Sartre, who, till then, had been fairly aggressive toward the other soldiers, suddenly developed a real instinct of solidarity with them."[61] Throughout his captivity, Sartre will be cordial and even happy.

A LOFTY CAPTIVITY

> *The world we have been torn away from . . . looks*
> *very small. . . . It has rejected us, and yet we feel as*
> *if we dominated it. . . . Everything lies at our feet.*
> —"MATHIEU'S JOURNAL"

FOR TWO months, from June 21 to August 24, in the barracks of Haxo de Baccarat, on the Meurthe River in the heart of Lorraine, between Strasbourg and Nancy, Sartre is kept prisoner along with 14,000 other soldiers. Captivity means hunger, even madness or oblivion. It means sleeping on the bare floor, squeezed in among hundreds of other bodies. It means the pillaging of the mobile guard's library and reading as the sole intellectual activity: Sartre reads Montluc's *Mémoires,* which bores him; an odd volume of Vaulabelle's *History of the Two Restorations,* which he finds very interesting because, "in it, I could retrace the traits of this new

Restoration—that of 1940—in which Pétain was playing the role of Louis XVII in occupied France";[1] and Jules Verne's *Around the World in Eighty Days.* Reading replaces writing as a means of escape. And yet, despite the endless waiting, Sartre remains optimistic, sure that he will soon be freed, and far from even suspecting that he might be sent to Germany.

The prison camp is a village with 25,000 inhabitants, all men. Its barracks are three-story-high wooden shacks containing roughly forty people per room. Its rules, laws, and curfews are in the hands of a few Germans—in high and low positions of authority—who wield power over thousands of third-class citizens, the prisoners. It has its rituals, its customs, its passwords, its slang: the Fritzes, the Frisés (Germans), the Revier (infirmary). It also provides a few distractions: music, theater, books. Its autarkical life teems with bribes of all sorts, favoritism, illegal trafficking, escape attempts. Contact with the outside world is minimal: the prisoners know little or nothing about the progress of the war or any other news. Now and then, a clandestine radio gives them a few vague and random details, often false or obsolete. Some of the prisoners have tasks that take them outside the camp, mostly to nearby monasteries. They always bring back wine and food and, at times, information, books, stories from the outside world.

"The paradox of our situation is that it is at once unlivable and easy to live," Sartre writes.[2] The life of the prisoner may reveal a charm that will later turn into nostalgia. Despite lice, fleas, bedbugs, the freezing winter—10° below (Fahrenheit)—and the scarcity of food, a new order is established in the camp, an order at once more cruel and more cohesive, more regulated and more protected than that of the outside world. An order punctuated by collective duties, mealtimes, curfews, group activities, Sunday walks, the arrival of Red Cross packages, mail deliveries. The camp protects while depriving. It suspends most social stakes: work, money, heterosexuality, politics. But it also creates new ones, on different grounds, just as it generates new privileges and new castes—that of the nurses, for instance, particularly detested because they constitute the aristocracy of the camp: They live apart, are better fed, have no lice, and can easily get both tobacco and sugar.

The first formality, and the first stage in the homogenization process, is the body search, which often involves the removal of most personal effects. Then, shaved, washed, and deloused, the prisoner is recorded on an identification sheet bearing his photo. All specificity, all social distinction is thereby erased. The second stage involves a brutal and abrupt introduction into the jungle of bribes and barters. The oldest prisoners, the Poles, for instance, grab you on arrival and offer you stale bread for your watch. Then begins the search for points of reference, familiar faces, cheap privileges.

Sartre feigns illness in the Revier, for a few weeks, just for a little more sugar and a few cigarettes. From the infirmary he is sent to the artists' barracks where his integration as a prisoner occurs by degrees. To face up to the Germans, to physical violence, humiliation, and arbitrary orders, the prisoner must merge with the others to become part of the whole: "We are so numerous, so anonymous, so indistinguishable, we needn't be afraid of anything: threat has become a mere ceremony."[3]

Sartre entered the camp in a cattle wagon in September 1940; he would leave it on foot, in March 1941, discharged thanks to false papers. In between, he endured the hardest part of the war, a period of profound mutation, a few decisive months, from which he managed to emerge active and militant, mixing with others after the solitude of the phony war. "In the stalag, I rediscovered a form of collective life I had not experienced since the Ecole Normale—in other words, I was happy."[4] His first impression was pleasant: it had to do with the topographical location of the camp. On top of Mount Kemmel, it dominated the city and valley around it, crossed by the Moselle River. "The sensation of living on a mountain overlooking a city is very strong in me . . . somehow I confuse the altitude of my location with some sort of moral superiority: everything at my feet."[5] "It's odd to think that freedom is *down there*, below me. To be prisoner on top of a mountain, what a paradox! . . . The world we have been torn away from looks very small from this eagle's nest: like a toy. It has rejected us and yet we feel as if we dominate it. . . . Everything lies at our feet: the red roads of the Palatinate, the flat, sinuous glint of the Moselle, and the nation of our conquerors. . . . But for the moment our gaze is freer than we are, freer than that of the town jailers. It soars, it is contemptuous, and yet we are here."[6]

The phony war exhausted him, he wrote and wrote. His captivity revives him; he is happy, much as he was at the ENS. Both experiences, college and prison camp, took place in closed institutions, male communities. "We were in constant communication, night and day . . . even the toilets had no walls, and when you have to use them along with several other people, the notion of an elite disappears."[7]

Others are devastated, crippled by the camp experience; Sartre, on the contrary, thrives on it, developing new talents, new activities, new strategies of survival. What does he like in the camp? "The feeling of being part of a mass,"[8] so much so that when he escapes, he does it reluctantly.

The German *Feldwebel* and his adjutants don't joke about discipline, law, hierarchy. "It's an order. Period." An absurd order, followed by no discussion, no explanations, no negotiations, with two alternatives, submission or punishment, a kick in the ass, a bayonet poked in a buttock, spit in the face. The structure of this sort of institution is classic: the authority of a small group tyrannizing, oppressing, insulting many people. For the first time in his life, Sartre comes face to face with concrete, tangible repression. One must accept the curfews, the doorless toilets, the codfish soup, the lice, the fatigue. A failed escape attempt can prove fatal. Two solutions: either submit passively and wait for the end of the war, or become a strategist and use one's talent and imagination to improve one's daily existence. Sartre opts for the latter. He gets himself a spot in the infirmary, among the privileged. Then, palming himself off as a playwright, he moves on to the artists' barracks. He sings, writes, puts on plays, acts, composes, lectures, teaches, plays the fool, and, finally, escapes with false papers.

But if Sartre thrives on the heights of Stalag XII D, it is also because of his sense of complicity with the other prisoners. "The adjutant we've nicknamed Pilchard likes to slap us. . . . What surprises, discourages, and exasperates the Germans most is our lack of discipline, our inertia. . . . At curfew, we stay out in front of our barracks, calm, enjoying every stolen minute. . . . Pilchard screams, his voice hoarse with anger; those who are closer to him go in, only to come out again as soon as he turns his back; the others wait, then disappear the moment he approaches. He retraces his steps: we are all back in front of our doors. . . . After ten minutes, he loses his head and begins to lash out; everybody runs away. . . . Our attitude is a form of defense against debasement. . . . There are other ones, from utter immobility to childish giggling."[9] On such occasions, captivity is like being in a summer camp, where the wearing out of authority is the supreme pleasure, the ultimate prize: we are prisoners, but we are still men. In the process, the image of the enemy, the German, changes: from stereotype it becomes a live subject, redrawn by direct experience, "a mixture of bad faith, tremulous tenderness, pedantic proselytism and utilitarianism."[10] The French have been assigned their image as well: "malicious and shrewd . . . the Parisian kid who always manages to slip through the fingers of the big German brute. . . . 'They can beat us all they want, but in the end we'll fuck them over.' "[11]

"Last night, for instance, I actually enjoyed getting kicked in the ass. . . ."[12] Suddenly and for the first time he confronts the humiliations of childhood in the capriciousness of a German soldier: "I had lingered behind, way after curfew time. . . . As I was sneaking back to the barracks along a side alley, the eye of a torchlight hit me full in the face. . . . The sentinel started to shout and threaten me with his bayonet. I immediately understood that he did not mean to poke it into my belly but rather that he was toying with the idea of sticking it in my buttocks: he was waiting for me to turn my back on him. I did, slowly. Never before had I been so aware of all that impotent flesh gathered at the small of my back. At last he gave me a big kick in the ass, which propelled me into the door. I was still laughing when I got back into my room. I told my buddies: 'I've just received the damnedest kick in the ass!' They all burst out laughing."[13]

His buddies are many: mostly priests—the only intellectuals in the camp; a few real friends—like Marc Bénard, a journalist from Le Havre; and then, of course, a number of chance companions, like "Braco,"[14] a stocky little man from the Ardennes, shrewd as a monkey, who owes his nickname to his extraordinary talents as a poacher, and who likes to tell everybody, in an almost incomprehensible, and probably mythomaniac, jargon, that he has just killed his wife because she cheated on him during the phony war. . . . This illiterate is also one of the secret leaders of the camp; he can juggle his two or three German words well enough to communicate with the enemy and is defter than anybody else at bartering both clothes and food. Between Sartre and Braco, a strong complicity is immediately established, based on mutual admiration of their rigorously complementary talents. Sartre devotes several pages of his journal to this "ugly, filthy little man, with sparkling, intelligent eyes . . . who is here under a false name, and spends his time stealing, pillaging, bartering, and, all in all, working very hard to amass a small fortune that he will blow as soon as he is freed. If we place our orders with him eight days in advance, he usually gets us what we've asked for. . . . For a while, he considered protecting me; he knew I was a teacher and thought that, given the opportunity, I might be able to testify as to his good character. He gave me some tobacco, twice. The third time, I refused it."[15]

But Sartre does not appreciate the "phalanstery of inverts" he ends up with in the artists' barrack, a mixture of musicians—such as Lebâtard, conductor of the camp's orchestra and a member of the Paris Conservatory—self-styled impresarios, such as Chomisse, and athletes of all sorts, wrestlers, boxers, fighters. . . . "Chomisse, you didn't know where that sort of fellow came from. They said he used to open the doors of taxis outside the Gaumont Palace cinema. It's not impossible."[16] Among these alleged artists, there are a few "who didn't play the game . . . who profited from [others' confidences] for their own advantage—those were the ones I disliked in the first place, and they might become real enemies." It is for the others, for his friends, that Sartre plays the role of entertainer, jokester, the life of the party: "In the evening . . . I'd tell stories, I'd sit at a table in the middle of the hut and talk and they were very much amused. I told them any old crap, playing the fool."[17] Later, while describing these evenings to Jacques Laurent-Bost, he adds, "I'd tell my buddies a bunch of funny stories before they went to sleep. And to make sure they were really listening to me, now and then I'd call their names, one by one. When everybody had failed to answer, I knew I could also go to sleep."[18]

During the winter of 1940 he again dons a pair of boxing gloves to face, in an official bantamweight bout, one Gaillot, a young printer from the provinces. During the first round, the philosopher has the upper hand, but in the second, the printer moves ahead. "I was overcome with fatigue," he explains, "because it was years since I had boxed and I had the worst of it. The result was a draw. Which I found disappointing, because Pardaillan did not have drawn matches."[19]

Sartre goes to work every morning, after coffee, to the headquarters of the 42nd division. Father Marius Perrin, the head of the barracks, has a large, heated office. Together, they discuss Malraux, Heidegger, and Rilke. They become friends, exchange books, share meals, introduce each other to other possible friends. Sartre is encouraged to reread Bossuet's Sermons, kindly lent by Father Espitallier, a professor of rhetoric in Lyon. He returns the book unconvinced but, nevertheless, glad to have been able to check his theory about classicism. For his part, he offers to introduce Perrin to Heidegger: a copy of Being and Time is sneaked into the camp by Father Etchegoyen, who works outside, in a monastery where he has struck up a friendship with an anti-Nazi German priest. Every morning, Sartre spends two hours discussing German phenomenology with Perrin next to the stove, in the headquarters of the 42nd division.

Sartre feels at ease with the priests despite the interminable arguments about faith. "It is quite advantageous to have faith," Father Espit tells him one day. Sartre pulls his pipe out of his mouth and, jumping up from his chair, asks, "What do you mean, 'to have faith'? Do you own faith the same way I own this pipe? Or do you mean that faith entertains, with you, its owner, some sort of magical relationship? Wouldn't you rather say that, by becoming a believer, you assume a fundamental attitude? You are a priest, and every morning, before saying Mass, you must remember to renew your priestness."²⁰ Espit admits he has not expressed himself adequately and thanks Sartre for this "lesson in spirituality." A few minutes later, he tells a friend, another priest, that Sartre is "a being like no one else, a kind of prophet." Most of the other prisoners have family ties outside the camp, heavy responsibilities, obligations, definitive bonds. The priests don't. As for Sartre, he is like one of his floating balloons, without a string, without moorings. What he discovers, in the stalag, is responsibility more than confinement. "Captivity brings us back to a horrible innocence, a total lack of responsibility. . . . We are not responsible for being here: We are here because we can't get out. The mind can rest!"²¹

"A witness, always a witness. Witness of others and of oneself. . . . Till the war, I had never done anything: I used to juggle harmless old ideas in front of a bunch of kids. Every month, the administration paid me a certain amount of money that seemed to have absolutely no relation to my babbling; I had a steady, private income and the bad conscience of a true consumer. I went around in circles, lending myself at times, but never giving myself: I was like a virgin who keeps herself for some extravagant betrothal; I had rejected all suitors because they weren't handsome enough, and particularly the Spanish Civil War, because it was not *my* war."²² In the middle of the camp's miniature society, Sartre's social paralysis starts to loosen up. For Christmas 1940, under pressure of circumstances he becomes a playwright. In six weeks, he manages to write the play, choose the actors, direct the rehearsals, take care of the production, provide scenery and costumes. He is sorry only for having to postpone his courses on Heidegger till January. Sure of himself and in total control he announces his subject, freedom, and his plot, a Christmas mystery. And he immediately gets to work, preferring, for this occasion, to write in the din of his barracks rather than in Perrin's office. He draws an outline of the play then casts the main roles, convinced that the physical personality of the actors must, in some way, affect the imagination of the author. For the main roles he chooses Henri Leroy, Marc Bénard, and Father Feller. They begin copying their parts while Sartre is still writing the main text. Rehearsals take place in the hangar—*die Halle,* as the Germans call it—that Father Boisselot has been able to get from the camp commander for a number of recreational and didactic purposes, including Mass. Sartre attends all the rehearsals and even manages to get from the Germans some colored paper fabric for the costumes.

On the evening of December 24, everything is ready. There is a brief accordion prelude. "Good people, gentlemen, I am going to tell you about the strange and wonderful adventures of Bariona, the Son of Thunder. This story takes place in the days when the Romans were masters of Judea, and I hope that it will interest you. While I am telling you the story, you may look at the pictures behind me: they will help you see things as they really were. And if you like my story, pray be generous. Now let the music play. We're going to begin."[23] The plot of the play is simple: Bariona wavers between despair and hope, between his mistrust of the Messiah announced by the Magi, and new, more constructive and dynamic possibilities. He ends up convincing his people to resist the Romans: "My faithful friends, Christ's soldiers," he shouts in his final speech. "You look ferocious and determined, and I know you'll fight well. I want you to die joyfully. . . . Come on, drink a slug of wine; I give you permission, and let's march against these mercenaries of Herod. Let's march, drunk with songs and wine and hope."[24] Prolonged applause, and the entire company comes out for a bow, including the author himself still wearing the costume of Balthazar, the black magus. Later, Sartre will speak of this strange experience that saw him in the double role of author and actor, on a stage, in front of a huge, literally captive audience: "As I addressed my comrades across the footlights, speaking to them of their state as prisoners, when I suddenly saw them so remarkably silent and attentive, I realized what theater ought to be: a great, collective, religious phenomenon . . . a theater of myths."[25] Elsewhere, he will also explain how, on that occasion, and through the intermediary of Bariona, he hoped to touch the prisoners' most sensitive spot, their resistance to the Germans. As soon as the play is over, Sartre changes and rushes off to join the camp's choir group to sing, under the baton of Father Espitallier, the hymns and responses of Christmas for the midnight Mass.

"It snowed all night," Father Marius Perrin writes on the following morning. "All is white. There are very few tracks on the ground. . . . Not a soul in sight this Christmas morning. . . . I haven't even seen Sartre yet: he deserves to sleep late this morning! Leroy has also gone back to sleep. The entire camp seems to linger in the arms of Morpheus. . . . I should probably say a few words about what's already on everybody's lips. I was really curious to see what Sartre would put together for Christmas. Thank God, he was able to keep his head. He pleased us without hurting himself. This *Bariona* has nothing of the classical Christmas mystery. There is no Virgin, there is no Child . . . except, perhaps, implicitly. . . . Bariona's men go away, maybe to die, but then they'll die so that the hope of mankind won't be murdered."[26] Corporal Pierre's reaction to the play is quite different: "Sartre has written an anti-Semitic play and has had the camp's theater company perform it," he notes, referring to a few provocative lines: "Of course, you Jews, you don't know how to keep yourselves warm. . . . You're real savages. . . . Most of your fellow believers . . . do not even know their birthdate. They were born the year of the great flood, the great harvest, the great storm. Real savages. I'm not hurting your feelings, am I? You're a cultured man even if you are a Jew. . . . Do you want to know the truth? The Jewish people are still children. For its own good, we would like to see somebody knock some sense into the head of the Jewish nation."[27] It is important, however, to know that these words are uttered by Lelius, the Roman civil servant, and that, as such, they should be read with a certain irony. On the other hand, was it really the right place, the right time, and, particularly, the right audience for speeches like these?

Sartre wrote about the play thirty years later: "I turned out *Bariona,* which was thoroughly bad but which did have a dramatic idea. . . . The Germans didn't understand [the play]. They just saw it as a Christmas play. But the French prisoners got the point. . . ."[28] "Though I took my subject from the mythology of Christianity, that does not mean that the trend of my thinking changed even for a moment when I was a prisoner of war. It was simply a matter, agreed on with my fellow-prisoner priests, of finding a subject most likely to appeal to both Christians and nonbelievers that Christmas Eve."[29] The experiment turned out to be more important than it had seemed at first: "[*Bariona*] gave me a liking for the theater."[30]

But now Sartre clashes head-on with Marcel Bucard's fascist group, which has just come together under the auspices of the Kommandantur. "Two hundred prisoners have already joined," Sartre writes on November 25. "I won't let it happen here. In fact, I have already bawled some of my people out. . . . But they are lukewarm, both pros and cons. They are all victims of the democratic illusion; they consider Gilly and his clique the stars of the camp. They don't like him, but they find him amusing and respond to his fame. They like to see him go by in his boots and a tarboosh that flattens his arrogant, pale face. . . . The moment they see him approach, they start elbowing each other. . . . He is certainly another one of those who have found their chance in the camp. These will be the best days of his life."[31] Sartre is already very sensitive to a softness, a consenting passivity that he hates. He immediately attacks those who have gathered around fascist ideologies and who, a year later, will become the Rassemblement National Populaire of Marcel Déat, strong and numerous enough to engage in an open demonstration within the camp. Meanwhile, he also argues with the communists. One day, he invites Marius Perrin to a meeting in the artists' barracks, a meeting that will eventually turn into a harsh political debate between the two of them and some communist students, on the topic of the German-Soviet alliance, which is, according to the PCF, merely one of Stalin's tactical stratagems, necessary to break the back of fascism, before the inevitable advent of socialism, democracy, and the Soviets. The argument fails to convince Sartre, who pulls no punches in his attack on the means used to achieve that end. Perhaps he is thinking of Nizan and the recent slanders that have followed his resignation from the Communist Party.

"Yesterday, I had a long conversation with Espit, Sartre, and Leroy," Marius Perrin writes at the beginning of 1941. "Sartre does not like what is happening in France; but he is reserved about de Gaulle. . . . He has no liking for any regime; that of the fascists horrifies him: power in the hands of the *salauds*. . . . As for the 'Republicans,' he sees them as old fogeys, only able to parade along with old war veterans. Besides, they are all cryptofascists. He does not regret not having voted for them, but thinks it is time to act. . . . The problem with free men is that they always let others have their way, and these others take advantage of it. He has decided to leave his ivory tower and plunge into the fray."[32] These projects will soon become more concrete. During the same discussion, Sartre begins to elaborate his ideas and sketch a program. "It is impossible to join a party: they are all rotten, including the communists. . . . On the other hand, there is room for a new kind of association, which could be called 'the party of freedom.' It would be open to all free men, whatever their philosophical convictions. His program is ready," Perrin adds, "at least in its broader outline. It owes a great deal to both Fourier and Saint-Simon." In a month or two, Sartre will put the outline into political practice.

His journey is almost over. He has realized the importance of action, without suppressing his disgust for parties, bureaucracies, and collective endorsements. He is perfectly aware of his own limitations: "If I ever joined a party," he writes in "Mathieu's Journal," "I would do it out of such self-conscious generosity that it would be immoral. The Communist Party is right to mistrust intellectuals."[33] He feels the need to act but remains independent. At the stalag, he has struck a balance. He has discovered others, the way an ethnologist discovers a primitive nation. He has analyzed them, observed them, interpreted them. With them, he has shared hardships, privations, vexations. He has talked to them, tried to communicate with them at all possible levels. He has undergone the glorious, inevitable test of general leveling and adopted survival strategies. He has discovered society from both ends and experienced the realities of authority, insubordination, and solidarity; in the midst of the barbed wires of a sordid German camp, he has also encountered a few marginal, lost individuals who have seemed to him far more pleasant than the three companions he had during the phony war. He has managed to achieve a real deliverance. Where others have fallen to pieces, he has braced himself and has learned to live. Before disappearing, he tells Marius Perrin, "We are freer here than across the street."[34] And, in his journals, we find a rather prophetic sentence, written shortly after his arrival at the camp: "We do nothing, of course; we are the passive subjects of a metamorphosis."[35]

LATER, ASKED about "what prisoners read" for a large survey, he gives a long answer, full of nostalgia: "I loved *Au pays des tigres parfumés* [In the Country of Perfumed Tigers] a book about India by a certain Dekobra, a totally ridiculous book, which I read with passion because it took me out of Germany. . . . I also read a number of detective novels, Nerval's *Filles du feu*, Sophocles' plays . . . and a few poems by Rilke and Carossa, in German. But my biggest discoveries were [Paul Claudel's] *The Satin Slipper* and [Georges Bernanos's] *The Diary of a Country Priest*. These are the only two books that had a real impact on me. . . . I read them by chance. I was never able to find the books that I would have brought along had I known I was going to spend so much time there. But during those totally inactive days, when daydreaming was our only means of escape, though we knew it was better not to mull over the past, reading acquired a charm and a power of fascination such as I had not experienced since childhood. We could read just about anything with a passion, and our days would inevitably be marked by our readings: there were Somerset Maugham days, Nerval days, even Dekobra days."[36]

Sartre was released in March 1941, thanks to a fake medical certificate, which declared him "affected by a partial blindness of the right eye, entailing difficulties of orientation." He managed to recover a manuscript that had been confiscated by a German officer and, ten days later, found himself back in Paris, stunned and almost sorry. "I left for a reason," he later explains, "though I did not really want to. But I told myself: 'I have to, just to prove a point.' "[37]

Stalag XII D, in Trèves, will forever retain, for him, the sweet aftertaste of nostalgia: he will remember it with the tenderness of the fetishist. In the summer of 1953, during a trip to Amsterdam, he takes a detour through Germany to show Simone de Beauvoir the remains of the Black Square, *die Halle,* and the wooden barracks, on top of Mount Kemmel, overlooking the town.

"SOCIALISM AND FREEDOM"

P ARIS, APRIL 2, 1941. A whole year since he has set foot in the capital. What is it like that day? An operetta stage set? An unbearable nightmare? A fantastic novel? Road signs point every which way, confusing everything, offering new destinations to new actors: the Kommandantur, the Deutsches Institut, the Wehrmachtsgottendienst. . . . Gray-green uniforms, boots, military caps, red flags with black swastikas, military cars, military salutes: an invasion. "We are freer here than across the street," Sartre had told Perrin fifteen days earlier, while still at Trèves. His mind reels: his camp companions, Braco's accent, the morning rituals, framed, regular, familiar—and here, these anonymous men who have invaded, raped, desecrated his city. He is thirty-six, and it's spring, and he is

160

back home, but Paris has changed, and he has changed . . . Crazy!

First evening out, the stranger in his home town, before he looks up old friends, automatically walks into a café: "Suddenly, I experienced a feeling of fear—or something close to it. I couldn't understand how these squat, bulging buildings could conceal such deserts. I was lost; the few drinkers seemed more distant than the stars. Each of them was entitled to a huge section of bench, to a whole marble table, while I, to touch them, would have had to cross 'a gleaming wooden floor' that separated us. If these men, shimmering comfortably within their tubes of rarefied gas seemed inaccessible to me, it was because I no longer had the right to place my hand on their shoulder or thigh, or to call one of them 'fathead.' I had rejoined bourgeois society, where I would have to learn to live once again 'at a respectful distance.' This sudden agoraphobia betrayed my vague feeling of regret for the collective life from which I had been forever severed."[1]

Before facing the real challenges that await him, he must get reaccustomed to the places, the distances, and the relationships between free men. The first and coziest stop is at 23, Avenue de Lamballe, in the 16th arrondissement, where his mother and stepfather live: bourgeois comfort, attentive maid, dinner. After it, he feels as if he has suddenly been immunized against the dizzying, paradoxical atmosphere of freedom. Should he look for Simone de Beauvoir? Leave a note in her mailbox at the hotel, and then go wait for her at the Café des Mousquetaires, on the Avenue du Maine?

SINCE JUNE 1940, France has lost both its autonomy and its integrity. Pétain signs the armistice with Hitler, de Gaulle appeals from London: "France has lost the battle but France has not lost the war." The country is cut in two: north zone/south zone, Pétain's men/incorruptible patriots. In fact it has shattered into a thousand pieces. Politicized writers either cling to their party lines, the ideologies of their groups, or become resigned, in which case they become like everybody else, forlorn, more isolated than ever. During the first months of the German Occupation, writers wander aimlessly, following earlier causes, the meanderings of their psychological profile, their ideological, social, geographical, and professional bent, their families, their age, their generation, their adventures in the army. Gide is softly pessimistic. Drieu loves only winners. Saint-Exupéry wavers in front of Pétain and fears de

Gaulle. Malraux is on vacation. Breton leaves for New York. Aragon writes occasional poems. . . . As for the Gallimard offices, it's like a political tower of Babel.

The big news in the Paris literary life is German censorship, which, obeying laws of its own ideology, bans or approves everything French writers publish. Rather, everything they *have* published: the first "Otto list," in force since September 1940, is a catalogue of all French books that may not be sold, listed by publisher: from *Nouvelle Revue Francaise* / Gallimard—Malraux's, *Man's Hope* and *Le Temps du Mépris*; Nizan's, *Chronique de septembre*; Denis de Rougemont's, *Journal d'Allemagne.* Sartre is spared, just as he will be in the second list of 1942. The German budgets for ideological propaganda are staggering. They need three organizations—the German embassy, the Deutsches Institut, and the Propagandastaffel—to succeed in their plan: the purification of French literature from Jewish, communist, Masonic, and other vermin. All these organizations are overseen by the French antennae of Alfred Rosenberg and various Nazi agents sent from Berlin to carry out specific missions in Paris.

Among the actors who now rule French literary life, Karl Epting, Karl-Heinz Bremer, and Gerhardt Heller had already tasted the joys of French culture during their stays as German lecturers in French provincial towns. As for Sieburg, nicknamed "the handsome Friedrich," he has become a celebrity since Grasset translated his book *Is God French?* Otto Abetz, the dashing, refined thirty-five-year-old ambassador who, before the war, had militated in favor of a Franco-German rapprochement, returns to the occupied country intoxicated with Francophilia and married to a Frenchwoman. The writer Ernst Jünger will choose his words carefully to describe, in his journal, the delight of German literati in Paris: "Paris, April 6, 1941. A rainy Sunday. Went twice to la Madeleine whose steps are stained with the green leaves of boxwoods; had lunch and dinner at Prunier's. The city is like an old familiar garden, now abandoned, but still known in all its paths and alleys."[2] These new actors feel no qualms about deriving pleasure from a city, a culture whose exoticism has long visited their dreams. Playing the artists and the esthetes, they go from Prunier's to Tour d'Argent, from the Ritz to the Hotel George V, savoring wine, champagne, and foie gras, like civilized ethnologues abandoning themselves to the customs of the natives.[3]

"I came back to France with the idea that other Frenchmen did not realize all this—that some of them, those who came back from the front and were liberated, realized it, but there was no one to make them decide to resist."

Sartre needs only one brief dip into occupied Paris to be convinced of the need for direct action. "That's what seemed to me the first thing to do on coming back to Paris—to create a resistance group; to try, step by step, to win over the majority to resistance and thus bring into being a violent movement that would expel the Germans."[4] This metamorphosis baffles his friends, especially Simone de Beauvoir, who, "quite taken aback by the rigor of his moralism," describes their first conversation and his new behavior in great detail: "Did I buy things on the black market? A little tea occasionally, I told him. Even this was too much. I had been wrong to sign the paper stating that I was neither a Freemason nor a Jew. Sartre had always asserted his ideas, not to mention his likes and dislikes, in a most dogmatic fashion, whether verbally or through his personal actions. Yet he never formulated them as universal maxims. . . . The first evening he gave me yet another surprise. He had not come back to Paris to enjoy the sweets of freedom, he told me, but to *act.* How? I inquired, taken aback. We were so isolated, so powerless! It was precisely this isolation that had to be broken down, he said. We had to unite, to organize a resistance movement."[5]

Sartre is still not aware that the Resistance had already started, during the summer and the fall of 1940. By December 1940, the word "resistance" had established itself: "To resist, this is the cry that issues from all our hearts, distressed by the disaster that has befallen our country . . ." Thus the first underground paper, *Résistance,* announces the appeal of the National Committee of Public Safety, which has founded it. Backing the committee is the group known as "The Museum of Man," founded by two scientists, Boris Vildé and Anatole Levitsky, later joined by Léon Maurice Nordmann, the lawyer, and the writers Claude Aveline, Jean Cassou, and Henri Abraham, Jean Zay's former private secretary. The group will go on with the publication and the distribution of its clandestine pamphlets till February 1942. There are demonstrations on November 11, 1940, commemorating the victory of 1918, and, on the part of "collabo" youth groups, the looting of shop windows on the Champs Elysées, followed by numerous arrests. There are publications such as the weekly of the French Resistance *Libération,* as well as *La Vraie France* or *Sous la Botte,* from spontaneous little groups, most of which will be demolished during the Resistance's toughest winter.[6]

On the communist side, isolation and confusion reign. Only a few oppositionists of the hard line—which has totally endorsed the German-Soviet pact—are busy preparing a few publications.

Within this complex political climate, where militants of all tendencies are forced to rely exclusively on their own individual initiatives, Sartre's determination is comparable, in its intensity, to the first pamphlets and the first demonstrations of the autumn of 1940. A novice in politics, only recently returned from captivity, he takes his first steps in the expression of a brutal anger. Thus, his friends' surprise; Sartre hardly mentions his recent past.

" '*A* JUDGMENT OF fact has to do with what is. A value judgment has to do with what should be . . .' If I remember correctly, these were the first words he dictated. It was the spring of 1941, and we had just started studying ethics": Jean-Bertrand Pontalis, a philosophy student at the Lycée Pasteur, witnessed the unexpected return of his professor. As an approach to philosophy it was a brutal and radical change. "His words were cutting."[7] The new Sartre is austere: three-piece suit, a reserved distance instead of the legendary camaraderie . . . and total silence about current events: "For a few months," Pontalis goes on, "he did not say a word about Vichy, our defeat, the stalag he had just left. But the subject he gave us for our dissertation was 'Remorse.' " New clothes, a new look help protect the heavy underground work that's going on at the same time. The violence of the resistance fighter is disguised by the changes in the professor: the day when Pontalis and his friend Bourla tear up a poster of Pétain in their classroom and are dragged in front of the principal, Sartre disapproves of their gesture without repudiating them. "That's when I first understood the real difference between a 'gesture' and an 'action,' " Pontalis explains.

A handful of people have gathered within the brownish walls of the shabby hotel room, overlooking a narrow street, right behind the Gare Montparnasse. A few hours earlier, Jean Pouillon has received an urgent phone call from Jacques-Laurent Bost: "Sartre has just come back from the camp. He's at the Hotel Mistral." Only the intimates have been called: Bost and Olga, Pouillon, Beauvoir, and Wanda. Sartre speaks for a long time. They must get rid of the Germans. They must observe, convince, win as many people as possible over to the Resistance. They must proceed by word of mouth until they attain their ends—not quite a well-conceived political scheme or a precise plan of defense against the Occupation. Sartre is simply continuing his discussions with the priests in the stalag. He is enthusiastic, convincing, optimistic: he is sure that spontaneous revolts will keep cropping up in isolated groups, mutually reinforcing each other, despite the risks of clandestinity and of repressive measures.

After the "family" it is the turn of close friends: Maurice Merleau-Ponty, who, for a few months, since the beginning of the academic year in 1940, has been working at the formation of a group named "Sous la botte" (Under the Boot). He is surrounded by his own students from the Ecole Normale: Jean-Toussaint Desanti, a twenty-six-year-old candidate for the *agrégation*, and his wife Dominique, a student of history at the Sorbonne; François Cuzin, Simone Debout, and Yvonne Picart, young, brilliant, and heavily politicized philosophers. They have written their pamphlets together with a few scientists from the Ecole, the most militant, such as Raymond Marrot, the mathematician, a libertarian totally disappointed with the communists . . . and Georges Chazelas, a twenty-four-year-old physicist of the class of '37, and his younger brother Jean, a student of medicine: two big, strong men ready for head-on action. These are the people who have concocted those urgent, caustic pamphlets advocating sabotage and resistance, in any possible form, without any exclusion, sectarianism, or delay. Midway between the "Sartre family" and "Under the Boot" are his former students, such as Jean Kanapa and Raoul Lévy: they have kept in touch with their professor, both while he was a soldier and while he was a prisoner, often visiting Simone de Beauvoir and the other members of the "family." Lévy considers himself a "Gaullist, because," as he explained to Beauvoir in 1940, "it was crucial that the French government went into exile, like the Dutch government." "You speak like an Englishman," she reproached him.[8]

"Sartre said a few words about his captivity then asked us: Well, what shall we do? Have you started doing something?"[9] The first meeting with the veterans of "Under the Boot" took place in a messy room of the Hotel d'Egypte, Rue Gay Lussac. Dominique Desanti remembers: "It was on the first floor, and we entered through the window, which gave us the illusion that we could escape more easily in case the police decided to arrest us. We were still innocent then." Between the two groups, there is a clear understanding: to fight the Vichy regime and all collaborators, and to dissociate themselves, on the right, from the Gaullists, and, on the left, from the communists and their ridiculous pact. They decided to call the group "Socialisme et Liberté" (Socialism and Freedom), because, Sartre explains, they must look ahead and elaborate a global plan for liberated France. They must open the way for the future, and organize socialism in view of the freedom that will come to power once fascism is defeated. Sartre views the end of the war as imminent. "Oddly," Dominique Desanti notes, "he, a mature man, seemed much more optimistic than we who were ten years younger."[10]

"Hitler is deporting our men," Sartre writes. "This is a situation we cannot accept. If we accept the Vichy regime, then we are not men: no compromise is possible with the collaborators. We must immediately start rebuilding a society where freedom will not be an empty word." Dominique Desanti types this text on a stencil. Then she takes it to Chazelas and Marrot, at work in the basement of the Ecole Normale. Cellar 50 is their secret domain, where—among crates and the instruments of a physics lab—they have installed their printing equipment—an old manual mimeograph machine, with ink and stencils, paper stolen from the physics laboratory, bottles of ink and gasoline, and screwdrivers and hammers, just in case. That particular day, while they are busy printing, the door opens. "Who's there?" a hysterical voice shouts. Chazelas recognizes Uchamp, the school bursar, a "notorious collabo," and runs to unscrew the light-bulb. A few seconds of panic. Marrot whispers in his ear: "There is only one solution, you have to kill him!" Then, suddenly, from the staircase, they hear a voice, a miracle, the bursar's secretary: "Monsieur Uchamp, Monsieur Uchamp, come quick, you're wanted on the phone, it's urgent." "That endless Sartrean treatise on freedom, all three pages of it," forty-two years later Chazelas still sighs. "It was a very bad joke to put us in such a situation for that sort of text. . . . Others did not know freedom as a philosophical tract but rather as a kick in the ass."[11]

Comical comings and goings, paradoxical situations, slapstick: the adventures and trials of the group often assume the chaotic appearance of a comic strip. Bost and Pouillon are upset because the mimeograph machine they have installed in Pouillon's mother's living room has begun to stain the carpet, so they move it outside, to the garden. A few days later, the two friends are turning the crank of the machine and collating bundles of secret pamphlets still wet with print under the bright spring sun and the puzzled eyes of passers-by. On another occasion, while walking to a meeting at La Coupole,

Pouillon realizes he has lost his briefcase. Where did he leave it? Did he leave it in a subway train? That would be disastrous. Everything is in that briefcase: names, addresses, telephone numbers of all their comrades, not to mention the bundle of pamphlets! General panic ensues till the following day when the briefcase is finally tracked down, on the shelves of the Lost and Found Office on the Rue des Morillons.[12] On yet another occasion, Georges Chazelas is operating the mimeograph machine in the house of the grandfather of one of his comrades, on the Rue du Ranelagh. The writer François Coppée has kindly agreed to host his grandson, Pierre Strauss, a student of medicine, and his friends for an afternoon. Suddenly, the doorbell rings: it is the Gestapo coming to seize Coppée's books. Someone sits on the mimeograph machine, someone else on the wet stencils, Strauss hurries to the stove to burn the most compromising pamphlets but succeeds only in tipping it over.[13] These are the acrobatics of the clandestine, when every action is a risk. A risk that, at times, can be very real and costly. On June 15, 1941, for instance, Georges Chazelas, exhausted by a night of work, decides to glue some posters on the wall of the school of medicine: it is a call to sabotage by means of bombs and grenades. At 6 A.M. he is arrested and will spend six months in jail.

Despite all the fears, the group grows and evolves. By June 1941, there are about fifty people—professors, students of letters, science, medicine, engineering—working for "Socialism and Freedom." How to minimize risk? How to confront the police with a strong line of attack? From now on, all meetings will be held by "cells." Each cell will consist of five members each of which will have the task of creating a new cell, also consisting of five members, and so on. This form of proselytism proves very effective: from one meeting to the next, from the Hotel d'Egypte to the Luxembourg Gardens, plans become clearer, functions become more diversified, points of view multiply, and discussions are more and more heated.

Marrot is an anarchist, Merleau-Ponty already a Marxist, Sartre a Proudhonian and resolutely anticommunist, Rigal a Trotskyite. Sartre refuses to give in to any sectarianism: he thinks it is crucial that the Marxists have a chance to express their views. "He rolled a cigarette, struggling with the strands of ersatz tobacco that kept piercing the paper," Desanti recalls, "stuck his cigarette into his mouth and launched the age of dialogue and multilogue, which he then pursued for years: 'All right, then, the editorial will be alternately written by a Marxist and a non-Marxist.' This type of decision entailed constant confrontation that would have been quite banal in times of peace, but not so now. In this room with locked windows, as a measure of protection against the possibly hostile ears of the passers-by, Sartre laid the foundations of what was going to become his own fight. His refusal of Marxism and of anticommunism was later to pit him against Camus. The decision to tolerate the insults of communists and not to abandon avant-garde organizations was made during a meeting in the Latin Quarter in 1941."[14] This sort of maneuvering is fairly difficult at a time when communist militants are having such trouble decoding the often contradictory orders they receive. "We hold out our hand to the goodwill of all French citizens," the manifesto says, while the underground *L'Humanité* of June 20, 1941 inveighs against the Gaullists and their "reactionary, colonialist" movement.[15] These ideological differences are, of course, accompanied by tactical differences, and provoke endless discussions among the most radical members, the unconditional partisans of direct action, like Raymond Marrot, Desanti, Chazelas, and others. "If we see a German train loaded with ammunition we blow it up," they say with gravity. "So, why shouldn't we start with the German Library 'Rive Gauche' on the Boulevard Saint-Michel?"[16] "We should try to locate the positions and the deployments of the German air force and sabotage them."[17] On another occasion it is Alfred Péron's cell that proposes "to reconstruct a detailed map of the Renault factories and pinpoint the points to attack and those to spare."[18]

For their part, the women are involved in specific, monitored operations. On the day they learn who is going to be on the train of French writers bound for Weimar, Simone de Beavoir inquires, "Who should smash Brasillach's face in, me or Debout?"[19] Dominique Desanti asks, "Should we distribute some pamphlets among German soldiers? There's a big difference between a German and a soldier." Only Sartre supports her proposition, which immediately gets bogged down. Merleau-Ponty reopens the question a little later: "And what if the German occupation lasts for a long time? thirty, forty years, for instance," he wonders. "I should try to write a few articles that might speak to them, convince them."[20] How far are they willing to go? Tanks and other heavy weapons could be used in a commando operation aimed at freeing an occupied village. "Do you know how to make a bomb?" Pouillon asks Bost. "Maybe we could learn how." A few months later, they will already be talking about *boîtes à sardines,* plastic explosives.

June 1941: the brave young soldiers of "Socialism and Freedom" do not spare themselves. The intellectuals compose texts and quarrel over editorials; the militants type, print, distribute, glue posters, stick pamphlets into mailboxes, gather clandestine information. For this, they often have to turn to the services of a sympathizer, such as Jean Rabaut or David Rousset, who, from the Ministry of the Interior, where he is in charge of international publications, has direct access to radio information in all languages. "Unfortunately," as Simone Debout remembers, smiling, "their information concerning future events often turned out to be incorrect."[21] The relationship between Sartre and Jean Cavaillès—that great intellectual of the Resistance who will end up in front of a firing squad—was more secret and much more serious. "Today, I have to ask you to behave most cautiously," Sartre whispers to Raoul Lévy before taking him along to the Hotel des Terrasses, Rue du Val de Grâce, where Cavaillès lives. Sartre and Cavaillès: both Normaliens, philosophers, Germanists, Protestants, in-situ initiates to Weimar Germany. But, as it will appear within the next few months, their attitudes toward political action are very different. In the meantime, however, Raoul Lévy sees a grave, authoritarian Cavaillès confronted by a Sartre, who is full of devotion and admiration "like a young boy." Lévy, a twenty-year-old student, represents the "Sartre group" to Cavaillès, that is, he is in charge of conveying information and secret messages. "In fact, I only did it once," Raoul Lévy remembers. "I was ashamed; the information I had to transmit seemed so ridiculous." And, indeed, the sheet Lévy handed to Cavaillès contained only two bits of news: the first was a statistical survey concerning the reading of pro-German papers in occupied territory. Raoul Lévy did not know that the actual information was encoded as figures with three decimals. All he could think about was the lack of proportion between Cavaillès's mathematical genius and the scientific value of that survey, for which they had questioned at most fifteen persons! The second bit of news concerned the unequivocal presence of German tanks in the Rambouillet forest, a fact that called for the immediate intervention of the British air force.[22]

Before breaking up for the summer, they decide to take stock of the situation. To respect ideological alternation, the two spokesmen of the group, Sartre and Merleau-Ponty, each compose a text. The purpose of these documents is to disseminate the ideas of "Socialism and Freedom," and to rally other intellectuals and other Resistance movements, over to their group. Merleau-Ponty proposes a text of some twenty pages; Sartre finishes his: a hundred pages of close handwriting, a real constitution for postwar France. "It was a profession of faith," reports Simone Debout, who read and reread the two documents, which she was supposed to take south, before she destroyed both in the toilet of a train for fear of being searched. "Sartre's text," she continues, "set out a program for the future state based on heavily Proudhonian and hugely anachronistic ideas. He already displayed that verbal virtuosity for which we admired him so much. We had all read *Nausea*, and we were all aware of his stature as a man of letters." "It was his first try at ethical and political expression," Jean-Toussaint Desanti adds. "According to him, our immediate actions would have no meaning if we did not simultaneously elaborate a long-term social, ethical, and political perspective for a France liberated from the Nazis."[23]

How to get a clear idea of Sartre's first political document when all ten copies have disappeared? How to analyze the remnants of this constitution, to measure the weight of its 110 to 120 articles, which, it seems, covered all sorts of economic and political structures, and even touched upon the Jewish question? Among other things, influenced by his recent reading of Marx, he proposed creating a currency that would be based on labor and would establish the value of an object according to the time it took to produce it. He also proposed to form a new parliament, which would democratically represent every trade and professional body. Then there was a scrupulous description of the judiciary, which he saw as totally separated from the executive, a new proposition for a different form of military service, and a set of elaborate principles for a more successful foreign policy. All we can gather about that document comes from the memory of the few who read it: Raoul Lévy, for instance, who, despite his "immense admiration for Sartre," found it painfully close to a "parody of an electoral platform."[24]

Did Sartre's first political contribution foreshadow some of his future stances? He already wished to engage in a worldwide political project of concrete action. "Sartre already thought," Jean-Toussaint Desanti explains, "that the moment one posited the ethical and ideological premises for a movement of this kind, and formulated a project of political development for a specific time in the future, one was automatically propelled toward an action that had already attained its aim. But he was not clearly aware of, nor particularly concerned with, the difficulties entailed by the transformation of these reflections into real political practice, whose modalities had to be controlled day by day."[25] And yet, apparently, he had given careful attention to certain details: he had devoted a whole article to the condition of teachers in postwar France and had gone so far as to consider the possible requirements for obtaining a sabbatical leave for personal work or some other research. Despite the broken or missing pieces of this mosaic, it is fairly clear that the lost text was also a continuation of the discourse held by Sartre the prisoner, that is, the Proudhonian, Saint-Simonian, and even at times the Fourier-ist spoken of by Perrin. It also certainly contained some of the main themes that will re-emerge later on and that already revealed some of the traditions of the French left, of a current that could be classified as anarcho-syndicalism.

Meanwhile the "Central Committee of the 'Sartre group' "—as Simone Debout's friends ironically call it—has decided to send him to the South to look for, meet, and convince a few famous writers, such as Gide and Malraux, to join "Socialism and Freedom."

"*I*T WAS permissible to send parcels from one zone to the other, so we forwarded our bicycles and luggage to . . . Roanne. . . . Then we booked tickets to Montceau-les-Mines; we had been given the address of a café there where we could find someone to get us through the border." Simone de Beauvoir, on this trip with Sartre, narrates. "We were hardly clear of the town before Sartre's front tire went flat. I can't think how I ever came to embark upon this adventure without having learned about repairing punctures, but the fact remains that I did not know how to. . . . It was years since Sartre had been for a bicycle ride of any length, and after twenty-five miles or so he was in very poor shape."[26] Two Parisians riding their bikes on the bumpy roads of Free France: Roanne, Bourg, Lyon, Saint-Etienne, Le Puy, the Cévennes, Montélimar, Arles, Marseilles, Grasse, Grenoble, Auxerre . . . Two weeks of extraordinary physical effort, of nights in a tent, of days fraught with bike accidents and political meetings. "Sartre far preferred bicycling to walking; the monotony of the latter bored him. . . . He enjoyed sprinting on hills . . . ; but on the flat he pedaled so indolently that several times he toppled off into the ditch. 'My mind was elsewhere,' he remarked on these occasions."[27]

"It was quite a feat to come all the way up to our house by bike," Marie Kaan remembers. "We lived in a small village, Saint-Etienne-de-Lugdarès, on a steep mountain at the junction of three départements, Gard, Lozère, and Haute-Loire."[28] Since the Ecole Normale, Sartre has been the friend of Marie's husband Pierre and his brother, André, who are both philosophers; André had once been a communist and was going to develop one of the solidest Resistance networks in the center of France; hence his meeting with Sartre. Sartre shows him his project for a constitution and details the activities of "Socialism and Freedom." "Under a pine of the Cévennes, I heard one of Sartre's most beautiful lessons," Marie Kaan remembers—"a kind of improvisation on the role of the unions in free France."[29] The two men try to imagine what could emerge out of the union of all the Resistance movements: a new and original leftist party that would respect the freedom of the individual. One night with the Kaans, and then they head south.

Marseilles, August 1941. Jean Rabaut, who had worked with the peripheral Trotskyites of "Socialism and Freedom," meets Sartre and Beauvoir in a post office: "Sartre, lantern in hand, was looking for men to join the Resistance. Which Resistance? He was not sure. . . . But he was looking for contacts. He had just seen, or was going to see, the socialist Daniel Mayer, who worked in Marseilles."[30] Beauvoir wrote later: "Did he have any broad policy to suggest to the group, any specific tasks to give them? Daniel Mayer asked us to address a letter to Léon Blum on the occasion of his birthday. Sartre left him, somewhat disappointed."[31] Later, Mayer will explain that he had acted that way to test Sartre, who, till then, had no political past.

According to Beauvoir, "Sartre had written André Gide's name down on his list, with an undecipherable address scribbled beside it: Caloris? Valoris? Surely this must be Vallauris. . . . We called in at the Town Hall to ask for André Gide's address. 'Monsieur Gide the photographer?' said the clerk. This was the only one he knew. . . . I . . . scrutinized my Michelin map. . . . Light suddenly dawned: Cabris."[32] Gide had left Cabris for Grasse. At the café the militant philosopher finally meets the octogenarian esthete. Two years earlier, Gide had asked Adrienne Monnier to organize a dinner so he could be introduced to the author of *The Wall*;[33] and Sartre had almost accepted Paulhan's proposal to write a text for a special issue of the *NRF*, a "Homage to Gide," to come out in November 1939. "I would like to write something about his journal . . . that is, unless you'd rather I wrote of Gide as 'the experimenter of the novel'—but that wouldn't interest me nearly as much."[34] Then the mobilization had put a sudden stop to Sartre's critical impulses.

Nothing convinces Gide to join "Socialism and Freedom" and Sartre does not insist. "Alas, I doubt France will ever get on its feet again," Gide wrote in his journal on May 6, 1941. "I'd find its collaboration with Germany quite acceptable, even desirable if I were sure it was honest. I even go as far as to believe that, despite the painful humiliation it entails, a German subjection might be preferable and less prejudicial to us than the kind of discipline proposed by Vichy,"[35] Even had Sartre reminded this old humanist that the Soviet Union's entry into the war at the end of June made sympathy with the communists much easier, would Gide really have sympathized with Sartre's activism? Just a few days before Sartre's visit Gide wrote a few pages in his journal that echo the Parisian estheticism of Ernst Jünger: "I cannot imagine a better view than the one I enjoy all day long from the window of my room at the Grand Hotel. In front of me, I have the town of Grasse, dominated by the cathedral whose tower cuts across the line of the distant mountains, and the harmonious disorder of its houses, stepping down, in tiers, all the way to the deep ravine that separates me from the town. . . . If I could start again from zero, I think I'd try to fill my life with more adventure."[36] But, clearly, he does not feel this was the time for adventure: Sartre finds only a writer stagnating outside all action, lost on another planet. "Sartre told him he had an appointment to see Malraux the following day. 'Well,' Gide said as they parted, 'I hope you find him in a good mood.' "[37] Then he sits at his table and writes to Roger Martin du Gard: "I don't know what will come of it, because Malraux does not like Sartre's literature at all. But Sartre knows that."[38]

André Malraux lives near Saint-Jean-Cap-Ferrat, at the Cap d'Ail, in the villa Les Camélias with his new friend, Josette Clotis, and their baby. "They lunched on chicken Maryland, exquisitely prepared and served," Beauvoir writes. "Malraux heard Sartre out very courteously, but said that, for the time being at any rate, action of any sort would in his opinion be quite useless: he was relying on Russian tanks and American planes to win the war."[39] Later, Malraux will explain that in June 1940 he was ready to go to London and that he had sent a message to that effect, but it had never arrived.[40] Malraux will participate actively in the Resistance only three years later, in 1944. For the time being, he spends his days in the sun, with his family. His baby's godfather is none other than the novelist Drieu La Rochelle, who is not yet a fascist and a collaborator and who paid them a visit three months before Sartre—the same

Drieu whom Malraux has just recommended to Gide and who is already packing to go to Weimar in October. These are the meetings of the Gallimard authors in Free France. While the Resistance is getting organized, and d'Astier de la Vigerie creates *Libération* in the South, and the young students of *Défense de la France* are refining their underground activities in Paris, the Paris literati refuse to listen to Sartre and prefer to spend the end of the summer of 1941 watching Mediterranean sunsets.

Disappointed, Sartre and Beauvoir stop at Colette Audry's in Grenoble: Malraux sees no reason to act, since, according to him, France is already "out of it all." Unless in fact it is, they discreetly surmise, because he does not wish to play the role of the anonymous hero. There, they also meet Simone Debout: "Malraux is not interested in what we are doing," Sartre informs her, "besides, it would have been impossible for the two of us to get along; we need only one leader."[41] Back in Paris, Sartre details his various failures to the Desantis. Their prestigious envoy, so optimistic only three months earlier, is now quite contrite.

After its failure to develop a movement in the provinces, after the negative responses of the people in the South, and, particularly, after the arrests of two comrades, "Socialism and Freedom" will limp along only until the end of 1941, a few months longer in the case of certain cells. "Don't trust Sartre; he is a German agent," was just one of the lies that the communists had spread throughout the southern provinces to discredit the head of the group. It was also "learned" that he had been freed from prison camp thanks to the direct intervention of Drieu La Rochelle, and that he was a henchman of national socialism, just like his mentor, Heidegger. . . . In other words, wallowing in their paranoia, the communists had decided to turn Sartre into their ideal scapegoat; after all, hadn't he been Nizan's childhood friend, and, as such, wasn't he also likely to be a potential spy? Given these conditions, how could Sartre have joined forces with the communists?

"Resistance," Sartre will explain later, "implied very strict and important norms, such as secret work or special and dangerous missions, whose underlying meaning was the building of another society that was to be free. It followed that the ideal of the individual's freedom was the free society for which he was fighting."[42] Simone de Beauvoir remembers the interminable discussions she had with Sartre all through October before the physical death of the group: "I agreed with his view that to make yourself responsible for someone's death out of sheer obstinacy is not a thing lightly to be forgiven. Sartre had brooded over this plan of his for months in the stalag, and had devoted weeks of his time and energy to it after his release, so it hit him hard to abandon it; but abandon it he did, though his heart told him otherwise."[43]

What was ultimately responsible for the failure of the group? Was it its ineffectiveness, its inexperience, its fragility? Was it its lightness and its impotence in relation to the rise of the two larger Resistance movements started, on the one hand, by the Gaullists and, on the other, by the communists? Was it its inner instability? Its refusal to continue running absurd risks? Violent communist attacks? The extraordinary torpor of the writers and other esthetes who had been counted on to swell its ranks? Yvonne Picart was arrested, deported, and never came back from Drancy. Alfred Péron disappeared and apparently died in one of the camps. And, before the group dissolves, there are a few more close calls: at the Ecole Normale, for instance, where Simone Debout and Jacques Merleau-Ponty have to rush to hide bundles and bundles of pamphlets on the roof. Simone Debout is sent as a liaison to tour all the Parisian groups, a mission from which she will return intensely disappointed: "They were all very earnest," she remembers, "but as noncommittal and nonrevolutionary as possible. After this mission, I left them and went back to work for the communists, who were infinitely better organized."[44] In October, the Sartre "family" meets Jean Cavaillès at the café La Closerie des Lilas. "But," Jean Pouillon explains, "we were not an organized Resistance group, we were just a bunch of friends who had decided to be anti-Nazis together, and to communicate our convictions to others. Besides, at a moment when Resistance movements were really beginning to get structured, a group like ours, isolated and with no exterior contact, couldn't possibly stand the test. And then, of course, wasn't the interest of our pamphlets more in their very existence than in their content?"[45]

Gradually, the various tensions and pressures to which the little group was prey end up destroying it. First of all, as Raoul Lévy points out, there were inner tensions caused by the strong oppositional fringe that existed within "Socialism and Freedom." "Born of enthusiasm," Maurice Merleau-Ponty wrote many years after, "our little group contracted a fever and died a year later, of not knowing what to do."[46] And indeed, starting in June 1941, with the Soviet Union's entry into the war, and the active mobilization of the French communists, the group ceased to have any impact, and particularly so given its intention to provide a "third option" between two powerful Resistance machines: the Gaullists and the communists, two structured organizations that drew their strength from both their ideological potential and their manpower. In the spring of 1941, Raoul Lévy had been charged with two missions that required utmost prudence: he had to establish contact with, on one side, the Trotskyites and, on the other, the communists. The Trotskyites had already predicted the USSR's involvement in the war. The communists wanted to receive some purely quantitative information about the group. The two meetings proved fruitless.[47] "Socialism and Freedom" was swept away by the active Resistance and the short-term political strategies of contrary political currents. At that particular moment, Sartre will refuse to cooperate with either the Gaullists or the communists, unlike all the other members of "Socialism and Freedom," who will gradually be absorbed into the ranks of the PCF. This unilateral nonalliance is particularly important in light of Sartre's political trajectory.

M ost of the former members of "Socialism and Freedom" spent the end of the war in the Free Zone, in the Resistance, often on the side of the PCF. Asked about the change of strategy decided by Sartre after this failure, everybody agreed on one point: Sartre had reacted realistically, adopting what, given the circumstances, was the wisest possible attitude. In fact, the attempts to rally Gide and Malraux to their cause that summer were probably premature, as was the expectation of creating other support groups. In other words, "Socialism and Freedom" could not survive as an alternative political movement at a time when most isolated writers, unlike Sartre, preferred to sit and carefully observe what was going on rather than plunge into immediate action. Pushed into the great void between Gaullists and communists, but still persevering and stubbornly faithful to his "third option," Sartre will also fight, but in his own way. His combat will be more ideological than political since it ultimately renounces all direct action and moves away from all the great currents of the Resistance. The PCF will never forgive him for having missed this first rendezvous with politics, perhaps because, having gotten involved before them, he had not waited for the prevarications and orders of any party to give free rein to his hatred of the Nazis.

"This is it," the Desantises thought the moment the USSR announced its entry into the war. Today, they add, "We were already ripe for the PC." They join it in 1943, after moving to the Free Zone and becoming active members of the Resistance. They leave "Socialism and Freedom," believing that Sartre "had gotten lost in the quicksands of action, because he had neither the preparation nor the competence nor the means to realize the clandestine project he had concocted."[48] Georges Chazelas will also join the Communist Party upon his arrival at Montluçon in 1942; then he will become the military coordinator of the Resistance for the département of Allier, and will finish the war freeing Moulins and Vichy with ten thousand men under his command. He remembers those few clandestine months in Paris with bitterness: "It did not help me take intellectuals seriously. Sartre had a great deal going for him: a famous name, a large following, but he was unable to spur them to action, even though he was certainly better placed than most to succeed. They struck me from the very beginning as fairly childish: they were never aware, for instance, of the extent to which their prattle jeopardized the work of others." And then he adds, "Even though they learned how to reason at the university, I can assure you that, when it came to political action, they were quite unable to think. Besides, Sartre was definitely not made for this sort of clandestine work, a fact that he himself realized toward the end."[49]

Raoul Lévy lived in the South till the end of the war, choosing to cross the frontier during the worst of the racial laws, when all Jews were ordered to wear the yellow star. He left Paris in June 1942, after Sartre had asked him to prepare a line of reflection for the group, something between a political analysis and a summer homework assignment. The subject: "The State in Hegel." Lévy will never do it. He will come back to Paris for only a few visits at the end of the war, and then will also join the PCF, just as his schoolmate at the Lycée Pasteur, Jean Kanapa, had. Today, Raoul Lévy is willing to talk about his experience with the group, but does it with a neutral voice, laced with a touch of bitterness, convinced that all in all the project was fairly negative, "an outlet for the anger we all felt every time we read the German papers," he explains, but "mere chitchat around a cup of tea." He is still convinced that Sartre was a political illiterate, totally unable to decipher the papers of the times, and that the essential motives for Sartre's commitment were more likely to be found in "a philosophical need to integrate history into his reflection than in a true and spontaneous interest."[50]

Freed from the German-Soviet pact at the end of 1942, the communists open up to broader alliances and, coming out of their sectarian exile, start looking for useful contacts. Then, quite naturally, they seek Sartre out, to ask him to join the national committee of writers and to contribute to the underground paper *Les Lettres françaises*. But, till then, they are quite suspicious of him, because he was a friend of Nizan, who had been accused by Maurice Thorez, head of the Party, of being a "rotten dog and a cop" for defecting from the PCF; because he is a pessimistic, decadent, petit-bourgeois writer, as *Nausea* clearly proves; because he might have been released from his prison camp thanks to the help of the Vichyists, including Brasillach; and, finally, because he is rumored to be "the friend of a demi-collabo."[51] As a result of these suspicions, when Jean Paulhan suggests Sartre to Jacques Decour as a possible contributor to *Les Lettres françaises*, the latter responds with an official and absolute refusal.[52] This scene took place at the very beginning of 1942, just before Jean Decour was executed. Sartre will not begin working for them till they open their doors to a much broader range of alliances, toward the end of 1942. But, despite the occasional moments of collaboration, Sartre's relationship with the French communists will always be fraught with a certain duplicity. The duel between them will last forty years. At this point, it has just begun.

Sartre soon finds himself, neither an organizer nor a figurehead but simply an extra.[53] Before leaving clandestine action, Sartre made a serious mistake: he agreed to write an article for *Comoedia*, the collaborationist weekly; in fact, according to Simone de Beauvoir, he may even have agreed to write an editorial for them on a regular basis,[54] and hence to work for a paper that, every week, exhorted its readers to familiarize themselves with Germany, to love Kleist and Hölderlin, in short a paper that was trying to give credit to the thesis that all was well in France, France was having fun, its cultural life was thriving. No trace of the war, no trace of Nazi occupation. "Max Jacob is dead," a paragraph announces on the first page, no further data, no mention of the Jewish writer's deportation. Nevertheless, at the request of the editor-in-chief of the magazine, René Delange, Sartre agrees to write a piece about *Moby Dick*. This mistake will result in at least one beautiful formulation: "No one more than Hegel and Melville has sensed that the absolute is there all around us, formidable and familiar, that we can see it, white and polished like a sheep bone, if only we cast aside the multicolored veils with which we've covered it."[55]

A YEAR LATER, in Paris, the French police start arresting the Jewish population. That's when Jean-Toussaint Desanti decides to engage in the armed struggle on the side of the communists: "That morning, in 1942, the Jewish children did not scream. They did not even cry. They simply waited, surrounded by the police. They were there, that's all. They didn't ask anybody to help them. And yet, I remember, as I was walking I kept telling myself: 'I must get back the [gun] I gave to M. at the end of last year. I hope he's taken good care of it and hidden it properly . . .' That was my only 'practical,' explicit answer."[56]

IMPASSE

"GIVE THEM shit, and they'd eat it!" The owner of the café, a blue apron tied around his hips, grumbles while puttering around his stove. This evening he has received a shipment of bad ersatz coffee, which the customers have drunk without raising an eyebrow. Winter 1941: on the left sidewalk of the Boulevard Saint-Germain, as you walk toward Saint-Michel, is the Café de Flore, with its mahogany tables and its mirrors, its red chairs and its columns, its banal décor with classical proportions. M. Boubal, the owner, knows how to get coal and tobacco better than anybody else. Through the black market? Nobody knows, nothing is ever sure in a period when anarchy seems to rule the distribution of food and commodities. Heat makes the Café de Flore the most coveted spot of the quarter. Seated close by the stove, Sartre writes. With his round, horn-rimmed glasses, his briar pipe, he has been working here for at least three hours, hardly ever raising his head. As soon as he arrived, he asked for a cup of tea with milk, which he immediately drank down. And that was it. Now and then, he jumps up from his chair, rushes to pick up the cigarette butt some other customer has just crushed on the floor, opens it up, drops the tobacco into his pipe and smokes it. Wrapped in an extraordinary fake-fur coat that's much too large and much too short, he looks like a strange little animal, squat and round, in constant motion. Nor does he seem to care that Boubal does not like to see customers sitting at his tables for hours in front of one order. Things will change the day somebody phones the café asking to speak to M. Sartre, and that little ball of fur and ink answers, "Here."[1]

Sartre's territory, during his first German winter in Paris is reduced to a triangle: Montparnasse, Passy, Saint-Lazare. Montparnasse: it is the Hotel Mistral, sad and dirty, between the Avenue du Maine and the Rue de la Gaîté, and the Café des Mousquetaires, where he drinks his *"jus"* (coffee) in the morning. Passy: M. and Mme Mancy's residence, 23 Avenue de Lamballe, an elegant street that meanders toward the Seine from Balzac's old house. There, he always finds a welcoming table, tended by a housekeeper who spends all her days in lines for food. Saint-Lazare: the Lycée Condorcet, where he has been teaching since the fall of 1941. Within these three points: Saint-Germain and the Café de Flore, his headquarters. His meetings are limited to his "family": Olga, Wanda, Bost, and a new recruit, Lise, a student of Simone de Beauvoir's at the Lycée Camille Sée, who refuses to go back to live with her parents. The combined salaries of two civil servants are barely enough to feed all these people: 7,000 francs a month for two is a lot, but 7,000 francs a month for six is really not enough. Even in the Category D restaurants, the cheapest dishes use up quite a few food coupons. It is Simone de Beauvoir who manages the group's economy, gathers all the food coupons, and even cooks. Next door to Sartre's room, at the Hotel Mistral, she finds a room with a kitchen: a windfall. Determined, methodical, she uses her imagination to track down food shipments. The first meal she prepares consists of a turnip choucroute, which she tries to improve by pouring canned soup over it. The cook is delighted with her success. "Sartre said it wasn't at all bad," she remembers. "He could eat practically anything, and on occasion went without food altogether. This cost him little effort; I was less stoical."[2]

At the end of the afternoon, the little "family" gathers again at M. Boubal's. They are joined by former students who have now become good friends, and, occasionally, by new ones. They say hello without really knowing each other, they meet according to obscure rules and mysterious laws: duos, trios, quartets. "When I was chatting at the Flore with Olga or Lise, when Sartre and Wanda went out together, when Lise and Wanda were having a tête-à-tête, none of us would have dreamed of joining their table. People found this behavior preposterous, but to us it seemed both natural and obvious."[3] By and by, they make the acquaintance of other regular customers at nearby tables, including a certain Mouloudji, who writes poems, and his friend Lola, an energetic redhead. It is life at close quarters, open to all. Work and love take place in broad daylight, and anyone can intrude at any point. No private property, no compartmentalization, no secrets: a social life down to its barest essentials, or almost.

· · ·

The winter of 1941–42 was very hard. The cold broke all records: no Parisian could remember a single winter, except perhaps the previous one, that had been quite so bad. Food and coal were rationed more and more strictly each month. Meat was already down to twenty grams a day per person, potatoes to seventy. The sidewalks were covered with snow for several weeks, the streets frozen and flanked by snowdrifts: the capital had become a real ice field. At first these climatic excesses were interpreted as a natural consequence of the German invasion, one more element in a logical series, a catastrophe among others in a brutal war that disfigured everything. Then, spring arrived, the snow melted, and the icicles that kept dropping from the roofs added their dangers to the others. But by now the Parisians were used to both the cold and the Germans, though they were still somewhat irked by a new feature of this period, which rendered their daily life even more ambiguous, like a dream one can't quite pull out of. The Germans had decided to impose their European Central Time onto France, with the result that night, postponed for two hours, lasted till nine in the morning. With curfew at six in the evening, and the frequent alerts that forced one into underground shelters or the nearest subway stations, daylight hours kept shrinking away.

On one side, privation; on the other, invasion: every Parisian must learn to handle a wallet that's constantly getting fatter with all sorts of papers. First of all the Ausweis, a new identity card with its *"gultig bis zum,"* its German validation mark. Then the bread and meat coupons, whose ration points can be detached only by the baker and butcher, and the coal coupons whose tiny squares have to be punched by the appropriate person as well. Then there are coupons for detergents and tissues, for shoes, tobacco, and fuel—pink or blue. To remain on the list for coupons, you have to sign up regularly, keep informed about new shipments of rabbits, turnips, and dandelion greens, and choose the best times to avoid the hustle and interminable lines in front of the dairy shop.

At the time, Sartre wrote, "We were never as free as under the German Occupation. We had lost all our rights, and, first of all, the right to speak; we were insulted every day, and had to keep silent. . . . and everywhere, on the walls, the papers, the movie screen, we were made to confront the ugly mug that our oppressors presented to us as our own: but this is precisely why we were free. As the German poison seeped into our minds, every just thought we had was a real conquest; as an omnipotent police kept forcing silence upon us, every word we uttered had the value of a declaration of rights; as we were constantly watched, every gesture we made was a commitment."[4] The failure of his first political endeavor and the constant presence of the Nazi oppressor only add fuel to Sartre's fire. Most people would have sunk under a comparable failure, others would have changed direction. Strong in his hatred of the oppressor and determined in his self-respect, Sartre braces up. His project for an anarcho-syndicalist constitution has floundered. Quickly, he shelves it and starts looking for something else, not elsewhere but within himself. In a mad, swirling, centripetal movement, he recoils, digs like a mole, blind and stubborn, under the wall of the impasse he is in.

Of daily life in Paris, he wrote, toward the end of the 1940s, "First of all we must forget all the clichés. No, the Germans did not walk up and down the streets of Paris gun in hand, nor did they ask civilians to move aside, or get off the sidewalks when they passed. Quite the contrary: in the subway, they often offered their places to older women, and generally went gaga over children and stroked their cheeks. . . . Still, we should not forget that the Occupation was a daily matter. . . . For four years we had to live with the Germans, fused, as if drowned with them in the collective life of the big city. . . . We looked at them as if they were pieces of furniture more than men. . . . And yet there was an enemy—the most detestable enemy —but he had no face. . . . We did not speak too much of him; we hid our wounds as we hid our hunger, partly out of dignity, partly out of prudence. It looked as if the city had several secret wounds through which it kept bleeding away as if by an internal and inscrutable hemorrhage. . . . Just try to imagine this perpetual coexistence of phantom hatred and of an enemy who's a little too familiar for us to hate."[5]

He lowers his head and charges, like a ram. Infuriated, whipped up, stimulated by the obstacle, he gathers all his energy and writes, writes, writes. Nothing to eat: he'll be happy with bread. Nothing to smoke: he'll look for cigarette butts on the sidewalks or under the tables of cafés. It is a sort of madness, a sort of drug: hunched over, absorbed, and alone, he fills up one sheet of paper after another, like an automaton. He mulls over his failures, his abortive meetings with Gide and Malraux, reconsiders them, analyzes them. He turns in on himself and tries to find a way to profit from his dead ends. No sooner has he become aware of his error than he's back on his way. The others haven't even waked up yet. His blind hatred grows stronger by the day, the better to hit the enemy who, in the last few months, has been raging all over the place. On June 22, 1941, Hitler sends his troups to fight the USSR. In September 1941, the French right and the far right harden their position and create the League of French Volunteers Against Bolshevism, better known as the LVF (Ligue des volontaires français). Huge recruiting posters are glued all over the city along with the sign: "Jews are forbidden to stop in front of this poster." In September 1941, the exhibition "The Jew and France" opens at the Palais Berlitz. The French fascists are in seventh heaven. Communist militants, freed of all scruples by the sudden rupture of the German-Soviet pact, begin their terrorist actions. On August 22, 1941, at the Métro Barbès, a German officer is killed with three bullets. This is all it takes. General von Stülpnagel, head of the German military forces in France, demands immediate action. Pierre Pucheu, minister of the interior for the Vichy government, agrees to invent retroactive laws that condemn innocents, particularly Jews and communists. Punishment is swift: on September 16, 1941, eight innocent prisoners are executed in Paris; on October 22, 1941, ninety-eight innocent prisoners are killed.

" *I* HAVE DONE *my* deed, Electra, and that deed was good." On June 3, 1943, the auditorium of the Théâtre de la Cité is all abuzz. It is the dress rehearsal of Sartre's first play, *The Flies*. The performance has been scheduled for the afternoon so as to avoid the possibility of power cuts. Large cast, production by Dullin—work between author and director has not been easy. Orestes returns to Argos and finds it choking on remorse: ". . . the people here held their tongues . . . they said nothing . . . they held their peace," Jupiter repeats, trying to describe the obsession and cowardice of the whole town in front of its king's death. "My good man was in the fields, at work. What could I do, a woman alone? I bolted my door." Mixed reactions, turbulence, in the audience. The fascist writer Rebatet boos. People murmur when the men of Argos plead, "Forgive us for living while you are dead." Orestes has come back to avenge his father. He will kill Aegistheus and Clytemnestra, the traitress, his own mother, and he'll try to convince his sister Electra to side with him. "Some men are born bespoken," he says during the first act. "And there are others, men of few words. . . . I have done my deed, Electra, and that deed was good . . . [I'm] neither slave nor master, Jupiter. I *am* my freedom. No sooner had you created me than I ceased to be yours."

The audience is dismayed and troubled by the character of Orestes. The stiffness of the costumes, the inflexibility of the armor, the fixity of the masks and the emphatic, ancient gestures of the actors also puzzle them.

"The real drama, the drama I should have liked to write," Sartre explains later, "was that of the terrorist who, by ambushing Germans, becomes the instrument for the execution of fifty hostages."[6] The allusion to the horrors of the summer of 1941 is evident, as is Sartre's stand in the debate that pits the partisans against the critics of innocent deaths. One must assume responsibility for one's actions even if these cause unjust murders. Just as one must also do one's best to "extirpate the disease of repentance, this maudlin complacency in remorse and shame." Sartre lets his hatred pour out and thus indicts both the Vichy spirit and the taste for self-flagellation. Is this a first step out of his impasse, the first expression of his theory of political commitment? And yet, the idea of *The Flies* had started as a game. One day, Olga, then an aspiring actress, had told him that, according to the great actor-director Jean-Louis Barrault, the best way for acting students to get a really first-rate part was to find someone who would write a play for them.[7] The idea interested Sartre. Still excited by the experience with *Bariona,* Sartre soon started imagining a play about the house of Atreus. By the summer of 1941, he was already working on it, first on the beach of Porquerolles, then at the least comfortable tables in the inns of the Jura, as he was biking back to Paris.

The production is a failure, the theater almost always empty, the performances often interrupted, the reception generally lukewarm. "The play leaves me perplexed, despite the undeniable beauty of some passages," Roland Purnal, the respected critic of *Comoedia* writes, carefully avoiding any political allusions. The "collabo" papers are downright nasty. Only Michel Leiris, writing for the underground *Les Lettres françaises* under a pseudonym, discusses the play's "great moral lesson": "Orestes refuses to be a king and leaves his native city forever, followed by the flies that had infested it since its king's death. . . . Orestes commits a murder that leaves him totally without remorse and with a feeling of fulfillment, because, for him, it was not a matter of vengeance or personal satisfaction but rather an act of freedom. . . . Orestes has broken the vicious circle and paved the way that leads from the kingdom of necessity to that of freedom."[8]

Yet the play's lukewarm reception was probably more a function of its philosophy than of any flaws in the production. By now the Paris audience, fed on Jean Giraudoux and Jean Cocteau, is accustomed to modern remakes of Greek plays. Jean Anouilh's *Antigone*, in modern dress, is performed during the same season, and the public has gotten used to hearing gardeners address gods as "guys." But Orestes and Electra are not as comprehensible as Antigone, or Vermorel's Joan of Arc (in a play that was a great success during the Occupation); the conflict they embody is not nearly as clear. "Just as in Sophocles," Sartre writes, "none of my characters is either right or wrong." And this is probably the real reason for the audience's perplexity. Joan of Arc confronting English soldiers in Nazi uniforms is an obvious allegory of the Resistance. Sartre's project, on the other hand, was perhaps a little too intellectual. "My intention was to revive the French people, to restore their courage," the author explains. He wanted to defy German censorship without risking its veto; this gave him a very thin margin to maneuver in at a moment when the moralist Vichy censorship seemed much more far-reaching than the political censorship of Paris. This little paragraph from *Comoedia* is a clear index of the unease caused by the play: "The production of *The Flies* at the Théâtre de la Cité has provoked different reactions among artists. For the most part, critics have been quite severe. . . . Nevertheless, *The Flies* has had profound repercussions both among the intellectuals and the young, who, for the first time, have come into contact with a new world and have thus felt a sense of discovery. We intend to open up a debate over this controversial play in one of our next issues."[9] But the debate was never opened up. Less moderate, the critic André Castelot, of *La Gerbe*, expressed his unmitigated disgust for the play and its author's obvious "predilection for the abject."[10]

Discussed as a political play, *The Flies* nevertheless remains a pioneering work in Sartre's career as a playwright. "If *Nausea* had not been published," he will later write, "I would have gone on writing. But if *The Flies* had not been performed, I wonder whether I would have gone on writing plays, since my main concerns kept me so far from the theater in those days."[11] His professional involvement in theater dates back to his first meeting with Dullin, who had been Simone Jollivet's companion since before the war. This near "family" relationship is fostered by frequent Sundays in the country at "the Dullins," even though Simone is overtly "collabo" and anti-Semitic. Despite the inevitable tensions between playwright and director, Dullin gave Sartre a crash course in theater. "Dullin conveyed to me . . . that a play for performance must be precisely the opposite of an orgy of rhetoric . . . in the theater you can't pick up your marbles and start again; for when a word is not one which can be taken back once it has been spoken, you must very carefully withdraw it from the dialogue. . . . After the rehearsals of *The Flies*, I never saw the theater again with the same eyes."[12] At once an enthronement and a deflowering, *The Flies* is already very far from the amateurism of *Bariona*. Even without considering its impact, a performed play is, no less than a book, a literary event that involves a public, provokes confrontations, produces reactions, opinions, conversations, rumors. In a letter dated June 23, 1943, Jean Paulhan expresses his delight: "Yesterday we saw *The Flies*. I found the play marvelous and Mauriac very unjust. This city is so full of remorse one would think we were in Vichy. And the masks were beautiful."[13] From this point on, escaping from marginality, Sartre moves closer and closer to the center of French literary life.[14]

*E*XACTLY CONTEMPORARY with *The Flies*, both in its composition and publication—June 1943—is his 722-page philosophical text, *Being and Nothingness*, conceived and written by a Sartre haunted by the intensity of the events of 1942. That year had started badly, with the exhibition "The Bolsheviks Against Europe" and the first trains of Jewish deportees to the camps. The period of Nazi seduction was replaced by one of Nazi severity. In May 1942, Darquier de Pellepoix was elected superintendent for the Jewish Question in the Vichy government. He immediately ordered that all citizens of "Jewish origin" wear a yellow star, which they could obtain by redeeming three fabric coupons. Two months later, the same citizens were forbidden entrance to all public places: cafés, cinemas, theaters. These laws were generally and frequently transgressed in Sartre's milieu. Few yellow stars showed up at the Flore; on the other hand, right around the corner there were denunciations, anonymous letters, and, particularly, the constant terror of a sudden police raid with its identity checks that often resulted in an immediate transfer to Drancy. It was the beginning of a horrible chain of events that first showed its shadow in July 1942, on the day of the great raid that brought most of Paris's Jewish population to the Vélodrome d'Hiver, in the 15th arrondissement. The operation was poetically christened "Spring Wind" by the French police, who executed the German orders with almost excessive zeal. Immediately after the failure of the French volunteer service in Germany and the "changing of the guards," the Vichy government decided to show more clout and create the "compulsory work service" [the "service du travail obligatoire," the famous STO], a civilian draft for all French males between 18 and 50. Those who refused to submit to this forced labor in Germany had no other choice than to move to the South.

France is covered with posters and notices; the asphyxiating, implacable Nazi ordinance has taken hold of the country like a bird of prey. In the middle of all this, Sartre works. NO ISRAELITES ALLOWED INTO THIS BUILDING; CHILDREN'S PLAYGROUND, NO JEWS ALLOWED; or, in the words of the publicity campaign for the film *The Jew and France,* "Every Frenchman must learn how to recognize a Jew if he wants to protect himself against the Hebrew influence." As Nazi horrors increase by the day, so does the ardor of the writer, as if every new sentence he writes were stolen away from the occupying forces, a small shred of freedom they shall not have.

France is seized by "Judeo-Bolshevik" phobia. Two communist intellectuals are executed: in May, Georges Politzer and in July, Valentin Feldmann. Posters all over the streets, notices all over the subway: everything is done to spread the terror. On vacation, Sartre writes: first in Paris, then at Le Havre, where he is spending Easter with Marc Bénard, a friend from the stalag. He keeps on writing during bombings and alerts. In August 1942, he is writing on the summit of the Tourmalet pass, "sitting in a meadow, with a writing pad on his knees and a strong wind blowing."[15] But, most of all, he writes in Mme Morel's comfortable house, near Angers. Sartre's room is quite large, with exposed roof beams and red floor tiles. He hardly ever leaves it since his hostesses come up to him for the evening meal and often stay till after midnight. Now and then, Simone de Beauvoir tries to drag him outside. When she succeeds, they take a walk along the Loire or ride their bikes through the country. But they always rush back to listen to the BBC news in Sartre's room. "First setback for von Paulus's troops in Stalingrad," they hear on Christmas: this is the first good news since the Allies' landing in North Africa.

"THERE WILL be a few boring passages, but there are also a few spicy ones: one concerns all holes in general, and the other focuses on the anus and love Italian style. The latter should make up for the former."[16] This passage from a letter to Beauvoir is meant to describe the first draft of *Being and Nothingness,* a book that had taken shape in the boredom and the cold of the phony war. According to Paulhan, it comprises "a kilo of paper," making it very useful, during the hardships of wartimes, to measure precise quantities of fruit and vegetables. However, a more serious look at the 722 pages of text indicates that here is a key to Sartre's entire life and works. As a declaration of the absolute supremacy of subjectivity over the world, *Being and Nothingness* is a profoundly Cartesian work, another stage in the odyssey of a solitary consciousness that will underlie all of Sartre's work up to 1943. *Being and Nothingness* will return to, explain, and further flesh out this key concept: the pride of consciousness facing the world, origin of one's absolute freedom. A consciousness that is at once a merging and a wrenching away, a freedom that is at once a fever and a discipline, a state of permanent criticism, a mistrust of all fixed and crystallized social roles: these are the stages through which one can attain and understand the motives at the basis of Sartre's relationship with politics, art, society, and morality. This is also how, later, one will be able to understand the very particular ties of familiarity and estrangement that Sartrean reflection combines with Marxist thought, and that will later provoke his numerous refusals of traditionally accepted social norms.

War will play the role of incubator for all these tendencies, while at the same time allowing the readings of Heidegger to assume their place within Sartre's thought. As he wrote in his *Diaries* in February 1940: "[Heidegger's] influence has in recent times sometimes struck me as providential, since it supervened to teach me authenticity and historicity just at the very moment when war was about to make these notions indispensable to me. If I try to imagine what I'd have made of my thought without those tools, I am gripped by retrospective fear. How much time I gained!"[17]

Obviously, the radicalism of *Being and Nothingness* has something to do with the political severity of 1942, the increasing repressions with Sartre's libertarian explosions. Already before the war, he had shot his first darts at the French philosophical tradition, which he globally defined as "essentialist," and he had absolutely rejected the French current after pitting the German phenomenologues against the Léon Brunschvicgs, the André Lalandes, the Emile Meyersons, the French popes of "pulp" or "digestive" philosophy, as he liked to call it. In *Being and Nothingness,* he also drastically rejects all social labels: "How then shall I experience the objective limits of my being: Jew, Aryan, ugly, handsome, kind, a civil servant, untouchable, etc.

—when will speech have informed me as to which of these are *my* limits?"[18] Because, he goes on to say, the alienation, the self-mutilation, and, in fact, the inauthenticity of the individual are all born out of his acceptance of these social labels. "Here I am—Jew or Aryan, handsome or ugly, one-armed etc. All this I am *for the Other* with no hope of apprehending this meaning which I have *outside* and, still more important, with no hope of changing it."[19] "In a more general way the encounter with a prohibition in my path ('No Jews allowed here') . . . can have meaning only on and through the foundation of my free choice. In fact according to the free possibilities which I choose, I can disobey the prohibition, pay no attention to it, or, on the contrary, confer upon it a coercive value which it can hold only because of the weight which I attach to it."[20]

In the dead end of direct, subversive action, strangled by unbearable daily repressions, Sartre suddenly sees the unacceptable. Of course, when he elaborates his theory of freedom, he is in the realm of full philosophical abstraction, but the situation out of which and under which his elaboration takes place is nonetheless concretely historical. It is in Nazi France that he shouts, loud and clear, his appeal to authenticity and responsibility and his denunciation of all forms of bad faith. Just as it is under the crazy pressure of this daily gagging that he develops the morality of the writer, magically extracting, from the darkest period of oppression, an appeal to freedom and individual anarchism.

The work was published in the summer of 1943, but during that whole year it was mentioned only in an article by René-Marill Albérès in *Etudes et Essais universitaires* (University Studies and Essays). The reviews appear later, slowly: three the following year, nine in 1945, and more than fifteen in 1946, while Sartre delivers his famous lectures. Once could hypothesize as to why, at first, the book goes practically unnoticed: the philosophical language, its ponderous speculations, the date of publication. And yet, once it gains notice, the appearance of such an enormous "bastard" takes the philosophical world by surprise. The treatise combines the classicism of its language, its reliance on other philosophical texts, its body of reference, its Cartesian logic, with a presentation that is revolutionary: "It is certain that the café by itself with its patrons, its tables, its booths, its mirrors, its light, its smoky atmosphere, and the sounds of voices, rattling saucers, and footsteps which fill it—the café is a fullness of being."[21] At odds with the prevailing university tradition, here is a new philosopher who uses the "triviality" of daily life to explain his theories. The followers, the fans, the real readers slowly emerge.

This is, for instance, the case with André Gorz, who will meet Sartre for the first time in Switzerland, in 1946, and will remain one of his most faithful friends: "When I first plunged into *Being and Nothingness,* I was totally fascinated with the novelty and complexity of its discourse, but did not understand much of it. Then, by sheer perseverance and constant immersion in that big thing, I finally got quite infected, adopted its terminology, and elevated it to the stature of an encyclopedia that tackled everything, and had an answer for everything. In short, I began living in a universe whose frontiers were *Being and Nothingness.*"[22] The writer Michel Tournier remembers *Being and Nothingness* in similar terms: "In the fall of 1943, a book fell onto our desks. . . . There was a moment of shock, then a slow rumination. It was a massive, bristly work, overflowing with irresistible power, full of exquisite subtleties, encyclopedic, superbly technical and traversed throughout by an intuition that had the clarity of a diamond. . . . No doubt was allowed: we were given a system."[23] Another Sartrean follower of that time was Olivier Revault d'Allonnes, a diligent Sorbonne student who remembers being quite startled "by this voice from the outside, which, among other things, had the nerve to label as 'essentialist' all the philosophies then being taught. A voice according to which philosophy could be expressed in a novel, in a language that everybody could read, written on the table of a café. Of course, cafés are not the only places in the world, but, on the other hand, there are certainly more cafés in the world than Sorbonnes."[24]

"THE SENTENCES in *The Stranger* are islands. We bounce from sentence to sentence, from void to void." Enthused by Camus's novel, Sartre devotes a twenty-page article to it: a precise, thorough, didactic, luminous piece. Secretly, he already sketches a sort of kinship that mesmerizes him. "*The Stranger,* a work detached from a life, unjustified and unjustifiable, sterile, already forsaken by its author, abandoned for other present things. And that is how we must accept it, as a brief communion between two men, the author and the reader, beyond reason, in the realm of the absurd."[25] Camus provides Sartre's first occasion for boundless praise: Sartre places him next to Hemingway and Voltaire. It is a case of mutual recognition, reciprocal speculation: Camus has already praised *Nausea* and *The Wall,* and some of his critical sentences could as easily have been applied to his own characters. "A man," he writes, "analyzes his presence in the world, the fact that he moves his fingers and eats regularly—and what he discovers, at the bottom of the most banal fact, is his fundamental absurdity."[26] It is not surprising that the two men should feel a certain kinship with each other: they display the same attitude, the same refusal of mystical or moral values, the same pessimistic radicalism. Four months after Sartre's article on *The Stranger,* on the opening night of *The Flies,* Albert Camus introduces himself to Sartre. Sartre continues contributing his reflections on contemporary French writers to *Les Cahiers du Sud,* the Resistance magazine published in Marseilles. He develops his own literary panorama, awarding points and structuring the field. Parain, Blanchot, Bataille all pass under the scrutiny of the master, who, at the end, after an exhaustive analysis, gloriously avows, "With the American writers, Kafka, and Camus, the contemporary novel has found its style."[27]

*F*ROM THE impasse of politics, the prolific, polyvalent, Protean writer finally re-emerges. By the start of the summer of 1943, he has elaborated a new framework, deepening his thought. He begins publishing new hard-hitting, merciless works, as in an article on Drieu La Rochelle, an article that brims with hatred: "He's a long, tall, sad kind of guy with a great big battered head and the faded look of a young man who didn't know how to grow old. . . . Drieu wanted the Fascist revolution the way certain people want war because they don't dare break up with their mistresses."[28]

"A WRITER WHO RESISTED, NOT A RESISTANCE FIGHTER WHO WROTE . . ."[1]

"*M*Y SHOES, spattered with white soap and toothpaste, deposited themselves next to a beautiful pair of untreated leather shoes belonging to Delannoy."[2] July 2, 1943, Pathé-Cinéma studios: a business meeting. Jean Delannoy, the movie director, is having a look at the screenplay Sartre has written for him. The production of *The Flies* has greatly expanded Sartre's small circle beyond the ambit of students, disciples, and readers who have loved

Nausea and *The Wall*. Delannoy, Leiris, Camus are a few of his new friends.

In the summer of 1943, with Mussolini's fall, the war takes a different turn. This is the third phase of the confrontation, and yet the civil war within France continues with mad brutality. Resistance networks are restructured and now absorb all opponents of the STO into their ranks; in the meantime, the ardor of the militiamen is on the rise. The first militiaman to be shot by the Resistance has been buried on April 24, 1943; two months later, the troops of Déat's RNP look impressive in the Pierre-de-Coubertin Stadium. On July 14, somber Paris is the stage of merciless confrontations: militiamen, with their blue shirts and basque berets, strut behind their flag along the Boulevard Saint-Michel. Their own policemen beat up anyone who refuses to salute; women in flowery dresses, their fists clenched, scream, "Lynch him!" Images of civil war follow one another more and more rapidly. On July 14, 1943, the Resistance students of *Défense de la France* distribute five thousand copies of their underground paper in the subways. The crowd is panicked. What else could one expect to find in a country that, just a few months earlier, decided to hand over to the enemy some of its most prominent politicians, such as the socialist Léon Blum, Edouard Daladier, and Clémenceau's adviser Georges Mandel?

Also on July 14, 1943, Editions de Minuit publishes a large collection of underground poetry, *L'Honneur des poètes*. "It is high time to proclaim," Paul Eluard writes in the preface, "that the best poets are simply ordinary men, since the best of them keep insisting that all men are or could be poets." Is this period particularly propitious for a poetic flowering? Literary life survives on the artificial respiration supplied by the underground press: in February 1942, for instance, Editions de Minuit publishes *Le Silence de la mer* by Vercors, the pseudonym of Jean Bruller, and, in August 1943, *Le Cahier noir* by Forez, the pseudonym of François Mauriac; then there are underground newsletters and newspapers such as *Les Lettres françaises*, and *L'Arbalète* in Lyon, *Fontaine* in Algiers, *Les Cahiers du Sud* in Aix, *Poésie 4* in Villeneuve-lès-Avignon. Literature adjusts its forms to the state of emergency: emphatic forms, lyrical forms. Poetry seems best for transmitting these messages of hope. "Paris a froid. Paris a faim/Paris ne mange plus de marrons dans la rue/Paris a mis de vieux vêtements de vieille/Paris dort tout debout, sans air, sans le métro . . ." (Paris is cold. Paris is hungry. Paris no longer eats chestnuts in the street. Paris is wearing an old woman's old clothes.

Paris sleeps standing in the stifling subway). Eluard issues the painful weather reports of a German Paris, while, under the name of François La Colère, Aragon writes fiery Alexandrines: "Vous pouvez condamner un poète au silence/Et faire d'un oiseau du ciel un galérien/Mais pour lui refuser le droit d'aimer la France/Il vous faudrait savoir que vous n'y pouvez rien . . ." (You can condemn a poet to silence and put a bird in a cage, but to refuse him the right to love France, that, you must know, you cannot do). The floodgates of emotion are open, the poetic fiber is hardening, the cult of France and patriotic ideals are in full bloom: "Entendez, franc-tireurs de France," Aragon will also write, "L'appel de vos fils enfermés/Formez vos bataillons, formez . . . , Assez manger le pain des larmes/Chaque jour peut être Valmy" (Listen, resistance fighters of France, listen to your jailed children. Start forming battalions. No more eating the bread of your tears, when every day could be a Valmy).

"A detachment of the Regent's militia enters a crowded street." Sitting alone at the Flore, Sartre writes. "Their faces hidden by their caps, their torsos erect in the dark shirts crossed by shining shoulder belts, automatic weapons in holsters, the men advance in a loud hammering of boots." The hand stops, hesitates a while; the writer raises his head, his eyes quickly survey their surroundings. Then, furiously, the hand resumes its mad race across the paper. "Leaning against the door of a shabby house, two big young men watch the troops go by with smirks on their faces. Their right hands are sunk in their jacket pockets."[3] A brief flash of satisfaction crosses the face of the philosophy teacher. He gets up, walks around his table, goes outside, inspects the sky, comes back in. The summer of 1943 has begun poorly. The weather's been bad, dismal gray sky, cold and wet autumnal afternoon. This is an odd season for Paris. Sartre can't sit still. His pipe, his inkwell, his pen are resting on scattered sheets of paper, his eyes roam. This contretemps is going to infuriate Wanda, to spark one of her brutal rages, one of those crises that she blames on her Slavic ancestry. It's true, he has promised: during the three weeks Simone de Beauvoir spends in the South he will be entirely at the disposal of Olga's younger sister, and will do whatever she wishes. She has asked him to help her rehearse the role of Molly Byrne in Synge's *The Well of the Saints,* and he has obeyed. She has asked him to wait for her in the squalid dressing rooms of the Théâtre de Lancry, while she is rehearsing. He has agreed but not without qualms: has he become one of those men who dote on young actresses, waiting for them in the wings? The day of the opening, he tolerated a crisis of tears and anger, and finally consented to do as she had asked him, and not see the play till the third performance. And now, on the very evening she expects to see him in the audience, he is forced to remain at the Flore, waiting for the arrival of Merleau-Ponty. It was Sartre's only chance to avoid an interminable line to buy a train ticket; he could not refuse the "Pontaumerle" 's kind offer to pick one up. But now he has to wait for him at the Flore.

What else is hidden behind the nervous tremor of his hand, whose writing is increasingly less round and often slides into the left margin? Beauvoir would not be very pleased if he missed his train and, with it, their appointment at Uzerche, on July 15. "Bye, bye my little Beaver," he is writing to her, "I'm kissing you with all my might, my beloved Beaver: I love you with all my heart."[4] And Wanda is probably going to cry because he has not kept the promise that he would devote all his time to her, and he will have to console her. Or is it Dullin's laconicism that worries him? The discomfort he detected in the director's voice the previous evening, on the phone, has been bothering him all day: did he really intend to limit the performances of *The Flies* to one a week starting next September? It would be ridiculous! In three days, he'll dine at Férolles with Wanda and demand an explanation. And then tomorrow's meeting is certainly contributing to his anxiety: the second day of work with the Pathé team is going to be decisive. Either they accept his screenplay, with the psychological coloring he has added to please Giraudoux, and sign the contract—in which case he'll soon receive a check for 37,500 francs, ten times more than his monthly salary as *professeur agrégé*— or they refuse it, and that will be a big disappointment. So many projects are tied up with the outcome of tomorrow's meeting! Fortunately, thanks to Delange, he has found Simone de Beauvoir a source of income for 1944—which could have been a problematic year given the termination of her appointment at the Lycée Camille Sée. She is going to work for the radio, with a salary that will range between 1,500 and 2,000 francs a week. If everything goes well, they can change hotels and Wanda, Lisa, Olga, and Bost can move in with them.

Prosaic worries for a man who has reached a turning point in his career as a writer, the critical moment when everybody seems to want him. One more day and he's reassured; his screenplay is accepted, a contract for three more is signed, the check is in the mail. The following Thursday, at exactly the same time, he meets Beauvoir at the Hotel Chavanez, at Uzerche, above the Vézère, and gives her the inner tubes she needs for her bike. Together, they pedal along the sumptuous serpentine roads above the gorges of the Tarn and sleep in barns, amid bales of hay. They appreciate the relative abundance of the South; peasants offer them milk, eggs, apple pies. They brave rain, wind, and other terrors, as when a sudden storm drowns the two bikes they have parked against a wall and sweeps away the manuscript of Sartre's latest novel. He has to chase after it, shaking with laughter under his yellow raincoat, blinded by his wet glasses. Then, after recovering all the pieces, he dries them and spends a great deal of time trying to rewrite all that has been erased by the rain.[5] They move on toward the friendly lights of the Loire and the welcoming comfort of Mme Morel's home at La Pouèze. There, they share moments of euphoria when, on the radio, they hear the news of Il Duce's demise and the withdrawal of the German forces toward the eastern front. In the middle of August, Sartre makes a short train trip to Paris for a reunion of the National Committee of Writers.

THE Comité national des écrivains, CNE, did not get in touch with Sartre till the beginning of 1943, after the communists' change of tactics. Till then, he had been a suspect, bourgeois, negative individual whom Jacques Decour could not stand. Decour had repeatedly told Paulhan as much, and Paulhan could not change his mind. Then, the wind had turned, Decour had fallen, along with a few others, thus becoming one of the heroes of the PCF, and, since Stalingrad, the communists gradually abandoned their initial sectarianism in favor of a more open approach. Sartre suddenly became a coveted prey to the promoters of this new phase. And he knew it well. During the first reunion of the CNE, he immediately made a point of telling Claude Morgan that he had found the pamphlet, which had been circulated against him in the South, quite reprehensible. "So," he noted with a smirk, "it would seem I am a henchman of national socialism because I have quoted and worked on Heidegger's phenomenology. If I'm not mistaken, the promulgator of this idiocy is a certain Marcenac." Very much embarrassed, Claude Morgan promised that he would immediately warn the comrades in the South against any repetition of such regrettable "errors."[6] Once their differences were ironed out, they got down to work. Sartre cooperated as best he could, proposing a number of articles for the underground review *Les Lettres françaises,* trying to find points of agreement in their discussions, avoiding conflicts.

These meetings take place at Edith Thomas's, 15 Rue Pierre Nicole, in the Latin Quarter. The initial little group has become much larger: at the collective meeting of February 1943, there are twenty-two, writers as various as Gabriel Marcel, Paul Eluard, Raymond Queneau, Jean Guehenno, Father Maydieu, Leiris, Jacques Debû-Bridel, Mauriac. All rivalries and ideological divergences have to be patched up before work begins. And that's no small task. How can Mauriac, for instance, forget for one minute that he is working with the very man who, before the war, had wounded him so cruelly? And can Sartre himself, who has avoided membership in all organizations, who spit on the literary orthodoxy between the two wars, be comfortable in this milieu?

There are practical problems, concerning paper, printing, and distribution; and there are tactical problems: "Shall we publish in *Comoedia* in order to infiltrate that rag, or refuse to so they won't be able to use us later as an alibi?"[7] "Was it wise," Debû-Bridel wonders a few years later, "to accept so many risks and endanger so many lives just to publish a few pages of anonymous literature? And particularly at a time when, as part of the Resistance, we could have all been involved in more useful tasks (sabotage, intelligence). To blow up a train was an act of war and, as such, a justifiable sacrifice."[8] But what function could a poem have? But then, an underground pamphlet with a few patriotic poems that had been parachuted onto a field had later been found, illegible and stained with blood, on the body of a dead soldier.

The sixth issue of *Les Lettres* is a real patchwork: its table of contents includes the poem "La Chanson des franc-tireurs" (The Song of the Resistance Fighters) and two polemical essays titled "L'Ecran français" (The French Screen) and "La Littérature, cette liberté" (Literature, This Freedom). Who could have detected behind these two anonymous texts, poorly printed side by side, the authorship of Aragon and Sartre? Till October 1943, *Les Lettres* is just a small square pamphlet of cheap brown paper, typed in old-fashioned characters, poorly laid-out. The articles are not separated from each other by a space but by a series of short lines drawn with the help of a ruler, and their titles are handwritten in capital letters in order not to be confused with the main body of the text. The very existence of this underground paper has the value of combat: four mere sheets in violation of the paper censorship, the ban on writing, all totalitarian muzzling. And, on these seedy sheets, the anonymous words—weapons?—of the greatest living French writers. It is a strange battle. Inaccuracies, typos, irregular publication dates.

Thanks to Georges Adam, it is printed and published every month, and gradually gets bigger: first four pages, then eight, with a circulation of twelve thousand copies!

Some of the contributors wax lyrical, others patriotic, still others lapse into pathos: only Sartre, like a solitary knight, will resort to pure hatred. "He was soft and cowardly," he'll say of Drieu, "without physical or moral energy, an 'empty suitcase.' . . . He had a wild time, took drugs—but moderately, anemically."[9] Or else, aiming his sword at Rebatet and the magazine *Je suis partout* (I Am Everywhere), he will inveigh against those "tenors, nearly stripped of any talent, who, like Céline and Montherlant, soon lost the little vigor and charm they once had, unless, like Brasillach and [André] Thérive, they never had any to begin with." Unstoppable, haughty, disdainful, he loves to finish off an adversary: "Isolated, terrorized terrorists, hopelessly enslaved to the Germans, scared at the sound of their own voices shuddering in the silence. . . . It is obvious that they don't like to write and that, in fact, they hate literature because, at bottom, they know that they have no talent."[10] Others will choose poetry, an emotional appeal, the cult of the homeland. Sartre will choose to sentence the enemy to death, preferring frontal attack, using all his resources and personal tastes, believable and authentic to the end.

He is with them, yet he is elsewhere. Nobody quite understands his place, his intentions, his position: he is always there when needed, but afterward he immediately goes back into himself. Through Kanapa, the communists keep harping on his isolation. The former student of the Lycée Pasteur turns his old professor into a dubious character, a certain Labzac, who spends the years of the German Occupation talking about the communists behind their back. "[They] have a real persecution mania," Kanapa has him say. "They see the Gestapo everywhere, traitors everywhere. They even had the nerve to investigate us! Just like vulgar cops! In fact, they have the mentality of cops."[11] This is just a sketch of a few tensions that will later become violent. On his side, Vercors wishes Sartre's attitude were more univocal: he would like to get some of his stuff for Minuit, where even Mauriac has published, but he is bothered by the fact that the Germans did not forbid the performance of *The Flies*. On the other hand, he would have also liked to see Camus accept his offer and give the manuscript of *The Stranger* to him rather than to Gallimard. A few reservations about Sartre, but no acrimony, no real resentment.[12]

*H*E IS there, yet elsewhere. During those years, Sartre is an underground figure, unknown by his contemporaries and maligned by those who reproach him for his absenteeism. In 1943 the Lycée Condorcet puts together a list of "leftist" professors, which includes the linguist Crouzet and the principal himself: one by one, they are all removed. Sartre stays. What does this mean? It is enough to read the report of the latest inspection to learn that the Vichy government had decided not to let him "carry on" much longer. Gilbert Gidel, director of the Académie de Paris under the Vichy government, writes on March 17, 1942. "By omitting mention, among his works, of the two books he published for the *NRF*, *The Wall* and *Nausea*, M. Sartre leads me to believe he has understood that, whatever the value of those two works, they are not of the sort a professor, that is, a man in charge of young souls, should write."[13]

During these underground years, around the spring of 1943, in Paris, Sartre renews contact with Pierre Kaan. Kaan has become the secretary of the National Committee for the Resistance (CNR) and as such works closely with Jean Moulin, particularly in the South. In May 1943, he is in Paris on a mission he deeply believes in: to remedy the sluggishness of the CNR, whose plans of action are neither direct nor effective enough, and to create some groups devoted to technical action and sabotage (AGATE). During his time in Paris, Kaan also meets with a few members of the Vélite network, among them Pierre Piganiol, Pierre Mercier, and Raymond Crolant. Through the intermediary Roger Wybot, these Normalien scientists had established contact with London very early and had won some renown for their clandestine work under the direction of Cavaillès himself. Sartre meets Kaan on several occasions and offers him his support in the creation of these sabotage groups.[14] The AGATE groups will soon establish several outposts, one in Corrèze, under the direction of Mercier, one in Paris, with Bertrand and Sartre, and a third one, consisting of an irregular corps of "Liberté" students, under the direction of Mercier's brother and Philippe Wacrenier. There are three urgent tasks: to create a network of information, to constitute a few security groups for the protection of people in danger—such as Pierre Brossolette—and to organize sabotage operations.

Croulebarbe Square, in the thirteenth arrondissement of Paris: contacted by his childhood friend, Pierre Kaan, Pierre Piganiol meets Pierre Isler, a professor of German, who is pushing a baby carriage to appear above suspicion. Together, they wait for a third arrival previously contacted by Isler. Sartre comes up, with his inseparable pipe; he seems in a hurry. No introduction is necessary; they speak as they walk. "Words are fine," Sartre tells them; "but now it's time for action. This does not mean that I am endorsing the London [Gaullist] ideology; on the other hand, there are times when a writer must succumb to the word of the canon since, in periods of crisis, the writer becomes speechless. I am here to confirm what I have already told Dupin [one of Kaan's pseudonyms]," he explains. "I have contacted some friends who have a large cache of weapons in the quarries of Villejuif and Arcueil." Projects follow: they must blow up a few German barges loaded with weapons, they must place bombs on the Vernon locks. "We have weapons," Sartre explains, "we have a few hiding places, and as soon as we have the means we'll launch a few more terrorist actions, like blowing up freight cars. I have a few interesting ideas. Later, we'll have to recruit men to relay messages and maintain contact with London. . . . As for me, I'm ready. I'm sick and tired of feeling muzzled." They set an appointment for the following month at La Coupole. "No need to play games," Isler whispers in Piganiol's ear. "You know who he is." "No," the latter admits, "but it's not going to be easy to wear that face and those eyes underground." "It's Sartre," says Isler, "and Kaan tells me that, despite his talent and courage, he doesn't have a very good reputation within the CNR. He's been severely criticized for the way his play was put on."[15]

What would Sartre have become in the AGATE group? Forty-one young men of the irregular force "Liberté" were shot to death. Then, in December 29, 1943, Pierre Kaan was arrested in Paris, as he was planning the attack on the Vernon locks with the Mercier brothers; he was sent to a concentration camp from which he never came back. Crolant also dies in 1945. Sartre's revolutionary zeal and his underground activity seem to end in 1943 with the failures of AGATE and Pierre Kaan's disappearance.

THE "top secret" file that arrived at Algiers in May 1944 and later re-emerged among the papers of Georges Oudôrd, head of the Resistance group "Cochet," is the only token of Sartre's presence in the underground. It is a text titled "La Resistance: la France et le monde de demain—par un philosophe" (The Resistance: France and the World of Tomorrow—by a philosopher), bearing, handwritten, the mention "Jean-Paul Sartre, Normalien, member of the National

Front." In the same file, there is a text "by a Resistance intellectual," attributed, also in handwriting, to "Albert Camus, . . . political [illegible] writes for the underground press."[16] Sartre could not remember ever having written such a text, but he admitted that all the ideas in it were his. And yet this text had been chosen by the Comité général des experts, the CGE [General Committee of Scholars], which, since its creation by Jean Moulin, had taken surveys on the potential of Resistance intellectuals.[17] The text is tainted by the remorse that followed the demise of "Socialism and Freedom," and its pessimism clearly shows us a Sartre who, after the disappearances of Cavaillès, Cuzin, and Kaan, is no longer the innocent man who dove headlong into action: he has been wounded, he has learned. It is already a postwar Sartre who speaks here, in the same voice we'll hear throughout 1944, a voice that was born during the months that preceded the Liberation. It is a voice at once lucid but disappointed, bitter but stimulating, a voice that has examined reality, and, for the first time, says "we." "We" means the French Resistance as opposed to that of Algiers or London.

This is the first expression of the writer's political will, accompanied by the analysis and synthesis of the witness who wants to speak. "We live in anguish," the voice says, "every day we lose a little more hope. . . . Our resistance is more or less ineffective. . . . Nobody in France *reads* our pamphlets. . . . Why murder the village butcher who is a collaborator when [Joseph] Darnand is alive and well and nobody thinks of killing him? . . . So many mistakes: not a day goes by that innocents are not assassinated in the Haute-Savoie. . . . Most of the time, our struggle resembles a disorderly bustle. . . . And, little by little, this vain fight is wearing down France's strength. . . . The warnings of the BBC or Radio Algiers often sound frivolous to us. . . . Impotent, we watch the thinning of the French population. . . . On the whole, the French Resistance is purely negative: we know *against whom* but not *for whom* we are fighting. . . . France is fighting in the dark . . . which explains the bitter resignation that characterizes this current phase of the Resistance: we are fighting because there is nothing else we can do, because our human dignity demands that we fight."[18]

Testimony, assessment, the will to look at things as they are, to resist all mystification: Sartre's voice is serious and its disappointment is real. Gradually, these general descriptions are replaced by much sharper criticism and more concrete proposals. A drastic refusal to slip toward either the Gaullists or the communists—as with

"Socialism and Freedom"—and a deliberate orientation toward a third-line politics: these are the two points that keep coming back. "Most Frenchmen," the voice continues, implacable, "are neither capitalists nor communists: they float. . . . There is no common measure between the useless courage of the Resistance and the fate that's awaiting us; even admitting that attacks and sabotage might hasten victory, we still don't know whom we are in fact helping. Nothing is more depressing than being unable to foresee the consequences of our actions, no matter how close they may be. . . . The young Gaullist who operates a clandestine radio may well end up hastening the advent of communism. The death of the young communist who was shot yesterday may well contribute to the re-establishment of the capitalist democracy he detests." And, leaning against its rejection of all political institutions, the voice concludes its monologue on an unexpected note of hope: "The French begin to understand that the only way to change man is to change the collectivity within which he lives, and they want to change it according to the principles of justice. . . . A socialist state and individual freedom cannot go hand in hand, that is for sure. But there are other forms of socialism, without considering the fact that any socialist structure that does not aim at the freedom of the individual and the recovery of human dignity would be utterly nonsensical. Today we have hit rock bottom: now we can start hoping. Any government-in-exile that is aware of the difficulties we are struggling with, and that chooses as its watchword the realization of concrete freedom by means of the collectivization of all means of production, would automatically win over the majority of France. It would also give a positive faith to the Resistance: with a message like this, France would find a new politics and a new dignity; and it would be able to find itself a new place in the world."

A strong, vibrant, unwavering voice. Never mind if he still considers his political activities secondary to literature: he has taken the crucial step. Activism, theoretical debates, meetings, realizations of all sorts, participation in organized committees, wavering between communists, Gaullists, and Trotskyites, Sartre's political awakening involves all sorts of approaches, trial and error, discussions with students, the decision to write exclusively for underground papers or the reviews of the Free Zone, the choice to publish only some of his texts and put his novels on the back burner . . . and, of course, and above all, the search for a place in the political life of France—a place away from all constituted groups, a place that no existing structure can provide and which, hence, he must build himself—and for a voice different from that of both poets and patriots. It is a very plausible project since he has become, after all, a full-fledged citizen of the Parisian "republic of letters."

*H*IS CONTRACT with Pathé has ensured financial well-being, and by the fall of 1943 the Sartre "family" is going to feel the difference. First they will all move away from the seedy walls of Montparnasse to the Hotel de la Louisiane, on the Rue de Seine, only a few steps away from Saint-Germain-des-Prés. Sartre and Beauvoir live on the same floor. She has a large room with a divan, a massive table, a kitchen, and a view of the rooftops. He has a tiny, bare room at the other end of the hall. The "little ones," Nathalie Sorokine— a former student of hers—and Bourla—a former student of his— live on the floor below. Before this, they lived in Beauvoir's hotel on the Rue Dauphine. But now Sartre has gotten rich and everybody can take advantage of the Rue de Seine. They eat their meals together, and are often joined by Olga and Bost, who have stayed at the hotel on the Rue Jules-Chaplain, behind La Coupole. Mouloudji and his friend Lola la Brune have also taken a room at the Louisiane. Lola immediately becomes very popular by washing and ironing the shirts of the other tenants at a time when soap is still rationed.[19]

"It made a great change in my life when the circle of our acquaintances suddenly expanded." After two years of austerity and voracious solitary writing, Simone de Beauvoir is the first one to feel she is coming out of a tunnel. She almost won a literary prize for her first novel and by now, she and Sartre are a true writer-couple. In the fall of 1943, a new era starts, with literary dinners, and a new image imposes itself on the circle of writers and friends, the image of an extraordinary couple: the Beaver, as they call her, a methodical fast talker, with her harmonious face and porcelain eyes, a full head taller than Sartre, the indefatigable live wire. They are received by the Leirises, and welcomed by the Queneaus, and they return the invitations according to the imperishable laws of the code of social reciprocity. They see a lot of Camus: they love his laughter and his talk, his ease, his gallantry of the Mediterranean male whether he is simply speaking to women or grabbing them by the waist to drag them along into the most impeccable double steps they have ever seen. At the Leirises, Quai des Grands-Augustin, they are introduced to one of the most beautiful of all collections of contemporary art: Ernst, Miró, Picasso, Juan Gris, and, for the first time in their lives, they listen with delight to the anecdotes of old surrealists. They particularly appreciate Queneau's response to Sartre's question as to what he has kept from his surrealist days: "The feeling I was once young!" And, taking advantage of Mme Morel's gifts and of Zette Leiris's occasional surprises, Beauvoir learns to be a hostess. "The quality's not exactly brilliant," Camus thanks her, "but the quantity is just right!"[20]

And, at last, they manage to dissipate some of the tension accumulated during curfews, rationings, and the general repression, with the help of a few delicious moments of utter hilarity. The way to all these encounters has been paved by earlier intimacies, reciprocities, and mutual recognitions. Camus has reviewed *Nausea* and *The Wall*, Sartre has reviewed *The Stranger*, Leiris has reviewed *The Flies*, Sartre has appreciated *The Age of Man*. A game of mirrors, which, almost by necessity, has brought their literary destinies together and initiated their friendship. Regular meetings, the CNE, cocktail parties, outings together: there is a cohesion here that Simone de Beauvoir will remember almost in the terms of a manifesto: "We agreed to remain together forever in league against the systems and men and ideas that we condemned. But their defeat was imminent, and our task would be to shape the future that would then unfold before us: perhaps by political action, and in any case on the intellectual plane. We were to provide the postwar era with its ideology."[21]

The publication of *She Came to Stay*, Simone de Beauvoir's first novel, the story of a couple that is in fact a trio, gave the readers and the public at large the sense of penetrating the heart of an intimate secret. Suddenly, the couple Sartre/Beauvoir became an actor in a transparent private life. The throes of Sartre's passion for Olga—or, rather, of Pierre's for Xavière—were here fully, if fictionally, deployed along with the trio's—Beauvoir/Sartre/Olga's—desperate attempt to master all feelings of jealousy and possessiveness. As the author admits, the novel provoked at once "curiosity, impatience, sympathy," and played, more than any other literary work, an extraordinary promotional role, as it deliberately unveiled and, indeed, even exhibited what traditional couples prefer to hide, particularly so when what is involved is an experience that transgresses the bourgeois code. On the other hand, the novel also sealed one of the most important aspects of the couple: their professional cooperation. Beauvoir had long played the role of Sartre's privileged interlocutor both with her endless readings of and commentaries on "Melancho-lia" and, later, *Nausea,* and with her discussions of the various theses of *Being and Nothingness.* When Sartre started theorizing on free-dom along nearly stoical lines—"One can always be free," as he used to put it—she asked, "What is the freedom of the women in a harem?" to which he admitted, "Well, yes, in the end there is always one who is freer than the others, but the difference is minimal."[22] Similarly, and with the same spirit of reciprocity, Sartre had con-tributed to the birth of *She Came to Stay,* at a moment in which both writers were grappling with their own novelistic techniques. Later, he had submitted the manuscript to Paulhan, whose first reaction had, unfortunately, been less than positive. He had decreed that the manuscript was to be rewritten from top to bottom, at which Sartre, moved by the expression of despair on Simone de Beauvoir's face, had gently concluded, "In that case, you needn't change anything."

*I*N THE meantime, the professor of philosophy continues teaching at the Lycée Condorcet: three half-days a week, which he spends discussing all sorts of subjects with his students, provoking them, teasing them. The students in the class of *hypokhâgne,* bored stiff by their professor, are impressed when they hear that the author of *The Wall* is lecturing next door. They immediately ask the principal's permission to complement their teacher's interminable explications of *The Critique of Pure Reason* with a few sections taught by Sartre. For two years, they will walk from their class into that of this friendly teacher who, sitting on his desk, juggling texts and quota-tions, speaks of literature, cinema, theater, and philosophy. When-ever Jean Balladur, now an architect, speaks of his career, he never fails to mention that once he was Sartre's student. "He was abso-lutely dazzling. He had the clearest diction and an uncanny way of plunging into the heart of the matter and immediately grasping it with his formidable intelligence."[23] Sartre still retains the reputation of a teacher unlike any other: a small man staggering under the weight of a full briefcase, which he inevitably opens during written examinations to pull out sheets of paper, which he then methodically fills with his distinctive handwriting; a small man, who started his classes without roll calls or any other form of authority, his hands in his pockets, just as if he were meeting a bunch of friends—"Have you seen Clouzot's latest movie?" "Balladur, how's your reading of Hemingway coming along?"—and would then suddenly delve into a discussion of the meaning of the beyond in Heidegger and Hegel. "A donkey is a restive animal, you have to hang a carrot in front of his nose to make him walk: this is Heidegger's image of the beyond. We all have "possibles" indefinitely looming in front of us. With Hegel, instead, we always manage to nibble on the carrot."[24] He makes the transition from daily life to philosophy without any difficulty, as if they were just two aspects of the same thing. He gives his students the pamphlets of the CNE, tells them about Munich and the citizen's duty to assume the historical project of his country, and then concludes with a talk on cowardice. On Wednesday afternoon, as they cross the Rue du Havre, right in front of the Gare Saint-Lazare, he invites them to have a drink. Then, with a few of them, he moves on to end the afternoon at some other place. Thus, when he was eighteen, Balladur met Giacometti in his workshop and Camus at the Flore, attended the opening of *The Flies*, and enjoyed a lecture Sartre delivered for some Dominicans, during which he was questioned about *Being and Nothingness* by Gabriel Marcel, among others. "In which category do you put a rose, that of the in-itself or that of the for-itself?" somebody asked, at which Sartre, embarrassed, got all tangled up in theoretical explanations.[25]

Teacher and students engage in a smooth, friendly exchange. He accepts with humor their academic pranks, as when he schedules a written exam on December 4 for his "taupe" class—the class that prepares students for the Polytechnique and the Ecole Centrale and in which philosophy is not one of the more important subjects. He does not have the vaguest idea that he has accidentally fallen smack in the middle of a powerful "taupe" ritual, the celebration of Sainte-Barbe's Day, during which, for generations, "taupins" have turned the world upside down. "Sainte-Barbe pray for us," the teacher hears his class answer somewhat excitedly the moment he opens his mouth to announce that time is up. The following week, as they get their exams back, the "taupins" find, much to their surprise, that they have been caught at their own game: topping the humor of his students, who have written their exams either from right to left or in the shape of a spiral, Sartre has corrected everything conscientiously, including the exam of a nonexistent student (of whose nonexistence he is perfectly aware), thus showing them all that the chief joker of the Rue d'Ulm still lives.[26] The teacher is sometimes ironic, sometimes gruff, always provocative. "You are lazy, Balladur, you never work, you'll never amount to anything!" he keeps saying during the year, but, on the final report, he marks "excellent."[27] The end of his class creates a traffic jam as students crowd around him in the first-floor gallery. According to rumor, Sartre would even have allowed his students to skip class in order to celebrate the anniversary of the demonstration of November 11, 1940 with the French Resistance students.

Could Sartre's students—adolescents during the war—avoid noticing the openness, availability, and generosity of a teacher to whom they could tell all they want and of whom they can ask whatever they please? One day, Balladur asks him to receive a friend of his; son of Turkish parents, emigrated Jews, the young Robert Misrahi has just read *Being and Nothingness* and would like to meet its author. "Come to the Flore between four and five," Sartre tells him. They discuss philosophy, talk of private matters; the wearing of the yellow star has just been made mandatory and Sartre is worried. "Come back to see me, I like talking to you." By and by, meeting by meeting, Sartre learns that the young *bachelier* is thinking of leaving his studies to earn a living doing odd jobs as a porter, delivery boy. . . . "You must prepare your *agrégation*," Sartre tells him. Soon Sartre is paying Misrahi a monthly "salary," which continues till the day of his *agrégation*. [28]

Sartre is praised by the authorities of the school, the inspectors, the principals. Inspector André Bridoux, who visits the class on January 30, 1943, appreciates his "extraordinary knowledge and understanding of the texts, the clarity of his expression and the breadth of his views," and lingers particularly on some "extremely suggestive connections, as when M. Sartre shows that the progression toward being that one has to trace from Descartes to Spinoza is again retraced, in contemporary philosophy, as one goes from Husserl to Heidegger."[29]

And yet neither his pedagogical capacities nor his passion for his students can stop another natural process: by now, the writer has taken the lead over the teacher, who is soon going to hand in his resignation. He has all sorts of projects ahead—cinema, theater, journalism—which inevitably draw him away from the academic world. During the years of the occupation, the "Resistance writer," disguised as a teacher, has come a long way.

SPIRITUAL LEADER FOR
THOUSANDS OF YOUNG PEOPLE

"*T*HREE EGGS and a bag of noodles": nutritional details have become a leitmotif of both conversations and correspondence throughout occupied France. Simone de Beauvoir learns that Sartre has finished his bread coupons and that he had to borrow 700 grams of bread from Wanda; that, due to a delay in the arrival of noodles, he has received a bunch of potatoes instead; and that, thanks to a Swiss admirer, Jean Lescure, the editor of the journal *Messages*, he has managed to get the most precious of all staples: fifty grams of blond tobacco sent especially for him via—maximum refinement —diplomatic pouch. The longer the German occupation, the harsher the privations and more violent the clashes it provokes. "A thriving black market . . . unspeakable privations . . . scandalous profits," Charles de Gaulle writes in his *War Memoirs* during the spring of 1944.

*A*T THE same time, the militia are waging a merciless war on the Resistance. On January 31, 1944, the Vichy government has put its militia in charge of "locating all the centers of hostile propaganda, finding the leaders of hostile forces, and repressing all antigovernment intrigue and demonstrations." The mission is often carried out with excessive zeal by a special branch of the militia, the "irregular guards," real military groups egged on by the violent speeches of Darnand, who has declared open war against all the members of the Resistance. Armed directly by the Germans, these fascist groups foster civil war in every region of France: the Red Easter of the Jura, the massacres at Ascq, and the execution of twenty-three "foreign terrorists" condemned during the "trial of the red placard"; their photos, posted throughout the Paris subway, summon all civilians to denunciations. . . . The little group at the Hotel de la Luisiane is also going to suffer. "One night there was such a violent explosion I thought the heavens had fallen. . . . Sartre came and dragged me out onto the hotel terrace. The horizon was glowing a fiery red, and the sky was the most fantastic sight. . . . This noisy chaotic spectacle lasted over two hours. Next morning we learned that La Chapelle station had been blown to bits and was surrounded by great mounds of rubble; bombs had fallen just outside the Sacré-Coeur."[1]

The largest French cities are bombed: hard hit, Le Havre will lose, among other things, the Hotel Printania. The noose is tightening. One day, Mouloudji, devastated, announces that Lola and Olga Barbezat have been arrested during a raid on the apartment of some friends, members of the Resistance. On their behalf, Sartre contacts someone who is on good terms with Pierre Laval, head of the Vichy government. But it takes time. Both Lola and Olga emerge a few weeks later, from the Fresnes prison.[2] Soon there is a real "family" drama, concerning Sorokine and Bourla, the "little ones" who stay in the same hotel: "They are so sweet," Sartre writes to Beauvoir, away on a skiing trip. "They always set a place for me at their table: a plate, a bowl, a spoon and a knife on their spotted tablecloth. It's touching."[3] She is tall, blonde, sleek, he, with black curly hair, intense, proud of his Spanish-Jewish origins. Two nineteen-year-olds, in love with life and literature. "One must trust the void," Bourla used to say after his experiences with writing poetry. He was sure of the imminent defeat of Nazism. Beauvoir writes: "One day Sartre . . . asked him what he would do in the event of a German victory. 'A German victory does not figure in my scheme of things,' he replied decisively."[4] The day they hear of Bourla's arrest, the entire Sartre "family" is stunned. A long wait, and the intervention of a German who claims he'll save him for several million francs: the money is found, and Beauvoir accompanies Sorokine to Drancy, where across the barbed wire she can greet a man she believes is her Bourla, still alive thanks to their "German friend." But they soon discover that they have been duped by the German and that Bourla was killed shortly after his arrest. Again, Beauvoir: "Bourla had been a close neighbor of mine, and I had taken him to my heart: besides he was only nineteen. Sartre did his honest best to convince me that in a sense every life is complete at its end, and that death at nineteen is no more absurd than death at eighty."[5]

As physical brutalities increase daily, Sartre continues his ascent through the highest literary spheres, alternating genres: cinema, theater, literary criticism, novels, political articles. . . . Is there a hierarchy in all this? "I've finished the Parain article and with delight returned to my novel," he writes one day; "it is so much more amusing than speaking of language."[6] From this moment on, it will be a constant to and fro between moments of pure enjoyment—fiction—and moments of speculation—criticism. Badgered by Paul-

208

han—"I'm eagerly awaiting the rest of the Parain article"[7]—the literary critic continues to dissect French literature. Does Paulhan relish his perfect control of this double game that sees Sartre publishing with one hand and stabbing away with the other? Paulhan appreciates Sartre's inability to pull punches, his capacity to sketch, today, the limits and frontiers that literature will reach tomorrow, and the way in which he follows his intuition in promoting new writers: after Camus, he has now passed to the scrupulous examination and dissection of, in turn, Blanchot, Bataille, Parain, and Ponge. "Not all the discontented can direct their anger against language. In order to do so they must have first attributed a particular value to it. Which is what Parain and Ponge have done. Those who thought they could detach concepts from words have given up and have chosen to apply their revolutionary energy elsewhere. Not so Ponge and Parain who, having already defined man by his language, got trapped, like rats, because language has no value whatsoever. We can assume that this is where they started despairing: their very position precluding any hope. We know how Parain, haunted by a silence that kept eluding him, went all the way to the extremes of terrorism then backtracked toward a more nuanced rhetoric. Ponge's path is a little more sinuous."[8]

SARTRE ALSO discovers the pleasures of a social life: literary events, invitations, new encounters, and opportunities. February 1944: on the jury of the Prix de la Pléiade with Malraux, Eluard, and Camus, he obtains the success of his protégé, Mouloudji. The ceremony is followed by a dinner in honor of the winner at the restaurant Le Hoggar. March 1944: literary meetings and discussions among literati in Marcel Moré's apartment: Sartre speaks with Pierre Klossowski, Jean Hyppolite, and Father Daniélou of the meaning of sin in Bataille's thought. April 1944: for the first time, Sartre asks for a sick leave from the Ministry of Education. And then, finally, there is Jean Grenier, who, leaning toward Simone de Beauvoir at the Café de Flore, asks her the fatal question: "Madame, are you an existentialist?"

Another special evening, the culmination of a series of events, will remain forever engraved in the memories of our two writers and their entourage. It all started in the spring of 1944 with the play Picasso had just finished, Le Désir attrappé par la queue (Desire Caught by the Tail). Leiris had liked the play, a distant parody of the avant-garde works of the twenties, and had proposed a reading of it with Camus as the director, Sartre in the role of Round End, Leiris as Big Foot, Dora Marr as Fat Misery, and Simone de Beauvoir as The Cousin. . . . There were several rehearsals and, finally, on the appointed evening, the Leirises' drawing room filled with theater people, such as Jean-Louis Barrault, painters, including Georges Braque, writers like Armand Salacrou, Bataille, and Georges Limbour, and others, including Jacques Lacan and Sylvia Bataille.

Intoxicated by the atmosphere and the alcohol, the amateur actors stay after the rest of the guests have gone. They start singing and soon it is curfew time. Leiris proposes, "Why not spend the night here?" Inside, songs, music, close friends. Outside, no noise, no movement, no light. The intoxication of being the only ones up, of being together, singing and laughing against the imposed silence and Nazi order. Sartre goes to the piano and plays his two favorite pieces: "Les papillons de nuit" (The Butterflies of Night) and "J'ai vendu mon âme au diable" (I Sold My Soul to the Devil). This party, the first in a series of many, lasts till five in the morning and binds Sartre and Beauvoir to Picasso and Dora Marr, while bringing them closer to Salacrou and his wife, and Bataille. In this surrealist circle, Sartre and Beauvoir would find a youth they had never had.[9]

Soon, they became full-time actors in the artistic life of Occupied Paris: two funny, energetic actors; two inventive and spontaneous hosts, whether they receive their guests in their hotel rooms or in the houses of friends, at Bost's in the country, or at Camille's. It is here, in her beautiful apartment, that, one evening, their collective imagination goes wild: "We constituted a sort of carnival," writes Beauvoir, "with its mountebanks, its confidence men, its clowns, and its parades. Dona Marr used to mime a bullfighting act; Sartre conducted an orchestra from the bottom of a cupboard; Limbour carved up a ham as though he were a cannibal; Queneau and Bataille fought a duel with bottles instead of swords; Camus and Lemarchend played military marches on saucepan lids, while those who knew how to sing, sang. So did those who didn't. We had pantomimes, comedies, diatribes, parodies, monologues, and confessions: the flow of improvisations never dried up."[10]

*A*FTER ALL the attacks on individual freedom, after the food restrictions, the curfews that keep getting earlier, alerts, bombs, and an increasing number of friends who have been executed, there is, for a while, a perhaps illusory sense of freedom and fun. A nocturnal escapade, temporary recklessness, and life goes on: theater, cinema, politics, Sartre's schedule is full. Maybe even too full: he risks overdoing it. "As for my moods," he writes at the time, "I was a little hurt to see my screenplays rejected: I'm so used to being praised of late that when I'm not I feel lost."[11] And, indeed, on this occasion he is not praised. "Discouraged by the mediocrity of the screenplay we got at Pathé, I decided to pay Sartre a visit," Jean Delannoy remembers.[12] Sartre's passionate involvement with the movies is still alive; we remember the speech he delivered on Prize Day at the lycée of Le Havre, and his interest in cinematographic discourse, which he enthusiastically conveyed to his students. "Good editing can bring together and interlock the most unlikely scenes," he explained to them. "We were in the fields, but now we are in the city; we think we are going to stay here for a while, but in fact we are already back in the fields. . . . Remember Abel Gance's *Napoleon.*"[13] Cocteau, Pagnol, and Prévert had made the transition to the screen, but Sartre's experience was much more mixed. "Wretched failures," he will himself say of most of his work for the movies. And, in fact, he always will remain a stranger to the world of cinema. He is awed and fascinated by it, just as he is fascinated by all avant-garde techniques, but he must stay awkwardly behind the windowpane, an unhappy spectator. His position of outsider is obvious in an article he wrote in April 1944 for *Les Lettres françaises clandestines,* about postwar cinema. It is a didactic, flabby, rather indigestible piece. "We are going to examine a particular case that is going to show how, for the moment, cinema cannot move out of the direction that has been imposed upon it": discourse, method, academic rhetoric, where have the sparkle, the virtuosity, and the elegance of the critic gone? And whom is he trying to convince when he outlines a traditional concept of the movies, and then maintains that "it alone can speak the language of the crowd, just as it alone can claim the exceptional role of 'art of the crowd' "? The "new" models he proposes are simply those of his childhood, which he defines as "the great pioneers of cinema, the Griffiths, the Cecil B. deMilles, the King Vidors, the Eisensteins." This frustrated relationship with cinema indicates some of the limits of Sartre's intellectual voracity, and his occasionally abortive megalomania. If he believes he has the necessary intellectual tools to speak of cinema, and the passion, the culture, and the technique to enter the world of screenplay writers, he is also hindered by a major handicap. While other writers, such as Cocteau, Pagnol, Prévert, have made the transition to cinema, Sartre seems less versatile, perhaps due to his academic training and his penchant for scholarly rhetoric. Nevertheless he tries to have an impact on contemporary cinema, "this giant," as he puts it, "which we have chained and forced to paint miniatures," because, he adds "we are afraid of it."

He continues to write screenplays and immediately produces two. *Les Jeux sont faits* (The Chips Are Down) and *Typhus,* and, shortly after, a third one on the Resistance. They all share the themes of *The Flies* and *No Exit*— his next play, already being written—the same concern for current events, the obsession with sick cities, closed places, and the unbearable malaise of the inhabitants. Ottawee, a city in the Malayan archipelago, is decimated by an epidemic. "It's awful," Nellie cries, "to stay in this city, steeped in typhoid, where death lurks behind every corner. . . . I don't have a penny, I don't have a home, I don't even know where I'll sleep tonight."[14] He works on the synopsis with the screenplay writer Nino Frank, who is quite surprised by his approach: "It was the first time that I had worked with a dialogue writer who thought in terms of shots rather than scenes and who wrote his dialogue very quickly, concisely and precisely; his work was strangely instinctive and, therefore, quite cinematic."[15] The technical cutting is left in the hands of Jean Delannoy. Cuts, ellipses: the two writers admire the talent of the director, but the end result disappoints them. "Circumstances lose their sharpness, edges are blunted, every possible exaggeration is erased. The director is constantly exercising his authority, reminding us of his knowledge of the public, the canons of Hollywood, the demands of the screen. . . . Sartre signaled to me not to insist, then, as we were leaving together: 'I'm sick of this screenplay. Let him do what he wants. The important thing is that it be filmed.' "[16] It is filmed, ten years later, as *Les Orgueilleux* (The Proud). *Les Jeux sont fait* will also come out, in 1947.

The screenplay on the Resistance will never be filmed, and yet Sartre believed in it. In an article he spoke of the subjects that he thought postwar cinema should broach: "Nobody but us could speak, about the deportations, the executions, the combat of soldiers without uniforms. . . . It should not be a propaganda movie. . . . The director who has the courage to undertake such a project should start thinking about it now, gathering all sorts of information: he would have only to show things as they were . . . paint a large social fresco that will give back to cinema the breadth and the power it has lost."[17]

*F*AILURES HERE, successes there, disappointments with cinema, satisfactions with theater. On May 27, 1944, *No Exit* opens at the Théâtre du Vieux-Colombier, midway between Montparnasse and Saint-Germain. The cast includes Tania Balachova and Michel Vitold, directed by Raymond Rouleau and Gaby Sylvia. It is quite an event, particularly so considering that it had started as a joke: Wanda, like her sister, had also expressed the desire to act in a play written by Sartre, and so had Olga Barbezat, whose husband would eventually organize a tour through the provinces. To these two female roles, Sartre had added a male role, which he had proposed to Camus, who was also to direct. The only task Sartre had imposed upon himself was that of producing three roles of equal size so as not to favor any of the actors. The rehearsals had started around Christmas 1943, either in Beauvoir's hotel room or at Camus's. There had been highs and lows and a mild flirtation between Camus and Wanda. "The Russian soul we have explored down to its deepest recesses is still somewhat unfamiliar to him," Sartre writes Beauvoir, denying any jealousy on his part. "He is quite taken by her, speaks of her 'genius' and of her 'human value.' "[18] And then there was a serious episode: the arrest of Olga Barbezat. The rehearsals had to be interrupted. Then the director of the Vieux-Colombier had gotten interested in the play, and the rehearsals had been resumed, with professional actors, this time, and an established director.

"I asked myself," the author remembers, "how one could keep three people together and never let one of them get away and how to keep them together to the end, as if for eternity? Thereupon it occurred to me to put them in hell and make each of them the others' torturer."[19] This anecdote should remind us of the atmosphere of the war and the stalag fence, of the psychology of the prisoner of war. The philosopher Jean Cazeneuve had just sent a manuscript on the subject to the Presses Universitaires de France, from the camp where he was locked up, and Jacques Merleau-Ponty had reviewed it in the underground paper *Combat*: "One could compare the chapter 'Horizon limité' to the hell imagined by Sartre in his *No Exit*, a prison where there is nothing but walls, corridors, and more walls, and no outside."[20]

Balachova, in a dark dress, her face even sharper than usual below a silk turban, is Inez. With short hair, a white strapless gown, and long black gloves, Gaby Sylvia is Estelle. Between these two women, between these two types of women, elegant in his thirties and his suit, Michel Vitold is Garcin. Three individuals meet in a Second Empire drawing room in hell. Pneumonia, a gas stove, twelve bullets through one's chest. Thus begins this ballet of attraction and hatred in front of a terrifying eternity and the irrevocable presence of the other two, the unbearable ghetto of their trio: "Hell is—other people!" Garcin cries, and the formula quickly seduces the audience. Inez, exasperated by the couple Garcin-Estelle, screams, "Very well, have it your own way. I'm the weaker party, one against two. But don't forget I'm here, and watching. I shan't take my eyes off you, Garcin; when you're kissing her, you'll feel them boring into you. Yes, have it your own way, make love and get it over. We're in hell; my turn will come." Garcin to Estelle: "Give me your lips."[21]

"We judge ourselves with the means other people have and have given us for judging ourselves," Sartre later explains to dispel all misunderstanding of his famous formula. "If my relations are bad, I am situating myself in a total dependence on someone else. And then I am indeed in hell."[22] But, beyond its atmosphere, its formulas, and its dramatic impact, the production of *No Exit* inaugurated a specifically Sartrean technique, a technique very characteristic of his talents. Performed a year after the publication of *Being and Nothingness, No Exit* can easily be seen as a version of the same text for the public at large. The lexical and theoretical austerity and the academic references of the former are translated into the theatrical agility of the latter, abstract thought into shimmering illustrations. "My big book was told in the form of short nonphilosophical tales."[23] From his beginnings as a writer, he has carried on simultaneous dialogues with different audiences, he has had twin moorings in theater and philosophy.

The collaborationist press insults the play because of its "immoralism."[24] R. Francis inaugurates the long list of insults with which Sartre will be copiously honored after the war: "We all know M. Sartre," Francis writes. "He is an odd philosophy teacher who, after publishing *The Wall* and *Nausea*, has specialized in the study of his students' underwear. . . . He has some sort of faithful 'claque,' and every time he raises his leg, whether it is on a book or on stage, a small troupe of young men and impotent old men run over to the spot and sniff it. Then they show their delight by wagging their pens over paper."[25] On the other hand, Claude Jamet, of *Germinal,* is very much impressed: "After Anouilh, Jean-Paul Sartre is certainly the most important event in contemporary French theater."[26]

Now he has everything he needs to succeed. Since the spring of 1944, he has had his partisans and his detractors, his enthusiastic accomplices and his rabid enemies. Literary celebrity doesn't require much more, and he has already provoked similar movements of opinion among French writers: Gabriel Marcel, for instance, who, while greeting the "extraordinary success" of the play, regrets its "Luciferian theme," which "will not contribute much to the restoration of our country."[27]

"Have you read Sartre?" Paulhan anxiously writes to Jouhandeau. "It's Giraudoux upside down."[28] Back from the performance, Jean Guéhenno, tells his *Journal des années noires* that everything in the play has disgusted him: its "horrors," its "infernal evocations," the "provoking and falsely cynical divagations of irresponsible characters." "Who is ever going to pull us out of this swamp?" he concludes.[29] Paulhan's letter and Guéhenno's *Journal* are quite eloquent: minimized by the former and totally misunderstood by the latter, to them Sartre already belongs to a different world. If these two prewar literati look at this "objet Sartre" with mistrust, considering it again and again from every angle without being able to classify it according to any known standard, and wondering, perplexed, as to what sort of product it might be, it is probably because, with *No Exit,* Sartre does indeed become unclassifiable. When Paulhan says that Sartre is "Giraudoux upside down," he already admits that one of the limits of contemporary French literature has been crossed and that a new topography of postwar French literature has been sketched. Guillaume Hanoteau, author of a book about the "golden age of Saint-Germain-des-Prés," is particularly impressed by the extraordinary advertising campaign that accompanied the opening of *No Exit.* "There is no doubt," he writes, "that *No Exit* was the cultural event that inaugurated the golden age of Saint-Germain-des-Prés."[30]

On June 10, 1944, a week after the opening of *No Exit,* Sartre delivers a lecture on dramatic style, under the auspices of Jean Vilar, the actor and director who will later found the influential Théâtre National Populaire (TNP). The lecture touches on the plays of Camus and Armand Salacrou, two colleagues present in the room. Then Sartre stands back to enjoy the heated discussion that follows, which involves, among others, Vilar, the great actor-director Jean-Louis Barrault, Jean Cocteau, and Camus.[31] By the end of June, his students at the Lycée Condorcet are surprised when they see him walk into the classroom with his hands in his pockets. The bulging suitcase has gone, the pages he used to fill have been published, the notebooks that kept piling up on his desk have been completed. At the end of June 1944, Jean-Paul Sartre, the writer, decides that his career as a teacher is over.

*I*N THE meantime, the Allies have landed in Normandy, and the first real signs of liberation are reaching Paris. On June 7, 1944, at five in the morning, after a party at Camille's, Sartre and Beauvoir, coming out of the subway, notice an incongruous detail: at the Gare Montparnasse, all the westbound trains have been canceled. They haven't yet learned anything from the radio. Simone de Beauvoir: "The days that followed seemed like one long holiday. People were happy and laughing, the sun shone, the streets had never looked gayer! . . . I would drink ersatz 'Turin gin' outside the Flore with Sartre and our various friends, or stroll along to the Rhumerie Martiniquaise, where we got equally ersatz rum punch. But we were building our future, and blissfully happy."[32] And yet the months of June and July were going to produce their own list of violence and death: the massacre of the entire population of a village near Oradour-sur-Glane; the assassination by the militia of Jean Zay, former minister of education; the arrest of Georges Mandel. The last German parades in Paris: the Champs-Elysées once again witnesses the passage of one of the most famous SS armored divisions under the proud eyes of Generalfeldmarschall von Rundstedt, and of the "Kommandant von Gross Paris," von Boineburg-Lengsfeld. The final combats double in violence; the settling of scores often ends in blood. The underground network "Combat" to which Camus belongs, and to which he has often brought Sartre, is gradually falling to pieces; it is necessary to take preventive measures: Camus suggests Sartre change his address, and, as a result, they spend the last summer of the war partly at the Leirises' and partly at Neuilly-sous-Clermont. "On August 11 the papers and the radio announced that the Americans were on the outskirts of Chartres," Beauvoir writes. "We hastily packed up and mounted our bicycles. The main road, we were told, was out of the question. . . . So we took a side road, which brought us out at Chantilly by way of Beaumont. Despite the blazing sun we pedaled along feverishly, gripped by the sudden fear of finding ourselves cut off from Paris: we had no wish to miss the actual Liberation."[33]

"*I*T BEGINS like a party and yet, today, the Boulevard Saint-Germain, deserted and intermittently swept by the fire of machine guns, affects an air of tragic solemnity. Almost despite oneself, one remembers those old Sundays, those Sundays of peace, when people gathered at some fair, or some sporting event, and then suddenly there was a serious accident. The light dresses would be stirred by an invisible eddy, as faces, white with fear and yet still vaguely gay, leaned over a body bleeding under the sun. A party: three red Sundays in a row . . ."

This witness to a present that is taking shape during the days of the Liberation of Paris is none other than Sartre. Recruited by Camus, he inaugurates a series of articles ("A Walker in Insurgent Paris") for the front page of *Combat*: "In the quietest neighborhood, every two or three minutes, one can hear the sharp snap of a rock hitting a stone: it is a gunshot. . . . Then, suddenly, coming from one doesn't know where, the volley of a machine gun. These noises are inexplicable: the Germans are no longer around, and the FFI [the official forces of the Resistance] are far away. Nobody is trying to solve the mystery. People look at each other and seriously say: 'Someone's being shot.' And that's that." It is a euphoric moment, Sartre's appointment with History. His city again looks like a stage set, just as it did when he got back from the stalag. And, once again, it's for real. "On the Boulevard Saint-Germain, at the corner with the Rue de Seine, civilians are killed every two hours. . . . Who could stay locked up in his room when Paris is fighting for its freedom? . . . Danger is unforeseeable: at three in the afternoon it is here, at four it is there. Why should anyone try to avoid it? I think there is grandeur in such a destiny. This is what gives Paris its extraordinary physiognomy."[34]

Others get excited and, like Claude Roy, express their lyrical delight. "The French flag is now flying over the Sorbonne, liberated from the traitors of the intelligence, from the intellectual Nazis. A student kisses his girlfriend. It is the best day of our life. The crowd sings *La Marseillaise*. It's the best day of our life. A young girl opens her arms in the air, laughs, dances. It's the best day of our life."[35] Sartre has a ringside seat at the liberation of his city. This playwright in love with Greek theater assumes the role of an actor in History: narrator, bard, teller.

"There is a geography of insurrection: in certain areas, they have been fighting relentlessly for four days; in others (Montparnasse, for instance), everything is almost disturbingly calm. But it is difficult to draw a map of fighting Paris. . . . The crowd is weighed down by some sort of inertia: they are still hoping that Paris will be evacuated without bloodshed, and waiting for the arrival of the Allies as if they were a gift. A few people venture all the way to the Boulevard Saint-Germain and come back disappointed: the flag with the swastika is still flying over the Senate. 'They' are still there. . . . Only an old man who cannot run stays on the boulevard, the Germans aim their guns at him. . . . He rushes to the door of a nearby building, and starts banging on it with all his might, hoping it opens. But the door remains closed, the Germans shoot, and the man falls. . . . This is enough to transform the crowd. Their snug dreams of a pacific evacuation are shattered . . . and they are no longer just a bunch of civilians; now they must take sides. . . . The war is still here, under the sun."[36] "On Wednesday, every hour brought the news of the Americans' arrival at Versailles. But, each time, a refutation dispelled our joy. Somebody called Versailles: they were not there. Then, suddenly, that Wednesday, the BBC announced that Paris had been freed. A friend and I listened to the news flat on our stomachs because heavy gunfire was just then hammering our building: we couldn't help finding the announcement somewhat surprising, even annoying. Paris had been freed, *but* we could not leave our building; *but* the Rue de Seine, where I lived, was still blocked."[37] "At last, the guns fell silent and Paris went to sleep. But, at dawn, the following morning, the streets are black with people. They are fighting over the morning papers. . . . On the Rue de Rennes, leaning against a flag-draped balcony, a woman applauds. Flat on the ground, hidden by a French tricolor, a man shoots between his legs; another man holds a child in his arms and smiles. The child is a doll that hides a gun. The hatred that gnaws at these hearts stretches its shadow over the entire city."[38]

At last, it is the real Liberation. "Eight days ago, revolt flared every hour; I was in this same Rue de Rivoli: It was empty. . . . Today, *they* are here, and in a few minutes *they* are going to parade by. I am on a balcony, on the Rue du Louvre. Facing me is the heavy mass of the Ministry of Finance. Below me, the crowd shines in the sun. I have never seen so many men at once. . . . I have never seen a more bizarre or more beautiful parade. It does not have the organization and pomp of our big military reviews. At first sight, these colorful cars, covered with weird badges and white paint, remind one of a shabby carnival, a war carnival. Men and women holding streamers parade slowly in their vans, as if they were Mardi Gras floats. . . . We hear the first shots, then a few more. In the tense, almost tragic atmosphere that has followed six days of blood and glory and the arrival of all these armies, they do not surprise me at all. I'd even go so far as to say that they seem to fit right in with the celebration."[39]

Saturday, August 26, 1944: all Paris is in the streets. De Gaulle, Marshal Leclerc, and the political leader Jacques Chaban-Delmas are parading along the Champs-Elysées and then come the tanks of the American Second Armored Division. The city exults. Young Frenchwomen give themselves to American soldiers. From his balcony at the Hotel du Louvre, Sartre watches the head of the temporary government pass, standing in a tank. That evening, over dinner, at the Leirises, with Jean Genet, whom he has just met, he listens to Patrick Waldberg, in an American uniform, tell of his arrival at Dreux, at Versailles.

Besides writing, Sartre moves through Paris like a madman: an appointment with Camus at the paper, lunch with Salacrou on the Avenue Foch, a reunion of the Comité National du Théâtre at the Comédie Française, where he spends his days and his nights. These days will provide material for his articles for a long time to come: "The Republic of Silence,"[40] "Paris Under the Occupation,"[41] "What's a Collaborator?"[42] "The End of the War,"[43] "The Liberation of Paris: An Apocalyptic Week."[44] As a privileged witness who has arrived at the right moment, Sartre explains the mood of occupied Paris. "Will people understand me if I say that the horror was intolerable but that it suited us well? . . . What London experienced in pride, Paris experienced in shame and despair. . . . We have never been as free as we were under the German occupation. . . . We would like you to understand that at times the occupation was worse than the war. Because, during the war, everybody can behave like a man, whereas, in this ambiguous situation, we couldn't really act or think. . . . The end of a war leaves man naked, without illusions, abandoned to his own forces, realizing, at last, that he can count only on himself."

"DAILY LIFE, in Paris, is not yet normal," the American expatriate Janet Flanner writes toward the end of 1944. "Even though, now, there is hope. The population of the capital is still a mass of restless individuals, each walking alone with his own memories, under a steady wintry rain."[45] Long meetings at the CNE: old scores are settled, the question of purges gives rise to violent debates. Back from their respective exiles, writers stake out their positions. Their opinions differ as, for instance, when they discuss Pucheu, an ex-Normalien, Pétain's minister of the interior, responsible for the retroactive laws. Camus is officially against the death sentence and would like to see his article published on the editorial page of *Les Lettres françaises*. Eluard and Morgan disagree with Camus: "If we have the right to forgive those who have hurt us, we do not have the right to forgive those who have murdered innocent people."[46] The debate concerning the "collabo" critic Robert Brasillach will be similar.

"The first meetings concerning the purges," Hanoteau remembers, "were indescribable: everybody had his private bête noire, some personal enemy. Mauriac wanted Edmond Jaloux's skin; Aragon hoped we'd denounce and shoot Armand Petitjean."[47] As Jean Lescure remembers: "The discussions concerning Breton's articles for *Comoedia* were interminable, and all the more so in that there was no clear-cut standard."[48] In this confused gathering of different generations, literary tendencies, and political appurtenances, French literature is like a gambling table where anything goes: the cards have been dealt and the stakes are high. It's where the main lines of the postwar future are going to be drawn; the storm has swept away all models. Mauriac, Malraux, Gide, Rolland, Martin du Gard are obsolete. A new generation emerges out of these postwar purges.

"Aragon was Grand Master of the Purges," Debû-Bridel remembers. "He would have gladly purged most cases, except for the former 'collabos' who had rallied to the PC."[49] French writers take positions on purges according to laws that are often hard to decipher: Paulhan and Mauriac are the partisans of mild purges; Camus's opinion varies case by case; Vercors sides with the toughest ones and goes so far as to propose purges for the publishers as well; Sartre opts for a lesser violence. On one occasion, Vercors and Pierre Seghers flare up: publishers are more guilty than writers; a thorough cleanup should start with institutions, not individuals. Paulhan tries to defend Gallimard. Aragon pays a visit to Gaston, who retorts "Come on, Louis, as you know full well I'm only a poor paper dealer!"[50] Gallimard appeases Aragon with promises and Aragon withdraws from the debate. The publishers will be spared; Vercors and Seghers, in the minority, resign from the committee. As for Sartre, he has been lukewarm on this question; he is elaborating a theory on individual involvement and individual responsibilities, and, incidentally, Gallimard has just agreed to finance his projected review, *Les Temps modernes*.

"We wanted to construct an ideology for the postwar age," Beauvoir remembers. "We had precise projects. . . . Camus, Merleau-Ponty, and myself, we would draw up a team manifesto. Sartre was determined to found a review that we would all direct together. . . . We had reached the end of the night, day was breaking, side by side, we were starting again from zero."[51] The editorial committee of the review will consist of Aron, Paulhan, Albert Ollivier, Merleau-Ponty, Sartre, and Beauvoir. At the end of 1944, Vercors, who has just started a new review, *Les Chroniques de Minuit*, for the Editions de Minuit, asks Sartre to be his editor-in-chief in order to fight, with him, against the last vestiges of nazism: "Too bad," Sartre answers, "I have just founded *Les Temps modernes.*"[52] Another sign of the times: Sartre and Camus both refuse to work for the review just launched by Editions du Seuil, *Esprit*, which they consider too "Christian." In a letter to Gide, Paulhan gives a clear picture of the tensions within that first committee: "Sartre has just finished writing a manifesto for *Les Temps modernes*. Its Marxist side seems fairly solid, but its metaphysical one sounds rather chimerical. Flaubert was wrong not to condemn the repressions of the Commune, and Proust never should have spoken of heterosexual love. So be it and God save the so-called literature of commitment! Unfortunately, Sartre can only extricate it from Marxism by pivoting on a notion of human freedom that's a hundred times lighter than Albertine. I have agreed to be on the committee of a review, which, by its very nature, is doomed to be boring and false. But in literature anything goes."[53]

Excitement, effervescence, the settling of old scores. Throughout the fall and winter of 1944, Sartre will prefer the meetings of the review to those of the CNE. "The CNE?" Paulhan writes to Raymond Guérin. "What's this sudden craze for sociability? Camus has resigned! Sartre never comes. I am officially hibernating. . . . It has been discovered that it was only a way for communist politics to hide behind the names of Mauriac, Duhamel, etc." And, in a letter to Eluard: "What the hell can I do in a committee where no one shares my opinions? . . . It is a question of knowing whether the honor of a writer allows or orders him to denounce other writers. Personally, I don't think so, and that's that. . . . Neither judge nor spy."[54] Like Paulhan, Sartre will soon also tire of these punitive meetings and will choose to move ahead rather than judge the past.

But he will not join organized groups. He does not attend the debates of *Action* at the Mutualité on December 20, 1944, where Pierre Hervé, Maurice Kriegel-Velrimont, Pascal Copeau, and Jean-

Daniel Jurgensen are trying to pull together a unique Resistance organization. Sartre does not feel at ease with that sort of thing. He is again having problems with the communists. In response to a series of articles that attacked "existentialism," he issues a statement in *Combat:* "What do you reproach us for? To begin with, for being inspired by Heidegger, a German and a Nazi philosopher. Next, for preaching, in the name of existentialism, a quietism of anguish. I too shall speak all by myself for existentialism. Have you even defined it for your readers? And yet it's rather simple. . . . Man must create his own essence: it is in throwing himself into the world, suffering there, struggling there, that he gradually defines himself. . . . anguish, far from being an obstacle to action, is the very condition for it. . . . Man cannot will unless he has first understood that he can count on nothing but himself: that he is alone, left alone on earth in the middle of his infinite responsibilities, with neither help nor succor, with no other goal but the one he will set for himself, with no destiny but the one he will forge on this earth."[55]

He could not have been clearer in his answer to Marxist ideology; the two areas are well defined. Sartre defends individual life as a daily creation—"we are to ourselves our own work of art"—in a radical project that sees the individual as pure creativity, as a bursting forth, an emergence. The theory of *Nausea* has been inseminated by the war. The isolated prewar path has crossed that of History. The man who stood aside has now moved to the center.

S ARTRE'S PLUNGE into the waves that followed the liberation of Paris creates a wave of its own. And it is Sartre, the intruder, the outsider, the marginal, who, along with Camus, is going to lead it. He commands a strategic position, where everything is getting reorganized, with all the resources that he has accumulated in the publishing and theater worlds. He already has a certain renown, and now he is symbolically taking possession of Paris, where literary life is a desert. His notions of radical pessimism, revolt, insubordination, and absolute solitude have met the mood of the times in the emptiness left by the war and can now bloom. After the failure of "Socialism and Freedom," he has found a new impetus. And from the failure came two novels, a philosophical treatise, two plays, five screenplays, eleven literary articles, eight pieces of reportage, three political articles plus one on the movies, as well as his correspondence, his notes, his notebooks.

In 1944, Sartre is still profiting from the weight and the social value of philosophy. Availing himself of this privileged position, the Nor-malien, the *agrégé,* this pure essence of elitism, is going to enter the French intellectual world wearing seven-league boots. With the superhuman strength of his will, his work, and his talents, he is going to leave a mark on everything. Legitimized by philosophy, he is going to invade all related fields: cinema, theater, the novel, criticism, journalism, politics. He is going to try to annex them, brandishing the philosophical tool as if it were an irresistible sword. The ap-proach will prove effective with the more traditional fields such as literary criticism and the novel, but not quite as much with cinema, journalism, and politics.

In a country exhausted by war, this is a moment of extreme receptivity: men like Paulhan and Guéhennos are puzzled by Sartre. But to the postwar generation, Sartre is a hero of his time. It is not surprising that the discussions and the regulations of the CNE bore him. He is elsewhere, in the future. Enthused by his radicalism, his permanent transgression of conventional models, his café life, his transparency, his marginality, so shocking to the bourgeois, a great part of French youth is ineluctably attracted to Sartre. "A Social Technics of the Novel," the lecture he delivers at the Maison des Lettres on the Rue Saint-Jacques in the fall of 1944 draws all the students and critics who have liked *No Exit.* It is an apology for the "American approach" to the novel. "It was the first time," Michel Butor remembers, "I had heard of Virginia Woolf, Dos Passos, Faulkner. . . . I am sure that a good deal of the problematical in my novels has evolved out of the reflections prompted by that lecture."[56] Thus, an entire lineage is naturally born out of the ideas of the lecturer, who, as he puts it, absolutely refuses to "go on forever retelling the loves of Babylas and Ernestine."

Young Alexandre Astruc has already devoted a twelve-page article to Sartre's oeuvre. "Events that enchant us are fairly rare in the world of French letters. . . . Sartre's first books seem precisely such an event. . . . What makes his revolt new is that it is radical, aiming at the very basis of existence. . . . So, from Lucien Fleurier to Orestes, we witness the drawing of one of the most exact images of man in literature."[57] Dragging followers and admirers in his wake through the general chaos of an eroded country, Sartre seems to know where he is going; the heroes of his novels and his plays have already become models. Given the context, Paulhan's half-humorous proph-ecy is hardly surprising: "Sartre is becoming," he announces to his friend Jouhandeau at the end of 1944, "the spiritual leader for thousands of young people."[58] At the beginning of December 1944, Bost appears in the courtyard of the Hotel Jules-Chaplain, behind the Café le Dôme, in Montparnasse, screaming, out of breath, "Camus wants you to go to America for *Combat!*"

FROM BUFFALO BILL TO FDR:
THE FIRST TRIP TO AMERICA

SATURDAY, January 11, 1945. The DC-8, military flight 137279, takes off from the Paris airport bound for New York. The eight French journalists aboard, ranging in age from twenty-five to sixty-five, have been invited by the U.S. State Department to spend two months in America. On the list of passengers, one name is immediately suspect to State Department employees: Andrée Viollis, special correspondent of the communist daily *L'Humanité* and *Ce Soir*. At sixty-five, she has written on India, China, and the USSR. Considered a dangerous communist, she will be closely watched by FBI agents throughout the entire journey. In fact, they must keep track, as precisely as possible, of the slightest movements of each member of the group, and report them, under the heading "Internal Security," to their superiors. Less suspect are MM. Denoyer of *France-Soir*, Pizella of *Libération*, and Sartre of *Combat* and *Le Figaro*. At Lyon, they have been joined by Robert Villers from Grenoble, Jean Terquelin from Marseilles, Louis Lombard from Paris, and Etiennette Bénichon from Toulouse.

This is Sartre's first flight, his first trip outside Europe, an interminable crossing—two days, three stops, more than twenty-four hours in the air, in a nonpressurized aircraft. On route he dreams of *Manhattan Transfer*, of hanging out with the Scotch-Irish worker Mac, somewhere between Chicago and Goldfield, Nevada. "American tendencies in Dos Passos . . . the American man . . . immigrants and the American melting pot . . . behaviorism . . . man seen from outside . . . journalism . . . the importance of newspapers . . . the novel-report . . . precise notes, pushed to the brink of boredom, on all that is general in an individual . . . absolute objectivity . . . never judge . . . impressions of the crowd and, through these, of the world

. . . the masterpiece: the declaration of war seen through Eleanor's eyes . . . the world as a series of points of view . . . the individual steeped in the world . . . how little man is among men."[1] Winter 1932, Le Havre, in the room of La Lyre Havraise: that is where he had first expressed his enthusiasm, his passion for Dos Passos, and his students had immediately mobbed him to know what to read, what to buy . . . Not easy back then: *Big Money* had not yet been published in France, and Beauvoir, slowly and patiently, had translated whole pages of each volume of the trilogy for him, in her fine handwriting slightly slanting to the right. Then, they had lived their lives as an American novel, telling each other about their days, in Dos Passos style, assuming the role of Mac, or Bud, or the reporter of the *Chicago Tribune*. "Such a simple, effective procedure: all you have to do is narrate a life in the style of American journalism, and the life becomes a social text," he was to write later, in 1938, in that breezy article for the *NRF*, which ended, "I regard Dos Passos as the greatest writer of our times."[2]

Sartre's love affair with America had begun with the magazine heroes of World War I, his collection of nearly five hundred issues, which constituted a mythic encyclopedia of that prodigious country. Little by little, America had become his El Dorado, his exotic alternative to the stifling atmosphere of the French provinces. Seated in the back of the Café Victor in Rouen, or at the Guillaume Tell in Le Havre, Sartre, Beauvoir, and their friends would play at decimating these somnolent provincial capitals with fictional grenades and guns borrowed for the occasion from American novels, movies, and detective stories.

He would soon land in New York, soon see Manhattan. Meanwhile, the plane was rocking and the other journalists were talking about the American war effort in a jargon totally different from his own. His mind kept drifting, imperceptibly at first, then more and more insistently, toward the heroes of *Sartoris*, to old Bayard, young Bayard, old John, young John, to plane accidents during World War I, and to that heavy, slow, deaf, stubborn grandfather. . . . A scene kept haunting him, that of old Bayard dragging his chair near the rusty coffer, slowly pulling a number of objects out of it till he finds a huge, brass-bound Bible which he slowly opens. "Bayard sat for a long time, regarding the stark dissolving apotheosis of his name. Sartorises had derided Time, but Time was not vindictive."[3] Waltz of names, waltz of places, Memphis, Quentin, Benjy, Simon, their love-hate relationship for the old South, the silence, the gestures, the

boredom of that country with its "rich people, decent and uncul-
tivated, who have neither work nor leisure, prisoners on their own
land, masters enslaved to their own negroes, forever bored, forever
trying to fill in the time with their useless gestures."[4] More air
pockets, and Sartre remembers what he wrote in the *Nouvelle Revue
Française* just before the war: "Faulkner's monologues remind one
of plane flights fraught with air pockets: at each pocket, the hero's
consciousness lapses back into the past and rises again only to fall
once more."[5] He knew that, once in the United States, he would be
looking for its blacks, its proletariat, its underdogs, and all the powerful contradictions that rendered this country, even before he had
arrived, slightly hateful yet extraordinarily desirable. He was also
going to look for all the signs of the future that this country was
clutching within its claws. "When we were twenty, around 1925,"
he will later write, "we had heard of skyscrapers. In our minds, they
symbolized the fabulous wealth of America. We had discovered
them with wonder in movies. They were the architecture of the
future just as movies were the art of the future and jazz the music
of the future."[6]

Sartre is ill at ease with the other journalists: a feeling he will have
throughout the journey even though, on the surface, he plays the
game. His irritation at their conversations during the flight from
Paris to New York will continue for the rest of the trip. And he will
remain out of place even in his fascination and his excessive wonder
as he approaches New York in one of the large airport limousines.
At first, New York appears to him as a nocturnal snowy city, straight
out of a fairy tale. "It all shone and was full of lighted shops . . . open,
lighted shops with people working in them—they were barber shops
—at eleven at night. You could have your hair cut or shampooed or
get a shave at eleven at night." Sartre's exploration of the New
World starts with the Plaza Hotel, off Fifth Avenue at Central Park
South. He has dreamed of Mac and the Bowery, of Dos Passos and
Faulkner, and instead he has unexpectedly landed in a scene from
The Great Gatsby. Crumpled, tired, and hungry, worn down by five
years of war, curfews, and food shortages, punchy from their long
journey and the time difference, their feet in shoes with cardboard
soles, the eight find themselves in front of the revolving door of the
Plaza. Inside, in the lobby, as if in a dream, they brush against the
tuxedoes, gowns, diamonds, furs, perfumes, and laughter that float
toward the ballroom. It is midnight in New York City, January 12,
1945: two different groups, two different worlds meet. "It was abso-

lutely as though I were rediscovering peace," Sartre will later remember. "They didn't realize that there was a war on."[7] Sartre spends his first night in America in a room with Robert Villers, the youngest member of the group; they will remain coupled throughout the trip. In the morning, they wake up to a sumptuous breakfast served on a silver platter: pastries, omelettes, coffee steaming in its silver pot, and a wealth of strawberries with cream. Then Sartre goes out, alone, to discover New York.

"Without any transition, I found myself at the corner of Fifty-eighth Street and Fifth Avenue. I walked for a long time under the icy sky. It was a Sunday in January 1945, a deserted Sunday. I was looking for New York and could not find it. As I kept walking along this coldly unimpressive avenue, I felt the city was drawing away from me, like a ghost. . . . Maybe, what I was looking for was a European city. Thus, slowly venturing inside the city, my myopic European eyes were trying to find in New York something to cling to, anything: a row of old houses suddenly blocking the street, a street corner, an old, time-worn building. In vain: New York is for far-sighted people, people who can focus to infinity."[8] A wealth of cultural references and cerebral discoveries blurs the physical confrontation between the hapless pedestrian and his mythical city. Troubled, though delighted, savoring an exquisite unease, Sartre discovers the large yellow cabs, so easy to hail, the ineffable rationality of topography, the constant presence of sky and space. And yet, during this first ambiguous meeting, Sartre does not really touch the city: it eludes him, alluring and restive, refusing, for the moment, to be tamed by him.

The representatives of the Office of War Information (OWI), hosts of the prestigious guests, are shocked at the sight of such a strange group in such a pitiful state. The demi-heroes look more like bums. The OWI does its best to transform our eight honorable survivors into normal human beings. A delegation is put in charge of their appearance: during a long walk down Fifth Avenue they are gradually, and as if by magic, provided with food, clothes, and shoes. Sartre emerges from a store smiling beatifically in his new pin-striped suit. The famous old sheepskin jacket he was wearing on his arrival, in which Henri Cartier-Bresson had immortalized him leaning against the Pont des Arts, smoking his pipe, is gone.

Quickly, the eight guests are caught in a whirl of ceremonies, invitations, and meetings, starting with the French community of

New York. Centered around the OWI, the Ecole Libre des Hautes Etudes, which had successively been headed by Henri Focillon and Jacques Maritain, was accustomed to welcoming the cream of the European intelligentsia: Alexandre Koyré, Georges Gurvitch, Theodor Adorno, Herbert Marcuse, Bertolt Brecht, Thomas Mann, Etiemble, Marc Chagall, Alexander Calder, Fernand Léger, André Masson, Yves Tanguy, Claude Lévi-Strauss, and Pierre Schaeffer. Exile, distance, and American hospitality remove all sorts of conventional barriers and allow new ties to be formed in an atmosphere of exalted freedom. New York's French community goes out of its way to welcome the eight travelers: everybody wants to talk to them, they are treated like celebrities, real heroes. Introduced by Denis de Rougemont, Sartre is often invited to dinners at Consuelo's—Saint-Exupéry's widow—who lives in a handsome penthouse, previously decorated for Greta Garbo, that overlooks the East River. There, he meets W.H. Auden. Elsewhere, he encounters Calder and Léger, re-establishes contact with the Gérassis, consorts with other artists —such as Tanguy and Masson—and even attends private screenings, including *Citizen Kane.*

"Those guys who had just landed in New York," Henriette Nizan writes, "were so eager to possess America, and us with it! They were starved. At first, New York was like a country fair for them: they kept drifting from parties to banquets, from one woman to the next, from bottle to bottle."[9] For these rare birds—the first Resistance journalists to visit the United States—this enthusiastic American welcome was a little like a revenge, a response to the triumphal entry of American soldiers into liberated Paris, to the kisses of French-women. Eight French journalists, drunk with the wild welcome of this rich country, live ecstatically the second episode of the Liberation. "They had left alone, without their wives," Mme Nizan writes, "after all those years of deprivation; next to their serious American hosts, they looked rather bizarre. Their life here was going to be a parenthesis, a sort of one-night stand, which made them look like Martians, inconsequential."

On January 20, at five in the afternoon, they have their first press conference in a small room at the offices of the OWI. "The two women, wearing extravagant black hats, are already seated behind a table when the six men walk in: three are tall, two average, and the last is small; the eyes of five out of six are adorned with the same uniform: a pair of round horn-rimmed spectacles. Viollis speaks of her clandestine activities: the composition and dissemination of articles and pamphlets for the CNE, in Paris, before she escaped to the Drôme. Bénichon talks about the unity of the different Resistance movements, and of the "meaninglessness of their ideological differences." But it is Denoyer who has the strongest impact: preceded by his reputation for having won the Strasbourg Prize for the best prewar articles on America and a fellowship from the Rockefeller Foundation, he has numerous admirers in the audience. In his elegant English, he speaks of the bombings and the complex reconstruction of large provincial cities such as Rouen and Le Havre. But, above all, he salutes the friendship between France and America. "We know all we owe to countries like Great Britain and the USSR, but America played a decisive role in our life: we all know that without her we would not be here today. Our task, during our stay in your country, will be to observe and understand you so as to provide France with a more precise and more exhaustive image of her surest allies." There follows a barrage of questions: "Were all the members of the Resistance communists?" Villers answers: "François Mauriac is definitely not a communist, nor should we forget that one of the most influential clandestine papers was *Les Cahiers du Témoignage chrétien*, founded and directed by a priest." Much to the surprise of the American journalists, Sartre remained totally silent throughout the two hours of the press conference, his eyes drifting here and there, clearly bored.

Just a month earlier the *Atlantic Monthly* had published his article on the French Resistance, the first on the subject to appear in English translation: "The Republic of Silence." The biographical note stated that he was "the author of *The Wall* and several philosophical essays, and one of the leaders of the CNE, that he had devoted himself to underground activities with sublime courage, establishing contacts among literati of different political stripes, organizing illegal publications, in short, representing, along with Aragon, Eluard, and Paulhan, the most brilliant tendencies of postwar French literature." Sartre had been awaited with curiosity and interest, and his silence was received as an unbearable mark of disdain at a time when only Saint-Exupéry, among contemporary French writers, had achieved renown in New York—*War Pilot* had been praised by the critics and, in 1942, *Night Flight* was made into a movie. To most Americans, the man who had disappeared in flight on July 31, 1944, was still the most prestigious French writer.

. . .

"De Gaulle Foes Paid by U.S., Paris Is Told": the first page of the *New York Times* of January 25 bears a rather alarmist account of Sartre's first article from America, just published by *Le Figaro* under the headline "French Journalists in the U.S.: France As Seen from America, by Our Special Correspondent Jean-Paul Sartre." This first article causes innumerable letters of explanation to go back and forth across the Atlantic. The invitation of the eight journalists by the State Department has taken place in the rather complex and confused framework of Franco-American relations established between the armistice of 1940 and the Normandy landing of 1944—an extremely subtle framework within which de Gaulle was resented and often violently attacked.[10]

"Never forget," de Gaulle had written in 1943, "that the whole affair will take place not between us and [General Henri] Giraud, who is no one, but between us and the government of the United States." After the landing of the Allies in North Africa and Admiral François Darlan's assassination, it is clear that the nomination of Giraud as Darlan's successor is a U.S. maneuver. "Washington is desperately trying to have Giraud pass as the head of the French Resistance," de Gaulle bitterly remarks. The long opposition between the two French generals will be only the visible tip of the iceberg: it seems—as the research of contemporary historians tends to confirm—that Giraud was a pawn that the Americans used to counter the communist threat they saw in the person of de Gaulle. In June 1943, Eisenhower invites both de Gaulle and Giraud to meet with him and demands that Giraud be kept in the post of commander-in-chief. Roosevelt comments, "Both the British and the American governments oppose letting de Gaulle have full authority over the French army at this time because they do not know what he might do." American pressure on the internal affairs of France becomes so heavy toward the end of 1943 that de Gaulle brings it up with Churchill: "Why do you seem to think that I should present my candidature for power in France to Roosevelt? There is a French government. And, in this field, there is nothing I can ask either of Great Britain or of the United States." Tensions continue till the landing of June 6, 1944 when the U.S. government has to admit the mediocrity of its pawn, Giraud, who has no sense of politics and no support. His hand somewhat forced by the situation, in July 1944 Roosevelt finally invites de Gaulle to the White House. "He can't easily forget four years of mistrust and arguments," the general writes of Roosevelt in his *Memoirs*, upon his return. As for Roosevelt, he will note that "de Gaulle is very touchy about anything that concerns the honor of France." General Douglas MacArthur had recently confessed to a French journalist, "As an American and a soldier, I am ashamed of the way in which my country has treated your chief, General de Gaulle. The shame with which my country has covered itself in that sad North African affair won't be easily washed away. I can't help expressing all my disgust for Roosevelt's, and Churchill's, attitude toward General de Gaulle." Perhaps the warm welcome extended to the French Resistance journalists was an attempt by the U.S. government to "wash away the shame" of which MacArthur spoke.

"The welcome we have received here is brotherly and moving," Sartre explains in one article, but then he adds, "Americans love France. But they have two images of France and two ways of loving it." In a deliberately antagonistic fashion, he announces that, in order to understand the "real meaning" of their journey, one should first have "a brief historical account of the Franco-American relationship as it has been lived by the people of this country since June 1940," and he then launches into just such an account. He is relatively tactful, and even finds a way to save face for the U.S. Government by revealing its partial innocence in the whole matter. And yet the simple mention of this shameful period is enough for some Americans to react angrily.[11]

Sartre's thesis rests on what he defines as the division of America: two camps opposed to each other in their perception of either a "frightened France" or a "revolutionary France." In a way, he is providing an explanation for those campaigns in the American press, which, at the beginning of 1943, as a mark of their hostility toward Giraud and his team, had revealed the persistence of prison camps in Morocco and the preservation of anti-Jewish laws in Algeria, despite the American landing. In the *New York Herald Tribune* of January 19, 1943, Walter Lippmann had even demanded the immediate replacement of the American envoy Robert Murphy, whom he denounced as the official responsible for these sinister affairs. In his article, Sartre will refer to Lippmann by name as well as to other Americans who, availing themselves of the American tradition of freedom of expression, had alerted the public to the misdeeds of the Giraud administration and American intervention in French internal affairs. Sartre also favorably mentions the Gaullist association "France Forever," which however represents only a small percent of the French population in the United States. Then, he talks about the press: "I do not want to mention names, but there [are] certain French journalists, at first Gaullists but then bought by high finance or subsidized by the State Department, [who] published a newspaper in French that did great damage to our cause." This little sentence would evoke an avalanche of letters and clarifications from both sides of the Atlantic and every side of the political chessboard.

Some American journalists found Sartre's article guilty of "lack of tact." One of these was the Paris correspondent of the *New York Times,* who immediately sent his paper a response in which he wondered whether the article in question was "a wise move." "Some of these observers are impressed by the fact that, just when France wants so much from America in the form of arms and supplies, the entire American aspect of Gaullism should be so conspicuous on both sides of the Atlantic."[12] At this point the editor-in-chief of *Le Figaro* chimes in to reassure the *Times* of his warm, pro-American feelings. Geneviève Tabouis—editor of the paper *Pour la victoire,* which Sartre accused of hindering the cause of the Resistance—is cut to the quick and full of indignation; in an open letter to the editor of the *New York Times* and in a long article for her paper, she expresses her anger at what she considers "an insult not only to the French writers who have found refuge in this country since 1940, but also to the American Government and to the American people." Without refuting anything, she criticizes the lack of politeness of this "anti-American clique," official guests of the U.S. government, and particularly of Sartre who, instead of "reporting on the American war effort," wastes his time launching "a violent diatribe against a number of Americans, friends of France."[13]

Sartre immediately responds with his letter to the editor of the *Times:* "I have never lost sight of the fact that I am a guest in the United States. . . . I know that your paper has defended our cause. I want to assure you of one thing. The criticisms that I have made and will continue to make will stem from a spirit of deep friendship for the United States. I will continue to report under my own responsibility all that I like and that attracts me in your country. I didn't have to wait to reach New York to feel a deep affection for all I know of your country. I am not saying all this only because of your soldiers who are fighting to defend our borders, which no Frenchman will ever forget, but also because men of our generation have been influenced by your literature, and because during the Occupation we turned our spirits toward you, the greatest of all free countries. I hope that these few words are sufficient to dispel a misunderstanding that is painful to me."[14] He deliberately assumes a stance against American financial powers and the pro-Giraud group in New York—already in trouble since one of its members, Henri de Kerillis, has just been accused of collaborationism—a position that some are going to see as a further "false step." For, however banal, Sartre's assertions are in direct violation of the ethical code tacitly in force among journalists, which demands the respect of group solidarity. Determined to keep the most absolute independence of mind, in his articles home, Sartre will continue to describe the "civil war" between the supporters of Giraud and those of de Gaulle in New York. He will speak of this "new Dreyfus affair" that is "dividing the best families," will recall the change of mind of the State Department, which "supported Giraud for military reasons," and will describe the enthusiastic welcome that de Gaulle receives in America, as a real "victory," which "signifies the triumph of one image of France over the other."[15]

The incident is immediately seized upon by the Gaullists in New York, who, under the auspices of Henry Torrès, are members of "France Forever" and publish the weekly *France-Amérique*. "It looks as if we are smack in the middle of a typical Sartre incident," Torrès writes. "As concerns the great writer, we maintain the very favorable impression of him we had before his arrival: he has given proof of his faith in Anglo-Saxon democracies under the most oppressive circumstances, thus jeopardizing both his freedom and his life." Regarding his colleague Tabouis, he adds: "Hush, hush, Madame Cassandra! My dear Geneviève, in the name of an old friendship, which has often made me tolerate your shortcomings, please allow me to tell you something: you lack the attributes to teach a lesson to one of our Resistance heroes. . . . You have insulted General de Gaulle for months and years, you have refused to recognize the existence of a Resistance and, under the pretext of your love for America, you have tried to separate it from France."[16]

And, in the wake of this incident, the eight journalists—those "heroes" who "for four years had not only risked torture but, with their underground papers, had also insured the free circulation of information"—are received with great emotion in the offices of "France Forever," where they are admired for "the way in which they speak of hunger, cold, destruction and pain as if they were daily companions, without melodrama."[17] "What to say about Jean-Paul Sartre?" the article goes on to wonder. "Despite his brilliant literary successes, he has remained a modest, charming, simple man. In his

recent journalistic efforts, the great writer has once again shown us
that he will not play around with the truth."[18] The reception was
followed by a banquet at the restaurant Chez Félix. Presided over by
Guérin de Beaumont, the general consul of France, it lasted well past
midnight, due to innumerable mutual toasts to both France and
America.

Meanwhile, not terribly interested in the details of the American
war effort, completely independent of conventional journalism, in
search of his own dreams, Sartre continues his discovery of America.
Camus will never tell him, but he is disappointed that the articles
Sartre sends *Combat*— which got him the job to begin with—are
more technical and bland than the ones he sends to *Le Figaro*, which
are much more elegant and picturesque. But Sartre is bored and
awkward when it comes to writing about Franco-American politics,
just as he is brilliant and exciting when he speaks of literature.
"What's new with French literature?" Denis de Rougemont asks
him on his arrival. "Well right now there are two great writers,
Albert Camus and Simone de Beauvoir." "Albert Camus?" "Yes,
Camus. He is an Algerian writer, a 'pied-noir,' and my absolute
opposite: handsome, elegant, a rationalist."[19] And, delighted, Sartre
hurries to prepare his first lecture.

In a veritable ode to Camus, Sartre talks of the old guard—Gide,
Giraudoux, Anouilh—and the new: Camus, Cassou, Leiris. "After
publishing many clandestine articles," he says, "often under very
dangerous conditions . . . they have gotten into the habit of thinking
that writing is an act, and have developed a taste for action. Far from
believing that the writer has no social responsibility, they demand
that he be always ready to pay for what he writes. In the underground press, every line that was written put the life of the writer
and of the printer in danger. . . . For all these young writers, to speak
is a serious matter, and to write even more so. Since they know that
their works automatically commit the reader, they want to commit
themselves completely to their works. And this is why everybody in
France today speaks of 'committed literature.' " Sartre speaks in a
terse, firm voice, without a trace of lyricism. He speaks without
emotion, hands in his pockets, serious and attentive. "In Camus's
somber, pure work one can already detect the main traits of the
French literature of the future. It offers us the promise of a classical
literature, without illusions, but full of confidence in the grandeur
of humanity; hard but without useless violence; passionate, without

restraint. . . . A literature that tries to portray the metaphysical condition of man while fully participating in the movements of society."[20] Here, Rougemont joins in: "This idea that man is at once free and responsible—" he begins. "I know perfectly well where I took it from," Sartre interrupts. "From *Politique de la personne*, Rougemont, 1934."[21]

*H*ow to understand a foreign country without a mastery of its language? How to ask for directions in the street? How to speak of literature, cinema, politics? How to read the papers? Till now, Sartre has visited only French émigrés who have helped him in the transition. What kind of America can he perceive on his own, without outside help? Aside from the architecture, the landscape, the music, he must be helped with everything else, and this is a situation he does not like: "When you don't know what to answer," one day he tells Pizella, who shares his handicaps, "just say 'fine.' It can be applied to everything—women, men, whisky, health, weather, music, cinema, cuisine, the army, the air force, civil or commercial aviation, roller skates, or a stab in the back."[22] Sartre, too, increases his English vocabulary. Soon, he'll be heard ordering a "whisky on the rocks" or a "whisky and soda," or answering, "Why not?" In the meantime he continues to survey New York, gradually adjusting, discovering new languages, new means of communication: "Walls speak to you," he discovers. "To your right, to your left, there are billboards, neon signs, large shop windows. . . . Here you see a woman with a distraught face offering her lips to an American soldier; there, it is an airplane, throwing bombs and, under the image, the words: 'No more bombs, just Bibles.' "[23]

Gradually, his love dance with the city changes: the two partners are slowly getting accustomed to one another. "I love New York. I have learned to love it. I have gotten used to its massive blocks, its large perspectives. . . . My eyes . . . run immediately to the horizon, looking for buildings lost in the mist, mere volumes, an austere frame for the sky. The moment one's eyes learn to encompass the two rows of buildings, which, like tall cliffs, flank a large artery, one is fully rewarded. . . . I have learned to love its skies, the avenues of Manhattan. . . . It has taken some doing, but now I can say that I have never felt as free as in the middle of a New York crowd."[24] A full-time citizen of New York, he appreciates the rituals and customs that cement a thousand cultures together: the weather forecasts on the radio announcing hurricanes, storms, and blizzards; the fear of direct gazes; the respect for other people's turfs; the great rhythms of crowds, the flow that drowns you and carries you beyond mere walking, transforming you into a full-time member of this large club, at once too selective and too democratic, into, as Claude Lévi-Strauss puts it, "this texture riddled with holes. . . . It was enough, to choose them [the holes] and to slip into them to discover, like Alice on the other side of the mirror, a variety of worlds, all so enchanting as to seem unreal. . . . Nowhere else more than in New York, could one find, at those particular times, easier means of evasion."[25]

In the meantime, the group has moved to Park Avenue, between 49th and 50th Streets, the Waldorf-Astoria, elegant art deco emblem of the thirties, covering a whole block with a perfect fusion of European between-the-wars taste and American gigantism: 1,800 rooms, a tower six hundred and twenty-five feet tall. . . . The largest hotel in the world, according to the brochures. But in some ways the journalists' most exciting discovery is the barber shop in the basement where for $4.50 each, the men are massaged, deep-cleansed, and shaved, their faces wrapped in hot then cold towels, the height of New York luxury and exoticism.[26] "Like every European today, at first I was struck by the wealth of New York, and then, little by little, I began distinguishing the signs, if not quite of privation, of some austerity." And here Sartre lists the various restrictions that burden the population, like the "brown-out," where the lights of the city are turned on to only half their capacity. "Of course, any Frenchman accustomed to the gloomy nights of Paris couldn't but be struck by this profusion of lamps, neon signs, street lights. But the American used to prewar luxuries feels a certain sadness weighing over even the livelier districts. . . . In short, I have gradually begun to recognize, beyond the opulence that stuns all Frenchmen, the first signs not of discomfort but of a careful, parsimonious economy."[27] Shunning official receptions and fashionable cocktail parties in favor of the working-class dance halls of Times Square and the movie houses of Broadway, Sartre begins to decipher another American reality, to conjugate sadness, comfort, and angst, among the sailors who, dreamy and remote, dance the jitterbug and the kids who fight in the streets. Once he has adjusted to the city, he will also be able to distinguish the different atmospheres of different districts and different avenues, to recognize the "mournful elegance of Park Avenue," "the cold luxury and stucco impassivity of Fifth Avenue," "the gay frivolity of Sixth and Seventh Avenues," "the food market that is

Ninth Avenue," "the no-man's land of Tenth Avenue," "the wretchedness of the Bowery."[28] He will go to night clubs, movies, and will look for jazz.

His students at the Lycée Pasteur, particularly the pianist Jacques Besse and Bernard Lamblin, two real jazz fans, had bemoaned the fact that Sartre was not a passionate follower of the most avant-garde tendencies of jazz—he knew nothing about hot jazz or boogie-woogie. They had found the reference to "Some of These Days," in *Nausea* somewhat specious. Sartre learned a great deal from them, and now he is in New York. Seven years earlier, Charlie Parker, then eighteen, had left Kansas City to go to the Savoy, in Harlem, to listen to Chick Webb's drums and Art Tatum's piano. Soon, he had found himself playing with Kenny Clarke, Dizzy Gillespie, Lester Young, and Thelonius Monk in sordid joints along 118th Street. While Sartre was in New York, Charlie Parker was one of the pillars of the famous 52nd Street, the street where, during the war years, seven clubs had opened, all in a row. The "Bird" was performing at Jimmy Ryan's, at the Onyx, at the Famous Door, at the Three Deuces, in this oneiric space between Fifth and Sixth Avenues, which featured such jazz greats as Sidney Bechet, Howard McGhee, Coleman Hawkins. It was the street of jam sessions, the street where bebop was born; years later, it was renamed "Swing Street."

"I found out in New York City that jazz is a national celebration," Sartre writes, still reeling from his nights at Nick's Bar. Suddenly he is aware of the artificiality of French jazz, "a pretext for a few tears in good company." In one of the sacred places of the New York night, he writes of the "national celebrants": "They sit down in a smoke-filled room, beside sailors, tough guys . . . whores, and women of the world. . . . No one talks. . . . There's a big man blowing his lungs out trying to follow the gyrations of his trombone, a merciless pianist, a bass player slapping his strings without looking at the others. They speak to the best part of you, the most unfeeling and most free, the part which doesn't want sad songs or sprightly ones, but a moment of deafening explosion. They make demands on you; they don't baby you."[29] He stays there, among his underdogs, forgetting both Plaza and Waldorf-Astoria; he stays there, in New York, exactly where he had dreamed he would be. "Jazz is like bananas; it has to be eaten on the spot," he writes.

He is often seen, particularly at the One-Two-Three bar, on 52nd Street, in the company of a smiling young woman about his height. Between the two wars, while she was an actress in one of the theaters

236

on the Rue de la Gaîté, in Montparnasse, Dolorès V. had often noticed a group of intellectuals sitting at a table in either Le Dôme or La Coupole, and had learned that one of them was the author of *Nausea,* which she had not read. Since the beginning of the French broadcasts for OWI, she had been in charge of the *"show féminin,"* which she prepared, wrote, and read every day with marvelous aplomb. Her low, well-modulated voice united the purest Parisian humor and the most unabashed New York expressions. Her spontaneity, generosity, directness, and informality were extraordinarily popular in the offices of the Voice of America. André Breton, who had published some of her poems in his journal *V.V.V.,* was particularly sensitive to her beautiful oval face, the purity of her smile, her refreshing nonchalance, her permanent good mood, her natural culture, her extreme honesty, and the way she passed from frivolity to gravity. She was his ideal companion whenever, accompanied by Lévi-Strauss, Georges Duthuit, and Max Ernst, he visited the antique shops on Third Avenue to buy a stone mask from Teotihuacan, or the dealer in South American knickknacks on 55th Street. At a moment when John Dos Passos and Koyré were asking to meet Sartre, Dolorès was still confusing his name with that of a sculptor, Raoul Del Sarte, whom she had once known. Sartre will meet her for the first time on a day when he and his group are invited to the offices of the OWI for a series of interviews.

"In front of my office there was a long line of French journalists waiting to enter the recording studio," Dolorès remembers. "At the very end of the line there was this little gentleman, the last and the smallest. At some point he knocked against something and dropped his pipe, then he picked it up and that's when we started talking. I don't remember what we said to each other, but whatever it was, once it was said he asked me whether we could see each other again."[30] Sartre tells her about Simone de Beauvoir, Olga, Wanda, Bost, Le Havre, he tells her everything, at length. "He was in a state of constant effervescence," Dolorès says. "He kept telling all sorts of stories to amuse you and draw you into his life. He was always looking for the things that could please you, going out of his way for you, and always giving his very most." He asks her a thousand questions about her life in New York. She helps him read the newspapers, translates his conversations, shows him the places she loves. She takes him to the Russian Tea Room, that beautiful, glossy place with its red curtains and waiters dressed as cossacks, where, behind a glass of vodka and a vatroushka, they watch famous people eat.

"Look, Stravinsky," she once said. "And there, further down, half hidden behind her hair, Garbo." And he didn't believe her, refused to recognize that they were in fact there, so unimpressed was he by famous faces.

"*D*OLORES GAVE me America," a sixty-nine-year-old Sartre will tell Simone de Beauvoir in 1974. But it is the State Department whose duty it is to show the country to its guests, and a particularly elaborate itinerary is concocted for them. For eight weeks, they travel aboard a military plane—a B-29 bomber—chartered exclusively for them. From north to south, east to west, from Quebec to New Orleans, from Philadelphia to San Francisco, from Detroit to New Mexico, they crisscross the misty American sky of this winter of 1945.

Smiling and relaxed, they are initiated into an experimental technique for the desalination of seawater. Smiling and tense, they board one of the patrol boats that had landed in Normandy, then visit the Twentieth Century-Fox studios in Hollywood. Frazzled and worn out, binoculars around their necks, they follow the maneuvers of tanks and armored cars at a U.S. Army training camp in Virginia. They participate in a debate at the University of Manitoba. They attend a concert of classical music, a posh cocktail party given by the *Chicago Sun,* and a meeting of midwestern farmers. They visit a parachute factory, a naval operations base, the Pittsburgh Chamber of Commerce, a Boeing factory, the dam at the Tennessee Valley Authority, and an infantry school in Georgia. On February 11, their pilot, ignoring the stormy weather, plunges into the Grand Canyon and follows it for 300 miles of narrow meandering, almost grazing the stone walls, revealing to his terrified passengers natural sculptures in pink and purple, Gothic cathedrals and lunar landscapes, finally to reach the end of the tunnel in the blue sky of New Mexico, on the strange plateau between Albuquerque and Taos, where they find the mysterious Indian cities of pink earth and the soft cubes of adobe houses.

On January 31, in Baltimore, they listen to Lawrence Drake, the secretary of the Committee for Postwar Redeployment, describe his plan of action. On February 21, in Chicago, they meet the local press. On March 3, in Washington, they are again questioned at length about food shortages during the German Occupation, try to correct the false information published in a not very scrupulous American press, denounce the "slanders" of Geneviève Tabouis, and predict heavy French dependence on American exports in the years to come. Also in Washington, during a cocktail party given by Walter Lippmann, they unconditionally maintain that de Gaulle is "the right man at the right place." On March 11, in Washington, in chambers of the House of Representatives, they hold a press conference after a banquet in their honor organized by the Foreign Affairs Commission. The press honors them with headlines, photos, and articles, reminding the public of their courage, heroism, and determination, and amply quoting from all the new information these ambassadors of an underground and unknown war have brought with them. Thus, the American journalists learn that the STO systematically requisitioned all young men between the ages of twenty and twenty-five, that the Gestapo killed a hundred thousand innocent civilians, seventy-five thousand in Paris alone, that the press changed and renewed itself under the influence of the Resistance, and that the entire French population was now eagerly awaiting the visits of many Americans in the future.[31]

And, the highlight of the journey: their visit to the White House, on March 9, and their meeting with President Roosevelt. A press conference is followed by private conversations. "As he shakes our hands," Sartre writes, "I look at his brown earthy face, so very American. . . . He does not look at all like his photos. What strikes one first of all is the profoundly human charm of this long face, at once hard and delicate. . . . He smiles at us, he speaks to us in his low, slow voice. He loves France: in his youth he biked all over its roads." The French journalists express their desire that the "high clouds that still hover over the two countries" will soon entirely dissipate. This is a perfect opportunity for the American president to publicly erase and somehow annul his long and powerful mistrust of de Gaulle; indeed, Roosevelt tries to explain that the supposed frictions between the two governments are merely an invention of the press, citing as proof the particularly cordial relations between himself and de Gaulle when de Gaulle visited him in the United States. The eight journalists reproduce these assurances in their entirety for the French public. Sartre titles his article for *Le Figaro*, "President Roosevelt Tells French Journalists of His Love for Our Country."[32] The trick has been played, the trip has paid off, the "heroes" of the French Resistance have accepted the tacit regrets of the American president, who is doing his best to wipe the slate clean by insisting on the warm wishes he wants the eight messengers to convey to the general. "We are good friends," he concludes. Does the general ever get the message? It does not really matter since Roosevelt dies less than a month later.

He stubbornly ignores weapons, bombers, tanks, hydroplanes. He is equally silent about receptions, social functions, idyllic scenes, pro-forma courtesies. His articles from America will never figure in the pantheon of his most brilliant works: flat, flooded with numbers, indigestible, they describe at length industrial enterprises whose ramifications they seem to ignore. Thus, a very scrupulous piece written for *Combat* tries to convince us that the Tennessee Valley Authority is a "democratic effort" since, "it attempts to bring together both individual initiative and private enterprise into a vast cooperative centered around a strictly limited state organization."[33] Elsewhere, he indulges in long didactic digressions about the unions: his readers learn to distinguish between the AFL and the CIO; they learn the form that what they call "the class struggle" assumes in the United States; they find a description of the American boss, "who never quite represents a particular social class," and a few vivid portraits of workers: "I have crossed the workrooms," he writes, "during their fifteen-minute break and was struck by the dreary stupor on their faces."[34] We learn at the end of another article, "on the American streets, a worker can't be distinguished from a bourgeois: there are no exterior class signs."

His reports from Hollywood on American cinema are more involved and authentic. "Los Angeles, March 11, no blackout. In the evening, the city sparkles with all its lights over a stretch of forty miles, like a long trail of milk. . . . Hollywood has changed. . . . The old stars, the ones we know in France, no longer want to act. . . . Other stars have been mobilized: Robert Montgomery, James Stewart. . . . The newer stars, Jennifer Jones, Ingrid Bergman, Betty Field, less well-paid, don't have the glamor of their predecessors. The foreign visitor's first impression of Hollywood is that American cinema, the cinema he has dreamed of during four years, has lost some of its vitality. . . . I haven't found anything that could stand up to *Hallelujah, The Crowd, The Fantastic Cavalcade.* It seems as if, with peace, something has been lost. And yet, something has also been gained." Sartre has long conversations with Vladimir Pozner, a Hollywood writer, and gathers the necessary information to write technical articles about screenwriters and sneak previews.[35] "We have had silent films and then the talkies. Now we are witnessing the renaissance of the intellectual film," Pozner tells him, and Sartre mentions *Casablanca, Tomorrow the World,* and *The Searching Wind* as examples in an article for *Combat.* "I attended the private screening of a movie by a French director, the admirable *The Southerner,* which Renoir has adapted from a novel about small Texas farmers and which has not yet been released in New York. . . . Growing up, American cinema has lost its grace, its childish charm, its joy in expression. But it has gained other qualities, including a taste for historical accuracy."[36]

On the racial problems of the South he is vibrant and impassioned. The individual excursion—with which each of the eight completes the tour—brings Sartre to Texas and New Mexico. Villers and Pizella, for example, choose a less sociological, more political trip: they go to the Pacific islands to meet General MacArthur and return to France triumphantly with a scoop, a confidential message for de Gaulle. "The misery of the farmer is nowhere more profound than in some regions of Texas and New Mexico," Sartre writes. "America is a colonial country, and it is precisely to our French colonists in Morocco that, despite the differences, I would like to compare American workers."[37] Later, back in France, he will further refine this new awareness of racial injustice. Articles, essays, lectures, even a play will bear the traces of a social outrage that grew out of the trip abroad. The dockers of Le Havre and their grievances before the creation of the Popular Front had never been able to stir him to action, just as French elections had never much interested him. It is far from home, far from his daily reality and his sociohistorical connivances, that his first endorsement of a purely social cause takes place.

"In this country, so justly proud of its democratic institutions, one man out of ten is deprived of his political rights; in this land of freedom and equality there live thirteen million untouchables. . . . They wait on your table, they polish your shoes, they operate your elevator, they carry your suitcases into your compartment, but they have nothing to do with you, nor you with them; they are concerned with the elevator, the suitcases, the shoes; and they carry out their tasks as if they were machines. . . . They know they are third-class citizens. They are Negroes. Do not call them 'niggers,' you'd hurt their feelings. . . . In the South they constitute an essentially rural proletariat. Sixty-four percent of the entire Negro population of the United States is employed in domestic or agricultural chores. . . . Segregation is practiced everywhere in the South: there is no public place where one sees Negroes and whites mix. . . . They sit apart in trains and trolleys; they have their own churches and their own schools, much poorer than those of the whites; even in factories they often work in separate rooms. These pariahs have absolutely no political rights."[38] The article continues implacably, as flat as a legal document or a declaration of war. This is probably one of the most unexpected consequences of the trip organized by the State Department.[39]

What Is Literature?, *Anti-Semite and Jew*, *The Respectful Prostitute*, these are some of Sartre's works that, in the months to come, deal with the reality he has discovered in America. His recent awareness of the black problem is enhanced by his friendship with the American writer Richard Wright, whose autobiographical novel, *Black Boy*, was published in March 1945. Wright was born in Natchez, Mississippi, three years before Sartre. At the beginning of 1945, he would confront two ostracisms at the same time: that of the American Communist Party, which he publicly abandoned—"Today, I no longer consider the Communist Party as a viable means for social change"—and that provoked by a daily, insidious racial segregation in allegedly enlightened Greenwich Village. "When the war is over," he wrote in his journal of January 20 and 21, 1945, "and if I have the chance, I want to leave the racial hatred and other American pressures, to go live in a foreign country where I can devote all my time to my work."[40]

Sartre was not yet aware of the problems Wright was going through at the time; he met him only later in Paris. But he did witness a number of shocking scenes in the United States. One occurred while they were traveling by Pullman between Baltimore and Philadelphia. They had barely started eating dinner when two black army officers approached the maître d' and asked for a table, which they were immediately and brutally refused. Aware of how this fact disturbed the French guests, the interpreter who was traveling with them in turn approached the maître d'. After a short, discreet discussion, the two officers were seated at the back of the car, but a pink curtain was delicately drawn between them and the rest of the patrons.[41]

"On February 7, X telephonically contacted the office and said that one of the French journalists had observed the posters of the Nazi spies recently put out by this Bureau, and wanted a copy of the poster. . . . Subsequently came to the office and was given copies of the poster, stating that . . . did not know what this journalist wanted to do with it." "On February 24, X telephonically advised our office in Washington. . . . X is in possession of a report of the visit of this group to the airplane plant in New Orleans manufacturing PBY flying boats. This report reflects that the journalists were interested primarily in employee welfare, the percentage of women workers employed, and the production lines. They likewise expressed great interest in the uses to which the PBY ship is put. . . . These individuals appeared to be above the average in intelligence and spoke excellent English, some of them, but did not display much technical knowledge." The FBI men don't miss a single stop, emphasizing with great relief that the visit to such and such a factory of amphibious engines "has not yielded any confidential information." Quite ironic for our Nick Carter fan that his every movement will be recorded: it will be known that at the Washington Statler he shares room W 808 with Villers, that at the Hotel Saint Anthony, in San Antonio, he is alone in room 327, and that, "on March 1st, Jean-Paul Sartre has not followed the program organized at Schenectady, and has instead left the city in the afternoon on a train that seemed to be bound for New York City."[42]

*A*ND, INDEED, Sartre once again distinguishes himself from the rest of the group. After the official journey is over, he returns to New York City. He savors the pleasures and the freedom America affords and is apparently not too eager to return to French political reconstruction. He again meets Henriette Nizan and informs her of his intention to put a stop to the communist campaigns against Nizan. She tells him that, since 1941, she has been teaching *Nausea* in one of the courses she offers at the New Jersey College for Women, an extension of Douglas University. It is the first time Sartre's work has been taught in an American university.

He tries to find some authors for Gaston Gallimard, who has given him carte blanche to sign book contracts. He has dinner with the publisher Jacques Schiffrin, who, forced to leave France, the Editions Gallimard, and his own collection, La Pléiade, because of the racial laws, is now working with Kurt and Helen Wolff at Pantheon Books. He again meets one of his old schoolmates from the Ecole Normale, Jean Albert Bédé, who is now teaching at Columbia University. He gives a few more lectures on contemporary French literature. He has an interview with poet Archibald MacLeish, at that time an assistant secretary of state; he again meets Dolorès and finally returns to Paris in May.

243

"My life was to be a series of adventures, or rather one adventure," Sartre explains in 1974, recalling his childhood dreams. "That was how I saw it. The adventure took place more or less everywhere, but rarely in Paris, because in Paris you don't often see a Redskin leap out with feathers on his head. . . . So the necessity of adventures compelled me to conceive of them in America, Africa, and Asia. Those were the continents made for adventure. . . . So I began to dream that I would go to America, where I'd fight with roughnecks and come out of it safely, having knocked around a fair number of them."[43] He saw some Indians, he saw some gangsters, he was even received by the president and admired his collection of small donkeys, the emblem of the Democratic Party, in all sort of shapes and materials: rubber, marble, plastic, clay. That was reality; Buffalo Bill and Nick Carter remained dreams.

THE SARTRE YEARS
1945–1956

PARIS: THE ERA OF EXISTENTIALISM

URING THE spring, summer, and fall of 1945, the French found
in their newspapers a quantity and continuity of information
that the recent freeing of the press and the greater availability
of paper rendered more gripping than ever. They learned about the
gas chambers and crematory ovens, "located in a brick building right
outside the barbed wire," as Jacques-Laurent Bost, special correspondent from Dachau, wrote for *Combat.* "Above the gas chamber
door there is the inscription 'Shower.' " They learned that, on May
7, at 2:41 A.M., Germany had unconditionally surrendered. They
learned about the beginning of the Pétain trial and about Paul Valéry's death, which occurred on the same day: while the eighty-nine-
year-old marshal was protesting his innocence and refusing to
answer questions, the seventy-four-year-old poet was receiving the
honor of a state funeral. Writers played a powerful yet delicate role
in both the settling of the national scores and in the washing of the
country's dirty laundry, a role that showed them, in turn, as heroes
and as scapegoats: winning here what they lost there, and constitut-
ing a new national category as responsible and as exposed as the
soldiers and politicians. For a few heated months, men of letters were
going to become men of action.

During the summer, fall, and winter of 1945, the French followed
the gradual sketching of a new social order and the reconstruction
of a new national equilibrium out of the still hot ashes of the old one
—a reconstruction that involves the selection of promising new
actors and the demise of old ones. "If Pétain has ever given of
himself, it was surely as a whore," Albert Camus writes in *Combat.*
"And certainly not to France." "No man has ever betrayed his
people in such a foul manner," Paul Reynaud declares. "Pétain has
plotted against the state," M. Herriot writes. General Weygand,
Edouard Daladier, Léon Blum take the stand. Pétain's trial lasts into
August. On August 15, 1945, he is sentenced to death. Two days later,
General de Gaulle, president of the provisional government, com-
mutes the sentence to life imprisonment. It is a show trial and a
laughable sentence since a few men are publicly assuming the re-

sponsibility for the behavior of a much larger group of people and for an ideology that will continue beyond them. Then there is the Laval trial, and on October 15, Pierre Laval, former head of the Vichy government, faces the firing squad. Finally, in November, the great trial against war criminals begins in Nuremberg, and Otto Abetz is temporarily jailed in the Strasbourg citadel. After a stormy trial, the academic Abel Hermant is sentenced to life imprisonment. On December 3, 1945, in Paris, the publisher Robert Denoël, who has published Céline, Rebatet, and Hitler, is murdered on a street near his house. A few days later, Louis-Ferdinand Céline is discovered and arrested in Copenhagen. The "bad" are eliminated, the "good" are hailed. In the wake of these purges, a new race of writer-heroes emerges. On November 22, General de Gaulle nominates André Malraux as his minister of information: in the press conference that follows, he makes a point of recalling the duties of writers vis-à-vis politics. A few days earlier, Romain Gary has received the Prix des Critiques for his first novel, *Education européenne,* and has also seized that opportunity to remind the public of his recent past as a Gaullist in London, as a man of letters in uniform.

"Parisians have been lining up to vote," *Combat* announced on October 16, 1945. "The Constituent Assembly has been elected," the headlines of the following day proclaimed. When, in November, General de Gaulle announced the composition of his government, few were surprised at the alliance it proposed: Maurice Thorez and other communist ministers were in it. Members of the Gaullist and communist Resistance were going to rule the country together, in a rather precarious balance. During the spring, summer, and fall of 1945, the French learned from their newspapers how to read France according to a new scale of values. This included the problems of daily life, such as new bread rations, and the frequent power cuts in the capital: "Due to lack of power, cafés and restaurants will be closed three days a week," it was timidly announced at the end of December. It was also announced that publishers would receive 40,000 tons of paper in 1946 and that, consequently, students wouldn't be able to buy new books till the end of the year.

The autumn of 1945 saw the reopening of the literary season. Like the political field, the artistic field had been decimated. The CNE meetings had worked hard, the previous year, trying to decide if only writers were to be punished or if publishers should, too. The issue was settled with a call for moderation, which did not, however, rescue Brasillach from the firing squad on February 6, 1945. That year, the Prix Goncourt was given to an unknown young novelist, Jean-Louis Bory, for his novel *My Village Under German Occupation*. The Prix Interallié went to the communist writer Roger Vailland for *A Strange Game*. On the stage of the Théâtre Hébertot, *Caligula*, the new play by Camus, was unanimously hailed. The title role was marvelously played by an unknown, twenty-three-year-old actor, a student of the Conservatory, whom Simone de Beauvoir described as "an angel": Gérard Philipe. Meanwhile, at the Théâtre du Carrefour, Olga Dominique (née Kosakiewicz) was acting in *Les Bouches inutiles*, Simone de Beauvoir's first play. "A natural," Robert Kemp described the young actress in the theater column he wrote for *Le Monde*.

Every day, the newspapers would announce new books, shows, talks, and lectures. Roger Caillois spoke about the Argentinian Republic since the revolution of June 8, 1943; Maurice Rostand about Sarah Bernhardt. A pastor publicly wondered "What to Rebuild?" while a professor of chemistry announced two topics: "The Discovery of Gas Lighting and Its Consequences" and "The Respective Situations of Natural and Artificial Rubber." Parisians even had the privilege of hearing about French Corsica, the America of 1945, and the years between 1935 and 1945, the truth about ten years of history. Nothing, in the announcements of *Le Monde*, under the heading "Lectures," distinguished these titles from the flat and laconic one a reader might have noticed on Monday, October 29, 1945: "Conférence Maintenant: on Monday, October 29, at 8:30 P.M., in the Salle des Centraux, 8 Rue Jean Goujon (Métro station Marbeuf), M. Jean-Paul Sartre will speak: 'Existentialism Is a Humanism.' "

It had cost the two organizers of the Club Maintenant, Jacques Calmy and Marc Beigbeder, a great deal of money to place this announcement in *Le Monde*, *Combat*, *Le Figaro*, and Emmanuel d'Astier's *Libération*. Surely, they'd never be able to fit the rental of the room into their budget. Their advertising campaign involved their wives who posted a few bills in the most prestigious bookstores of the Latin Quarter, Montparnasse, and Saint-Germain-des-Prés. Beigbeder was quite optimistic, but Calmy was worried: "With a title like that! Existentialism!" Beigbeder had paid Sartre a visit and, together, they had decided on the title "Existentialism Is a Humanism," which, after the antihumanistic tirades involving *Nausea*, had at least the merit of paradoxical provocation![1]

An unprecedented cultural success. Scrimmages, blows, broken chairs, fainting spells. Box office destroyed: no tickets could be sold.

Beigbeder and Calmy were, by turns, satisfied, worried, terrified, embarrassed, devastated, and helpless before this tidal wave. Gaston Gallimard, Armand Salacrou, and Adrienne Monnier came. The crowd, packed together, nervous and irritable on this hot October evening, forbade anybody to enter. Only once did they make an exception: when they saw Jean-Louis Barrault and Madeleine Renaud approach, only then did social deference replace blows and wounds. Sartre had come alone, by subway, all the way from Saint-Germain-des-Prés. When he turned onto the street and saw a dense, threatening crowd congregated in front of the Centraux building, where he was supposed to speak, he said to himself, curious, "Probably some communists demonstrating against me," and considered turning on his heels. But then, on second thought, he walked on, more out of professional integrity than from any desire to confront that human tide, which he believed hostile, and, without conviction, made it to the entrance. How many of those two or three hundred listeners had ever seen his face? Sartre was certainly not the kind of person who would say, "I am Sartre, please, let me pass." Sartre did not say anything; he merely let himself be dragged back and forth, from right to left, in the rhythm of nudges, kicks, and blows; he let himself be carried, now slowly, now more brutally, all the way toward the front of the room: the journey from the door to the platform on which he was supposed to stand lasted over a quarter of an hour. Finally, one hour behind schedule, in an overheated, overcrowded, overexcited room, the lecturer began to speak.

He spoke without notes and as long as possible with his hands in his pockets. He started by defending existentialism against the attacks of the communists—who called it "contemplative philosophy, philosophy *de luxe,* bourgeois philosophy"—and against the attacks of the Catholics—"the underlining of human ignominy, the exposure of everything sinister and slimy." Then, he briefly explained his purpose: to clarify the meaning of "humanism," and, thereby, to try to define "existentialism" as "that doctrine which makes human life possible." The lecturer admitted his puzzlement at how fashionable the term "existentialism" had become, so much so that "it has lost all meaning. . . . In fact, 'existentialism' is the least scandalous and most austere doctrine, suited strictly only to technicians and philosophers." Having thus defined his domain and closed it to intruders, critics, and other intellectual thieves and having thus reinstated his favorite field, philosophy, he launched into a real philosophy course, as technical and austere as he had promised, despite the heterogeneity and worldliness of the audience, the broken chairs, the fainting spells. He respected the outline he had drawn the moment he had agreed to deliver the lecture, and did not deviate from the rigorous elaboration of his argument. The Schweitzers would have appreciated the uprightness of his behavior, his ease with success, and the simplicity which, that evening, prevented him from playing to the crowd.

His listeners submitted to his rigorous and precise analysis of the theories of Jaspers, Gabriel Marcel, Heidegger, Kierkegaard, Kant, and Auguste Comte, as well as to an avalanche of references to Voltaire, Diderot, Dostoyevski, Zola, Stendhal, Cocteau, and Picasso. It was a well-argued, interesting, varied, and sober performance. He stressed the themes of individualism, responsibility, angst, commitment, solitude, and returned to a few stock formulas such as "Existentialism defines man by his actions"; "It tells him that hope lies only in action, and that the only thing that allows man to live is action"; "Man commits himself to his life, and thereby draws his image, beyond which there is nothing"; "We are alone without excuses. This is what I mean when I say that man is condemned to be free." He added that existentialism was "a doctrine based on optimism and action." He had managed to invent the complex definition of "existentialist humanism" and, above all, to introduce a new kind of individual with whom everybody could identify, "the European of 1945," an individual whom he placed at the center of the world, and whom he endowed with the power to understand "every project, even that of the Chinese, the Indian, or the black." This magical European of 1945 was going to become very popular. Because of lack of time, Sartre's lecture was not followed, as had been planned, by a debate with his critics. When he had nothing more to say, he left.

The following day, around noon, Marc Beigbeder met him at the Café de Flore to apologize for the poor organization of that memorable evening, and to inform him of the plight he was in: although they had agreed on a fee for the lecture, at the moment the Club Maintenant was saddled with a huge bill—rental of the room, ads in the papers, damage to the premises, including a big bill for broken chairs that the owner of the Centraux had already compiled . . . Sartre interrupted, "As for my fee, forget it! Besides, it looks like we were a success!" he added, showing him the articles in the morning papers he was perusing over coffee and croissants.

"Too Many Attend Sartre Lecture. Heat, Fainting Spells, Police.

Lawrence of Arabia an Existentialist," was the title of Maurice Nadeau's article in *Combat*. Nadeau and a good number of the other reviewers delighted in describing the panic and excesses of the crowd. They spoke of "elbow fights," a "nonexistential angst," the fear of "dying of suffocation," and the repeated interventions of "those venerable old men who get immediately booed when they mention the police"; they spoke of the boos and screams—"a *No Exit* situation"—and the heat that dissolved make-up, clothes, bodies. Justin Saget, the reporter of *Terre des hommes,* carried away by his love of movies, drew a comparison between the modest room at the Centraux and Groucho Marx's ship cabin in *A Night at the Opera*, and between the deck of the *Bounty* at the moment of the mutiny and the lecturer's platform, ending with a eulogy to Sartre—oh, the shade of Jean-Baptiste—as "a great captain, the only master on board, the perfect master of his men, who appeared on the platform like foam on the crest of a wave." Did such lyrical outpourings detract from the impact of that unique evening, or did they rather contribute to turn it into the forerunner of modern "media events"? Each newspaper had something to say on the crowd that was "a mob rather than an audience," the "fifteen fainting spells," the "thirty broken chairs," and the "victory" of the lecturer. If the bellicose, comical, and nearly fantastic elements of that evening made the critics happy, the lecture itself was perceived by everybody as "a university course," "too scholarly," and the lecturer was unanimously praised for his "cool," his "courage," his "grit," his "personal magnetism," and the "impact of his mere presence."

From that day on, and much to everybody's lingering puzzlement, Sartre became a public figure. The lecture was remembered as the cultural event of 1945. In his novel *L'Ecume des jours* (1947), Boris Vian recounts the adventure in burlesque fashion by having a certain Jean-Sol Partre fend his way through the crowd with an axe, all the way to the platform, while his fans arrive by hearse, parachute, and the sewers. It will be a crucial text for the elaboration of the Sartrean legend. Vian's satire, however, fails to provide any real explanation for the unexpected tidal wave of that evening. All the more unexpected considering that, the same evening, at the Théâtre du Vieux-Colombier, in Saint-Germain—where *No Exit* had been performed a year earlier—Julien Benda, author of *The Treason of the Clerks*, had delivered a lecture in a large, comfortable, and totally empty room. The Sartre phenomenon had been born.

Throughout the fall of 1945, the name of Sartre, whether alone or alongside those of his friends on the literary scene, was relentlessly hammered into the mind of his compatriots. "Existentialism? I don't know what that is. My philosophy is a philosophy of existence," he had declared only two months earlier during a symposium in Brussels. But in October 1945, overwhelmed by both the press and the very public that had appropriated the term, Sartre himself used it, giving in to what, by then, had clearly become a new fad. Of course, Sartre was a man of formulas, and his work allowed everybody a niche of his own. It could be read in several ways; it could respond to several needs: *Nausea, The Wall, Being and Nothingness, The Flies,* and *No Exit*—to mention only his literary works—were providing the Sartreans of 1945 with new tools, new formulas, new models, and, particularly, new heroes, for all sorts of uses and situations.

*A*ND YET, the first step had already taken place a month earlier with the joint publication of the first two volumes of the trilogy *The Roads to Freedom*: *The Age of Reason* and *The Reprieve*. Their publication had been immediately followed by the first issue of Sartre's review: *Les Temps modernes*. After *Nausea*, a philosophical novel, and *The Wall*, a collection of short stories and novelistic extracts, *The Age of Reason* was awaited as Sartre's first real novel, and all the more so in that his talents as a critic and a theoretician had already enjoyed great success, and his readers were anticipating judging the novelist in relation to his literary theories. The mechanisms of Sartre's mind, that's what people were going to look for in *The Roads to Freedom*. "The only thing left to do for a writer who can do what he pleases with his pen," André Rousseaux wrote in *Le Figaro*, "is to make a name for himself with a big novel, one of those copious, abundant novels once the norm in America." The imminent publication of the two first volumes of *The Roads* was already assuming the traits of a challenge, a bet, almost a gamble.

The Age of Reason, originally called *Lucifer*, was conceived immediately after the last sentence of "The Childhood of a Leader"— the final story in *The Wall*—even though its elaboration went quite slowly. Sartre planned and began the manuscript at the very beginning of 1939. He kept writing it during the first months of the phony war, and concluded it by stages, between December 31, 1939 and the end of the summer of 1941, endlessly writing then erasing the words "The End." Then he had the urge to publish the finished manuscript: "The book should come out in October [1940],"² followed by sudden scruples: "Sartre shelved his manuscript because no publisher would have dared touch such a scandalous thing," according to Beauvoir.³ After all, his characters had really *lived* with the soldier-writer of the phony war; he had been close to them, observed them, seen them, loved them, spent time with them, remembered them in all his letters, and, finally, put them on a stage and watched them move, react, tremble. Ivich, Boris, and Mathieu became the fictional homologues of Olga, Bost, and Sartre. Then he started the second volume, *The Reprieve*, which he wrote between 1942 and November 1944. Though they had been conceived and executed during two very different periods, both volumes were made available to the public on the same day, and were an immediate success. The hazards of war had worked in Sartre's favor.

In September 1945, at the end of the war, the French were introduced to the adventures of a character, Mathieu Delarue, the hero of *The Roads to Freedom*, who resembled Sartre as a brother—same age, same profession, same way of life. And they followed him, both in *The Age of Reason* and *The Reprieve*, through the months of June and September 1938, as he wandered from café to bistro, from bistro to night club, forever accompanied by his growing disillusionment, his desperate romanticism, his anarchism, his marginality, his esthetic of failure, his frustrating self-consciousness, his individualism, his freedom. With him, the age of reason, far from springing out of a rupture, still partook of a certain adolescence. He floated easily between his last mistress's abortion and the rebuffs of the student he courted, receiving and dealing blows in a life without frills, heroism, or pretense.

"My intention was to write a novel about freedom," the novelist explained. "I wanted to retrace the path followed by some people and social groups between 1938 and 1944. . . . I decided to tell *The Age of Reason* in an ordinary way, by simply showing the structured relationships that link a few individuals. But then come the days of September 1938, and all the barriers collapse. . . . In *The Reprieve* we'll find again all the characters of *The Age of Reason*, but now they are lost in a crowd." And, referring explicitly to his models Zola, Dos Passos, and Virginia Woolf, he concludes, "I picked up their project at the very point they had left it off, and tried to find something new in it. Only the reader can tell me whether I have succeeded or not."⁴ There is pride in this profession of public faith, in this open and blunt declaration of his intentions.

"Jean-Paul Sartre has definitely taken his place among the greatest French writers of our day. . . . His powerful talent has affirmed itself with rare brilliance": Louis Parrot for *Les Lettres françaises*. "If Sartre's ambition was to force the doors of literary history, he has succeeded. . . . Like all great novelists, he also enjoys the privilege of having a universe of his own": Gaétan Picon for *Confluences*. "The masterpiece of the contemporary novel": Maurice Nadeau for *Combat*. Maurice Blanchot: "This meeting of a philosopher and a man of letters, both equally excellent, in the same man is a direct outgrowth of the way in which both philosophy and literature have made him receptive to such a meeting." In *Le Monde*, Emile Henriot aims his barbs at the "professor of existentialism and admired master of a good part of today's youth," and then warns the reader against a "disgusting book that exhales the obnoxious odor of latrines." "If books could smell," Louis Beirnaert follows suit in *Etudes*, "one would have to hold one's nose in front of Sartre's latest books. . . . Sartre's objective is, very clearly, to show life through its excrement and lower the value of existence to the level of the gutter and the dump." As for André Billy, in *Le Figaro*, he despises the language of a novel that "has caused a scandal with the daring and the crudeness of its portraits, the limpness of its characters, and the pessimism and disgust with life that it exudes." He is joined, on the side of the moralists, by Claude Benedick, of *La Marseillaise*, who sounds the alarm: "It is at once strange and disquieting to witness the emergence of a theory that justifies all sort of excesses at a time when courage and discipline are more necessary than ever. This theory is, of course, particularly dangerous when it is promoted by one of the most powerful writers of his generation."

An increasingly complex image of this uncommon man of letters, of this talented philosopher begins thus to develop between the Sartre who is perceived as a "danger to French youth," and the Sartre who has been raised to the level of the "giants: Balzac, Zola, and Proust" (Pierre Maulet, *Renaissances*).

Mathieu Delarue, this character conceived in 1938 at the time of the Munich agreement, developed on the eve of World War II, remodeled and refined in the course of the phony war, and, finally, perfected during the first months of the French Resistance, became a paradigm of the postwar period. Mathieu Delarue appeared in 1945 and brought along with him all the historical challenges of the prewar period: the nonchalance, the deceitful calm of June 1938, the growing tensions of September. With his hesitations and his choices, he offered the perspective of a thirty-five-year-old man on a prewar period that, as of 1945, had not yet been analyzed or reconsidered.

The publication of the two volumes of *The Roads to Freedom* in September 1945 produced such an avalanche of articles because it occurred at a strategic moment during the renewal of the French press after wartime censorship. The regulations of August 26, 1944 started the age of freedom and provoked a real revolution in French journalism: hundreds of new publications and extreme competition. The three ministers of information who succeeded one another in 1945—Pierre-Henri Teitgen, Jacques Soustelle, and André Malraux —witnessed the birth of thirty-four dailies in just one year! "The revolution that has transformed the French press," Raymond Millet writes in 1946, "still astounds the rest of the world; it has no precedent. No other country has ever witnessed such an extensive renewal!"[5] At the same time, Camus, in *Combat,* warns, "The value of a country can often be measured in terms of its press . . . we have found the means to start the revolution we have so long desired. But we have yet to carry the day."[6] Well prepared and well under way, the Sartre phenomenon that exploded in the fall of 1945 became an ideal product for this starved press, the first real media product of the postwar period. Starting with his first essays, published in *Combat* and *Le Figaro,* Sartre's history will become entangled with that of the French press, and this almost uninterruptedly till the day of his death. But more than just a media product born out of the euphoria of an exalted liberation, Sartre became also an actor, and a central one at that. The first issue of *Les Temps modernes,* the review he directed, came out in October 1945.

"*T*HE MOST important event of the week is, without any doubt, the first issue of *Les Temps modernes,* " a critic in *Le Figaro* notes on November 3: "We had all expected it to be the review of the third party. Next to those two large families of acolytes—the Marxists and the Christians—who try to play a role in the rapid change of beings and things, *Les Temps modernes* proposes its own path. It really looks as if now our literary life, like our political life, has its 'three heroes.' " A similar comparison could not fail to arouse public interest at a time when de Gaulle and Thorez were going to govern side by side, and when the political scene was split between the socialists and Gaullists, on one hand, and the communists, on the other. Symbolically, *Les Temps modernes* was already assuming traits that belonged neither to one side nor the other, but were rather, unmistakably, Sartre's own.

The public waited for the first issue of *Les Temps modernes* as much as it had waited for the first two volumes of *The Roads*. The review, announced as a monthly, had a sober, indeed almost austere cover —red and black letters alternating against a white background—a classic format—6 by 9 inches—a title that alluded to Sartre's Chaplinesque tastes, and a large editorial board: Raymond Aron, Albert Ollivier, Michel Leiris, Jean Paulhan, Beauvoir, and Merleau-Ponty. The editor-in-chief was Sartre. Among the review's innovations, an announcement, in bold type, at the end of the table of contents, that the editor-in-chief "receives every Tuesday and Friday from 5:30 P.M. to 7:30 P.M."

Doubtless what most appealed to readers of that first issue were Sartre's "Présentation" and his first article, "The Nationalization of Literature." His Présentation was immediately recognized as a manifesto. "The writer has a place in his age," he wrote. "Each word has an echo, as does each silence. I hold Flaubert and Goncourt responsible for the repression that followed the Commune because they did not write a single line to prevent it. It was none of their business, you may say. But then was the Calas trial Voltaire's business? Was Dreyfus's sentence Zola's business? Was the administration of the Congo Gide's business?" Accusations, diatribes, appeals to honored ancestors, outright condemnations, formulas: a pure manifesto. Six years after the attack on Mauriac, this was far more violent, the work of a "headhunter," according to one critic. Sartre hammered out his program and definitions: to change at once man's social condition and the conception he has of himself; to bring literature back to what it once was, a social function; to turn *Les Temps modernes* into a research instrument; to encompass all literary genres: from poem to document, from report to inquiry; to consider our time as a "meaningful synthesis" and to envision its different manifestations with a "synthetic mind"; to welcome all those of good will and to serve "committed literature." The age of "committed literature" had a resounding start.

Such an avalanche of Sartrean statements could either irritate or convince. It irritated some, like Gide, who had escaped Sartre's massacre by a hair: "The manifesto of *Les Temps modernes* is quite disturbing," writes Gide, still unwilling to engage in a frontal attack and be kicked in the teeth like the rest of his colleagues. "I truly hope that, after literature he will also 'commit' painting and music."[7] The famous author of that masterful slap that was the *Retouches à mon 'Retour de l'U R S S'* " (Revising My "Return to the USSR"), Gide ironically provokes his adversary, by recalling, not without condescension, his own experiences in the "country of the Soviets." "I remember," he wrote, "an exhibition of Russian painting in Tiflis. There wasn't a single work that did not shun personal value in favor of political commitment; even in the edifying choice of subjects." Some grind their teeth, others give their warmest approval. "The match promises to be exciting," the critic of *Le Figaro* jokes under the heading "Sporting News." "Lots of Sartre in the news. An overflowing presence: novels, theater, lectures."[8] "As for being a premier intellectual, Sartre's not bad," the critic of *Terre des hommes* writes, "a born writer, endowed with uncommon resources."[9]

*T*HE SARTREAN products that saw the light in the fall of 1945 developed ideas that had been ripening for some time: while *The Age of Reason* was conceived before the war, the idea for *Les Temps modernes* had been formulated with Beauvoir and Merleau-Ponty, and later with Camus and Leiris, in the wake of the discussions held by "Socialism and Freedom," and, more urgently, after its failure. The arrests of Yvonne Picart and François Cuzin had moved Sartre to reassess the reality of political action and to reconsider his own limitations. The review was the result of this new awareness. Aron, Paulhan, and Ollivier, however, would soon resign from the editorial board. "I really don't see how this review can help being boring and false. But in literature, everything helps," Jean Paulhan had written to Gide as early as December 10, 1944; all he would grant Sartre was limited attention, a wait-and-see attitude, and minimal participation. The *Nouvelle Revue française*— compromised by Drieu's political stance during the Occupation—had earlier been discontinued.

With the creation of *Les Temps modernes*, Sartre began settling down; he became the editor-in-chief of a review, ran a prosperous business, received sympathizers: he held real power. After the intellectuals, his first fringe of readers, he had reached the public at large with his articles and, particularly, his plays, and with *Being and Nothingness*, the culmination of the philosophical texts he had produced between the two wars, he had also infiltrated academia. And now, in 1945, he was returning to the public with two novels, a review, and a number of lectures. The conquest was global, "synthetic," as he himself liked to put it, a total seizure of power. He shocked and disgusted the right-thinking bourgeoisie, relic of a France that years of rampant Pétainism had kept behind the times. He offended the communists, who now proudly occupied the seat of honor in the French political arena. But, in the fringes of the "third party" that had been hailed by the critic of *Le Figaro*, he fascinated and seduced: people fought to meet him, to know him, to watch him think. Thanks to Sartre, in 1945, a writer was no longer simply a man of letters. He became, among other things, a juggler of ideas, a thinking animal.

*I*T WAS just such a wonder that, on October 29, at 8:30 P.M., drew four hundred people to the hall of the Centraux, on the Rue Jean-Goujon. His "intellectual acrobatics," according to Maurice Nadeau, fully justified this interest.[10] Would Sartre have been so surprised if he had realized the size of his audience, the devotion of his followers, the power and resonance of his voice, and the legitimacy it had by now achieved?

During the years of failure, the cursed cycles of 1935–38 and 1941–42 —as an intellectual he had operated in a void. Now in 1945 he could let his talents multiply and flourish, freely. But what an incredible naïveté lay behind the incredible output. He is all involved in a dialogue with himself, then with the rest of the world. The two steps are not necessarily related: Sartre was neither a demagogue nor a hypocrite. He was determined to succeed, and did, crushing others in the process with the incredible superiority of his talents and his megalomania, but the results surprised him. The Protestant in him was responsible for the astonishing simplicity with which he accepted his success till the end. It pleased him, naturally, but it did not interest him: he preferred to move on, plowing his furrow, incessantly listening to his ongoing interior dialogue, and delighting in the increase of his possibilities, in the range of his explorations and his conquests thanks to a phenomenon that he had called "magical": knowledge.

If, during the fall of 1945, Sartre and his existentialist products gave the impression of a real invasion, of a flood, it was simply because they reached all possible publics. Simultaneously accepted and recognized by both academic thinkers and the public at large, he was thus able to bring the notion of commitment into a field from which it had always been absent: philosophy. And could connect the notion of freedom with that of being simply by using the passwords of the milieu, the most scholarly philosophical rhetoric.

Some time after the first lecture, the organizers of the Club Maintenant planned a purely philosophical evening. They invited the philosopher Jean Wahl to deliver a "Short History of Existentialism" and other philosophers to counter his arguments. Thus, Nikolai Berdiaev, Georges Gurvitch, and Emmanuel Levinas devoted a whole evening to the analysis of the roots of existentialism—Kierkegaard, Husserl, Heidegger. "I haven't yet read *Being and Nothingness,*" Levinas confessed, "but I suspect that the new philosophical excitement contributed by Heidegger's thought is based on the distinction between *to be* and *being,* and the investment of being with the relation, movement, and efficacity that had, till then, resided in existing. . . . When, in his novels, Sartre italicizes the verb *to be,* when he underlines *am* in: 'I *am* this suffering,' or in 'I *am* this nothingness; he is insisting on the peculiar transitivity of the verb to be."[11]

R EAD OR neglected by his peers, Sartre became the object of debates, analyses, interpretations, and commentaries that they could not ignore. Soon a book, *For or Against Existentialism,* gathered together both detractors and sympathizers. Besides "family" members Colette Audry, Francis Jeanson, Jean Pouillon, Jean-Bertrand Lefèvre-Pontalis, there were, on the side of the critics, Emmanuel Mounier, Roger Vailland, and Julien Benda. "Existentialism?" Benda wrote. "It is simply the modern form of an eternal philosophical stance."[12]

Sartre imported into the French novel techniques borrowed from the American novelists he had praised, and into French philosophy the currents he had found in Germany and in Denmark with Kierkegaard. Heir to the solidest French intellectual tradition, he subverted its classical models with tools made abroad. "French novelists won't enrich our literature by discovering America" was the immediate defensive reaction of all right-thinking people, in this case represented by the weekly *Samedi soir,* which, for years to come, was to turn Sartre into the bête noire for an entire segment of the French population. In the words of this newspaper, he is a crook, counterfeiter, traitor, a bandit who pollutes, bastardizes, and prostitutes the French cultural heritage: "Touraine is not peopled with Negroes who spend their time singing spirituals and drinking Jamaica rum to drive away the ghosts. Dijon does not look like Chicago, nor do Parisians walk around drunk on whisky."[13] Latent xenophobia, rabid protectionism, cultural hypernationalism: the last live and active tendency of the Pétainism of 1940 survives by scapegoating Sartre.

The simultaneous publication of a novel and a play by Simone de Beauvoir further sharpens their quills: it is evident that Sartre, "this academic brat, who raises his head from his books to enflame the studious tables of the Café de Flore with the fiery breath of a literary revolution," and Beauvoir, this proper young woman, brought up according to the best standards of the French aristocratic tradition, are trying to corrupt French youth. "Shady hotels, drunken nauseas, abortions, dreary nights, stale love affairs: the novels of Sartre and Simone de Beauvoir confront us with the seamier side of existence. They attempt to uproot the French novel from the bourgeois universe in which it has almost constantly been from *La Princesse de Clèves* to Laclos, Stendhal, Proust, and Giraudoux. Here, politeness, elegance, refined feelings, harmonious language, all those ancient characteristics of the French novel have been irrevocably discarded."[14]

Corruption, filth, depravity, debauchery, atheism, treachery, moral license, countless other vices: a whole panoply of flaws is invoked by upright citizens to denouce Sartre's circle, so pernicious in both its intentions and its effects. "To the hairy adolescents of Saint-Germain-des-Prés," the same weekly goes on, "he is the 'master.' For all right-thinking citizens, he is a 'murderer.' But what in the world has M. Sartre done to so stir our souls? It's simple: he has spread a new fashion throughout the living rooms of both banks, a fashion centered around a rather nebulous philosophical abstraction, a doctrine of German origin that goes by the barbaric name of 'existentialism.' Nobody knows exactly what it means, but everybody speaks of it over tea. We have not witnessed such a promotional triumph since Barnum."[15] Of course, no analysis of the doctrine in question is ever volunteered: readers are only, repeatedly, told that it comes from abroad and alters and disfigures the purity of French culture.

"Celebrity for me meant hatred," Sartre later admits. And, in fact, he owed much of his notoriety to the hysteria of *Samedi soir*. Even the Church of France eventually became involved and, toward the end of the forties, innumerable sermons warned all believers and followers against the diabolical dangers of "existentialism." "Existentialism is a worse danger than rationalism" became a frequent refrain.[16] Such formulas and distortions contributed to the diffusion of Sartre's name among the populace. The "enemy within" became the "existentialists" with their false creed "existentialism" and their mentor was Jean-Paul Sartre; the center of their sinister activities, the amusement park where they could be observed at play, was Saint-Germain-des-Prés. The formula was easy and it worked wonders: soon a whole legend full of sensationalism was built up around "Sartre and the great Sartreuse." Thus began the quest for the most scabrous, the most outrageous, the most sordid details concerning the private life of the two monsters, an activity that provided a good part of the French population with an outlet for all the tensions accumulated during the war years, an easy revenge against the triumph of the Resistance. The "existentialists" were an ideal postwar prey. The public was told that Sartre lived at the Hotel de la Louisiane, on the Rue de Seine, "in a penumbra of spilled ashtrays and scattered clothes," as the article further indicated before indulging in an explanation of how the very name Louisiana evoked "memories of the Civil War, negro spirituals and handsome Confederate soldiers." It also appeared that Sartre enjoyed inviting young women up to his hotel room to have them smell a Camembert! "A few years ago," another anecdote ran, "a hapless customs officer asked the author of *Nausea,* on his way to America, to open his suitcase. The officer plunged his hand in a mess of clothes and underwear, pulled out some garment or other, and, gasping for air, told the author 'Quick, quick, move on!' "[17] Often the attacks involve more serious allegations: "Existentialism is also an excellent business: Today, the existentialists ... invade theaters, bribe the press, enslave the publishing houses, publish a review whose title, *Les Temps modernes,* has been borrowed from Charlie Chaplin, and try to convince American capitalists that they hold a monopoly on French thought." It is believed that "Sartre wants to impose his doctrine and his rule over the entire world."

This was the tack employed by *Samedi soir*: "Beware, the enemy is right outside your door!" "Current decadence of show business ... the Parisian public has the shows it deserves ... the crushing responsibility of the public."[18] Or else, a little later: "After literature, even cinema is gnawed by the worm of politics."[19] "Montparnasse is resting on its laurels. ... Where can one go? To Saint-Germain-des-Prés, of course, to bump up against a few existentialists."[20] "If you want to be published, you must be *swing* [sic], frequent cafés and dance the *jittersburg* [*sic*]."[21] Guilt, protectionism, nationalism, all the old phantoms return. Hitlerian nostalgia and xenophobia: "The Only Photo of Eva Braun and Hitler," announced the head-lines of *Samedi soir* on July 7. "Himmler died in the arms of a Jew," another article claimed shortly after. As for racism, that was a daily treat: "Mouloudji, the child of sorrow and the errand boy of existen-tialism, will have his revenge," one read on February 1, 1947. Jean Genet was portrayed as the "jailhouse angel," in another article, which mentioned his close friendship with Sartre. On November 24, 1945, it was announced that, in Montparnasse "only Le Dôme has seen the return of some of the Israelites that the German occupation had dispersed; they have come back to look for their coreligionists." Sartre's name was next to de Gaulle's in a news item that proclaimed them as the two French best-sellers in the United States. "Much to their surprise, people abroad have learned that the French often forget material problems to engage in passionate arguments about existentialism."[22] The spite and irony of foreigners was, of course, invented in order to reopen the wound of nationalism. In the fall of 1945, France split once again in two, as it had done in June 1940, at the time of the armistice, and it split along precisely the same lines: one side cloaking itself in the ample folds of a moralistic, conformist hypocrisy, thus protecting itself against its new enemies, the existen-tialists, its new oppressor, foreign philosophy, and its new obsession: Sartre and his hordes of followers.

"*W*HAT DO you think of existentialism?" a journalist asked Ro-main Gary after he won the Prix des Critiques. With a short embarrassed laugh he answered that he did not know what it meant, since he had had very little contact with French literature for the past five years. "There is no doubt about it," Pierre Fauchery writes in *Action*. "There is a small existentialist world; very closed and nar-row, a sort of freemasonry."[23] "Existentialism has become a kind of catchy tune," André Billy added. "It is impossible to go out to dinner without being pulled aside by a pretty young woman, who, in a tone of shy intimacy, will ask you the ritual question: 'Would you please tell me what existentialism is all about?' "[24] "I am not an existential-ist," Albert Camus explained.[25] "Camus is not an existentialist," Sartre confirmed.[26] "What is existentialism?" Henry Magnan seri-ously wondered as he asked the philosopher Jean Beaufret to indulge in an historical explanation for *Le Monde*.[27]

Existentialism, like faith, cannot be explained, it can only be lived. . . ." In her *Petit Catéchism de l'existentialisme pour les profanes* (Little Cathechism of Existentialism for Laymen), Christine Cronan offered an accelerated, hypervulgarized course in existentialism, a digest for every occasion: key words, various manifestations, philosophical origins. The book sold like hot cakes. Now everybody could speak of existentialism. "Question: What is existentialism? Answer: Existentialism is the belief that man creates himself through his actions. Question: Who has brought existentialism up to date and made it fashionable? Answer: Jean-Paul Sartre. Question: What is the basic premise of existentialism? Answer: That existence precedes essence." From the most elaborate and sophisticated products to the simplest, thinnest by-products, the fashion of existentialism kept on growing, spreading along a series of concentric circles, and reaching, circle by circle, what Sartre would later call "the total public." Or as Christine Cronan put it, in verse, "In your commitment you will incite/ All humanity. . . . Relentlessly you will create/ By your acts alone."[28]

In no time at all, existentialism began to represent, haphazardly, and for no apparent reason, a philosophical current, a way of life, a "religion," and thus became a vast category that could accommodate just about everything French society had rejected as deviant, marginal, dangerous, anarchic. Soon the term "existentialism" grew to encompass all the new ideas circulating at the time. The result was a ridiculous mixture, the pure product of media speculations, the unrecognizable bastard of a collective paternity, all quite extraneous to *Being and Nothingness,* or any other work by Sartre. From German phenomenology, we had thus moved on—much too fast—to an "ism," a meaningless word that everybody seemed to understand, a presumed philosophical movement that everybody seemed to know, a vague and nebulous daily behavior that everybody seemed to adopt.

*I*T IS not surprising that Sartre would balk at the uncontrolled skid that this sudden and much too brutal fame wanted to impose on him. Later, he will have to pay for it, but for the moment, he is caught and deformed by this new role. No longer able to control what people say about him or to repudiate the remarks attributed to him, he is stuck in an infernal machine. Soon, he will even have the impression that his own creation is eluding him, that he can no longer quite understand it. In three months, and solely because of his own literary production, he has managed to be compared with the most famous men of letters, those very ones who had enjoyed the most intense relationship with the people. The Sartre who is accused of corrupting the nation's youth is compared to Socrates. The Sartre of the cafés, the messianic bohemian, is another Diderot. The Sartre of political commitment speaks, almost despite himself, for Hugo and Zola. If he entered the world of legend as the old lecher luring his virginal prey with a piece of Camembert, he is now quickly evolving, and not without some humor, into the composite offspring of a variety of centuries and a number of forebears, writers, philosophers, men of action. The geographical center of existentialism is perceived as Sartre's neighborhood: Saint-Germain-des-Prés. Gradually, over the past five years Sartre and his group have moved from Le Havre, then Laon, then Montparnasse toward a new center, which, for at least ten years, beginning in 1945 will become, or rather become again, the absolute center of the cultural and literary life of France and even the world. Saint-Germain-des-Prés was often called a village, because of its church, its square, and the narrow streets on both sides of the Boulevard Saint-Germain. And it had layers of cultural tradition—of erudition and adventure, of pleasure and revelry, of science and criticism, of Molière, Diderot, the Benedictine monks and the surrealists. It had sheltered monks, clowns, scholars, actors, revelers, painters, deputies, poets, and writers. Each configuration of this magical place had inscribed itself on the previous one: when, in February 1941, Sartre decided that it would be more comfortable to write near the warm stove of Père Boubal than in his hotel room, he inherited, almost in spite of himself, this tradition.

*I*N THE winter of 1941, Sartre, Simone de Beauvoir, and their friends established residence at the Café de Flore. Before this, in 1938 and 1939, they had met in Montparnasse, either at Le Dôme or at La Coupole, or else, further out, at Les Mousquetaires, on the Avenue du Maine. Larger, less intimate, more open, Montparnasse did not provide them with the absolute guarantees of security they needed in those difficult and clandestine times—whereas at Père Boubal's Flore, one could work for whole days near a coal stove, behind thick curtains, which, in that rigorous winter, also saved a good deal of money. Smaller rooms, the proximity of narrower village-like streets and of their new hotels had attracted them to Saint-Germain-des-

Prés at the same time that a restless, intense, and nonconformist postwar generation was replacing the quarter's prewar regulars. After the Liberation, in 1945, aspiring actors and young intellectuals got into the habit of having their coffees at the Café de Flore or the Deux Magots, or a grog at the Rhumerie Martiniquaise, or a beer at the Reine Blanche. Soon, to people in their twenties, the area became synonymous with disenchanted nonchalance, frenzied freedom, and the discovery of excess. The public space of a café and the intimate corners of a village were the privileged places in which one could speak freely and abandon oneself to dreams and chance encounters. A new society was born of this flexibility, these mixtures, these various meetings.

Sartre and the new fauna of Saint-Germain-des-Prés shared a number of attitudes and tastes, including a form of exoticism centered on blacks and jazz, an esthetics of angst, a hunger for new experiences, the cult of populism, and the subversion of traditional values via language. When, toward the end of 1946 and the beginning of 1947, the cellars of Saint-Germain-des-Prés, now rediscovered, were invaded by bebop dancing and jazz musicians and drew to their sleepless nights all those who found an answer, a sympathetic esthetic, or simply a provocation in the exaltation of the senses, the press wasted no time in dubbing the cellars *caves existentialistes,* thus blending a life-style—Sartre's—and a philosophical theory—also Sartre's—with the behavior of a whole generation, without bothering to verify that they knew each other or were even aware of each other's existence. It did not matter that Sartre hardly ever visited the cellars. All that mattered was that both Sartre and this new generation criticized traditional values, and that both shared a liking for jazz, discussions in cafés, free love, a bohemian life, and a certain disenchantment. "Those young people have nothing to do with me, and I have nothing to do with them," Sartre kept insisting, somewhat exasperated.

"Don't go looking for existentialists at the Flore. They are no longer there. Now they have taken shelter in cellars. . . . That's where the existentialists, probably waiting for the atomic bomb they so love, drink, dance, make love and sleep. Existentialism has ripened so fast that it is already divided by a class struggle. Today one can easily distinguish between rich and poor existentialists." Barely eighteen months after the famous autumn, *Samedi soir* is featuring a special issue, a cross between an exhaustive, if maniacal, anthropological handbook and a scandal sheet. The whole thing is introduced by a photo of a couple: they are young, attractive, they both lean against what might well be the entrance to a "cave." The low slant of the flaky wall and the lit candle the man holds in his hand are meant to suggest it. Both wear identical gray clothes, androgynous uniforms, and look totally inoffensive, indeed quite sweet and contemplative, twenty-year-old children. In their faces one may recognize two stars of the postwar period: Juliette Gréco and Roger Vadim. *"Caves existentialistes," "rats de caves existentialistes,"* "existentialist suicides," "rich existentialists" and "poor existentialists," "young existentialists" and "old existentialists," both noun and adjective are declined *ad nauseam,* just as had happened for "snob," "enragé" (angry), and "branché" (in the know). The term soon loses its precise meaning, only vaguely designating a certain group of people moving within an ambiguously defined perimeter and sharing a few nebulous characteristics.

That Sartre had, some time earlier, written a song for Juliette Gréco did not help matters. And the fact that he not only knew the trumpet player Boris Vian but had invited him to write a column, "the liar's news," for *Les Temps modernes* further complicated them, while Sartre's well-publicized weakness for young women and actresses somehow justified all sorts of weird matings and wild guesses. Although seldom seen at the Bar Vert, at the Tabou, at the Club Saint-Germain, at the Canne à Sucre, at the Montana, at the Mephisto, Sartre was nevertheless cast as the intellectual-in-residence, and his name was associated with the changes in Saint-Germain-des-Prés—from the age of the café to that of the "cave," and then from that of the "cave" to that of the boîte, or nightclub. And then, one day, the fashion ended. Why? Saint-Germain had never been, despite its revolutionary vocation, a popular neighborhood, like Montmartre. "It never had a Rue de la Gaîté," Jacques Prévert guessed. "Besides, how could it have become a real 'quartier' without any whores or peanut sellers?"[29]

*I*MMEDIATELY AFTER his return from America in the spring of 1945, Sartre learned something that his discreet and thoughtful mother had hidden from him during his absence: his stepfather, Joseph Mancy, had died on January 15, 1945. Without the slightest hesitation, the forty-year-old Poulou rushed back to his "petite maman" and, together, they moved into an oldish apartment at 42 Rue de Bonaparte, on the corner between the church of Saint-Germain-des-

Prés and the Rue de Rennes. In the living room, among the false Louis XVI furniture, an upright piano on which, every morning, the four hands of the two Schweitzer heirs delighted in playing Schubert lieder and Chopin waltzes. The son had his own bedroom with a narrow single bed, a bureau, and a desk, right in front of the window that overlooked both the church and the square. Mme Mancy found a maid to help her with the housework and to wash and iron Poulou's shirts. But, for the rest, she herself took care of the famous man that her son had become, with both admiration and awe for this "ugly duckling" she had brought into the world. She behaved like the perfect mother, sweet, loving, exceedingly helpful. To her friends, she often expressed her surprise at the hostile criticism her son would now and then receive, but she never dared express the slightest reaction in front of Sartre himself. Indeed, what a difference between "the head of French existentialism" concocted by the media and the man who, sitting at the upright piano, took such pleasure in deciphering Schubert with his mother!

"THE SPIRITUAL leader of thousands of young people," as Paulhan had called him after *No Exit*, had, just a year later, become the talk of French society. What he had brought to the cultural life of his country was a real rupture; things, after him, would never be the same. "Who will replace the hero of the novel?" Nadeau wondered in *Combat*. "Will it be an event, as Sartre thinks? Only the future will tell."[30] To some, Sartre represented the rape of French thought by foreign trends. Whatever he set out to do smacked of heresy. Everyone recognized the connection between Sartre and the end of a certain era in French literature, the death of a prewar past. But, while the critics were wondering about the future of his review, of his novels, of his literary theory, or of his *Morale*— announced by *Being and Nothingness* — Sartre was about to disappear from the scene.

Perhaps only the journalist from *Terre des hommes* who had noticed the dedication of the "Présentation des *Temps modernes*: To Dolorès" suspected something. "Though written for the general reader," he pointed out in his article, "this introduction is dedicated to a certain Dolorès."[31] Indeed, despite her absence or maybe because of it, the woman Sartre had met in New York six months earlier had gradually acquired such a hold on him that he not only had dedicated this text to her but was already planning a second visit to America to see her again. This presented no difficulty in that he had been bombarded with requests to give courses, lectures, and interviews there. By December 15, he was ready to go, to abandon enthusiastic followers and journalists for a love affair that would take place thousands of miles from Paris.

NEW YORK

"*T*HE LITERARY lion of Paris bounded into Manhattan last week for a brief lecture tour," *Time* announces.[1] On January 28, 1946, the magazine has already put Sartre under the heading "Foreign News," section "Europe," subdivision "Existentialism." The lion arrived in New York via cargo ship, after an adventurous eighteen-day journey on a wintry sea. To see Dolorès again, he had managed to arrange a tour of lectures throughout the United States, but he could not afford plane fare. His dedication of the "Présentation des *Temps modernes*" to Dolorès was the gesture of a determined, daring, impatient, romantic, utopian lover. He had written Simone de Beauvoir in July 1945: "A letter from Dolorès pleased me a great deal. Its tone is very proper, since she has not yet received the one that I sent her via Knopf, but in fact she writes me to tell me to please write. She had to temper this with studied rigor, but, behind the words, there is a nice warmth."[2]

So, toward the middle of December, at Bordeaux, Sartre boards one of the beautifully named Liberty ships: "You must realize," he writes Beauvoir, "my Liberty ship is just a cargo ship—worse yet, a military cargo ship." The crossing takes three weeks, and the wind and constant pitching "create a void in his head." His days are endless since he cannot read and can barely write. He curses the monotony of the sea, the bad weather—"awful, stormy weather, and in the middle of the storm some engine problems"—and the captain, who's about to send an SOS. But, above all, he curses his fellow travelers, who, having recognized his name on the labels stuck to his suitcases, have been plaguing him with all sorts of stupid questions. "They fight over my books and then they give them back to me in terrible condition. They're all Pétainists and collaborationists. Some of them dream of a nice little dictatorship in France. What they say is so mindboggling; one day I had to leave the table in utter disgust because [one of them] had started ridiculing and slandering people like Vercors." In vain, he tries to elude his neighbors, impatience, and boredom, the "boredom between sky and sea," with empty gestures, flimsy flirtations, and memorable drunks. One morning he is found snoring away in a lifeboat where he took shelter to flee God knows what terrible danger. "The Brazilian consul's wife has been putting the make on me for eight days," he complains in another letter.[3]

"December 16, 1945. Good and subjectivity: Good must be done. This must mean that it is the end of an act. . . . But never mind whether Good *is* or is not. What matters is that it *must be through us.* . . . Monday, December 17 . . . This sad street I am walking through, with its big barrack-like buildings . . . it stretches as far as my eyes can see, it is my life, it is life. And what about my loneliness in Bordeaux? It was *the* loneliness, *the* renunciation of man. A problem: there are two orders. . . . Why should salvation necessarily be the fruit of a new process that automatically annihilates the previous one? Let's think. What we here call 'authenticity' is in fact a first project, or an original choice that man makes by himself when choosing his Good."[4] This is a philosopher dealing with the most intimate meandering of his thoughts, almost physically struggling with his ideas, unable to stop thinking or noting down his thoughts during the eternal internal debate that sees him constantly going back to his theoretical projects, making new notes, adding a recent anecdote—in short, a philosopher at work. And this despite the fact that he is in love, that he is seasick, that he is uncomfortably stuck on a freighter in bad weather among hostile people. And, to top it all, he is still uncertain of his reception once he gets to New York.

Because Dolorès, for whom he is undertaking this irksome journey, is not yet conquered. "I fell in love with him only during his second stay," she will tell us much later. In the meantime, the philosopher-in-love is stuck on an absurd military cargo ship, in the middle of New Year's Eve celebrations with a bunch of French conformists, haunted by thoughts of his mythical Dolorès. In the midst of a shipboard tryst, he is seized by remorse: "I've put an end to a ridiculous affair that had neither rhyme nor reason," he writes Beauvoir, "and had made me waste my time for someone I don't even respect and who would certainly have caused me great trouble had it all gone as I wished." Besides, he adds, the affair "was not nice toward Dolorès, and, I risked ending up, pitifully, disgraced."[5] Sartre is madly in love with Dolorès. Yes, the existentialist at the summit of his glory to whom *Time* magazine dedicates a cover story, with a flattering portrait—which for Dolorès will remain "Sartre's best photo"—with the incisive caption "Philosopher Sartre. Women Swooned," this man is in love.

The article is accompanied by a caricature by Jean Effel: a faun with philosophical aspirations, steeped in the reading of a huge book by Sartre, is asked by his acolyte, a centaur: "Do you get it?" "A little." But if the caricatures were imported from France, the photographs are left to Americans. And indeed, William Leftwich's Sartre, introduced by the caption as the latest Parisian craze, a womanizer, and an irresistible seducer, looks so clean, so handsome —a slightly aloof contemporary hero, a charmer despite himself. The collar of his white shirt goes perfectly with his pin-striped suit and dark tie; the neck is long, the mouth sensual, the nose regular and well delineated, the eyes are large and clear behind perfectly serious, round horn-rimmed glasses, the forehead is broad, the hair neatly combed and parted on the side, the one visible ear is big: in short, it is the portrait of a classically sensuous face. Even the strabismus is barely perceptible: the particular angle the photographer has chosen has transformed it into a slight enlargement of the pupils. By what strange miracle had the eye of an American photographer been able to find the right angle and draw out of Sartre's face some of his mother's traits: his seriousness, his sensuality, his beautiful clear eyes, his large mouth, in short, precisely those characteristics that so many had found ugly? A Sartre in full metamorphosis after the disappointments of his return from Berlin when both his work and his sentimental life seemed to have fallen to pieces and he was getting fat and he was very much aware of the first signs of aging—the incipient baldness he had coyly dubbed "embaldment." Here he was, a decade later, France's favorite son in the arena of Manhattan, elegant, handsome, successful, looking younger, and in love!

" 'Avant-garde' magazines all over the country," Dorothy Norman wrote in the *New York Post*, "are beginning to bulge with articles by or about the brilliant French writer Jean-Paul Sartre. The communists attack him. The anti-Stalinist *Partisan Review* applauds him. *The New Yorker* smiles. The fashion magazines begin to record the Sartre 'trend.' "[6] *Harper's Bazaar* commissioned from Simone de Beauvoir an intimate portrait of Sartre, which it then published under the provocative title "Jean-Paul Sartre: Strictly Confidential" at the moment of his arrival in New York. "He detests the country-side. He loathes—it isn't too strong a word—the swarming life of insects and the pullulation of plants." Beauvoir did not do things by halves. In no time, the American public discovered a number of secrets about the daily habits and most intimate tastes of this new hero, such as his hatred for greenery and his disgust for raw meat.

*W*ANDA ESCORTED him on the train from Paris to Bordeaux; the Brazilian consul's wife had courted him on the ship from Bordeaux to New York; Beauvoir had herself introduced him to the American public, and in New York he was expected by a Dolorès who was going to use all her talents to seduce him. What a dream! All his women were there, present, mindful, active, fully supportive of his glory—more than all the little fiancées of the Luxembourg Gardens Charles Schweitzer had dreamed of—all the eyes of those kindly, loving women that he would keep seducing, careful not to lose a single one. In the winter of 1946 he reigned, happy, in the middle of this feminine galaxy, heedless of both future sacrifices and broken promises. But now Dolorès alone stimulates the fantasy, the genius, the polymorphous inventions of this talented lover: songs, poems, letters, walks, compliments, surprises, conversations, burning questions, complex emotions. "He had a unique way of loving you," Dolorès remembers. "He put everything he had and everything he knew into it; he did his utmost to listen to you and understand you, and love you. He used all his intelligence and all his talents, and he inevitably succeeded in winning you over."[7] Once he had conquered, he would abandon himself entirely to his conquest. "You'd learn everything about him," Dolorès continues. "Absolutely everything. When he was in love and wanted to seduce you, he would keep on talking, questioning you, getting inside you . . ."

For two and a half months he lives with Dolorès: he shares her days, meets her friends, accompanies her to her favorite places. And on weekends, for two solid days, they stay cloistered in her apartment, for a married woman, even if she is living by herself, can seldom elude the gossip of doormen in certain respectable New York buildings where liveried men escort one from cab to the elevator and then to one's door. Dolorès calls him "the prisoner," teasing him about the hazards of his condition. "Here life is sweet and uneventful," he writes Beauvoir. Work, love, and appointments. Walks, jazz clubs, quiet bars. Weekends in the country at friends of hers. The forty-year-old Sartre finally possesses New York through Dolorès. This is her "gift of America." Dolorès, petulant, blossoming, generous, displays all her talents. Effortlessly, she produces the most sophisticated and delicious aspics, integrating her gastronomic gestures into the swirl of life, with the flourish of a real stylist. Dolorès and Sartre, a radiant couple, wander around the city, talking and joking in French slang, like two happy, rowdy children.

"Things here are the same as in Paris," he writes to Beauvoir, "everybody speaks of me and drags me through the mud. I suppose it's my fate."[8] And indeed, right-thinking Americans, alerted by the arrival of this "bleak philosophy of pessimism derived by a French atheist from a Danish mystic,"[9] were more than ready to defend themselves, with all the strength of their ethical virtues, against the infiltration of this Gallic virus. "At the time," Henri Peyre remembers, "the whole thing was blown out of proportion. In America, existentialism had a very bad reputation as a literature of defeat." Peyre, back from Cairo in 1939 to direct the prestigious department of French at Yale, and on his way to becoming a key figure in French literary and academic life in America, had invited Sartre to deliver a lecture at Yale. "Hearing that Sartre was coming to Yale," he continues, "a businessman complained to the president of the university and the chairman of the French department: he was afraid that Sartre would end up demoralizing the whole university. I talked to him myself and tried to explain to him, a businessman, how and why existentialism was a perfectly moral philosophy." Despite these misgivings, 250 people, Yale professors and students, attended Sartre's lecture, which repeated, among other things, the themes of "Existentialism Is a Humanism." "He was clear, luminous, unaffected, very affable when it came to answering questions, very cordial, very simple."[10] Sartre was particularly impressed by the army of "Sartrean exegetes" he found in the French department; besides Henri Peyre there were Jean Boorsch and Kenneth Douglas. They had already read everything, assimilated everything, and knew what questions to ask. Thus, they came to talk about the "intellectual hero" in the French novel—an exotic phenomenon to most Americans—to which Victor Brombert would later devote a marvelous book.[11]

Sartre went back to Yale and, this time, spoke of the influence of American writers on France, and, particularly, on his generation: "We were crushed," he explained, "without knowing it, by the weight of our tradition and our culture. Without a past and without help, American writers have forged, with barbarous brutality, a few

274

tools of incalculable value. . . . We have used, in a conscious and intellectual manner, what was the product of talent and unconscious spontaneity. . . . Soon, the first French novels written under the Occupation will be published in the United States. We are going to give back to you the techniques you have lent us. We will give them back to you digested, intellectualized, less efficacious, and less brutal —consciously adapted to suit French taste."[12] Two years later, the prestigious *Yale French Studies* devotes a whole issue to Sartre and existentialism.[13]

Then Sartre gave a talk at Harvard, where Jean Seznec, an old fellow student, taught: he introduced him to Harry Levin, famous among scholars of comparative literature. During dinner, just before the conference, Sartre expressed the desire to modify the theme of his talk; initially, he had planned to discuss the French approach to American novelists—"whom I didn't think he knew all that well," Levin notes. "But, you see," Sartre explained, "just before leaving Paris, I read *The Plague*, by Camus, and loved it. I would really like to talk about it, just off the top of my head." "And so he did," Levin remembers, "he stood in front of his audience and talked about *The Plague*, and it was an extraordinary talk, eloquent and enthusiastic."[14] Daring acrobat or classical lecturer, Sartre continued his tour from Yale to Harvard, from Princeton to Columbia, from New York to Toronto, from Ottawa to Montreal—he even spoke at Carnegie Hall.

And the more crowded his lectures, the more intrigued the American public, mostly thanks to the press since few of Sartre's works had yet been translated into English. Those who did not read French had to depend on the reports of others—professors, critics, anyone who could read the original in order to give them an idea of the totality of his work. By January 1946, his only texts published in English were two short stories, "The Room" (Hogarth Press, London, 1939) and "The Wall" (*Chimera*, summer 1945), one play, *No Exit* (Horizon, London, 1945), and some of his articles, like "The Republic of Silence" (*Atlantic Monthly*, December 1944) and the English version of the "Présentation," "The Case for a Responsible Literature" (*Horizon*, London, 1945 and *Partisan Review*, New York, summer 1945), and an article commissioned by *Vogue* and published in May 1945, "New Writing in France." Shortly after Sartre's trip to the United States, *Partisan Review* would publish an excerpt from *Nausea* and the article "A Portrait of the Anti-Semite," which had appeared in *Les Temps modernes* a short time earlier.

"Sartre is going to talk at Carnegie Hall? I'll be sure not to go. He's one of those types the Ecole Normale is wont to produce now and then: perfectly capable of turning out an essay of fifty pages on any subject at all in a weekend. . . . And fifty good pages at that!" This is how Marcel Duchamp, cynical and paradoxical, had introduced Sartre to Lionel Abel. Yet, a few days later, Duchamp was in one of the first rows of Carnegie Hall listening to Sartre's lecture on new tendencies in the contemporary French theater. Organized by Charles Henri Ford, editor of *View*, the evening turned into a real celebration: what the lion of French literature had to say about the renewal of the theater in postwar Europe mattered minimally since it was Sartre people had come to discover and appreciate, not his lecture. And appreciate they did, particularly when, warmed up by the cocktails that followed, he began joking about his linguistic incompetence and generally carrying on. "He told us, at once," the journalist of *The New Yorker* writes, "that he approves of New York without qualification: 'Here there are no restaurants of an exclusively intellectual clientele,' he said 'so it's easy to keep out of fights!' . . . Sartre has made two trips to the United States. . . . He first arrived in January 1945 . . . [and] stayed four months . . . travelling all over the place, and quickly concluded that he would like the country immensely if he were not under the constant necessity of visiting war factories. . . . This time he came on a mission for the Service of Cultural Relations of the French Government. . . . 'I had to lecture,' he told us, 'but I have liked lectures better than factories.' "[15]

So, what the American public noticed was something that no text could have conveyed: his human warmth, his humor, his capacity for contact. They also noticed something his photos did not show: "that he was small, stocky, with strong shoulders and a large chest." Lionel Abel, for instance, was struck by "the evident virility that emanated out of his way of speaking, by his physical strength and his attitude in front of pain," and, more particularly, by his extraordinary powers of communication. "Once you've heard him talk in public," he added, "you can't help wondering whether he could ever find himself short of words."[16] Also present at Carnegie Hall that evening, William Barrett would later write innumerable articles on Sartre for both the *Partisan Review* and the *Atlantic Monthly* as well as the famous book *What Is Existentialism?*[17] which was published the following year. "I barely shook his hand," he tells us nearly forty years later. "What I remember is that the hall was absolutely jam-packed and that there were quite a few American surrealists. Sartre was wonderful with his oratorial brio. Of course he was also preceded by the reputation that the press had created for him. But what really fascinated us was the polyvalence of his writing. It was quite unique to find a philosopher of that caliber who was also a novelist—however disappointing—a playwright, a journalist, an essayist. . . . Yes, it was all this that really got us."[18] Irving Howe, who would also, eventually, write a good deal about Sartre, was particularly interested in the extraordinary appeal of the Sartrean image: "the independent intellectual, outside of all institutions, free of all determinism," even though "it was somewhat difficult for us to think along similar lines, and particularly for what concerned politics since, here, the communists did not amount to much whereas the PCF was in power: we had a completely different analytical point of view."[19]

But Sartre was criticized for his meetings with the group from the *Partisan Review*. They invited him to lunch at a restaurant on West 56th Street and there he met Hannah Arendt, William Phillips, Philip Rahv, and Lionel Abel. They planned an exchange of articles with *Les Temps modernes*, commissioned a few texts from Sartre himself, discussed politics—of course, they all agreed about Stalin, but William Phillips was quite disappointed with the dogmatism of Sartre's arguments. "Camus was much more direct," he would explain later.[20] Sartre's later connections with the PCF would further disappoint some of his American friends. But at this lunch, Sartre was quite a success when it came to answering questions about his French colleagues. Camus? "Yes, he is a friend, a talented writer, a good stylist, but definitely not a genius," he answered. This seemed to please both Philip Rahv and Hannah Arendt, who immediately felt freer to express their misgivings about *The Stranger*. "On the other hand," he added, cutting everybody short, "we do have a real literary genius in France: his name is Jean Genet and his style is like Descartes's!' "[21] Shortly thereafter the *Partisan Review* devoted an article to Genet.

Sartre did not meet the refugees of the Frankfurt School, such as the philosopher Max Horkheimer, who was then teaching at the New School for Social Research in New York. Horkheimer had in fact told Norbert Guterman that, according to him, Sartre was just a "crook and a racketeer in the world of philosophy." "Besides," Guterman remembers, "hadn't he already admirably maneuvered his own publicity? And hadn't he, in fact, refused to write an article for *Life* because it did not pay well enough?"[22] Nor, apparently, did he meet the large number of American sociologists and anthropologists who taught at the University of Chicago, even though their research was fairly close to his own. The sociology of daily life that he had repeatedly broached in *Being and Nothingness* might well have seduced men such as Talcott Parsons, Herbert Blumer, Alfred Schutz, Gregory Bateson, C. Wright Mills, Kenneth Burke, and George Herbert Mead. *Being and Nothingness* would not be translated into English for another ten years and, till then, only Herbert Marcuse would refer to it, in a 1948 article: "Sartre's existential analysis was a strictly philosophical analysis seeing how it totally disregarded the historical factors that constitute empirical concreteness."[23] The sociologist Erving Goffman in 1946 was barely in his twenties, still studying philosophy at the University of Chicago with professors such as Herbert Blumer and William Thomas. And yet, there were already a few striking similarities in the philosophies that underlay their respective researches and their fields of investigation: the interest in social marginality, at the origin of Sartre's ethico-political combat, was to Goffman the stimulus for daring investigations in microsociology. "Sartre had elaborated," Erving Goffman will tell us in 1982, "a sociology à la George Herbert Mead. In *Being and Nothingness,* for instance, he had a few passages of pure ethnology, but he did not really influence us in any significant way. While we were pursuing our studies, he had not yet been translated. When we were finally able to read him, we were already formed."[24] They will remain parallel, related, familiar to one another and to their readers: Goffman plunging into the observation of society with all its differences and its deviations—the asylum, the prison—all its monstrosities; Sartre getting involved in the same phenomena but as a philosopher and a militant moralist. They share the same outlook, stripped of any complacency, raw and straight, directed to the real, the existential.[25]

*S*ECOND STAY in America: it is the opportunity to create a Sartrean outpost at Dolorès's, an extension of *Les Temps modernes.* She sorts out his correspondence, organizes his schedule, files articles, receives all his friends passing through New York. Soon everyone has his own Sartre: professors of philosophy or literature, journalists, politicians, novelists, playwrights—Arthur Miller, for instance, who, though he never met Sartre in person, still remembers the media trails left by his passage, the "absolutely fascinating" personality revealed by the press, and the feeling of "profound identity" that he felt toward Sartre the playwright. "In America, we have a tendency to write very realistic plays," he explains, "but his had the addition of philosophical and psychological analysis, which here are absolutely forbidden."[26]

Back in Paris, Sartre immediately began writing a manuscript directly related to the experiences he had just gone through, with the tentative title of "Tableautins d'Amérique" (Little Pictures of America), but nobody knows what happened to it. The only trace of it may well be Sartre's introduction to the special issue of *Les Temps modernes* devoted to the United States, published in the summer of 1946. "There are great myths," he writes, "that of happiness, that of freedom, that of triumphant maternity; there is realism, there is optimism. . . . There is the myth of happiness, there are enticing slogans inviting you to be as happy as possible as soon as possible . . . movies with a happy ending . . . a language fraught with optimistic, nonchalant expressions like 'have a good time,' 'enjoy,' 'life is fun,' etc." After mentioning American taboos and American racial segregation, he concludes on a nostalgic note about "the strange, tired tenderness the faces of New Yorkers assume when the first lights are turned on on Broadway."[27]

"I want to comeback, I'm being killed by passion and lectures." At the end of February 1946, Sartre writes to Simone de Beauvoir to tell her that he is postponing his return, citing as reasons money problems, things to buy: he will come back by plane on March 15. In his letters to her he often enumerates his problems hoping to inspire a little sympathy: "Dolorès's love for me is frightening. . . . Really, her passion literally scares me, and particularly since I am not very much of an expert in this field."[28] Sartre has mastered the language of a part-time Don Juan. Lies, promises, apologies, presents, trips: all to preserve his open unlimited harem. In fact, at the very moment he is telling Beauvoir about his discomfort at Dolorès's love, he is leaving Dolorès with a very clear promise: "He told me: 'Come on, we'll get married, and that's that,' " she will tell us later, "without even considering that I was already married. And he really wanted to accept the offer of his friend at Columbia and stay in New York with me for two years. But I was not sure that, with his language problems, he'd really like to live in New York."

WHEN SARTRE got back to Paris, on March 15, 1946, the major topic of discussion between himself and Beauvoir was Dolorès. "Sartre talked to me a great deal about Dolorès," she writes. "At present, their attachment was mutual, and they envisaged spending two or three months together every year. So be it: separations held no terror for me. But he evoked the weeks he had spent with her in New York with such gaiety that I grew uneasy . . . suddenly

I wondered if Dolorès was more important to him than I was.
. . . According to his accounts, Dolorès shared completely all his
reactions, his emotions, his irritations, his desires."[29] In her jealousy
for an affair that doubly eluded her since it was taking place in New
York, Simone de Beauvoir confronted Sartre with the eternal question "Her or me?" which Sartre answered with a masterpiece of
ambiguity: "I am extraordinarily fond of Dolorès, but you are the
one I am with!" Was he mad, perverse, cynical, opportunistic, cruel,
sadistic, or simply clumsy? He could speak of the one to the other
with the utmost transparency whenever he wanted to communicate
his happiness. But he could be decidedly ambivalent when it was
time to defend himself. The stratagems of Sartre-in-love, of the
polygamous Sartre, would delight all those who, caught in the middle of two or three lives, were unable to find adequate arguments.
He did pull it off, but there was a price.

"I will also tell you about Dolorès. . . . It might be difficult for
you to imagine her curious mixture of fear and determination, profound pessimism and trivial optimism, passion and caution, timid-
ity and grit. . . . When she is happy she can be as innocent and
candid as a child."[30] Was he simply mad or was he cruel when he
wrote these words to Beauvoir? Was he mad or was he cruel when,
back from America, he went around telling everybody how
Dolorès was the most wonderful woman in the world and how she
would soon come join him in Paris? In the extraordinary candor of
her love for her son, coupled by her very conventional view of
marriage and emotional stability, Mme Mancy kept asking questions of everybody who had been in New York and had met
Dolorès. One day, she approached Henriette Nizan and, lowering
her voice, asked her, "What about this Dolorès, do you think she
is right for Poulou?"[31]

IN THE ENGINE ROOM

FROM 1946 to 1949, Sartre publishes nonstop: *Existentialism and
Humanism* (March 1946), "Materialism and Revolution"
(June), "New York, a Colonial City" (July), "Introduction to
the United States" (August–September), *Anti-Semite and Jew* (November), "Calder's Mobiles" (fall), "Cartesian Freedom" (Decem-

ber), "Writing for One's Age" (December), *Baudelaire* (January 1947), *What Is Literature?* (serialized through the year 1947), "Les Faux Nez" (March), "Nick's Bar, New York City" (June), *The Chips Are Down* (September), "The Tribune of *Temps modernes*" (October), *Situations* (October), *Theater* (October), "*N*-Dimensional Sculptures" (December), "Black Presence" (December), "Faces" (January 1948), "Giacometti: In Search of the Absolute" (January), *Dirty Hands* (March), *Situations II* (spring), "Black Orpheus" (spring), the Preface to *Portrait d'un inconnu* by Natalie Sarraute (spring), "Consciousness of Self and Knowledge of Self" (April–June), *L'Engrenage* (November), a series of articles on the Rassemblement Démocratique Révolutionnaire (March–December), an interview with Georg Lukács (February 1949), an answer to François Mauriac (May), *Situations III* (June), "The Birth of Israel" (June), "Black and White in the United States" (June), the introduction to the *Thief's Journal* by Jean Genet (July), *Troubled Sleep* (August), a report on Haiti (October), "The Last Chance" (December), as well as numerous other articles and interviews that appeared in France, Europe, North and South America, and unpublished talks he gave in Switzerland, Italy, Great Britain, Germany: more than forty works in less than four years. The genres included lectures, essays, plays, articles, introductions, radio broadcasts, biographies, philosophical speculations, screenplays, songs, novels, reports. The themes ranged from esthetics, literature, ethics, politics, and philosophy to travel, art, and music.

To describe those years Jacques Audiberti suggested the images "Sartre and his five brains," or "a truck parking everywhere with great commotion, in the library, in the theater, at the movies."[1] "When I heard him whistle, I knew he was writing philosophy. When he looked happy, it was a novel. And when he didn't even bother to hide a foul mood, it was either a play, an article, or politics": this according to Jean Cau. Among the different products of those lucky years, the texts he wrote for his own pleasure and the ones that he wrote out of duty, the texts he scribbled in just a few hours on the corner of a table and those he locked himself into whenever he had the time, there is coherence as well as variety and seeming disparity. His more scandalous texts were not his favorite, nor were the most popular ones the best thought out; as for the best-sellers, they were never the ones he cared the most for. In the end, everything has a very simple and yet very complex underground organization: only consideration of all the texts—the published and the unpublished, the past and the present ones—along with all the actions, articles, and theories, reveals the unique and personal structure of Sartre's engine room.

U PON HIS return from his second trip to America, in the spring of 1946, Sartre's system changed, a change registered by involuntary gestures, determined by an evolving underlying system coupled with various exterior pressures. From artisan, he was becoming a professional. The engine room is, of course, the central chamber of this formidable system, a hidden place, a secret, intimate, extremely sophisticated environment, where, between the ironworks and the furnaces, in the middle of an extraordinary heat, the pistons keep going, relentlessly. Watching over the whole, the master, the engineer, constantly on the lookout, between the turbines and the boiler room, the engines and the assembly line, fixing, chipping in, supporting his crew, a genius and a madman, drunk on the vapors and infernal heat, pushing all the machines to the utmost, particularly his own—coffee to stay awake, orthedrine pills to keep the speed up, whisky to relax—a strong, stocky, energetic, witty, stimulating forty-year-old man, an indefatigable drinker, smoker, and good-timer. While the weekly *Samedi soir* keeps gossiping about the "pope of existentialism," and the *salauds,* between pear and cheese, entertain themselves with his various vices—the smell of his hotel room, his overflowing ashtrays, his unmade bed and its sinister effluvia—and poke fun at his "troops," the Sartrean edifice takes shape according to models, rhythms, and laws that it will preserve to the end. Everything is now happening elsewhere, far from the lice-ridden, smelly hotels. Not far from the cafés and the "caves" but higher up, the way he likes it: on the fourth floor of a clean oldish building, in an apartment overlooking the church, the square, and the Rue de Rennes. The engine room is yet higher up, but close by. That's actually the place where everything is planned and creation takes place.

It all begins with the acquisition of a secretary: one day, a Sartrean *khâgneux* comes to offer his services. A great admirer of Mathieu, from *The Roads to Freedom,* seduced by the image of a teacher who likes to hang out with his students, he meets Sartre at the café, approaches him, speaks to him. Sartre immediately likes Jean Cau, his spontaneity, his insolence, his fiery cockiness, his raw strength, his rugged southwestern accent, his large, strong hands, his roguish eye, and his impatience, like that of an animal ready to spring. He is in his twenties and has just come out of the *khâgne* of Louis-le-Grand where he has shared his readings and his thoughts with boys like the filmmaker Claude Lanzmann, and the philosopher Gilles Deleuze. He likes to stress his feisty proletarian background and the raw and colorful accent of the Aude. As Sartre's secretary, he spends all morning sitting in a small study on the Rue Bonaparte, answering the telephone, sorting the mail, managing finances: "a great boss," he'll say later, "incredibly generous and trusting."[2] He must shuttle between the Rue Bonaparte and the office of *Les Temps modernes,* making appointments, managing projects, sorting out offers. . . . The team of Sartre and Cau will last eleven years, from 1946 to 1957. Another advantage in Cau's favor: during the war, in Carcassonne, he met Robert Gallimard, whom he sees again in Paris at a cocktail party to which he went with Sartre. "What are you doing here?" "I'm Sartre's secretary." This encounter will accelerate the flow of information between publisher and author to the point where Robert Gallimard—the "leftist of the family" and a contemporary of Cau —an extraordinarily shrewd, quick, direct, warm man, becomes and remains Sartre's publisher. Jean Cau is variously seen as "a genius," "a bit shady," "in love with Sartre," even "abominable and vulgar." After his departure, Jean Cau will speak of Sartre only rarely and with great affection and only when he is unable to dodge the question. In the spring of 1985, he will come out of his silence to devote twenty pages of his book *Croquis de mémoire* to Sartre—a very moving, discreet book, with a number of vivid passages but no real analysis: a perfectly smooth pebble, impossible to grasp.

Meanwhile at 42 Rue Bonaparte, the stronghold of another century, the main character at a functional level is Mme Mancy. Among her false Louis XVI furniture and behind her lace curtains, she takes care of all their material needs with the help of her Alsatian maid: purchase of clothes, choice of ties, washing and ironing white shirts, food, cleaning. Discreet, unobtrusive, charming, Mme Mancy lives in awe of the "world's wonder" she has created, bedazzled by her extraordinary son.

Next to this beautiful and proper sexagenarian, who, for the next twenty years, will again bask in her son's affection, there is, of course, Simone de Beauvoir, now nearing forty in the splendor of a mature beauty, set off by her eccentric, often folkloristic, clothes, her Castilian hairdos, her complicated earrings, and her unimpeachable taste in colors. Beauvoir is the linchpin of the system, at once its oil, its fuel, its wheels; she is also a masterpiece of organization, an admirer, a creator, a colleague, and an active, indefatigable interlocutor. Since the middle of the thirties, she has read and reread, advised and supported the first writings of a man who was caving in under the weight of his depressions and of philosophical systems that were far too heavy and too awkward for fiction. A convinced and yet autonomous disciple, a feminist, she knows how to keep her own balance: with her own work, at once a double of Sartre's and yet totally her own. Beauvoir is the manager who oversees everything that goes on between the Rue Bonaparte and *Les Temps modernes,* indispensable, efficient, a stable presence.

And then there is the "family," with its male members called the "Sartrean guard" and the "barons of the regime." They are almost all former students, devotees, close friends. In 1946, these are Jacques-Laurent Bost, Jean Pouillon, and J.-B. Pontalis. Claude Lanzmann joins them six years later. With the possible exception of Pontalis, they will stand by Sartre till the end. Like Cau, these barons, this young guard constitute an efficient buffer zone between Sartre and the world: they turn away intruders and welcome potential new recruits. Like Beauvoir, they expand and disseminate the master's thought via lectures, articles, novels, essays. They also serve as models, particularly Bost, whose slightly stiff elegance, princely ease, awkward charm, linguistic impertinence, and constant transgressions will always fascinate Sartre. Bost, half younger brother, half spiritual son, Olga's husband, may well be the most Sartrean of the barons, certainly the only one who will enter Sartre's oeuvre as the character of a novel, the model for Boris in *The Roads.* The Bost who brought his anecdotes and his life to the Rue Bonaparte and who will faithfully and devotedly remain in the Sartrean orbit from 1935 to 1980—his "sterile" satellite, as some dubbed him—will thus be immortalized by Sartre. Sartre's family keep him in contact with the outside world, while ensuring the endurance of *Les Temps modernes* and of the Sartrean oeuvre: they turn his plays into screenplays, supervise adaptations, translate, explain.

Then after the barons, a loose circle of friends: at times intimate for several months, at times absent for several years, at times fervent followers, at others sworn enemies. Also consisting of former students, this third group entertains, with the barons, a relationship that, for some time, will be fairly intimate—lunches, evenings out, frequent rendezvous. But the moment they leave the Sartrean orbit, they become autonomous and often break definitively with the ensemble of the system—as do Cau, and Raoul Lévy—unless they maintain a violent conflictual relationship with it, whether public, as in the case of Jean Kanapa, or tacit, as in that of Robert Misrahi or Jean Genet. Thus, several former students will contribute a new perspective to *Les Temps modernes* then leave the Sartrean space either out of inadvertence or simply out of exhaustion. Among these are Albert Palle, Jean Balladur, and Nathalie Sorokine (now Nathalie Moffat). Recruited by the barons and in contact with them, these old students from Le Havre and Rouen, or from the lycées Pasteur, Condorcet, and Molière, all eventually end up in the pages of *Les Temps modernes,* delighted at having been asked but soon much too busy with their own personal activities to remain under the Sartrean spell.

As strong, as solid, and as tenacious as the family are the women. Former girlfriends of Sartre, ladies of the court, whether still in love with him or not, they will also faithfully follow the course of the Sartrean oeuvre. The most visible among them are his actresses, his interpreters, his muses: Olga, Bost's wife, Electra in *The Flies;* Wanda, Sartre's mistress, Estelle in *No Exit,* and, a little later, Evelyne Rey, Claude Lanzmann's sister, in *The Condemned of Altona.* Similarly inspiring and inspired, in 1946, Juliette Gréco will receive from Sartre the famous present of "La Rue des Blancs-Manteaux," a song written by him for *No Exit.* Thus Juliette Gréco was born, at the age of twenty, a black elflike presence, a charming young woman, fragile and talented, exactly to Sartre's taste. He gave her the initial push, supported her beginnings, lent her his own books to help her find her own repertory.[3]

Installed at the moment when existentialism and Sartre's popularity had reached their zenith and his credibility could no longer be disputed, the engine room, with its unique organization and administration, has accumulated a maximum of symbolic energy. The output of the period 1946–49 is unquestionably one of the most abundant and diversified. Getting its impetus from the explosion of 1945, it soon turned Sartre into a very rich man. Plays, novels, essays, articles, are all sold abroad. Translations, adaptations, theater productions: *The Flies* is performed in Stockholm and Berlin, *No Exit* in Montreal and New York, excerpts from *Nausea* are published both in London and in New York, and the "Présentation des *Temps modernes*" appears simultaneously in Berlin, London, and Rome. His articles and lectures are highly compensated. In short, Sartre has become an export item and, much to the surprise of *Samedi soir,* more in demand than de Gaulle. During this period, his promotion is also assured by the publisher Louis Nagel, previously the agent for his plays. When François Erval, one of Nagel's editors, decided to publish the famous lecture of October 29, 1945, Nagel found a clever layout for it—the text would appear on the right half of the page, the subtitles of each paragraph on the left half, and an unpublished discussion of the whole at the end of the volume—which artificially inflated the contents enough to publish them as a book. "Several hundred thousand over forty years," Nagel answers when asked about the sales of this opuscule, which was translated into eighteen languages and which, much to Sartre's horror, soon became a sort of "bible of existentialism," Sartre's "little red book," a vulgarized abridgement of *Being and Nothingness*.

"I made Sartre," Nagel assures us. "If I had not had the idea of publishing *Existentialism and Humanism*, he would have remained the intellectual leader of a small clique. The little book I published was very cheap. Students could buy it, and that gave Sartre a huge public. I was also the one who convinced Sartre to leave the hotel, financed his apartment on the Rue Bonaparte, and signed a contract with him for a very high monthly salary. . . . One day, I was walking down the Boulevard Saint-Germain with one of my lawyers: he pointed at the cafés and at all the people sitting in them and said, 'Louis, your empire!' "[4] Sartre published four books with Nagel. Simone de Beauvoir and Maurice Merleau-Ponty also gave him several manuscripts, and, for a while, there was even a chance that he would publish *Les Temps modernes*. But the relationship between Sartre and Nagel deteriorated very rapidly and, after insults and reproaches, ended in a courtroom. Nagel's interest in Sartre was only one more sign of the latter's marketability.

Of course, Sartre spent the money—more than he had ever seen before—in his own way. He walked around with pockets full of bills, which he would then scatter all over the table whenever he had to pay a check; he left huge tips to the waiters, and always insisted on paying for everybody. In 1946 alone, for instance, he supported Wanda, Robert Misrahi, and several others with a monthly salary. Every month, his budget was seriously tapped by a series of checks that might involve, in addition to the regular "salaries," the payment of Wanda's doctor or Kanapa's hospital bills or of Bost's taxes. Thus, in the center of the engine room, there is the Sartrean manna, a solid gold treasure that the engineer generously metes out in one form or another. Though he has always refused to sacrifice his personal life to traditional patterns—such as marriage, apartment living, procreation—the ties he has formed with a number of close friends fully deserve the title of family. And, within this network, he will behave like a pelican father till the end of his days, giving and taking, delighting in giving but probably also in the power this gave him over others. "It makes me look like a big shot to pull out a fat bundle," he will later admit to Michel Contat. "And yet I'm not a big shot. No, I think I like having a lot of money on me because it corresponds in a certain manner to the way . . . I wear my everyday clothes, which are almost always the same, and the way I have my glasses, my lighter, my cigarettes with me. It is the idea of carrying as many things with me as possible that define my whole life. . . . The idea, therefore, of being entirely what I am at the present moment and of not depending on anyone, of not needing to ask anyone for anything, of having all my possessions at my immediate disposal." And then he concludes: "When my grandmother gave me money, she would always say: 'In case you break a window, you'll have a few cents on you' . . ."[5]

The silence of the apartment on the Rue Bonaparte smells of beeswax. In the morning, they work: Cau in his corner, Sartre in his, every morning, without exception. In the afternoon, Beauvoir comes to occupy the studious lair now vacated by Cau. She either writes or reads while Sartre sits at his piano to decipher a Beethoven sonata, or a prelude or fugue from the *Well-Tempered Clavier.* "One can be very fertile without having to work too much," he will later state. "Three hours in the morning, three hours in the evening. This is my only rule . . . Even on vacations."[6] Lunches and dinners are generally devoted to close friends, friends, or mistresses. Never a dinner out, never a social gathering. He meets people only informally, either at the Flore or at the Deux Magots or at the restaurants where he has lunch. People recognize him, greet him, stop to have a word with him, to ask him a few questions.

"NOT ONE Frenchman will be free so long as the Jews do not enjoy the fullness of their rights. Not one Frenchman will be secure so long as a single Jew—in France or *in the world at large*—can fear for his life."[7] Two years after the end of the war, when France was still numbed by the weight of Nazi persecutions, of denunciations, compromises, and a still widespread cowardice, when people still couldn't or wouldn't speak of the Jewish martyrdom,

Sartre took the initiative. He grabbed the enemy by the collar, looked at him with a nasty grin, then punched him in the nose: *Anti-Semite and Jew.* "The anti-Semite has chosen hate because hate is a faith. . . . The anti-Semite readily admits that the Jew is intelligent and hard working. . . . Many anti-Semites—the majority perhaps—belong to the lower middle class of the towns; they are functionaries, office workers, small businessmen, who possess nothing. . . . The anti-Semite flees responsibility as he flees his own consciousness. . . . For the anti-Semite, what makes the Jew is the presence in him of 'Jewishness.' . . . One of the elements of his hatred is a proud sexual attraction toward Jews. . . . A destroyer in function, a sadist with a pure heart, the anti-Semite is, in the very depths of his heart, a criminal."[8] This short, taut essay, published in November 1946 and written in a simple, direct style, took everybody aback. In fact, it developed an idea Sartre had already sketched in 1939,[9] and foreshadowed a philosophical monument in progress since the previous year: the famous *Morale,* announced in *Being and Nothingness.* Sartre did not expect *Anti-Semite and Jew* to have such an impact. "I see the oppressed (colonized people, proletarians, Jews). I want to free them from oppression. Those are the oppressed who touch me, I feel involved in their oppression; only their freedom can grant me mine": Jean-Paul Sartre, *Cahiers pour une morale.*[10] This six-hundred-page draft will remain unpublished until 1982. And yet, composed between 1945 and 1948, it holds the key to Sartre's works of the period by focusing on the essential themes of the system. "It's the world I want to possess . . . its totality," he had written a few years earlier in his *War Diaries* "I want to possess it qua *knowledge.* My ambition is myself alone to know the world. . . . And, for me, knowledge has a magical sense of appropriation."[11] At the center of the Sartrean project there are two themes, two passions: the world and oneself. Not a narcissistic, egocentric self, but rather oneself-and-the-other, oneself as seen in its relationship to the other, whether the other be a great man or a bastard, a celebrity or a misfit. Two themes, two passions, and two tools, philosophy and literature, each fighting for supremacy of expression. Because here, the aim is to find the all-encompassing text, a total genre that would at once integrate and go beyond all other possibilities. Things have not changed much since 1928 when, stretched out on the cot of his room at the Ecole Normale, he was wondering: literature or philosophy? Literature and philosophy! But the negotiations are still not over; they will never be over.

Hidden, powerful, huge, the great *Morale* was the only text that, in those years, produced perky moods and joyous whistles. Like an underground rock, a pedestal, a root, it was the supreme foundation, the springboard from which Sartre launched into an exploration of the world: first theoretical, via ethics and philosophy, and then, shifting from reflection to practice, concrete. This to and fro between the theory of the philosopher and its practical applications, what some will call his political practice, will eventually result in a perfectly indissociable whole. The *Morale* covers everything and, in turn, gives way to a number of corollary texts, polymorphous variations such as his essays on the oppression of Jews and blacks, and his articles and lectures on the same theme, and his works for theater: *The Victors, The Respectful Prostitute,* and, of course, *Dirty Hands,* exemplary mirror of the Sartrean oeuvre in which ethics and politics find themselves bound up in sharp contradiction and at the same time in a relationship of complementarity. The *Morale* also leads to two screenplays—*Les Jeux sont faits (The Chips Are Down)* and *L'Engrenage (In the Mesh),* both perfect illustrations of his philosophy; several "dialogues" with Marxism such as "Materialism and Revolution" and *What Is Literature?*; the broadcasts of "La Tribune des *Temps modernes,*" the articles and lectures on the Rassemblement Démocratique Révolutionnaire, and a few passages in the third volume of *The Roads to Freedom.*

*A*NOTHER LONG dialogue of Sartre will focus on "oneself and the other" or "oneself in the other." In 1947, this dialogue produced his *Baudelaire* (dedicated to Jean Genet), an important, strong, and largely misunderstood book in which Charles Baudelaire appears as Sartre's double, his kin, his brother. That same year, it also produced articles on Alexander Calder, Giacometti, and Genet, and the beautiful lecture on "Kafka, a Jewish Writer" which he delivered on May 31 at the French League for a Free Palestine, with its commentary on the themes of the absent father and the hated stepfather. Nor should we forget a long, unpublished work—almost five hundred pages—on Mallarmé, which he wrote during 1948 and 1949: "Mallarmé . . . our greatest poet. A wild, impassioned man. Yet so self-controlled that he could kill himself with a simple movement of his glottis!" Sartre will state later, after the publication of an excerpt from the text. And then he will add, "His was an all-embracing commitment—social as much as poetic."[12] Later, in the same vein, he will write *Saint Genet, The Words,* and the enormous *Flaubert (The Family Idiot)* as well as numerous portrait articles on Merleau-Ponty, Camus, Nizan, Frantz Fanon, Patrice Lumumba, Tintoretto: all self-reflective investigations, biographical inquiries in the mirror. From the tales of anonymous lives that he wrote for *Les Temps modernes* all the way to the famous theory of the universal singular ("For a man is never an individual; it would be more fitting to call him a *universal singular.* . . . Universal by the singular universality of human history, singular by the universalizing singularity of his projects, he requires simultaneous examination from both ends"[13]) up to the gigantic incomplete *Flaubert,* Sartre's autobiographical quest will be relentless. From these bountiful years, the three essential titles are *Baudelaire,* the most personal and intimate, the feistiest and the most violent, the first of his biographical works in the tradition of ethical combat; *Anti-Semite and Jew*; and the work of Sartre's that sold the most in France, the play *Dirty Hands.*

A few images, a few vignettes from the album of a rising celebrity: the scandal provoked by the torture scenes in the play *The Victors* on the stage of the Théâtre Antoine, resulting in the suppression of some passages and, starting with the second performance, the introduction of a warning to the audience. The alarm of some, the deputy Frédéric-Dupont for instance, when the word "putain" (prostitute) first appeared on the playbill—not for long as it was immediately transformed into a "p" followed by three dots. The outrage of Parisian pro-Americans at those scenes in the same play that overtly exposed anti-black racism. Céline's venomous spittle, tit for tat, in his "Agité du bocal," a response to *Anti-Semite and Jew*: "damned rotten ass," "bloody little shitbag," "those bulbous eyes . . . that hook . . . that slobbery sucker: is it a cestode?" The fashionable snapshots taken during the presentation of his movie, *The Chips Are Down,* at the Cannes Film Festival, wherein the author, in a white shirt and pin-striped gray flannel suit, flanked by Micheline Presle, the lead actress, and Jean Delannoy, the director, cordially answers the questions from an elegant press. His incredible meeting with actor François Périer, who, after a performance at the Théâtre des Ambassadeurs, sees a small gentleman hurrying in his direction waving a manuscript: "Here, I have written a play. I have proposed the role of the boy to several actors who are not interested. So, I have thought of you." At first Périer recognizes the face without recognizing Sartre, but as soon as he has finished reading the manuscript of *Dirty Hands* he calls the Rue Bonaparte, rushes over, rereads in front of its author the entire role, concluding with "Non. Récupérable." (No. Salvageable.) with a blank voice instead of "Non récupérable" (Unsalvageable). Périer will forever be grateful to the author, who chose not to point out the blunder and provided him with the tragic role he had not yet had the opportunity to perform.[14]

The friendship with the Vians, Boris and Michelle. His first quarrels with Camus. His squabbles with Mauriac, culminating in the Catholic novelist's famous advice: "Our philosopher must listen to reason. Give up politics, Zanetto, *e studia la matematica.* "[15] The repetitive and boring formulas involving "existentialists," Saint-Germain-des-Prés, and Sartre. Innumerable business trips through Europe, with lecture tours and their press conferences. Infinite debates, symposiums, and other forms of public exposure. Sundry leisure trips: Italy, the Netherlands, Italy, Scandinavia, Italy, Algeria, Italy, and so on and so forth. The various female friends among whom he has to parcel out his time: "I'll meet you at the Deux Magots at ten. I'll be with you till noon. The problem is that to Wanda 'until the 24th' means something completely different from what it means to you. So, not to spoil things, I think we'd better leave it to her. It will help the general mood."[16] And, finally, his various projects, always new, always unexpected, like writing a detective novel or a large study of the French Revolution.

"When I consider that the objections leveled against Plato in the fourth century are very similar to the ones leveled against existentialism today, I can believe in the universal nature of man."[17] Where was Sartre when he wrote these lines in his *Morale,* some time in 1947? Where was the Sartre who could presumably be spotted at any time of the day in one of the cellars of his existentialist kingdom? He was elsewhere, of course, far away, shuttling between Plato and Socrates, in his favorite place, in the company of great men.

HARD TIMES WITH GROUP POLITICS

THE LAST phase, the last stage of these auspicious years is militant action. Since the end of the war, each of Sartre's texts has included an appeal to political commitment. As time goes by, the "night watchman of the intelligence" (to use Jacques Audiberti's expression) confronts the various political parties, judging, attacking, criticizing them in countless articles which are immediately translated into English, Spanish, and German, before himself jumping into the arena.[1] As his stance becomes clearer, he begins to focus on a deliberate criticism of the French Communist Party. "If it should be asked whether the writer in order to reach the masses," he writes in 1947, "should offer his services to the Communist Party, I answer 'no.' The politics of Stalinist Communism is incompatible in France with the honest practice of the literary craft."[2]

The communists' counterattacks get increasingly violent. "Jean-Paul Sartre, a false prophet," Roger Garaudy writes in December 1945, and accuses existentialism of being a "literature for gravediggers," sheer "metaphysical pathology": "All thought divorced from action is sick," he states, "this sickness, today, is called existentialism . . . the middle classes delight in Jean-Paul Sartre's intellectual fornications."[3] Then, Jean Kanapa, Sartre's former student at the Lycée Pasteur, takes up the cudgel, in his book *Existentialism Is Not a Humanism*: "He is a dangerous animal who likes flirting with Marxism . . . because he has not read Marx, even though he knows, more or less, what Marxism is." He compares *Les Temps modernes* to "a bunch of bored bourgeois with bitter eyes, prolific pens, and desperately, lamentably flabby arms."[4] The previous year, with all the zeal of a recent convert, Kanapa had ridiculed Sartre in his novel *Comme si la lutte entière* (As If the Whole Struggle), in the guise of a certain Labzac, a disagreeable, ambiguous character.

In postwar France, where the communists control one section of the new tripartite government, Sartre soon becomes public enemy number one of the PCF. His texts anger them: his professions of faith smack of manipulation and his novels of moral depravity. In "Materialism and Revolution," Sartre had proposed a revolutionary philosophy that would fight for the reconstruction of socialism and the advent of a new humanism. A "revolutionary humanism" that would emerge, he maintained, "as truth itself, humiliated, masked and oppressed by all those who have a reason to elude it." In the same piece, he had also settled a few scores with "the naïve, stubborn scientism of M. Garaudy," with the fears and the dead ends of the communists, and with the "crisis of the Marxist mind, which can't find anything better than Garaudy as its spokesman."[5] This strong, and perhaps too hasty, criticism of dialectical materialism in the end amounted to the proposition of a third philosophical-political course.

Also in 1946, Sartre had gotten passionately involved in another frontal attack against the communists over the "Nizan case." The friend of his adolescence died near Dunkerque, on May 23, 1940, a year after his resignation from the Communist Party. In between the communist underground press had launched a slanderous campaign against him. Maurice Thorez, the PCF general secretary, himself had contributed to it with insults against a comrade who had been a member of the party for over eleven years, and the coeditor-in-chief of the daily *Ce Soir*. By 1945, the slanders were still going on, and mention of Nizan's name—the name of, to use Thorez's words, that "traitor," "that filthy dog in the pay of the Ministry of the Interior" —was no longer permitted in the ranks of the PCF as if its mere utterance would be a contamination. Sartre had been kept informed of all the developments of this unpleasant story: in New York, he had met Henriette Nizan, had become the guardian of her two children, Anne-Marie and Patrick, knew of the demands for an explanation they had addressed to both Maurice Thorez and Louis Aragon, and was aware of the cowardice implied in the total absence of an answer. Finally, he had also read, in the handwriting of the communist philosopher Henri Lefebvre, a tacit acceptance of treason as a permanent feature of Nizan's life and oeuvre. So, in 1947, he decided to head a group of intellectuals and publish a press release expressly addressed to the PCF:

"We are often told that Jacques Decour and Jean Prévost died for us . . . but the name of Nizan, one of the most brilliant writers of his generation, is never mentioned . . . some people whisper that he was a traitor. . . . Well, if that was the case, why don't they prove it? If we receive no answer and no evidence, then we shall publish another press release proclaiming Nizan's innocence."[6] Guy Leclerc's answer in *L'Humanité* merely reiterated his attacks against the "traitor to his own party," the "traitor to his own country," who had "helped the agents of the fifth column in their criminal politics."[7] For Sartre, Aron, and others, this was a call to action.

*I*N THE meantime, *Les Temps modernes* had become a sort of meeting place, an exclusive club, which, each month, gathered the most prestigious signatures of the leftist intelligentsia of both Europe and America: Francis Ponge, Samuel Beckett, Philippe Soupault, Maurice Blanchot from France, Alberto Moravia, Elio Vittorini, Ignazio Silone, Carlo Levi from Italy, and Richard Wright and

James Agee from the United States. In it, one could also find the contributions of the composer René Leibowitz and the economist Pierre Uri, and articles by Boris Vian, Raymond Queneau, Michel Leiris, Jean Genet, Violette Leduc, and Nathalie Sarraute. To these were amiably associated names of a lesser caliber, the friends and students who were making their debuts in the magazine: Raoul Lévy, Robert Misrahi, Jean Cau, Jean Balladur, and Nathalie Sorokine. The intention announced in the "Présentation" of October 1945—"we shall be hunters of meaning"—which allowed for the coexistence, next to literature, of documents, narratives, and reports, had also, finally, taken a concrete form in the shape of anonymous documentary narratives. The life of a disaster victim, the life of a Jew, the life of a French bourgeois, an Israeli magistrate, the life of a German, the life of a French foreign legionnaire, the life of a prostitute: each story tried to give an idea of both an individual and a society, with the "micro-social" playing the role of symbolic revealer of the "macro-social." "If the Truth is one . . . seek it not elsewhere but everywhere," Sartre will also write several years later,[8] returning to the idea of examining our times in their totality, as a meaningful synthesis. *Les Temps modernes* also publishes two special issues, in August–September 1946 and August–September 1947, devoted to the United States and to Italy, respectively. The magazine pushed its explorations of the world still further when, in the fall of 1947, its editorial board was asked to present a weekly radio broadcast, "La Tribune des *Temps modernes,*" allowing the group to reach a much larger public, including listeners who would not necessarily read a magazine.

Alphonse Bonnafé, former colleague and friend from the lycée at Le Havre, had brought the possibility of the broadcasts to the attention of the Ramadier government. There resulted a series of more or less chaotic discussions centered on the proposition of the "third option," Sartre's idée fixe since the Liberation. Sartre, unable to choose between bourgeois idealism and Marxist materialism, had first come up with the idea of a third option in "Materialism and Revolution," and had again insisted on it in *What Is Literature?* Between the USSR and the English-speaking bloc, he will opt for a socialist Europe: "As for a socialist Europe," he explains, "there's no 'choosing' it since it doesn't exist. It is to be made."[9] This "third option," becomes the refrain of "La Tribune des *Temps modernes*": "It is necessary to campaign against the belief in the inevitability of a Russian-American war," Sartre explained in an interview with

Louis Pauwels, on the eve of the broadcasts. "Historical inevitability," he continued, "is constantly on people's minds. And so we enter the world of this inevitability with our hands and feet tied." Then, returning once again to his episodic definition of the writer's role in today's society, he declared, "Committed writers must move from writing to such 'relay' arts as radio and cinema."[10] These are the same views he has already expounded in *Les Temps modernes,* the same advocacy of so-called minor arts (versus "noble" arts), the same plan for an all-inclusive exploration of all forms of expression, without exception; the writer's place, according to him, is in the very center of a galaxy, which he proposes to explore in all directions. A broadcast analysis of contemporary political life was just another tool, and the quantity of current political events, whether international or French, would provide the group with constant food for discussion.

Since the referendum of October 21, 1945, when the French had voted for a tripartite regime—MRP (Mouvement Républicain Populaire)–SFIO (Section Française de l'Internationale Ouvrière)–PCF—the political balance had had time to collapse. The temporary agreement reached in the wake of the Liberation had not lasted long: the Fourth Republic was rapidly been torn apart by deep conflicts, each party resuming, much sooner than expected, its prewar political line. On January 20, 1946, General de Gaulle, the head of the government, had left his post as a result of constitutional conflicts with the Assembly; but the speeches that he delivered on June 16, 1946, from Bayeux, and on March 30 and April 7, 1947 from Bruneval and Strasbourg, indicated that he meant to remain on the political scene. Then, on May 5, 1947, as a last stage in postwar reconstruction, the communist ministers had resigned from the government after refusing to pass a vote of confidence. At this point, the tripartite regime that had endured since 1945 definitively caved in, leaving the socialists quite willing to pursue the experience of power despite the communist departure. In the meantime, on the international front, the threat of a Cold War between Americans and Soviets was becoming more and more a reality. The cooperation brought about by having a common enemy in the Nazis had been frittered away, and Europe was going to bear the brunt of this rupture. In June 1947, the proposal of the Marshall Plan marked the beginning of the Cold War: Molotov immediately rejected it, while in Europe the various political parties either opted for the Atlantic Alliance or for the Soviet Union. In France, the socialists endorsed the Marshall Plan, thereby widening the gap between themselves and the PCF. The end of the tripartite regime, the beginning of the Cold War: in France, political tensions finally gave way to the social troubles that kept cropping up throughout 1947. The strikes of the Paris press, in January and February, were followed, in July, September, and November, by large strikes in other professional arenas, such as public transport, which, in turn, entailed confrontations with the police and the threat of employing reservists against the communist-run, major trade union, the CGT. The country was in turmoil.

In the middle of this difficult political situation, and these troubled social conditions, General de Gaulle decided to found the Rassemblement du Peuple Français (RPF). The strength of this new party would be tested in the fall of 1947 in the municipal elections of October 19 and 25. The first round marked an extraordinary breakthrough for the new Gaullist movement and the collapse of the MRP: 38 percent for the RPF, and only 10 percent for the MRP, which, since 1945, had lost almost two-thirds of its support.

"JEAN-PAUL Sartre and his colleagues present 'Les Temps modernes' . . . [music] . . . The subject of today's broadcast is Gaullism. Our panelists will be Jean-Paul Sartre, Simone de Beauvoir, Maurice Merleau-Ponty, J.-B. Pontalis, and Alphonse Bonnafé." On Monday, October 20, 1947, the experiment in "free radio" began. It was the day after the first ballot and the Gaullist landslide. Charles de Gaulle, was, of course, the butt of this eager team's irreverence and irony. Merleau-Ponty, as usual the most rational of the group, undertook a precise analysis of de Gaulle's latest speech, and, particularly, of the section on foreign policy. "This is a new aspect of de Gaulle's politics," Merleau-Ponty explained. "The politics of French grandeur having floundered, he is now defining another one . . . : from now on we shall pledge military alliance to the United States. I wonder whether it is serious even to contemplate the active participation of France in a war" at the side of the United States. But Merleau-Ponty's intervention, the only serious and well-argued segment in the whole broadcast, did not last long. Sartre compared the new leader to Pétain: "Marshal, General: It does not make any difference. Both belong to the army, to the silent majority, both are eloquent orators, both Catholic, both believe that sovereignty comes from above, both have given themselves to France." In the past six months, the electoral campaign of the RPF had relied on the cult of personality, and the photo of the general was now posted on every wall. Many people had condemned the glorious, even miraculous, return of this leader of one sector of the Resistance, and had criticized his violent anticommunist declarations and the unequivocal way in which he proposed himself to the country, evoking, as the alternative, a nearly planetary catastrophe. But Sartre and his friends went way beyond mere criticism, or a mere condemnation of the general. "When one looks at those RPF's posters glaring from every wall of the city," Bonnafé said: "You know what I'm talking about, the huge portrait of the general . . . the little mustache, the heavy eyelids . . . not to mention the lock across the forehead . . . It's all there, I tell you! And the people who pass by say: 'But that's—' " "Don't say it!" another panelist interrupted him.[11]

The broadcast was not well received in Gaullist circles. In fact, it caused a scandal. General Pierre Guillain de Bénouville and Henri Torrès, a lawyer, both members of the RPF, responded to it the same day on the radio. A new show was announced for the following day: a debate between the two Gaullists and Jean-Paul Sartre, with Raymond Aron as moderator. Years later, Aron remembers: "When I got to the room and saw Sartre sitting on one side and, on the other, Bénouville and Torrès, all busy insulting him, I wondered what I had gotten into since the situation was obviously a stalemate. What could I do? I couldn't possibly support Sartre: to compare de Gaulle to Pétain was one thing, but to Hitler! . . . I couldn't defend that. On the other hand, I was certainly not going to side with the others and hurl insults at [Sartre]."[12] So, the debate never took place, and everybody went their separate ways. "The Gaullists demanded an open discussion," Simone de Beauvoir writes about the event. "Sartre accepted, but the two Gaullists and Aron refused."[13] "My words weren't nearly as violent as some have made out them to be," Sartre remonstrated. "A citizen has the right to say what he thinks, always. . . . I feel no hatred for the person of General de Gaulle. How could I? I don't even know him."[14] The audience for this stormy encounter could hear only Torrès's voice: "Monsieur Sartre's broadcast about General de Gaulle was an attack on the probity and the dignity of the spirit. . . . The author constructed a false de Gaulle, which he then compared to Pétain and Hitler; such a thing could only deserve the contempt of the public. Given the circumstances, there was no need for an answer. Such an infamy deserved only silence."[15]

According to the press, the insults the lawyer had hurled at Sartre were so violent that the philosopher could not possibly have defended them. "Monsieur Torrès behaved so violently and so vulgarly that there was really no point in my responding: in short, he refused the debate I had requested," Sartre explained to the journalists the following day. As for Pierre Loewel, the Gaullist journalist, he was incensed that "a writer, master of his language, and a philosopher, master of his thoughts, could lower himself to playing the clown."[16] Albert Ollivier, a former colleague on *Les Temps modernes*, considered Sartre and his side as "virtual fascists,"[17] while Paul Claudel's reaction was memorable: "Monsieur Sartre does not like General de Gaulle's looks: is he happy with his own?"[18] This unexpected event monopolized the attention of the press for over a week. "They pretend I compared de Gaulle to Hitler," Sartre defended himself. "That's false. I merely compared the electoral propaganda of the RPF to that of the Nazis."[19]

The long quarrel between Sartre and Aron grew out of this pathetic and outrageous misunderstanding, out of these deliberate anarchical excesses. Aron's presence on the editorial board of *Les Temps modernes* had lasted less than a year, and even then rested on a very shaky consensus; nevertheless, Aron had had the time to write a few articles, which he stood by several years later, among them one concerning the Pétain trial, published in 1946. But this rather futile incident provoked a long silence between the two men: Aron remained convinced of having saved Sartre's face whereas Sartre was sure that Aron had come to the meeting only to side with the Gaullists.

"*LA* TRIBUNE des *Temps modernes*" lasted less than a month after these stormy beginnings: the fall of the Ramadier government dealt the final blow. In the meantime, however, Sartre and his colleagues proposed a series of debates on themes such as "Liberalism and Socialism," "The Socialist Crisis," "Trade Unions and Social Conflicts," "The Real Meaning of Workers' Claims," "Communism and Anti-communism." With their jokes, their often oppressive unanimity and their frequently drawn-out discussions, these broadcasts brought new life and a hitherto unknown style and air to French political debate.

The *Temps modernes* group could boast of a large audience that wavered between passionate interest and violent hatred. On November 3, the program was devoted entirely to answering letters, both of congratulations and of insults, in itself clear evidence that their listeners were at least as numerous as their readers. In the course of its nine broadcasts, the group's stance did not change very much. Sartre: "We are on the side of the workers . . . and, in principle, we sympathize with the parties that represent them. . . . the PC has, since the Liberation, shown a great deal of hesitation. . . . For the most it seems to have concentrated on the demolition of centrism, that is, of the socialist party in power." Pontalis: "We are unable to see hope either on the side of Gaullism or on that of communism. . . . some people have been speaking about a third option." Merleau-Ponty: "We don't have many weapons, and particularly not powerful weapons, we only have the weapon of truth, and that is the one we shall employ." Their interventions grew more and more political and more and more concerned with current issues. The program scheduled for December 8 was to be called "Two Appeals to International Opinion," but it was never broadcast because, in the meantime, the Schuman cabinet had replaced the Ramadier government and suppressed "La Tribune des *Temps modernes.*" Instigated by Claude Bourdet, editor-in-chief of *Combat,* Emmanuel Mounier, of *Esprit,* Georges Altman of *Franc-Tireur,* and David Rousset, among others, these two appeals were meant to alert public opinion against the escalation of the Cold War and to propose an alternative to the politics of the great powers, in the form of a socialist Europe. Sartre had enthusiastically endorsed the program, but, among his colleagues, Pontalis had remained somewhat skeptical: "Do you really think we are the right people to form another party?" he had anxiously wondered. "No, we are not speaking of a party," Sartre had answered. "In the first place, many signatories, including myself, would be absolutely unable to adhere to a party, it would be an absolutely preposterous vow . . . we would be the first to laugh at it."

*I*N NOVEMBER 1947, Sartre had signed two appeals to international opinion composed by some leftists he felt close to, expressing Europe's refusal to be a pawn in the Cold War while insisting on a socialist European identity. A few months later, he was again contacted by Georges Altman and David Rousset: pursuing the political analyses that had resulted in those two appeals, they were now planning to found a political movement and wanted Sartre to join them. He agreed. On February 27, 1948, the entire French press published the committee's statement calling for a Rassemblement

Démocratique Révolutionnaire—or RDR. The steering committee included Rousset, Sartre, Paul Fraisse from *Esprit,* Altman, Daniel Bénédicte, Jean Ferniot, Bernard Lefort, Charles Ronsac from *Franc-Tireur,* and Roger Stéphane. These were joined by four members of Parliament and six trade unionists. Soon, the press would begin to refer to it as "Sartre's and Rousset's party." This was Sartre's first experience with party militancy since "Socialism and Freedom." For eighteen months, he would find himself in the arena of political action along with leftists of every stripe: Trotskyites, leftist Christians, socialist youths, socialist dissidents, communists, ex-communists, Marxists, non-Marxists, and workers.

At the center of the organization, two groups: one was centered around Altman and his daily newspaper, *Franc-Tireur,* with a circulation second only to that of *Le Figaro,* and a readership that was mostly blue-collar or recent middle-class and generally non-communist; the second group consisted of several people, most of them connected with the *Revue internationale*— founded after 1945 by Claude Bourdet, Gilles Martinet, Rousset, Gérard Rosenthal—and represented a broad spectrum of the left, ranging all the way from the Trotskyites to the most extreme wing of the SFIO. All their analyses focused on the inadequacy of the trade unions, a general discontent with the traditional political parties, and the disintegration of militancy. Recent events related to the Cold War had challenged the validity of these issues, and the idea of seeking Sartre's support was an excellent strategic move. "One of the concepts that immediately seduced me when you came to see me," he will later confess to David Rousset, "which was at the very basis of the formation of this movement, was that of establishing the premises—long forgotten by the existing parties—of a real democratic organization within a political group."[20] In a period of looming political crisis, the RDR represented the desperate dream of various dissidents disappointed with the parties of the left but still hopeful of finding an active and honorable political solution, a dream that had already repeatedly been entertained by a fringe of socialist and communist oppositionists: the nostalgic dream of a return to a theoretical purity, which the socialist party of Marceau Pivert, the PSU, and the New Left would all vainly try to realize in a series of abortive alliances spanning the period between 1930 and 1960. In this thirty-year search, the RDR would represent the stage "1948."[21] In 1948, the militants of this particular left felt more than ever like passive hostages in the hands of politicians they no longer believed in, the toys of calculating, self-interested political parties. What brought them together was their discontent and their rejection of the PCF and the SFIO, the USSR and the USA. Cornered by the urgency of this choice, all these adherents of different sectors of the left and the extreme left—former prisoners, former deportees, former Resistance members, various dissidents, seasoned militants, inexperienced intellectuals, old trade unionists, well-meaning students, instinctive leftists—met and decided to work together. They all shared the dream of a real democracy, of a collective political practice in constant renewal, of a unique experiment whose time had come.

"There are millions of us in France, millions in Europe and the rest of the world. Millions looking for the same path. Survivors from hell, Resistance refugees, militants, sympathizers, or comrades from all the movements that believe in social emancipation, we think that the world has paid for its deliverance from Hitlerism dearly enough to know that there is no salvation outside of the respect and the preservation of man's rights and freedom." This was the somewhat lyrical beginning of an appeal that newspapers and pamphlets spread all over the country, an appeal to the responsibility of men against political regimes, an appeal to democrats and revolutionaries: "It is not true that men have to choose between large political blocs," the text went on before concluding: "It is up to France to awaken the world with Saint-Just's hopeful cry: 'Happiness is a new idea in Europe,' completed by the appeal Marx launched a hundred years ago: 'Workingmen of all countries, unite!' In 1948 as in 1848, let us repeat the appeal to a new freedom reinforced by social justice." The explicit reference to the revolution of 1848—as opposed to that of 1789—was a reminder of both its centenary and its import, which, for the RDR, was none other than "the incarnation of the socialist ideal," here sealed by the handshake between Louis de Saint-Just, the radical, the pure, the intransigent, and Karl Marx. At this time there was troublesome news coming from the East: Klement Gottwald had seized power in Czechoslovakia, his "coup de Prague" ending the political alliance of communists, socialists, social democrats, and Christian democrats, shattering the hopes of an eventual reconciliation between the two blocs.

On March 10, 1948, in Paris, the RDR holds its first press conference. Among the panelists are two intellectuals, Rousset and Sartre, and two trade union militants, Jean Rous and Léon Boutbien. Gradually, their answers define a particular direction. "Most Europeans already seem to have chosen their conquerors. We are fighting a war by proxy," Sartre raps out his speech in a voice that the eighty journalists crowded in the room know well. "The RDR refuses to endorse one side because of fear of the other. We would like to cleanse the situation, and to establish contact with other European democratic groups to put Europe at the head of peace." As Rousset further explains, "What we want is a large mass movement, not monolithic, but animated from below by open discussions. . . . We side with the workers and the middle classes who fight for their survival. . . . The originality of the RDR resides in that it is a gathering and not a party." Its aims: "We need fifty thousand members in Paris, within a month."[22]

Welcomed with irony by its political neighbors, but supported by newspapers such as *Combat* and *Franc-Tireur,* and magazines such as *Esprit* and *Les Temps modernes,* the RDR kept on growing throughout 1948, as if propelled by the threats of World War III, in themselves enough to justify the group's existence. Meanwhile, the communists, speaking through Etienne Fajon, Pierre Hervé, and Pierre Courtade, denounced the RDR's "complicity with the Americans." "One cannot solve the problem of war and peace," Courtade wrote, "with wordplay and false candor."[23] The socialists, on the other hand, analyzed the various components of the new movement with great skepticism, and, only a few days after its creation, Gilles Martinet published his own conclusions in *Bataille socialiste*: the enterprise was given, at best, a very short lifespan. Martinet reminded his readers of the RDR's heterogeneous composition, its almost total lack of cohesion ("Logic would have demanded that the alliance be made on the basis of belief rather than on collective action"), underlined the limits of its concrete proposals ("a hodgepodge of perfunctory and disparate doctrinal formulas, an avalanche of propagandistic propositions"), and, finally, accused it of a total lack of political knowhow, citing, as evidence, the pious vows, abstract wishes, chimerical projects, and "intellectual delusions" of its members: "You will split up into a bunch of cliques," he prophesied. "You say: 'We are millions,' but, in fact, you are only a few hundred. . . . It is surely not your literature that will renew the self-confidence of disoriented workers." He concluded the piece with a master stroke: "Socialism cannot be 'rethought' *with* Jean-Paul Sartre, it can only be rethought *against* him."[24]

The first large meeting of the RDR took place on March 19, 1948 in the Salle Wagram. Among the participants were Georges Altman of *Franc-Tireur,* Paul Fraisse of *Esprit,* Jean Rous, Rousset, and

Sartre, who was the last to speak: "The main objective of the RDR is to join all revolutionary claims with the idea of freedom . . . and to gather effectively the men of this country, whether producers or consumers, into neighborhood committees, town committees, factory committees, where they will find a concrete way to bring about the satisfaction of their demands." Before reminding his audience of the motives underlying the organization of the RDR, he analyzed two examples and evoked two types of drama, that of hunger and of war: "Hunger in the belly and freedom in the heart," he began. "Hunger, mere hunger, is already a legitimate complaint to the man who wants to be freed of all that prevents him from being a man."[25]

Through the first months of the RDR's life, the recruiting was quite impressive: the creation of various committees seemed at once flexible and efficient, the concept of a leftist group that did not have any of the handicaps of political parties was a true novelty, and, finally, the ideals of peace and freedom and a socialist Europe were very attractive. Groups and committees started springing up throughout the greater Paris area and then all over France. The first issue of the bimonthly paper *La Gauche–RDR*, edited by Jean Ferniot, came out in May. It looked as if the movement was under way. It received letters: Richard Muller, general secretary of the railroad union for the eastern region, was delighted: "At last some hope and a certainty . . . I am sure that the faith that animates those men will stimulate all the workers who long for better days, in a France led by true democrats." Guy Jezouin, from Avignon wrote: "Just a few days ago, a few friends and I came across your manifesto. It was great to read something like that at a moment when everything looks so grim. We resigned from the SFIO a few months ago."

The manifesto, a press conference, and the first meeting in the Salle Wagram all received encouraging responses. Sartre's presence among the first rank of the militants was crucial in gaining support. He received numerous letters, pro and con. "The guiding idea of M. Sartre and his acolytes," *Rassemblement*, the official paper of the Gaullist RPF, explained, "is to replace the wicked myth of war with the good myth of peace." *Le Monde* adopted a wait-and-see attitude but recognized the "undeniable nobility" of the manifesto and the "moving sincerity" of its authors. "Let's greet them with sympathy; we'll never have enough dreamers among us."[26] And Raymond Aron wrote some sensible words in his analysis of the RDR's birth for *Le Figaro*. In an article devoted to the "contradictions of communism," he tried to find the reasons for the decline of intellectual

Stalinism, and then concluded: "The RDR, from *Franc-Tireur* to *Les Temps modernes,* is trying to occupy the place left vacant by the Stalinists. Between bureaucratic despotism and capitalism, they are trying to pave the way for revolutionary romanticism, disillusioned by many failures, but always ready to re-emerge."[27]

Around June 1948, *La Gauche–RDR* doubled the number of its pages: "Palestine, South Africa, Czechoslovakia . . . Where in the world are Freedom and Democracy?" Charles Ronsac wondered, while David Rousset, considering the decline of socialism and the isolation of the communists, maintained that the RDR could "fill a great void." A new meeting was planned for June 11, just before the summer holidays, in the auditorium of the Sociétés Savantes. The meeting was marred by violent incidents; RPF groups had come to demonstrate against the leftists. That evening, Sartre spoke with passion—"European youth unite! Shape your own destiny!"—addressing himself to the generation he had always favored. "We men in our forties, we do not have the right to tell the new generation what to do; we haven't done our job well enough to feel justified in doing so. I am not here to give advice but rather to tell you what I have learned during a few trips through Europe." And, having captivated his audience, he added, "By creating Europe, this new generation will create democracy. With the constitution of a federation and the implementation of a movement that transcend all frontiers, European youth will finally be able to have *its* future, *its* peace, *its* true freedom."[28] Paul Fraisse spoke of the "school of freedom": "The RDR will do its best to enforce the promotion of public education, the only school of freedom." With their revolutionary romanticism and antagonistic stances against their immediate political neighbors, the leaders of the RDR kept insisting on the same themes. The attack by the RPF "commandos," of which they had just been the victims, was clear evidence that, in barely three months, they had become the enemies of the young Gaullists, dangerous enemies, worthy of their attention. How else, in fact, explain the presence of fifty young men armed with bludgeons and brass knuckles and shouting "Long live de Gaulle" and "Down with the pigs," and who had tried to break into the rooms where Sartre, Rousset, and Rosenthal were speaking. "This meeting must go on," the latter announced as he heard the brawl raging outside the doors. "We refuse to call the police. We will protect democratic order by ourselves."[29]

Another sign of the RDR's success after its first three months of existence was the recognition it received from abroad. The *New York Herald Tribune* published a three-column interview with "Jean-Paul Sartre, a revolutionary democrat." For the leaders of the RDR during the last few days of June 1948, everything seemed possible, even the construction of a revolutionary Europe that would vie with the two other world powers, a "free European socialist federation," a "vast international assembly whose first act would be the launching of a charter for a worldwide revolutionary democracy."[30]

Around the same time, Sartre, Rosenthal, and Rousset engaged in a number of debates later published under the title of *Discussions on Politics,* providing a retrospective analysis of the situation of French political parties and an explanation of how the RDR had managed to slip through the meshes of this tight network and woven its own web among the leftist parties, thus winning over its own supporters —who could still retain their membership in another party—and uniting various social strata generally separated by politics. These discussions, occurring as they did in the salad days of the Rassemblement, show us a Sartre and company intoxicated like all revolutionary leaders who read, in the increasing number of their supporters, the nearly sacred sanction of reality, the unquestionable evidence of their success. Did Sartre, Rosenthal, and Rousset believe they had become another Lenin, Luxemburg, Liebknecht? Basking in the beneficial effects of their revolutionary illusions, they progressively deferred the limits of all their analyses: the various councils would compile long lists of claims, on the model of the revolutionaries of 1789; and the management committee would remain in constant contact with them, just as each subcommittee would remain in constant contact with the others. The idea of a "totally democratic operation," which had seduced Sartre from the very beginning, was now becoming a real objective, along with a number of other projects such as the elaboration of an ideology that would bind together all the leftist parties already represented by the RDR or of the "common aim" defined by Sartre: "the integration of a free individual into a society conceived as the union of the free activities of the individual."[31] Among all the reservations and criticisms provoked by the RDR the only one that really struck home was Aron's tag of "revolutionary romanticism" repeatedly debated and denied by the three revolutionaries.

After a euphoric birth and a dazzling takeoff, the RDR reached its peak at the grand meeting in the Salle Pleyel on December 13, 1948, its real moment of glory, when it displayed all the most evident

2.

◄ 1. Sartre, photograph by Gisèle Freund, 1939.

2. The Sartre farm at Puifeybert (Dordogne).
3. Thiviers: Sartre's family home is located on the right, at the beginning of the street; across from it, below the balcony, is the Chavoix pharmacy.
4. Jean-Baptiste Sartre, Jean-Paul Sartre's father, as a student at the Périgueux lycée, around 1885.
5,6, and 7. Ecole Polytechnique: three students from the class of '95—Jean-Baptiste Sartre (5), Georges Schweitzer (6), and Joseph Mancy (7).
8. Les Bouvines, the battleship on which Jean-Baptiste served as a lieutenant.

3.

4.

5.

6.

7.

8.

9.

10.

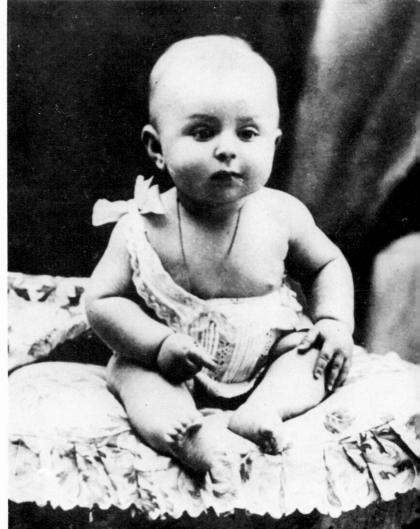

11.

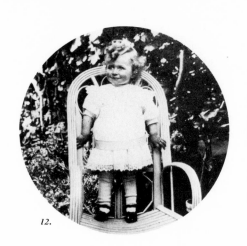

12.

13.

14.

9. *Anne-Marie Schweitzer, Jean-Paul Sartre's mother, around the time of her wedding.*
10. *Jean-Baptiste Sartre around the same time.*
11. *Jean-Paul Sartre, "Poulou," when he was a few months old.*
12. *Poulou at one-and-a-half.*
13. *Anne-Marie and Poulou after Jean-Baptiste's death.*

14. *The "Schweitzer quartet" in 1913, on a visit to Pfaffenhoffen. Left to right: Charles Schweitzer, Sartre's grandfather; Anne-Marie; Emile Schweitzer, Sartre's uncle on his mother's side; eight-year-old Poulou; Sartre's uncle and aunt Biedermann; Louise Schweitzer, Sartre's grandmother.*

16.

17.

15.

15. *A portrait of the child by his mother, 1913. "I am round-cheeked, and my expression displays a kindly deference toward the established order; my mouth is puffed with hypocritical arrogance: I know my worth."* (The Words)

16. *1919–20: third-form students at the La Rochelle lycée. Sartre is in the front row, second from the left, seated on the floor with his arms crossed.*

17. *As a sixth-form student at the Lycée Henri IV.*

32. *April 2, 1948: Sartre greets the novelist Francis Carco at the opening of* Dirty Hands.
33. *The same day, with François Périer, creator of the role of Hugo.*

33.

34. *At the Pont-Royal with Dolorès V., Jacques-Laurent Bost, Jean Cau, and Jean Genet.*
35. *At Simone de Beauvoir's, a meeting of the editorial board of* Les Temps modernes: *Jacques-Laurent Bost, Simone de Beauvoir, Claude Lanzmann.*

30.

31.

30. *With Boris and Michelle Vian and Simone de Beauvoir.*
31. *Sartre and Beauvoir during a broadcast of "La Tribune des* Temps modernes."

29.

29. *Sartre in 1946. Photograph by William
Leftwich, published in* Time.

27.

28.

25.

26.

25. ⟨⟩ 16, 1944: at the reading of Picasso's play Desire Caught by the Tail. *Standing, left to right: Jacques Lacan, Cécile Eluard, Pierre Reverdy, Louise Leiris, Zanie de Campan, Pablo Picasso, Valentine Hugo, Simone de Beauvoir, Brassaï; and, at their feet, Sartre, Camus, Michel Leiris, Jean Aubier.*
26. *October 16, 1944: a demonstration at the Père-Lachaise cemetery in memory of the victims of the Nazis. Sartre is a member of the committee of the Front National du Spectacle.*
27. *The Café de Flore in 1945.*
28. *January–March 1945, during Sartre's first trip to the United States. The eight French journalists pose at the San Antonio airport. Left to right: Etiennette Bénichon, François Prieur, Louis Lombard, Sartre, Pierre Denoyer, Andrée Viollis, Stéphane Pizella, Robert Villers.*

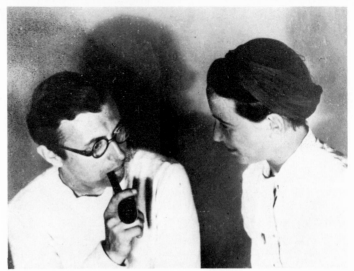

23.

24.

21.

22.

21. *Summer 1929: Sartre firing a rifle. To his left, Hélène de Beauvoir; to his right, half hidden, Simone de Beauvoir; next to her, Fernando Gherassi, the painter.*
22. *1930–31, at the Le Havre lycée.*
23. *Sartre and Simone de Beauvoir on vacation at Juan-les-Pins.*
24. *During the phony war, Sartre, a second-class soldier in the meteorological corps, uses a telescope to observe a balloon held by Corporal Pierre.*

18.

. 19.

20.

18. *Ecole Normale Supérieure, 1927: a walk on the roofs. Sartre is sitting on the chimney. In the front row, Henriette Alphen and Paul Nizan (second and third from the left); standing behind them, second from the left, Daniel Lagache.*

19. *Ecole Normale Supérieure, the 1925 student revue, "La Revue des deux mondes ou le désastre de Lang-son": Sartre, seated, is playing Lanson to Sylvain Broussaudier's Dupuy.*

20. *The same revue: Sartre as Lanson with Daniel Lagache as Dona Ferentes.*

34.

35.

36.

38.

37.

39.

36. *June 1954: at the National Library of Leningrad.*
37. *Fall 1955: during their trip to the People's
Republic of China, Sartre and Simone de Beauvoir
have tea with Marshal Zhen Yi.*

38. *July 1957: in the Piazza San Marco, Venice.*
39. *February 1960: meeting with Fidel Castro, in Cu*
40. *At his window—42 Rue Bonaparte—
overlooking the café Les Deux Magots.* ▶

43.

42.

41.

44.

41. *September 1959: at the Théâtre de la Renaissance during the rehearsals of* The Condemned of Altona, *with Evelyne Rey and Serge Reggiani.*

42. *November 1, 1961, during the Algerian war: a silent vigil against racism, on the Place Maubert.*

43. *Last moments of calm, at a Montparnasse café, before the rejection of the Nobel Prize.*

44. *1965: at La Coupole with Arlette Elkaim.*

45.

46.

47. 48.

45. *November 9, 1966: at a press conference against apartheid.*

46. *Spring 1967: during his trip to Egypt, Sartre pays a visit to a Palestinian refugee camp.*

47. *March 21, 1967: Jewish and Arab students welcome him at the Lod airport.*

48. *During a visit to Kibbutz Merhavia in Galilee.*

49. *March 23, 1968: at the Mutualité with Joseph Kessel and Laurent Schwartz, during a meeting of intellectuals against the Vietnam war.*

50. *February 11, 1969, at the Mutualité: on the lectern he finds the message "Sartre, be brief. . . ."*

51. *June 26, 1970: hawking* La Cause du peuple.

49.

50.

51.

52.

53.

52. *At his worktable with Robert Gallimard,* 222 *Boulevard Raspail.*
53. *1978, 29 Boulevard Edgar-Quinet: a meeting of the editorial board of* Les Temps modernes. *Left to right: Jean Pouillon, Benny Lévy, Claire Etcherelli, François George, André Gorz, Beauvoir, Sartre, Lanzmann.*

54. *June 1979: at the Elysée with Raymond Aron, in support of "A Ship for Vietnam."*
55. *September 27, 1979: at the Père-Lachaise cemetery, during the funeral of Pierre Goldmann.*
56. *February 1980, Boulevard Edgar-Quinet: in the shadow of the tower.*

56.

55.

57. *April 19, 1980: Sartre's funeral.* ▶

signs of success. The event was highlighted by a panel featuring Sartre, Camus, Breton, the American Richard Wright, the Italians Carlo Levi and Guido Piovene, intellectuals from India, Madagascar, Vietnam, Spain, and Morocco, as well as the RDR leaders themselves, Rousset, Altman, Bourdet, and Rosenthal. This meeting of intellectuals from all over the world—deliberately, if awkwardly, titled "The Internationalism of the Mind"—gathered together more than four thousand people. One by one, each writer expressed his disgust at fascism and his faith in freedom. "Human ambitions can no longer be satisfied by the existing parties," André Breton asserted, while Camus set forth the idea that the world was in disgrace and governments were in the hands of inquisitors before announcing the formula: "Better be wrong and murder no one than be right in a slaughterhouse." Carlo Levi, author of *Christ Stopped at Eboli*, declared himself convinced that "all the movements in favor of a revolutionary democracy will soon be only one movement." Sartre insisted once more on the need to unify Europe: "All the men who have gathered here today believe in Europe. They share the same fears and the same hopes. . . . Any attempt to unify Europe becomes suspect the moment it is initiated by governments or high political figures. This initiative must come from the European masses." The German Theodor Plievier spoke of the youth of his country who, he reassured his audience, "no longer dream of a German hegemony, having finally understood how that dream was at the origin of the country's fall. After the understandable apathy that followed the demise of the Nazi regime, German youth are again becoming interested in politics, in the broadest sense of the term." Richard Wright then launched into a diatribe fraught with all the contradictions that had perpetually plagued him: "These two nations, Russia and America, believe they represent human freedom, and the human mind is sacrificed to these two beliefs. Man is scared, unable to choose." Then, remembering the real purpose of his presence there, he swerved in another direction: "Writers and artists, listen to me: the leaders of the world are waging a war against you! They don't need you in the society they are contemplating."[32]

There was considerable behind-the-scenes discord. According to David Rousset, "Merleau-Ponty had been invited but Camus had intervened. He would not attend the meeting if Merleau was present. And since Camus was much more popular, we had to choose him over Merleau."[33] And, as for the tenor of the contributions, one did not have to be a scholar to realize that it concealed a rather fragile, superficial, banal consensus: of course everybody was for peace and against war, for telling the truth over lying, and for Europe over the other two existing world powers.

The real assets of the movement lay elsewhere: in its attempt to establish a dialogue with certain groups of workers—the striking miners of the North, for instance—in its numerous attempts, by trial and error, to introduce the country to a true democratic experience, and in various other microscopic experiments that would reappear twenty or twenty-five years later in phenomena such as the student revolution of 1968 and the self-managing enterprise of the Lip watch factories in Besançon—to cite two examples in which Sartre himself took part. Already in 1948, with the RDR, he militated in favor of two experiments he really cared about: popular universities and training courses for North African workers. One day, invited to speak by a few Moroccan students, he found, for the first time, the third-worldly tones that would a few months later become his trademark: "A Frenchman can attend a Moroccan meeting only with a feeling of guilt," he began. "Moroccans are oppressed. . . . But it is France who oppresses them, not the French masses. Of course you must have been told about France, the country of freedom, every time you had to fight for it against a foreign power. You were being fooled. Many of you were killed for the sake of imperialism, but you thought you were dying for freedom. . . . You are right to accuse France. . . . You are right to complain. . . . When you fight for your freedom, you also fight for the freedom of mankind and, therefore, for our freedom. But we will not be really free as long as we aren't able to say: "There is not a man on earth who is oppressed because of us."[34]

Had the RDR been only the first awkward step toward the assertion of certain political problems—national independence, European identity—or an occasion for the demonstration of certain social problems—immigrant workers, secular education, the third world —that would have been enough to justify its existence. For, in the final analysis this idealist mobilization, spurred by the threat of World War III and an impossible choice between East and the West, humiliated by the degeneration and the passivity to which Europe had been forced, and stimulated by the blockade of West Berlin, was a healthy reaction. But, according to Rousset, it was premature.[35] "It was my first real political move," Sartre explains, "and I must admit it was not the most felicitous: our ideas were fairly vague; all in all, I would say it was a new version of that 'third force' so many people wanted to create in France."[36] A rather negative final assessment.

THE DEFINITIVE rupture between Sartre and Rousset occurred when, for financial reasons, the latter turned toward the U.S. trade unions the AFL and CIO. With their help and that of American intellectuals such as Sidney Hook, he organized the International Day of Resistance to Dictatorship and War on April 30, 1949. On January 29 and 30, Sartre had missed the meeting of the of the RDR's management committee, during which twenty-five members had elaborated the various stages of the group's insertion into the Socialist Movement for the United States of Europe, and had discussed tactics and candidates for the cantonal elections of March 20, 1949. Sartre was also absent from the demonstrations of April 30. April 30 had been planned in response to the initiatives of the recent peace movement, now entirely in the hands of the communists. Delicate negotiations had taken place between certain members of the RDR—Fraisse, Rous, Bourdet, Rousset—and some communist intellectuals, among them Laurent Casanova, in an attempt to reach a possible agreement, some common purpose. The result of these efforts was a total failure, with the communists leaning toward Moscow and the RDR toward Washington. At around the same time and for similar reasons, there was a rift between Sartre and Rousset. "Realizing that we had been had," Sartre explains, "Merleau-Ponty, Richard Wright, and I refused to attend a meeting to which had been invited a few well-known American anti-communists, like Sidney Hook, and during which some people praised the atomic bomb. . . . we demanded an emergency meeting, which took place a month later."[37]

June 28 and 29, 1949, were devoted to the first national congress of the RDR. Seventy delegates attended to "exchange points of view in a brotherly fashion, in the total independence of their respective thoughts,"[38] as *Franc-Tireur* diplomatically noted. According to Sartre, "It was a violent congress; some ex-communists and Trotsky-ites reproached Rousset for his connections with the United States. . . . The RDR fell to pieces. A large majority wanted to work with the communists, while a small minority favored the United States."[39] And, indeed, if the name of Sartre is still in the RDR archives, it is partly because of the motion he and some friends presented before the final reckoning: the "Chauvin-Sartre motion." Besides Sartre, a member of the managing committee, and Jean-René Chauvin, a member of the Paris council, the endorsers of the document were Henri Sack, a former militant of the German Communist Party, Henri Massein, a Trotskyite, and Georges Gousseau, who later joined the Socialist Party. "Today, the RDR is over a year old," they essentially stated. "Where does it stand? The odds seem to be against it. After a promising start, recruiting has come to a standstill. . . . we have started losing our supporters: entire sections have resigned, others have been stripped down to the bone. And yet, at the same time, the management committee has continued to plan its meetings and spectacular demonstrations . . . which would be all right if recruiting were still going on. But, since that is not the case, a large gap has developed between a totally stagnant base and a management committee that keeps addressing the masses, Europe, the world— everybody, in short, except its own militants. . . . The direct democracy on which the whole organization was supposed to rest now exists only on paper. The problem has never been tyranny, however, but anarchy."[40] There is anger in this self-criticism, as well as frankness. The lack of internal democracy was only one of the problems; ideological differences, contributing to the tug of war between Moscow and Washington, constituted another. "Not only does the RDR not reject any joint action with the Communist Party," the motion maintained, "but it supports every link between communist and socialist workers whenever there is a question of defending the immediate interests of the workers."

Before the national congress, the management committee had formed a commission to outline a "project of general orientation" for the RDR. The commission included Altman, Dechezelles, Fraisse, Parisot, Rosenthal, Rous, and Sartre. Its conclusions: The RDR had failed to "organize a real militant collectivity" or to define "the structure of its organization," but it had succeeded in being the "organizing and dynamic center of several democratic and labor movements" representing a broad spectrum of the non-Stalinist, left.[41] Sartre left the movement in October 1949, reproaching Rousset for having evolved "too much to the right." All the papers commented on this event: "After a brilliant beginning," Le Monde noted, "the RDR has fallen asleep, weakened by inner conflicts. . . . Sartre's defection is evidence of the movement's inability to solve its internal quarrels."[42] To turn Sartre into the barometer of the RDR was, to say the least, excessive: one more token of the French media's stubborn, daily pursuit of the philosopher. "Nauseated by Politics, Sartre Leaves the RDR," read the headlines of Samedi soir, not known for its interest in political news. The day of the congress, Sartre was in fact nowhere to be found: he had just left for a tour of Mexico, Guatemala, and other countries, accompanied by Dolorès.[43]

By this time, the movement had only about two thousand adherents in all of France; not many, considering it was over a year old. According to Paul Fraisse, Sartre was a "very generous financier" —he had given a total of 300,000 francs—but an inadequate "committee member."[44] On the other hand, his name had certainly been crucial in drawing foreign support. When, in February 1949, a group of young Italians expressed their desire "to correspond with *La Gauche–RDR,* whose program they "fully endorsed," they specifically referred to Sartre: "In one of his articles, Sartre urges young Europeans to become the interpreters of their own life. In the last twenty years, not a single government has been able to give its youth real democratic institutions that would allow them to get rid of dogmatic formulas."[45] Sartre's favorite generation, the "twenty-year-olds" to whom he had addressed his speech, had answered his appeal, as it would for years to come.

Once the experiment with the RDR was over, Sartre limited himself to very occasional political interventions until the end of 1949. Two of these are worth mentioning. First he supported Garry Davis and his movement of World Citizens. In September 1948, this World War II U.S. Army Air Force pilot had publicly torn up his U.S. passport to convey his disapproval of the Cold War and then entered the UN building in New York to demand a new "world citizenship." There followed press conferences, expressions of solidarity, meetings, petitions: several French writers decided to mobilize in his behalf, including Breton, Camus, Queneau, Vercors, Paulhan, Emmanuel Mounier. At first, Sartre held back. But in June 1949, as his relationship with the RDR rapidly deteriorated, he agreed to "engage in a dialogue" with Davis and the World Citizens, and began by offering them a well-argued criticism of their projects. According to him, the whole idea of a world government was much too utopian and idealistic, but he would gladly remain a "friend and an ally" of the movement.[46]

His second political intervention was a lecture that brought together all his reflections and experiences from 1946 to the present in an original new formulation. Delivered on April 24, 1949, at the Centre d'Etudes de Politique Etrangère and titled "A Defense of French Culture in the Name of European Culture," it purported to show the impact of politics and the economy on culture with the help of numerous examples: "The relationship between cultures is, to a certain extent, determined by the relationship between powers," he stated. Then, trying to determine the identity of French culture in relation to American culture, he spoke of impermeability and used all the anecdotes of his last lecture tour to show what it was that distinguished European intellectual writers from U.S. writers. "I would say that what characterizes European culture is a struggle against evil. . . . European writers have always fought against power, against established ideology, and for social justice. . . . Whereas in America a writer and an intellectual are two separate things, in France a writer is by definition also an intellectual. . . . There is an American virus that risks contaminating us quite soon, and that is the pessimism of the intellectual. . . . Do we have the means to save the most essential elements of our culture?" he wondered after evoking the specter of a French culture threatened by American hegemony. "Yes, we do," he answered optimistically, "provided we constitute a 'cultural unity,' and inaugurate a 'European cultural politics.' " He illustrated his fears with an image that "occurred to me during my European journeys": Voltaire, Kierkegaard, and Kafka buried under an avalanche of indigestible Yankee novels. "It is only by aiming at a European cultural unity that we will be able to preserve French culture; but this cultural unity will mean nothing, will be mere empty words, unless it is part of a much larger and deeper effort toward the realization of European political and economic unity."[47] An obvious product of his reflections, observations, and political analyses, this lecture is also a perfect synthesis of Sartre at his moment of glory. The status of the writer, the status of Europe, cultural and political projects are here mixed in a very personal program. These will be his last reflections of this kind before he leaves, for a time, the political arena.

"Sartre really made an effort," David Rousset believes today. "Maybe Altman and I were wrong when we went to him before launching the RDR: his presence had a few very positive effects. He was very direct in his dealings with the militants, but he always retained his almost papal dogmatism. I believe this is what finally hindered his participation in political action, because, despite his lucidity, he lived in a world that was totally isolated from reality. . . . He was very much involved in the play and movement of ideas, but not so much in events. . . . No, he was never terribly interested in the world. Rousset pauses for a second, thinks, then, pursuing his train of thought, he adds: "Yes, that's it, Sartre lived in a bubble."[48]

After the failure of "Socialism and Freedom" in 1941, the arrests of his friends, and the dangers of underground political action, Sartre had needed a pause. After the failure of the RDR, the experiment of a libertarian, intellectual democracy, and a second realization of the discrepancy between intellectual peculation and concrete militant action, Sartre needs to pause again. He finds himself in a second impasse. From now on, his political interventions will no longer be those of a militant belonging to a specific movement or group, but rather those of a sympathizing intellectual who lends his support from the outside. After his resignation from the RDR, he retires from the field of political action. Now it is time to measure the full extent of his commitment and the limits of abstract dreams, of those few months of "revolutionary romanticism," to use Aron's unsympathetic definition.[49]

THE IMPASSE REVISITED

"SOMEDAY YOU'LL be able to open the dictionary and read SARTRE, Jean-Paul, famous twentieth-century preface-writer." Thus he would now and then joke about what seemed to have become a new career. After the failure of the RDR, all the engines had slowed down. "Sartre had practically given up all political activity," Beauvoir writes. "He dabbled in history and economics, reread Marx,"[1] and wrote prefaces. Among the many authors prefaced, cautioned, enthroned by Sartre, "Sartronized": Louis Dalmas for an essay on Yugoslavian communism; Juan Hermanos for an essay on Franco's regime; the composer René Leibowitz for his analysis of the artist's commitment to a "nonsignifying" art; Roger Stéphane for his *Portrait de l'aventurier*; the Nagel guides of Scandinavia, where Sartre had traveled; and, later, Henri Cartier-Bresson for his photos of China, where Sartre had not yet traveled. What did these baptismal gestures mean for a man who had always refused real paternity? Although he had never procreated, he nevertheless had a rich and large progeny: his readers, his followers, his devotees, who were first "Roquentized" and then "Sartronized." "Sartronization" became a sacrament that could be bestowed only after due application and a thorough examination of the applicant's files by members of the "family." The case of Nathalie Sarraute, first on this list, is one of the most interesting: her second novel, *Portrait d'un inconnu*, was published in 1947 with an eight-page preface by Sartre. "Sartre was wonderful to me," she will later explain. "After the Liberation, he read my latest manuscript and decided to write a preface for it. 'It's a difficult book,' he told me, 'you'll have difficulties finding a publisher.' He was right. But even with his preface, in 1947, at a time when he was so famous that carloads of tourists would constantly file by the Deux Magots in the hope of catching a glimpse of him, my novel was refused by everybody. I finally found a publisher who managed to sell four hundred copies before pulping it."[2]

The activity of preface writer makes far more sense that it may at first seem: Sartre's prefaces were very dynamic and gave him the opportunity to develop ideas, modulate them, clarify them. They allowed him to explain his notion of commitment in so-called abstract arts (Leibowitz); to complete the article he wrote in 1938 against Mauriac, by opposing the good faith of writers to God's point of view (Nathalie Sarraute); to resume the theme of commitment in both its ethical and political aspects (Roger Stéphane); and, in 1950, to assume a public stance in favor of Tito and the Yugoslav experiment (Dalmas). They also allowed him to bring new friends, allies, and accomplices into the Sartrean sphere.

Another symptom of his celebrity, his credibility, his acquired capital was the increase in requests for advice and for appointments. Bernard Pingaud had direct experience of the multiple seductions exercised by Sartre's personality and oeuvre. Pingaud attended Lycée Pasteur, but not in Sartre's class, then he wrote a first novel, *The Phoenix*, which one of his friends proposed to show Sartre. "He read the manuscript, then he asked me to meet him at the Flore," Pingaud remembers. " 'I have read it. You have talent,' he told me. 'But why are you trying to be so lyrical? You are dry. Cultivate your dryness. You will never be lyrical, but come back to see me if you feel like it.' "[3] Pingaud published his novel in 1946, read *The Roads*, and began to write a study of Sartre, which, with the help of the rightist writer Pierre Boutang, he then transformed into a pamphlet, *Is Sartre Possessed?*, jointly signed Boutang-Pingaud. In it, the two authors reproached Sartre for not being lyrical enough, for being too terse and dry! Later Pingaud would join the editorial staff of *Les Temps modernes*.

Sartre managed to attract many young, postwar French writers, both from the right and the left. He drew anarchists, libertarians, premature leftists, and even such rightist "hussars" as Roger Nimier, who dedicated his first novel, *La Prisonnière*, to Sartre. Similarly, when Louis Pauwels published his first novel, *Saint Quelqu'un*, in

1946, he introduced his hero, Jousselin, as a totally "Roquentized" being, also partly influenced by Meursault, Camus's *Stranger*. By 1946, there is already a sure Sartrean posterity. "I have only loved serious writers," Roger Nimier writes to Jacques Chardonne in 1953. "Bernanos, Chardonne, Sartre. We must go back to Sartre. We have been unjust to him."[4] On another occasion, he will hail Sartre's "social role," which he compares to Voltaire's, before adding, "His image, recomposed, is that of a destroyer, and yet, first prize for intelligence, and second certificate of merit in obscenity."[5]

313

THE MOST famous and certainly the most complex of Sartre's visitors was Bernard Frank, who wrote of their relationship (between 1951 and 1953) in a number of his works. He left his first manuscript with the concierge at the Rue Bonaparte, and then waited, anxiously, for a favorable answer. "When Sartre summoned me over to tell me that I was a writer," Frank writes, "I realized that for him it was a discovery whereas for me it had long been a certainty. His surprise, his joy, his congratulations displeased me. . . . But now I can find a thousand justifications for them. . . . Sartre was incommensurably kind . . . the interest he showed his visitors was generally very useful."[6] The meeting measured up to the expectations of this twenty-one-year-old writer: a year later, Sartre asked Frank to direct the literary page of *Les Temps modernes*. So, in less than a year, this unknown but promising writer found himself on Sartre's team and, indeed, in the very bosom of the little family. "Sartre informed me . . . that for the first six months I would be there on trial. . . . I felt as if he was turning me into a young, scrupulous, but somewhat too vivacious, maid, who is suddenly entrusted, not without some misgiving, with the black feather duster that's been taken out of the hands of an old and cranky servant whose tics and grumbles have been driving the whole house crazy." After a first, euphoric phase—"I liked the role of the irregular, the mercenary that I played for *Les Temps modernes* . . . it fit my nature," Frank writes—the relationship started deteriorating: his articles were rejected, his new novel, *Les Rats*, was panned in *Les Temps modernes*, and by none other than Jean Cau. The staff of *Les Temps modernes* had failed to appreciate, in the novel, Frank's criticism of what he called their "strange *collective* solipsism." A certain amount of friction or jealousy between Frank and Cau became the subject of Frank's next book.[7]

The sociologist Michel Crozier also contributed a few articles to *Les Temps modernes* between 1951 and 1952: "I was young and unknown. I sent my article to them as one would throw a bottle into the sea," he writes. "But *Les Temps modernes* liked my prose and asked for more."[8] Was this another example of the flexible structure, the openness, and the accessibility that Sartre seemed to encourage in everything he undertook? "No," Crozier answers, and explains his disappointment. "I did not expect to become famous overnight, but I did hope I'd be given some attention, find a few people I could talk to, stop feeling completely isolated. In short, I hoped I'd be considered as part of a living milieu. But at *Les Temps modernes* I only found snobbism, rivalries, and pretension. Its milieu was as cold and as impersonal as a political party or a university."

At about this time, Sartre decided to write a preface to Jean Genet's works. Introduced in 1944 via Cocteau, Genet had become a devotee of the Sartre family, a friend of sorts, accompanying members of the group on outings and dedicating his book *The Thief's Journal* to Sartre and Beauvoir. Sartre had praised Genet on both visits to the United States, had dedicated *Baudelaire* to him, and had written, in March 1946, a promotional insert for *The Miracle of the Rose*: "For Proust pederasty was a destiny . . . for Genet it is a choice. . . . the author has chosen theft and prison, love and the consciousness of Evil. He teases the reader and he shows off, but he never abandons himself completely; his art keeps the reader at a distance. It is thanks to this if, at the bottom of this remote world, in the hell of solitary confinement and drug pushers, we still find a man."[9]

Gradually, the preface to Genet grows into a monstrous hybrid. It keeps on swelling, imbued with all of Sartre's passions, till it reaches 690 pages! And Jean Genet will be imprisoned, within these pages, as the Sartrean hero par excellence. Genet has known all the social curses: illegitimacy, public assistance, delinquency, imprisonment, homosexuality. He has lived them all and transformed them into a work of art. He has crossed society from every margin, in every direction, impermeable to its norms, beyond its scorn and its sanctions, but also beyond its bonuses and its acknowledgments: a perfectly independent being on which social anomie has absolutely no hold; completely autonomous, the creator of his own system of values, his own universe, the way Sartre had tried to be in his complex disputes with Jean-Baptiste, Charles Schweitzer, and Mancy. *Saint Genet* could be a double of Sartre, but a successful double whose life is in itself a work of art: an

esthetic of provocation, of sublimation, of the most rigorous aso-
ciality, in the supreme alternation between humiliation and challenge, between stigmatization and omnipotence. The tug of war
between society and this sort of individual is generally frightful,
but Genet came out of it whole, triumphant, and indifferent. "Eva
Peron's canonization by the pope," Cocteau will write after reading Sartre's book, "and Genet's by Sartre (another pope), are the
two mystical events of this summer."[10]

Following Sartre's directions, Jean Cau had shown the huge manuscript to Genet before it was published. If Genet had found fault
with it, he could easily have spoken up, just as he could have kept
it, lost it, or even burned it. But he did not. He tacitly accepted it,
and also accepted all its consequences. The readers of this unusual
book could thus witness the meeting between two individuals who
represented the two opposite poles of French society, two individuals differently determined by their birth. The Normalien, weighed
down by his readings, his cultural references, his sophisticated theoretical tools eagerly drawn to the bastard, the jailbird, the misfit, the
homosexual.

"I became a traitor, and remained one," Sartre will later write in
his autobiography, *The Words*. The capacity for treason that he
perceived in Genet, many-voiced, insatiable, and permanent, under-
lies the whole of *Saint Genet*. "The deftest, most intelligent lesson
in phenomenological ontology of its time, quite French,"[11] Jacques
Derrida will decree, alluding to the psychoanalytical-biographical
ambitions of the text, and Sartre's greed for the person and the
oeuvre of Genet. It was nearly a rape. The theme of bastardy evoked
in him a more radical version of the fatherless orphan, just as the
themes of theft, jail, and homosexuality evoked those of social subversion, treason, and marginal violence, though at a much more
concrete, more experiential level. The notion of "praxis," crucial in
Sartre's philosophical reflection, thus gradually takes shape. In her
introduction to *Search for a Method*, Sartre's English translator,
Hazel Barnes, says that Sartre uses this Greek word for "action" to
signify "any meaningful or purposeful human activity, any act that
is not mere random, undirected activity."[12] Still implicit, embryonic
in *Saint Genet*, this notion will be applied to politics by the following
year and then, in 1960, will be analyzed and elaborated in the *Critique
of Dialectical Reason. Saint Genet* marked a new stage in the dynamics of Sartre's work, an intersection between the (auto)biographical

path—*Baudelaire, The Words, Flaubert*— and the philosophical one
—the *Morale* and the *Critique of Dialectical Reason.*

316
Cocteau's journal sums up the complex and confused reception of
the book. "As all real books of criticism, it is a monumental portrait
of Sartre, for which Genet is only the bronze or the stone. . . . it
represents Genet no more than the Statue of Liberty, in New York,
represents American freedom. . . . Sartre acquits Genet. . . . Finished
Sartre's book. The last chapters sloshed on in a nauseating mud. Too
bad. . . . I feel uncomfortable as I am leaving the book. Who can
swallow such a thing? Sartre makes it, thanks to a perfect cohesion
of style and concept. . . . he has the nobility of a clinician, is honest,
loves his subject. It is scary, disgusting . . . but not embarrassing. And
there is something else. The will to be the center of attention in
literature, and render everything else insipid."[13] Others joined the
debate: "Sartre did not want to wound Genet; he only wanted to
stake his honor on his head, like William Tell," quipped Olivier
Larronde.[14] Mauriac was simple and direct: in *Le Figaro,* he described Genet's work as nothing more nor less than a "turd." As for
Paul Claudel, in *Les Nouvelles littéraires,* he had found an article by
Robert Kemp, titled "Repugnances," about a book by Sartre and one
by Céline. Both books, as all of Claudel's oeuvre, were published by
Gallimard. So he wrote a rather bourgeois, awkward letter to "Dear
Gaston," intimating that the proximity of those two texts in the same
prestigious catalog was physically unbearable to him. "The author
[Sartre] who proposes this individual to the admiration of his own
devotees," Claudel writes, "has the dubious taste of applying to him
texts by Saint Theresa and Saint John of the Cross. It seems you are
the publisher of such books; I hope they'll bring you some money.
But unfortunately you won't have much time to enjoy it because,
whether you like it or not, one of these days you'll have to pay for
them. In the meantime, I wonder what you feel at the thought that
one day your grandchildren might recognize the name of their
grandfather indelibly engraved on the covers. Please accept my most
doleful regards."[15] We don't know whether Gaston Gallimard's
descendants were indeed shocked by the juxtaposition. To Robert
Gallimard, Sartre's own editor, it was all quite ridiculous. Besides,
Claudel had not even read *Saint Genet.*

Georges Bataille published an enthusiastic article in *Critique*:
"This interminable study is not only one of the richest books of our
time, but also Sartre's masterpiece. . . . It leaves you with a feeling
of confused catastrophe and universal deception, but it also manages

to cast some light on the situation of man today, revolted, unhinged. . . . Sartre's flaws have never been more obvious; never before has he left his thoughts drone on at such length, never before has he closed himself off so utterly from the discreet pleasures of chance that cross life and furtively light it up: he paints horror with complacency."[16] As for Genet, he wrote to Cocteau: "You and Sartre have turned me into a monument. I am somebody else, and this somebody else must find something to say."[17] "Jean has changed since the publication of Sartre's book," Cocteau notes. "He looks as if he were trying at once to follow it and to escape it."[18]

W RITTEN AT the same time as *Saint Genet,* Sartre's seventh play, *The Devil and the Good Lord,* was performed for the first time on June 7, 1951, and ran uninterruptedly till March 1952; it was the major event of the theater season. "This play may be regarded as a supplement or sequel to *Dirty Hands,"* the author writes in an introductory text, "although the action takes place four hundred years earlier. I want to show a character as alien to the spirit of his age as Hugo, the young bourgeois in *Dirty Hands,* and equally torn by contradictions." Simone Berriau, the director of the Théâtre Antoine and a dynamic, seductive businesswoman, given to wearing wide-brimmed hats day and night, convinced Sartre to write the play, and kept him going whenever he felt like giving up. Louis Jouvet, a legendary figure in the French theater, took on the play as his last production, and died two months after the premiere. The lead actors were all major figures in the French theater. Pierre Brasseur starred as Goetz. Jean Vilar, founder of the Théâtre National Populaire, took the role of Heinrich. The great Maria Casarès (famous as Death in Cocteau's film *Orphée),* with her hypnotic presence and burning voice, was Hilda. Wanda, alias Maria Ollivier, played Cathérine. The rehearsals began before Sartre had finished writing; Simone Berriau demanded last-minute cuts; Sartre and Jouvet had their disagreements; preparation of the costumes and sets took countless hours; Sartre worked under the pressure of time, Jouvet under the pressure of impending death and Berriau under that of an impossible schedule, all of which helps to explain the tensions and energies that accompanied this mad project.[19] It became an obsession, as was always the case when Sartre wrote a play, but this time it obsessed a dozen or so people simultaneously. "Sartre maintained," Simone de Beauvoir writes, "that when Simone Berriau wandered around the theater, her hands mechanically imitated the movement of a pair of scissors."[20]

"Jouvet is waiting for Sartre," was the title of a critic's article four months before the opening of the play. And the journalists enjoyed themselves speculating on this confrontation between giants, on the outcome of the struggle. The evening of the premiere, a member of the audience booed so loudly that he had to be dragged out of the theater and into the nearest police station, where he told the chief: "I hate Sartre. He is a criminal. He poisons our youth. We must shoot him like an evil beast."[21] This troubled climate was fostered by those critics who saw the play as "a war machine set against God," or "a ridiculous blasphemy." Mauriac dubbed Sartre, "the providential atheist," and Thierry Maulnier declared, "There is no Good Lord." Others reproached the play for not knowing whether to be intellectual, philosophical, metaphysical, boring, chatty, or verbose. Elsa Triolet said that it made her think of Ghelderode; others mentioned Claudel. But one notes, above all, in the reactions of the contemporary critics and the performances of the actors, the idea of the death of God. In his introductory text, Sartre had provided a few keys: the sequel to *Dirty Hands,* heroes cut off from the masses . . . Roquentin, Lucien Fleurier, Orestes, Hugo, Genet, now Goetz: the identical questions, the same freeze-frames, a Sartre in search of himself, in search of the connection between the individual and his actions, his world, a morality. In fact, *The Devil* was a crucial link in Sartre's philosophical reflection, a link that Simone de Beauvoir later elucidated in *Force of Circumstance.* Her familiarity with Sartre's philosophy, both in its genesis and in its various manifestations, and her privileged acquaintance with the unpublished manuscripts the writer composed at the same time, allowed her to propose an "internal" interpretation of the themes and the ideology of the play: "In fact, Sartre was once more confronting the vanity of morality with the efficacy of *praxis.* This confrontation goes much further than it had in his previous plays. . . . In 1944, Sartre thought that any situation could be transcended by subjective effort; in 1951, he knew that circumstances can sometimes steal our transcendence from us; in that case no individual salvation is possible, only a collective struggle."[22] Goetz will be Genet pushed to the extreme of evil in his quest for the absolute, as well as the incarnation of the growing dialogue between Sartre and Marxism after the failure of the RDR and the impotence of reality. "I had Goetz do what I could not do," Sartre will himself admit.

*T*HE LEAST known and most ambitious work of these years, abandoned for no clear reason, was undoubtedly the manuscript that went by the title of "La Reine Albemarle ou le dernier touriste," an unfinished, unpublished novel which, according to Simone de Beauvoir, was supposed to be the *"Nausea* of Sartre's maturity." He had written the first hundred pages of the text in a little notebook with a black moleskin cover on which was a label with the title "La regina Albemarle o l'ultimo turista." This Italian title implies more than mere personal pleasure at writing a few words in Italian: the manuscript was written in Italy, about Italy, and around Italy, the country Sartre visited most frequently and with the greatest pleasure. Naples, Venice, Milan, Turin, but, particularly, Rome. His daily schedule was as perfectly organized in Rome as it was in Paris. Breakfast was followed by a few hours of work in a café. Then, toward the end of the day, he'd take a walk, and look for some piazzetta, some outdoor restaurant, one among the thousands the city harbors. Long walks along the Tiber, toward Piazza Navona where he liked to sip his evening Scotch and indulge in the bitter, rich flavor of a *tartufo con panna*— his favorite chocolate treat—or toward Campo dei Fiori and Piazza San Eustachio, where one can drink the best coffee in Rome, the densest most bitter espresso, under the gaze of a deer head mysteriously protruding from the façade of the church.

Sartre loved Rome with all the greed and passion of a romantic. Starting in 1946, he visited every year for several weeks. He stayed either at the Hotel Minerva, overlooking the small square where a miniature elephant carries a huge obelisk on his back, at the Hotel Senato, on the Piazza del Pantheon, or at the Hotel Nazionale, the ritziest, in front of the Parliament. There, starting in the 1960s, he will reserve a suite—"rooms 94 and 95" as the doorman mechanically announces when one mentions the writer's name—with balcony and air-conditioning for himself and Simone de Beauvoir. Roman delicacies, cobblestones, flower markets, ocher façades, fountains, fig trees, smells of sewage, pizzas, and roasted coffee, cars nudging pedestrians, mixing with them, honking, but above all, eyes, aggressive, inquisitive, caressing, almost protective, eyes that seize you, possess you, and immediately consecrate you as a Roman pedestrian. Sartre roams the city, a happy stroller in search of familiar smells and tastes. In Rome, after the first excitement produced by the announcement of his arrival, he could be again an anonymous citizen, rarely recognized in cafés, seldom bothered, and hence free to sit at a table and abandon himself to his passion, his "voyeurism," as he was used to doing in Paris before the war, and as he had done in Le Havre and in Berlin. He would sit in front of a glass of white wine and watch the movements of the crowd, people coming and going, pretty women. *"Un espresso," "Un whisky," "Un gelato," "Grazie, grazie,"* and he was all set. A magical, corrupting city, an anonymous crowd, an unknown language. He could let himself go in his favorite places, in a freedom of movement that his celebrity no longer allowed him in France. He felt protected by the language barrier, an indulgent fog that infantilizes and lulls.

"One of the charms of Rome," Simone de Beauvoir writes, "is that since 1946, the unity of the left has remained intact. This is exactly what Sartre had tried to do."[23] And indeed, it is onto Rome, and onto Italy that Sartre will eventually project all his political and cultural phantoms. To him, the Italian Communist Party (PCI) is a miracle, the anti-PCF, the party of freedom and of potential, just as Italy is a magical country, the "country where people laugh in the streets."[24] He finds the Italian communist intellectuals uncommonly open and easy to talk to and understand, because they live in a country where it is still possible to choose and where to fight with and for the proletariat does not necessarily lead to a major compromise; a country where, crucially, a committed work of art could remain a work of art. For Sartre, there is no comparison between the numerous books produced by the French communist writers of the fifties and the beautiful novels of Elio Vittorini, Carlo Levi, Ignazio Silone, and Alberto Moravia—as if Roman magic, Tuscan harmony, and Piedmontese elegance were in themselves enough to safeguard their authors from all dogmatism and arbitrariness.

"I was supposed to work on the screenplay of *No Exit*," Moravia remembers, "but Sartre did not seem to like my interpretation of the play, and he was probably right. We were to meet at a small café in the Piazza Colonna. There, I told him how delighted I was to meet the author of *Nausea* and 'The Childhood of a Leader.' "[25] By 1946, Moravia, a lover of Flaubert and the surrealists, perfectly at ease in the correct, rich French he had learned from his governess Mlle Durand, had already written eleven novels. Two years younger than Sartre, he had already broached the theme of the alienation, the indifference, and the hyperlucidity of the individual in his novel, *The Time of Indifference,* published in 1929, ten years before *Nausea.* There are intimate ideological ties between the two men even though Moravia, who, "as a citizen," is not afraid of offering his outside, indiscriminate support to the PCI, will always oppose the idea of Sartrean commitment. "In my mind, the artist's quest for the absolute has always been in radical opposition to the politician's quest for the relative," he says.

In Rome, Sartre visits Carlo Levi, Renato Guttuso, and dines with Palmiro Togliatti, the leader of the PCI. He finds he can talk with them; he has more things in common with them than with his French homologues. In the cafés of Rome and Venice, he finds again the eyes and the pen of the voyeur for "La Reine Albemarle," just as in Le Havre he had found them for *Nausea*. "Italian women still have the spontaneity Stendhal so admired," he writes. "I like the way they enter a restaurant or a dance floor. Our women are constantly looking for an attitude. They are not."[26] He writes "La Reine Albemarle" as he would a journal: day by day, watching himself closely. He invents the concept of the "antitourist," tells an anecdote that occurred to him in a gondola, in Venice, then analyzes it until it becomes significant: thus he discovers that the antitourist has some traits of Roquentin's, an older Roquentin, perhaps, but still knocking about. "The sadness of Venice is like a cold day, sweet but piercing, slowly seeping down to one's bones. . . . In Venice one can only be an amateur, an artisan . . . one's life, as well as one's vision can only unfold at short range, as it were, minute by minute. . . . Venice resembles the haunting mind of someone who's unable to untangle himself from the web of his bad faith. . . . Depressing . . . And then there is the water . . . gradually one swells up."[27] He jots down a few details to which he is particularly sensitive: "These Italians are all addicts, dope fiends . . . with their forty kilos of pasta a year . . . I've heard that thirty coffees a day could kill." The attraction of the addict, the dope fiend, for a country of addicts and dope fiends. The slow outlining of a potential novel, an aborted novel.

The text written in the notebook with the moleskin cover is mirrored by another manuscript, another approach to "La Reine Albemarle": thirty pages long, this astounding text relates a fantastic Roman encounter in a foggy, oneiric atmosphere whose eerie sonority bears no similarity to Sartre's usual tones. The narrator butts against a number of monstrous, shapeless creatures, which eventually turn out to be incarnated memories, concrete souvenirs. Thus, for instance, he realizes that the proportions of a particular house are "more or less the same as those of our barracks at the Stalag XII D: it held 158 of us." This deformation of proportion and nearly magical recall of previous, lost proportions, as well as the coexistence of the monstrously huge and the grotesquely tiny, are typical phenomena of waking dreams, hallucinations. This is again obvious in another fragment: "Rome is empty . . . a midget, a woman, comes toward me dragging her slippered feet. At last! I was about to believe I was a ghost. But, as she goes by, she casts a fearful glance at me, and, in her eyes, I see she is not sure I am not one."[28]

According to the most knowledgeable "Sartrologists," the manuscript amounted to some five hundred pages, and so far only a hundred of them have resurfaced. At the request of the weekly *France-Observateur,* Sartre authorized publication of a few pages—which were later reprinted in the fourth volume of *Situations* as "Venice from My Window," and "A Bed of Nasturtiums." "It is raining. All big cities look alike under the rain. Paris is no longer in Paris, nor is London any longer in London, but Rome remains in Rome. . . . Thirty centuries have impregnated the walls with phosphorescence: I walk under the rain among sweet solar clearings. Romans run through these wet suns laughing. . . . I turn around a devastated Pantheon; the . . . obelisk is supported by a very unhappy elephant; this African mishmash hails the glory of Christianity. Here is Rome: it emerges from the water, already dry, a whole bloody ossuary."[29]

Sartre has left quite a few traces in Rome; at the Hotel Nazionale, for instance, or near the large synagogue, at the entrance of a restaurant where, at least till August 1984, one could read this mention: "Piccioncino alla Jean-Paul Sartre, ricetta di Jean-Paul Sartre." But, despite the elephant of Piazza Minerva, and the young pigeons of the restaurant, Sartre abandoned "La Reine Albemarle" to her magic and her myths, and, with her, the notion of a great novel: this will neither be the first nor the last time Sartre gives up on an unfinished manuscript, but the abandonment of "La Reine Albemarle" marks a precise end. When Sartre resumes his political activity, two or three years later, he will embark on a radically different phase, contributing to his role as a writer with other goals and ambitions.[30]

*F*OR THE time being, isolated and stubborn, he reads, writes, and plays music, mostly at Simone de Beauvoir's. In the course of these years he neither participates in public discussions nor delivers even a single lecture. Instead, he turns in upon himself and rediscovers an esthetics of solitude, of ascesis. Nor is it surprising that he should spend so much time with Beauvoir: his relationship with Dolorès has been over since June 1950, barely a year after their long trip to Central America, the trip for which he had missed the first and last congress of the RDR. They had gone to Mexico, Guatemala, and Haiti, where they had attended cockfights and witnessed voodoo rites, then to Cuba, where Sartre met Ernest Hemingway for the second time, at his house, La Finca. The two writers spent the entire evening speaking more about author's rights, percentages, foreign sales, and translations than of literary theory or existentialism. Dolorès was peculiarly silent all evening. Sartre failed to appreciate Mrs. Hemingway's repeated efforts to make something special happen between the two men of letters. Later, in her memoirs, she will note how that dinner of August 27, 1949 had fallen short of her expectations: "I had hoped to get an overview and an analysis of existentialism. . . . Instead, they spoke like two businessmen."[31] Dolorès finds neither the evening nor the trip, for that matter, particularly memorable. Apparently, Sartre was often morose and grumpy: obviously not their best time together.

Their affair ended like all the others: Sartre proposed to keep it going, and offered an apartment and regular meetings—a contract for a lifelong friendship. Dolorès refused. Later, she spoke of "incredible cruelty" without accusing anybody; she spoke of "destruction," of "the destruction of several lives," of "thoughtless acts," all the while refusing to attribute any guilt; she spoke of "will power and implacable harshness" among the people of Sartre's circle who were hostile to their relationship. "She was the only woman who frightened me," Simone de Beauvoir told Sartre in 1974. "She frightened me because she was hostile."[32] A short time after his break with Dolorès, Sartre got involved with Michelle Léglise-Vian, who had just left Boris Vian. They were often spotted, relaxed and happy, in the bars of the Left Bank. Michelle, with her golden hair, her sweetness and precision was always ready to lend her proficiency in English to such and such a translation, such and such a meeting. Always present, always fragile, she never broke with Sartre.

Crucial years, years of reflection and rearrangement. In February 1951, André Gide dies. We remember his famous "Who is this new Jean-Paul?" when he first discovered Sartre after reading "The Wall" in the NRF in 1938. We remember their first meeting, brought about by the photographer Gisèle Freund, as well as Sartre's visit to Gide, in the summer of 1941, when he was trying to draw famous recruits to his small Resistance group. We also recall Sartre's salute to the writer of decolonization in the declaration of war that was the

"Présentation des *Temps modernes*," as well as Gide's perplexed grimace after Sartre's appeal to commitment. And yet, in the summer of 1950, they were together in Gide's garden at Cabris, in Provence. Comfortably sunk in two huge armchairs with excessively soft backs, they posed for a sequence of a documentary on Gide. When Gide died, just a few months later, Sartre devoted a short article to him in which he praised the virtues of the octogenarian writer: "The same man dared publish the profession of faith of a *Corydon*, the indictment of the *Journey to the Congo*. He had the courage to ally himself with the Soviet Union when it was dangerous to do so, and greater still, he had the courage to recant publicly, when he felt, rightly or wrongly, that he had been mistaken. Perhaps it is this mixture of prudence and daring that makes him exemplary." The daring of the independent, the logic of contradiction and constant research, the courage of subversion, and a strong bias for truth at whatever cost: this is what Sartre praised in his "The Living Gide," all the while emphasizing that, unlike so many others, Gide was an "irreplaceable example because he chose . . . *to become his truth.*" And he added, as if speaking of himself: "Every truth, says Hegel, has become so. We forget this too often, we see the final destination, not the itinerary, we take the idea as a finished product, without realizing that it is only its slow maturation, a necessary sequence of errors correcting themselves, of partial views that are completed and enlarged."[33] This farewell to Gide will be a paving stone, however small, in the long road of Sartre's bio- and autobiographical investigations.

In the meantime, *Les Temps modernes* grew to include a few new collaborators, some fairly close to the PCF. Among these, Claude Lanzmann—who will become an intimate—Marcel Péju, Bernard Dort. Also in the meantime, the magazine denounced the labor camps in the USSR, with an editorial by Merleau-Ponty titled "The Days of Our Lives": "If there are ten million concentration camp inmates—while, at the other end of the Soviet hierarchy salaries and standard of living are fifteen to twenty times higher than those of free workers—then . . . the whole system swerves and changes meaning; and in spite of nationalization of the means of production, and even though private exploitation of man by man and unemployment are impossible in the USSR, we wonder what reasons we still have to speak of socialism in relation to it."[34] In short, Soviet labor camps were "still more criminal because they betrayed the revolution." Merleau-Ponty's denunciation was very scrupulous, very ethical: he made a point of underlining the fact that, nevertheless, Russia remained "not comparable to other countries," and that it was only "permissible to judge it when one has accepted its undertaking, and then only in the name of that undertaking."[35] Of course, it was still a public accusation, but it was a warning uttered against the author's will. Merleau-Ponty's article contains an ambivalence, an inability to condemn radically, and yet, a desire to do so despite a vestige of confidence and hope. The condemnative aspects did not escape the communists. "Our friends in the Party weren't able to digest the article on the camps," Sartre will write. "Right was on our side and this was our feast. Their insults didn't bother me in the least: rat, hyena, viper, polecat—I rather liked this bestiary. It took me out of myself."[36] A new conflict, new insults, new ambiguities. But why so many scruples on the part of *Les Temps modernes* if it was not in the name of the workers, of the homeland, of socialism, of what they called the "communist values"? Because, Merleau-Ponty added, "We have the same values as a communist." And then, he explained: "People will tell me that the communists have no values . . . they have them *in spite of themselves.*"[37]

S ARTRE CONTINUED to share these "communist values," whether real or fictional, during the years of his second impasse. He immediately agreed, when contacted by Claude Roy and Jean Chaintron, to back Henri Martin, a communist sailor who had been arrested in May 1950 and condemned to five years in jail for his political activity against the war in Indochina. Sartre was among those public figures to sign the plea for mercy that was submitted to the president of the Republic and he additionally demanded a private audience with the president, Vincent Auriol: "Henri Martin's case," he declared as he was leaving the Elysée Palace in January 1952, "reflects the discomfort of a whole generation at odds with a society it no longer approves, when it has to deal with principles and aspirations that are quite different from those society wants to impose on it."[38] Sartre also agreed to participate in a collective work that would attempt to reconstruct the whole affair in its minutest details. Henri Martin's case was emblematic of all the causes that Sartre had endorsed: it involved an individual who had been incarcerated unjustly, and it expressed a clear opposition to the war in Indochina. Sporadic riots, guerrilla activities, sham agreements, and a resumption of the warfare continued throughout 1945. In 1946 things got even worse, and by December Ho Chi Minh had resumed his underground activities, announcing that it was imperative to free Cochin China from the French "by any means available." After the vague hope that the conflict could be controlled politically, the guerrilla war picked up again. In France, the news from the front showed French troops flailing in front of the tenacity and stamina of Ho Chi Minh's men. General de Lattre's death, in 1952, confirmed the humiliation of the French army in this remote, costly, and absurd war. Some soldiers, among them the young Henri Martin, experienced this absurdity in person. They saw the sham; they were not fighting against the Japanese army now but rather against the Vietnamese people, who were desperately trying to protect their independence with all the means at their disposal. Henri Martin's case and the Indochinese war were precisely the kind of causes on which Sartre would never compromise. He had long been concerned with the struggle against colonialism, and now he took an active interest in the question of Vietnam.

According to some, the Martin case was Sartre's own Dreyfus or Calas affair, and yet his own text on the question, some hundred pages of it, part of a collective work published by Gallimard in 1953, is relatively unknown. The book is now out of print, impossible to find. Framed by the analyses of Michel Leiris, Hervé Bazin, Jean-Marie Domenach, Jacques Prévert, and others, Sartre's defense speech is like a bronze statue, a tribute to a positive hero: good son, good student, good Resistance fighter, good worker, good sailor. Martin's model life is simplified, purified down to the brightest, most basic colors and the most naïve outlines. His letters to his family from the Bay of Along show the gradual change in this uncommonly analytical sailor.

"My dear parents," Henri Martin wrote from Saigon. "We can be proud of today's toll: one child dead and one woman wounded, without considering all the other bodies we have left in the ricefields. . . . Now that we have killed his child and wounded his wife, our Annamite is certainly going to turn to the Viet Minh, if he isn't already one. This is how we pacify them. Aside from this, peace everywhere. This is all for tonight. Lots of kisses, Henri."[39] No lyricism, but much indignation; no real literature, but much more than just literature in this long and awkward account, full of contained outrage and honest shock. Sartre worked like a public prosecutor, checking every little piece in his files.[40]

Voltaire had gone through a similar process after duly collating all the pieces of the Calas file. He had also been vehement in his defense: "What?" he had shouted. "While philosophy and ethics are supposed to instruct mankind, we condemn an innocent man to the wheel with a majority of eight votes over five, and charge fifteen hundred pounds to transcribe the drivel of an abominable tribunal?! And we want the widow to pay!?"[41]

The Martin affair had a deep resonance in Sartre's memory. The letters sent from the Bay of Along dated "On the Mekong . . . 1947" couldn't have failed to remind the silent orphan in him of the letters, dated 1895, that Jean-Baptiste had also sent from the Bay of Along to his family in Thiviers. They too spoke of pagodas, burning junks, and bloody battles. Henri Martin had revolted in the very same sites where Sartre's father, also with some disgust, had fought and fallen fatally ill. Henri Martin wanted to undo the works of conquest that Jean-Baptiste and his men, on board the *Jean-Bart* and the *Descartes,* had carried out in the very same place, fifty years earlier, in the name of those primitive populations that Vice-Admiral de Beaumont so yearned to civilize.

PIGEONS AND TANKS

ROME, SPRING 1952. Sartre was back for a few weeks' stay in a hotel. This time he was with Michelle Vian. While continuing his Roman walks, he also worked on two manuscripts: "Mallarmé" and "La Reine Albemarle." These few weeks away from France, after an impasse lasting two years, were almost like an exile. Since the sobering death of the RDR, only Henri Martin's case had been able to draw him out of his torpor. But perhaps that was a sign that, at the first good opportunity, he was ready to re-emerge. With the RDR he had gotten involved in a program rather than in a specific situation, in an ideological project rather than in direct action. Henri Martin's case clearly showed that he was ready at the first real emergency to offer all he had: his support, his pen, his name, his money, his own being.

In Rome, Sartre kept informed through both the Italian and French press, and he followed the most recent developments in the controversy surrounding the use of chemical weapons and the development of bacteriological warfare in Korea. He also learned that the PCF was organizing a demonstration to protest the imminent arrival in Paris of the American general Matthew Ridgway, the promoter of this new form of warfare. Henri Martin's case had moved the communist militants into a new phase where the feeling of national persecution was constantly fueled by news from America of McCarthy's witch hunt. In Rome, Sartre also learned that Police Chief Baylot had forbidden the demonstration against Ridgway— a year earlier, the same Baylot had declared, "A communist is a Russian soldier. Whether he knows it or not, that's what he is. The attitude we have adopted toward them is a direct result of this fact"[1] —and that, in the heat of the squabble, the communists had decided to disobey the prohibition. "It was real class warfare," Dominique Desanti writes. "For six hours we were involved in a real civil war."[2] The demonstration of May 28, 1952, will remain legendary in the annals of the PCF: twenty to thirty thousand people marching illegally through the streets of Paris, mobilized by a government that kept making blunders. One of these occurred precisely on the evening of the demonstration when Jacques Duclos, the secretary of the PCF in the absence of Maurice Thorez who was then in Moscow, was arrested in his car. He was returning home with his wife and a few pigeons—the gift of a militant from the provinces—which he meant to roast for dinner. The instructions of the Pinay government were applied to Duclos with unparalleled zeal: the presence of the pigeons in the acting secretary's car was interpreted as the sign of a communist plot against the state; clearly, they were carrier pigeons used to communicate with the militants. Duclos spent over a month in prison.

"I learned from the Italian newspapers of Duclos's arrest, the theft of his diaries, the farce of the carrier pigeons. These sordid, childish tricks turned my stomach. There may have been more ignoble ones, but none more revelatory. An anticommunist is a rat. I couldn't see any way out of that one, and I never will. . . . In the name of those principles that it had inculcated into me, in the name of its humanism and of its 'humanities,' in the name of liberty, equality, fraternity, I swore to the bourgeoisie a hatred that would die only with me. When I precipitously returned to Paris, I had to write or suffocate. Day and night, I wrote the first part of 'The Communists and Peace.' "[3] Beauvoir remembers, "Sartre was livid with anger."[4] Sartre's verbal violence and impulsive outrage reach way beyond the

French Communist Party, back to his past, his family, his stepfather, the *salauds*. These famous pages should be set next to others: together they will form the two limits, the parentheses, within which the dialogue between Sartre and the PCF will unfold during its four most friendly years. November 9, 1956: "It is not, nor will it ever be possible to resume any connection with the current leaders of the PCF. Each sentence they utter, each action they take is the culmination of thirty years of lies and of sclerosis. . . . Today, we go back to the opposition. . . . with our intellectual resources, we will try to help de-Stalinize the French Communist Party."[5]

Two key dates: July 1952 and November 1956: these two dates, these two declarations enclose the only period during which dialogue replaced insults in the troubled relationship between Sartre and the PCF. Four years of relative understanding, during which Sartre discovered the USSR, and devoted himself to congresses, debates, meetings, messages, answers, speeches, discussions, practically abandoning all literary production and subordinating—or so it seemed—his writing to the struggle on the side of the working class. Some observers were quite surprised by Sartre's sudden change. In fact, Sartre was simultaneously settling some personal scores and adjusting to the PCF's new revolutionary line. It was as if two insurrectionary strategies had suddenly met: Sartre, heir of the nineteenth century, hating the bourgeoisie the way it was hated then; and the PCF of 1952 preparing for a new civil war. Henri Martin in prison, Duclos in prison, the PCF victimized by a desperate government. In just a few minutes, all his previous grudges against the PCF were forgotten: Kanapa's barbs in the heyday of existentialism, Leclerc's obscenities at the time of *Dirty Hands,* the boos of communist militants when the play was turned into a movie in 1951, Alexander Fadeyev's insults at the Wroclaw congress. Sartre didn't even have to consider all this; his mind had never worked according to the logic of noncontradiction: he thought in cycles, believed in the relativity of urgency, loved open conflicts. The first product of his class hatred, the first installment of "The Communists and Peace," appeared in *Les Temps modernes* in July 1952.

"When the CRS [Compagnie républicaine de sécurité] charged into the miners, the rightist press published bulletins of victory: that is what made me believe that *Le Figaro* did not like workers. But I was wrong. I apologize to everybody and, particularly, to M. Robinet [editor-in-chief of *Le Figaro*]. Because M. Robinet adores workers. He just did not want to admit it—out of modesty, I suppose."[6]

The first sentences of "The Communists and Peace" are absolutely unequivocal. The Sartrean artillery sweeps through the bourgeoisie. His words lash out, his irony kills, his murderous violence and hatred fire all over the place: he lets his fury flare against the *salaud*, the oppressor, the enemy in the name of the humiliated and outraged, the working class generally represented by the PCF. Conflicts have always stimulated him, particularly when they seem insoluble; hatred has always electrified him, particularly when the enemies are many and complacent. First it was Robinet, then he took a potshot at Georges Altman, editor-in-chief of *Franc-Tireur*, who had worked with him at the RDR four years earlier. "You have spent so much time looking for the slightest flaw in the communist line," he tells Altman and his friends, the "rats," "that you have become shortsighted."[7] This is a very daring act of intellectual acrobatics: ruthlessly tearing himself away from his political friends and his own anti-Stalinist discourse, Sartre takes his post in a new territory, next to a PCF oppressed by "the police methods of a dying regime,"[8] and harangues his old friends. All this according to the logic of relativity and of contradiction, Sartrean logic: yesterday's enemy has changed; today he has become the martyr of a blind, bestial, cruel bourgeoisie.

"The Communists and Peace," three hundred pages in three installments published in *Les Temps modernes* between July 1952 and April 1954, confirmed his rapprochement with the communists. "Generally speaking—and only generally speaking—the voice of the docker is worth half that of the pharmacist, or half that of the sacristan, or half that of his brother-in-law, the town clerk."[9] With the help of statistics, he showed that "his" docker had been transformed into a "sub-man," "politically weak," "a second-class citizen."[10] Something very particular must have attracted Sartre to the PCF. Perhaps he identified with their transgression of a police order issued from the most authoritarian of bourgeois governments. Perhaps he liked the way the PCF refused to bow, flouted the humiliation, and challenged the right with its demonstration against the presence of Ridgway in Paris. In any case, the moment the Communist Party became at once the prey and the decoy, he had to back it. He wrote those texts like a machine, in white heat, with all the brutality of his hatred against the bourgeoisie, with all the rage, passion, and hatred that his own bourgeois past could inspire in him. "I have always thought against myself," he liked to say. His "self" being his bourgeois self, at once son, grandson, and stepson of the bourgeoisie. So, he supported the PCF of 1952, and the abused docker; he attacked the "rats" who had once been his allies, and, by so doing, killed the dormant bourgeois in him. At the same time, he elaborated his first analysis of revolutionary praxis: only the PC, he explained, allows the unorganized masses to acquire this praxis and thereby transforms them into a powerful, active working class.

331

*H*IS BREAK with Camus occurred at this time. Profoundly anchored in the political context of those violent years, the quarrel between the two men was often perceived as a conflict between rival writers. But that was hardly the case; in fact, their argument became all the harsher as Sartre kept clashing with the *salauds,* the bourgeois, the cowards, and the undecided. Camus bore the brunt of it. It was a definitive, cruel break, accompanied by public verbal attacks and insults. Had there always been some rivalry between the two writers? The postwar press had chosen to make them play the role of enemy brothers, which might have had an impact on their relationship. The hostility had gradually and insidiously manifested itself during the various stages of their parallel careers, of their defeats and successes. In the heat of discovery, their first greetings to each other had been almost gallant: Camus had saluted *Nausea* and *The Wall* in *Alger républicain,* Sartre had welcomed *The Stranger* in *Les Cahiers du Sud.* They had again met at the opening of *The Flies.* Sartre had written *No Exit* for Camus, both the actor and the director (but Camus was not involved in the production when it premiered). Camus had introduced Sartre to *Combat* and had sent him to America for the first time in his life. They had had fun together and had shared the same friends. Sartre had invited Camus to join the editorial board of *Les Temps modernes.* They were again together at the meeting of intellectuals organized by the RDR at the Salle Pleyel in December 1948: Breton, Sartre, Camus, Wright, Levi, and the others, all quite unable to hide their underlying disagreements behind their antiseptic speeches. And then they had often met again at parties, whether at the Vians or at some other mutual friend's. And yet, from the very start, they were doomed to come into conflict with each other. For, if these two stars of contemporary French letters were like twin brothers both in their social and professional trajectories as well as in their literary and political ambitions, they were the heirs of two very different backgrounds. Their styles, rhythms, and strategies were always different: Camus remained faithful to his cultural heritage, indeed quite haunted by it, whereas Sartre betrayed his, the way heirs often do, and tore up without the slightest hesitation the bourgeois contract under whose regime he had been born.

332

By 1952 it is difficult to believe that there were ever any real ties between Sartre and Camus. Perhaps their salad days, between 1943 and 1946, were only a fluke. Their first disagreement, which began during a party at the Vians, lasted from December 1946 to March 1947. Toward the end of the evening, when everybody was already quite high, Camus started attacking Merleau-Ponty about his article "The Yogi and the Proletarian." "Merleau-Ponty defended himself," Simone de Beauvoir writes, "Sartre supported him; Camus, shattered, left, slamming the door behind him; Sartre and Bost rushed out and ran after him along the street, but he refused to come back."[11] It seems it was Dolorès who finally reconciled them, but only temporarily. Their friendship, if there ever was one, was eventually eroded by increasing ideological disagreements. Even the amicable façade collapsed when, in the fall of 1951, Camus published *The Rebel*. At first, Sartre decided that, since he did not like the book, *Les Temps modernes* would not review it, but the editorial staff eventually managed to convince him to "cover" the event anyway. "The one of you who is least hostile to Camus's book should take care of it!" Sartre exclaimed. Francis Jeanson wrote the article, which was very unkind. Sartre backed him. Camus immediately sent Sartre a letter, which began with the formal "Monsieur le Directeur." He was hurt by the fact that his book had been criticized not by Sartre but by Jeanson, whom he did not even deign to mention by name, preferring to designate him by the anonymously distant "your collaborator." He even lashed out at him in a sentence that wavered on the edge of pathos: "I'm getting tired," he wrote, "of seeing myself, and particularly seeing old militants who have known all the fights of their times, endlessly chastised by censors who have always tackled history from their armchairs."[12] Camus had been deeply wounded, and did not attempt to pretend otherwise. And that may have been a mistake, maybe he should have hidden his wounds, his battered pride, his lachrymose narcissism. Sartre immediately seized on the ridiculous aspect of that attitude, and he answered Camus with a public letter, one of the most cruel and violent texts he had ever written. "My dear Camus: Our friendship was not easy, but I will miss it. If you end it today, that doubtless means that it had to end."[13] These famous first sentences shall never be forgotten. Sartre was lavish in emphasis, past subjunctives, exclamation points, question marks.

"Your combination of dreary conceit and vulnerability always discouraged people from telling you unvarnished truths. . . . I would have so much preferred that our present quarrel went straight to the heart of the matter, without getting confused with the nasty smell of wounded vanity. Who would have said, much less thought, that everything would finish between us in a petty author's quarrel?" Like most domestic scenes, this one was particularly painful because each party knew exactly where to hit, where it hurt the most. Sartre knew Camus's vanity was wounded, and that's exactly where he aimed. "Tell me, Camus, for what mysterious reasons may your works not be discussed without taking away humanity's reasons for living? . . . How *serious* you are, and yet, to use one of your old words, how frivolous! And suppose you are wrong? Suppose your book simply attested to your ignorance of philosophy? Suppose it consisted of hastily assembled and secondhand knowledge? . . . Are you so afraid of being challenged? . . . But I don't dare advise you to consult *Being and Nothingness.* Reading it would seem needlessly arduous to you: you detest the difficulties of thought." Suddenly, Sartre was telling Camus exactly how much he despised him.

Ultimately these ideological differences drove them apart. The whole argument, in fact, hinged on the question of freedom in the USSR. The staff of *Les Temps modernes* had opted for the denunciation of forced labor camps without advocating an anticommunist stance. If they were ready to attack oppression in Russia, they were also going to mention other countries, like America: "Let us denounce it everywhere or nowhere at all." Among all the ideological currents that coexisted at *Les Temps modernes,* Sartre chose to side with Merleau-Ponty in the nearly instinctive need to preserve, for a while longer, the image of a socialist country that differed from any other country. For Camus, instead, the denunciation of the various incarnations of Stalinism should have gone unhesitatingly to the very bottom of all its crimes. Sartre was a partisan of truth, but with an eye to extenuating circumstances. Camus believed in the equation of Stalinism and fascism. Sartre was trying, in a complex and sophisticated way, to find a possible compromise between ethics and politics. Camus was trying to conceptualize the same premises but in a much more antagonistic fashion. Sartre was opting for ethical pragmatism, Camus, more radically, for the refusal of all violence no matter what its origins and premises. Their perspectives concerning the role of ethics in politics were quite different: Sartre looked for the moral perspective in politics, but he also tried to reconcile it to the dimension of strategic choices (short term/long term; international strategy/national strategy; political advantage/political disadvantage, etc.); Camus, instead, entrenched himself behind his principles and moral strictures, and refused to bow to political polemics. Sartre tried to cope with reality while Camus invoked his ethical principles; no dialogue was possible between them.

Behind these *ad hominem* arguments and ideological disagreements, other antagonisms contributed to the relationship's pitifully quick deterioration. Sartre, the heir, and Camus, the upstart, were already opposed when they first shook hands in the lobby of the Théâtre de la Ville, for the opening of *No Exit,* in June 1943. Sartre was the pampered, dour offspring of the Schweitzers, with their diplomas, their culture, their music, their gold-trimmed, leatherbound book collections, their Protestant ethic, their pedagogical programs; Camus was the sickly child of Catherine Sintès from Chéraga, an illiterate woman who worked as housemaid in Belcourt, the proletarian district of Algiers. Sartre was a pretentious, self-satisfied student; Camus, a cultural refugee, saved from shipwreck thanks to his own talents and his teachers' discernment. Camus was self-taught, an eager learner; Sartre belonged to a cultivated elite. Camus will display the same tension, the same dynamism, the same cultural greed that Sartre had encountered in Nizan at the Lycée Henri IV. Sartre, for his part, will exhibit the passivity and indolence of all those who have never had to be streetwise. How could their respective experiences have vanished with a handshake? The paternalistic arrogance and spite of Sartre in 1952 had been there all the time, just as Camus's admiration for his colleague had always been marred by resentment. Their respective public images were so different from one another that they often approached caricature. Camus had no difficulty speaking of himself, analyzing his behavior, what he liked to call his "Mediterranean temperament"; Sartre was more discreet, jovial, to be sure, but certainly less narcissistic.

And then, of course, there were their professional rivalries: fundamentally totalitarian, both dreamed of dominating the same intellectual territory. They were both involved in the same means of expression: the novel, theater, philosophy, journalism, politics, literary criticism, cinema. Both were published by the same publisher. And, as if all this were not enough, their first novels dealt with similar themes, in similar tones: the absurd, indifference, distance, aloofness, savage individualism. The same territories, the same polyvalent attacks, the same tools, the same causes, the same time. As evidenced in the public response he wrote Camus in 1952, Sartre tried to exclude Camus from the philosophical context, to show that his rival could barely repeat, more or less literally, the few ideas he had inherited from Jean Grenier, his old teacher in Algiers. More at home in theater, and determined to show his supremacy in this field, Camus responded by sharply criticizing *Dirty Hands.*

The press at the time certainly played a major role in these conflicts by publicizing their personalities, their private lives, even their love lives. French literature had already known a few spectacular confrontations that had delighted the more bloodthirsty members of the public—Voltaire and Rousseau, Breton and Aragon—but none as odious as this one. Although Sartre locked himself up in utter silence until after Camus's death, Camus forced mutual friends to take a position. Many years later, when Sartre was asked about his friendship with Camus, he maintained it had been something of absolutely no consequence: "For two or three years I had really good relations with him. We could not go far on the intellectual level," he answered, "because he grew alarmed quickly. In fact, there was a side of him that smacked of the little Algerian tough guy, very much a hooligan, very funny. . . . we had good times together. His language was very racy—so was mine, for that matter—we told filthy stories one after the another, and his wife and Simone de Beauvoir pretended to be shocked."[14] "It was a missed love affair," concludes Robert Gallimard, who, somehow, managed to remain the friend of both.

"*F*INANCIAL ORDER translates into an orderly currency market, monetary order into economic order, political order into order in private behavior."[15] Thus spoke Antoine Pinay, the prime minister of the Fourth Republic, when the Parliament reassembled in 1952. "M. Pinay is laying the groundwork for a dictatorship," Sartre— who seized every opportunity, including the arrest of Alain Le Léap, leader of the CGT (Confédération Génerale du Travail), the main communist trade union, to speak out—answered in *Libération.* Having opposed the Indochina War, Le Léap had been found guilty of "demoralizing the nation." Sartre wasted no time in counterattacking: "That the war in Indochina is immoral is not just a communist opinion. . . . It looks as if our government is using anticommunism the way the Americans do."[16] After two years of silence, Sartre's voice was louder and clearer than ever. According to Dominique

Desanti, the three issues of *Les Temps modernes* published during the summer of 1952, and containing the articles comprising "The Communists and Peace" and the reply to Albert Camus, were "sold out in just a few days, both the first and the second edition. To students young and old, this was their master's rapprochement with the persecuted, mysterious, sullen PCF, the only party that, at the time, defended the causes of the proletariat, of protest against the war in Indochina, of peace."[17] "I had always thought," the new sympathizer declared, "that it would have been impossible to reconstitute the left, whose absence is now sharply felt in France, against the Communist Party. Today, I know that it is impossible to reconstitute it without it."[18] So, he supported the Communist Party because the government "wanted to prevent it from expressing itself." He moved toward it two years after having publicly denounced the existence of labor camps in the USSR, just a few months after the murder of the defendants of the Slansky trial in Prague, and on the heels of the affair of André Marty and Charles Tillon, expelled from the PCF over political disagreements. As an outside supporter, as a critical supporter, he did not have to endorse everything. If he made a move toward the PCF at that particular moment, it was, above all, because he would not accept that it could be reduced to silence by the government in power: this was an emergency.

The idyll between Sartre and the communists was publicly confirmed during the Vienna congress of December 12–19, 1952, at the gathering of the World Peace Movement. Since 1948, throughout the Cold War years, the communist intellectuals who had started the movement had mobilized a large number of international sympathizers. Vienna was the culmination of their efforts. "The congress took place under the sign of the 'Ode to Joy,'" Dominique Desanti remembers. "The 'Ode to Joy,' from Beethoven's Ninth Symphony, was going to be performed on the last day in front of hundreds of Vietnamese, Pakistanis, Hindus, Japanese, Chinese, men and women from all the countries of Latin America, Africans from both the North and the South, and, of course, delegates from all over Western Europe. France had sent dockworkers from Le Havre, sailors and metalworkers from Marseilles, sugar and textile workers, wine growers, miners, the mothers of large families, and young women who had left school only to end up unemployed. . . . The beauty of these congresses rested in the way they brought together different occupations, ages, classes, races, countries. . . . Solitary people were immediately caught up in the spirit of solidarity, and the workers in large firms felt bound by a brotherhood that transcended all frontiers. It was really a sample of the world."[19] Some, like Jean-Pierre Delilez, were less sensitive to the general euphoria and described it as something between an international supershow and a hokey political convention; it was held in the large hall of the Konzerthaus, brimming with gold and Hapsburg splendor, and its most noticeable guests clad in purple, magical, stiff as robots, were four high dignitaries of the Polish episcopacy, who, by their silence, tried to express their disapproval of their country's political regime.[20]

As for Sartre's presence in Vienna, some maintain that Aragon had forced his hand by publicly announcing that Sartre was going to attend, so that the latter had found himself trapped and unable to back out.[21] In any case, he was in Vienna and quite visible: he made declarations on his arrival and his departure, official speeches, declarations following the official speeches, declarations before his return, declarations after his return. It was Sartre "live," full of joy, as if he had just gone through one of the most extraordinary experiences of his life. And, indeed, these are more or less the words he used to describe it. During one of his many declarations, he spoke of the three events of his adult life that had meant the most to him, that had renewed his hope: the Popular Front of 1936, the Liberation, and the Vienna congress.[22]

Among the writers who attended were Jorge Amado and Pablo Neruda from Latin America and, from the Soviet Union, Ilya Ehrenburg and . . . Alexander Fadeyev, who had called Sartre a "hyena with a fountain pen" at the peace congress four years earlier. Sartre very quickly became the star of the event: he delivered the opening address at the inaugural meeting and was constantly surrounded by autograph seekers. Jo Starobin, the American communist journalist, reported: "The congress has exceeded all expectations. . . . This is probably due to the presence of Jean-Paul Sartre, the existentialist philosopher, once hero of the *New York Times Magazine*, and now embodying the greatest turnabout that has ever occurred in Western Europe. . . . He is now encouraging all men of good will to abandon the 'no-man's land of anticommunism.' "[23] In this assembly of mixed opinions—according to Beauvoir and Sartre, "only twenty percent of the participants were communists"[24]—in this huge Austrian fair where people had come to find whatever they wanted—human warmth, the popular union of all European countries, an exchange of ideas—Sartre felt perfectly at ease, indeed, as he put it, quite "happy." "When he got back," Gilles Martinet remembers, "Sartre

338

kept saying that this congress, the first he had attended in his whole life, had been a marvelous experience; he thought that the most positive aspect of such a congress was that it left its participants free to devote themselves entirely to debates, without any other worry; the workers, for instance, did not have to worry about preparing for strikes."[25] But Sartre also felt his usual ambivalence: "I can easily understand how some may have ignored or ridiculed the enthusiasm of the last day. It's part of the game." He admitted that "one could smile at a conviction rooted in an emotional response," while at the same time proclaiming, "Despite all the slanders, the Vienna congress will remain in history."[26]

In his inaugural speech, he had evoked his mistrust of the politics and thought of the times. "They are leading the world toward a massacre," he had said, "because they are abstract. They have cut the world in two and each half is afraid of the other. . . . Within this perspective, even men become abstract. Everybody is the Other, the possible enemy, not to be trusted. . . . What is new and admirable about this congress is that it has brought men together."[27] Nothing earth-shattering, no real "conversion," just a few sensible remarks signifying a refusal of all bloc politics. Sartre's most symbolic pledge of allegiance to the PCF took the following form: by paying hefty damages, and much to the distress of his agents and publishers, he managed to stop performances of *Dirty Hands* then playing in a Vienna theater.

Dirty Hands had already been the source of a number of problems: Sartre disapproved of the translation and adaptation of the play for the New York stage in 1949, and a trial resulted. In December 1948, the Soviet government had officially requested that performances of the play in Helsinki be forbidden, deeming it "propaganda hostile to the USSR"; and in February 1949, *Les Lettres françaises* had published a violently critical article by Ilya Ehrenburg, the latest in a series of similarly antagonistic pieces that had recently appeared in the communist press. Whether merely technical or unabashedly political, these misinterpretations and hostilities had turned *Dirty Hands* into a cursed play. Finally, at the Vienna congress, Sartre made the decision to forbid the performance unless approved by the Austrian Communist Party. Two years later he justified his move: "I do not disavow *Dirty Hands*, I only regret the way it was used. My play became a political battlefield, an instrument of political propaganda. Given the tense atmosphere of our time, I don't think that its performance in sensitive spots such as Berlin or Vienna would benefit peace."[28] Though he had the right to do as he pleased, according to the relativity of political emergencies and the pragmatism of his own ethics, some of his earlier texts would often get in the way and thwart his freedom of expression. But this time it was not some article in *Les Temps modernes* condemning the gagging of writers by the orthodoxy of some party, or a novel, or an essay: it was a play. Sartre was betrayed by the very genre of political theater: each new performance re-echoed throughout the contemporary political scene. Hugo's tirades, which, in 1948, were merely criticism of a PCF that was then strong and arrogant, became, in the context of the Cold War of 1952, a pro-American weapon, and, therefore, an encumbrance to their author. Trials and conflicts concerning *Dirty Hands* continued throughout the world until 1956.

In Vienna, Sartre drank vodka with Ehrenburg and Fadeyev, and amid all that Hapsburg gold, snow, and apple strudel, he agreed to go to Moscow. He even agreed, with Dominique Desanti as interpreter, to teach an elementary existentialism course for Alexander Korneitchouk's best students. All these meetings, all this dialogue, all these new friendships are rather insignificant next to his chastisement of *Dirty Hands.* To further stress the possibilities of dialogue with the PCF and to show the validity of the communist struggle, he even attended the meeting at the Velodrome d'Hiver meant to publicize the results of the Vienna congress and recall its major resolutions, in the company of Jacques Duclos. As everybody noted, and Simone de Beauvoir first of all, December 23, 1952, was going to become a memorable date: two familiar figures, side by side on the same platform, exchanging jokes; one small, fat, with a jovial round face and the reputation of an iron grip, Jacques Duclos, the pastry cook from the Southwest; the other small, thin, just as jovial, but also peculiarly enthusiastic, very much immersed in the discovery of the life of congresses, panels, speeches, a Sartre joyfully beginning his years on the lecture circuit.

*A*ND YET, besides the Vienna congress and the *Dirty Hands* affair, all of Sartre's struggles, during the first months of his relationship with the PCF are ethical. After Henri Martin's case and the Korean War comes the Rosenberg affair. And it is again an aggressive, wounded, resentful man who jumps onto the scene. *"I Rosenberg sono stati assassinati"*: once again, he hears the news in Italy. And once again, he stops everything he is doing and picks up his pen. He will dictate his article to *Libération* by phone, the day after. He is speaking directly to America. "The Rosenbergs are dead and life goes on. This is what you wanted, isn't it? . . . You already played the same trick with Sacco and Vanzetti, and it worked. But this time it will not. . . . You won't be able to turn the execution of the Rosenbergs into a 'regrettable incident,' or a judicial error. This is a legal lynching that covers an entire nation with blood and clamorously denounces the failure of the Atlantic pact and your inability to assume the leadership of the Western world. . . . You thought that the murder of the Rosenbergs was a private settling of scores. A hundred thousand voices kept telling you: 'They are innocent.' And you stupidly answered: 'We punish our citizens according to our law. This is none of your business.' Well, actually the Rosenberg affair is our business: when two innocents are sentenced to death, it is the whole world's business."[29] With a cold, brutal, insolent defense speech, he hurls his accusations across the Atlantic. "Decidedly, there is something rotten in America. . . . One day, maybe, all this goodwill will heal you of your fear: we hope so because we have loved you. In the meantime, however, don't be surprised if, from both sides of Europe, we scream: Watch out, America has rabies! We must cut all ties to her, or we'll also get sick."[30] It is not at all surprising to note that, in Washington, the FBI men, Nick Carter's sons, would be alerted by Sartre's article, "Animals with Rabies": "A letter of January 24, 1953 signed by the Comité pro Libertades Civiles (CLC) has informed its correspondents . . . that the movement of international sympathy formed to save the lives of the two Rosenbergs did not depend on just any political movement. The letter has also explained that the writer Jean-Paul Sartre has declared himself on the side of such a committee."[31]

This act of accusation against America, after the Rosenbergs' execution, was accompanied by "The Infernal Machine," a speech Sartre delivered at the Mutualité on May 5, 1953, during a debate on the Indochina War. This happened during the worst phase of the conflict, just before the advent of the Laniel government, which, by June 1953, would start turning things around. By then, France had lost all hope of winning and was looking for a way out that would save face. Sartre spoke of "useless massacres" and, among other things, declared: "Is it really that important to fight in order not to abandon Indochina to Ho Chi Minh and Mao Zedong when we all know that in the case of a French victory we would automatically relinquish it to Bao Dai and the Americans? Anyway, we are quite out of the race. And yet we go on letting our men be killed while killing Vietminh, for nothing, for air."[32]

*T*HE YEAR 1953 had been particularly rich in coups, countercoups, plots, and trials. January: the "doctors' plot" is made public in Moscow. Nine doctors, of whom seven are Jews, who are supposed to have confessed to the murder of Andrei Zhdanov in 1948 and to a conspiracy against high officials, are arrested. Four months later, the world will learn about their innocence, their tortures, and all the machinations invented by Stalin's regime. In Paris, André Marty and Charles Tillon are expelled from the PCF because of political disagreements. February: anti-Semitism flares again in the USSR. March: Stalin dies and, six months later, is replaced by Nikita Khrushchev—quite a lot to digest for our new convert still in the first blush of his discoveries. Now and then he was asked to justify himself—Mauriac, for instance, publicly questioned him about the doctors' plot and anti-Semitism in the USSR. "M. Mauriac worries about my silence," the editor-in-chief of *Les Temps modernes* laconically answered. "He needn't. If magazines seem quiet it is because newspapers talk too much."[33] Sartre's change of course was inevitably going to entail a certain number of modifications in the network of his relationships and to cause a few conflicts on a number of issues that he now considers in a different light—conflicts that often involved the staff of *Les Temps modernes,* or, at least, those of them who were less than enthusiastic about this new Stalinist direction, like Merleau-Ponty, Claude Lefort, and Etiemble. In February 1953, the latter, in charge of the literary column, received a violent letter from the editor-in-chief: "My dear Etiemble: In your note about the 'Two Standards' (*NNRF* [*Nouvelle Nouvelle Revue française*] March 1) I noticed the following sentence, on p. 528: 'To be perfectly honest, I prefer the frank *salauds* and the French *salauds* and the nazo-nazis to the stalino-nazis.' In other words, you prefer the followers of Hitler to the communists. The other day you asked me whether there was a limit to the freedom of our collaborators. I thought there was none. I was wrong. I now see a limit: you've shown it to me by exceeding it. It coincides with the limit of my esteem. I consider your article as evidence of a change of address. We will forward your mail to the Rue Sébastien Bottin. Yours truly, Jean-Paul Sartre."[34] Is this tone new to Sartre? Is it part of his determination to denounce all anticommunist hysteria? "Depressing to see all that bad faith in J.-P. S.'s letter," Paulhan writes to Etiemble. "By the way, I think you should answer it, and in the *NRF.* As soon as possible, please."[35]

The polemics with Claude Lefort, one of the pillars of the magazine and a close friend of Merleau-Ponty, were even more serious, more complex, more violent. The two men confronted each other in issue no. 89 of *Les Temps modernes,* April 1953: first Claude Lefort, with his "Marxism and Sartre," then Sartre, with his "Reply to Claude Lefort." This debate shows Sartre's specific place, isolated, in the middle of all the crypto- or para-communist currents of the postwar period—that is, the tradition of the French "second left," the one that keeps repeating, "The PCF, what a disaster!" Sartre was neither a Marxist nor a communist when most intellectuals of 1945 were either one or the other: This was his first missed rendezvous. He moved toward the Party in 1952, precisely at the moment when that very same generation of intellectuals was beginning to move away from it. This was his second missed rendezvous. All of Sartre's dialogues with the groups that were crossing the same waters along with him, as neighbors, registered these disjunctions. Sartre's polemics with groups such as "Arguments" and "Socialism or Barbarism" and with individuals such as Edgar Morin, Kostas Axelos, Cornelius Castoradis, and Claude Lefort, are part of this double rupture. So, when Lefort engages Sartre in a debate concerning the theory of organization and spontaneity and asks him whether the existence of a proletarian party is really necessary to the working class, Sartre answers "yes" according to the strictest Marxist orthodoxy. This will eventually prompt Morin to forge the admirable adjective "hypostalinist" in his analysis of Sartre's political foundations: if "hyperstalinism" fiercely denies the existence of labor camps in the USSR and blindly supports the Soviet Union, Morin maintains, "hypostalinism" accepts all the criticisms of the first so-called socialist country, without interrupting work for the advent of Revolution everywhere in the world. A sharper analytical look at this debate brings up another question: what if Sartre's unexpected involvement with the PCF, resuming once again a tradition inherited from the seventeenth and eighteenth centuries (in this case, that of the intellectual fighting for the masses), was meant to update that old frame of reference for the 1950s? This "holy alliance" lasted only four years, after which Sartre, somewhat orphaned, was again free to reinvent new forms of direct intervention.

SARTRE QUARRELED with Camus, Etiemble, Lefort, and, finally, with the man who had been closer to him than anybody else, Merleau-Ponty. This was the highest price he had to pay for his four-year long march with the French proletariat and for the pleasure of calling everybody else a bourgeois. Merleau-Ponty had been with *Les Temps modernes* from the very beginning, and had often been in charge of its editorials. Indeed, for a while, his and Sartre's functions in the magazine had been practically interchangeable. Both Normaliens, both *agrégés* in philosophy, both steeped in phenomenology, if each in his own way, they had first met at the Ecole Normale, in a rather bawdy manner. "At the time, the Ecole was up in arms against one of my classmates and myself," Merleau remembers, "because we had sung a few traditional songs that they had found too vulgar. For some reason or other, Sartre slipped in between us and our persecutors, and managed to pull us out of that ridiculously heroic situation unharmed."[36] In the winter of 1941 they met again to work together for "Socialism and Freedom." Together, they experienced the meaning of disorganization and of failure. Then they began to see each other regularly, at the wild parties that celebrated the end of the war. Together, they mapped out the future *Temps modernes.* Their collaboration thus lasted from 1945 to 1952, without any major conflict. The first serious disagreements between them started the moment Sartre began supporting the PCF. Before finally abandoning *Les Temps modernes* in 1952, Merleau wrote a farewell article, "Indirect Language and the Voices of Silence," which appeared in the June and July issues of the magazine. Ironically, at around the same time, their paths diverged once again: while Sartre was strengthening his ties with the communists, Merleau-Ponty accepted a chair of philosophy at the Collège de France. Later, in 1955, he published a book, *Adventures of the Dialectic,* which was made up of independent chapters, in one of which he developed a subtle and exhaustive analysis of Sartre's relationship with communism, "Sartre and Ultrabolshevism."

But the philosophical differences that underlay the reflections of the two thinkers were already there when they first discovered phenomenology. "We got a hold of [Husserl's] *Ideen* the same year," Sartre later wrote, "both by chance and by necessity . . . One day, he discovered what he had been looking for, *intentionality* . . . The same year, in Berlin, I also came across *intentionality* in *Ideen,* but what I wanted from it was more or less the opposite of what Merleau-Ponty had been looking for: I wanted it to rid consciousness of all its slags, of all its 'states.' . . . we were both quite true to ourselves." What Merleau wanted from the notion of intentionality was direct access to spontaneity, whereas Sartre used it to pave the way to a new notion of freedom. "Spontaneity, freedom," Sartre continues, "the difference between the two means nothing and everything: these two words connected our respective births, childhoods, choices to the objectives of our thoughts. Later, when we quarreled . . . we always had to go back to the initial terms and then gradually retrace the way down to the terms of our disagreement."[37] By 1952 their divergences had reached the point of no return. In his definition of "ultrabolshevism" (in *Signs*) Merleau-Ponty points at the contradictions, the subtleties, and the specificities of Sartre's position. The last sentences about Sartre's "ultrabolshevism" are prophetic: "One cannot at the same time be both a free writer and a communist," Merleau-Ponty writes, "or a communist and an oppositionist, the Marxist dialectic which united these opposites will not be replaced by an exhausting oscillation between them; they will not be reconciled by force. One must then go back, attach obliquely what could not be changed frontally, and look for an action other than communist action."[38] These lines were written in the spring of 1955. Eighteen months later, after the Soviet invasion of Hungary, Sartre was already looking for a line of action other than the communist.

I N AN interview published at the same time as *L'Affaire Henri Martin*, Sartre further defined his concept of the intellectual. "Henri Martin's case, as well as the Rosenberg case," the journalist Serge Montigny asked him, "raise the problem of state injustice. Do you really think that we should fight against such an injustice only in the Western camp?" "Absolutely not," Sartre answered dryly, "we must fight it wherever we can do so efficiently. Which does not mean that we can fight it everywhere with the same means. Whether we want it or not, and whatever our attitude toward the United States, we are part of a 'bloc,' that is to say, of a complex organism." And he proceeded to compare the Rosenberg case—"unfortunately European indignation does not have much weight in American internal affairs"—with the Slansky trial, a "denial of justice," against which, however, he did not react publicly: "It would have been pure formality." He justified such abstentions by invoking the Cold War, which, he maintained, had the tendency to transform certain protests into real "acts of war." Then, recovering his legendary assurance, he came up with a formula that became the title of the article: "The duty of an intellectual is that of denouncing injustice wherever he sees it."[39] The first part of the interview, with this formula, appeared on the first page of *Combat* next to this bit of news—an interesting familial juxtaposition: "Albert Schweitzer and General Marshall, Nobel Peace Prize. Oslo, October 30.—The five members of the Nobel committee have awarded the prize for peace this evening. Albert Schweitzer, the Alsatian doctor, director of the hospital of Lambaréné in Gabon, receives the prize in 1952 . . ." Two Schweitzers, "Uncle Albert" and "Poulou," opposed by their respective ethical stances, became neighbors thanks to the hazards of news and layout. "We have often worked for the same causes but with different principles," Poulou wrote his "dear uncle Albert" ten years later.[40]

The years that followed marked an even more drastic turn in Sartre's comradeship with the PCF: these were the years of his first trip to the USSR, as well as numerous congresses and gatherings of the peace movement, such as the one in Knokke-le-Zoute, where he met Brecht, the one in Berlin, where he delivered a speech to protest the H-bomb, the one in Helsinki, where he repeated more or less the same things he had said in Berlin, and, finally, the one in Venice where he cemented his ties with the Italian communists. These were also the years of his trip to China, and of his nomination as vice-president of the France-USSR association. Sartre also met Chaplin and Picasso, Heidegger and Lukacs, Togliatti, Moravia, Silone, Ungaretti, Guido Piovene. He met the poet Viteslav Nezval in Prague, Constantin Simonov and Lili Brik in Moscow, visited Elsa Triolet at Knokke-le-Zoute, and lunched with Aragon in Paris on the day of Stalin's death. Thus, he modified his network, acquired new friends, new habits, new means of expression. This is the Sartre of the Cold War, of four particular years fraught with discoveries, congresses, official journeys, public interventions, speeches, petitions.

He put a foot into the network of communist and procommunist writers, found his way into the peace movement, and was caught up in the system: he was grabbed, swallowed, sought out . . . unable to refuse invitations and proposals. Elsa Triolet invited him to visit her at Knokke-le-Zoute, where he also met Simonov, who, in turn, invited him to Moscow, where he met . . . etc., etc. The appeals of the working-class party were, to him, a duty, a necessity. If, at the time of Saint-Germain-des-Prés, and with the help of the little family, he had been able to establish a relatively effective protection system, his comradeship with the PCF was going to demolish all defenses, with the help of Sartre himself, who, maybe sensing the temporariness of his closeness to the working classes, became very accessible, perhaps too much so. One remembers the story of the "carrier" pigeons, his determination to keep up his internal debate, the obsessive violence with which he tried to kill the bourgeois in himself, in thinking against himself to the limits of exhaustion. This game continued the whole time he spent with the communists. We also remember the coffee-orthedrine period, in 1947, when, fiercely involved in writing, he pushed himself to the limits of physical endurance. Now, he discovers other drugs, other stimulants: whisky, pills of all kinds, as if he finds pleasure in personal abuse, excess, and self-brutalization, at all levels—physiological, psychological, intellectual—exhausting himself in a furious duel that, after all, concerned only himself. In 1954 he had an attack of arterial hypertension, and his doctor immediately ordered a long period of rest, which, of course, Sartre did not observe. He forced himself to meet the most impossible deadlines, playing with fire, driving himself to the edge. This was the most altruistic as well as the most suicidal period of his life. He accepted too many prefaces, made too many speeches, took too many trips. The totalitarian machinery of the Communist Party gave him no reprieve. This was the time of his first trip to the Soviet Union.

By the time he reached Moscow, he had attended a parade, celebrated the anniversary of the union of the Ukraine with Russia, visited universities, factories, museums, churches, mosques, met students and workers, technicians and writers, nurses and doctors, discussed contemporary Soviet painting with intellectuals, and bluntly admitted his aversion for this sort of art.[41] But he had admired the equality of the social system and the pride of the workers. He had answered all the questions the workers had asked him about France, witnessed the cultural progress of the illiterate women of Uzbekistan, attended the performance of a popular play in a kolkhoz, read and appreciated the The Thaw, Ehrenburg's latest novel, and agreed to allow the staging of The Respectful Prostitute in Russian. He listened to the reproaches that a group of workers had leveled against the writer Simonov, whose latest novel had failed to please them, he discovered that, in that country, "privileges did not exist," he discussed with a student of philosophy the new Soviet philosophy and the possibility of assimilating it to an ideological plurality, he had applauded all peace efforts, and he raised his hat to a culture that reconciled scientism and Marxism. He had crossed the country from Moscow to Tashkent, from Leningrad to Samarkand, and, accompanied by colleagues such as Ehrenburg and Simonov and by a permanent interpreter, he had visited Simonov's dacha, where he had drunk too much. "There is a total freedom of criticism in the USSR," he declares as soon as he is back in a series of interviews with *Libération.*

D URING THE 1930s, the ritual of "returns from the USSR" had become a literary genre in itself: declarations, articles, essays, conferences, his assuring everybody that the USSR was really different from any other country. Barbusse, Aragon, Malraux, Nizan, Jean-Richard Bloch, Gide, and many others, on their return from the Soviet Union, had all expressed their opinions, one by one and each in his own way. Whether they were mere tourists, like Barbusse or Malraux, or party members, like Aragon or Nizan, they all saw and told, and they all came back profoundly shaken by the experience. Some had to modify their whole system of perception to describe this mythical country, this paradisiacal land where it was believed, by someone like Nizan for instance, that even the problem of death had been solved! Some of those returned from the USSR were fanatical, others were more realistic and damning—such as Gide's formidable slap, when, in 1938, back from his second trip to the country and a regal reception, he wrote his implacable *Retouches à mon "Retour de l'URSS,"* a definitive denunciation of pro-Soviet mythology. Besides, the Stalinist trials and purges were already well under way and, in the West, some people had begun to criticize the entire system. Nizan had spent all of 1934 in Moscow, as a very active permanent member of the Communist Party and, upon his return, had paid the usual tribute in declarations and conferences. And yet, it is precisely during that year that his belief had begun to flag. In Uzbekistan and Georgia he had noticed the flaws and the discrepancies of the system: the problem of nationalities had not been solved, nor that of freedom of expression, nor that of equal opportunity. He swallowed bitter pill after bitter pill until, four years later, he resigned from the party.[42] Exactly twenty years after Nizan, Sartre was going through the same ritual, his own first return from the USSR. To say that Sartre astonished his audience would be an understatement. His enthusiastic declarations dumbfounded all those who, like him, still had reservations concerning communist practices, ethics, and excesses. Sartre abandoned himself to the most incredible Soviet panegyric, to the most emphatic, the most extraordinary, the most naïve and unexpected declarations.

Simone de Beauvoir maintains that he was exhausted by all sorts of excesses, hypertension, and his ten days in the hospital. She also maintains that he never reread the text of his interviews with *Libéra-tion*. But how can one suppress a series of five long, enthusiastic, and retrospectively embarrassing interviews when what Sartre published in the newspaper *France-URSS*, and repeated in his subsequent speeches throughout 1954 and 1955, entirely reconfirm what he had said then? Between July 15 and 20, the first and third pages of *Libération* gave French readers a totally euphoric account of Sartre's return from the USSR, with photos as evidence. "Jean-Paul Sartre's Impressions of His Trip to the USSR": this generic title covered five articles on five subjects: "Total Freedom of Criticism in the USSR," "From Dostoyevsky to Contemporary Literature," "Belonging to the Elite is Not a Sinecure," "Soviet Philosophers Are Builders," "Peace Through Peace." The information had been gathered in shorthand by the journalist Jean Bedel during an interview that had lasted over two hours.

"Do you have the feeling," Bedel asked Sartre, "that the Soviets are currently undergoing a change? I am alluding to what some Westerners call 'the Malenkov age'?" "Yes," Sartre answered, "they are indeed undergoing a change and they are glad to talk of it. I can't possibly take Lazareff's articles seriously." Clearly, Sartre's main concern was to disengage himself officially from the American-style journalism of Pierre Lazareff in *France-Soir*. Sartre's public condemnation of Lazareff started a conflict that would develop into several episodes. "The Soviet citizen has full freedom of criticism," Sartre said, "a criticism, that does not hinge on men but on measures. It would be a mistake to believe that the Soviet citizen does not speak and keeps his criticism bottled up inside himself. That's not true. He criticizes much more and much more effectively than we do. Whereas the French worker might say, 'My boss is a pig!' the Soviet worker will say, 'Such and such a measure is absurd.' The difference is that while the French worker is likely to vent his objections in a café, the Soviet worker will voice them publicly, and will take full responsibility for his criticism during an official meeting. . . . Even when his criticism is particularly bitter he will have a positive aim in mind. What is true of the workers is true of everybody."[43]

"Do you have the feeling," the journalist also asked him, "that the Soviet citizen is a particular kind of man?" "They consider themselves as such," Sartre answered, and then illustrated his assertion with examples and anecdotes: "The first thing to keep in mind, I think, is that in the USSR, one is immediately part of a society, from infancy. You can see seven-year-old children playing in a pioneers' camp, and dance and have fun on a construction site right below a huge poster of Stalin. On one side, you have drawings representing the main heroes of the Resistance during the Occupation . . . on the other the heroes of Fadeyev's novel, *The Young Guard.* One has the impression that from the age of seven onward, children are surrounded by the social: their reflection is fed by it, their imagination fueled by it."[44] Then, quite brutally, after such indiscriminate praise of the exciting functions of young pioneers' camps and Stalin's portraits, Sartre had expressed his doubts as to Ilya Ehrenburg's latest book: "Have you read *The Thaw?*" he had asked the journalist. "It's a strange book. [Ehrenburg] is very critical of the Corneille side of today's Soviet hero. . . . It's the story of a young woman who loves Alexander Blok's symbolist poems and has to force herself to love the social, committed poetry of her contemporaries. The novel has been sharply criticized." Sartre seemed weighed down by the softness, the complacency, the very intellectual lethargy he had so often and so violently condemned. When the journalist asked him whether social privilege was as widespread in the USSR as in Europe: "No," Sartre answered without hesitation. "At most there is a little kernel of elitism that risks deteriorating into social stratification because of its origins. . . . But such a stratification can only affect a very small portion of the current society." "Did you tell this to them?" Jean Bedel asked him. "Yes," the writer answered, "and they had no difficulty admitting it. As I said, if they are ready to accept any kind of constructive criticism it is because they are perpetually criticizing themselves as a means to progress. This is what people like Lazareff have failed to understand."[45]

Thus, the list of Soviet beauties and unknown wonders unfolded implacably according to the logic of the cheapest sentimentalism, eighteen months before the 20th Party Congress, the great defeat, the public revelation, in front of a huge international tribunal, of all the crimes committed under Stalin. "Do the Soviets wish to visit foreign countries?" Jean Bedel asked. "No, not to come and visit," Sartre replied. "There are a few exceptions, but they really have no desire to leave their country. I've asked a number of them: 'Why wouldn't you come? You often misjudge us.' But the idea does not particularly tempt them. They don't feel like traveling right now. They have lots of things to do at home."[46] Then Sartre outdid himself in his predictions concerning the future of the relationship of France and the

USSR: "The USSR is a great nation, which, in thirty years and with huge sacrifices, has gotten industrialized, has built its own culture and continues to march forward. If France keeps on stagnating as it is now, before 1966 the standard of living in the USSR will be far superior to ours."[47] Sartre's only reservation about the USSR concerned the teaching of philosophy in the universities: "They do it the way French religious institutions teach Kant, Hegel, or Marx: a teacher explains their ideas, shows their mistakes, or what it is believed are their mistakes, raises a few objections, and then dispatches them."[48] Obviously, the citizen, the literary critic, the writer, and the journalist in Sartre had all been unconditionally seduced by the USSR. The only one to resist was the pedagogue, personally at variance with relatively obsolete teaching methods, traditional, repetitive, monological, so different from the critical dialogue he had always practiced in his own courses.

"This series of controversial interviews is not going to end here," the newspaper announced after the last interview. "We have received a letter from Mme Hélène Lazareff and M. Pierre Lazareff severely reproaching M. Jean-Paul Sartre for having called them into question by name."[49] By attacking the Lazareffs, Sartre had provoked not just the powerful press but the world of the press in general. Soon this conflict, which opposed an intellectual to the class of professional journalists, assumed considerable proportions.

Sartre's declarations caused a general outcry. Jacques-Francis Rolland humorously recounts the stunned reactions that Sartre's astonishing turnabout provoked within the party. Apparently, Sartre's statements "enthused the comrades. . . . All over the section one could hear remarks like this: 'If he keeps on at this rate, soon he'll be at the door begging for a membership card.' Laffont appreciated the joke, but not without re-establishing a certain distance: 'Easy, now. True, he's made some progress, but he's still full of shit.' "[50] The general impression was that Sartre was probably having fun playing a self-destructive game in which, alone against the world, he kept praising the USSR with the net result of finding himself more and more isolated. Everybody was on his back: his former colleagues from the RDR, who could not understand the reasons behind what they saw as an inadmissible turnabout, this sudden acceptance of what they had always denounced together; his friends at *Les Temps modernes,* such as Merleau-Ponty and Claude Lefort; his political neighbors, members of a radical but institutionalized left, such as Gilles Martinet, and the entire staff of *France-Observateur,* including

Roger Stéphane and Etiemble. At the time of the RDR Sartre had continuously criticized communist morality as conformist, the "morality of the petty bourgeois."[51] Then he had written *Dirty Hands*, where he again insisted on freedom of judgment, critical individualism, the salvation of the solitary fighter. And now that the great mass of communist militants and the great tide of communist intellectuals of the 1950s were beginning to wake up and to question communist ethics—from the "doctors' plot" to the Slansky affair, from overt anti-Semitism to the detention camps—Sartre, alone in his logic, moved closer to the PCF. Just in time to see everybody else move away.

"After my first visit to the USSR in 1954, I lied," he declared twenty years later. "Actually, 'lied' might be too strong a word: I wrote an article—which Cau finished because I was ill—where I said a number of friendly things about the USSR which I did not believe. I did it partly because I considered that it is not polite to pour shit on your hosts as soon as you are back home, and partly because I didn't really know where I stood in relation to both the USSR and my own ideas."[52]

As a token of gratitude for his declarations, or as a thank you for his praise of the USSR, in December 1954, just six months after his return, Sartre was named vice-president of the France-USSR association. So, for two years, his name and prestige lent credit to an organization that was profoundly connected to the Communist International, its promotional enterprises, and its various committees. He assumed this new role with the same zeal he had displayed during the two previous years. As an echo to this official, public life, his work as a writer continued, whether overtly or covertly, often taking unexpected turns but always intimately connected to the official program.

During the period of his association with the PCF, he wrote two plays, *Kean* and *Nekrassov,* performed in 1953 and 1955, respectively, the screenplay for the movie *The Witches of Salem,* and in 1953, he also published some ten pages on Mallarmé—the remains of a 500-page manuscript he had written between 1947 and 1949. Speeches, petitions, responses, articles, impressions, and prefaces replaced, at least in quantity, the literary texts of the previous years; his brush with the PCF had sterilized the man of letters, or, at least, so it would seem. He became a guarantor, a proselyte, a traveler, a hawker, a peddler with a good loudspeaker, a signatory, an orator, a benefactor. And yet, in the wings, the turbines were still running, as relentlessly as ever as the writer worked on unpublished texts, reordering old manuscripts, experimenting, selecting, shelving notebooks with moleskin covers, reopening huge files.

Of Sartre's plays, *Nekrassov* is certainly the most furiously sympathetic to the PCF and the most polemical. It is probably also his most Manichaean text, and his most dated: a sequel to his return from the USSR. Presented at the Théâtre Antoine, under the auspices of Simone Berriau, the play was immediately attacked by both the bourgeois press and other groups of various persuasions. The issue *Nekrassov* raised hinges on the relations between the major press and politics in general and, in particular, the PCF. The very choice of this theme provoked both indignation and anger among the journalists, as if a taboo had been violated. Sartre admitted, "It's a flawed play."[53] "What I have tried to do in *Nekrassov* is to write a satirical play . . . a certain sort of press is already crying out before it even knows what my play is about and before it has been hurt."[54] "My play is very clearly a satire of the procedures of anticommunist propaganda."[55] "Some papers refuse to accept the publicity my play offers them—perhaps the price is too high."[56]

The character of Jules Palotin, alias Jojo the Suspenders, editor-in-chief of a newspaper with a wide circulation, *Soir à Paris,* was particularly offensive to the majority of the press: it was not difficult to recognize caricatures of Pierre Lazareff and his paper, *France-Soir,* which Sartre had already publicly attacked a year earlier. A last-minute change had slightly blunted the sharpness of the parallel: initially the actor who was supposed to play the main role was Louis de Funès, whose smallish stature further underlined the resemblance with Lazareff, but he was replaced by Armontel, who was quite tall. Despite these efforts, meant to minimize any physical resemblance that might further incriminate Sartre, everybody was outraged, beginning with Françoise Giroud, who wrote a scathing review of the play for *L'Express.* By and by the whole of the Paris press—except the communists—came to the rescue of *France-Soir. Paris-Match, L'Aurore, Le Figaro:* nobody wanted to be outdone. The play was accused of being simplistic, childish, ridiculous, silly, wrong. Pierre Macabru: "A thick-ankled farce, repartees as heavy as boulders, the elegance of a rhinoceros: Jean-Paul Sartre's play tramples on the spectators for four solid hours. It is a superhuman test. . . . The production is totally mindless. There may be reasons for it, but Sartre doesn't have any."[57]

But *Nekrassov* also had a few important defenders, among them

Gilles Sandier, Jean Cocteau, and Roland Barthes. *"Nekrassov,"* Sandier explains, "was neatly strangled at birth. . . . *Le Figaro* summoned its readers to demonstrate against the play without even having seen it, just basing its judgment on hearsay. The entire press went at it. . . . hiding its rage behind false condescension. In this sense, the play hit the mark."[58] Roland Barthes was even harsher, discovering the "famous myth of the separation of genres" at the heart of a debate that was archaic and hypocritical and which vainly sought to figure out whether the play should be seen as a farce, a comedy of manners, a satire, a revue, or a burlesque. Barthes fully committed himself to a vehement defense of Sartre's writing in the play, which, according to him, at times was "as dazzling as Beaumarchais's." Because, Barthes added, "by separating social good from social evil without any class sophism, Sartre has touched the bourgeois soul where it hurts . . . unfortunately for our critics, who are so much in need of magnanimity, Sartre has painted a political universe and not a moral one. . . . *Nekrassov* reveals the global servitude of the press in power and turns its brutal clarity into a celebration: the joy of recognizing the truth of what one merely sensed, after all, isn't that the very point of comedy, the catharsis of satire?! . . . I feel better at the thought," Barthes lyrically concluded, "that every evening, for a time, which I hope will be as long as possible, *Nekrassov* will bring some relief to all those Frenchmen who, like me, are stifling under the bourgeois malady. 'I have a France-ache,' as Michelet used to say: that's where *Nekrassov* helped me."[59] When the play was again put on, first in 1968, by Hubert Gignoux, at the Théâtre National de Strasbourg, and then, in 1978, by Georges Werler, at the Théâtre de l'Est, in Paris, the controversy flared up again, as fiercely as before. Sartre's relationship with the press remains a very sensitive area, seldom explored before. Never fully accepted as a peer, and often suspected, Sartre was made to pay for an influence that his fellow journalists had often found too threatening, polyvalent, totalitarian. The journalists' case became even stronger when, barely a year later, Sartre's "primary pro-Sovietism," as François Chalais called it,[60] also proved fairly limp.

With *Nekrassov* and its blunt attack on the French press, Sartre had opened a whole new file concerning the relationship between the press and a certain type of writer. There had been a golden age, when Gide, Aragon, Malraux, Nizan, Camus, could walk the straight line betwen journalism and literature, the novel and the feature article, at times to the point of been able to have a high position at a major paper, as had been the case with Camus. Re-cruited by Camus, Sartre was first initiated to journalism during the liberation of Paris and then, later, during his trip to America, before he founded *Les Temps modernes.* On the other hand, his efforts in the field had not been particularly well-regarded by the connoisseurs, who generally considered them rather amateurish. His return from the USSR poisoned things: the tenor of his statements, his direct attack on the Lazareffs, and his implicit imputation of their compe-tence were enough to place Sartre in the role of the interloper, the aggressor, the colonizer, the peripheral apprentice who waltzes into a milieu of professionals to inform them that, after all, they really do not know what they are doing, and that they should let him, the professor, the philosopher, the novelist, the playwright, the literary critic, the orator, show them how to utilize the benefits of a journey abroad to their best advantage, how to analyze their own percep-tions, in short, how to be a good reporter.

Nekrassov is a writer's contribution to the fight for peace," Sartre had told Guy Leclerc of *L'Humanité.* "We undertook obligations in Vienna; now we must fulfill them. At a time when *détente* is grow-ing, when the Four-Power Conference is about to be held, one of the most powerful brakes on our hopes, on what we are trying to do, is what this sort of press is doing to poison the atmosphere. I wanted to set down its methods in black and white, to open the eyes of men of good will among its own readers."[61]

The other work Sartre wrote under this new influence, *The Witches of Salem,* a movie adaptation of Arthur Miller's play *The Crucible,* also allowed him to express his views against McCarthyism, more or less the same as those he had developed in the articles he wrote to support the Rosenbergs. It was a three-hundred-page screenplay, which was later turned into a movie with Simone Signo-ret and Yves Montand in the main roles, directed by Raymond Rouleau. Though the movie, released in 1957, was well received throughout France, neither *Nekrassov* nor *The Witches of Salem* would remain among Sartre's most memorable works. Rather, they will always be considered as part of a necessary ideological output, along with his speeches, his petitions, his declarations, and his pro-communist articles.

Sartre's literary production, however considerable during those years, will reach the general public only much later. *Kean,* for in-stance, the least political and politicized play he wrote during the Cold War period, provides one of the most singular characters of the

Sartrean oeuvre, totally isolated, the only literary voice, the only personal concession he made in the course of those problematic years. In this adaptation of the elder Alexandre Dumas's play, with its reinterpretation of the astonishing personality of the British actor, Sartre continues his long biographical investigation, exploring and describing a new kind of individual, an actor, for his gallery of portraits, which now includes Genet, Mallarmé, Baudelaire, and Kafka. To judge from the joy that emanates from *Kean*'s generous, nineteenth-century prose, Sartre had fun writing it. He captures the megalomania, Don Juanism, solitude, and formidable pride of Kean in a number of superb tirades, which Pierre Brasseur, the creator of the role, masterfully boomed across the stage of the Théâtre Sarah Bernhardt, in the fall of 1953. The themes, ideas, obsessions that emerged out of the dialogue between Sartre and Kean were extremely intimate. The themes of bastardy and treason attained an extraordinary depth in the play. "An illusion, a fantasy—that is what you have made of Kean. He is a sham prince, sham minister, sham general, sham king. Apart from that, nothing. Oh, yes, a national glory. But on condition that he makes no attempt to live a real life. . . . Do you understand that I want to weigh with my real weight in the world? That I have had enough of being a shadow in a magic lantern? For twenty years I have been acting a part to amuse you all. Can't you understand that I want to live my own life?"[62] In retrospect, *Kean* appears to be a last burst of existential psychology before Sartre's entrance into the collective world of communism, an attempt to find a balance between subjective creation and group militantism, between the writer, producer of sense, and the actor, interpreter of texts.

S ARTRE LOST the first five hundred pages of "Mallarmé," halted "La Reine Albemarle" midway, and started a history of the working world and a screenplay on the French Revolution, which he never completed. To these abortive projects one should probably add the various other projects he often mentioned and never wrote, such as the detective novel he once described to Jean Cau and to several others. During the four years of communist comradeship, Sartre's inner literary upheavals were particularly severe and violent. After the crisis that followed the war of 1939, these amounted to the second and last great metamorphosis in the life of the writer. With the vehemence of the Protestant out to destroy the bourgeois in himself, Sartre had rushed to the aid of Duclos and the PCF. He encountered this impossible system with both the devotion and the blindness of a soldier throwing himself into battle. In his attack on men such as Antoine Pinay and the police chief, Baylot, in his excessively idealistic praise of the USSR and the Vienna congress, and in the eagerness with which he tried to demolish the anticommunist press, there was the passionate zeal, the outraged innocence, and the panic of the man who is afraid of falling short of the role he has chosen for himself. In 1953, he started three new manuscripts, two of which he will ultimately complete: an autobiography, tentatively titled *Jean sans terre,* and finally published in 1963 as *The Words*; a philosophical text that took over the famous *Morale*— temporarily left to lie fallow—published in 1960 as *The Critique of Dialectical Reason*; and, finally, an illustration of the latter, a monstrous obese parenthesis, which will later, in 1971 and 1972, become his *Flaubert, The Family Idiot,* a monument in three volumes, 2,802 pages, and incomplete.

*T*O FULLY understand the extraordinary effort that went into the composition of *The Words,* and experience an obsession similar to the one Sartre must have felt while at work on it, one should touch the manuscript, handle its blue, white, and beige sheets, brittle and torn, read each of the lines that thickly follow each other for over three hundred pages. One should try to decipher its angry, rebellious, resilient scribble, twisting and slanting in blue across the page, leaving three lines here, crossing out the next five, then starting over again to be again erased till they reappear on the next page. One should taste the tension and the fierce determination that lurk behind each sentence, behind each erasure, behind each new trial, and wonder at the meaning of those two or three isolated words, or the suggestion of a sentence, dropped as if by mistake at the top of a page and abandoned there, vain relics of a passing thought. Hashed, rehashed, rewritten, reworked, chiseled relentlessly for nearly ten years, *The Words* is a unique text, the only work of Sartre that demanded such painful, passionate, physical labor. "This is the beginning. I have invested everything in literature. . . . I have been writing for exactly half a century, and for forty years I have lived in a glass prison. . . . I realize that literature is a substitute for religion. . . . I felt the mysticism of words. . . . little by little, atheism has devoured everything. I have disinvested and secularized writing.

One could say that my metamorphosis started with the transformation of my relationship with language. I have passed from terrorism to rhetoric: in my most mystical years, words were sacrificed to things; as an unbeliever, I returned to words, needing to know what speech meant. But it is hard: I apply myself, but before me, I sense the death of a dream, a joyous brutality, the perpetual temptation of terror. [For forty years, I have been thinking against myself—(Sartre crossed this out).] For fifty-one years I have written out of habit. . . . I have systematically undermined the bases, yanked religion away from literature: no more salvation, nothing can save, besides, that is no longer the question. . . . immortality is not the point: I write for my times. . . . old age has arrested all progress. . . . Here is my beginning: to recover from an illness, I have invested everything in literature . . . the consequence being that I have been writing for half a century. . . . I entered the orders in my eighth year, it happened by itself."[63]

The manuscript was written between "The Communists and Peace" and the reply to Albert Camus, the return from the USSR and *Nekrassov*. While, on the surface, he fought against the persecution of the Communist Party and of the working classes with both passion and fury, deep inside, he also fought with passion and fury against the entire Sartrean edifice: against the edifice erected by a crazy eight-year-old child to escape from the influence of his grandfather, against salvation via literature, against the immortality of genius. At eight, he had found, in himself, the means to stifle all the various pressures that the adults around him had shamelessly imposed on him. He had "withdrawn behind a screen" to "restart his own birth."[64] And now, at forty-eight, he was starting the operation again so as to move in a new direction. "Most of *The Words* was written in 1953," he will say later. "At that time of my life, all sorts of changes were taking place, and in particular I came to the realization that ever since I had first begun to write I had been living in a real neurosis. My neurosis—which wasn't all that different from the one Flaubert suffered in his day—was basically that I firmly believed that nothing was more beautiful than writing, nothing greater, that to write was to create lasting works, and that the writer's life ought to be understood through his work. And then in 1953, I came to the realization that that was a completely bourgeois viewpoint, that there was a great deal more to life than writing. All of which meant that I had to rethink the value I placed on the written word, which I now felt was on a whole other level than where I had previously placed it. From that point of view, I was, somewhere around 1953–54, cured almost immediately of my neurosis. And at that point I felt a strong urge to understand. . . . And so I wrote *The Words.*"[65] He will go back to this discovery, this new view of writing as a bourgeois notion inherited from the nineteenth century in the course of several interviews: "Writing was just another function,"[66] nothing more. He will again explain how he "had dreamed" for almost fifty years, how he had been "mobilized by an absolute," and how, now, starting with the 1950s, "the absolute had disappeared."[67]

RECALLING THE events of those four years—the fury and the passion, the rage against his old friends and, first and foremost, himself; his violent attacks on his closest ideological neighbors, to the right of the PCF, to the left of the PCF, inside the PCF; everybody's surprise at his apparent and inexplicable radical conversion—and re-examining his surface behavior in the light of his underground maneuvers, shed light on some of the Sartrean logic at work then. The Cold War, the politics of superpowers, the refusal of a world war, the disgust with the Korean War, the outrage at the persecution of the PCF had conspired to push Sartre toward this critical comradeship. It was May 28, 1952. He had abruptly left Rome and all its magic without being at all aware of the nature of the system in which he was already becoming entangled. It is October 23, 1956. He is again in Rome when he hears of the uprising in Budapest, of the invasion of the city by Russian tanks, and of the Soviet repression. If, in 1952, he had left Rome to hasten to the rescue of the PCF, now, in 1956, he again leaves Rome to hasten to the aid of the oppressed Hungarians. Duclos's pigeons and the tanks of Budapest elicited from him the same devotion, the same passion, according to the same Sartrean logic: that of the relativity of emergencies. "I condemn the Soviet invasion wholeheartedly and without any reservation. Without putting any responsibility onto the Russian people, I nevertheless insist that its current government has committed a crime. . . . And the crime, to me, is not just the invasion of Budapest by army tanks, but the fact that this was made possible by twelve years of terror and imbecility. . . . It is and will be impossible to reestablish any sort of contact with the men who are currently at the head of the PCF. Each sentence they utter, each action they take is the culmination of thirty years of lies and sclerosis. Their reactions are totally irresponsible."[68]

Within the immense Sartrean galaxy, the PCF has become a shard, but it was an essential stage, after which nothing will ever be the same. The writer has to die to give birth to the intellectual in the service of the wretched of the earth. "The philosopher and his beggars," as Jacques Rancière later puts it. From that moment on, Sartre will become something else, in total rupture with the child-king, the crazy child—as he will tell us in *The Words*— and in yet more radical rupture with his nineteenth-century, Schweitzer heritage—as he will tell us in *Flaubert*. But he will never really tell us anything more. He will settle all his scores with himself, jettison his family heritage, and dedicate his life to the persecuted. The last phase of the Sartrean production is already planned by 1956: he has made a decision and he will stick to it. He will join Socrates, Plato, Rousseau, Voltaire, and Marx in the tradition of philosophy that tries to rescue society. In 1956, he is fifty-one, "a man who's been waking up cured of a long, bittersweet madness."[69]

IV

A MAN WAKING UP
1956–1980

For the last ten years or so I've been a man who's been waking up, cured of a long, bittersweet madness, and who can't get over the fact, a man who can't think of his old ways without laughing and who doesn't know what to do with himself.

—THE WORDS

YOU'RE TERRIFIC

WAS THE France of the fifties really *formidable* (terrific)? And what about the French, who were just waking up to modernity; were they also terrific? The word was certainly all the rage. Charles Aznavour and Gilbert Bécaud used it in their songs; schoolchildren employed it all the time, like a magic wand: shortened and abused, "C'est formid" became, with "C'est sympa" or "C'est sensass," the key word for every enthusiasm, every conquest.

"You're terrific." Jean Nohain's famous voice repeated every day on the radio and later on national TV. This journalist, in his mid-fifties, imposed his style, his baldness, his good-natured optimism, his famous voice, and his hyperbole onto postwar France and its hunger for new forms of communication. As a popular entertainer, Jean Nohain soon won the hearts of his audience with his radio programs and his game shows such as "Queen for a Day" and "You're Terrific." He would lend his mike to the appeal of a needy French family and then, with his contagious, paternalistic voice, would exhort his "terrific" listeners to come to the rescue. In no time, his office would be piled high with canned goods, furniture, clothes, and medicine, and the needy family would suddenly find itself submerged in all the riches this privileged, if illusory, moment of national generosity and warmth could pour over them.

To the rhythm of Jean Nohain's weekly miracles, France kept on dreaming and unwittingly sliding toward the age of consumerism. Various forms of initiation, collective apprenticeship, group admissions: the door to modernity was open to all. The latest models of cars invited people to taste the joys of speed: the 4CV, pride of the Renault factories, the Frégate, the Trianon, the Versailles, the Dyna Panhard, all round and soft, totally devoid of edges. And then, of course, there were the first wonders of refrigeration, formica, plastics. And the most important dinner guest was Pierre Sabbagh, the first anchorman of the eight o'clock news for three hundred pioneer viewers of French TV. But was the France of the fifties really that terrific?

"**Y**OU'RE TERRIFIC," Jean-Paul Sartre parodies Jean Nohain, in an article he publishes in the April 1957 issue of *Les Temps modernes.* "Newspapers are courting us," he states, "they want us to believe that we are good. Whenever radio and television want some spare change, they title their programs 'You're Terrific.' . . . But we are not terrific, nor are we honest: this illusory community of honest folk is limited to the readers of *France-Soir.* And if we refuse to investigate French truth, when we are perfectly capable of piling up our old mattresses on our 4CV to unload them at the feet of Jean Nohain, it is simply because we are afraid. Afraid of seeing our naked faces. This is our lie."[1] When anti-Semitism was in its larval stage, Sartre had set the cat among the pigeons with *Anti-Semite and Jew.* Ten years later, he roughs up the idol of the French petite bourgeoisie. Sartre reappears brutally; the paradoxical, lucid philosopher rolls up his sleeves and starts shattering idle dreams and inane complacency. After his pro-Soviet canticles, this is how he recovers his voice and his punch.

"First lie . . . Second lie . . . Guilty. Double guilty." In May 1957, with his negative version of "You're Terrific," Sartre also sounds the alarm on Algeria, or, rather, he re-emphasizes the message of a brochure that had been published a few months earlier, *Des rappelés témoignent,* denouncing the looting and torture taking place in Algeria, revealing the full corruption of the French army in its colonial excesses. "We are sick, very sick," Sartre insists. "Feverish and prostrate, obsessed by old dreams of glory and the foreboding of its shame, France is struggling in the grip of a nightmare it is unable either to flee or decipher. Either we'll see things as they are or we will die."[2] Sartre initiates a trial that involves the entire country.[3] Invoking the specter of 1945 and "collective responsibility," he assumes the garb of the public prosecutor to stir up dormant cowardices, awaken good consciences, probe live wounds. In a few lines, he sketches the France of 1957, underlines the contrasts, points out the contradictions and exposes the famous "You're terrific," the formula of the year, as noxious, vulgar, obscene.[4] In his article, Jean Nohain, the magician of France, the perverse healer who injects the whole country with a lethargic serum, becomes the stand-in for the Mollet government, which, aware of the torture occurring daily in Algeria, continues to sweep the dirt under the carpet. "Never evading any sacrifice, [the Mollet government] has set the Queen of England on the throne of France for three days. . . . Meanwhile, however, in Algeria, a gang of stubborn men kept doing their job: there are no holidays for butchers."⁵ "The queen has left; now she is resting up at Windsor Castle. We remain silent, but we know those documents. How many mattresses will we have to pile up on the Place de la Concorde to make the world forget that children are being tortured in our name while we choose to remain silent?"⁶ This is a typically Sartrean parallel: Queen Elizabeth II, whose coronation, three years earlier, had been followed in all its obsolete pomp and circumstance by every Frenchman with a TV set, and Jean Nohain, requesting mattresses for the indigent Lambda family, become one and the same thing, and Sartre incriminates both.⁷ So, for the peace of mind of the French people, this painful African truth is suppressed, along with other nightmares and collective shame. "We will be caught in an abominable trap," the writer predicts, "and what's more, in an attitude we have ourselves condemned."⁸ Indignation, exaltation, urgency—"It's still time . . . It's still possible"—before the final injunction: "Let's look at the truth, it will allow us either to condemn our crimes publicly or admit them lucidly. . . . This is the evidence, this is the horror, ours: we won't be able to see it without tearing it away from us and crushing it."⁹ Sartre will repeat this strong, urgent, outraged text often, with minor variations on the same theme, rasping obsessively on collective guilt, the disease of silence, playing this role, his role, to the hilt.

"*FORMID*," "*impec*," "*sensas*": like their French counterparts, Algerian schoolchildren in their light smocks enjoyed using the new lexical treasures of the fifties, which allowed them to be in sync with pop songs and the launching of Sputnik. While Jean Nohain patted the French on their collective back, France was already feeling the first throes of the vain effort that was going to tear it apart for the next eight years. The Algerian war was infecting the entire country. From Dunkerque to Tamanrasset, the colonial edifice that had once seemed so prosperous, and solid, was ineluctably caving in. The schoolchildren of El-Biar, Ouargla, and Tlemcen were taught that their country had a large granitic massif, Le Massif Central, at its center, and was irrigated by a number of rivers like the Loire, Vienne, and Garonne, but they knew nothing at all about the Djurjura, the Arach, or the Mitidja Plain. These same schoolchildren were forced to love and, declaim the poems of Du Bellay or the great speeches of classical theater while they ignored everything about Ibn Kaldoun or Queen Kahana or the poet El-Manfalouti. Since 1830, when General Thomas Bugeaud had, in the name of France, taken Algeria away from Abd-el-Kader, a politics of assimilation had been implemented all over the country, and French had officially replaced Arabic, thus automatically diffusing a reduced and reductive imported culture. Moslems, Berbers, Jews, and French farmers had thus coexisted for over one hundred and twenty-five years by the time the "Metropolitan French," as they were known in Algeria, started to notice the first signs of the profound troubles that were upsetting a population of seven million people.

Suddenly the entire Algerian lexicon—obscured by a quarter century of French occupation—and a culture, history, and geography that have been stifled for a century and a quarter, impose themselves on the attention of a shocked France. Words such as *Aurès, djebbels, douars, oueds,* and *fellaghas* begin to coexist with "rebels," "outlaws," "maintenance of order," in the newspapers. November 1, 1954 will remain the symbolic date of the explosion. "Various attacks have taken place throughout Algeria," François Mitterrand, minister of the interior in the Mendès-France government, explains six days later. "These attacks are either the work of individuals or of small isolated groups. Certain measures have been taken by the governor general of Algeria, M. Roger Léonard, and the minister of the interior has put supplementary police forces at his disposal. Total calm reigns over the general population." The culprits are identified as "terrorists," a word that has not been used since the Occupation. After the fall of Dien Bien Phu, Mendès-France had signed a peace treaty with Indochina and, had also granted internal autonomy to Tunisia. But he had been unable to settle the Algerian question. There, he had inevitably butted against the interests of the "pieds noirs," among whom he was known as the "Empiremonger."

Soon Edgar Faure succeeded Mendès-France and Guy Mollet succeeded Faure, while, in the general governorship of Algeria, Roger Léonard succeeded Edmond Naegelen and Jacques Soustelle succeeded Léonard. Finally, in February 1956, Robert Lacoste was named resident minister of Algeria. Over a period of less than six years, more than seven politicians had tried to cope with this embarrassing affair—rendered all the more embarrassing in that every week brought more disconcerting information as journalists kept chipping at the whitewashed façade of French Algeria. In the long run, they ended up demolishing the accepted political line: "Algeria is France"; "Together, Algeria and France constitute a unity that nothing could ever compromise"; "From Flanders to the Congo, there is only one law, French law."

Massacres in the north of Algeria in August 1955 had led to thousands of victims both among the Europeans and the Moslems. The journalist Robert Barrat decided to investigate. First, he met with Soustelle, then general governor of Algeria, and with a few Algerian leaders, the famous *fellaghas* of the FLN. Then, he tried to establish some contacts between the "rebels" and the representatives of French law, but in vain. After his article "A French Journalist Speaks with Algerian Outlaws," was published in *France-Observateur*, he was arrested on orders of Soustelle, and then released on orders of Faure —a typical example of the incoherence and the vacillations of the French government at the time. But Barrat's documentation was soon supported by that of Francis and Colette Jeanson, who, in their *Outlaw Algeria*, showed in great detail the complete failure of the so-called process of integration that had been attempted over years and years of colonization. They also demonstrated the political, historical, economic, and cultural validity of these supposed "outlaws" pursued by French parachutists throughout the *djebbels* of Kabilia. The Barrat file, the Jeanson file: gradually *L'Express*, *L'Observateur*, and *Le Monde* began lending more and more space to voices who spoke of the intolerable "Algerian truth." In the fall of 1955, after the first few burning articles by Barrat and Jeanson, some intellectuals opposed to the continuation of the Algerian war created a Comité d'Action. It brought together people of all persuasions, Christian intellectuals such as André Mandouze as well as communist militants such as Edgar Morin, Robert Antelme, and Dionys Mascolo. "We wanted to fight against the very principle of colonial war and for the rights of the people," the sociologist Morin will later explain.[10] Some writers soon joined the founders of the committee, including Roger Martin du Gard, Mauriac, Sartre.

S ARTRE AND Simone de Beauvoir had gotten acquainted with the Algerian reality during their trips. But they had not noticed much in the way of political turmoil when, in the spring of 1950, they had crossed Algeria on their way to Mali and Senegal. At Ghardaïa, they had admired the beauties of the Mzab. "We were opposed to the colonial system, but we had no *a priori* prejudices against the men who administered native affairs or supervised the construction of the roads."[11] But if there had been no drastic realization in the course of this trip, their hatred of colonialism, of all sorts of colonialism, had always been very strong and uncompromising. During the years of the RDR, Sartre had unconditionally denounced the oppression in Morocco. "You are right to accuse France," he had declared in front of a large audience of Moroccan students in Paris, in his first anticolonialist speech.[12] Later, during a congress of the World Peace Movement in Helsinki, he had again returned to the issue of colonialism. "The colonialist age is coming to an end," he had stated, while openly wishing that France would meet the demands of Algeria, Tunisia, and Morocco in a peaceful fashion.[13] It was a pious wish, still possible in June 1955, when it was uttered. Just four months later, however, a chain of events had made the word "peace" totally obsolete within the Franco-Algerian context. Sartre had gathered a great part of his information about the Algerian situation from Francis Jeanson's reportage. A staunch admirer of Sartre, particularly since 1945, Jeanson had devoted three works to him—some of the most thorough analyses of his texts—and had then remained within the sphere of influence of *Les Temps modernes*. Jeanson had developed an interest in Algeria after World War II, during his frequent journeys and through his contacts with nationalist militants. Via Jeanson, Sartre and the staff of *Les Temps modernes* had been kept informed, almost daily, of the series of events that had brought about the awakening of an Algerian political consciousness. Jeanson's book, *Outlaw Algeria*, appeared in the fall of 1955 and immediately caused a scandal. Shortly thereafter Sartre and Jeanson were divided over Sartre's article "Stalin's Phantom." Jeanson thought Sartre's condemnation of the communists was a little too caustic. Their quarrel lasted three years, with the regrettable consequence of cutting Sartre off, and *Les Temps modernes* with him, from his only direct contact with the Algerian crisis.

"This morning I was in Algiers. . . . I bring you the greetings of the Algerian revolution." Thus, lyrically, André Mandouze immediately plunged the meeting of the Comité d'Action at the Salle Wagram, on January 27, 1956, into a "very 1793" atmosphere.[14] Among the other speakers: Jean Amrouche, Robert Barrat, the poet Aimé Césaire, Alioune Diop, Dionys Mascolo, Jean-Paul Sartre. "For Abolition of the Colonial Regime," the posters stated. "For the Respect of People's Right to Govern Themselves." "For a Peaceful Solution to the Algerian Problem." Sartre dealt with the Algerian problem— which, in 1956, was not yet a war—in one of his strongest, most carefully reasoned lectures. "Colonization is not a coincidence of chance, nor the statistical result of a thousand individual enterprises. It is a system that was implemented toward the middle of the nineteenth century, started producing some results around 1880, began declining after World War I, and is currently turning against the colonizing nation."[15] At the same time, he attacked the "neocolonialist mystification" proposed by the partisans of an intermediary solution, that of a tamer French Algeria. "There are no good colonists and bad colonists," he insisted. "A colonist is a colonist."[16] He impressed his audience with the precision of his information, his effective recourse to the tools of economics. "In 1850 the colonists owned 275,000 acres; in 1900, 3,900,000; in 1950, 6,669,000. Today, the French state owns 27 million acres as so-called state lands. In other words, we have left 17 million acres to the Algerians: it took us only a century to take a third of their land away from them. . . . When French troops first set foot in Algeria, all *good land* was cultivated. . . . The history of Algeria is that of the progressive concentration of European landownership at the expense of Algerian property."[17] He recalled how at the end of the nineteenth century this system was reinforced by the creation of large colonial companies and by the theories of Jules Ferry, the apostle of "new colonialism." He condemned the importation of a capitalistic European economy into Algeria. "If this operation has continued into the twentieth century, as if pushed by the blind necessity of an economic law, it is because the French state has brutally and artificially created the conditions of capitalist liberalism in a feudal, agricultural country."[18] And he went on to denounce the blind Gallicizing process that, for instance, developed viticulture—which, between 1927 and 1932, had increased by 428,000 more acres, most stolen from the Moslems—"in a country where most of the population does not drink alcohol. On the land stolen from them, the Moslems used to grow cereals for the Algerian market. So, they were not only deprived of land, but also of their main source of nourishment. For the Moslem population, 1.25 million acres of good land, parceled up and entirely devoted to viticulture, are as good as nonexistent."[19]

Algerian agriculture, Algerian economy, Algerian demography, Algerian history: Sartre addressed them all, before getting to what he knew best: culture. "As for our famous culture, were the Algerians really so eager to acquire it? In any case, we certainly did not begrudge it to them. . . . We were all too willing to turn our 'Moslem brothers' into a population of illiterates. Still today, 80 percent of the Algerian population is practically illiterate. . . . Since 1830, Arabic has become a foreign language for most Algerians."[20] He concluded, "All of us Metropolitan French should learn our lesson: colonialism is gradually self-destructing. But, in the process, it is stinking up our atmosphere: it is our shame, it mocks our laws, it pollutes us with its racism. . . . We must help it die. Today, the only right thing we can possibly do is to fight at the side [of the Algerian people] in order to free both Algeria and France from colonial tyranny."²¹

The Algerian problem, the "African truth," was the first political issue to which Sartre devoted himself after his rupture with the PCF. On the other hand, this stubborn commitment to the Algerian conflict brought him back, almost automatically and in spite of himself, within the communist orbit since the fight against colonialism is a basic part of the Marxist project. And, in fact, toward the end of the fifties, his main target was less the Communist Party than General de Gaulle. Except for the pro-Gaullist articles he wrote in 1945, during his first trip to the United States, he will always oppose the general. De Gaulle came to power in 1958. In the period just before this, an excessively parliamentary, unpopular Fourth Republic had been worn out by the first Mediterranean crises. A series of governments had succeeded one another: Mollet, Bourgès-Manoury, Gaillard, Pfimlin. The agitations of the political right had stirred up the public: Pierre Poujade's nationalist speeches against "commies," "wogs," "pederasts," "empiremongers," and all the enemies of the "pied-noirs" and French Algeria, were applauded by full houses. The army, and particularly its Algerian contingent, still included a few resentful old soldiers who would soon voice their views. "Power can no longer be seized," de Gaulle stated, "it has to be picked up."²² De Gaulle's return to power was organized by a number of Parisian politicians headed by Michel Debré and by the Algerian army headed by General Massu.

"A great honorary man is hazardous to a nation, even if he hides in a remote village. He does not have to speak, his past does it for him. General de Gaulle had not said a word for quite some time, but his past was still with us." After the coup of May 13, 1958, Sartre begins his attack in an article for *L'Express* titled "The Pretender." He inveighs against the general's political resurrection, his image, his veiled deception, the speech he delivered on the evening of May 13 from Colombey-les-Deux-Eglises, where he lived. De Gaulle had solemnly declared, assuming the dramatic voice of the literary swordsman that the French will get used to over the next ten years, "The degradation of a state inevitably entails the progressive distancing of allied countries, restlessness in the army, national dislocation, the loss of independence. . . . Some time ago, our country put all hope of salvation into my hands. Today, it is facing a number of new trials, and I want it to know that I am ready to assume all the responsibilities of its government."[23] Sartre had immediately reacted against the image of the conventional, nationalist, Catholic, and militaristic France that was forcefully imposing itself through the personality of the general. "De Gaulle was waiting," Sartre writes in his article. "That silent mountain drew its strength out of our weaknesses: all our impotence and our contradictions converged in him." Throughout France, the left was well aware of the dangers implied in this overt reliance on an army man, including of course the threat of a military dictatorship. Sartre was very quick to detect the first menacing symptoms: "Since the sovereign is a general," he wrote, "the country obeys an army, which only obeys itself. Yes, indeed, our state is in bad shape."[24] Then, he wondered, "What would happen if Charles de Gaulle really had these extraordinary powers? What is he planning to do? What verdict will he return? . . . The solitude of this man, imprisoned in his grandeur, will forever prevent him from becoming the leader of a republican state. Or it will prevent any state of which he is a leader from remaining a republic, which amounts to the same thing."[25]

"Of Rats and Men," "Frogs Begging for a King": to illustrate the first months of the Gaullist government, Sartre availed himself more than ever of an animal lexicon borrowed from La Fontaine, thrilled at discovering in this new language—which the communists had already used against him, "jackal," "polecat," "stinking hyena,"—a cruel distorting mirror to hold up to the general. His response to the referendum of September 1958 is immediate: "If I quickly sketch the main lines of a program, it is not to propose them today but rather to ask all those republicans who are going to vote for de Gaulle on Sunday whether it is because of this that they are voting for him. Why do you pretend to vote for a program when, in fact, you are merely responding to a man? . . . Your candidate is more famous for the noble stubbornness of his refusals than for the scope of his economic and social awareness."[26] Sartre detests de Gaulle's idea of personal power, his particular relationship with the country. "Those who, *today,* believe that 'de Gaulle is the only one who . . .' are totally irrational," Sartre goes on. "If there is a man, in the entire human species, who alone knows, and if his knowledge gives him the right to become, however benevolently, our destiny, and if his actions are always valid and good for the sole reason that they express his essence, then the human species is in full dissolution: there isn't a single man left, just one superman and a bunch of animals."[27] And he concludes his tirade against the return of the "constitutional monarch" with an exhortation: "Let's face it: it is

impossible to cure the impotence of a country by putting all power into the hands of one man. . . . To vote 'yes' means you are dreaming. To vote 'no' means you are waking up. It's about time we decide whether we want to get up or go to bed."[28]

N EVER BEFORE had Sartre committed himself as deeply to a contemporary political combat. Never before had he assumed the role of political editorialist. More than a conflict between two men, this is a conflict between two models, two French traditions, both products of the nineteenth century: the Catholic, nationalistic, militaristic, conformist tradition versus the Protestant tradition of scholars, pedagogues, advocates of free will.

"You're terrific," Jean Nohain kept telling his delighted listeners. "France has overcome all internal and external tribulations, and is now marching toward a great destiny, a great posterity. . . ."[29] De Gaulle maintained every time he addressed the nation, his interminable arms sweeping the air. "We are all murderers," Jean-Paul Sartre answered them, pouring the venom of his radical criticism and skepticism into this orgy of self-congratulation. Sartre lived the fifties in a creative frenzy similar to his prewar period. To maintain that rhythm and keep the engines running, he pushed himself to the brink with too little sleep, too many cigarettes, much too much alcohol. In 1945, he was forty; the orthedrine pills he favored were a useful, necessary stimulant. With the years, however, his body had tired; work and other excesses eroded various parts of the engine. In the summer of 1954, fatigued and overwrought, weighed down by too much drinking, he had finally collapsed. His first trip to the USSR had ended in a Moscow hospital. He was prescribed moderation, rest, sleep, but Sartre was not a man to listen to doctors. This first crisis was followed by a second one while he was attending a rehearsal of his latest play, *The Devil and the Good Lord,* at the Théâtre Antoine with Simone Berriau, Beauvoir, and Bost. They were chatting over a drink. Glass in hand, Sartre was participating in the conversation, but, when he tried to put his glass down, he suddenly felt faint; leaning toward the table, he hesitated, his glass slipped out of his hand, fluttered in the air like a sick butterfly, and then landed on the rug. "Only Simone Berriau managed to keep her head," a close witness remembers.[30]

Painful for Sartre's friends to accept these first signs of weakness; even tougher for the little family. How could they possibly deal with a handicapped Sartre when he had always been so full of life and energy? Besides, who among them would have dared put a check on Sartre's overpowering personality, and on the increasingly insidious tyranny it exercised over him? And yet, the problem was quite obvious. Sartre's life had been more or less equally divided between, on the one hand, intense socializing—trips, rich meals, heavy drinking, drugs, and tobacco—and, on the other, the monastic austerity of a rigid work schedule. Work till noon at Rue Bonaparte. Twelve-thirty: one hour of appointments, scheduled by his secretary. One-thirty: back at Rue Bonaparte, with Beauvoir, Michelle, or some other woman. He could not stand people to be either late or early. For lunch, he would either go to La Coupole or Balzar by cab, or walk to Lipp or Akvavit, on the Rue Saint-Benoît. Two hours over a heavy meal, washed down with a quart of red wine. Punctually, at three-thirty, he would stop in mid-sentence, push away the table, get up, and run back to his desk at Rue Bonaparte. 1958 was exhausting, according to Beauvoir. Sartre's troubles became more and more frequent: sudden absences in the middle of a meal, short notes in a hasty, sick scribble, brief moments of frenzy, dizzyness, hypertension, congestion. When he felt really sick, and the doctor prescribed rest, he would opt for a compromise: less tobacco and fewer drugs for a week. Then, as soon as he felt better, he would start up again, reassured and delighted at his shrewdness and its success. But if the overall rhythm was preserved, his health kept failing and his days became increasingly shorter. To get out of this bind, Sartre decided to compress time; instead, he created a vicious circle. Sleeping pills would assure his sleep, Corydrane would wake him up, coffee and whisky would take care of the rest, so he could keep on working, the way a drowning man swims, frantically, desperately, knowing time is at his heels, ready to swallow him up.

In the fifties, Corydrane was the drug of students, intellectuals, artists. It was believed to supply talent, genius, lucidity. Its very composition was miraculous: aspirin got rid of fever and pains, amphetamine stimulated the nervous system. At once, it could calm down and work up, soothe and excite. It lent wings to the intellect. People could not do without it. In 1971, Corydrane was declared toxic and was withdrawn from the market. And yet, it looked totally innocuous: a pretty, discreet little tube containing twenty tablets, enclosed in a green-brown box. A product of the Delagrange

Laboratories. "Corydrane, tonic, analgesic, antipyretic," the box announced and then listed indications, directions, active ingredients: "Flu, coryza, algia, asthenia." "One or two tablets in the morning and at noon." "Each tube contains aspirin 50 mg; racemic amphetamine 144 mg." The whole terminated in a warning: "Do not exceed the prescribed dosage."

As soon as he was up, after a heavy meal and just a few hours of bad sleep, artificially induced by four or five sleeping pills, he had a cup of coffee and some Corydrane: first one tablet, then two, then three, which he chewed, while working. . . . By the end of the day, he had emptied a whole tube and produced thirty to forty pages of Sartre. When calm and smoothly linear—words clinging to one another—his spidery blue handwriting would unfold with vigor, leaning slightly to the right, often stretching upward, or dipping, but always under control. But, at times, it was like a storm, utter chaos, unfettered madness, monstrous words, twisted every which way, stretched to the breaking point, shrunk, bloated, unruly, drunk. This is how he wrote *The Critique of Dialectical Reason*: a wild rush of words and juxtaposed ideas, pouring forth during crises of hyperexcitement, under the effect of contradictory drugs, that would zing him up, knock him down, or halt him in between . . . up, down, stop, and so on and so forth in a constant struggle against himself, against his tired body, against time and sleep. Everything in excess. His diet over a period of twenty-four hours included two packs of cigarettes and several pipes stuffed with black tobacco, more than a quart of alcohol—wine, beer, vodka, whisky, and so on—two hundred milligrams of amphetamines, fifteen grams of aspirin, several grams of barbiturates, plus coffee, tea, rich meals. Heavy doses for a tough man, hyperlucid and nearly impervious to pain, who, however, would occasionally lapse into moments of absence, from which he then promptly re-emerged, ready to resume control, with vivacity and pride. Was he aware of the effort he was demanding of himself? Did he know that he was pushing himself to the brink, and past it? Did he realize that his behavior was a form of suicide?

"You see, my trusting in Corydrane," he told Beauvoir in 1974, "was to some extent the pursuit of the imaginary. While I was working, after taking ten Corydranes in the morning, my state was one of complete bodily surrender. I perceived myself through the motion of my pen, my forming images and ideas. I was the same active being as Pardaillan."[31] And he added, "I thought that in my head—not separated, not analyzed, but in a shape that would become rational—that in my head I possessed all the ideas I was to put down on paper. It was only a question of separating them and writing them on the paper. So to put it briefly, in philosophy writing consisted of analyzing my ideas; and a tube of Corydrane meant 'these ideas will be analyzed in the next two days.' "[32] Writing became a gamble against himself and the source of much pleasure, a mad, desperate, intoxicating private race. "Take care of my health?" he'd answer his friends. "What for, when life means watching oneself relentlessly!" And he would recall the longevity of the Schweitzers, all dying in their nineties, still strong. Sure of his genetic capital and his healthy background, he kept speculating on them, risking, gambling against himself.

*T*HE FIRST volume of the *Critique of Dialectical Reason,* published in the spring of 1960, was dedicated "To the Beaver," as had been *Nausea* and *Being and Nothingness.* In 755 pages, Sartre analyzed the difficult relationship between Marxism and Sartrean existentialism. All his other contemporary works, such as the essay on Tintoretto, and his ninth play, *The Condemned of Altona,* are rooted in the *Critique.* Philosophy had always occupied first place in the hierarchy of Sartrean values: we remember the passionate composition of *Being and Nothingness* during the Occupation, and, later, in the frenzy of the Sartrean years, between 1947 and 1949, that of the *Cahiers pour une morale*— which will remain unpublished till 1982. The *Critique of Dialectical Reason,* its conception and its composition seem to follow a particular pattern, which could be described as follows: like *Being and Nothingness* and the *Morale,* this work is the product of an empty period, a dead end, a rupture. In 1941 there was "Socialism and Freedom," in 1949 the RDR, and, finally, in 1956, the PCF: three experiences, three failures, three periods of latency and general reassessment followed by the production of a theoretical work. *Being and Nothingness* had followed the untimely disappearance of "Socialism and Freedom," the *Morale* was conceived at the moment of the first difficulties within the RDR, the *Critique* begins developing during the months that follow Sartre's rupture with the French Communist Party. The three main stages of a philosophical career: three theoretical works anchored in the failure of three political experiences. As if concrete action and philosophical speculation echoed each other on the same issues, the same questions, the same problems: two sides of one quest wherein philosophy finds its legitimization in its capacity to integrate and transcend reality.

"For the last fifteen years I have been looking for something," he explains to Madeleine Chapsal. "I was trying, if you like, to give a political foundation to anthropology. This project got bigger and bigger—it grew like a generalized cancer. Ideas came to me, and I wasn't sure what to do with them, so I put them anywhere—in whatever book I happened to be working on at the time. Now I've finished with that. The ideas are all in place. I'm working on something that will relieve me of all of them—the *Critique of Dialectical Reason.*"[33] Organic metaphors, metaphors of illness: to describe the process of his creation, Sartre once again relies, as at the time of *Nausea,* on a well-known device: metaphors of teeming life, pullulation, viscosity, animality. The same sort of metaphor keeps cropping up in the course of the interview with Madeleine Chapsal: "When one is writing works that are nonphilosophical, while still ruminating on philosophy—as I have been doing for most of my time over the past ten years—every page, every line suffers from hernia. Recently, when I felt I was writing a hernia, I found it better to stop. That's why I have all these books waiting to be completed." And retracing the connections between all the themes that haunt him and all the books that he is simultaneously writing, he underlines the echoes between his work on dialectic and his book on Flaubert. At the origin of the *Critique of Dialectical Reason* was an article commissioned by a Polish magazine, *Twórczosc,* dealing with the situation of existentialism in 1957. "Marksizm i Egzistencjalizm," was later published by *Les Temps modernes* as "Questions de méthode." To Chapsal's question, "Did you have to write about the *Dialectic* in order to be able to discuss Flaubert?" Sartre answers, "Yes. The fact that I couldn't stop myself discussing him in the Polish article proves it; and the fact that I transposed long passages from my book on him into the *Critique* confirms it. At the present moment the book of Flaubert is long and still not finished. But at least it now won't need a truss—I won't have any hernias."[34] We are allowed to penetrate an intimate, secret world, to become the observers of three sacred dimensions: the archeology, the architecture, and the alchemy of the creator. Old intellectual projects recouped and revised in the light of new interests. Games of mirrors between his different works, his two great passions: "I and the world" and "I and the Other." Along with various other speculations to decide which work will subsume and which will be subsumed, which hernia to keep and which to operate on. And of course, the systematic, methodical addiction to amphetamines and other chemical stimulants: coffee, alcohol, tobacco. Thus, *Flaubert*— whose first volumes will be published only in 1971—will be at once a parenthesis, an illustration, a development, an overcoming, and a synthesis of the *Critique*. Everything is linked and entangled in this sophisticated, complex, mobile mosaic.

*B*Y THE end of the fifties, there has been no radical change in the central mechanism of the engine room: despite a few arrivals and a few departures the infrastructure has remained the same. In the summer of 1957, after eleven years of work between the Rue Bonaparte and the offices of *Les Temps modernes,* Jean Cau resigns as Sartre's secretary and is replaced by Claude Faux. Till the Hungarian crisis, Faux had been a permanent member of the PCF and had worked in the shadow of other communist journalists and writers such as Aragon. After finishing his new novel, *Les Jeunes Chiens,* he had decided to send it to Sartre, who had immediately sent him a cable to tell him he was ready to talk about it. "I've liked your book," he had told him with a dry voice. "You love people ... that's important. . . . What are you doing now?" "Actually, I'm looking for a job." Then, while walking him to the door, Sartre had nonchalantly added, "By the way, I am looking for a secretary . . . if you have nothing better to do . . ."[35] Claude Faux assumed his post in the study at the Rue Bonaparte, where he would report every morning for the next six years. "First of all, I had to take care of a number of big financial hassles having to do with tax returns, etc. I had to look for money, beg publishers, request extensions from the internal revenue office, dodge possible seizures of property, etc., etc. . . . The financial expert I consulted on a number of precise points suggested we form a society, if nothing else to make the management of certain matters easier. Sartre didn't even want to hear of it. He stubbornly refused to deal with anything having to do with money. He saw it as a waste of time. And yet he was in constant need of it: to give it away, to help others."

*T*HE ENGINE room is fundamentally the same, but Sartre's "little family" keeps changing. New meetings, new feminine friendships. Arlette Elkaïm, an eighteen-year-old *khâgneuse,* calls up to talk to Sartre about *Being and Nothingness* for her philosophy dissertation. Cau, who answers the phone call, communicates her request to Sartre. At the end of the first interview, Sartre tells her to keep in touch. She does. "Little Elkaïm on the phone . . . can you talk to her?" Cau shouts in the direction of Sartre's study, a hand covering the telephone receiver. Thus, Arlette Elkaïm, with her black, intelligent eyes, her "doelike sweetness," and the wounds of a vulnerable, fragile Algerian Jew, becomes a frequent guest on the Rue Bonaparte. In 1965, Sartre adopts her. Another woman enters Sartre's life at the same time: Evelyne Rey, Claude Lanzmann's sister. A young blond beauty, Evelyne is elegant, intelligent, and extremely sensitive. She is also a political militant, an actress, and a journalist: as a member of Sartre's "family," she will have ample opportunity to develop all her talents. For her, Sartre will write a splendid part in *The Condemned of Altona.*

For some time now, the Sartrean family and its feminine corollary have been perpetuating and consolidating each other while slowly and imperceptibly evolving on their own. Beauvoir, by now a well-known feminist and writer, has moved to first place among women of letters. Her personal success has at once brought her closer to and distanced her from Sartre. With the publication of *The Second Sex* in 1949, and with formulas such as "One is not born a woman, one becomes one," she appealed to an entire generation. She is still autonomous, and fully so, when, in 1954, at forty-six, she earns the Prix Goncourt with her novel *The Mandarins.* Money, fame, autonomy: for the first time, she allows herself a few possessions; she buys a studio on a quiet street, by the Montparnasse Cemetery. She is also autonomous when she decides to have her own affairs, in total Sartrean transparency, with Nelson Algren and Claude Lanzmann. This opens up a whole new system of vacations by four—Sartre-Michelle, Beauvoir-Lanzmann—which, however, does not preclude the occasional tête-à-tête between Beauvoir and Sartre. All sorts of new combinations are tried. With *She Came to Stay* (1943), *Memoirs of a Dutiful Daughter* (1958), and *The Prime of Life* (1960), Simone de Beauvoir becomes the memoirist of the Sartre "family" and its times. She tells the public about the morals, customs, and behavior of the couple she and Sartre form and of the group they and their friends constitute. At the same time, she still provides Sartre with daily support: he never publishes a manuscript that has not first passed through her hands, that has not first been criticized and approved by her. Throughout her life, she will remain his most meticulous, most demanding critic. Precise, trustworthy, and endowed with an extraordinary memory, she listens to him, challenges him, dissects his arguments, trims his excesses, underlines weaknesses. Every time Sartre turns to her for an argument or advice, she has the right word, the best answer. And, unlike so many others, she will never flinch at his popularity. In fact, one of her greatest strengths is that she never shows either sycophancy or complacency in her daily confrontations with him.

Did she care about Sartre's mysteries, his need for compartmentalization? About the fact, for instance, that he asked Gallimard to print two copies of the *Critique* dedicated "To Wanda," whereas all the other volumes were printed "To the Beaver"? In all the functions "à trois"—Sartre, Beauvoir, X—she always imposed on the third one with her formal way of addressing Sartre, and her strange intimacy with him. If, at times, the couple Sartre-Beauvoir lunched with their friends, in more intimate situations, the tête-à-tête was the norm: on Tuesday, she would lunch with Pouillon; on Wednesday, she would dine with Lanzmann; while, at the same time, Sartre would share his meals with either Michelle or Arlette or Bost. All this, of course, would provoke a great deal of gossip. Thus, Sartre shared his emotional life with, in turn, Beauvoir, Wanda, Michelle, Evelyne, and Arlette: one after the other, he took them all to Italy, with obligatory stops in Rome, Capri, and Venice. With each he laughed, lived, had fun, always refusing to either break up or give up.

*I*N THESE ideal affective conditions—stable, permanent, and yet constantly renewed—the "corydraned" philosopher developed some hernias and trussed others, all the while furiously writing his *Critique of Dialectical Reason* and other satellite texts. Among these, the most intriguing may well be the essay on Tintoretto: one more link in the chain of Sartrean biographies, with *Baudelaire, Saint Genet,* and *Flaubert,* but also one more fragment of his Italian landscapes, such as "Venice from My Window" and "A Bed of Nasturtiums," and one more chapter of "La Reine Albemarle ou le dernier touriste," the novel Beauvoir had dubbed "the *Nausea* of his maturity."

The last relic of that unfinished masterpiece, the piece on Tintoretto, titled "The Prisoner of Venice," is an extraordinary little text, impish and haughty, not too unlike a comic strip. Sartre tackles the Venetian Renaissance with wit, verve, poise, and ease, indulging in a deliberately prosaic style, anachronisms, and caricature. He has always felt at home with great men, and so he assumes full responsibility for Jacopo and launches into an exhaustive apology aiming at his rehabilitation: "Jacopo waged a losing battle against a numberless adversary, grew weary, and died, defeated. And that is the essence of his life. We shall see it all, in all its dismal nakedness, if, for a moment, we brush aside the overgrowth of slander which blocks our way." Thus Sartre retraces Tintoretto's real life: "His life is the story of an opportunist gnawed by fear." And he goes on to remind his readers of the power struggle that opposed Tintoretto, the twelve-year-old son of a dyer, to the imposing figure of Titian, his master, the undisputed monarch of Venetian painting. The apprentice was thrown out by the master, "blacklisted." But, Sartre goes on, "Jacopo has been invested by an entire working-class populace with the mandate of redeeming through his art the privileges of the pure-bred Venetian." Clearly, Sartre has once again chosen to side with a man alone against institutions, power, and the *salauds.* "Jacopo's ambition was born suddenly; in all its virulence and diversity of forms, it was girded for war. But also, it had assimilated that merest thread of light, the possible. Or rather, that nothing is *possible.* . . . But Tintoretto wasn't interested in any of that. Each man has his own ascending force and his own natural habitat. He knew he had a gift, and he had been taught that this was capital. . . . There he was, totally mobilized for a lifetime, with nothing left to spare. He had become a vein to be exploited, until both miner and mine were exhausted. At about this same time, another glutton for work, Michelangelo, grew disgusted."

More and more sensitive to his new hero, the scriptwriter quickens the pace, stresses the contemporary traits: "Tintoretto's rebellion next struck at the roots of the system," "He had nothing but ridicule for the literati," "[He] was a mole, at home only in the narrow galleries of his underground dwelling," "Raphael and Michelangelo were employees, living in magnificent dependence. . . . Tintoretto was another sort," "Michelangelo, the counterfeit noble, and Titian, the son of peasants, were strongly attracted to the monarchy. But Tintoretto sprang from a milieu of self-employed workers. . . . a manual laborer, he was proud of his hands," "Venice imposed the maxim of the puritans upon her painters: *no personal remarks.* " Just a few pearls gathered here and there. A few bright, colored vignettes and sundry Sartrean memories, enough to lend magic to any text. The artist and his city, the artist and social repression, the artist and his choice of voluntary confinement and sublimated madness, the artist versus the moneyed, the bourgeois, his solitude, his anger, his pride: these are just some of its themes, so finely wrought, so precisely and yet so casually drawn that one forgets everything about the sixteenth century and its unusual men, speaking of whom Sartre still wonders: "Were these renaissance painters demigods or manual laborers? The only thing to conclude is that it all depended."[36]

"*T*HE PRISONER of Venice" ("Le Séquestré de Venise") appeared in *Les Temps modernes* in November 1957; *The Condemned of Altona (Les Séquestrés d'Altona),* his ninth play, was composed between 1957 and 1959: two texts concerning voluntary confinement in the same creative period. Madeleine Chapsal questioned Sartre on the subject: "One has the feeling," she told him, "that you are still more ill at ease in this gloomy society of ours than others, that you feel restricted in it, that it stifles you—and that you 'secrete' your work as a kind of refuge from it. This is why I asked you whether you felt 'sequestered.' " "No," he answered. "The sense of gloom in *Les Séquestrés* was essentially inspired by the current state of French society. It's a frightful wreckage—and like anyone else, I'm inescapably part of it. If I'm a prisoner—together with all who have said no and who go on saying no—it is of the present regime."[37] Indeed, despite the geographical and historical background of *The Condemned of Altona*— an aristocratic family, the von Gerlachs, in postwar Germany—the references to the political situation of contemporary France are quite obvious, so much so that one could easily read the piece as an allegory. The play deals with the passionate, brutal, unbearably intense relationships among Franz von Gerlach—a political prisoner, constantly oscillating between madness and lucidity, marvelously played by Serge Reggiani—his sister Leni —Marie Ollivier—his sister-in-law Johanna—Evelyne Rey—and his father—Fernand Ledoux. Seldom had Sartre delved so deeply into his own divagations, experiences, and phantoms: *The Condemned* is undoubtedly his most poignant, imaginative, and powerful play.

A hard, impenetrable face, a monocled right eye, straight and stiff in his SS uniform, Franz von Gerlach—"this new Hamlet, this Nazi Lorenzaccio," according to the theater critic Gilles Sandier[38]"— who first appeared on the stage of the Théâtre de la Renaissance on September 23, 1959, remains an unforgettable character, a legendary figure. In a post-Nazi Germany that has forgotten its bad conscience and has restored its economic balance, Franz, the heir of a never-clearly-Nazi aristocratic family of powerful Protestant industrialists, has refused to forget and has locked himself up in voluntary confinement. *The Condemned* is a sort of *No Exit* with five characters: the father, his two sons, his daughter, and his daughter-in-law. The guilt feeling that oppresses Franz contaminates the others at different levels. "The father and the son communicate from a distance without seeing one another," Sartre explained. "The movement. . . . I see here as a spiral." The past, in an invisible role, complements this oppressive quintet. "The characters are dominated, gripped by the past throughout, just as they are by each other. It is because of the past, their past, everyone's past that they act in a certain way. As in real life."[39] *The Condemned of Altona* is a contemporary tragedy whose task is to remind us of our cowardice and our responsibility for every massacre and every torture. Franz, in his moments of faked madness, when he speaks of crabs and addresses them, is a true advocate of collective responsibility in the world of the living dead. "What crabs? Are you mad? What crabs," he screams at Johanna, his sister-in-law. "The Crabs are men . . . I, the Crab . . . I turned the tables and I cried: 'Here is man; after me, the deluge, *you*, the Crabs.' All unmasked! The balconies swarming with Arthropods. You know that the human race started off on the wrong foot, but I put the lid on to its fabulous ill-fortune by handing over its mortal remains to the Court of the Crustaceans."[40] This passage reminds us of Sartre's experience with mescaline after his return from Le Havre, when, in his hallucinations, he saw himself pursued by lobsters and crabs, the sort of marine zoology that he abhorred on a dinner table. With its typically Sartrean obsessions, contemporary political echoes, and classical breath, *The Condemned* remains Sartre's most literary, freest, and most excessive play. The pressures under which it had been written were certainly partially responsible. First of all there was Corydrane, which he kept popping throughout that cruelly sterile 1958, if only because it gave him the illusion that he could recover lost time. Then there was Simone Berriau, who kept breathing down his neck to get the finished manuscript. And finally, as at the time of *No Exit*, there was his promise to two friends—Wanda, the old one, and Evelyne, the new one—that he was going to write a play for them. Professional, emotional, and physiological pressures: triply stuck, Sartre wrote like a madman. One can easily imagine what the atmosphere of the rehearsals must have been like, with

Sartre trying to keep the peace between two women equally eager to get the main role and doubly rivals for his affections. Sartre had been unable to finish *The Condemned* in the summer of 1958. But he finished it during the summer of 1959, in Venice, under very odd circumstances. After a month in Rome with Beauvoir, he was spending a few weeks in Venice with Arlette. They had started off at a good hotel but then, as finances dwindled, they moved to a small, noisy, seedy inn next to the station, a situation reminiscent of Le Havre. "It was terribly hot," Arlette remembers. "Sartre, barebacked, sweaty, and tired started reading me Franz's monologue, which he had just finished writing. . . . Actually, he did not so much read it as declaim it, in a very lyrical, very melodramatic way, imbued with the same kind of cheap romanticism that made him play an extremely tearful Chopin on the piano. It was so odd that it rather scared me: first for the style, then for the play. . . . I was afraid the end would mar the rest of the play. . . . Now I know I was wrong."[41] "Centuries of the future, here is my century, solitary and deformed —the accused. . . . The century might have been a good one had not man been watched from time immemorial by the cruel enemy who had that has sworn to destroy him, that hairless, evil, flesh-eating beast—man himself. . . . Oh, tribunal judges of the night—you who were, who will be, and who are, I have been! I have been! I, Franz von Gerlach, here in this room, have taken the century upon my shoulders and have said: 'I will answer for it. This day and forever.' "[42] In the full light of a Venetian summer, in the heat of noon, the barebacked playwright turned actor ended his reading and went to the post office to mail the last pages of the manuscript to Simone Berriau, Théâtre de la Renaissance.

This time, the critics were nearly unanimous in their recognition —to quote Bernard Dort—of "the generosity, the heroism of Sartrean thought . . . the passion for a history lived by man, our History, which inhabits Sartre and relentlessly torments him."[43] After the general outcry provoked by *Nekrassov,* four years earlier, this was a new start. "Jean-Paul Sartre Comes Back to the Stage After Four Years of Absence," ran the headlines of *Paris-Journal.* Others also spoke of a Sartrean "comeback," and still others, such as Gilles Sandier, applauded this "Socrates of playwrights," and his character, "this self-chastising executioner, this Lorenzaccio . . . darkly romantic, and fully responsible for the mistakes of his century."[44] With *The Condemned* Sartre ended his dramatic career. After it, there would be some adaptations, such as *The Trojan Women,* in 1965, and some revivals, such as *The Devil and the Good Lord,* at Vilar's National Popular Theater (TNP) in 1968 and *Nekrassov* at the Theater of East Paris (TEP) in 1974. But *The Condemned of Altona* will remain unsurpassed.

IN 1958, while working on *The Condemned* and finishing his *Critique,* Sartre was contacted by John Huston, who, in 1946, had staged *No Exit* in New York. Huston asked Sartre to write a screenplay on Sigmund Freud, paced like a detective story and full of adventures: something in the best Hollywood tradition, focusing on Freud's discovery of hypnosis and his first intuitions about psychoanalysis. It was a classic encounter: the European intellectual vs. the Hollywood director, two perfect caricatures of their respective worlds. Sartre and Huston were the same age, were leftists, and admired each other, although at a distance. Both were excessive in their creativity. Linguistic and cultural differences and various other misunderstandings, however, would eventually sabotage a project that was probably doomed from the start. And yet Huston's offer was very generous and Sartre accepted it without the slightest hesitation. He immediately asked Michelle Vian to translate Ernest Jones's huge biography of Freud, still unpublished in France, and reread *Studies on Hysteria* and *The Interpretation of Dreams.* Then he threw himself into the project with the same eagerness he had always felt for crazy endeavors.

Dr. Freud and Dr. Meynert, in a Vienna hospital, at the end of the nineteenth century. Freud and his fiancée, Martha, in a coach. Freud and his father. Freud and his mother. Freud and his Austrian students. Freud in Paris studying with Charcot. Sartre composed his scenes with the same historical, geographical, and cultural ease he had displayed the previous year in his study on Tintoretto. From the Venetian sixteenth century to the Viennese nineteenth century: nothing is impossible when one is named Sartre and has been brought up on the old, leather-bound volumes of Grandfather Schweitzer's library. "The first synopsis he gave Huston," Michelle Vian remembers, "already showed a great deal of work and research: he discussed the lighting, directed camera angles, described the costumes in great detail."[45] Sartre put into the project more passion and pleasure than anyone could have expected. On December 15, 1958, he sent Huston a ninety-five-page synopsis. A year later, he finished the final screenplay. Huston found it much too long and overbearing, and requested cuts and adjustments, at which point their relationship started souring. Sartre obeyed, then got angry. His text, shrunk and crippled, would eventually be reworked by Charles Kaufmann and Wolfgang Reinhardt, Huston's two assistants, and Sartre ultimately withdrew his name from the titles. In fact, he never even saw the movie, with Montgomery Clift in the title role, and always refused to consider that "bastard" as one of his products. "I want to give a hard time to my future biographers; I'll make them sweat blood"[46]: these words that he put into Freud's mouth he might have uttered himself.

Sartre and Huston were profoundly foreign to one another, both in their conception of the movie and in their history. The first evidence of their differences involved the $25,000 check Huston sent Sartre. An extraordinary sum for a French writer, the money was quickly accepted, and Sartre immediately produced a great quantity of pages, way more than he had ever been asked for. "Sartre agreed to write the screenplay for $25,000," Huston writes. "I phoned Elliot Hyman, who had been in on *Moby Dick* and *Moulin Rouge,* and without hesitation he put up the money." Later, referring to the half-completed project, he notes: "The money spent on it so far was a comparatively small amount for Sartre's services."[47] At the financial level, there were two completely different scales of value, the enormous disparity between the royalties of a European writer and the fee of an American screenwriter. But the misunderstandings and tensions involving the screenplay went deeper. "Sartre was a communist and an anti-Freudian," Huston writes. "Nevertheless I considered him the ideal man to write the Freud screenplay. He had read psychology deeply, knew Freud's work intimately and would have an objective and logical approach."[48] In fact, Sartre was far from knowing Freud well, let alone in depth. Huston was the victim of his image of the classic European intellectual. "Sartre was slow getting started," Huston goes on. "One day I received his first draft. As I recall, it ran well over 300 pages in French. Figuring a page a minute, it was more than five hours of motion picture. . . . It was simply too much to tell in one motion picture. . . . Some time later he sent me the revised version. I wasn't too surprised to discover that it was even longer than the first draft. . . . Obviously Sartre saw no reason why a movie should not last eight hours."[49]

The most memorable meeting took place in Ireland, on Huston's property at Saint Clerans, where Sartre and Arlette had gone to visit him just a few days after the premiere of *The Condemned,* in the fall of 1959. The purpose of the trip was to produce the final draft of the screenplay. Of course, nothing of the sort was even approached. "I haven't yet stepped out of this immense building," Sartre writes to Beauvoir. "My windows overlook a green prairie that seems to stretch for miles and miles. On the prairie, there are cows and a few horses, which our host, a cap on his head, rides every afternoon. He trots or gallops near his house followed by a small prancing donkey, which turns the ride into ridicule."[50] Huston's description of Sartre is hardly more flattering. "Sartre was a little barrel of a man, and as ugly as a human being can be. His face was both bloated and pitted, his teeth were yellowed and he was wall-eyed. He wore a gray suit, black shoes, white shirt, tie and vest. His appearance never changed. He'd come down in the morning in this suit, and he would still be wearing it the last thing at night."[51] Tit for tat: this is how Sartre describes his host: "Through this immensity of identical rooms, a great Romantic, melancholic and lonely, aimlessly roams. Our friend Huston is absent, aged, and literally unable to speak to his guests."[52] The mutual rebukes of two creators, two sacred monsters who have sized each other up. Two cultures at odds. For a week, under the same roof, two men are going to measure the depth of the gulf that separates them. In this Irish manor, as painters and carpenters work, guests meet without talking to each other—it is unclear whether they even speak the same language. "The last stop before the moon . . . that is the interior landscape of my boss, the great Huston," Sartre adds, somewhat intrigued by this crazy world whose language he cannot understand. "Huston isn't even sad," Sartre continues, "he is empty, except for those moments of childish vanity when he wears a red tuxedo, or rides one of his horses, or reviews his paintings and orders his workers about. It is impossible to keep his attention for more than five minutes at a time: he is unable to keep on working, refuses to think. . . . His emptiness is purer than death. . . . He refuses to think because it saddens him."[53]

Sartre finds himself dealing with a brutal illiterate, a visitor from another planet; Huston, with a thinking machine: "I've never known anyone to work with the singlemindedness of Sartre. He made notes —of his own words—as he talked. There was no such a thing as a conversation with him; he talked incessantly, and there was no interrupting him. You'd wait for him to catch his breath, but he wouldn't. The words came out in an absolute torrent. Sartre spoke no English, and because of the rapidity of his speech, I could barely follow even his basic thought processes. I am sure that much of what he said was brilliant. . . . Sometimes I'd leave the room in desperation—on the verge of exhaustion from trying to follow what he was saying; the drone of his voice followed me until I was out of earshot and, when I'd return, he wouldn't even have noticed that I'd been gone."[54] Misunderstandings, *malentendus*; Sartre had in fact noticed Huston was gone. "We are all sitting in the smoking room," the philosopher writes, "chatting, when, in the middle of a sentence, he ups and leaves. We'd be lucky if we saw him again before lunch or dinner."[55]

The most absurd moment of all occurred when, suffering from a terrible toothache, Sartre asked Huston to refer him to a dentist. "He took the first guy he found," Huston writes, "and had his tooth pulled. One tooth more or less was of no consequence to Sartre. The physical universe did not exist for him. Only the mind mattered. On the other hand, he kept popping all sorts of pills."[56] Their inability to communicate is even more drastic when Sartre receives a thick envelope from Paris containing various reviews of *The Condemned*. "He didn't stop to read it," Huston notes. "Before lunch, he drew aside for a moment to peruse its contents, but when he came back he didn't say anything about them. I had to ask him to show them to me to know they were positive. As I was watching that imperturbable monster sip his sherry, I could not help remembering the sleepless night I had spent waiting to know what the press and the public had thought of my father's role in *Othello*. "[57] All these scenes would be meaningless if they did not reveal the rigidity of these two chance collaborators, if they did not confirm what could be called their "cultural and human autism," and, ultimately, if they did not constitute a perfect Kafkaesque play, far more absurd than *No Exit* and *The Misfits* combined. And yet, as Sartre adds in one of his letters to Beavoir, "it is interesting to live this sort of shared solitude at least once in one's life. . . . I am not bored, but I can't figure out why."[58]

Between 1957 and 1960, he wrote his Tintoretto, the Freud screenplay, *The Condemned*. These are the hernias—whether commissioned or a direct product of the creator's imagination—which developed around the most fundamental manuscript of those years: the *Critique of Dialectical Reason*. "I'm in the process of writing a large philosophical thing," Sartre had mentioned, in passing, during a lunch with Robert Gallimard. "One evening the switchboard operator called me," the latter remembers, "and told me that Sartre was downstairs. I went down and found him in the lobby, sitting on an old sunken sofa, with a huge package under his arm. 'I just wanted to give you this,' he said and dropped the whole thing in my arms."[59] Typical of Sartre: to put his all into a manuscript, and then get rid of it as quickly as possible. And yet the *Critique* lies at the very heart of his philosophical thought, and his life, at the crossroads of his questions and his works.

Somewhere between 1947 and 1952, he had started a work on the French Revolution. He had gathered a great deal of material to write the individual biographies of each deputy of the Constituent Assembly, starting from the hypothesis that a whole is never just the sum of its parts. Left unfinished, this work was then easily assimilated into the *Critique,* as one of the numerous illustrations of this otherwise intensely theoretical text. Thus, Baudelaire, Flaubert, Freud, Robespierre, one by one, they will all be convoked to lend life to different pieces of this huge philosophical mosaic. Among the various and variously interesting concerns and analyses of the *Critique,* probably the most haunting, if not the most crucial, is the question involving the meaning of History—the long dialogue between man and History. Does man contain History or does History contain man? A question that is repeated in all the "hernias" of this period, in all the biographies, and all the reconstructions of these emblematic, unique individuals: Jacopo Tintoretto, Sigmund Freud, Franz von Gerlach. "So far, Sartre concludes, "we have been trying to get back to the elementary formal structures . . . and we have located the dialectical bases of a structural anthropology. . . . If the truth is *one* in its increasing internal diversifications, then, by answering the last question posed by a regressive investigation, we shall discover the basic signification of History and of dialectical rationality."[60]

The Condemned will be his last play, just as the *Critique* will be his last published philosophical essay. Despite the predominant theoretical tenor of the work and the small number of its real readers, the publication of the *Critique* again raised Sartre's market price. What was at the roots of its success? Fashion? Parisian snobbism? While finishing his manuscript, Sartre had accepted Jean Wahl's offer to deliver a lecture, at the Collège de Philosophie, on dialectics and other issues he addressed in his book.

The lecture took place at 44 Rue de Rennes, exactly opposite his own apartment. He entered the packed room around six in the evening, carrying a huge folder under his arm. "I am going to tell you what I am doing now," he started in a mechanical, hurried tone of voice. And he continued to speak without ever raising his eyes from the text, as if still absorbed in his writing. "He spoke for three quarters of an hour," Jean Pouillon remembers, "one hour, an hour and a quarter, an hour and a half, an hour and three quarters, without ever raising his head. All those who were standing, half of the audience, were exhausted. Some had already crumpled to the floor. . . . It was as if Sartre had completely forgotten about time."[61] At last, Jean Wahl signaled him to stop, and the philosopher picked up his papers and walked back to his study as abruptly as he had come.

*I*NTEREST IN the *Critique* continues past its publication. In the spring of 1960, Claude Lévi-Strauss asks Jean Pouillon to talk about it in the seminar he offers at the Ecole Pratique des Hautes Etudes. "This happened three months after the publication of the book," Pouillon remembers. "At first I refused, thinking that nobody as yet had the time to read the entire text. But then I changed my mind and proposed to divide my reading of the *Critique* into three two-hour seminars. Generally, my courses in anthropology drew about thirty people . . . but this one drew a real crowd. I recognized a few faces, such as, for instance, Lucien Goldmann's."[62] With *Nausea,* the *Critique* will remain one of Sartre's favorite works, one of the most important in his oeuvre.

Now Sartre is emerging into a new, more active stage of his life. Literature has acquired a new function for him: he is no longer obsessed with the notion of literary survival, and he confides his new definition of committed literature to Madeleine Chapsal. "If literature is not everything, it is worth nothing," he maintains. "This is what I mean by 'commitment.' It wilts if it is reduced to innocence, or to songs. If a written sentence does not reverberate at every level of man and society, then it makes no sense. What is the literature of an epoch but the epoch appropriated by its literature?"[63] He will discover this epoch very soon, in the spring of 1959. For the past two years, while Sartre was absorbed in his writings and his articles, Francis Jeanson was underground. He was running an FLN support network, whose task was to help Algerian militants acquire means of transportation, lodgings, and passports, to centralize the contributions of Algerian workers residing in France, and, finally, to publish an underground newsletter, *Vérités pour.* Sartre and Jeanson had quarreled in the fall of 1956, following their different analyses of the Hungarian uprising and the Soviet repression it had entailed. And yet Jeanson was perfectly aware of how desirable and useful it would be to have Sartre on his side. But they had argued and Jeanson had scruples. "One morning," he writes, "the urgency I felt to find this man and again face him, gave me a very plausible argument: *I did not have the 'right'* to let my scruples intervene between the cause we served and one of the men most suited to support it. We needed Sartre: I had to approach him, even though he might well say, 'Go to hell.' "[64]

Once the decision was made, a strategy was adopted: Marceline Loridan, a member of the network, would take care of it. She was solid, sure, and her prudence was legendary. Besides, she was a good friend of Evelyne Rey. So, Marceline would put Evelyne in charge of testing Sartre's eventual availability, his feelings toward support networks, his current attitude toward Jeanson. A meeting was scheduled and Marceline found herself at the Rue Bonaparte. "I have an important message for you on behalf of Jeanson," she began, somewhat apprehensively. "He immediately offered to follow me to Jeanson, who was then hiding in my apartment," she remembers. "He asked me about his health and whether his asthma had gotten any better. . . . We went by cab to the Rue Chéroy, where Jeanson was, and Sartre immediately agreed to work with us. I think," she adds, "he was intellectually ready to move in our direction."[65] And yet, that day, Francis Jeanson was ready for the worst: "Alone in that apartment, near the Théâtre Hébertot, I began envisaging all sorts of possible scenarios. When I heard the doorbell ring according to a pre-established code, I knew I was soon going to face the disappointed explanations of my messenger; but it was Sartre who first walked into the room. 'So, how are you?' he asked me, and, without even giving me the time to answer, went on, 'You know, I am a hundred percent behind you. Use me as you see fit: I have other friends who would also love to put themselves at your disposal. Tell me exactly what you need.' By the time he left, two hours later, I had an interview with Sartre for our underground paper as well as a number of addresses that would prove invaluable."[66]

"It is absolutely incredible," Sartre was quoted as saying in the interview that appeared during the summer of 1959, "that men of the left could declare themselves frightened by Algerian nationalism. . . . What should matter to you is that the FLN be allowed to envision an independent Algeria in the form of a social democracy, and to recognize, in the midst of this struggle, the need for agrarian reform."[67] This will be Sartre's central argument, for a number of reasons. First of all because, in the Sartrean hierarchy of the oppressed, the colonized have, by now, replaced the proletariat. "The proletariat has long entertained a number of generous ideas about our colonies. But generous ideas are often only words, totally in-effective when they are not backed by a real solidarity of interests. . . . *Today,* French workers support Algerian fighters because they realize that it is in their common interest to break the fetters of colonization."[68] This fifty-four-year-old man who is waking up, working, and letting the grating sound of his voice echo throughout a France that believes itself "terrific" has become, thanks to Jeanson, of real value to political struggles. Sartre on one's side means a hundred thousand followers, and Sartre has just offered his active support to an underground network that is fighting for Algerian independence. France will soon know what this means.

THE ANTI-AMBASSADOR

*I*N THE meantime, Sartre was surveying the world. Since the beginning of the thirties he had wanted to live and teach abroad. But he had stayed at Le Havre, then at Laon, and with Beauvoir had discovered the pleasures of tourism—Italy, Germany, Greece, Morocco—without ever really quieting his hunger for conquests. Knowledge, exploration, conquest: for him they were one and the same thing. His philosophical adventure had also a great deal to do with traveling. America, in 1945, had been his first big experience of this kind; he had begun to discover the world in this encounter of the other, in social and racial injustice. Then, for a while, traveling was replaced by writing: articles, statements, reporting. *Les Temps modernes* became a crossroad of sorts, the meeting point of those postwar cultures that were renewing themselves all over the world. Its special issues covered the United States, Italy, Germany, the USSR, and China.

Sartre's great journeys began much later than he had hoped and under very different conditions. But it is precisely by traveling from Peking to Moscow, from Rio to Jerusalem, from Prague to Tokyo, from Cuba to Rome, from Stockholm to Belgrade, from Cairo to Leningrad that Sartre was finally able to "possess the world." His travel album is impressive. In less than twenty years he became one of the French personalities best known abroad, a symbol. Few writers before him had had such a hold on the world. Only Voltaire, in his lasting relationships with Frederick II of Prussia, Gustav III of Sweden, Christian VII of Denmark, and Catherine of Russia, had played a similar role. A review of all the invitations and the meetings that brought Sartre to shake hands with Castro, Che Guevara, Mao, Khrushchev, Tito sheds some light on the fascination that foreign countries and foreign leaders felt for the French writer. In 1930, Sartre had hoped to be transferred to Tokyo: he would have to wait twenty-five more years before traveling to the Far East.

His visit to the People's Republic of China, from September 6 to October 6, 1955, was his first big eastward trip. It was this trip, moreover, that confirmed him and Beauvoir, both official guests, as a traveling couple. From this moment on, they would be ineluctably intertwined, in the eyes of the world, as two political globetrotters: everywhere they went they left the image of their legendary silhouettes. To Chinese photographers, Beauvoir appeared wearing a light shirt-dress with a flowery print and her usual French twist; Sartre, in a dark suit and tie, hands fidgeting, head vaguely leaning to the side, or bending forward, smiles uneasily. They are again side by side, again smiling, on October 1, 1955, while watching the parade in Beijing which, every year, commemorates the proclamation of the People's Republic. Purple walls, golden roofs, multicolored silk flags, a joyous flood of young pioneers, builders of dams, workers, peasants, artists, and writers representing all the provinces of China. Huge paper dragons, swirling and swaying in the air, children letting red, green, blue, and yellow balloons fly up in the sky, acrobats perched on barrels: for four hours, Sartre and Beauvoir watched the spectacle, listened to the national anthem—composed by a contemporary Chinese musician who had studied with Paul Dukas—and, finally, heard the official speech delivered by the mayor of Beijing, without, however, understanding a word of it. "We honor today," he said, among much else, "the glorious people's army that has freed our country." Again side by side, they ceremoniously, if silently, greeted Mao Zedong, shared the traditional cup of green tea with Zhen Yi, the vice chairman, around a lacquered table, and smiled to the photographers in front of the lake of Huang Tchu, the old Sung capital.

This trip to China had appealed to them the way all changes and new experiences always did. They were both eager to see with their own eyes what China was trying to accomplish, however upsetting it was for Western thought. Nor should these images of two happy tourists lead us to believe that their trip was limited to an exotic, picturesque tour. In China, they were going to meet History, to participate, directly, in the new experience taking place in that country. Even before knowing the country, Sartre had agreed to write the preface to Henri Cartier-Bresson's book *D'une Chine à l'autre* (From One China to the Other), and had pored over the photos of Chinese crowds, Chinese cities, and the Chinese countryside with the fascination of an explorer way before they had become a reality to him. In his preface, he had spoken of China with both knowledge and passion, as one would of a well-known, beloved country. "Cartier-Bresson," he wrote, "manages to suggest a phantasmal swarming, parceled into tiny constellations, the discreet but ubiquitous presence of death. Since I love crowds as much as I love the sea, I can't find anything scary or foreign in these Chinese multitudes. They kill, but they hide their dead in their breast and drink their blood as blotting paper absorbs ink: no one will be any the wiser. Our crowds are much angrier and more cruel."[1]

Then he moved on to more philosophical and political considerations: "Between the circular time of old China and the irreversible time of new China, there is an intermediary stage, a gelatinous span equally distant from both History and repetition: waiting. The sharp photos of old Peking are followed by heavy, dense images. Waiting. When the masses don't take care of history, they experience important events as interminable waiting."[2] Then, stung by the Chinese bug, as he had once been by that of antiquity or illustrious men, he concluded: "This album is an announcement: it announces the end of tourism. Gently, and with no useless pathos, it tells us that poverty is no longer picturesque, nor will it ever be again."[3] With the help of Mme Cheng, their guide and interpreter, they met and spoke with the artisans of old Peking, the aged servants of large cities, the local intellectuals. "Neither my own name nor Sartre's meant anything to them," wrote Beauvoir. "The newspapers explained that Sartre had just written a 'Life of Nekrassov,' and the people we talked to frequently expressed a polite interest in this work; then we would move on to gastronomy. This mutual ignorance restricted our conversations even more than the various political constraints."[4] China, in 1955, did not recognize these illustrious travelers.

"What characterizes today's China," Sartre said on the air, upon his return, "is that the wall of solitude has been destroyed. Nowhere have I ever witnessed such solidarity and such care. . . . Lack of professors? Never mind. Every Chinese who knows how to read will teach it to another Chinese. And I could quote a number of different examples. These masses, which we have often compared to anthills, are stirred by powerful concentric waves: they educate themselves, they tighten their bonds, they raise at once the level of production and that of friendship, they emancipate themselves. What struck me most about China is that friendship, there, is the reverse side of an economic necessity, the mainspring of production."⁵ As had already happened on his return from the USSR, in the summer of 1954, and as will again happen on his return from other trips, Sartre showed great kindness toward the country he had just visited. On this occasion, Sartre maintained more critical distance, even though, in 1955, he saw the Chinese people and the Chinese masses as the quintessence of the positive hero, harbingers of revolutionary hope for the entire world: "Between the two world wars China, exploited by foreign capitalism, crushed by a stupid feudal system, and devastated by the Japanese invasion, had lost all self-confidence. One must have been there to seize fully the bitterness concealed behind the objectivity of this famous sentence: 'We are intellectually and economically backward' [Mao Zedong]."⁶ And he finds it impossible to resist comparing the Chinese Revolution to the Russian one: "The USSR have never been a colonial country; they became industrial in order to defend the revolution. But China was a colony, and could again be a colony, and the reason why it has now become an industrial country is simply because it wants to be able to protect itself against colonialism."⁷

While Sartre was giving various accounts of his visit in his declarations, his discussions, and his articles, Beauvoir had decided to narrate those four weeks in a book, which she will title *The Long March.* What had they gathered from this first trip? That the Chinese Revolution was one of the most extraordinary political events of the twentieth century, the birth of half our planet, and that the history of the Western world was slowly beginning to wake up to the reality of another world, a more complete one. Unlike the Russian Revolution, the Chinese Revolution spoke of other continents, other people, and, in its wake, brought along all its exploited, unknown, oppressed brothers from Africa and Asia. The trip to China awoke Sartre to the problems of the third world and prepared both travelers for their future combats.

As of 1985, the only Sartrean texts translated into Chinese were one chapter from the *Critique,* an old version of *The Respectful*

Prostitute, and a few excerpts from the novels—published in literary magazines. And it was practically impossible to find any of them in either bookstores or libraries. In April 1983, *Clarity,* the newspaper of Chinese intellectuals, and *The Workers' Daily* devoted a series of articles to existentialism. "Arsenic Under Honey," their final definition, almost sounded like a condemnation. With a delay of nearly forty years, the Chinese were finally able to include, both in their dictionaries and in their conversations, "a word, new to China, that some seem to admire a great deal: existentialism."[8] At the beginning of 1981, a play by Sartre was performed in China for the very first time: *Dirty Hands.* "No sooner was the play publicly announced," according to Yao G., an intellectual from Fudan, "than the first three performances were sold out in less than two hours."[9] The public seemed to be spontaneously drawn by Sartre's name. There followed lively discussions about the personality of the philosopher, his behavior, his stances. Generally speaking, the Chinese public seemed more interested in the intellectual than in the writer. "A friend of the Chinese people is dead," the New China News Agency announced on April 15, 1980. If Sartre's works are still practically unknown in China, Sartre's name nevertheless elicited a strong response thirty years after the philosopher's first trip to the country.

*F*IVE YEARS after China, another country in upheaval demanded the presence of the two travelers: Cuba. Invited by the weekly *Revolución,* Sartre and Beauvoir would be the guests of the young Cuban Revolution from February 22 to March 21, 1960. In a sense, they were asked to be the official godparents of this newborn adventure, the guarantors of the Cuban experiment. "What we are doing concerns you: you must come and witness the progress of our revolution," Carlos Franqui, a journalist, had told them in Paris. They landed on the island toward the end of that same winter. Sartre had first come to the island with Dolorès in the summer of 1947, and visited Hemingway. Back then, still under the Batista dictatorship, Cuba could certainly not boast about the sociopolitical situation of its sugar and tobacco workers—the most disastrous in the whole Caribbean. Thirteen years later, Sartre met Fidel Castro, Raul Castro, and Che Guevara, then finance minister. For the eyes of the entire world, he presented his congratulations to the thirty-three-year-old lawyer who, with a bunch of students and intellectuals, had managed to seize power after six years of guerrilla war. The hugs and

handshakes that took place between the bearded giant in battle
fatigues, with the eternal cigar stuck in his mouth, and the small
philosopher in civilian clothes, with his surprised smiles, eloquently
announced Sartre's endorsement of the Cuban regime.

Everything in the Cuban experiment was likely to seduce Sartre:
its attempt to establish a direct democracy in an island of peasants
that was just waking up from years of Spanish colonialism and
dictatorship; its prodigious, supreme challenge to American imperialism, only a few miles from its frontiers. It was not difficult for
Sartre to measure the distance between the young law student and
his classmates and the American ninety miles away, and to appreciate the master/slave allegory it implied. Indeed all the young men
and women steeped in the romanticism of the extreme left that
characterized the sixties, whether in European or American universities, saw in the Cuban upheaval the perfect example of a cultural
and democratic revolution and, what's even more, one that had been
carried out in an atmosphere of joy and holiday. And then, of course,
there was Fidel Castro's charisma, his vigor, and his epic speeches
—often three, four, five hours long—which totally seduced his people because they told them about themselves: "I promise, to the
Cuban people, and, in particular, to all Cuban mothers, that I will
do my absolute damnedest to solve all our problems without shed-
ding one single drop of blood. I can swear to all Cuban mothers, that
not a single gunshot will be fired by their sons if not in self-
defense."[10] How could Sartre fail to respond to such romanticism?

In February 1960, he visited sugarcane and tobacco plantations,
met peasants, politicians, students, and journalists. Declarations, lectures, questions, discussions: it was a real Sartre-Cuba festival. "Can
there be revolution without ideology?" he was asked by a Cuban
student during a debate at Havana University. Sartre's answer was
as immediate and incisive as usual, but then he realized it had a few
lacunae and decided to mull over it a little longer. The newspaper
Lunes de revolución immediately offered him space on its pages, and
Sartre wasted no time in filling them with an article that appeared
the day of his departure: "Ideologia y revolución." An exercise in
Sartrean virtuosity, the article established some ties between the
theories and abstractions of the *Critique* and Castro's practice, the
concrete realizations of the Cuban Revolution. "A few months ago,
some Cuban friends came to see me in Paris; they spoke to me very
warmly about the revolution, but I was unable to push them to tell
me whether the new regime would be a socialist one. Today, I realize

I was wrong to look at it that way; but absence is often a source of abstractions and big words, symbols more than programs."[11]

"I saw Fidel on the podium, and his people in front of him. Castro started speaking . . . evening gradually came to veil their dark faces, then night fell." The philosopher analyzes his experiences and the anecdotes of his trip, bouncing questions, descriptions, and realizations off one another, in an attempt to understand the Cuban phenomenon, which, having started with a coup, "has seen all its objectives disappear one after the other, each time revealing newer, more popular, deeper objectives, in short, a more revolutionary aim." The philosopher questions his new direct experience, his meetings with revolutionaries; he accumulates information and modifies his previous theories. "I thought I could see, in the history of your struggles, the rigor of an idea," he writes. And later elsewhere: "That's when I understood that the enemy's maneuvers only accelerated an internal process that was already developing according to its own laws."[12] With Cuba we again confront a constant aspect of Sartre's personality: his periodic fascination with the myths of rebirth, renewal, and youth. These crushes seem to become more and more frequent with age; the seventy-year-old Sartre will be more and more easily seduced by twenty-year-old interviewers.

"The regime that has emerged out of the Cuban revolution is a direct democracy. . . . the Cuban revolution is a real revolution."[13] Back in Paris, Sartre wanted to speak of Sunday evening in Havana, of the carnival, of the enthusiasm of people when they recognized him in the street, of the favorable attitude the press had showed him, of his nocturnal meetings with the leaders of the revolution, and of *The Respectful Prostitute,* then being performed in a theater in Havana. The advocate of spontaneity was truly moved by Cuban euphoria, the youth of its leaders, the way in which the daily reconstruction of the country took place in an exhilarating atmosphere, heightened by white rum, Caribbean music, and general gaiety; it was "the honeymoon of the Revolution."[14] "The Cubans had fallen asleep one after the other, but Castro united them in the same white night: the national night, *his* night. . . . I watched them, somber, their heads held high, busy trying to understand everything. . . . [That night, Castro and I] talked for a long time, and, I am ashamed to admit, I was the one who had to be excused around one in the morning. Sleep was getting the best of me, I couldn't understand anything any longer. The air-conditioned study was kindly left to Simone de Beauvoir. All the other inhabitants of the governmental palace went to sleep in a communal room. Actually, not all of them: Castro, Raul, and Celia were not there. Celia was the first to come back, around two in the morning. Raul followed, at two-thirty. I could not fall asleep. I had stretched out on the bed without undressing, and was having trouble with the blanket, which I found a little too short. The screens of the open windows were all abuzz with insects; thus the night shivered on, till dawn, stirred by innumerable transparent wings. Now and then, the croaking of a toad would rise out of the marshes. Castro came back around three-fifteen."[15] A strange text, bristling with emotions, local color, and revolutionary intimacy, surprisingly sentimental and uncritical for Sartre. The series of articles titled "Hurricane on the Sugarcane" which he wrote for *France-Soir* upon his return are all astonishingly anecdotal, simple, even simplistic. One is reminded of the articles he wrote about America, in 1945, and about the USSR, in 1954: the same clichés, the same tendency to panegyric, the same analytical superficiality.

A few themes, nevertheless, emerge: the theme of youth, for instance, with all its corollaries—energy, passion, vital strength. "No old people in power!" he writes in an article dated July 9. "In fact, I haven't seen a single one among the leaders. Walking through the island and into the revolutionary headquarters, I have met only people who could be my children." Among these possible children, there is, of course Che Guevara, former leader of the revolutionary army and now president of the National Bank. "He was the most cultivated among them, and, according to Castro, one of the most lucid minds of the revolution. I met him: the sweetness and the wit he displays with his guests are clearly not put on for the occasion. . . . All these young people are a discreet homage to the kind of energy Stendhal so loved. . . . To stay up, at night, is a passion. . . . they stay up for no reason . . . and Castro more than anybody else."[16] And he recalls his wonderment when Ernesto Guevara told him he would see him at midnight, in his office, and Castro at two A.M. This struggle against oneself, against sleep, against rest also provoked strong personal echoes in Sartre. Thus, he experienced the Cuban Revolution, seduced by these new children he had adopted, lavishly meting out his analyses, his enthusiasm, his advice, his attacks against the Gaullist regime, Algerian colonization, and American imperialism.

On one side, the Cuban experience was one long spree, a honeymoon that, back in Paris, resulted in unabashed pro-Cuban propaganda. On the other side, however, one could hear a slight gnashing of teeth. A few Cubans had failed to appreciate the more fatherly side of Sartre, that of the "adviser." Some had found it outright pedantic; Fidel himself had often thought it somewhat overbearing. And Che was rumored to have declared: "Let Jean-Paul Sartre philosophize about revolution; we who carry it out have no time for theories."[17] The reactions of the French officials on the island were more predictable; they were exasperated and offended by this unexpected anti-French visit. And everybody was baffled by Sartre's determined refusal to answer any question concerning existentialism on the grounds that he had not come to Cuba to speak of literature. Despite his decision to move in a different direction toward action, most of the world still saw him as a man of letters.

This gnashing of teeth was audible elsewhere. The FBI's "secret" files on Sartre were immediately updated to include an account of the visit and of the philosopher's positive response to the Cuban regime. "In February 1960, Sartre and his wife [*sic*] went to Cuba as guests of the Cuban government. Sartre wrote a book, *Sartre on Cuba,* and an article by the title 'Ideology and Revolution.' He signed petitions, organized pro-Cuban campaigns for the press, offered to send "The Truth on the Cuban Revolution" to all those who might be interested in the question, and, finally, got together a number of trips to Cuba for groups of students favorable to the regime. Sartre described the Cuban Revolution as the most original he had ever witnessed and accused the United States of being a brainless nation."[18] Sartre and "his wife," as the prudish FBI agents insisted on calling Simone de Beauvoir, returned to Paris at the beginning of the spring. They were immediately updated on the alarming situation in Algeria.

Sartre's support of China and Cuba was very much related to the struggle he and his friends were waging on behalf of Algerian independence. Indeed, for the next few years, Sartre would back any movement of anticolonialist emancipation, wherever it took place. At the beginning of the summer of 1960, he was faced with a difficult choice: the support networks of the Algerian FLN needed his presence in France, but he had promised the novelist Jorge Amado that he would go to Brazil on a political trip. He carefully weighed the situation, consulted his friends, and then decided. His presence among the Brazilian masses was fully justified by his recent support of Cuba. Besides, his friends at *Les Temps modernes* would keep him posted. On August 15, with Beauvoir, he boarded a plane bound for Rio; their stay would last till November 1.

"You must come to Brazil to have a clear idea of the problems of an underdeveloped country," Amado had told Sartre and Beauvoir during a visit to Paris. The trip to Brazil would turn out to be their longest and most political. Amado and his wife carefully mapped out an elaborate touristic-political itinerary. Sartre and Beauvoir were initiated into the economy, architecture, literature, demography, gastronomy, politics, and agronomy of the country. They were shown tobacco, coffee, and cocoa plantations, oil-drilling centers, local markets, ultramodern cities. They saw *favelas, fazendas,* and *vaqueiros,* were introduced to the *candomblé,* and drank *batidas.* They visited Recife, Bahia, Olinda, Copacabana, Rio, Brasilia, São Paulo, Araraquara, Fortaleza, and Amazonia. The Indians kindly offered them feathered headdresses and bows and arrows. They met all sorts of Brazilian celebrities in all sorts of professional fields: Oscar Niemeyer, the architect, Oliviera de Kubitschek, the president of the republic, Rubem Braga, the publisher, Emiliano Augusto Di Cavalcanti, the painter, and the writers Paulo Freire and Josué de Castro, as well as innumerable students, academicians, journalists, workers of all trades, dockers, Samba teachers. And they penetrated into all the rural settings they had already encountered in Amado's novels and Freire's essays.[19]

"In Brazil, I want to be the anti-Malraux, to erase what he did when he put French culture at the service of the Algerian war." As soon as he got to Bahia, Sartre revealed the deeper intentions of his trip. Malraux, the great voyager of the Orient, the former revolutionary pilot of the Spanish Civil War, had, as of July 27, 1958, become the cabinet minister in charge of the "diffusion and distribution of French culture." As such, he had spent the summer of 1959 on propaganda trips throughout Latin America—Argentina, Uruguay, Peru, Mexico, Brazil—where he had delivered lectures, uttered proclamations, written articles, mostly advocating Gaullist politics, everywhere justifying the healthy presence of French power over Algeria. "Eight hundred thousand Frenchmen and a million Arabs have opted for France against thirty thousand fellaghas who believe in the Algerian FLN," he had declared in Buenos Aires. "To abandon Algeria means to murder our supporters. France will not let that happen."[20] These Gaullist propaganda trips had cost the Quai d'Orsay a great deal of money, and all the French ambassadors, consuls, counselors, and cultural attachés in Latin America had gone out of their way to ensure their success. Sartre's anti-Gaullist propaganda tours were organized by cultural centers, institutions, universities, political, and trade unionist associations, publishers and journalists, bookstores, and other random groups that belonged to the Brazilian left or extreme left. All these sympathizers of decolonialization were trying get the world's attention, and Sartre was their ideal spokesman, the perfect antithesis to Malraux. In Brazil, Sartre behaved exactly as he had six months earlier in Cuba, as the most honest and most vehement counterambassador of the French Republic. For this purpose, he assumed a new role, a new function: de Gaulle's scourge. "De Gaulle is an impostor," he declared in Rio, "and Malraux is an aide to the king and not the minister of French culture, which doesn't need a minister."

Among the subjects he dealt with in his innumerable lectures and roundtables, the Algerian war was, of course, the most recurrent. The representative of the interim provisional Algerian government (GPRA) representative in Brazil asked to meet him. "Together, we discussed pro-Algerian propaganda. We were in perfect agreement."[21] Everywhere, at the press conference in São Paulo, during a speech on "Youth in Today's World" that he gave at the Paulist School of Medicine, in his public declarations at the Institute of Brazilian Studies in Rio de Janeiro, everywhere he insisted on the same point: "There is only one definitive solution for Algeria," he declared in São Paulo. "Independence. Self-determination might yet be the best means to solve the problem, but only on condition that the FLN be given real guarantees." And in Rio: "The Algerian war is supported by groups tightly connected to the colonists, a population comparable to the old Cuban planters." And pushing the parallel between Algeria and Cuba further, he added, "This is why I, a Frenchman, tell you about a national flaw we have no right to hide. If we, old Europeans, want to remain the friends of young nations, we must recover our internationalist tradition, whereas underdeveloped countries can only grow by relying on and affirming their own nationalism."[22] The lecture he gave at the University of São Paulo drew more than 1,500 people: It was a real tidal wave comparable to the one at the Rue Jean-Goujon, which ushered in the age of existentialism. People, mostly students, poured into the room, smashing chairs, breaking down doors, invading the platform. After Sartre had presented his argument and then that of the FLN, questions started pouring in. One of them, in French, was in defense of French Algeria; the man was booed, shouted down. The session ended with a pro-Algerian demonstration. Elsewhere, Sartre criticized the Brazilian trade unionists for their passive and cowardly attitude toward the Algerian problem and, pushing them into a corner, exhorted them to engage in militant action: "What have you done on behalf of the Algerian people?" he asked them. "Nothing up to now. What do you intend to do? What can you do to help them in their struggle? Do you find it normal that your representative at the UN supports the French government in this crucial question?"

He kept drawing a parallel between Cuba and Algeria in all his speeches, though, according to some journalists, his general stance had somewhat changed since his Cuban experience. He praised the Cuban Revolution according to his own principles, no longer Castro's. He called himself a Marxist, criticized the current representatives of Marxism, and expressed the hope that today's youth might be able to introduce some anarchy into Marxism. This, however, did not prevent Sartre from citing the Cuban example to all his Brazilian audiences: "Cuba's main problem concerns its land and its peasants. . . . A problem you haven't yet solved in Brazil. . . . If we want the Cuban revolution to have some meaning it is important that all Latin American countries follow its example in their march toward independence. In other words, its real success depends on the complete solidarity of other Latin American countries . . . against U. S. imperialism."[23] Was Sartre aware of the consequences his speeches might have? of the dangers involved in his advocacy of an anarcho-Marxist revolution throughout Central America? Carried away by his own rhetoric, he turned himself into the interpreter and messenger of his hosts' tacit ideologies.

He got deeply involved in the Brazilian crisis, declaring before an audience of 1,200, "Brazil is at once a completely Western democracy and a dictatorship of ten million urbanites who take advantage of the extraordinary industrial growth of the country to lord it over sixty million poverty-stricken peasants. A Frenchman has the impression that in Brazil everybody is a leftist." Thus, praising, criticizing, lavishly citing examples from his most recent experiences, accompanying these with figures and philosophical references, Sartre pursued his American journey, provoking some, enchanting others, but always self-confident, as if it were perfectly normal that a European intellectual would come as an ally to encourage with his very presence the students and the politicians of developing countries. The newspaper *Ultima Hora* published a Brazilian translation of his Cuban reportage, "Hurricane on the Sugarcane," which a Brazilian publisher managed to turn into a booklet just a few weeks later. This little book, when it went on sale at the French-language bookstore in São Paulo, became the object of one of his most extraordinary autograph sessions: more than a 1,500 people invaded the bookstore. Sartre signed for several hours, and Simone de Beauvoir was often asked to add her signature next to his.

Upon their arrival at the Recife airport, Sartre and Beauvoir had been welcomed like two stars by a crowd of photographers, journalists, and admirers. The São Paulo airport, also invaded by a dense crowd, almost became the stage for a political demonstration. "Viva Sartre, Viva Castro," shouted the students. "Cuba sí, Yankee no," read the posters. More than 1,500 people attended his lecture on esthetics sponsored by the school of scientific and literary philosophy at São Paulo University. More than a thousand heard him speak on "Youth and the Problems of Today" at Araraquara University. More than a thousand journalists were present at the roundtable devoted entirely to political questions at the Institute of Brazilian Studies of Rio. And more than five hundred listened to his philosophical considerations in the dean's offices at the University of Bahia. No other visitor before Sartre had been able to provoke such an enthusiastic response among the Brazilian public. The São Paulo press alone published more than 250 articles on him during the week Sartre spent in the city. As for the Brazilian press, its numerous reactions were divided according to the political tendencies it represented. "Despite his talent," wrote one paper, "this material atheist . . . does not belong to the same lineage of the eighteenth-century 'philosophes.' Brazil does not need foreign ideologues or dangerous revolutionary propagandists." The *Diario Carioca* of Bahia spoke of a "Sartrean hysteria . . . all the more inexplicable in that, today, Sartre is little more than a shadow in Europe." The *Jornal do Brasil* went even further, "deploring the zoo," and regretting the fact that "one of the most fashionable writers of our times should come to a foreign country to criticize the government of his own country." But there were also enthusiastic papers, such as *Ultima Hora*, which was particularly pleased with the roundtables in which Sartre had participated with trade union leaders: "If Sartre could stay in Brazil for two years, the destiny of our country would be changed, and trade unionism would have a clearer idea of its future."

Needless to say, this trip did not sit too well with French officials, who immediately wrote long and exhaustive letters of protest to their foreign affairs ministers, and collected huge files relating the minutest details of the journey. It was already being rumored that Sartre had been invited to revisit Brazil in the spring of 1962. Nobody, neither the French officials nor the journalists nor the trade unionists noticed that Sartre was tired, sick, and often quite exhausted. As he was about to leave for Recife, he had suffered an attack of shingles, and his health did not improve during the rest of the trip. In some of his letters to his most intimate friends, he often complained about the innumerable visits and the endless obligations. He even complained of having become a bauble, a toy in the hands of his hosts, a writer-object, caught in his own celebrity, playing a double role: civil and obliging in public, harassed and disillusioned in private. Far from adhering to the impeccable façade that he offered to the eyes of the world, he was in greater and greater need of turning in upon himself and focusing on his own concerns.

"When Ben Kheddah visited Brazil in the fall of 1961," Beauvoir writes, "he was struck by the services Sartre had rendered to the Algerian cause. He told Lanzmann and [Frantz] Fanon how, when he landed, the authorities had wanted to keep him out of the country; but the students who had come *en masse* to greet him marched him out of the airport in triumph. And immediately began talking about Sartre."[24] Sartre's trip to Brazil, so intimately connected to his battle against colonialism and for the independence of the third world, and, thereby, with the situations of both Cuba and Algeria, was going to have multiple impacts on both France and the world. Lanzmann had already phoned Sartre and Beauvoir in Rio to warn them against flying back to Paris; better book places on a plane from Rio to Barcelona since the situation in France had recently become very serious, and Sartre had had something to do with it.

S ARTRE'S BACKING of China, Cuba, and the Latin American democracies was an indirect attack on the United States. Despite the numerous invitations he kept receiving from American students and the more liberal universities, he had repeatedly refused to go back to the United States. One of the reasons for this had to do with his rather complex relationship with the USSR and the Soviet bloc. In little more than four years—from June 1962 to September 1966—he had visited the USSR nine times, occasionally staying several weeks. Moscow, Leningrad, Kiev, Yalta, Odessa, Tbilisi, Estonia, Georgia, Lithuania, the Ukraine: generally accompanied by Beauvoir, Sartre had traveled through all the socialist republics of the Soviet Union. There were several reasons for these frequent trips. First of all, there was his connection with the COMES (the European Community of Writers), of which he had been elected vice president on March 14, 1962. Secondly, he had to go to Moscow to collect the royalties from all the translations of his works into Russian. Thirdly, he had a number of recent friends whom he could see only by visiting them there. On the other hand, his Soviet friends could use a French writer of Sartre's fame only according to the political and cultural directives of the party—at times quite open and favorable (as when Sartre, citing the example of Kafka, was able to show them the profit they could draw from the integration of Western and Soviet cultures), at others rigorous and nostalgic for the good old days of socialist realism. In the name of "cultural coexistence" Sartre agreed to engage in a number of discussions with foreign colleagues such as Giuseppe Ungaretti, Guido Piovene, and Ezio Vigorelli in Italy; Angus Wilson and John Lehmann in England; Hans-Magnus Enzensberger in Germany; and Nathalie Sarraute, Alain Robbe-Grillet, and Roger Caillois among his compatriots. The years of cultural liberalization initiated by Khrushchev were a period of relative broadmindedness and tolerance. But in 1964, when the party retrenched again behind the esthetic of socialist realism, Sartre made it his duty to assure his dissident friends, such as Ilya Ehrenburg and, later, Andrei Tarkovsky, the great film director, of his support.

The most expressive instance of the "controlled relationship" the Soviet Union entertained with Sartre occurred in the summer of 1964, when Khrushchev publicly flared up against the writers of COMES he had invited to his dacha in Georgia. "Since he had invited us," Beauvoir remembers, "we thought he would at least treat us cordially. Not the least in the world. He inveighed against us as if we really were the henchmen of capitalism. He hailed the beauties of socialism, and assumed all responsibility for the Soviet invasion of Hungary. Then, after this blast, he squeezed in a few civilities: 'Well, after all, you are also against war. . . . we can still eat and drink together. A little later, Surkov took him aside and told him he might have been a little rough on us. 'So what,' Khrushchev snapped back. 'They've got to understand.' "[25]

This icy welcome may have been a result of Maurice Thorez's recent visit to Khrushchev and his intimations that the writers the Soviet premier had just invited were all "dangerous anticommunists" and of the worst possible kind since they were also "leftists." Beauvoir insinuates as much. Sartre's well-known sympathy for Soviet Jews and other oppressed groups made him somewhat suspect to begin with. There was also the rumor that, in the summer of 1962,

Sartre had gotten involved with his interpreter, Lena Zonina, reputed to be "a remarkably intelligent, cultivated woman . . . a great beauty with large black eyes in a perfectly oval face . . . a mane of dark hair, a deep, husky voice, and a very mysterious, but intense, affective life . . . in short, a Slavic femme fatale."[26] Her university studies had been seriously handicapped because of her Jewish origins. Her role within the writers' union was not clearly documented, but she was known to be one of the oppositionists. She was Sartre's guide, and informant, on all his trips throughout the Soviet Union. It seems the French philosopher and his beautiful Soviet interpreter fell passionately in love with each other, according to the unwritten rules by which Sartre fell in love in every country he visited. The most compromising trace of their acquaintance remains Sartre's discreet dedication of *The Words* "To Madame Z" barely one year after their first meeting—too much for the Soviets, who took these three words to mean, among various other things: "Beware of me, Sartre. Don't touch that woman, I am her protector." Mme Z translated *The Words* into Russian.[27]

Sartre seemed to take some sort of impish pleasure in returning to the USSR. Did he feel committed to back the oppositionists? Or was it because, via trips and colloquia, he meant to re-establish an international network of committed writers opposed to U.S. imperialism? His interest in the PCF had been more instrumental than ideological. Throughout his complex relationship with it, he had always kept himself proudly on the outside, on the margins, observing it, absorbing it. Then he had overtaken and vampirized it. The strategy he employed toward the foreign regimes that interested him was very similar and just as personal: interest, conquest, overtaking, exploitation. Such was Sartre, at ease with Khrushchev and Castro as he had been with Freud, Kafka, Tintoretto, Baudelaire: calm, self-assured, the conqueror. Nor should one think him gullible, naïve, or inconsiderate: it would be a misunderstanding of the deepest meanings of his approach to the world. In his journeys, his meetings, his dialogues, he was trying—awkwardly, at times— to articulate and join several systems of values while, at the same time, fertilizing his original culture—which he amply criticized— with new compost he had found elsewhere. His encounter with Yugoslavian communism is an eloquent example. Ten years before his visit to Tito's country, he had agreed to write a preface to a book by Louis Dalmas. "Tito's communism is exceptionally important to us," he had written then, "because it aims at subjectivity not as a formal ideal but rather as an effective reality resulting from historical objectivism. . . . Tito's half-victory has reintroduced subjectivity among Yugoslavian leaders, thereby affecting also the Soviet leaders."[28] Delighted at having discovered a realization of his philosophical subjectivism, Sartre agreed to go to Belgrade. Any attempt at liberalization, any new interpretation of Marxism, seemed to him, *a priori,* in harmony with his own analyses. Significantly, Yugoslavia was the first so-called Eastern country to translate Sartre's entire oeuvre and to produce all his plays. Numerous Yugoslav intellectuals —who would later join the ranks of dissidents, such as Vladimir Dedijer—found inspiration in his writings. Invited by the union of Yugoslav writers, on May 13, 1960, Sartre and Beauvoir were officially welcomed by Marshal Tito. Their trip had a double objective: a series of lectures at the University of Belgrade as well as Sartre's overt endorsement of the Yugoslav experiment—his handshake with Tito, barely two months after the one with Castro, was the confirmation of the new image of himself Sartre wanted to project. The Yugoslavs gave him an enthusiastic welcome: two of his plays, *No Exit* and *The Condemned of Altona,* were performed during his stay, and he had the pleasure of attending both.

Later, when he is outside this particular orbit, Sartre will be the first to support the demonstrations and struggles of Soviet dissidents. He will publish Yevgeny Yevtushenko's long poem "Babi Yar" in *Les Temps modernes* and will repeatedly try to keep the West informed about human rights in the USSR.

Sartre's relations with Japan were less complex. Eleven years after his trip to China, he was again on his way to the Far East. All his works had long been translated into Japanese, they had been analyzed and studied in the universities and had generated a number of imitators: the opposite of what he had found in China. He arrived in Tokyo, on September 18, 1966, as a guest of both Keio University and Kazuho Watanabe, his editor at the publishing house Jinbun Shoin. "Sartre and Simone de Beauvoir arrived," Bernard Dufourcq, the current cultural attaché, remembers, "at the beginning of the autumn, while we were celebrating a 'French fortnight' in Japan. The new French-Japanese high school had just opened, and Tagasimaia, the department store, had organized a grand exhibition devoted to Napoleon, for which they had even been able to obtain, from the Malmaison, the cloak Josephine had worn on the day of her coronation. . . . Sartre and Simone de Beauvoir were given a triumphant, clamorous welcome."[29] While waiting for Sartre's arrival, the local press had numbered him among the three best-known French personalities in Japan, along with Napoleon and General de Gaulle. During the press conference he gave at the airport, Sartre smilingly confessed that never before had he been as besieged by quite as many cameras.

Several generations of Japanese intellectuals had already had the opportunity of appreciating Sartre's oeuvre. Some, such as the writer Oda Sakunosuke, had loved *The Wall* because of the new perspectives it brought to Western literature. *The Roads to Freedom* and the main tenets of Sartrean existentialism had then broken upon the tight nucleus of the Japanese intelligentsia, opposing orthodox Marxists to pro-Sartrean modernists. Later, Sartre's debates with the PCF had repercussions among Japanese intellectuals. Among the writers directly influenced by Sartre, one can cite Norma Hiroshi, Ohe Kenzaburo, Hanada Kiyoteru, and Nakano Shigeharu.[30] Indeed, Sartre's oeuvre—as he himself had ample time to realize—had all the requisites for success in Japan, where it had immediately found the best promoters: various departments of French literature —whose professors spoke a very elegant French, often learned while they were assistants at the ENS—and the literary supplements of the major newspapers, which often sold up to ten million copies. As Sartre discovered, Japan had an extraordinary cultural appetite for anything French, including a snobbish curiosity about the excesses of existentialism, a natural interest in the tradition of the "intellectual mentor" and in Sartre's view of the social role of the intellectual. Thus the themes of his lectures: "What Is an Intellectual?" "The Function of the Intellectual." "Is the Writer an Intellectual?" Huge audiences, careful, precise questions: the press covered the event with great benevolence. The more touristy part of the journey lasted another month, and the two guests took advantage of it to make frequent declarations urging Japanese writers to rise up against U. S. imperialism. If most people praised the intelligence and oratorical talent of the French writer, some responded with skepticism if not outright disappointment at his conception of the world, which they found quite "remote from the reality of contemporary life." Later, while Sartre was already entering his third political phase, his "leftist" phase, the Zengakuren student groups would often claim a relationship between their nearly illegal actions and Sartre's political activities. In twelve years, Sartre had visited Asia, Latin America, Africa, and numerous European countries. A year after Japan, it was the turn of the Middle East, where he would be a guest of both Egypt and Israel.

*F*ROM ITS inception, the trip to Cairo assumed the traits of an official political journey. And it was to be strictly evenhanded. The previous year, Sartre had expressed his "feeling of being torn between two friends, two loyalties in conflict with each other," between "his admiration for Israel's struggle against England, and his solidarity with the Arab world's quest for sovereignty and humanity." Claude Lanzmann, who was preparing a special feature on the conflict between Israel and the Arab world for *Les Temps modernes*, had taken care of all the local contacts: he was Sartre and Beauvoir's guide during the eighteen days they spent in Egypt. Officially organized by the Cairo daily *Al Ahram*, the program involved numerous meetings with avant-garde intellectuals and artists, political militants, trade unionists, and other representatives of the Egyptian intelligentsia. A special welcoming committee—consisting of journalists such as Hassaneim Haykal Lufti el-Kholi, the editor-in-chief of the magazine *El-Taliaa*, and writers such as Louis Awad and Tewfik el-Akim—had orchestrated their various activities. The Egyptian infatuation with the two visitors was obvious from the start: "The enthusiasm that the Cairo population seems to feel for Sartre," a newspaper noted at the beginning of the trip, "is very similar to the one the Paris population has shown at the Tutankhamen exhibition." At the University of Cairo, he again spoke of the role of the intellectual in Western society to an audience of two thousand, including the vice–prime minister, Saroit Okacha, who introduced him: "Jean-Paul Sartre represents the conscience of his times, the symbol of our most noble dream, of human fraternity." On this occasion, however, Sartre confused a great many listeners by the speed of his delivery.

Sartre attended numerous debates, meetings, social gatherings, even a performance of *The Flies* in Arabic. The journey assumed an increasingly solemn aspect that culminated in Sartre's meeting with the president of the republic, Colonel Gamal Abdel Nasser. The encounter lasted over three hours and was sealed by a friendly handshake for the benefit of the photographers. "I was very pleasantly surprised by President Nasser's personality," Sartre declared upon his return to Paris, "and sincerely deplore the image of him in the Western press."

And yet, the press conference right before Sartre's departure caused a few winces: journalists and observers knew that Sartre's Egyptian trip would be followed by an identical one in Israel, just as they were all aware of the sympathy the author of *Anti-Semite and Jew* felt for the state of Israel. So, they insisted on questioning him about the Palestinian problem, and Sartre was forced to beat around the bush, wavering between circumstantial pragmatism and what he called his own "necessary neutrality." He had just come back from a visit to the Gaza strip, the armistice line, and a talk with representatives of the Palestinian refugees. He deftly avoided all sticky issues by listening and gathering information rather than proclaiming his own opinions. "I have come here to learn, not to teach," he declared on numerous occasions. He also announced a forthcoming special issue of *Les Temps modernes* devoted entirely to the Middle East, and he made the point that both Arabs and Israelis would have the opportunity of presenting their positions without engaging in a face-to-face dialogue. Everybody noticed Sartre's embarrassing and somewhat disappointing effort to remain neutral, and his refusal to proclaim himself on the side of Egypt. On the other hand, everybody was surprised and greatly pleased when Sartre suddenly announced: "Until now I have refused to speak of socialism in connection with the Egyptian regime. Now I know I have been wrong." And he went on to interpret specific aspects of the Egyptian regime as a necessary, intermediary stage toward a more accomplished form of socialism. So, by the time he left Egypt, he had saved face but had not committed himself to any clear stance.

If the Egyptian press had been miffed at the proximity of the two visits, the Israeli press was no less baffled by what they called "flagrant tactlessness." And, indeed, Sartre's double trip was taking place under particularly tense political conditions—it was two months before the six-day war between Israel and Egypt—and in an idealistic, even utopian, frame of mind. How else could he have dared visit two staunch enemies back to back and cross, without qualms, the "sand curtain" separating them? Organized by Mapam, a party of the left, and the magazine *Outlook,* the trip through Israel lasted fifteen days and involved a program practically identical to that of the Egyptian trip: meetings with Israeli journalists, university professors, leftist writers; visits to the most culturally and socially relevant places in the country; lectures and debates; and, finally, political discussions and interviews. In their introductory articles,

Israeli journalists had not failed to remind their readers that Sartre was the author of *Anti-Semite and Jew,* which had been published in English in 1948 and in Hebrew just a few years later. Thus, from the very beginning, Sartre appeared as a "semitophile" writer, a friend of the Jewish people and of Israel in general. All the personalities of the country's cultural life mobilized to meet the two French writers: among these were the poet Avraham Shlonsky, the writers Gershom Scholem, who was originally from Berlin, and Nathan Shaham, the sculptor Dani Karavan, a number of journalists, deputies, trade union representatives, and government officials. Sartre impressed his hosts with his indefatigable curiosity, the relentless fire of his questions, and his intelligence—as one put it, "He's smart as a computer."

The most original aspect of this trip was the visit to the kibbutz Merhavia, in Galilee. For three days, Yehoshua Rash, the kibbutz secretary, led them on a tour of the most modern innovations of the agricultural cooperative. Beauvoir was very much interested in child rearing: "Why children's houses?" "How did a child who did not sleep in the same house as his parents develop?" she would ask, concerned. "It was a real experience for them," according to Rash. "They were very interested. They saw the kibbutz as a concrete realization of the kind of socialism they had themselves envisioned."[31] Sartre was particularly interested in the motivations of kibbutzniks: "What criteria does one admit as a motivation for work?" he inquired: "Public respect? The collectivity's welfare?" They visited the house that had once belonged to the founder of Merhavia, Meir Yaari, and in the large meeting room they questioned and answered some fifty kibbutzniks. They were particularly moved by Simone de Beauvoir: As she put it, she had finally discovered an institution that had come very close to establishing equality between men and women. Then, they left Galilee, its red hills and cypresses, and, after a brief stop in Nazareth, where they talked with a few Christian Arabs and some communists, proceeded to Jerusalem, to the same inevitable lectures on the same subjects, in the same inevitably crowded rooms: he spoke of "The Intellectual's Role in Contemporary Society," and she of "The Woman's Role in Contemporary Society." The only innovation in this endlessly repeated scenario occurred when Beauvoir, at the last moment, decided to change the subject of her talk. What she had been witnessing in Israel had shown her such an emancipated view of woman that she did not feel she had anything relevant to add to the subject—and this new situation became the subject of her impromptu talk. Sartre delivered his lecture as planned in front of a perfectly silent crowd. He certainly preferred the more intimate and outspoken group he met the following day.

"Six or seven of us met at Claude Fegelman's," Menahem Brinker remembers. "The group included Jeremihiaou Yovel, Ran Sigat, and myself: we were all writing our dissertations in philosophy. And that's all we spoke about for two hours: philosophy. Sartre would have preferred to hear our opinions of his *Critique* . . . but we had only read a hundred or so pages of it. So, we limited ourselves to discussing the relationship between *Being and Nothingness* and the *Critique,* the question of concrete relations with the Other. 'That search is over,' he told us. 'It no longer interests me.' " At which point, Menahem Brinker, then in his early thirties, launched into a much closer critical analysis of the work: "You like to present the *Critique* as a total refutation of your earlier philosophical stances. But, in fact, I think the *Critique* has many more points in common with *Being and Nothingness* than you would like to admit. And, even though you like to define it as an improved version of Marxism, I maintain it is an alternative to Marxism." "No," Sartre replied. "I might have exaggerated when I said that existentialism had died. But it is true that the *Critique* represents an entirely new beginning. *Being and Nothingness* was concerned with the question of being; the *Critique* deals with the notion of freedom. And now I believe that only a historical approach can explain man."[32] Sartre greatly enjoyed his discussions with this young exponent of local philosophy. Their dialogue was resumed a few years later when Brinker, who was then preparing an anthology of Sartre's philosophical texts, consulted Sartre about which texts to include and which concepts to pursue in his criticism.

As in Cairo, visits, lectures, and academic meetings were followed by political exchanges. Sartre and Simone de Beauvoir met Igal Alon, the secretary of labor, Zalman Chazar, the president of the republic, and Lévi Eshkol, the prime minister. These official meetings remained stiff and formal, whereas their interview with Moshe Sueh, the secretary of the Communist Party, turned out to be quite interesting. "What impressed us most," Gabriel Cohen, who was present that day, remembers, "was Sartre's totally concrete and political conception of the conflict between Israel and the Arab world. Because he had just come from Egypt, he was well acquainted with the situation. Lots of Israelis wasted a great deal of time trying to explain to him things he already knew perfectly well."[33]

The trip ended with the usual press conference, in Tel Aviv, on March 29, 1967. Friendly questions, witty answers, smiles, cordial exchanges: everything seemed to proceed swimmingly. Of course, there were a few linguistic snags: as usual, Sartre was pronounced "Sartère," and, as usual, Sartre pronounced every English word with a heavy French accent—his "meetings" always came out "may-tang." As usual, Sartre started off with an account of his current political battles, of the Vietnam War and the Bertrand Russell War Crimes Tribunal. As usual, he articulated his arguments slowly, with great poise and clarity according to a very personal technique that consisted in foreseeing all eventual objections and in dismantling them before they were actually uttered. As usual, Simone de Beauvoir spoke after him, as a true militant. She did not repeat Sartre's arguments, nor did she participate in the ideological debates that followed them, she merely limited herself to driving his points home. "If you want to help and support the Russell tribunal," she explained, "understand that we need money and that you can organize yourselves into committees."

Sartre behaved like a real ambassador when it came to a discussion of the Middle Eastern conflict. "Should Israel's right to exist," he was asked, "be put into question by the rights of Arab refugees, as you seemed to imply in Cairo?" And he was repeatedly questioned about Egypt, its perception of the war, the attitude of its "progressive" forces toward Israel, and so on. If he disappointed rather than shocked his listeners, it was because he confined himself to the prudent—and somewhat cowardly—position of the observer who wants to remain impartial. "Egypt," he awkwardly explained, weighing every word, "wants something that Israel refuses to give: the return of the refugees to their territories. Its position has certain demands, and, as such, it allows for the idea of war—even though such an idea was very seldom alluded to in front of me, except, perhaps, by a few Palestinians. On the other hand, all Israel wants is to be recognized by Egypt—a demand that seems to presuppose peace and the status quo. In other words, Israel's desire for peace presupposes a condition, and Egypt is determined not to negotiate with Israel except on the basis of another condition—"negotiate" might not be the right word—that is, only if a condition is met beforehand. This, of course, implies a more aggressive attitude. Do you see what I mean?" Then, he referred to the real context of the conflict: the tug of war between the superpowers. "You know," he stated, "that the Egyptians see you as 'imperialists' just as much as you see them as Russian subjects. . . . Both sides should try to relinquish such a counterproductive point of view."

Did Sartre disappoint his Israeli audience? "After meeting with Nasser and Eshkol," Guy Kessary, of the daily *Maariv,* asked him, "what is your personal, political, and ideological opinion of these two statesmen?" The audience laughed. Slowly, Sartre took the mike. "I am going to tell you the only thing I can tell you without jeopardizing my neutrality: I spent one hour and a quarter with Mr. Eshkol and three hours with President Nasser." The laconic humor and courteous ambiguity of this answer was immediately greeted by laughter and all sorts of smiles, but, later, it was harshly criticized by the Israeli press, weary of so much caution (and the implied preference for Nasser over Eshkol). The day after the press conference, *Al Quds,* a Jordanian daily in Jerusalem, published an open letter to Sartre signed by Khalil Sawahreh, a young Palestinian refugee: "How can you make so many concessions to Zionist ideas? Have you already forgotten the painful memory of your visit to the refugee camp of Gaza?"[34]

*T*ODAY, LONG after all those trips, the traces of Sartre-the-traveler are still visible in France and abroad. In Latin America, Africa, and most underdeveloped countries, Sartre is still known as the prophet of modern times, a legendary intellectual. "Sartre un mal nèg," ran the headlines of a Caribbean weekly the day after Sartre's death, hallowing, with this Creole formula the man they called "brother," a "great good man," an "exemplary individual," a hero. *El Heraldo,* a Colombian monthly, printed excerpts from Sartre's then unpublished manuscripts—such as *The War Diaries* and the *Cahiers pour une morale*—along with a photo of the philosopher on its cover.

The mythic place Sartre had acquired outside France during the sixties provoked a mixed reaction in his country. Some felt that by weaving a network of sure and trustworthy relationships in other continents, Sartre had dangerously increased his powers; by expanding the *Temps modernes* group onto an international scale, he had again secured foreign support; by developing his enterprise into a multinational with subsidiaries all over the world, he had instituted a company for the importation and exportation of leftist culture on a global scale. The innumerable photos of the philosopher's handshakes with statesmen only increased the misgivings of some of his countrymen.

In the meantime, the conflict between History and the colonial empires established during the nineteenth century was spreading throughout the world. Sartre was going to play an important role in the painful excision of Algeria from France, and particularly so during the final two years: 1960–62. General de Gaulle, who was well aware of the growing charisma of the traveling philosopher, behaved accordingly. He knew Sartre had become a fundamental cultural asset to his country as well as an eminently exportable item, however difficult to control. So, he handled him as if he were a grenade, with caution and diplomacy. He knew Sartre was the ambassador of the French counterculture, offering an image quite unlike the ones fostered by the Quai d'Orsay, roaming the world in total freedom, eagerness, and curiosity, weaving global networks, prestigious, dangerous, explosive.

UNTOUCHABLE

*T*HE YEAR 1960 was, in all respects, a key year in Sartre's life, a midlife year, halfway between the beginning of the Second World War and Sartre's own death. It was a year when the image of the writer slowly gave way to a newer one, that of the militant traveler: Cuba with Castro, Moscow with Khrushchev, Belgrade with Tito, Brazilia with President Kubitschek. It was a year rich in iconography, poor in literature, the beginning of a new public image, that of the intellectual as symbol. French society, torn apart by the Algerian war, focused many of its tensions on Sartre, who served as a scapegoat for some, a symbolic shield for others. "Shoot Sartre!" shouted demonstrators on the Champs-Elysées. "You do not imprison Voltaire," General de Gaulle said, a few months later, refusing to see in Sartre an ordinary French citizen. Even de Gaulle treated him as different: Sartre became untouchable.

*I*N FRANCE, people no longer spoke of the "Algerian conflict" but, increasingly, of the "Algerian war." Nearly everyone, it seemed, had something against de Gaulle: the French colonists and other nationalist groups felt betrayed; the *petits gars* of the French army, sent into the field, into the *djebbels kabyles,* felt either manipulated

or abandoned; leftists and some liberals were disgusted by the army's
techniques for handling the Algerian fighters, by the excesses and
patent lies that those in power used to cover themselves. During the
summer of 1960, French society was reshaping itself along stricter
lines, as is always the case in confrontations where the national and
ethical stakes are high. There was even talk of a new period of
resistance; new clans began forming on the model of their predecessors. For two or three years, several highly placed and fairly liberal
French officials had publicly expressed their concern over the severe
tactics used by the French army in Algeria, calling on the government to take up its responsibilities. René Capitant, a professor of
public law at the University of Algiers, had handed in his resignation
to the minister of national education to protest the "suspicious"
disappearance of one of his former students, Ali Boumendjel. Paul
Teitgen, secretary of the Algiers Police Headquarters, had followed
suit. "I have become convinced," he wrote to the prime minister,
"that we are involved in a situation, the anonymity and irresponsibil-
ity of which leads to war crimes."[1] A few days later, it was General
Paris de la Bollardière's turn; under such questionable ethical conditions, he refused to continue as commander of the Atlas Blidéen
sector. Vercors, former Resistance fighter and author of the unforgettable *Silence de la mer,* sent back his Legion of Honor medal to
the president.

The summer of 1960 was one of the most heated times of this latent
civil war. French intellectuals, taking up a public cause again, had
to prepare for battle, sharpen their pens, and concentrate their forces,
in isolation and semisecrecy. There were important troop maneuvers
at the edges of different schools of thought: surrealist writers, the
Temps modernes group, old communists, the *Lettres nouvelles* group.
They exchanged ideas, letters, strategies. They mobilized in a climate of general uneasiness and extreme suspicion. The key men of
these grand maneuvers were Maurice Blanchot, Jean Schuster, Dionys Mascolo, Maurice Nadeau, Jean Pouillon. In the spring of 1960,
while more and more young men called to Algeria were choosing
to resist, the press informed the public that on September 6, the trial
of the FLN support network would begin: "Mascolo had the idea
then," said Schuster, "of a collective declaration that, under pretext
of the trial, would support and justify the actions of all those who
refused to take arms against the Algerian people, that is, all who
actively helped that people shake off colonization."[2] A first draft was
worked out by the two initiators of the project and submitted to their

surrealist friends. In Paris they immediately gathered fifteen signatures in support. Maurice Blanchot rewrote nearly all of the first part of the text, making it more explicit, and titled it "Appeal to World Opinion." "We respect and deem just the refusal to take up arms against the Algerian people. We respect and deem just the conduct of the French citizens who judge it their duty to bring help and protection to the oppressed Algerians in the name of the French people. The cause of the Algerian people, which is decisively contributing to the destruction of the colonial system, is the cause of all free men."

Thus, between the offices of two journals, *Les Temps modernes* and *Les Lettres nouvelles,* with the publisher Julliard as intermediary, was born this provocative work that history would remember as the Manifesto of the 121. Sartre immediately submitted his signature, gave his backing, and offered all the help and support that his friends at *Les Temps modernes* could provide. "We met in July," says Mascolo, "at the bistro L'Espérance where he was having lunch with Simone de Beauvoir. Blanchot was there too, and we showed him the text and asked for his approval; we immediately got it."[3] This happened in July 1960. At the beginning of August, Sartre flew to Brazil with Beauvoir, entrusting the leaders of the group with his instructions. "Use me as you want," he said in his decisive voice to Lanzmann, Pouillon, Péju, and Bost before leaving on the plane for Recife.

"THE TRIAL of the network is supposed to begin on August 29," wrote Jean Schuster to Dionys Mascolo on July 14, 1960. "We have to come out just at the right moment, as the trial opens. Nadeau has seen the lawyer who will take care of it. I think that, with a bit of dexterity, it will cause quite a stir. Am very optimistic. Trying to contact [Françoise] Sagan through Simone de Beauvoir. At the moment, there are thirty signatures. Has to get to the printer on August 25. By then, I think we'll have a hundred or so signatures, two thirds of them pretty well-known."[4] During the six weeks of the traditional Parisian exodus, some fairly important letters were in the French mails: Schuster to Mascolo, Blanchot to Mascolo, Mascolo to Pouillon, Pouillon to Nadeau, Lindon to Nadeau. "The list continues to grow," writes Pouillon on July 29, "though we have met with a few refusals. As far as I'm concerned, I realize I have signed because of the conclusion, not the analysis, which I would have conducted differently. . . . Do you have answers from people like Morin or Duvignaud? I hope so, because they're officials and the officials I have contacted wouldn't like to be alone." "This is the sort of rhythm," notes Schuster on August 5, "that develops into a frantic questioning of state power and petrifies the official left and the strategic left." "Right now I have thirty-five names," Pouillon proclaims triumphantly on August 9. "I am waiting for another ten or so and hope that Blanchot, Nadeau, Péju, and you [Mascolo] will have more at the end of the month. I'll see Beauvoir tomorrow, and she'll write a note to Merleau-Ponty right away."

Name follows name: Robbe-Grillet, Alain Resnais, Pieyre de Mandiargues, Florence Malraux, Nathalie Sarraute, Simone Signoret, Michel Leiris, Vercors, Jean-François Revel, Edouard Glissant, Pierre Boulez—one after the other they all agree to support the enterprise. There are also refusals, some of which are surprising: Lévi-Strauss, Merleau-Ponty, Colette Audry, Edgar Morin, and others. While everyone is trying to collect signatures in an atmosphere of great confusion, Blanchot, always meticulous, proposes a new, more suitable title: "For lack of another, better one," he writes to Mascolo on July 26, "I would suggest 'Declaration for the Right to Insubordination in the Algerian War.' 'Insubordination,' perhaps that word seems a little too restrictive to you. One could be more forceful, 'Declaration for the Right to Insubordination and Desertion in the Algerian War.' But I think 'insubordination' might be enough since it signifies the refusal to assume military duty." It is time for secrecy, but it is also time for prudence; each word is weighed. Every decision involves clashes, tensions, and power struggles; the surrealists and the *Temps modernes* group may appreciate one another, but from afar. "*Les Temps modernes* has to come out on the 10th," writes Nadeau to Mascolo. "If not, we'll have to go back to the first idea: mimeograph and send to the newspapers. That way the text will be known before its publication in *T.M.* At any rate, I'll republish it in the October issue of *Les Lettres nouvelles* to show that they don't have exclusive rights. Quarrels are sordid. But are they going to plead copyright? . . . I'm not only thinking of us, but of Breton and others who don't have much sympathy for *T.M.* . . ." "I'm letting you know that *T.M.* believes they're going to be the first to publish the text, on September 10," he writes again. "Beware of sabotage!" Conflicts among groups that, though quite distant, have met for a few common political causes, but do not like being led by others. "All this is true," writes Schuster to Mascolo on

August 13, "just as it's true that the surrealists are the only ones who have a concretely revolutionary position with which to confront that of Stalinist intellectuals, from Kanapa to Aragon. Nobody forgives the surrealists, whether in 1925 or in 1960, for being the Jews of the intellect. . . ."

Could a job that called for a clockmaker's precision be carried out by such diverse personalities and yet be kept completely clandestine? There were, in fact, leaks, and Gilles Martinet's editorial, which appeared on August 17 in *France-Observateur,* dispelled all anonymity: "I have in front of me," he wrote, "the text of a manifesto signed by certain writers—André Breton, Jean-Paul Sartre, Alain Robbe-Grillet etc.—. . . extremely revealing . . ." The gossip started immediately. "A very serious matter!" "Quite a gaffe!" Where was the leak? Did the "official left," as Schuster called it, disapprove of this new undertaking, these fantasies of a "new Resistance"? The response from abroad is generally more positive, sometimes even frankly enthusiastic. "Elio Vittorini, who is here right now," writes Mascolo to Maurice Blanchot on July 31, "was just telling me that [the text] made him want to be French, that it was an *act,* an important act, and a true Resistance act, because the Resistance, before being an action and giving rise to a movement, or seeking to do so, was, had to be, a *no,* a refusal, a verbal action, a judgment." On September 4, 1960, *Le Monde* announced, "One hundred and twenty-one writers and artists have signed a declaration for the 'right to insubordination in the Algerian war.' " From the post office of the Rue des Saints-Pères, Mascolo had sent more than 2,000 envelopes containing a four-page newsletter with the text of the declaration followed by one hundred and twenty-one signatures. Since nothing was done carelessly in this affair, envelopes were sent to the Elysée Palace, as well as to the main ministries. But no journal could dare publish this text without risking confiscation. The issue of *Les Temps modernes*— which some had feared would claim full paternity of the affair—appeared in the month of October with two blank pages, provocative and insolent, a symbolic challenge.

On September 5, 1960, the "Jeanson network" trial opened in the permanent military court of Paris, on the Rue du Cherche-Midi— the same street where, seventy years before, the first Dreyfus trial had taken place. The two defense lawyers were Roland Dumas and Jacques Vergès. Sartre was in Bahia that day, but his shadow and symbolic weight were with the accused and in their lawyers' files. His renown had made him ubiquitous. Pouillon, Lanzmann, Bost, and the others were there in flesh and blood. It was as if the great traveler had allowed himself the luxury of being represented by the fine flower of his barony. "By the time the trial opened," Roland Dumas comments today, "the hundred and twenty-one signatures had already shaken public opinion and all the more so in that the great shadow of Sartre stood before them, like a shield, tremendous. His name alone tipped the scales over, pulling along the leftist intelligentsia, and initiating a reversal of public opinion."[5] Already allied with several members of the "Manifesto of the 121," such as Maurice Nadeau, for instance, Roland Dumas had worked out a defense strategy: he would use certain famous names, above all Sartre's. "How should we unleash Sartre?" he asked, convinced that Sartre was one of the trump cards of his defense speech, and that he could succeed, with Sartre's name alone, in mobilizing the intellectual forces of the country.

The trial of the Jeanson network was a masquerade, a farce, a circus, a political happening, a series of challenges of an insolence and a violence rarely seen in a courtroom, a vaudeville revue, and, on the part of the lawyers, a provocation of justice, the army, and the Gaullist government—in short, a platform for the partisans of Algerian independence to voice the implacable urgency of their appeal. Day after day, the presiding judge had to listen to the descriptions of torture the defense lawyers hurled at him, as one would insults, in order to expose the cruelties of the French army in Algeria. Vergès, in perfect form, relied on provocation. On one occasion, he referred to the minister of culture, Malraux, as an "old terrorist"; on another, he cried out "Vichy!" just as the presiding judge was trying to make his escape; in short, he kept blowing up the scandal to block the judiciary machine and make a mockery of the government—he even went so far as pushing his clients to summon the entire army to court. "I say that Private Second-Class Paupert *demands* that Colonel Argoud come to testify in person at the Jeanson network trial." Naturally, the French press gave lengthy accounts of these historic sessions. "People would line up in the evening," says Roland Dumas, "to attend the sessions of this trial, this great poker game . . . as if they were going to a show."[6]

After a procedural battle that dragged on until September 15, the most important phase of the trial actually began: the political discussion. Many important personalities came to the witness stand—personalities who were not suspected, *a priori*, of anarchism toward the state, but who had sent letters of resignation or returned their legion of honor awards in order to publicly dissociate themselves from the actions and gestures of the French army: Paul Teitgen, Vercors, Marcel Aymé, Jean Cassou. Harsh words were spoken: "Can the witness tell us," Vergès asked Paul Teitgen, "on the basis of reports that were presented to him by his subordinates during the performance of his functions: 'Alas, yes, there was torture in Algiers, there was torture every day, there was systematic torture,' or 'No, that is not true'?" The presiding judge, addressing Paul Teitgen, repeated the question: "Do you have any knowledge of excesses or torture?" Teitgen replied: "These excesses and tortures were the reason I resigned from my duties, your Honor. . . . I am sorry to have to acknowledge that certain disappearances were brought to my attention. . . . I am certain about them; and, to close the door on what are for me the most painful recollections, I wish that the rigor that has struck those with a troubled conscience may also strike those who are staining the honor of my country and of its army."[7] Paul Teitgen's testimony revealed, among other things, that some French soldiers, disgusted by the dirty police work they were forced to perform against Algerian militants, had chosen to desert and support the FLN. Thanks to the lawyers, the witnesses, and the press the situation was gradually but irrevocably turned around; the accusers became the accused and vice versa. The trial of desertion and in-subordination became the trial of the French army, its illegal prac-tices, and the misuse of its men in Algeria. "Twenty-five bizarre days," Marcel Péju remembers, "where everything was disconcert-ing, where judicial frenzy was succeeded by violence, where a bewil-dered court would constantly adjourn, reconvene, contradict itself, recant, sit night and day, or take a four-hour break to meet again for a seven-minute session, suddenly grant without debate what it had passionately refused for days, cut off everyone only to listen, the next day, to the most extraordinary speeches without the slightest reaction."[8]

The lawyers invoked Sartre's name whenever they could, which infuriated the presiding judge. "We should start the trial all over again; Sartre should be here," a lawyer would threaten. At which the judge, suddenly awakened by the hated name, would exclaim, "Watch out! Keep Sartre out of this!"[9] Nevertheless, the judge would have to hear Sartre's name again and again since Tuesday, September 20, was dedicated to the testimonies of the 121 manifesto signers. One after another, twenty witnesses were brought to the stand, among them Claude Roy, Vercors, André Mandouze, Jérôme

Lindon, Jean Pouillon, Nathalie Sarraute. Immediately after Claude Lanzmann's deposition, Roland Dumas asked to be heard: "I've just received a letter and a telegram from Jean-Paul Sartre, who is detained in Brazil on a lecture series. The telegram asks that his absence be excused and affirms his 'total solidarity' with the accused. Will you give me permission, Your Honor, to read the letter now?" The judge having agreed, Dumas began. "My dear Mr. Dumas: Finding myself unable to come to the hearing of the military tribunal— which I deeply regret. . . ."

This letter, dated September 16, 1960, which would provide one of the most spectacular moments in the trial by focusing all eyes on the great absent witness, had a long history. "Use me as you want," Sartre had said to his lieutenants before flying to Recife; the instructions were clear. Lanzmann and Péju had managed to reach Sartre in Rio by phone, to let him know the state of affairs at the beginning of the trial, and to tell him how useful his testimony, if only in writing, would be. After lengthy consultations on the phone, someone found an interview that Sartre had given to Francis Jeanson at the time of their reunion: Sartre's letter was then drawn up by the Sartrean lieutenants in Sartrean style, and typed by Paule Thévenin. Sartre's signature was forged by Siné, the cartoonist.[10] "If Jeanson had asked me to carry suitcases or to give sanctuary to Algerian militants and I could have done it without putting them in danger," read Roland Dumas, weighing every word, "I would have done it without hesitation. . . . Another fate has temporarily separated [the accused] from us, but I dare say that they are our delegates. What they represent is the future of France. And the authority that is about to judge them no longer represents anything."

The letter caused a general outcry and the press spoke about it for several days. It was as if, with this supreme provocation, Sartre had touched both the French government and all the citizens of the country. "A Bomb," *L'Aurore*'s headlines ran. "From the depths of Brazil, Jean-Paul Sartre has sent a scandalous letter and has insulted the French government." "Sartre has replaced Maurras with his anarchical dialectic," Alain Terrenoir, the minister of information, declared. "This suicidal dialectic pretends to speak for a misled or decadent intelligentsia. As long as it was only an intellectual game, it was possible to attach a limited importance to it. But now, the very basis of the national community is being put into question."[11] Thierry Maulnier, in *Le Figaro*, felt that "M. Jean-Paul Sartre had nothing left to do but to defend his position in the ranks of the FLN;

at least, there, he would be taking some risks."[12] *L'Express* also attacked him through the voice of Mauriac: "Sartre is inviting the French left to unite and compromise itself by associating with terrorists covered in both French and Algerian blood. . . . What madness! For, when it comes to Sartre one cannot say 'what foolishness!' "[13] "Jean-Paul Sartre's letter," added *La Croix*, "brings the whole trial down to the level of the lowest politics."[14] The deputy from Seine-et-Marne, M. Battesti, wrote a letter to the Chamber of Deputies demanding that the government start proceedings against the philosopher: "Does the government consider it normal that, while thousands of French youths are risking their lives to ensure the peace of Algeria, M. Jean-Paul Sartre can declare himself in favor of the FLN with impunity?"[15] Perhaps the most incisive commentary was that of Jean-Marc Théolleyre, a journalist at *Le Monde*, who had been covering all the debates from the outset of the trial. "Incendiary remarks," he commented, wondering whether, by this letter, which took such a "posture of defiance," Sartre was not, in fact, trying "to solicit charges."[16] That was precisely the case.

Indeed, charges soon began coming down onto the signers of the manifesto. Officials were suspended from their duties without salary, radio and television reporters were fired. Charges, searches, interrogations, the entire police system was mobilized to track down the culprits. On September 22, the prime minister, Michel Debré, got the Council of Ministers to pass a law increasing the minimum sentence of those encouraging insubordination or harboring insubordinates. "It is imperative," stressed the ordinance, "that we punish, with utmost severity, not only insubordinates but also those who incite them to avoid their duties. . . . These appeals . . . confuse the understanding of all those listeners who are particularly vulnerable to insidious and demoralizing propaganda . . . any encouragement to desertion will be punished. . . . As far as government officials are concerned, [the penalty imposed] severs all ties with public duties: its expiration will not allow the resumption of a previously occupied post." The following week, on September 29, the government struck with even greater force; in a new ordinance it authorized the suspension of any official speaking in favor of insubordination or desertion, or encouraging members of the army to disobey orders. "Nobody forces officials to enter the service of the state," commented the minister of information. Protests, messages of sympathy, scandalized communiqués, lists of supporters, passed through the newspapers and echoed in the media. The Union of North African Combatants protested "the scandalous nature of the so-called witnesses who ... are insulting our country," noting that "the name of M. Jean-Paul Sartre, previously linked to the milieu of Saint-Germain-des-Prés and to the idea of nausea, will now be associated, in the mind of French youth, with the idea of treason."[17] The right-wing group MP 13 attacked the signers of the manifesto, describing them as "a handful of degenerate intellectuals and girls aching for the exotic, the rich delinquents of a decadent society," concluding with, "It is to General Raoul Salan, Grand Master of May 13, that the princes of the Fifth Republic owe everything."[18]

In an open letter to the prime minister, the general secretary of the Centre National des Indépendants, M. Duchet, wrote: "Following the free publication of Jean-Paul Sartre's letter and the restrictions imposed on General Salan, I would like to inform you of the feelings of all those who love their country, respect the servants who serve it well, and abide by its laws. M. Jean-Paul Sartre, who has never brought us anything but subversive theories and sophisms, has been able to insult our army and France with impunity. He has publicly shown that to save the honor of his country, he had to violate its laws and aid its enemy. On the one hand, Jean-Paul Sartre can violate and denounce the most fundamental laws for the safeguarding and salvation of the nation, and on the other, one of our greatest and disciplined military leaders is punished for having evoked and upheld the same fundamental laws. I ask you to reconsider such deplorable attitudes, which, you know as well as I do, cause havoc in the army and the entire country."[19]

On the other side, the Committee for University Vigilance affirms that the "Manifesto of the 121" "publicly translates the will to deny the state the means of continuing the unjust war it is carrying out in Algeria. . . . We would like to assure [all signers] of our sympathy and esteem." The Republican Action Committee of Artists and Art Critics is unanimous in thinking that the signers' "righteousness, their disinterestedness, and their patriotism merit respect. They join all those who, for the honor of France, are requesting their discharge and liberation."[20] Thus, during the autumn of 1960, everyone seems to be taking stances, pro-Sartreans, anti-Sartreans, leagues of war veterans against teachers' associations, those nostalgic for the French Empire against actors' unions. *Les Temps modernes* is confiscated in spite of the two blank pages where the text of the manifesto should have been. France is in a panic, the government gets tougher. The scandal of the trial having reached foreign countries is echoed back to Paris: Italian, German, American, and British intellectuals mobilize for the famous 121 signers. Counter-manifestoes circulate among French intellectuals advocating law and order. "They want to destroy the soul of France," Professor Charles Richet of the Academy of Medicine writes. "In his impassioned delirium, Sartre has gone too far," states André Brissaud in the columns of *Le Figaro* on September 30: "The real France must be crushed so that there will be victory for the Sartrean France, the revolutionary idea of France that M. Jean-Paul Sartre has substituted for France, and which he prefers to France. In this Sartrean France, in this France of 'thinking individuals,' it is the FLN that is the true army, while the French army becomes the hated, unpardonable enemy, something like the inheritor of Hitler's army of the 1940s." In *La Croix*, Jacques de Bourbon-Busset observes that the trial has revealed something new: "The divorce between the majority of public opinion and those who are termed intellectuals. This is a serious symptom because intellectuals prepare a society for what is to come."[21]

The affair of the 121 brought back to memory two others: the Calas affair, the Dreyfus affair. And there were a number of reactions to the word "intellectual" itself: a new list of signatures approving the Manifesto of the 121 as well as the plan for a counter-manifesto. "It is the battle of intellectuals," *Le Figaro* announced triumphantly. "The manifesto of the French intellectuals: 260 against 121."[22] And score was kept, like a soccer match. There were announcements about the competitors: "The French intellectuals in the Sartrean camp," said the headlines of *L'Aurore*, "like all advocates of desertion, are impostors and traitors."[23] Other newspapers spoke of the "new treason of the mind." Still others acknowledged the courage of Sartre and those close to him. Thus, the newspaper *Réforme*, in an article titled "The Era of Militants," urged, "Sartre's analysis deserves to be heard. . . . He does not want current events to throw him once again over to the mild left; he thinks that the time has come to take risks. He urges young people to be insubordinate; he aligns himself with Algerian nationalists fighting for their country's independence. Rather than judging Jean-Paul Sartre, we should try to understand him."[24]

Important voices spoke out: Mauriac, as mentioned above; André Malraux, who thought it "better to let Sartre shout 'Long live the FLN' in the Place de la Concorde than arrest him and embarrass ourselves."[25] At the close of the meeting of the Council of Ministers concerning the sanctions to adopt against the 121 signers of the manifesto, General de Gaulle specified the spirit in which he hoped the sanctions would be applied, thus pursuing a policy of delegation of tasks within the government itself. Some were to act as hawks, some as doves. The chief of state, then, made a distinction between "civil servants" (whom he could not allow to go against the laws of the state) and "intellectuals" (of whom he spoke with detachment and benevolence, recalling the examples of Villon, Voltaire, Romain Rolland). "These people," he said, "caused great trouble in their time, but it is essential that we continue to respect their freedom of thought and expression insofar as this is compatible with the laws of the state and national unity." "De Gaulle: 'I Forgive Voltaire, But Not Civil Servants' " ran the headlines of *Paris-Jour* that same day. This sovereign generosity, this Gaullist gesture of appeasement, was one of the first steps in the canonization of Sartre.[26]

"Shoot-Jean-Paul-Sartre!" "French-Al-ger-ia!" "Lib-er-ate-La-Gail-larde!" "Po-wer-to-Sa-lan!" Monday October 3, on the Champs-Elysées, between six and seven thousand demonstrators meet at the corner of the Rue Washington. It is a few minutes after 7 p.m. They follow the Champs-Elysées toward the Arc de Triomphe and L'Etoile, to "give silent tribute to the dead, both civilian and military, who fell under the blows of the FLN" and to "protest the summons to treason." Six veterans' organizations had called for this rally: Rhin-et-Danube, the Veterans of the 2nd DB, Flanders-Dunkerque, the Veterans of the French Free Forces, the Veterans of the Expeditionaries of Italy, the National Union of Fighters and Sons of the Dead. Flags on golden flagpoles, medals, military caps, marchers in uniform. A hundred or so standard bearers leading the way, just behind men carrying wreaths. Members of the city council, their red-white-and-blue sashes across their chests, among them Jean-Marie Le Pen (who in the 1980s re-emerged as a leader of the racist, neo-fascist National Front), with his deputy's badge and green parachutist beret. Behind, the bulk of the group: young militants of the extreme right handing out leaflets. Ritual placement of the wreaths followed by one minute of silence in the presence of Marshals de Lattre and Leclerc. The demonstration quickly degenerates: a violent return down the Champs-Elysées, smashed windows, an attack on the offices of *L'Express*. That day, Sartre's name was used for the first time in a street demonstration as a symbol of all those "false French" who were pushing the government to "abandon" Algeria. A whole sector of the French population was turning him into public enemy number one. "Sartre, that's a monster," the weekly *Force nouvelle* commented a few days later.

A number of French people who had not taken sides before joined the battle and rebelled against the brutality of government sanctions. A handful of intellectuals and the notorious Manifesto of the 121 had brought over to their side all the troops of the left. The liaison committee of entertainers, the communist trade union CGT, the Christian trade union CFTC, the assembly of French cardinals and archbishops, radio and TV journalists, Centre National de la Recherche Scientifique (CNRS) scholars, students of the Ecole Normale Supérieure, the teachers of Corrèze, the National Committee of Writers (CNE), the Union of Critics, the League for Human Rights, each in turn spoke out against the sanctions adopted against government employees. Referring to key moments in the history of France, the communiqué of the CNE proclaimed: "The witch hunt introduced into France at the moment the battalions of the Wehrmacht were introduced into Sissonne and Mourmelon, was the preliminary to France's loss of face, and the ruin of France's international reputation. The only means of putting an end to this arbitrary behavior is to put an immediate end to the war in Algeria."[27]

De Gaulle had just put Sartre into the category of citizens whom the law could not touch: the intellectuals. The law would also look on his friends with favor. Jean Pouillon, employed as the *rapporteur* at the National Assembly, had been suspended from his office for six months without salary. But he was never prosecuted and, despite the repeated letters in which he affirmed that he had not only "solidarity" with but was also an "accomplice" of the accused, despite police searches and interrogations, he was not harassed further. "I'm convinced," he explains now, "when I think of the amount of information that the police could have assembled, that Sartre and his entourage were the objects of a special treatment. To lay hands on Arlette, to lay hands on Pouillon, would have been to lay hands on Sartre's name. His name was sufficient for our protection."[28] On September 9, the day after the first communiqué concerning the Manifesto of the 121, the daily *Paris-Press-l'Intransigeant* had run the headline "Jean-Paul Sartre, Simone Signoret, and 100 Others May Get Five Years". Barely one month later, things had been turned around: Sartre had become Untouchable, radiating the benefits of his class over the *Temps modernes* group and the members of the Sartrean family. Sartre's desk, at the Rue Bonaparte, was daily submerged by letters that were opened and read by his secretary Claude Faux: "We're with you. We support your action. What's your next move?" was their essential message.[29]

"The situation in France is extremely serious," Lanzmann had explained in his last telegram and in final phone call to Sartre before the latter's return from Brazil. "Under no circumstances should you land in France. Take the Rio–Barcelona flight." "It was absolutely necessary," Jean Pouillon explains, "to keep Sartre up to date on all the details of the political situation, to keep him from making hasty declarations to the press." On November 4, Sartre and Beauvoir landed in Barcelona. Bost and Pouillon drove down to meet them. The four met at the Hotel Colon, the same hotel from which, twenty-five years earlier, Paul Nizan and André Malraux had witnessed the great events of the Spanish Civil War. They made a quiet visit to the Barcelona museum, where, as Pouillon recounts, "Sartre gave an improvised lecture on the Catalan frescoes, a lecture so brilliant that the other museum visitors thought he was a guide." On Monday afternoon, they left for France. At the border, Bost took the lead, fearing an incident; he got out of the car and showed the four passports to the head customs official. The official looked over the names, the photographs, and, of course, insisted on meeting the bearers to verify their identities. "Please be good enough to enter, maître," he said to Sartre, bowing to the ground. "Maître, please take a seat in my private parlor. . . . Maître, may I offer you cigarettes, whisky, newspapers?" Uniformed police ran out to get cigarettes, whisky, newspapers. After three-quarters of an hour, the official returned. "Maître," he repeated, bowing again, "I am pleased to inform you that you can cross the border. . . . But before that, Maître, I have a favor to ask you: would you be willing to sign my autograph book?" Sartre affixed his signature on an already half-filled page. As soon as he had signed, he looked, out of curiosity, at the signature that was just above his. "General Raoul Salan," he read. Sartre and MP 13's Grand Master had both crossed the same border, half an hour apart, going in different directions.[30]

"We re-entered Paris by the backroads," recounts Pouillon, "after a stopover in Béziers and another in Tournus. At Pont-Saint-Esprit we met up with Lanzmann, who had come down after us. We arrived in Paris on either Wednesday or Thursday of the following week." In Tournus, Bost, Pouillon, and Lanzmann noticed the hatred that Sartre's mere presence awoke in a certain sector of the French population. As soon as the five of them entered the main restaurant in Tournus, Sartre in the lead, followed by Beauvoir, heads turned, people recognized them. The three lieutenants noticed the stares and heard the whispers: "That bastard . . . monster . . ." Even today, Pouillon speaks of the "hatred." "But the owner," he adds, "handed him her autograph book, visibly overjoyed to get Sartre's signature." In the space of one summer, Sartre's place in French society had acquired a symbolic power it had never had before. During the trip back, Sartre, Beauvoir and their friends discussed strategies. "Of course," Sartre said, "I am completely ready to be charged, like all the other signers of the manifesto." "By a chance coincidence," Pouillon concludes, "the charges were dropped the very day Sartre set foot in Paris."[31] "Judge Pérez, who was in charge of the dossier," Roland Dumas explains, "sent Sartre four of five summonses, followed immediately by a notice that the charges were being dropped! This little game lasted one month. French justice was wrong in wanting to treat all intellectuals as if they were petty truants; the attempt to intimidate them under the pretext of 'calming them,' was, of course, especially clumsy. To do this was to ignore the popular power they represented, to overlook the weight of the ideological baggage that backed the intentions of the 121."[32] Sartre had only one hearing before a commission of the judiciary police, and then waited in vain to be summoned before the examining magistrate. "In Paris, the commissioners started collecting our testimony," Sartre would later recount. "Supposedly, eight days later we were to appear in front of the examining magistrate. The evening before, the poor judge fell sick; eight days later he was still sick, and thus the joke ended. That's the last thing we heard about the charges brought against us, as signers of the Manifesto of the 121."[33]

On December 1, after having waited more than a month for the summons, Sartre decided to call a press conference: French and foreign journalists gathered at Beauvoir's home. "This time," he said, "it is obvious that they don't want us to testify or, at any rate, that they don't want us to plead guilty. Why? I have no idea. I know that there are others who, charged, have pleaded guilty and will be tried. If the government had withdrawn the case altogether, I wouldn't have disturbed you. I would have assumed they had finally seen reason. But since they have charged thirty of the co-signers and not the others, we, the others, find ourselves in an unhealthy situation and have to speak out against it. . . . They are using a double standard," he continued, "for two equally responsible sets of co-signers. This is an entirely unacceptable situation. If those men are found guilty, then we all are. If not, then let them withdraw the case. . . . I am telling the press what I would have told the examining magistrate: I am one of those who drafted this text, and distributed

it in order to collect signatures. I demand, then, to be charged.
. . . They have used my name for all sorts of dubious causes, I have
served as an alibi for freeing people who are in opposition not only
to the government, but also to democracy."[34] Sartre was denouncing
the internal contradictions of the governmental machine: orders and
counter-orders following each other, as the ball bounced back and
forth between the sternest ministers—Michel Debré, Alain Ter-
renoire—and the more moderate ones, such as Malraux. Sartre was
highly amused by the consideration that the authorities accorded
him, and did not miss a chance to speak out against their incoherence. This enormous fracas turned the country upside down, but in
December 1960, not a single printer having dared undertake the job,
the Manifesto of the 121 had not yet been printed. One day, Mascolo,
coming out of the Brasserie Lipp, met the deputy of the Fédération
de le Gauche Democratique Socialiste (FGDS) from Nièvre, François Mitterrand, and suggested to him, "If you could manage to read
the text of the manifesto during one of the sessions of the National
Assembly, the text will have to be reproduced in the *Journal Officiel*,
which would at once create a precedent and permit its definitive
publication." "Mitterrand answered neither yes nor no," Mascolo
says today, "and, apparently, did nothing."[35]

Sartre was active during the Algerian war because, called on by
Jeanson, he had agreed to give his total support and that of his group
to the network supporting the FLN, which he had not himself
created. He had similarly lent his name and all the assistance of his
group to the Manifesto of the 121. There again, he was a precious
support, not an initiator. As for the letter that Roland Dumas read
at the trial on September 20: it was not genuine but had been written
by others in Sartre's name. So, was Sartre really active, or simply
consenting, managed (and well-managed) by the members of his
group and other French intellectuals? Apparently, by then, he did
not need to decide or to act: he had become a shield, a screen, a
"national treasure," as Pouillon puts it, a fact that may well have
bothered him.

The political position that Sartre had acquired in the context of
the Algerian war brought him sympathizers from all over the world.
At the beginning of the sixties, in the centers of political consciousness that kept developing throughout Africa, Southeast Asia, Latin
America, and, of course, Europe, among the youth of the extreme
left who were mobilizing on behalf of China, Algeria, and Cuba,
Sartre was perceived as a theoretical foundation. He became, for a

while, the prophet of this new world that seemed to be awakening with a start and shaking off the chains of Western imperialism and colonization.

*T*UNIS, SUMMER 1960. A big empty room, its only furniture, a mattress on the floor. Claude Lanzmann and Marcel Péju, emissaries of *Les Temps modernes,* have come to meet Frantz Fanon. "He was ill," Lanzmann remembers, "but even in his terrible suffering, he denied that he suffered. He had already read the *Critique of Dialectical Reason,* and he spoke to us about it for hours and hours. He also spoke to us about the illumination provided by certain models from the heart of the country, paragons of self-abnegation, sacrifice, and dedication. His need to communicate was immense; he wanted, above all, to convince us that the "heart of Algeria" had become pure freedom, free of all prejudice. He told us that Sartre was a god. He spoke with a voice intensified by urgency; he spoke with the voice of illness (his leukemia, which would soon kill him), the voice of the Algerian revolution and of the African revolution. For he had already moved way beyond the Algerian revolution," Lanzmann continues. "He spoke of his visionary dream of unification for blacks of all countries. He dramatized the game of History, giving us clear evidence of the extraordinary moral stance he demanded. He had gone into the field, into hidden *wilayas* near the Algerian-Tunisian border, to meet the revolutionaries, give lectures, speak to them about the things he had read, including Sartre's work. One day he had also explained to them what he had liked in the *Critique* (published that same year). He had gone to shape the theoretical foundations of those groups, those militants among whom were men such as Colonel Houari Boumediene, Ben Khedda—the pharmacist of Bliba who would replace Ferhat Abbas at the head of the GPRA—Abdelaziz Bouteflika and Ahmed Medgui, the future minister of the interior. . . . All these people had the greatest admiration for Fanon."[36]

The arrival in Tunis of the two emissaries from *Les Temps modernes* initiated the Fanon-Sartre axis. Ever since 1948, Fanon had acquainted himself with Sartre's earlier work in favor of African minorities; he had read and particularly appreciated "Black Orpheus," Sartre's preface to an anthology of new black and Madagascan poetry written in French. "What did you expect," Sartre had written, "when you took away the gag that kept these black mouths shut? That they would sing your praises? These heads, which our fathers had bent to the earth by force, did you think that when they stood up again you would read adoration in their eyes?"[37] Sartre's reading of the poems of Aimé Césaire, Léopold Sedar Senghor, David Diop, Etienne Lero, Rabearivelo, Damas le Guyanais, and Brierre le Haïtien, was full of fury and magic as it meandered through experiences, evoking Paul Niger's line—"On Judgment Day Armstrong's trumpet will interpret man's sorrows"—analyzing the concept of "negritude"—"the triumph of Narcissism and the suicide of Narcissus"—examining the evangelism of black poetry trying to free itself from the "culture prison," and describing it as "Orphic" because "this unflagging descent of the black into himself makes me think of Orpheus going to Hades to steal Eurydice away from Pluto." Finally, in a vein similar to that of *Anti-Semite and Jew*, written during the same period, Sartre addressed his white contemporaries, provoking them, almost insulting them: "The white man has, for three thousand years, enjoyed the privilege of seeing without being seen. Today, these black men look at us, and our gaze returns and penetrates our own eyes; black torches, now, light up the world, and our white heads are nothing more than little lanterns swaying in the wind."[38]

Later, in his last works, Fanon would himself rely on Sartre's analysis of "negritude." This first meeting with Lanzmann and Péju was very satisfying for Fanon, who saw in it the concretization of his ties with the *Temps modernes* group. The journal had printed an excerpt from his still-unpublished "Year Five of the Algerian Revolution," and gave sustained support to FLN activities. "Algeria is not France," *Les Temps modernes* had publicly proclaimed in 1955, thus attacking the persistent notion of a French Algeria. Then it had published a series of articles on "Algeria: Myth and Realities," and one on torture and disappearances; and had drawn support to numerous French and Algerian militants who were either mistreated or imprisoned, such as Maurice Audin, Djemila Bouhired, Henri Alleg, and Francis Jeanson. . . . Moreover, Frantz Fanon and the *Temps modernes* group shared a disgust for the institutionalized left, always so slow to move. "At the dawn of the fourth year of the war for national liberation," Fanon would write in *El-Moudjahid*, "the French left is less and less a presence. . . . Many intellectuals, in fact almost all of the democratic left are falling apart and proposing their conditions to the Algerian people."[39] In May 1955, a famous special issue was devoted entirely to the French left. Fanon's "Intellectuals and Democrats Face the Algerian Question" shared its analysis and its anger with Sartre's "The Left in Question." The two men would meet some time later in the heat of the Roman summer. Meanwhile, events in Algeria were strengthening their ties.

Sartre and Fanon's first meeting took place in Rome during the summer of 1961, with days and whole nights of passionate and endless conversations; their mutual interests seemed inexhaustible. Fanon, feverish and agitated, questioned Sartre relentlessly. "With a razor-sharp intelligence," relates Beauvoir, "intensely alive, endowed with a grim sense of humor, he explained things, made jokes, questioned us, gave imitations, told stories; everything he talked about seemed to live again before our eyes."[40] Fanon had just finished writing his final book, *The Wretched of the Earth,* which would be published in France by François Maspero. Some time before this first meeting with Sartre, Fanon had sent an intense and eager letter to his editor, in which Sartre's name once again played a notoriously symbolic role. "The state of my health having improved slightly," Fanon wrote to Maspero from Tunis, on April 7, 1961, "I have decided to write something after all. I must say that I was asked insistently to do so by our own people. . . . Trusting that you'll satisfy my request, I would like to ask you to speed up the publication of this book: we need it in Algeria and Africa. . . . Ask Sartre to write a preface. Tell him that each time I sit down at my desk, I think of him who writes such important things for our future but who as yet has found no readers . . . at all."[41]

Sartre's preface to Fanon's *Wretched of the Earth* remains one of the texts that speak most eloquently in support of the third world. Some of its sentences, some of its formulations—flaunting the elaborate literary style that has already become the trademark of Sartre's writings—are unforgettable: "Why would Fanon care whether you read his work or not? It is for his brothers that he is denouncing our old hatreds, certain that we do not have any spare ones. It is to them that he says, 'Europe has put her paws on our continent; we must slash at them until they pull back. The moment is with us.' "[42] Further on, Sartre admonishes his contemporaries, harangues them: "Europeans, open this book. Enter it. After a few footsteps into its night you will see strangers gathered around a fire. Approach. Listen. They are discussing the fate awaiting your trading posts, and the mercenaries who are defending them. They may see you, but they will continue to speak among themselves without even lowering their voices . . . this indifference goes straight to one's heart."[43] This text, following the events of the summer of 1960, marks the end of an epoch, the end of one kind of Europe, the joyous slaying of a colonial system directly inherited from the nineteenth century. In this text, Sartre celebrates the emergence of an autonomous voice for the colonized, the official birth of a new political partner, the transformation of the oppressed into a peer who speaks to peers. In this long meditation on subject and object, in this analysis of the dialectic European/colonized, the master learns from the student, the father learns from the son, the European, finally, learns from the ex-colony. If Europe wants to be cured, Sartre says, it must accept this voice. Fanon's book, he explains, "did not need a preface, all the less so since he is not speaking to us. I have written one, nevertheless, so as to carry the dialectic to its logical conclusion. We, the people of Europe, we too are being decolonized, by which I mean to say that the *colon* in each and every one of us is being finally excised. Let us look at ourselves, if we have the courage, and let us see what's become of us."[44] "European," cries Sartre, "have the courage to read this book. . . . You see, even I can get rid of the subjective illusion. Even I, I tell you: 'All is lost unless . . .' Europeans, I am stealing the book of an enemy and am using it to cure Europe. Take advantage of it."[45] After having spoken of the Europeans to the Europeans, Sartre returns to Fanon. For him, he finds the most lyrical tones, the driest rhythms, his most frantic concision, his most intense prose: "We have sown our seeds in the wind; he [the colonized] is the tempest. Son of violence, he draws his humanity from it. We were men at his expense; he is making himself a man at ours. Another man, and a better one."[46]

The Wretched of the Earth was published in seventeen languages: more than a million copies. The book entered the ideological debate during a politically sensitive period—the end of the Algerian war—and offered itself as an emotional indictment. In a way, it was the political testament of a man about to die. The yoking of Sartre and Fanon became a sort of theoretical creed. Among the most powerful elements in the book, the most memorable is the reiteration and use of the term "third world." "The third world today stands in front of Europe like a colossal body . . . the third world must remake the history of man." "Third world" was used for the first time by Alfred Sauvy in 1952, in a daring parallel: third estate/third world. But, after the publication of *The Wretched of the Earth* the term "third world" spread everywhere.[47] When twenty-five years or so later, this concept was called into question, it was because the context in which it was conceived had been forgotten. It is important to recall, for instance, the beginning of the fifties when European leftist intellectuals, more or less influenced by Marxism, condemned the "misery" and the "underdevelopment" of the "third world" as tools used by American imperialism in its anticommunist campaign (as clearly evidenced by the fourth point in President Truman's 1947 address). The third-world rhetoric of the 1960s was nothing but a scream filled with hatred for the "imperialist" right, part of a rhetoric that was much too one-sided, much too schematic, much too idealistic perhaps, and certainly much too Manichaean.

On December 6, 1961, Fanon died in Washington. Sartre's preface to Fanon's last book was the first instance of a new genre, that of a funeral oration, in which he played the Bossuet of the twentieth century. On January 4, 1960, Albert Camus had lost his life in a car accident at the age of forty-seven. On May 4, 1961, Maurice Merleau-Ponty had also died violently at the age of fifty-four. In honor of these two, Sartre would publish two magnificent tombstones in *Les Temps modernes*: "Albert Camus Lives," "Merleau-Ponty Lives." In addition to these two pieces, Sartre agreed to write a preface for the new edition of Nizan's *Aden Arabie*, published by Maspero. This preface is another "tombstone." Nizan, gone at thirty-six; Fanon, thirty-six; Camus, forty-seven; Merleau-Ponty, fifty-four. In this Sartrean pantheon, four men who had died too soon were resurrected by his voice. One remembers the "life stories" published in the first issues of *Temps modernes,* and young Poulou's passion for the lives of famous men, which he experienced in his grandfather's library. And, of course, one thinks of his own autobiography, *The Words,* which he is now about to finish: "A whole man, composed of all men and as good as all of them and no better than any."

Sartre began to compose as soon as he heard about Camus's death: "[Camus] represented in this century, and against History, the present heir of that long line of moralists whose works perhaps constitute what is most original in French letters. His stubborn humanism, narrow and pure, austere and sensual, waged a dubious battle against events of these times. But inversely, through the obstinacy of his refusals, he reaffirmed the existence of moral fact within the heart of our era and against the Machiavellians, against the golden calf of realism."[48]

Written during a brief stay in Cuba, in February 1960, finished during the return trip, the preface to *Aden Arabie* appeared the following month. Since Paul Nizan's death, in 1940, his three novels, two pamphlets and various essays had been largely unavailable in bookstores. The man and his works had both disappeared. Maspero's idea would bring Nizan back to life twenty years after his physical and symbolic death. His childhood friend, Sartre, was appropriately put in charge of the mission. There had been a few missed rendez-vous between these two contemporaries who had never lived their political and literary lives together but had nevertheless ripened together in the same hothouse. Sartre wrote one of his most beautiful texts, just by letting his memories, from the Ecole Normale to World War II, dance on the page. Nizan became his pretext for introspec-tion, and Sartre, in a text of retrospective identification and symbolic appropriation, mythified at leisure.

"Finally came the Marshall Plan. The Cold War went straight to the heart of this generation of dancers and vassals. . . . These cellar rats became elderly, stupefied young men. Some grew gray, others bald, still others got a pot belly . . . I still see them at twenty, so vital and gay, determined to relieve us at the next shift. Today I see their eyes eaten away by a cancerous astonishment, and I think to myself, they didn't deserve this . . . Just where had their lives gone? Nizan can answer for the desperate as well as for the faithful. Only I doubt whether they are willing or able to read him: for a lost and con-founded generation, this vigorous dead man tolls the bell."[49] At full gallop, Sartre cuts through this century. More obsessed than ever before by aging bones and aging ideas, he retrieves his friend from formaldehyde, finds him still intact in his capacity for anger and hatred, and he brandishes him before the eyes of the world as the perfect model of the dead hero. It is ironic that, when they were both in their twenties, Sartre was the one who bristled with insouciance and "happiness"—a fact he himself liked to recall. When *Aden Ara-bie* was published in 1931, Sartre was able to perceive only the slightly lyrical and exaggerated delirium of his too-literary friend. Sartre rediscovered him only thirty years later, and made him into the spearhead of the young radicals of the day. "Who will speak to these angry young men? Who can enlighten their violence? Nizan. Year by year, his hibernation has made him younger. Yesterday he was our contemporary, today he is theirs. When he was alive, we shared his rages, but none of us, finally, was capable of 'the most simple surrealist act'; and now, here we are, old, having betrayed our youth so many times that it is only decent to ignore it in silence. Our old memories have lost their claws and teeth. Twenty years old, yes, I must have been twenty once, but now I am fifty-five."[50]

An attack on the PC, another one on the institutionalized left, a last one on scoundrels and traitors. At times, Sartre explodes: "Could the sons then be attracted by the left, that corpse, lying on its back and full of worms? This cadaver stinks. The power of the military, dictatorship and fascism are rising or will rise from its decomposition. One would have had to be very devoted to it, not to turn away in revulsion. It had made us, the grandfathers."[51]

In 1960, the anarchical grandfather Sartre offered his adopted grandsons the perfect model of his friend Nizan: an incorruptible, incisive militant, challenging the communists on their left flank, incapable of betraying the practical sphere in favor of the wooden language of bureaucracy, but, nevertheless, intense, radical, exalted, pure. Whether or not Sartre's construction was firmly founded, or whether the reality was true to the model, the image of Nizan had a future that went beyond anything Sartre might have wished. In the midst of the Algerian war, when the PCF (tagging along behind support networks and other forms of benevolent aid) kept criticizing Sartre, Jeanson, the Manifesto of the 121, and everything else they chose to fit under the disdainful heading of "provocations," this resurrection of Nizan was a real counterattack. Nizan became the ideal hero for all the passionate generations who found, in Sartre's portrait, a new type of activist, the ideal alternative to the fallen communist militant. At the Ecole Normale Supérieure, the cell of communist students adopted the name "Paul Nizan cell." From then on, every time a debate opposed Sartre to a communist (Roger Garaudy, for instance), one would automatically see, as Marc Kravetz says, "on one side, Nizan's brilliant preface writer, on the other, a cop."[52] The real Nizan was getting confused with Sartre's portrait of him, and the hallucination lasted a long time. "It is not a bad thing to begin with this naked revolt: at the origin of everything is, first of all, refusal. Now, will the old men be so good as to move aside, and let this adolescent speak to his brothers: 'I was twenty once, and I shall let no one say that it is life's most wonderful age.' "[53]

*A*LL EVIDENCE suggests that, if Sartre wrote of Fanon with euphoric empathy, Nizan with warm passion and nostalgia, and Camus with concern filled with sorrow, Merleau-Ponty was a true trial for him. "Sartre had a terribly difficult time writing this article," Arlette Elkaïm confirms today. "For him, it was a rite of passage. He spent the entire summer of 1961 working on it. He took a lot of

Corydrane and suffered a great deal. I think that his relationship with Merleau-Ponty was very complex and he hadn't yet come to terms with it. At times I was so worried that I wished he would drop the project altogether. This was the only time he couldn't quite erect a tombstone." The article appeared five months after Merleau-Ponty's death, in a special issue of *Les Temps modernes.* Sartre had had no trouble finding the words to bid farewell to Camus. If it was so hard for him to salute Merleau-Ponty, it was certainly because he had not yet concluded any debate—be it philosophical or political—with this truly Husserlian philosopher, who, just a few years earlier, had argued against him so brilliantly, and had dismantled the Sartrean mechanism with such precision in his essay "Sartre or Ultrabolshevism." Maybe, they had shared too many things—the Ecole Normale, philosophy, phenomenology, common friends, World War II, Marxist sympathies. All this made it difficult for Sartre to separate the ideological from the historical. With Camus, the ideological debate had been violent and straightforward. But Sartre had never truly answered Merleau-Ponty. Sartre had once greatly admired Descartes's thought, which "cuts and slices"; he was attracted by razor-sharp intelligences. And Merleau-Ponty had criticized him with that very sharpness. At the death of Merleau-Ponty, Sartre, bewildered, perplexed, was left with all the arguments he had been unable to develop earlier, facing Merleau-Ponty, now facing, above all, himself.

"I have lost so many friends who are still alive. No one was to blame. It was they. It was myself. Events made us, brought us together, separated us. And I know that Merleau-Ponty said the same thing when he thought of the people who haunted and then left his life. But he never lost me, and he had to die for me to lose him. We were equals, friends, but not brothers. We understood this immediately, and, at first, our differences amused us. And then, about 1950 the barometer fell: fair wind for Europe and the world, but for us, a gale knocked our heads together, and a moment later, it tossed each of us to opposite poles of the other."[54] During the 1930s Sartre had lost sight of Nizan and lost track of him intellectually. It was just then, during his discovery of phenomenology, that he had met Merleau-Ponty. "Socialism and Freedom" had drawn them together. From 1945 to 1950, the two philosophers shared political activities and concrete discoveries at both *Les Temps modernes* and in the RDR. The signature "T.M." at the bottom of the editorial page had long been the sign of their consensus. In 1952–53, they disagreed and then broke up over Stalinism. Merleau-Ponty resigned from *Les Temps modernes*. But, underneath these political disagreements, there were real theoretical discords—which they had never disentangled—that drove them apart. To suffer while composing his "Merleau-Ponty Lives" was, for Sartre, to attempt to clarify by himself an essential debate that had long remained suspended. This article may be Sartre's finest attempt to define his political trajectory in global terms. In it, he strives relentlessly to evoke, scene by scene, the most powerful moments of his relationship with Merleau: the composition of "The Communists and Peace," the Camus/Merleau-Ponty quarrel, the meeting of the Velodrome d'Hiver. He strives to relive each episode, each problem. "Beneath our intellectual divergencies of 1941," he admits toward the end, "so calmly accepted when Husserl alone was the cause, we discovered, astounded, that our conflicts had, at times, stemmed from our childhood, or went back to the elementary differences of our two organisms; and that, at other times, they were between the flesh and the skin; in one of us, hypocrisies, complicities, a passion for activism, hiding his defeats, and, in the other, retractile emotions and a desperate quietism. Of course, none of these were completely true or completely false. We quarreled because we put the same ardor into convincing, understanding, and accusing ourselves."[55]

Of course, Sartre could not completely hide his discomfort: it exploded on every page, and particularly in the first version, so guilt-ridden was he. It was a discomfort that finally found release in the last lines of the homage: "This is true, but it is also true that it was us, we two, who loved each other badly. There is nothing to be concluded from this except that this long friendship, neither done nor undone, obliterated when it was about to be reborn, or broken, remains inside me, an always open wound."[56]

Camus, Nizan, Fanon, Merleau-Ponty: in 1960 and 1961 Sartre settled accounts as well as he could with his four friends. In 1964, he would do the same thing with the secretary of the Italian Communist Party, Palmiro Togliatti, whom he saw frequently during his summers in Rome. This new esthetic escaped no one, especially not François Mauriac: "For the third time now," he writes on October 29, 1961, in his *Bloc-Notes*, "a text by [Sartre] inspires me—as a Christian. Now that the spotlights have turned away from him, he is closer to us, and we can finally measure his true stature. Perhaps he is no longer the 'philosopher of our time' but he has become a writer, as I understand that word, a man who uses writing to clarify his relation to the beings he has loved. Who would have said, fifteen years ago, that young Sartre, who seemed to have been put into the world in order to break everything and stain everything, would, one day, use his dialectic in the service of his heart and ours?"

*W*HILE HE labored over his funeral orations, Sartre continued his political activities, most of them centering on the Algerian war. The Organization of the Secret Army, the OAS, which was founded in February 1961, attracted all those who had been let down by the French empire: fierce partisans of a French Algeria, stung to the quick each time the president mentioned the "Algerian Republic" or the "Sovereign Algerian State." They were racists, violently determined to preserve a status quo that, in their eyes, was being eroded every day. On April 22, 1961, as a last desperate measure, Generals Salan, Maurice Challe, Edmond Jouhaud, and Henri Zeller tried to seize power in Algeria. A state of emergency was immediately declared throughout all French territories. Sartre was one of the first targets of the OAS attacks. His apartment on the Rue Bonaparte was bombed twice: on July 19, 1961 and on January 7, 1962. The offices of *Les Temps modernes* were also attacked on May 13, 1961. Sartre was not physically hurt by these explosions, but, his door at the Rue Bonaparte was destroyed, and many manuscripts and letters disappeared. He then moved to an apartment his secretary had rented for him on the Quai Louis-Blériot, facing the Eiffel Tower. While continuing to support the FLN, he took part in many political activities: on November 1, 1961, he attended a silent demonstration on the Place Maubert to protest the recent murderous repressions by the French police; on November 18, 1961, he participated in another demonstration, before attending a press conference at the Hotel Lutétia; on December 13, he was in Rome at a meeting for Algerian independence which was also attended by the Algerian leader Tayeb Boularouf; on December 19, in Paris, he participated in a particularly violent demonstration on the Place de la Bastille; on February 13, 1962, he marched to protest the police massacre that had taken place, a few days earlier, near the Charonne Métro station. To all this one can add various meetings in Rome, Brussels, and at the Mutualité, and depositions at trials where his voice and his prestige were needed —Georges Arnaud's trial in June 1960, and the Abbé Davezies's in January 1962. "The Algerian war was *his* war," Roland Dumas would say twenty-five years later. "The Spanish Civil War passed

Sartre by, as did the Popular Front. The Resistance? Yes, but so little. . . . He missed all the important political events of his time except the Algerian war, which was, in a way, the meeting of a great cause and a great personality."[57]

S ARTRE DID not attend the ceremonies that, on July 1, 1962, cele- brated Algerian independence because he was busy working on his autobiography. First published in two installments in *Les Temps modernes*— October and November 1963—*The Words* was brought out by Gallimard in April 1964. This book, which many felt was Sartre's masterpiece, was nearly missed by his regular editor. "One day, during lunch," says Robert Gallimard, "Sartre parenthetically told me: 'I'm in the process of writing my autobiography; an English publisher asked me for it.' "[58] At first, Gallimard gasped, though he knew that coming from Sartre, this was more an awkward move than deliberate treason. An hour later, the contract for *The Words* was signed. The book was published in the spring of 1964. It immedi- ately received unanimous critical praise. "Sartre Hates Jean-Paul"— "Who Is Sartre?"—"Sartre and the Impossible Biography"—"The Passion of the Explicable"—"Nobody's Son"—"Young Jean-Paul" —"Jean-Paul Sartre, Destroyer of His Childhood"—"A Work of Exorcism"—"The Anti-Hero and the 'Salauds' "—"Sartre Has Tricked Us"—"Me, I Say, and That's Enough"—"The Limits of Autobiography"—"What Does Sartre Think of It?"—"I Have Lived"—"Auto-Sartro-Graphie." Headlines poured forth as if they were covering a story for the gossip columns.

Everyone felt directly and personally implicated in the work. In an "Open letter to Jean-Paul Sartre," Alain Bosquet wrote to the author: "You have just given us a masterpiece. *The Words* reminds us that you are a writer, even though you have long tried to forget it. . . . We have the urge to cry out 'thank you,' in the name of this most beautiful and lasting gift: a harmonious use of the beautiful French language. . . . Beautiful, pretty, lovable . . . It does not matter! There you are now, converted to that prestigious status even if—and we fear this—it means you'll soon return to your demons: thought, good, evil, the desire to be useful to your contemporaries."[59] Except for the conservative Jean Dutourd, who found the style "vulgar," nearly everyone felt that Sartre had recovered the talent of *Nausea* and *The Wall*. Again and again, readers wondered why the writer had to use ironic distance to tell the story of his own childhood.

Coquetry? Supreme pride? Availing himself of the most sumptuous literary tools he had ever used, Sartre devoted two hundred and thirteen pages to celebrating the death of the notion of literature he had so much respected as a child: "What the hell is going on here?" Bernard Frank wondered. Everybody was similarly puzzled. The mode was altogether unexpected: self-critical, ironic, self-distancing. *The Words* was Sartre's official farewell to literature, his version of a childhood that he attacked with nostalgic rage, and appropriated with the supreme pride of the only child. At that time, in 1964, except for his family—Mme Mancy, who did not deprive herself of the pleasure of reminding him that he had "never understood a thing about his childhood," and his Aunt Adèle, who did not hesitate to write a scandalized letter about his wretched portrayal of the Schweitzers—nobody could have questioned his family portrait, the writer's interpretation of the sociocultural conditions that went into the genesis of the child-genius. No one knew what he had left out or why. No one could have undertaken a counterinvestigation or dismantled the skillful architecture of the book, with its incoherent chronology, its errors in dates. For instance, did the Sartre family move to the Rue Le Goff in 1917 or in 1919? Did the episode of jealousy in Arcachon happen before or after World War I? Sartre must have felt great joy in prancing about freely, as he did with his Nizan, through territories he believed to be his alone. "Private property," perhaps the only form of it he ever laid a claim to, was what these pages suggested.

The numerous interviews he gave to all those who asked for them did not make things easier for the critics. Scarcely had the readers had the time to ingest the two hundred and thirteen pages of *The Words* than Sartre came back in full force with additional interpretations, new formulas. This period of his life—from two to twelve— had been, until then, the most unknown, the most mysterious. Now it became the most illuminated, the most eloquent. His was a very elaborate self-defense strategy: one scarcely had time to admire the technique, the virtuosity, the general structure, to discover new data, locate leitmotifs, paradoxes, felicitous formulas, and already, Sartre had escaped. He had escaped to a place where no one, not even those closest to him, could enter. In his discretion, he never spoke of this secret place. He had found the best way to mislead his pursuers: a verbal hyperlogorrhea that said a lot about little and left a great deal unsaid.

"It is the story—mine—of a man of fifty, the son of petty bourgeois, who was nine years old on the eve of 1914 and who had already been marked by this first prewar period. Between the two wars, he pursued his studies far, but continued to live in ignorance of his life's meaning. He was the plaything of mystification, until, one morning, he woke up to find that one could become the plaything of circumstances."[60] Since the beginning of his work on *The Words*, since 1955, he had shared certain themes of the book with the press. "I am not sorry nor do I disown my earlier work," he explained to Jacqueline Piatier, of *Le Monde*. "There isn't a single work of mine that I disown. . . . What I was sorry about in *Nausea* was my distance from it. I stayed outside my hero's pain, preserved by my neurosis, which, through writing, brought me happiness. . . . But, had I been more honest with myself, I would still have written *Nausea*. Then, I still lacked a sense of reality. I have changed since. I have served a slow apprenticeship. . . . I have seen children die of hunger. In front of a dying child, *Nausea* has no weight."[61]

What no one could know by reading this fluid text was that the manuscript of *The Words* had been belabored, had been the object of many drafts, reformulations, corrections, cuts, revisions . . . and Corydrane. It had demanded a great deal of patience, the patience of an artisan, such as Sartre had never had before and would never again have with any of his works. One day, aware of the limits of his own capacity for self-analysis, Sartre had said to Pontalis: "You know, J.B., I'm in the process of writing my autobiography, *Jean sans terre*. I record my dreams and try to interpret them, but I don't think I can go deep enough by myself. I'm wondering whether I shouldn't undergo . . . psychoanalysis . . . with you, maybe." He had said it in passing, without really dwelling on it. Twenty seconds, at most. "I don't think you should do it with me," Pontalis had gently answered. "I know you too well, Sartre." The matter had rested there. Twenty-five years later, J.B. Pontalis would agree, for the sake of this biography, to work on the dreams that Sartre used to dictate to Arlette Elkaïm upon waking. Most of these dreams seemed to focus on the question of immortality, incompletion, recognition: "I had to give a four-part lecture in a foreign country. I left after the third part, wondering whether they understood that I had not finished" reads the dream of December 7, 1960. December 21, 1960: "I was at a banquet organized by a foreign university where I had spoken the previous evening. Beside me was the president of the university, who told me 'We've set aside funds to erect a statue in the garden.' 'I know,' I answered, 'but in a few years I'll either be forgotten or too well known.' " January 12, 1961: "A very famous black musician to whom I had been listening kept repeating the same bars 152 times. I did not think he should have repeated the same bars so many times, and said to myself: 'He must really have a devoted public to be able to do that!' " "Dreams from on high," Pontalis would comment. They were an astonishing counterpoint to Sartre's repeated claims that he cared neither about his audience nor about his fame and his posterity. They had therefore remained secret, sheltered from all fierce analysis in Arlette's small notebooks. Sartre never underwent analysis, not even with Pontalis. A quarter of a century later, however, Pontalis would humorously agree to give us a hint of his interpretations, but professional discretion prevented anything more. "I always interpreted 'Jean sans terre' as 'Jean sans père.' . . . And by the way, you know that Sartre called me 'J.B.' like everyone else. . . . So, what was his father, Jean-Baptiste Sartre, called? J.B. . . . Interesting."[62]

The literary surprise provoked by *The Words* was followed soon after by another surprise on an international scale: his refusal of the Nobel Prize in October 1964. A surprise that must have seemed almost a paradox to any outside unacquainted with Sartrean logic. And yet in the context of the path Sartre had chosen for himself this move makes perfect sense. "Double for Jean-Paul Sartre," runs the headline of *L'Aurore*: "1) He Gets the Nobel 2) He Refuses to Accept It." This interesting combination provoked many contradictory opinions, as was usual when it came to Sartre. The major right-wing papers reacted with chauvinism, proud that such an honor should have been granted to a Frenchman and congratulating themselves for the decision of the Nobel committee. In a column of *Le Figaro*, Thierry Maulnier, of the Académie Française, wrote that Sartre was, nonetheless a "gold medal." "Whether or not one agrees with Jean-Paul Sartre's thought," he added, "it is certain that no French writer of his generation, and perhaps no writer of his generation anywhere in the world, has enjoyed or continues to enjoy a reputation and a public equal to his among the contemporary intelligentsia. . . . Sartre's fame depends on the work of a philosopher, a novelist, a dramatist, a critic, a political and even a polemical writer."[63] On the front page of *Le Monde*, in his daily column, the writer Robert Escarpit gasped with astonishment at Sartre's refusal of the prize: "Sartre to the Stake," read his brutal headline. "Sartre is wrong. And now he's trapped."[64] Of course, there were also wicked tongues. André Maurois in *Paris-Jour*: "Coat and tails do not suit him and one must dress up to receive the prize." Or better yet: "He wants to avoid making

Simone jealous." In *Rivarol*, the former collaborationist writer Lucien Rebatet wrote: "Each of Sartre's decisions is a combination of truisms, sophisms, priggish pedantry, evasions, pride and fear, mixed with an indefatigable genius for crankishness. But, whatever one might say about Sartre, he has never done anything for the money. And that, at least, puts him above that old moneybags in Malagar [François Mauriac], who is, on all counts, truly repugnant."[65] There were, also, those who explained that Sartre had refused the prize to get more publicity, and that he was refusing it because Camus had gotten it before him.

That Camus should have received the prize before Sartre made perfect sense, given Alfred Nobel's will: he had wanted to award the prize to works with "humanist and idealist tendencies." Similarly, Roger Martin du Gard had received it before Gide. The French Nobel prizes in literature between Gide and Sartre: Mauriac in 1952, Camus in 1957, Saint-John Perse in 1960. Strangely enough, after Sartre's refusal, the Swedish Academy awarded no more prizes to French writers (not counting the Francophone Irish Samuel Beckett) until Claude Simon received it in 1985. Did the academy interpret Sartre's gesture, which had not been intended to cause a scandal, as an insult? Was Malraux, who did not receive the prize in 1969, a victim of Sartre's refusal?

The 1952 Nobel winner, François Mauriac, once again gave a tribute to Sartre's gesture in his *Bloc-Notes*: "He has given his reasons to the city and to the world without inflating his words, keeping a most appropriate tone, as should a well-educated bourgeois who knows what is due to honest people who award you such a laurel. But above all, Sartre has been able to avoid ostentation: this was the danger of his gesture. . . . This great writer is also a true man, and therein lies his glory. . . . A true man: one does not find them everywhere, not at the editor's desk nor in publishers' offices. It is because he is a true man that Sartre can touch even those most alien to his thought and most hostile to the side he has taken." Mauriac's analytical clarity points, mostly, to one thing: the Nobel, even though refused, brought back a few old friends who had chosen to keep their distance from the more recent Sartre. "I interrupt myself here," Mauriac goes on more and more lucidly, "to brag and admire myself for honestly admiring this philosopher who, as a first step in his literary career, tried to wring my neck."[66] It was as if a rejected Nobel were worth more than an accepted Nobel, and, retrospectively, justified all Sartre's mistakes, all his excesses. René Naheu, his friend from the Ecole Normale and by then director of UNESCO, wrote an article in *Le Figaro:* "Would I have been surprised, forty years ago, at the beginning of our friendship, if someone had predicted that one day he would receive this great distinction? Not in the least. And I understand and completely accept the reasons for his refusal." He was praised, supported, congratulated.

But there was more to the story of Sartre's refusal than it had at first appeared. Sartre had found out, from an article in *Le Figaro littéraire* that the Nobel committee was about to award him the prize. He had immediately written to inform the committee of his irreversible decision not to accept it, and to ask them to revoke their choice and not to make it public. In the upper right-hand corner he had affixed his name, address, and the date, 14 October 1964. What followed was extremely polite, gentle, and handwritten, to avoid any suspicion of untimely self-importance. "Monsieur le Secrétaire," he wrote. "From sources that were only today brought to my attention, I have found out that this year I might have the good chance of being awarded the Nobel Prize. Although it is *presumptuous to assume the outcome of a vote* before it has taken place, I am nevertheless taking the liberty of writing you in order to clear up or avoid any possible misunderstanding. I would first of all like to stress, Monsieur le Secrétaire, my profound esteem for the Swedish Academy and for the prize which has honored so many writers. However, for personal and other, more objective, reasons, which it would not be appropriate to explain here, I wish not to appear on the list of possible laureates as I cannot and do not want to—not in 1964 or ever—accept this great distinction. Please accept my apologies, Monsieur le Secrétaire, and my most sincere respects."[67] By an unfortunate combination of circumstances, this letter did not reach its destination in time. Sartre had addressed it to the "Nobel Foundation," where it was received by an official, who forwarded it, without opening it, to the secretary of the Swedish Academy, who had just left on vacation. The decision to name Sartre as the Nobel Prize winner in literature for 1964 had been made *before* the vacation and was officially announced on October 22. Dr. A. Osterling, a member of the Swedish Academy, made the following announcement: "The Nobel Prize has been awarded this year to the French writer Jean-Paul Sartre for his work, which, in the spirit of freedom and in the name of truth, has had a great impact on our era." Later, a message from Stockholm tersely added: "The nominated laureate has just informed us that he does not wish to accept this prize. The fact that he is declining this distinction does not alter in the least the validity of the nomination. The Academy announces that the awarding of the prize cannot take place." The Swedes managed to remain sober and dignified even in the face of this unprecedented refusal.

The official announcement, on October 22, immediately unleashed a mad pursuit of Sartre through Paris. He tried as well as he could to escape journalists, photographers, camera flashes, and microphones, and relied on his publisher to decide on the best defense strategy. It was Carl-Gustav Bjurström, the Swedish writer, editor, and translator, who was granted the only interview. Claude Gallimard and Bjurström had met seven years earlier, when the Nobel was awarded to Camus. In the Gallimards' view, Bjurström was absolutely reliable. Sartre, Bjurström, and Claude and Robert Gallimard met at the Café L'Oriental, Place Denfert-Rochereau. Having dispatched photographers and journalists, Robert Gallimard loaded the other three into his car and rushed to the Mercure de France, where Simone Gallimard's office served as a welcome asylum. "I got ready to ask Sartre the questions I had prepared," says Bjurström, "but even before taking off his coat, he was off like a gun and deep into a lecture. I had no choice but to write like a madman, trying to leave nothing out."[68] Back at home, Bjurström drafted Sartre's statement in two versions, one in French and one in Swedish, and at the end of the day, went to see Beauvoir to have his text approved. "Sartre and Simone de Beauvoir reread the document together, corrected two or three things," Bjurström explains, "and then Sartre made a gesture that, retrospectively, seemed to me of the utmost civility: at the bottom of the French text and in his own hand he added the note 'translated from the Swedish.' To him it was extremely important not to offend the Swedish people: his statement was first meant for Sweden, and only then addressed to the world." This text, Sartre's only official act of clarification, was in fact intended for the Swedish Academy.

"I am terribly sorry," he said, "that this affair has taken on an appearance of scandal: a prize is awarded and I refuse it. The only reason for this is that I was not informed early enough about what was being planned. . . . I was not aware that the Nobel Prize is awarded without asking the recipient's opinion, and I thought I still had time to avoid it. . . . The reasons I am refusing to accept the prize have nothing to do with the Swedish Academy or the Nobel Prize itself, as I indicated in my letter to the Academy. I'm doing it for two kinds of reasons: personal reasons and objective reasons. . . . My refusal is not an improvised act. I have always declined official distinctions," and he cited as examples his refusal to accept the Legion of Honor after the war, and a chair at the Collège de France in the 1950s. "The writer must refuse to let himself be transformed by institutions, even if these are of the most honorable kind, as is the case here." Then he spoke of the "objective reasons," largely political in tenor: "Today, the Nobel Prize appears to be a distinction reserved to writers of the Western bloc and rebels of the Eastern bloc. . . . I do not mean to say that the Nobel Prize is a 'bourgeois' prize. . . . I know that, in itself, the Nobel Prize is not a prize limited to the Western bloc, but it is what one makes of it. . . . The only possible combat on the cultural front should aim at the peaceful coexistence of the two cultures, that of the East and that of the West. . . . I am particularly sensitive to the conflict between these two cultures. . . . Nevertheless, of course, I hope that 'the best wins,' that is to say, socialism."

This was all the explanation Sartre gave to the public, the Nobel committee, and journalists worldwide. And of course to the publishers of his works, who well knew that this first refusal of the Nobel Prize was, in the end, the best advertisement of all. The 250,000 crowns awarded to the laureate, was what "tormented" him the most. "With the sum the laureate receives, one could support a number of important organizations and movements. Personally, I would begin with the Apartheid committee in London." Robert Gallimard heard him also speak of the Tupamaros. But he refused the prize, and the money. Now, however, with twenty years of hindsight, it is possible to give a new interpretation of this gesture, quite different from the perfunctory explanations offered by Sartre himself. He refused the Nobel Prize for ethical reasons he did not feel like elaborating in a newspaper. His text was merely a shield: "personal reasons," "objective reasons," a seemingly complete explanation. Who understood that then? In a beautiful article from 1966, at once insightful and tender, Max-Pol Fouchet took up the real problems. "The Sartrean sorrow is not what his adversaries believe it is. I see it in the latest editorial of *Les Temps modernes*: an admirable elegy for Togliatti. . . . All Sartre's isolation is in this text. Why shouldn't the Swedish Academy have insisted on naming him laureate? No one as much as he has shown, both in his texts and in his acts, the solitude of the revolutionary writer. . . . We know a number of leftists who would have accepted the prize without feeling that they were taking part in a suspect 'collaboration'. . . . But M. Sartre *must not.* He who denounced the lie of worldly and external self-importance, was he going to take the road he had chosen for the protagonist of 'The Childhood of a Leader'?"[69]

Referring to the funeral oration for Togliatti, Fouchet was illuminating one of the most misunderstood Sartrean quirks: in an evasive gesture of freedom and pride, Sartre had refused to be embalmed alive, to be made into a living statue and prematurely canonized, even though he wove lyrical funeral wreaths for those friends who had died, definitively offering them monumental places in his pantheon. With *The Words,* with the rejected Nobel, he brought to completion the collection of events that made him Untouchable, while contributing to his seemingly endless contradictions.

In 1963 and in 1964, Sartre was famous throughout the world: he was the man of scandal, man of wisdom, man of freedom, man of truth. He was the one who had refused the Nobel, a hero, the one nothing could touch. But never, during his entire literary career, had he had as few contacts with other intellectuals, his contemporaries. In Paris, in the Latin Quarter, he seemed rather a has-been. In 1963, 1964: Sartre's image had noticeably changed in the French intellectual sphere. Some dated the change to the debate at the Mutualité, on December 9, 1964. Organized by the newspaper *Clarté,* the meeting addressed the question "What can literature do?" It brought together, besides Sartre and Simone de Beauvoir, writers from the *Tel Quel* group such as Jean Ricardou and Jean-Pierre Faye, and still others such as Yves Berger and Jorge Semprun. "It seemed that Sartre was then at his zenith," says Louis Audibert, then a *khâgneux* at the Lycée Louis-le-Grand. "When he came to the podium, he was greeted with cheers; but, at the same time, there was a sense that others, Foucault, for example, were quickly taking his place."[70]

That's when the rupture that was increasingly separating Sartre from the intellectual currents of his time might have occurred. Disappointing discussions, mechanical political involvements, frequent refusals of direct confrontations: Sartre seemed to be drifting. He did not seem to take much interest in the currents that emerged in the 1960s: Lacanism, formalism, structuralism—he followed none of these paths. It was disappointing, then, to hear Sartre or those close to him utter formulas that minimized the importance of Michel Foucault—"a positivist in despair"—or that, in the name of History, passed up ethnography, linguistics, and psychoanalysis. Even though at the time France was excited over Lévi-Strauss, Barthes, Lacan, Althusser, and Foucault, Sartre refused to confront their fertile methods of investigation in any way whatsoever, let alone with the open mind that would have been so useful in such a confrontation. He gave an interview to *L'Arc* that many still remember today, twenty years later: "Philosophy represents totalized man's struggle to recapture the meaning of totalization," he said. "No science can replace it, for each science applies itself to a well-delineated aspect of man. . . . Philosophy is the investigation of praxis, and as such, the investigation of man. . . . the important thing is not what one does with man, but *what he does with what one has done with him.* What one has done with man, these are the structures, the signifiers, that the social sciences study. That which he does is history itself. . . . Philosophy is the hinge."[71] Once again, Sartre took up and reaffirmed the same philosophical credo, in a statement of principle that is both weak and globalizing. In this way, he managed to bypass any debate with the epistemologies of rupture and logical empiricism. "He could never stand a confrontation," Raymond Aron had already observed, referring to the Sartre of the twenties. Indeed Sartre could never stand to look directly at many of the esthetic and intellectual movements that were akin to his own thought. By denying them or appropriating them—"the radical impulse to overtake" of which Pierre Bourdieu speaks—he passed them by, untouched and ill at ease. Among the things he bypassed were the group "Socialism or Barbarism" and the formalism of the sixties, without actual effrontery, without actual antagonism, but with a kind of uneasiness similar to what he had shown after Merleau-Ponty's death.

Sartre's bizarre relationship with psychoanalysis is even more symptomatic of his slippage into isolation. When in 1966 he was questioned about Lacan's statement that "the unconscious is the discourse of the other," Sartre salvaged psychoanalysis via intentionality: "There is no mental process that is not intentional," he affirmed, "or that is not bogged down, deviated, and betrayed by language; but, reciprocally, we are the accomplices of these treasons which constitute our depth."[72] Only years after this declaration, a radical and definitive conflict was to terminate Sartre's false debate with psychoanalysis. Only one opponent managed, it seems, to corner Sartre—but only once—in a true intellectual confrontation, and that was Louis Althusser. In 1960 or 1961, Alain Badiou had asked Sartre to give a lecture at the Ecole Normale. Jean Hyppolite, the director at the time, had suggested they invite Canguilhem and Merleau-Ponty to listen to him. The "cayman" of philosophy, Louis Althusser, was, of course, also there, with all his students. "Sartre spoke of the 'possible in History,'" Régis Debray tells us, "then

Althusser answered him. It was Althusser, for once, who held the more dialectical position, embracing Sartre's thought. 'The Sartrean cogito,' he said, 'was difficult to maintain within a Marxist conception of History.' "[73] According to Régis Debray, then a student in philosophy, Althusser won this round. Canguilhem noticed in particular the "treachery of the questions that Althusser's students asked."[74] The Sartre-Althusser debate remains an extraordinary moment, one that none of those present ever forgot. Unfortunately it was never published.

Several years later, Sartre adapted Euripides' *The Trojan Women* for the Théatre Nationale Populaire. As he had done with *The Flies*, he took ancient tragedy and set it in a contemporary political context. Troy was the third world; the enemy was Europe. The Trojan chorus, like a long lament, an obsessional plaint, expressed the mothers' sorrow. Allegories, lyric incantations, this great oratorio on war and oppression was one of the plays that developed public interest in popular political theater. "The dominant theme of my play," Sartre remarked, "is the condemnation of war in general, and of the colonial enterprise in particular." Michael Cacoyannis directed, with a cast that included, among others, Eleonore Hirt, Judith Magre, Françoise Brion, and Nathalie Nerval. "Europeans, you are massacring Africa and Asia," said the women of the ancient chorus, full of dignity and ceremony. "Barbarians," they continued, "they know now that they died for nothing." In this pure and poetic play, Sartre achieved an acutely personal form of expression; after all, his familiarity with Greek myths had begun early, in his grandfather's library, as soon as he had learned how to read.[75]

*A*FTER THE two bombings at the Rue Bonaparte in 1962, an era was over: the apartment was sold. Sartre moved into a small studio at 222 Boulevard Raspail, just to the right coming from the Boulevard du Montparnasse and Le Dôme. It was a modern studio in one of the top floors of a modern building: one big wall full of books, a great leather armchair and a long worktable, thick and old—the kind of table used for meals in a convent—laden with manuscripts. From the table, one could see far into the distance, toward the Eiffel Tower. This new abode was Sartre's farewell to Saint-Germain-des-Prés, to the postwar period, to the existentialist explosion—his return to Montparnasse, where, from then on, all those close to him would meet: Beauvoir, Bost, Lanzmann, Arlette, Michel, and even Mme Mancy, who rented a small hotel room nearby. Somewhat later,

André Puig replaced Claude Faux as Sartre's secretary and Gorz replaced Marcel Péju on the editorial board of *Les Temps modernes.* In January 1965, Sartre decided to adopt Arlette Elkaïm. He lost two friends, Evelyne Rey, who committed suicide in 1966, and Simone Jollivet, who died in poverty on December 12, 1967. The postwar period and Sartre's forties were really over. Now in his sixties Sartre was feeling the losses, deaths, changes—perhaps these were some of the things that made him want to adopt Arlette. "So that, when I'm old, you'll push my wheelchair," he had told her when they were visiting Capri. With Arlette, who was in her thirties, Sartre was, in a way, showing his faith in the future. He knew that, whatever might happen, she would take care of the publication of his posthumous works.

The Untouchable had completed his journeys and sown his ideas. The Untouchable had embalmed his peers, woven wreaths for the dead, had made himself a great man on the corpses of others, and then had refused to let anyone freeze his work in a prize, in a label. The Untouchable had shelved literature as an accessory. He was now over sixty. He would soon sink into a kind of anarchistic jubilation, and curl up into the shell of his old fake-leather jackets in his tiny studio. The uneasiness that he showed during his trips, his distance from his former identity, the bad articles he agreed to write because he did not know how to say no, are nothing but early warning signs of the old age for which he was readying himself, more than ever attracted to social effervescence, younger generations, true friends, real discussions, real confrontations. The years when Sartre was the Untouchable will remain those of his apogee. The public will have a hard time understanding the new Sartre: a small old tramp carelessly wandering from the Closerie des Lilas to La Coupole, with "nothing in his hands, nothing in his pockets."

BETWEEN FLAUBERT AND THE MAOISTS

EVERY MORNING, toward the end of the sixties, the inhabitants of Montparnasse could watch Sartre go by on his daily rounds —breakfast at the café on Boulevard Edgar-Quinet, lunch at La Coupole, around three in the afternoon, then he would buy *Le*

Monde at the newstand on the corner of Raspail and Montparnasse. But nobody would have ever guessed that the famous little pedestrian with such regular habits was about to finish the last of his great crusades, a literary crusade he had been leading on the pugnacious intimacy of a messy table, covered with thousands and thousands of sheets of paper he had accumulated in the last thirty years. On the other hand, the inhabitants of Montparnasse had certainly noticed that he had changed his sartorial habits and had definitely abandoned his shirt and tie for a strange leather-and-knit jacket he wore over a colored polo shirt. The Nobel Prize had conferred on him a sort of anonymous celebrity by virtue of which he was simply Sartre— whether respected or feared, loved or hated. Back in Montparnasse, the sexagenarian writer went on with his life, an odd life, a double life more or less equally divided between his political and his literary activities.

The huge manuscript on which he has been working for so many years will grow bigger, in quality and in quantity, than anything he has written before. *Being and Nothingness, Saint Genet,* and the *Critique,* his heftiest tomes, are going to look like mere sketches next to his *Flaubert,* still in progress. One day, to both Sartre and his readers, they will retrospectively look like the major stages of a constantly evolving oeuvre of which *Flaubert* will be the supreme achievement. The first two volumes of *The Family Idiot* will be published in the summer of 1971. The third in 1972. Altogether, they will total 2,802 pages. They will be immediately followed by two more volumes of *Situations,* the eighth and the ninth. Among his last publications, these will be the most meaningful to him. And yet, none of them will arouse the interest of the critics, they won't sell well, and will hardly be read. Sartre's popularity has already started to flag. In the meantime, however, *Flaubert* is occupying every day, fully absorbing his attention. Sartre's connection with the student riots of May 1968 is an invention of the press, pure illusion. At that moment, Sartre is elsewhere, back in 1831, under the "bourgeois" monarchy of Louis-Philippe; he is with Flaubert, in a boys' school, somewhere between Rouen and Croisset, already resisting established authority.

Flaubert, music, his "family," and the various appointments his secretary, André Puig, schedules for him: Sartre channels all his energies into his writing, more vehemently and urgently than ever before. His visibility is limited to intermittent appearances prompted by his political commitments. On February 2, 1967, in Paris, he delivers a lecture against the Vietnam War in the name of the Russell tribunal he is heading; on May 2, he is in Stockholm; on May 19, he is back in Paris, on the platform of the Mutualité; on October 27, he is in Brussels, and the last week of November in Roskilde, in Denmark. On March 23, 1968, with Joseph Kessel and Laurent Schwartz, he participates in a demonstration of intellectuals against the war in Vietnam. In August 1968, with Bertrand Russell, he supports the boycott of the Olympic Games in Mexico City, and on December 19, 1969, he gives a press conference to denounce once again the "American massacre of Vietnam." During this entire period, he will continue to attack the Americans with both force and dedication. But he will also attack the Soviets: since the Algerian war and his collaboration with leftist groups, his anti-Stalinist and anti-Soviet criticism has been on the increase. "This is a real aggression, what international law would define as a war crime," he declares from Rome, in August 1968, after learning of the invasion of Prague by Soviet tanks. "Today, the Soviet model is no longer valid, stifled as it is by bureaucracy. On the other hand, the model that was evolving out of Czechoslovakia is very appealing. More than a mere expression of socialist civilization, Prague represents a hope."[1] A few months later, he officially accepts the invitation of the Czechoslovak Writers Union to attend the opening of his play *The Flies*, but in fact he goes to display his solidarity with them. "I've discovered great courage here, a solid reasonable hope that manifests itself in measured, conscious attitudes. Those who believe that the Czechoslovaks have been defeated are wrong. Despite the accidents of last August, the path they opened last January, after years of preparation, is strictly Marxist, and thus quite different from other liberal or bourgeois movements. It reveals the model for a more sophisticated form of socialism based on its democratic essence."[2]

These declarations in favor of the liberal endeavors of Czechoslovak intellectuals reassured Sartre's listeners in Prague, who, five years earlier, had been quite disappointed by the philosopher's participation in a Kafka conference sponsored by the Charles V University: "To us, he was like a pope or a Messiah," Ilios Iannakakis remembers. "A thousand young people had invaded the amphitheater to listen to him despite the innumerable police barriers. We had all read *The Roads to Freedom*. They had been banned from all our bookstores, but we had copied them by hand. We were even willing to forgive his flirtation with Marxism. . . . He walked to the podium and started speaking about socialist realism! We couldn't believe our ears. That day, Czechoslovak youth mourned the loss of Jean-Paul

Sartre."[3] After his declarations during the summer of 1968, and his subsequent winter trip, Sartre re-established his ties with Czechoslovak dissidents.

He increasingly committed himself to anti-Stalinist criticism and the defense of human rights. On January 7, 1971, for instance, during a short speech he gave at the Mutualité, he personally pledged his support to all persecuted Soviet Jews who were forbidden to leave the country. The following October, he reconfirmed his stance and signed a petition demanding that Soviet jews be allowed to emigrate. Also in 1971—because, among other things, of a dispute involving the dissident poet Herberto Padilla—he ended all connection with Castro and the Cuban regime. But, until the storm of 1968, Sartre was mostly concerned with the Vietnam War as the president of the Russell tribunal, representing intellectuals, lawyers, and union leaders from France, America, Germany, Great Britain, Pakistan, Japan, Austria, Turkey, and Italy, who met either in Sweden or Denmark and gathered documentation for the trial of "American war crimes." In Stockholm, Sartre spoke of genocide: "The American government is not guilty of having invented modern genocide, nor even of having . . . chosen it from among other possible and effective replies to guerrilla warfare. . . . The American government is guilty of having preferred, of still preferring a policy of aggression and of war, aiming at total genocide, to a policy of peace. . . . It is guilty of continuing and intensifying the war. . . . It is guilty, it admits, of knowingly carrying on this *cautionary* war to make genocide a challenge and a threat to peoples everywhere."[4] In his support of Vietnam and his condemnation of the American government, Sartre did not spare either his voice or his pen: he continued to express his opinions as a philosopher, an economist, an advocate, and an historian. And, of course, as a writer: "The documents contained in this book," he wrote in his preface to an album of war photographs, "amply demonstrate how the Vietnamese defend our dignity. What I see in the eyes of these men, women, and children attacked by the most powerful nation on earth is neither fear nor discouragement but anger."[5] After the Algerian war, this battle in favor of the Vietnamese FLN drew Sartre, as well as numerous student groups, away from daily French reality. May 1968 will bring them all back to it. But, in the meantime, Sartre is somewhere between Washington and Saigon, between Flaubert and the FLN that's fighting along the seventeenth parallel, between Croisset and Stockholm, desperately trying to alert people, until he will finally turn to de Gaulle himself.

"Dear Sir," he wrote on April 13, 1967, "Please allow me to draw your attention to the following facts. The tribunal formed last November under Lord Russell's initiative is planning to hold a second meeting in Paris between April 26 and the beginning of May. Up to now we have had no reason to believe that the French government may be against it." Written on squared school paper, in blue ink, this is probably the most relaxed and least conventional official letter he had ever written: his first letter to General de Gaulle. What he wants of him is very simple: a visa for Vladimir Dedijer, a Yugoslav member of the tribunal—a visa that the French government had previously denied him. "I want to believe, dear sir," the philosopher goes on, "that my fears are not justified and that our government will grant a visa to both Mr. Dedijer and all the other members of the tribunal who might find themselves in a similar situation, as well as to all those people who would like to be witnesses at the trial." "Mon cher Maître," the president replied by return mail to justify his refusal to let the tribunal meet on French territory. Things didn't, of course, end here. A few days later, in the course of an interview with *Le Nouvel Observateur,* Sartre exploded: "Only café waiters who know I write have the right to call me 'Maître.' If the president has found it convenient to address me by that title, it is simply because he wanted to stress the fact that he was speaking to the writer and not to the president of a political tribunal he refuses to recognize." And then, in a last outburst, he added, "Paradoxically, all these obstacles they put in our way further legitimize the existence of our tribunal and clearly prove one thing: people are afraid of us. Of course, not of Bertrand Russell, who is ninety-four-years old, nor of myself, who am pushing seventy, nor of any of our friends. If we were just a dozen intellectual simpletons playing at judging the world, they wouldn't bother us. So, why do they fear us? Because we are bringing up an issue that no Western government wants to confront: that of war crimes, which everybody wants to retain the right to commit."[6] This was the last battle Sartre led on behalf of the third world: after the Vietnam War, he would turn his attention back to France.

*I*N FRANCE, the Gaullist era is nearing its end. The regime instituted by the general in the wake of the Algerian affair in 1958 is now confronting a great wave of antiestablishment activities. A new university for the offspring of the postwar baby boom was under construction in Nanterre, on the western outskirts of Paris, in a large vacant lot that belonged to the army, next to a bunch of shantytowns inhabited by immigrant workers from the Maghreb. The first courses were taught in 1965. It is thus not surprising that the first outbursts of violence by students should start here. These ostracized students, these outsiders, aware of their marginal position, will be the first ones to register and express the troubles and contradictions of French society. Sporadic strikes, occupation of buildings, police repression, street demonstrations, and *contestation* increase, becoming more and more political. In May 1968, French society will experience its most violent shock since the beginning of the twentieth century. From May 18 to June 7, nine million citizens are on strike, and on May 13, 1968, the tenth anniversary of de Gaulle's return to power, one million two hundred thousand people demonstrate in the French streets—a human tide that no one seems able to stop. Politicized by the Algerian and the Vietnam wars, and violently opposed to the practices of Western communist parties, the French students try to find new revolutionary models elsewhere— in China, with Mao, in Cuba, with Castro, or in the more theoretical ideas of workers' cooperatives and permanent revolution inspired by Lenin and Trotsky. Whether Marxist/Leninist, pro-Chinese, anarchistic, or anarchistic/unionist, or Trotskyites, the movements of the extreme left will produce their theories, their political practices, their leaders, and their troops with the extraordinary speed of a fire in a windstorm. Their complaints against all bourgeois "watchdogs," the established left, the communist traitors, and the rotten capitalists will, in a very short time, involve all of French society, including communists, trade unionists, and workers.[7]

"France is bored," Pierre Viansson-Ponté, a journalist for *Le Monde*, wrote in a now-famous article on March 15, 1968. "It refuses to participate in any of the turmoil currently shaking the world. . . . Our young people are bored. Students demonstrate and fight in Spain, Italy, Belgium, Algeria, Japan, Germany, and even in Poland. They feel they have to conquer something, to protest something, and, at the very least, to confront absurdity with something equally absurd. . . . In France, the arguments, homilies, and apostrophes of our politicians appear rather comical to our youth. . . . General de Gaulle is bored. . . . Only a few hundred thousand people in France are not bored: unemployed workers, jobless youths, small farmers crushed by progress, and forlorn old people. . . . Isn't there any other alternative between apathy and incoherence, a deathly quiet and a rabid storm? The real aim of politics should not be the management of the common good in the least bad possible way. . . . it should be the opening of new horizons, a spur to action, even if it should take some pushing. . . . Ardor and imagination are as necessary as well-being and expansion."

Sartre was not bored. Steeped in his *Flaubert,* he continued his routine existence punctuated by visits to his "little mother," in her hotel on the Boulevard Raspail, to his adopted daughter, Arlette, in a flat close to La Coupole, to Michelle Vian, on the Boulevard du Montparnasse, to Wanda, on the Rue du Dragon, and, of course, to Beauvoir, whose duplex was only a five-minute walk away from his own studio. Every Sunday at noon, he had lunch with his mother, a ritual he enjoyed very much: pork roast with mashed potatoes and a strange cake called *étouffe coquin.* That year, thanks to Arlette, he rediscovered music: she was studying the flute and piano and was taking voice lessons. Every time Sartre paid her a visit, after his lunch at La Coupole, he would sit at her piano for one, two, three hours, and, at times, even longer, playing and singing along with Arlette as he once had with his own mother. One day, without any preparation, he played the entire score of Pergolesi's *Stabat Mater,* without making a single mistake. He loved playing Gounod's *Faust,* and, particularly, the song of the King of Thule, one of his favorite arias, and he would sing along with great brio. And there was also a good deal of Bach, Mozart, Wagner, Chopin.

The leaders of May 1968 saw Sartre as a writer, no longer an initiator and even less a mentor. "Some people thought Marcuse was our intellectual leader," Daniel Cohn-Bendit explained a little later. "It was a joke. None of us had read Marcuse. Some had read Marx, of course, and maybe Bakunin, and, among contemporary thinkers, Althusser, Mao, Guevara, Henri Lefebvre. The political militants of March 22 had all read Sartre . . . but their movement was not inspired by any author in particular."[8] "My relationship with Sartre has always been passionate," Alain Geismar admits. Since 1958, he had endorsed Sartre's anti-Gaullist texts: he is the one who initiates both Sartre and Simone de Beauvoir into the events of May. "Herta [a friend from March 22] and I got to Simone de Beauvoir's apartment around two in the morning," he remembers. "We were both delighted at the interest they were showing in our action. They made us talk for a very long time, maybe two hours, trying to find out what was going on and treating us like friends, with words of encouragement, disbelief, and admiration. . . . And yet, I didn't feel there was a real exchange going on between us. They listened to us, but didn't really *hear* us."[9]

That evening, Sartre was, in fact, elsewhere. Deep in his *Flaubert*, he followed the events from the outside, understood them, and, now and then, even supported them, recognizing, in them, ideas close to his own. How could he have failed to respond to euphoric slogans that put language, desire, and freedom in power? "Run, comrade, the old world is at your heels." "We want nothing to do with a world where starvation can only be swapped with boredom," one read on the walls of universities. "Let's go after bankers, cops, priests, and sociologists!" the walls of the city answered. A profusion of words, speeches, pamphlets, posters—every mouth had its say, everybody talked with everybody else. This new awareness, initiated by students, spread to all sorts of professions, all sorts of social milieus: radio and television journalists, the actors of the Théâtre de l'Odéon, high school students, bankers, metalworkers, farmers, fishermen, women, Folies-Bergères employees. They all began questioning their status, their salaries, and the hierarchy that governed them, buffeted by the words and formulas that swept France for months. Suddenly France was no longer bored. "Power is in the streets!" "Let's go all the way!" "The great spring cleaning!" "The imaginary is real!" "Be realistic, ask for the impossible!" "Life without boredom, pleasure without whoredom!"

"The solidarity we are here pledging to all the student movements in the world—movements that have suddenly upset the so-called leisure society so perfectly represented in France—is, above all, our answer to all the lies with which all the institutions and political organizations (with hardly any exceptions) and all the organs of the press and the rest of the media (with even fewer exceptions) have been trying, now for months, to alter said movements and to pervert them by ridiculing them." This text, almost a manifesto, was published in *Le Monde* on May 10, 1968. It was signed by Sartre, Blanchot, Gorz, Klossowski, Lacan, Lefebvre, Nadeau, and it intervened in the conflict between students and political power at a crucial moment: on the very eve of the night of the barricades, the very climax of that entire period. Sartre also, individually, expressed his unequivocal support of those students some had already described as "madmen." "These young people do not want to share the future of their fathers, that is, our own," he declared on Radio Luxembourg, "within a set of themes we know all too well . . . that is, a future that has clearly revealed our cowardice, our weariness, our sluggishness and servility, and our total submission to a closed system. . . . Whatever the regime, violence is the only thing remaining to the students who have not yet entered into their fathers' system and who do not want to enter into it. . . . For the moment, the only anti-establishment force in our flabby Western countries is represented by the students, but I hope that it will soon spread to all our young people. . . . Meanwhile, it is up to the students to decide what form their fight should assume. We can't even presume to advise them on this matter because, even if one has spent an entire life protesting, one is inevitably a bit compromised in this society."[10]

A few days after these declarations, Sartre met the anti-establishment leader of March 22, Daniel Cohn-Bendit, and their encounter was immortalized in the pages of *Le Nouvel Observateur.* Sartre played the role of the intelligent, enthusiastic journalist who, with his friendly questions, tries to stimulate his subject, to push him toward some clarity: the fear of the sudden relaxation of the movement with the approach of vacations, their relationship with the workers, etc., etc. . . . Sartre touched on a number of crucial issues and then concluded: "The most interesting aspect of your action is that it gives power to the imagination. Your imagination is as limited as everybody else's but you have more ideas than your fathers. . . . The working class has often imagined new ways to fight but always according to the particular situation it found itself in. . . . Your imagination is richer, and the formulas one reads on the walls of the Sorbonne prove it. . . . You have been able to create something that has astonished, upset, and denied all that has turned our society into what it is today. This is what I'd call the extension of one's potential. Don't give it up."[11]

Sartre's most interesting opinions concerning May 1968 appeared in two articles published by *Le Nouvel Observateur* at the end of June, "The Bastilles of Raymond Aron" and "The New Idea of May 1968." The two texts related Sartre's experiences as a teacher and a student, then attacked Raymond Aron's attitude. Through the authenticity of their personal testimony, these texts became true endorsements of the movement. They also indulged in a typically Sartrean description of the various characters in the event—sketches, caricatures. The students? "Quite unlike the image we have of them: Despite their radical attitudes, they are not troublemakers who want to smash everything into a thousand pieces." The current political regime? "The politics of cowardice . . . a call to murder. De Gaulle's decision to create committees of civic action is precisely that. . . . The president's invitation to murder has nothing to do with the students' violence. The old man got angry only when Mitterrand and Mendès-France called his political power into question. Till then, he was vaguely benevolent, unable to understand what was going on but willing to wait for the storm to blow over, sure that he could eventually bring everything under control." University professors? "They are always the same—even in my time—people who have written a dissertation they keep on reciting for the rest of their lives. But they fiercely cling to the little power they have: that of imposing, in the name of knowledge, their own personal ideas on others without allowing them the right to question them." Knowledge? "An elusive thing, never exactly what we think it is, always put into question by new observations, new experiences, new, better methods of approach." The university? "It should produce questioning men. . . . But we still have those ridiculous little islands, ex-cathedra courses, taught by men who have only answers." The scapegoat of both articles was Raymond Aron, Sartre's old schoolmate at the ENS. "When an aging Aron," he wrote, "endlessly repeats the main tenets of a thesis he wrote in 1939 to his students, without letting them express any criticism whatsoever, then he is exercising a real power that, however, has nothing to do with anything worthy of the name of knowledge. . . . We must abolish the current system. . . . We can no longer believe, with Aron, that to spend hours at one's desk, alone, thinking the same things for thirty years, is an intellectual exercise. Each teacher must agree to be judged and questioned by his pupils. . . . Now that France has had the opportunity of seeing a naked de Gaulle, it is time that students be allowed also to see a naked Aron. And he should not get his clothes back until he has agreed to be questioned."[12]

What had got into Sartre? Why did he turn Aron into the scapegoat of May 1968? And why did he have to go back to his twenties to do it? "You have no idea how many idiocies I was taught when I was a student," he writes. "I remember Gurvitch . . . and Brunschwig—we attended his courses at the Sorbonne because we found them more ingenuous than most. . . . Today, the university is no longer what it was thirty or forty years ago. . . . We weren't many, and, unfortunately, we considered ourselves an elite." The events of '68, disputing, as they did, academic pedagogy, static knowledge, note taking, and ex-cathedra courses, were clearly responsible for these nostalgic flashbacks in a man who, generally, shunned all sorts of reminiscence—the role of so many grandfathers endlessly re-

461

counting their wars, their salad days. "Why I mostly reproach the people who insult our students is that they fail to see that they are trying to express a new claim, the right to sovereignty. In a real democracy, all men must be sovereigns, that is, they must be allowed to decide what to do, not by themselves, each in his own corner, but in the company of others."

While Sartre was thus expressing his notions of democracy in the pages of various weeklies, he was also testing his limitations in public meetings with students. On May 20, 1968, he spoke to them in the amphitheater of an occupied Sorbonne. As soon as they heard about it, thousands of young people invaded the venerable, gold-trimmed room, heedless of all security considerations. Arlette, who accompanied Sartre, remembers it: "An incredible confusion, a smoky mess. Sartre was very tired, and not particularly eager to talk. He swayed as he walked. Physically he was not at his best." Nevertheless, once he was on the platform, nobody could have guessed it. Complete anarchy, the joy of unleashed talk, a downpour of questions, on all sorts of subjects: "What do you mean by democracy in a class society?" "What about the situation in Tunisia?" "Do you think that the French left could have, if not seized power, at least put itself in the position to do it?" "Do you think there are some cultural forms that should be junked?" Relentless, the audience kept pushing the philosopher to talk. "The French Communist Party has grown stiff and sclerotic. No action is any longer possible from it. That's why France has so many stereotypes of the left. The CGT likes to follow, so it followed your movement. Above all, it wanted to avoid the wild democracy you have created in the face of all the old institutions. What is happening now is a new social concept based on true democracy, a fusion of socialism and freedom."[13] All codes abolished, everything was possible in that incredible confusion. The chairman tried to put some order into the discussion without having any real control over it. "Comrade Sartre, are you on the side of the fighting workers?" He was asked by somebody in the front rows. Then a TV camera appeared, blinding the speaker with its lights. The commotion suddenly increased. "Shut down that damn camera!" "It's a documentary for the factories." "Shut it down! Jean-Paul agrees." (No one in Sartre's most immediate circle of friends had ever called him Jean-Paul.)

He answered all the questions without, however, making any new declarations. His was mostly an act of supportive presence. He did not say much except that he was there in total intellectual communion with them inside this symbolic Bastille, the Sorbonne, they had seized from established power. "You must reinvent your tradition," he added, "a tradition worthy of this cultural revolution." This was his statement of solidarity, his only advice. The last question embarrassed him: "Comrade Sartre, what do you think of Marcuse's theories?" "Look, this is hardly the place to talk about it. He is a philosopher. . . . Marcuse believes that the only elements that can change a society are marginal. 'Our hope can only come from the hopeless,' he writes in his latest book, *One-Dimensional Man.* Not only do I agree with him, but I think this is one of the meanings behind student revolts." His voice went on, slow and poised, lingering on the words it wanted to stress. "I'm going to leave you now," he finally announced despite the shouts and the protests. "I'm tired. If I don't go now, I'll end up saying a bunch of idiocies. I like this kind of informal debate between students and writers. This is only the first one, but I am sure there will be other ones. Goodbye." Outside the room, in the hallways and in the main yard, more people had been able to hear him talk, thanks to the loudspeakers that had been installed on the capitols of all the columns, behind every door. Raphaël Sorin had brought along his uncle, Elias Canetti, who happened to be passing through Paris. "Canetti listened to Sartre from the yard of the Sorbonne," Sorin remembers, "but we couldn't hear much. All we could really hear and recognize was Sartre's voice, symbolic and precise. Canetti thought that very few writers could have had such an extraordinary appeal to students."[14] Despite his advanced age, sixty-three, Sartre had an impact on the students who had gathered at the Sorbonne. But a few months later, a little snag, a minor event, showed that his power of persuasion was also quite limited, and his influence much less real than it had seemed.

"Sartre, be clear, be brief: we have to discuss the adoption of a number of regulations." These words were scribbled on a sheet of paper, abandoned on the lectern of the Mutualité just before Sartre's speech on February 10, 1969. Sartre saw it before he started to speak. A few days earlier, he had been contacted by Jean-Marcel Bouguereau, Jean-Marc Salmon, and André Glucksman: would he be willing to participate, with Michel Foucault, in a meeting to protest the expulsion of thirty-four students from the university? He might also want to say a few words about the new law concerning academic reforms proposed by Edgar Faure. "Sartre immediately agreed to come," Jean-Marcel Bouguereau remembers. "He asked us to show him all our files so as to have a clear idea of the situation. We dropped them off at his door one evening, and he spent the whole night browsing through them. He drew a lot out of them for his statements."[15] That day, the Mutualité was crammed with students; on the platform: professors and student representatives. It was a rather banal meeting whose agenda involved a number of debates concerning attitudes to adopt in response to the government's latest measures. "I immediately realized I had nothing to do there," Sartre wrote just a few days after the meeting. "What measures to adopt —that was none of my business; they should have discussed this with their peers."[16] Sartre knew exactly how to explain this first gesture of scorn on the part of his favorite public. He was Sartre, true, but what was Sartre to a crowd of twenty-year-old students who had probably never even read him? And what could he say in a meeting whose main participants seemed to have so little in common with him—different age, different class, different interest. Hadn't he already given them all his moral support? And wasn't that all he could offer them? "I simply told them that they should fight the press on its own grounds, and tell the workers, and even the petit bourgeois why they refused the Faure Law. But I disappointed them, and I know why: their friends had been judged arbitrarily and they wanted to answer violence with violence and not waste their time analyzing some law." Did February 10, 1969 mark a definitive decline in the popularity of the writer? "Sartre . . . be brief."

Not only did Sartre remember the lesson, but he also spoke of it publicly, playing the role of the devil's advocate against himself. He addressed refractory parents: "Your children are your only future. It is up to you either to massacre them or let them save you, because, I can assure you, you won't be able to save yourselves. In any case, remember that if your children are revoluntionaries, it is because their destiny was shaped by your cowardice. They won't explain this to you. . . . Their words poured out last May, they got drunk on them, and now they have nothing else to say to those hardened, rotten, battered children we call adults. We will explain it to you. But who is 'we'? A few adults who are either less rotten or more aware of their rot."[17] These words are reminiscent of his preface to Nizan's *Aden Arabie*. And Sartre, the Untouchable, newly put into question by his eternal friends, Sartre, the historical monument whose marble has just been chipped, Sartre manages to find a way out of this regrettable incident: he assumes the role of the mediator between the students and their fathers. He, who could be these rebels' grandfather, immediately assumes the role of the doting elder and sides with the grandchildren against their parents. We remember his boxing matches, and the picnics on the beaches of Le Havre, when he enjoyed toughening his students—then only five or six years his junior. We remember his glasses of beer and his long discussions with the young men from the Lycées Pasteur and Condorcet, thirsting after knowledge. He had always, even in his forties and fifties, looked for the approval and the company of the young. Indeed, those exchanges seemed to provide him with the opportunity of relentlessly putting himself into question, an often painful process, which, however, he never eschewed, probably because of his "famous Sartrean masochism." At the beginning of the 1968–69 academic year, he was again contacted by Geismar, about a newsletter sponsored by different leftist organizations on the theme May Is Still Alive. Geismar explains, "I wanted to pursue that crazy talk I had with him that night in May and know whether he was willing to work with us in what we called the 'movement.' We had lunch together, and I asked him whether he wanted to contribute to our newsletter, *Interluttes* [Inter-struggles]. . . . I realized there was a misunderstanding between us: he spoke of May as if it were a positive coalition of opposing groups trying to achieve a consensus . . . whereas, in fact, we were living through the rebirth of these groups as they metabolized into a real movement, but as a difficult search."[18] Through exchanges and discussions, several years later, they finally did find a consensus and some common tools.

And yet these images of Sartre in his worn fur-lined jacket, speaking at the Sorbonne and the Mutualité, these images of a man always ready to endorse certain political causes are far from giving us an idea of the life he leads or of the interests that absorb him in the course of these years—'68, '69, '70. The center of his life throughout this period, his only true passion, is his monumental *Flaubert,* which he is now on the verge of finishing. Despite all appearances, his interest draws him neither to the events of May—by now he is back on the margins—nor to surface militarism—to which he lends himself rather mechanically. His real and only passion is this *Flaubert,* on which he has now been working for over thirty years and on which he has accumulated thousands and thousands of partially filled pages that he is no longer able to organize.

The reconstruction of *Flaubert* initiates another period of hard work, tension, and drugs. He again turns to Corydrane, as he had done during the composition of the *Critique.* He becomes nervous, difficult. At times he bends his arms and flaps them repeatedly in the air, as if they were a pair of cropped wings, a most disquieting tic. He drinks and smokes, as is his wont in moments of stress. Some of his closest friends resort to all sorts of stratagems to calm him down. Arlette has a little notebook in which she makes him jot down, and sign, a number of promises: that he will never touch Corydrane again; that he is done with both alcohol and tobacco. She even sorts out his papers and types them up to give them some semblance of order, some clarity. As for Beauvoir, as usual she reads and rereads everything he writes, methodically erasing, correcting, commenting according to a tacit agreement she will always respect.

"*F*LAUBERT REPRESENTS for me the exact opposite of my own conception of literature: a total disengagement and a certain idea of form, which is not what I admire. . . . [Flaubert] began to fascinate me precisely because I saw him in every way as the contrary of myself. I found myself wondering: 'How was he possible?' " In an interview with the English journal *New Left Review,* a year before the publication of *The Family Idiot,* Sartre tries to enumerate the various reasons that pushed him to undertake such a project.[19] "Why Flaubert?" Jacqueline Piatier, a journalist with *Le Monde,* had already asked him in 1964. "Because he is the opposite of what I am," Sartre had answered without the slightest hesitation. "I need to rub against everything that puts me into question. 'I have often thought against myself,' as I wrote in *The Words.* That sentence has never been understood, some have read it as an avowal of masochism. But, in fact, that's precisely how one should think: always questioning one's own assumptions."[20] Flaubert will be the ultimate evidence of the extraordinary endurance of the most fundamental Sartrean project.

So, Flaubert, and particularly "young Gustave," as he likes to call him, is the exact opposite of Poulou, "the little boy who is sure of himself, who . . . has had all the love that a child needs in order to become an individual and a self that dares to affirm itself."[21] Thus, the first three volumes of *The Family Idiot* are a thorough, maniacal investigation of Gustave's early childhood. Sartre delved into the individual careers of Flaubert's father, mother, older brother, and younger sister, into the social and economic characteristics of the family, into the historical events of the times, to find an explanation for the "oddity" of Gustave: a sandwich-child, a dolt, unable to read

466

at seven but already writing letters and books at thirteen. "Achille [the older brother] must have been a child prodigy.... And Caroline, the last born, learned without even trying," Sartre writes in the first pages of *The Family Idiot*. "Gustave is squeezed between these two marvels—inferior to both, he doesn't look good."[22] Weaving the most meaningful elements of Flaubert's family life with the more determining elements of national history, Sartre wrote an enormous book that reads like a collection of adventure stories. "As for the veracity of this work," he admits to Arlette, "I can't say. When I was a child, I used to tell myself stories, and I never really stopped. This might be the last story I'll ever tell myself."

If young Gustave is the opposite of Poulou, they have nevertheless walked together, hand in hand, from the very beginning. Sartre first read Flaubert when he was eight. Then he read him again at the ENS and at Le Havre. Then he rediscovered him intimately during the long, boring months of the "phony war." He reread *Sentimental Education* and devoted a few devastating pages of his notebooks to the "falsely beautiful style of Flaubert," delighting in picking on the "embarrasingly crass Norman wit," "the congenital weakness of the verb, dragging along its banality," the "platitudes," the "most infelicitous effects."[23] Sartre's relationship with Flaubert always wavered between love and hate, in full literary intimacy. During the Occupation, Sartre plunged into Flaubert's correspondence. He had already made up his mind, in 1943, that he would start writing on Flaubert. Besides the more personal reasons behind this decision, Flaubert seemed to provide him with a set of problems and a background that were crucial to his ongoing research. So much so that when, in 1954, he and Roger Garaudy undertook the project of comparing methods on a common subject, Sartre immediately thought of Flaubert. "In three months," Sartre will later say, "I filled twelve notebooks. What I did was both rapid and superficial, but I was already using psychoanalytic and Marxist methods. I showed the notebooks to Pontalis . . . and he said to me, 'Why don't you turn this into a book?' I went to work and produced a study of about a thousand pages, but abandoned it around 1955. Some time afterwards, I told myself that I couldn't go on abandoning my projects in the middle. . . . I decided that for once in my life I would have to finish something. I have continued to feel this need, this resolve to carry something through to the very end. The *Flaubert* has kept me busy for ten years, and though, naturally, I had other things to do, I can say that after I finished *The Condemned of Altona*, I worked on nothing else."[24] Sartre's relationship with Flaubert can hence be summed up in a few dates. 1943: the initial decision; 1954: its concrete implementation; 1956: the rough draft; 1960–70: its actual, daily composition. Before completing the final version of the book, which was then published in the spring of 1971, he had finished at least five manuscripts.

Sartre's interest in young Flaubert also came from the wealth of available information. "Few people, either in literature or in history, have left so much information about themselves. Flaubert's correspondence fills fifteen volumes, each over six hundred pages long."[25] And this without considering innumerable other documents, such as the Goncourts' journals, George Sand's letters, and, of course, Flaubert's early works, his "autobiographies," as Sartre liked to call them. A gold mine, yet untapped, that was going to beckon Sartre as a remote, unknown land draws a daring traveler or explorer. Young Gustave would be his Far West, a Far West that stretched from the boys school in Croisset to the family flat on the Rue du Gros-Horloge, in Rouen.

To tackle Flaubert, Sartre availed himself of all the methods and approaches he had already tried out. The main purpose of his project was "to abandon all the theoretical analyses that inevitably led nowhere, and try to produce a concrete example of what one could do."[26] The study of young Gustave, his innocence, his hysteria, his backwardness, and his clumsiness profited from all previous Sartrean researches, from *The Psychology of Imagination,* through *Being and Nothingness,* to *Search for a Method,* his entire philosophical oeuvre. "To me," he stated, "the study of Flaubert represents the continuation of one of my early works, *L'Imaginaire* [in which] I had tried to prove that all imaginary objects (the images) were an absence. Starting from Flaubert's life and art, I try to explain the relationships between the real and the imaginary. . . . at the bottom of all this, there is, of course, the question 'What was the *imaginary social world* of the dreamy bourgeoisie of 1848?' "[27] This new biographical endeavor would subsume and resume all the ones he has undertaken before, from Baudelaire to Tintoretto: it would be the absolute dream that, according to Sartre, is nurtured by every author.[28] "How can I study one man," he wondered, "with all these methods, and how are all these methods going to interact in the course of my study? [From this standpoint] my study of Baudelaire was inadequate, even bad. . . . My study of how Genet was conditioned by the events of his objective history is, similarly, very, very insufficient."[29] Thus, young

Gustave profited from the summit meeting of two specific approaches, Marxist criticism and psychoanalysis. "I would like my readers," the author admitted, "to be able to feel, understand, and know Flaubert's character both as totally individual and totally representative of his times."[30]

So, forty-five years later, Sartre returns to the very same concerns that had first assailed him during his years at the ENS when, for his advanced degree, he decided to deal with "The Image in Psychological Life: Its Role and Nature." The meaning of Sartre's oeuvre and of his creative project rests in the connection between that early text and the long, continuous research that, from 1927 to 1972, will keep digging away at the same basic problem, around the same root, relentlessly: how to explain the emergence of the symbolic within the social according to a radically phenomenological method? Or, in other words, how does an individual imagination articulate itself within the context of social imagination? *The Family Idiot* will not only be the consummation of Sartre's oeuvre, the culmination of his research, the conjunction of all his critical methods, but it will also lend extreme coherence to all he wrote in the course of his life.

"I would like my study to be read as a novel, because it really is the story of an apprenticeship that led to the failure of an entire life. At the same time, I would like it to be read with the idea in mind that it is true, that it is a *true* novel. . . . Even though I have done nothing else for several years, I have enjoyed writing the *Flaubert.*"[31]

According to Gallimard's sales figures, by 1985, the first three volumes, in the boxed hardback edition, had sold 27,000 copies, a surprising figure for a text that Sartre had announced as the most important of his entire oeuvre. Even more surprising was the poor press coverage the book received. Apparently, a friend of Sartre's, the editor at a major French weekly, told the author about the perplexity of the editorial board; they were unable to find a reviewer since all the people they had approached had balked at the size of the task. Could Sartre suggest somebody?

"Sartre . . . be brief." For a few years, Sartre had been quite marginal. Structuralism, Lacanism, Althusserianism: not one of these new trends had elicited any response, recognition, criticism from him. And this was not because he disapproved of his new colleagues—Louis Althusser, Jacques Lacan, Michel Foucault, Roland Barthes, Claude Lévi-Strauss—the new stars of the Latin Quarter. Not in the least: Sartre would always be very civil toward them, neither for nor against. He was simply not there. He accepted them, coexisted with them, let them be. But he remained silent. He was silent when Althusser buried young Marx's manuscripts. Silent when Lacan initiated the grand debate on language. He uttered only a few words when Foucault published his two masterpieces on madness and prisons. He was absent as if his contemporaries' intellectual concerns were quite extraneous to him: "A whole man, composed of all men and as good as all of them and no better than any," he had written at the end of *The Words*. And yet, when he wrote those words he was all alone, merrily pursuing his own personal project, his absurd, anachronistic dialogue with great men, with Flaubert, with eternity. Undaunted, he questioned the nineteenth century in a solitary exploration of the phenomenon of creation. Was Sartre no longer interested in his times? His times were no longer interested in Sartre. It was a little like a divorce, a great silence, a slow drifting apart.

Flaubert also meant historical commuting between the nineteenth and the twentieth centuries. Sartre's feet were stuck in the crises of the twentieth century, but his head was turned backward, toward the revolution of 1848, witnessing, day by day, the strikes, petitions, demonstrations that had shaken the bourgeoisie of Rouen in 1830. Did he feel closer to the students of May 1968 or to their counterparts in 1831? His work inevitably involved him in a comparison of the two historical situations. In the summer of 1968, sitting at his long, crowded table in front of the open window, Sartre writes of the student revolt in Rouen. In 1831, Louis-Philippe has gotten rid of Lafayette, thus opening the door to the reaction. And, indeed, just a few days before Flaubert entered the boys' school at Rouen, there was a real test of strength between the students and the administration. The official reason for the conflict was that the students refused to confess every morning. "My deepest respect," Sartre notes, "to these fourteen-year-old kids who had the courage to concoct such a strategy when they knew full well that they were going to be expelled for it. First they confronted the chaplain, then some other school official, and, finally, the headmaster, who expelled them. As they had hoped, this provoked a general outcry. Fourth-year students threw rotten eggs at the assistant headmaster and two of them were thrown out. The following day, at dawn, all the day students in the same class gathered and swore to avenge their classmates. The day after, at six in the morning, the boarders let them into the school: together they proceeded to occupy the buildings. In 1831! From the roofs of their fortresses they bombarded the building where the disciplinary committee had convened to decide what measures to take. In the meantime, the headmaster was kneeling at the feet of the oldest students, begging them—successfully as it turned out—not to support the occupants. The fourth-year students failed to obtain the reinstatement of their classmates, but they received the authorities' assurance that the people who had occupied the buildings would not be punished. Three days later, they realized they had been duped: the school was shut down. Just like today."[32] Thus the author kept drawing parallels between the historical reality of his book and his own times. And yet, during his encounter with Cohn-Bendit, when he was repeatedly pushed to draw the same kind of parallels, he had limited himself to a few laconic statements. Speaking of the workers' mistrust of students, he had noted: "Such a mistrust is not natural. It is an acquired trait. It did not exist at the beginning of the nineteenth century. . . . it appeared only after the massacres of June 1848." "In Billancourt," Cohn-Bendit had kept pushing him, "the workers prevented the students from occupying the factories."[33]

Fully absorbed by Restoration France, the riots of 1831, and the revolutions of 1848, Sartre was at once present and quite absent from the events of May 1968. He was about to start a thorough investigation of the sexuality of his victim, examining bit by bit every single detail to understand once and for all how Flaubert could, for instance, identify so thoroughly with Madame Bovary. "Flaubert's entire art," he explains, "resides in his sadomasochistic relationship with his characters. . . . He writes from inside his characters, and yet he speaks only of himself."[34]

But what, in fact, was this *Flaubert*, which some read as a monstrously stretched version of the *Critique of Dialectical Reason?* If, indeed, it was meant to be the summa that, all things considered, it would seem to be, then we must remember that it was an incomplete summa. Of course, all Sartre's works might be considered unfinished: *Being and Nothingness* is still waiting for its *Morale*, *The Roads to Freedom* their fourth volume, and the *Critique* its second part. The "Mallarmé" is also unfinished, as is the "Tintoretto" ("The Prisoner of Venice"), and, of course, the *Morale*. On the other hand, of all Sartre's works, only the fourth and fifth volumes of *The Family Idiot* — the first one bearing on *Madame Bovary*, and the second one barely sketched—were to remain unfinished for purely physiological reasons. In 1973, Sartre became blind and, thus, unable to write. And yet, with what ardor had he spoken of his new book! And with what certainty had he foreseen its completion just a few months before blindness struck him. "I've been working on my Flaubert for too many years ever to abandon it. I will finish it because it would be absurd not to, particularly considering that maybe, one day, and quite independently from its literary value, this book might prove useful to a lot of people. Who knows what culture will be like, later."[35] But he would never finish this book he cared for so much. The will of the writer would be defeated by his health, by the sudden night that fell on his left eye and swept away both Flaubert and Emma. "*The Family Idiot,* my most total failure," he would later explain, "has gone to join all my other truncated works. I wonder why I always plan books that are so much longer than the ones I actually write." And then, in a rare moment of abandon, he added, "One must always reckon with the life of writers: it always affects what they write, in one way or another, interrupting it, halting it. It is quite sad for an author."[36] Sartre would not finish his *Flaubert* any more than de Gaulle would complete his term. The president of the republic, abandoned by his people at the referendum of the spring of 1969, resigned, as expected. When he died, two years later, Sartre brutally noted, "I've never held him in any esteem."[37]

*I*NCOMPLETION, recognition, immortality: three important themes of *The Words.* The obsessions that appeared in the dreams of an age: Sartre would have liked to analyze them: he had briefly mentioned it to Pontalis, but then they had never spoken of it again. The editorial board of *Les Temps modernes* had opened up to psychoanalysis and had decided to publish certain texts proposed by J.-B. Pontalis even though Sartre kept maintaining that "the unconscious did not exist." And then, one day, in 1969, following a dispute over an article, Pingaud and Pontalis—"the right of *Les Temps modernes,* " as Sartre later dubbed them—left he editorial board. "I missed a meeting of the editorial board and then learned that the text was going to be printed," Pontalis calmly recalls. "I also learned that, after the decision was made, Sartre had added, 'This is going to piss off Pontalis.' Apparently, the board, in typical corporate fashion, had decided to back Sartre . . . in the end we reached a compromise."[38] Pingaud and Pontalis violently opposed the publication of a piece titled "The Man at the Tape Recorder," which the editorial board of the magazine had, however, decided to print. The compromise of which Pontalis speaks allowed for the publication of three different letters, signed respectively by Sartre, Pingaud, and Pontalis, next to the controversial text, after which, the two oppositionists would leave the review. "Psychoanalytic Dialogue" was the title of the piece on page 1824 of the April 1969 issue of *Les Temps modernes*. It appeared in the section of "Testimony," along with a brief explanation: presumably, the text —the transcription of a tape-recorded psychoanalytic session—had reached *T.M.* by mail.

"A.: Stay where you are, doctor! You're going to stay there and you're not going to pick up that phone; you're going to stay where you are and above all don't start threatening me with the lockup.

"Dr. X.: I won't threaten you if you leave this room.

"A.: I won't leave this room! I'm calling you to account. I mean it—and you'd better be able to account for yourself. I'm not doing this just for me, but in the name of . . . Come on now—sit down; don't let's get angry. You'll see? . . . You won't get hurt. I'm not going to bugger you!"

Fifteen pages of verbal violence and tension, the power struggle between analyst and analysand straining every line. "I am not a 'false friend' of psychoanalysis but rather a critical fellow traveler," Sartre explains in his text, to back up what he characterizes as a "liminal situation." Then, he attacks: "Analysts can explain the motives of all 'passage to action,' but have never bothered to consider the act that interiorizes, transcends, and maintains its morbid motivations in a tactical unity. They should reintroduce the notion of subject." This is the whole point: what Sartre refuses in the analytical situation is the objectification of the patient, of the client. "In England and Italy," he goes on, "A., the undisputable subject of this brief story, would find a number of legitimate interlocutors: there, a new genera- tion of psychiatrists is trying to establish a relationship of reciprocity between their patients and themselves . . . hopefully, one of these days the more orthodox psychoanalysts will also join them. In the meantime, let me introduce this 'dialogue' as a benign and beneficial scandal." Three years earlier, Sartre had agreed to write a preface to *Reason and Violence* by R. D. Laing and David J. Cooper, two antipsychiatrists' approach to some of Sartre's texts. "What particu- larly appeals to me in your book," he had written, "is your constant attempt to implement an existentialist approach to mental patients." Pontalis's reaction is terse: "What interests me is that Sartre should be fascinated by A.'s revolt against his feudal oppressor. But to conclude from that tragicomical fragment that it is time for all analy- sands either to follow the watchword read to Censier—'Analysands arise!'—or to emigrate to Italy seems to me rather excessive." This first consequence of May 1968 within the microsociety of *Les Temps modernes* was magnified by the press and further confirmed the leftist image Sartre liked to project.

*A*T FIRST, absorbed by Flaubert, Sartre had played only a minor role in the emergence of new leftist groups: he had mostly limited himself to attending a few meetings, expounding his own personal ideas like a distant echo. Neither mentor nor point of reference to the actors of 1968, he was merely a slightly worn-out fellow traveler, an old bourgeois humanist. The most sectarian, rigorous Maoist groups, those who, led by Althusser, turned to the original Marxist texts in order to dismantle all later interpretations and restore the real revolutionary principles, enjoyed ridiculing, in their papers, the practices of the stardom of intellectuals. Besides, they saw Sartre's Marxism as much too individualist and personal— a vague, pseudo-idealistic deviation—and profoundly mistrusted him. Their theoretical references were Lukacs, Marcuse, the first texts by Georges Lapassade, and, particularly, Althusser's work. They had read Sartre, but with skepticism. "As for me, nearly two years after May 1968," Sartre will later explain, "I was still trying to understand what had happened. I had not quite understood what they wanted, nor what role old fogeys like me were supposed to play. I had followed them, I had congratulated them, I had spoken to them at the Sorbonne, but it did not mean anything. I only began understanding them later, when I had a closer relationship with them."[39] This closer relationship begins when the Maoist groups start feeling harassed: their papers are constantly seized, their editors-in-chief are repeatedly arrested by order of Raymond Marcellin, the minister of the interior. Despite the political and intellectual distance that separates them from Sartre, they nevertheless decide to turn to him to shield themselves with his name and his prestige. On March 22, 1970, Jean-Pierre Le Dantec, editor-in-chief of *La Cause du peuple*— published by the Maoist group Proletarian Left—is arrested and his paper is seized. He is immediately replaced by a new director, Michel Le Bris, who is also arrested ten days later. The Maoists' problem is fairly simple: either they are going to let the minister of interior strangle them with his own hands, or they're going to find a way out, and Sartre is the way out.

But Alain Geismar refuses to see this appeal to Sartre as a last-resort stratagem. "Those who did not confine themselves to the notion of the proletariat in the narrowest sense of the term were hoping to find in him some exchange with a new kind of intellectual. So, the simplest thing was to approach the quintessence of the Intellectual and see whether such a thing was possible. Of course, Sartre's presence would have brought us other advantages, but we could easily have found another solution. . . . He made us feel as if our appeal were a great honor for him, and yet agreed to maintain the highest discretion about it. . . . On our side, we absolutely wanted him to commit himself, which he did, starting with that very lunch, by getting involved in a discussion with us."[40] The lunch in question took place at La Coupole on April 15, 1970: it included Sartre, Pierre Victor, and others. On April 28, 1970 Sartre agreed to become the editor-in-chief of *La Cause du peuple*. On September 23, he accepted the same position at *Tout*, the paper of the VLR (Vive la Révolution) group, and on January 15, 1971, at *J'accuse*. In the meantime, Parliament had passed the law against demonstrators, which, in turn, had allowed the minister of the interior to dissolve the Proletarian Left, on May 27, 1970. The alliance between Sartre and the Maoists was thus determined by circumstances, indeed almost demanded by them, without any prior ideological agreement. Logically, it could have had rather depressing consequences. Instead, for two full years, Sartre shared the militant life of his new Maoist comrades and fully lived a new radicalization of his political activities, wrote articles, paraded, testified, occupied factories.

La Cause du peuple was a four-to-eight-page sheet whose red and black characters on beige paper emphasized the aggressivity of its arguments. *"La Cause du peuple*, a revolutionary, proletarian, communist paper,"* the full title stated in between an effigy of Mao and a hammer and sickle. Sartre's name appeared on the last page, with the rest of the editorial board, but it was also appended, along with Simone de Beauvoir's, at the bottom of all the other pages, like a seal, a token of the inviolability of the publication. However, the alliance between Sartre and *La Cause du peuple* had its limits, as evidenced by the following detail. "Jean-Paul Sartre has decided to occupy the position of editor-in-chief of *La Cause du peuple*, " stated a box in the issue of May 1, 1970, "and he explains why in the following letter." "We must stop the maneuvers of the government which aim at the total ruin of this paper through confiscation and the spreading of rumors insinuating that its articles are a call to murder," Sartre allegedly declared. "By assuming the functions of editor-in-chief, I hereby affirm my solidarity with all those actions aimed at the expression of the revolutionary impulse that animates the masses. If the government wants to hand me over to the law, my trial will be political."[41] But a week later, the next issue of the paper carried the following correction: "Sartre's letter should not have read 'I hereby affirm my solidarity with all those actions,' but rather, 'I hereby affirm my solidarity with all those articles.' " Just a small detail, but enough to clarify the extent of Sartre's cooperation with the Proletarian Left: he would lend it his pen, yes, but would maintain a healthy distance from its political actions.

When Sartre allowed the paper to use his name as a shield, the titles had already become particularly violent and their style had assumed the tone—at least since December 1969—of frenzied proletarian romanticism: "We are the new partisans," they affirmed, thus participating, like everybody else, in the collective invention of an historical psychodrama. "Death does not blind the eyes of the partisans!" "Let's tear out the bars of our brothers' prisons!" And, to drive their point home, they shouted: "Long live the new Resistance!" "We want to overturn the capitalist system and build a proletarian France," was a relentless slogan whose counterpoint, on the last page, was a quotation from Mao: "The five continents rise up in thundering storms." A great crusade to track down bourgeois ideology, denounce it, fight it, and replace it with proletarian ideals; the determination to reveal, among other scandals, police abuses, the censorship of the press, and exploitation and hierarchical structures within factories; an appeal to proletarian violence as the only weapon with which to counter capitalist violence and stop the tyranny of the bosses and the police, and the illegal appropriation of capital by the state or the employer. A Marxist doctrine revised and amended by the Chinese Revolution, along with a great nostalgia for the Resistance. By the time the Maoists of the Proletarian Left had found a shield in Sartre, they were already well into the second year of their struggle.

What kind of an impact could a weary philosopher, who spent his days dissecting the neuroses of the most bourgeois French writer of the nineteenth century, have at the heart of this new ethics of revolutionary heroism? "A deputy can be lynched," "A boss can be imprisoned," the new partisans asserted. "Little bosses can be curbed." "The struggle for freedom should be waged in anger." One of the leaders of the Proletarian Left asked Sartre in December 1972, "Have you always been in control of the revisions of your thought?" His name was Pierre Victor, a pseudonym for Benny Lévy, who would eventually become Sartre's last secretary. "What bothers some of us," he continued, "is that you could be writing something more useful for the movements of May '68. . . . instead, you keep writing *Flaubert*. . . . wouldn't it be more appropriate if you wrote a popular novel?"[42] If Sartre had to confront new contradictions in his politics as well as in his writing, the Maoist groups did not miss any opportunity to remind him of how much he differed from the ideal revolutionary intellectual. Accusations, reproaches, all sorts of attacks: Sartre was not spared by his comrades. In their eyes, Sartre, at the age of sixty-seven, should have given up his book and the entire theoretical edifice he had constructed to become another kind of intellectual, with other projects, other manuscripts, other ideological premises. "I've been studying Flaubert for several years," he answered his questioner, "with techniques and methods I have tried to change. I don't think the masses would want to question that. [If I don't give up my work on Flaubert] it is simply because the three volumes I have already written need a fourth one. I have recently reread them and, at every page, I realized the work needs a conclusion." "But your theoretical interests," his interlocutor insisted, "don't you think they could move a little closer to the ideological demands of the revolution?" "Do you really think it is that simple?" Sartre replied wearily. "It is not enough for them to ask me to do it, I must also know what a popular novel is . . . and whether, in fact, it can be useful in 1972. . . . Were popular novels useful in the nineteenth century? Besides, you know, there is also my age. I'm old. I'll be very lucky if I manage to finish *Flaubert*. If I do, then I could possibly try my hand at a popular novel . . . but I need time. Since you demand my contributions fairly often, I have less time for myself. . . . There are lots of things one could do for you. . . . But, at sixty-seven, the most I can wish for is that I have enough time to see the revolution. The future is limited. And you ask me to begin a new literary career at my age!"[43]

This difficult exchange shows us a tenacious Sartre as determined as ever; clearly, nothing in the world could make him abandon his *Flaubert*. Tenacious, yes, but also tired; for the first time, he speaks of his age, his failing health, impending death. He sounds as if he had finally resigned himself to the evidence that even Sartrean pride, at sixty-seven, has a limit. He is no longer the same man who used to push himself as far as possible with the help of Corydrane and whisky, now, he has to take better care of himself, he must protect himself and admit he is tired. "[May '68] has come a little late for me," he admits in the course of the same interview. "Had it come when I was fifty, it would have been much better. . . . To do the kind of work you are demanding of me I should indeed be fifty. . . . The best time to get something out of a famous intellectual is when he is forty-five or fifty. You see, I can't even accompany you through an entire demonstration because one of my legs is no longer that good."[44] Quite an admission for a man who has always been known for his resistance to pain, and who never spoke of his limitations. "Anyway, I will only be operative for at most three or four more years. After that, if I went on mingling with active people, I'd have to be pushed around in a wheelchair, and I'd be in everybody's way. Age turns you into a Chinese vase. I'm not afraid of admitting it." Despite the difference in age, ideology, and experience that separated him from his Maoist comrades, Sartre shared with them a certain "concept of direct democracy"; this was, essentially, what had brought and bound them together. Through them, he would have the opportunity to try out various new theoretical approaches to political reality, and to test the limits of the revolutionary press.

Since May 1968, a number of well-known intellectuals had mobilized and were continuing to do so with appeals, protests, demonstrations, and other expressions of their opposition to the government in power. Sartre was often accompanied by Michel Foucault, with his polished skull, the gravel-voiced Maurice Clavell, and the lanky Claude Mauriac, François's son. But Sartre was alone when he was attacked by the French press for having agreed to be editor-in-chief of *La Cause du peuple*. The Gaullist paper, *La Nation*, explained it as a pathetic act of belated stardom: an aging intellectual's need to be in the limelight promoting himself. As for the communists, *L'Humanité* saw Sartre as having made a terrible mistake by endorsing the "vulgar provocations" of the left. Nothing new, hence, in the images of Sartre fostered by the two presses. Only one article tried to find a calmer, less polemical interpretation of this new Sartrean incarnation. Published in *Le Monde*, its title was "M. Jean-Paul Sartre and Violence," and its author was Raymond Barrillon. In Sartre's gesture, he appreciated "the risk run by a man who intends to remain faithful to himself," and saw a perfectly logical stage of Sartre's "political career," which, since the Liberation, had consisted of "a coherent sequence of motivated refusals," answering his "permanent need to put his solitude at the service of the oppressed, the solitary, the minorities." Then, he noted, "Whether we approve of it or condemn it, such a commitment deserves to be taken seriously. The Sartrean revolt deserves some reflection. We cannot laugh at a man who commits himself to a new cause at the very age in which most of his contemporaries would rather espouse a mellow philosophy of 'comprehension,' oblivion, and indifference."[45] With his respect for this combination of two sorts of values, on one side age and experience, on the other generosity and coherence, Barrillon drew a new portrait of old Sartre. His was the first public portrait of a new character who was beginning to impose himself on the media, of a new Sartrean role that would last until his death.

No sooner has Sartre agreed to protect the Maoist papers with his own inviolability, than events begin to overtake Sartre and his "family." On May 25, 1970, at the Mutualité, Sartre presides over a meeting to protest the arrest of the two previous editors-in-chief of *La Cause du peuple*, Jean-Pierre Le Dantec and Michel Le Bris: the paper will not be outlawed, but the court judges the two editors guilty. The decision of the court is immediately followed by unrest and violent demonstrations. On June 4, 1970, Sartre and his friends decide to found the Association of the Friends of *La Cause du peuple*, using Simone de Beauvoir and Liliane Siegel as fronts. On June 20 and 26, the association organizes a spectacular event: the distribution of the paper in the most popular districts of Paris. Both Sartre and Simone de Beauvoir are there, as well as a number of journalists, such as Jean-Edern Hallier and Jean-Francis Held, and theater figures, such as Samy Frey and Patrice Chéreau. Robert Gallimard, Eric Losfeld, and Claude Lanzmann will witness the whole thing in the role of "anonymous passers-by." The photographer from Gallimard shoots the entire event. First in front of the Alesia church, in the fourteenth arrondissement, and then on the Grands Boulevards, between the Rue du Faubourg-Poissonnière and Boulevard Bonne-Nouvelle—right in front of the billboard of the Cinéma Rex, advertising *La Vengeance du shérif*, a grade B western starring Robert Mitchum—Sartre and the twenty-seven other wild hawkers start pushing the paper on the passers-by.

"Read *La Cause du peuple*," "Read *La Cause du peuple*," Sartre approaches people, trying to interest them in the paper. "Read *La Cause du peuple*." He is timid at first. His voice is as resonant as usual, but somewhat faltering. "Read *La Cause du peuple*." More and more people come out of their offices, and Sartre starts taking heart in his new role. His voice acquires volume, assurance, even resonance.

"Read *La Cause du peuple.*" In ten minutes, Sartre has become an excellent hawker: he has guts, he almost screams. "Read *La Cause du peuple!*" Observers disguised as passers-by notice the strange metamorphosis. "He did his job like a real newsboy," Robert Gallimard remembers with great admiration. Then, the police arrive and drag them all off to the nearest station. After an hour and a quarter of identity checks, Sartre is released. "Double Standard!" run the headlines of *La Cause du peuple* on July 10. Sartre gave his own version of the story on the air: "Nothing happened. They arrested us and then questioned us because we were distributing *La Cause du peuple*, which, as you all know, is not a legal paper but rather a paper that is illegally seized every week. Then, they took us to the police station where we were treated very well indeed." "Were you trying to get arrested?" a journalist asked him. "No," Sartre answered. "In fact, I'm delighted I was released. It will allow me to take the stand at the trial of those who have been detained. I'm only trying to force the government to face its responsibilities."[46]

Did Sartre achieve his aim? He angered, bothered, and annoyed people, but did he manage to go as far as he did in the fall of 1960, during the Algerian war, when he became everybody's target? The fall of 1970 joined that of 1960 in the cyclical power struggle between Sartre and the minister of the interior. But this time Sartre went even further in his public provocation. The Geismar trial in which he was a witness opened on October 21. But he did not show up; instead, he sent a cable to the two magistrates of the 17th criminal court that read: "The chips are down, and I don't mean to say anything more than I usually do when I'm in a court. It is more important for me to take my stand in the streets, in the court of public opinion." And, indeed, that day he took his stand in the street, a deliberately provocative act by which he was trying to prove that state justice was only a ploy. On October 21, 1970, Sartre gave us the first in a series of images: a small, old man, wearing a white sweater, a beige leather-and-knit vest, and, on top of it all a lumber jacket with a fake fur collar, standing on a barrel of oil, holding a mike in his hand and haranguing the workers coming out of the Renault Billancourt factories. That same Wednesday, at 2:30 P.M. he spoke on the Place Bir-Hakeim: "Comrades, at this very moment I should be in the witness stand at the Geismar trial, but I prefer to give my evidence to you. . . . Geismar, the defendant, is the people. That is, the people who, having discovered the violence they are capable of and the strength they have, rise against those who want to enslave them.

. . . but there is another reason why I have come to talk to you: I'm an intellectual and a century ago we would have been allies. That gave us a considerable power. But at the beginning of this century, that alliance ended. We must bring it back into existence. Not so that the intellectuals can advise the workers, but to constitute a new united mass that will change the point of view of the intellectuals, as well as their own action, thereby creating a solid and unbreachable union. The very fact that you are willing to listen to me is a good beginning. We'll have to meet again. For the moment, I will only say: Free Geismar!"[47]

"The workers did not bestir themselves," André Guérin explains in the article he wrote for *L'Aurore*. "Sartre's audience consisted only of the few Maoists he had brought along. . . . The spectacle of that tired man obstinately playing the role he has chosen for himself must have been rather depressing. When will he understand that one cannot pursue forever the image of Saint-Germain-des-Prés with its ponytailed Valkyries, hoping to receive applause for a repertory of recantations that's getting more labored day by day. A dimwit with no other resources could be forgiven for it. But Monsieur Jean-Paul Sartre is still a great novelist and an eminent playwright."[48] From Raymond Barrillon and his respect to André Guerin and his insults, from *Le Monde* to *L'Aurore*, French journalists kept looking for the right words to reconcile the different elements of the Sartre puzzle: on one side, a coherent generous old man; on the other, a worthy aging writer who's become somewhat distressing and rather rowdy —almost a caricature: a weary-faced philosopher, wearing a lumber jacket, making a barrel his platform, and calling with his microphone to mostly uninterested workers.

"We said the summer would be hot, and so it was. Now we say that the autumn will be a scorcher. It must be, and it will be!" In the fall of 1970, the leaders of *La Cause du peuple*, force the issue. In the meantime, Sartre has also become editor-in-chief of the paper *Ce que nous voulons: Tout*, published by the libertarian Maoist group Vive la Révolution, among whose members is also Roland Castro. "I agree to be the editor-in-chief of *Tout*," Sartre wrote, "just as I have already agreed to be that of *La Cause du peuple*. These two papers do not agree on many points, nor am I necessarily in agreement with all they publish. But this is secondary; the ridiculous, shameful trials the government keeps staging for the hawkers of *La Cause du peuple* clearly show that the ruling class means to suppress the revolutionary press. Since I haven't yet been found guilty in any of the trials currently under way," he concluded, "I put myself at the disposal of every revolutionary paper so that I may be able either to force the bourgeoisie to bring me to court on political charges dealing with the freedom of the press, or, in case they again find me not guilty, to unmask the deliberate illegality of the repression."[49] Though *La Cause du peuple* and *Tout* were involved in similar struggles against the same enemies, their styles were completely different. *Tout* was a large, gaudy, polychromatic paper that excelled in insults and published a large variety of articles on subjects ranging from politics to sex: the anarchical bent was certainly more evident there than in the more dogmatic and sectarian *La Cause du peuple.*

After Geismar's trial and the barrel at Billancourt, other struggles greeted Sartre's clamorous return to the political scene. On December 12, in the city of Lens, Sartre chaired a popular trial to protest the deaths of sixteen coal miners, victims of a mine explosion in the North. "Who's responsible for the murders of Fouquières? The case was dismissed at the superior court and entrusted to an exceptional tribunal because bourgeois justice is not justice. . . . Justice can only emanate from the people."[50] Then, in February 1971, he launched a campaign against the conditions in French prisons. Michel Foucault, Jean-Marie Domenach, Pierre Vidal-Naquet, and others organized an investigative committee. They were going to follow and support the various hunger strikes that kept cropping up all over the country: in Melun, Toul, Limoges, Nancy, Thionville, and elsewhere. "What is a prisoner?" Sartre asked during a press conference on January 5, 1972. "It's a man who's detained against his will. Why is he detained? Because he has dared revolt against our sinister society. . . . We are constantly lied to. A fearful government keeps concealing information from us. We are oppressed, exploited, but at least we can go back home to sleep. They can't, because they have been detained."[51] Sartre also moved against racist attacks aimed at immigrant workers. He demonstrated, along with Foucault, Maurice Clavel, and Claude Mauriac at La Goutte d'or, in Paris, in Ivry, and in the southern suburbs, and headed a delegation to the Place Vendôme, in front of the Ministry of Justice.

Then, on February 14, 1972, he returned to the Renault factory in Billancourt. He was supporting a hunger strike initiated by a number of workers who had recently been fired and were trying to get reinstated. Till then, the strike had not been publicized. "At 3:30 P.M.," Jean-Pierre Barou remembers, "Sartre boarded a Renault van rented by the Maoists . . . the ride was silent, except for two wooden benches that kept banging against each other. Then, the driver announced: 'We've gone through the door'."[52] Thus, Sartre was smuggled into Seguin Island, in the company of a few journalists and several Maoist militants. They were supposed to uncover the secret of this so-called nationalized factory, rumored to be like a forced labor camp. The small group was immediately, and somewhat violently, thrown out by the guards, and the press gave a great deal of space to the event. And yet—and here Barou's report allows us to understand the whole affair—if Sartre trespassed onto state-owned property a second time, it was less out of provocation as such, as some believed, than to draw attention to an action that, without his intervention, would have been totally ignored. "At noon," Barou remembers, "Pierre Victor briefed him on the impasse that confronted the Maoists and the plan of operation for that afternoon. Sartre was still working on his *Flaubert*. . . . he put down his pen just to come down to meet us. . . . he listened to Pierre Victor. . . . 'You are our last chance.' . . . Sartre was not surprised, I can still hear his warm, rasping voice say: 'All right.' "[53]

But, despite his unfailing support of this kind of political action, and his protection of three Maoist papers—in January 1971, he had also become the editor-in-chief of *J'accuse,* which later merged with *La Cause du peuple*— the relationship between Sartre and the Maoists was not very good. If these two years of militancy gave him the opportunity to detach himself completely from the P"C"F—as most leftists liked to call it—they were also fraught with tensions. When, in the summer of 1970, Sartre was interviewed by Jean-Edern Hallier and Thomas Savigneau, he tried to define the status and mission of the revolutionary intellectual as opposed to the classical intellectual and, as an example, used his recent experience with the Maoist revolutionaries: "The editorial direction of *La Cause du peuple* radicalized me," he said. "Now I consider myself available for any correct political tasks requested of me. It wasn't as a liberal defending freedom of the press that I took over direction of *La Cause du peuple.* . . . I did it as an act that committed me to the side of people with whom I got on well but whose ideas I certainly don't entirely share. Yet it's not a purely formal commitment." But, when he was asked to express his opinion of the revolutionary press, its systematic and often arguable amplification of seemingly minor news, he became a little more reticent. "As I see it, the revolutionary press should give a true account not only of successful actions, but of unsuccessful ones too. As long as you keep up a triumphalist tone, you stay on the same terrain as *L'Humanité,* which is something to be avoided. There are certain old techniques of lying, which I do not like. . . . What needs to be told, of course, is the truth. . . . What is even more serious is the fact that the bourgeois press tells more of the truth than the revolutionary press, even when it's lying. The bourgeois papers lie less. They just lie more skillfully. They manage to discredit, but they stick to the facts. It's terrible to think that the revolutionary papers, far from being more truthful than bourgeois papers, are less so. But what is also necessary is that we—who are also the masses—learn to live with the truth. Revolutionaries don't want to know the truth; they have been brainwashed. They live in a sort of dream world. We have to create a desire for the truth, in ourselves and in others."⁵⁴

This critical lucidity was, thus, not very indulgent, but that did not stop him from pursuing his march alongside the Maoists until 1973, that is, for as long as *La Cause du peuple* kept going and he could see. "Those were tense times," Pierre Victor will later note. The paper underwent another crisis during the aftermath of the Bruay-en-Artois crime, when some of its members, wasting absolutely no time, accused a bourgeoisie they considered guilty *a priori* since the crime involved the murder of a working-class girl. "Beginning of the debate on *La Cause du peuple* : self-criticism," Sartre wrote. "In 1970, *La Cause du peuple* had a few new voices. Today, it has become as self-righteous and edifying as a charity group. Of course, it still has a radical address, but it has also gotten into a few bad habits that will be hard to shake off. For instance, it should be better informed about its enemies, know their reasons, their tactics." And Sartre signed his piece, adding, to his name "in agreement with the rest of the editorial board."⁵⁵

*A*S IMPORTANT as the activism, revolutionary journalism, theoretical debates, and denunciation of the government in power that Sartre engaged in during his Maoist years, was the sense of comradeship and warm conviviality he experienced within a political group. "I've been in contact with both communists and Trotskyites, but without any sense of camaraderie. We spoke of politics, and that was that, whereas with the Maoists I had a true human relationship. When we spoke with each other, we were just a bunch of guys who had decided to do a couple of important things together but could as easily have met to go to the movies or something similar. I was constantly talking philosophy with Benny. . . . I was drawn to the moral conception of action and human relationships. That's what the Maoists were for me."[56] Camaraderie and metaphysics seem to have been the main values Sartre discovered among the Maoists. Paradoxically, his discussions with them brought him back to philosophy. These young students, who could easily have been his grandsons and from whom so many things separated him, made him rediscover the joy of philosophical exchanges, a joy similar to that which, fifty years earlier, he had experienced in his talks with Nizan, Aron, Beauvoir, and, a little later, Merleau-Ponty. He got along particularly well with Benny Lévy, alias Pierre Victor: their respective political views shared similar problems. "I'm not a Maoist," Sartre would repeatedly maintain. "Violence, spontaneity, morality: for the Maoists these are the three immediate characteristics of revolutionary action."[57] He also spoke of their radicalism and their extremism, which, from his Flaubertian retreat, seemed to Sartre the requisites of all political action. Thus, it is with outright jubilation that Sartre watched the dusty, old France of the sixties, the France that had been ruled by a man of the nineteenth century, de Gaulle, collapse under the blows of various leftist groups. "The students and workers discovered that the old bourgeois society was finished, and could only protect itself from certain death with billy clubs," he will later explain.

What traces will this Maoist period leave on Sartre's career? First of all, the friendship with one of the leaders of the Proletarian Left, Pierre Victor. A Normalien and a philosopher, from 1973 on, until Sartre's death, he will be both his final secretary and his closest confidant. Secondly, the Lip adventure: workers occupying a watch-making factory, over a year's experiment in self-management, the euphoria of concrete action, the elation resulting from the implementation of direct democracy in self-management. And, last but not least, the *Libé* adventure. In June 1971, Sartre and a few others decided to create, first, a revolutionary press agency, Libération, and then the daily *Libération,* whose first issue would appear on May 23, 1973. To see the project through, he even temporarily abandoned his *Flaubert.* To him, the *Libération* experiment was like a new book, a concrete application of his backing of the leftists, a tribute to his Maoist years. "I'm going to abandon literature and philosophy for six months," he declared. "I want everybody to know that I want to do everything I can for this paper." Already in his first public speeches in May and June 1968, he had inveighed against one of the greatest villains of French society, the bourgeois press. "French public opinion—like all public opinion—" he had declared then, "is stupid because it is poorly informed, and the reason why it is poorly informed is because the press does not do its job." And then he had spoken about the establishment of committees of revolutionary action "in front of the newsstand, on the Raspail-Montparnasse corner"; about spontaneous discussions on the sidewalk, the birth of public agitations "that do, on the streets, the job the press should do."[58] And, to conclude, he had retraced the development and stressed the excesses of the revolutionary press and other small publications, which he would later analyze for the short-lived anarchist journal *L'Idiot international.*

From this moment on, Sartre will devote himself to two kinds of writing simultaneously: via *Flaubert,* he will analyze and exorcise the problem of literary writing, the ceremonious writing inherited from the nineteenth century; via *Libération,* he will delve into journalese and the invention of a more colloquial style that will become the trademark of the paper. Thus, his writing will bridge two different worlds, yesterday's and tomorrow's, and two projects at once complementary and antagonistic: the liquidation of the acquired heritage, and the invention of a new form of writing. *Libération* was an avant-garde adventure insofar as the project involved the quest for yet unknown modes of information, experimentation, real risks, and various challenges at all levels, technical, financial, and ideological. Sartre contributed money—the 30,000 francs he had received for a collection of interviews with Philippe Gavi and Pierre Victor, *On a raison de se révolter* (We Are Right to Revolt)—ideas, and time to bring this adventure to a successful conclusion. He participated in the press conferences that announced the creation of the paper; he went to Lille and Lyon and agreed to take part in a radio program, "Radioscopie," where he did his best to speak as little as possible of himself and as much as possible of *Libération.* With this adventure he found the perfect outlet for the ideas he had developed in his political experience at the side of the Maoists. "We believe in direct democracy," he explained, "and we want people to talk to people. . . . We are looking for a way to use the more charismatic aspects of colloquial, popular speech to create a new kind of writing . . . we must reinvent gestures, intonations. . . . if we could develop a style out of them, a particular style for all the articles of *Libération,* I think the paper would be a sure success."[59] And he recalled the emotions that the enthusiastic response of workers, strikers, and demonstrators had elicited in him when they were first told about the objectives of the paper. "We want to consult the actual participants in an event, we want them to speak for themselves." Popular financing, popular language, a democratic management: *Libération* seemed to embody the ideal counter to power that all the other revolutionary papers had dreamed of since 1968. Delighted at the realization of this dream, Sartre will stake everything on it, including his *Flaubert*, thus proving to the world that both projects were equally important to him. Both projects will still be equally important to him when, in the fall of 1973, having become blind, he will have to abandon both at the same time. Suddenly he can no longer read, no longer write, no longer work.

*B*ETWEEN FLAUBERT and the Maoists, Sartre will conclude another phase of his life. In the fall of 1945, he had been dragged out of the silence following World War II by the extraordinary explosion of a press in full renaissance. Then, during the fifties and the sixties, he had followed its various movements: he had created *Les Temps modernes* and, immediately after the opening of his play *Nekrassov* had gotten involved in the confrontation with Lazareff. *Libération* was the upshot of all the dialogues, whether successful or not, Sartre had maintained with the press of his age. At the same time, he will also conclude the most pragmatic stage of his political quest. After the experience of the RDR, in 1947, he had cut himself off from any political endeavor within the context of a given party. From that moment on he would offer his external support to various organizations, particularly the PCF. In 1970, in response to the Maoists, he had discovered a leftist, slightly anarchical, sphere of influence, and the pleasure of tailgating the communists from the left by offering his support to a variety of small social initiatives, which, since the thirties, had bound him to a then-abstract idea of direct democracy. He had imbued all the journalistic and political experiments that he had undertaken by the side of the leftists with both his past experiences and his passion. And he had worked for them, chaotically and sporadically, during the moments of rest his principal activity would allow him. At sixty-seven, his body, worn by many abuses, had started to tire. And yet, at the time, nobody perceived that his work was nearly over.

"The Cancer of the Nation," ran the headlines of *Minute,* a weekly of the extreme right. "Send Sartre to Jail!" Considered responsible for some articles that had appeared in the leftist press under his name, for *Minute* he immediately became the scapegoat of a changing France. "Beware, this man could be an addict," the editors of *Tout* had captioned a small photo of Sartre they had attached to an article that dealt with new methods of drug detection. "We would like to draw the attention of doctors and cops," the caption went on, "to the fact that our editor-in-chief seems to display all the symptoms of addiction: slovenly attire, equivocal demeanor . . . hangs out with other notorious drug addicts . . . is wont to hide in unusual places: the back of bars, political platforms, backrooms."[60] As for unusual places, from that moment on, Sartre would be hiding on the Boulevard Edgar-Quinet, where he will spend the last part of his life. The owner of his apartment on the Boulevard Raspail having asked him to leave just as he was becoming blind, he had to find a new apartment. He also had to find a new secretary, and get used to a new set of new habits that will remain with him until the end. On January 30, 1969, Madame Mancy had died, at eighty-nine. Her death was a real blow. Sartre refused to pay any attention to the management of her papers and other relics. Just as he was unable to show any interest in his new apartment, its furniture, or the transportation of his manuscripts.

IN THE SHADOW OF THE TOWER

" *I* WAS supposed to meet Arlette in a hospital for disabled actors, where she was working as a volunteer. This took place in a country where she was playing some revolutionary role on behalf of the peasants. I found myself on the corner between the Rue Jacob and the Rue Bonaparte, and was about to enter the Rue de l'Université to reach my destination. That's when I realized that I'd forgotten something, maybe my gloves, and turned on my heels. Suddenly, it started pouring and thundering, a real storm. I couldn't feel the rain, but everything had gotten completely dark, as if night had fallen, and I couldn't see a thing. A worker was walking behind me. . . . For some reason I mistrusted him. He told me, "Can't see a thing. . . . What a storm!' I answered something like 'Yes, indeed,' though I knew that I could at least see the porch of my house. . . . Then I woke up."[1]

Sartre had this dream on a Friday morning, February 10, 1961, after a night at Arlette's. She had immediately recorded the dream in a little notebook. This was about the time that Sartre was thinking of undergoing psychoanalysis with Pontalis. Why did he dream of total darkness twelve years before he actually went blind in the autumn of 1973? Why didn't the rain wet him? What is the meaning of the hospital for disabled actors? Why thunder? Why a storm? Why the forgotten gloves? Why did he mistrust the worker? Why, despite the darkness, could he see the porch of his house? In the fall of 1973, Sartre entered the years of darkness.

"MY OCCUPATION as a writer is completely destroyed. . . . The only point to my life was writing. . . . Everything in my past, in my training, everything that has been most essential in my activity up to now has made me above all a man who writes, and it is too late for that to change. If I had lost my sight at the age of forty, perhaps it would have been different. . . . Without the ability to read or write, I no longer have even the slightest possibility of being actively engaged as a writer. . . . What will no longer be accessible to me is something that many young people today are scornful of: style, let us say the literary manner of presenting an idea or a reality. This necessarily calls for revisions. . . . I can no longer correct my work even once, because I cannot read what I have written. . . . I was in the habit of writing alone and reading alone, and I still think that real intellectual work demands solitude. . . . In spite of everything, this dependence is hardly unpleasant."[2] On June 21, 1975, his seventieth birthday, Sartre agreed to answer Michel Contat's questions for an interview, which would appear in the *Nouvel Observateur* as "Self-Portrait at Seventy." Nothing complacent or optimistic about this interview: in typically terse Sartrean fashion, Sartre gives a flat, cruel assessment of his physical deterioration, his handicaps, the new challenges he is trying to face. Sartre did not ask for this interview, but he accepted it: he agreed to talk about himself, and so he did, honestly, in the name of transparency. Others would have perhaps avoided a similar situation, but Sartre abandoned himself to it entirely, in a low, clear, serene voice. Naturally, and without the slightest trace of sentimentalism, he sentenced himself to a desperate, hopeless situation.

From the autumn of 1973 on, the writer disappears, but the man lives on for almost seven more years, always groping through darkness, except for those rare moments in which he experiences the illusion of some lateral vision: a few forms moving through a thick fog. His right eye has been blind since the age of four; at sixty-eight, he also loses his left eye. Hypertension, arterial thrombosis, triple hemorrhages at the base of the eye, weak arteries, lowering of resistance due to age, numerous excesses of tobacco, alcohol, and multiple drugs: the diagnosis is clear. The blindness that thus cuts short his life as a writer is only the inevitable culmination of his chronic hypertension, losses of consciousness, sudden episodes of amnesia, frequent losses of balance, and problems of circulation in the arms, the legs, the brain. His body, long abused, is abandoning him prematurely. But, though he has grown totally dependent on others for his daily needs, he has yet to tame his legendary pride before he can fully resign himself to this new situation: "Don't worry, I can see. I can see," he often protests, either to convince himself or so as not to be a burden to others. He is equally dependent on others for his intellectual life, and so his only contact with the outside world will be through the voices of those who read him books and newspapers.

From now on, he experiments with a new form of collective speculation. He lives according to the rhythm of others, resigning himself to the loss of autonomy and control over his own decisions. And he does it, and does it simply. A simplicity that, in a man of Sartre's pride and power, is more moving than surprising. According to all his friends, he behaved stoically, accepting the result of his excesses without either resignation or regret. Indeed, he would always try to elude his blindness by relying on the little lateral vision he had, looking for the best angle from which to capture light and perceive forms. One day, in Rome, he quite surprised Simone de Beauvoir: a cab had picked them up at their hotel to drive them to a restaurant both knew well. "This is not the best way to get there," Sartre noted after five minutes, thus showing that he was much more present than anyone would have thought.

Although his life as a writer had been, as he put it, "destroyed," he kept on pursuing different types of intellectual activities until the end. Throughout the last seven years—aside from the more or less long periods during which he lapsed into nearly total torpor or amnesia—he let his mind slow down, but never quite allowed it to take a complete rest, not for as long as he had the physical power to keep it moving. Every morning, he worked at some project or other with Pierre Victor, and, in the summer of 1974, he began a long series of recorded interviews with Simone de Beauvoir—"We are going to question each other on our respective lives," he had proudly told Robert Gallimard—for a project that, in some way, was the continuation of *The Words*. His new apartment on the Boulevard Edgar-Quinet was the headquarters of his new, collective intellectual life and pursuits.

*B*OULEVARD Edgar-Quinet is a strange street: it's a bit like the countryside, with its spacious central sidewalk; it's somewhat morbid, with the gravestones and purple orchids of the Montparnasse Cemetery, whose western wall it flanks; and it's noisy, from daybreak on Wednesdays and Saturdays, the market days: fruits and vegetables, fish, meats, cheeses, exotic produce, prices shouted out . . . a madhouse. Boulevard Edgar-Quinet is a strange street that unfolds between Boulevard Raspail and the Gare du Montparnasse, rooted in the old Montparnasse and emerging into the most recent additions of the 1970s: a fifty-five-story tower, the railroad station, the commercial center, and the large Inno department store, the first of its kind in the capital. And yet, Boulevard Edgar-Quinet is probably the most Sartrean street in Paris: less legendary than Place Saint-German-des-Prés, where he spent his best years, but, nonetheless, more authentically Sartrean. On his return from Le Havre, all the hotels he checked into were in this area: Avenue du Maine, Rue Delambre, Rue de la Gaïté, Rue Cels. Close to the cafés of Montparnasse, this quarter, with its whores and seedy bars, was—as Prévert points out—still truly popular by the end of the thirties. It is here, on the popular Boulevard Edgar-Quinet, that Paul Hilbert—the hero of "Erostratus," one of the short stories in *The Wall*— chooses to open fire on the crowd. Sartre's last two addresses, first Raspail and then Edgar-Quinet, have gradually brought him closer to Erostratus's corner. Significantly, in 1980, his body will be buried in the Montparnasse Cemetery, immediately to the right of the entrance on Boulevard Edgar-Quinet, just beyond the wall.

Number 29 Boulevard Edgar-Quinet is an especially ugly modern building with a narrow vertical front and a backyard jammed between the Inno department store and the Montparnasse tower, whose gray mass chokes everything around it. It is one of those anonymous buildings that demand an acute sense of orientation from residents and visitors alike, as they work their way through lobby after lobby, along corridor after corridor, all romantically designated by a letter and a number, A1, A2, A3, etc. Once in the right lobby, the visitor has to find the correct elevator, and then the correct corridor. All of it in the shadow of the Montparnasse tower. Of course, Sartre never really saw the apartment, the building, or the Montparnasse tower, but he certainly had an idea of the complexity of the itinerary that led him, from the street, through various lobbies, hallways, and the garden, to the elevator that would finally land him on the tenth floor of the A2 section. His friends must certainly have described it to him. They probably told him that it looked like a cross between the sinister dormitory of an Eastern European university and a low-income housing project on the outskirts of town. They probably even told him about the shape of his apartment, also oppressed by the relentless presence of the Montparnasse tower, though, on a clear day, one could also catch a glimpse of the Eiffel Tower. "I no longer like it here," Sartre complained during a spell of depression. "This is where I no longer work."[3]

Number 29 Boulevard Edgar-Quinet, which Sartre no longer liked—and probably never did—will become the control center of all his activities: business meetings, editorial board meetings for *Les Temps modernes,* interviews, assignments. And the kernel of the Sartre "family" will soon concentrate there: Arlette will relieve Michelle, who has just relieved Wanda, who has just relieved Hélène Lassithiotakis, who has just relieved Simone de Beauvoir. All these women Sartre has so deftly kept separate till now will finally meet, or, at least, pass each other as they take turns at Sartre's side, making sure he is comfortable, refilling his prescriptions, keeping him on the right diet. Similarly, despite his blindness, the summer holidays— which Sartre always religiously observed on the academic calendar —will unfold according to the schedule he had concocted after World War II: three weeks with Arlette, in the house he had bought for her in the Midi; two weeks with Wanda, either in Capri, Venice, or Florence; and one month with Simone de Beauvoir, at the Hotel Nazionale, in Rome, where they spend most of their time talking into the tape recorder. To his new Greek friend, Hélène, he devotes one or more extra weeks either in Athens or on some Greek island. These are the main women and the main geographical reaches of Sartre's old age: though blind and short of breath, when with a woman, he is still able to summon up enough pleasure to eat a *cassoulet,* or a smoked sausage, or a ripe Muenster. But in Paris, only Beauvoir and Arlette take turns spending the nights with him; all the others are confined to the day, at such and such a time, according to a very precise, inflexible schedule. Every Friday and Sunday evening he sits with Arlette in front of his TV set to "watch" one of the films offered by the Cineclub, a program he refuses to miss even in his blindness. They sit close to the set, and, with her soft, low voice, Arlette tells him what is happening on the screen, describing the movements and expressions of the actors. Otherwise, she reads to him, either a long sixteenth-century Chinese novel—a favorite of his—or Claude Manceron's *History of the French Revolution*. With Beauvoir, he listens to all the records—she has a record player—they bought together. In his apartment he has a small radio, on which he often listens to the programs of France Musique.

His blindness has put a stop to his piano playing, but it has simultaneously increased the time he spends listening to other people's music. In 1977, he gives a long interview about music to Lucien Malson, of *Le Monde*, in which he returns to the themes he developed in the fifties when he wrote a preface about René Leibowitz. He speaks of "extra-European" music, of "proletarian music," of the difficulty of speaking about meaning in music; he opposes music to politics and draws a parallel between music and madness; then he admits that, for him, who studied music sixty years earlier, the note was and still remains exotic.[4]

In the meantime, he continued to be approached for signatures, petitions, interviews, financial support. The movie *Sartre by Himself*, filmed by Alexandre Astruc and Michel Contat in 1972, was being edited for release in the fall of 1976; in it, he spoke of himself and his life, surrounded by his friends from *Les Temps modernes*. The collection of interviews he had put together with Gavi and Victor, *We Are Right to Revolt*, whose rights belonged to *Libération*, had been published in paperback by Gallimard; Michel Sicard was working on a special issue of the review *Obliques* devoted entirely to Sartre; a colloquium on his oeuvre was being organized at Cerisy-la-Salle in Normandy; having completed their monumental bibliography of Sartre's writings—published in 1970—Contat and Rybalka were polishing up the first volume of the Pléiade edition devoted to his novels; his friend John Gérassi kept asking him questions for a biography he was preparing; Jean-Pierre Enard's booklet, *Le Dernier Dimanche de Sartre* (The Last Sunday of Sartre), was about to be published; the review *L'Arc* was publishing an article on him; the September 1975 issue of *Le Magazine littéraire* was devoted entirely to him; the tenth and last volume of *Situations* was going to come out within the year along with a paperback edition of *Being and Nothingness*. A revival of *Nekrassov*, staged by Georges Werler at the

Théâtre de l'Est in Paris, was planned for the following year. And then, of course, there were more foreign translations—*L'idiot de la famille,* for instance, in German and English—adaptations of his plays, and innumerable requests for interviews with foreign students at work on his novels or his philosophy. In other words, the Sartre factory was still operating, even though in slow motion, still delivering Sartrean products and by-products, which no longer sold quite as much as they used to. "Today, people speak of me as if I were one of the living dead," he told Victor in January 1977. "I died with my *Flaubert,* and maybe even a little before that. . . . I kept on writing but nobody read me anymore."[5]

*I*N SPITE of all these symbolic deaths, Sartre went on living and thinking. And, since it was now useless to do it alone, he started doing it with others. Thus, he embarked on a few new projects that were supposed to become part of his oeuvre. In Rome, he continued his taped interviews with Beauvoir. For the last seven years of Sartre's life, Pierre Victor would come to the Boulevard Edgar-Quinet punctually every morning to work with him. Sartre's decision to take Victor on as a secretary happened almost by chance, under the pressure of circumstances, and gave the impression of being an act of solidarity. Victor—whose real name was Benny Lévy—was the stateless son of an Oriental Jewish family that had left Cairo in 1957, during the Suez crisis. His citizenship status was fairly precarious—"one of the most objective reasons for my paranoia," he will later confess, "but not the only one"[6]—and particularly so since, given his political activities, he was more than likely to come into contact with the police. This is why he had assumed the pseudonym of Pierre Victor, which remained his only political identity until 1980, why he would often go to his appointments wearing a false beard and sunglasses, why he would seldom sign his articles, and, in short, why he had acquired the troubling, mysterious image of the occult and powerful Maoist leader, energetic but invisible. The director of the École Normale Supérieure, Robert Flacelière, had, in vain, repeatedly requested the naturalization of his student; the president of the republic, Georges Pompidou, another eminent "archicube," seemed determined to refuse it. "I am ashamed of being French," Flacelière apparently sighed after one such refusal. Then *La Cause du peuple* dissolved, the Maoist movements were about to follow suit, and, every month, Victor had to report to the police to validate his situation. "Geismar decided to tell Sartre," Lévy remembers, "though it was Liliane Siegel who actually made the proposal." It would be very helpful if Sartre could employ Victor as his secretary, with a monthly salary. Sartre agreed immediately: "You'll help me finish my *Flaubert,*" he told Victor. By the fall of 1973, his sight was nearly gone, and the unexpected appearance of this exciting, intelligent young man was a godsend.

"Of all the people I have known," Sartre said to Michel Contat, in 1975, referring to Victor's dual role as an intellectual and a militant activist, "he is the only one who completely satisfies me from this point of view." "He appreciated the radical nature of Victor's ambitions," Simone de Beauvoir would later write on the subject, "and the fact that, like Sartre himself, he wanted everything. 'Of course you don't attain everything, but you must want everything.' Perhaps Sartre was mistaken, but if so it is of no great importance. That was how he saw Victor."[7]

If the decision to employ a new secretary seemed ideal to most members of the Sartrean family, some, such as Arlette, weren't all that much in favor of it. "There was already Puig," she explains, "who used to come to my apartment every morning to work as a secretary: making appointments, sorting out various requests, taking care of the author's rights for adaptations, etc. When he heard about Victor, he said sadly, 'And now, what's going to happen to me?'" Besides, she was afraid Victor might become Sartre's own Ralph Shoenmann, Lord Russell's last secretary, who, at the Vietnam War Crimes Tribunal, had shamelessly passed off his own opinions as those of his employer.[8] Simone de Beauvoir, instead, was favorable to Victor at the beginning. "He had to be coaxed a great deal before he accepted the job," she now notes. "But he was a young militant who knew Sartre's work very well and had a decent smattering of philosophy: Sartre was immediately conquered by this mirage and so he staked everything on him. And I am fairly sure that, at least at the beginning, Victor felt some real affection for Sartre: He was soon aware of how much he needed him. I don't think at that moment he had any bad intentions in this regard. He did exactly what Sartre expected him to do; it was later that things changed."[9]

Who was this Pierre Victor, whose name was totally unknown to the public until it appeared next to Sartre's at the head of the discussions they would jointly publish in three consecutive issues of *Le Nouvel Observateur,* in March 1980, just a few days before Sartre's death? Who was this would-be philosopher, who used to phone Robert Gallimard and laconically request a certain number of books to read to Jean-Paul Sartre? "When I first knew him in 1970," Sartre would later explain, "his thinking was quite far from mine. He came from another intellectual tradition—Althusser's Marxism-Leninism, which had formed him. He had read some of my philosophical works, but he did not agree with them completely. Then I had the good fortune to work with him on an idea which was solid, which held together, and which opposed mine without rejecting it completely. That is the condition for a real relationship between two intellectuals, a relationship which allows them both to move ahead."[10] The contest between these two intelligences will go on relentlessly, following Sartre's own crises and contemporary political events. "When I came to Europe, after 1956," Lévy remembers, "my problem, shared by most Jews in a similar situation, was that of 'figuring out' where I was, and what France was to me. . . . Sartre helped me solve it, when I was fourteen or fifteen: through him, I felt part of the French language."[11]

Without a country, but with French as his native tongue, Victor's integration began through Sartre's books. Then he received other signs of yet more concrete solidarity; his job as Sartre's secretary granted him a resident's card, and, later, Sartre's direct appeal to the president of the republic, Valéry Giscard d'Estaing, gave him a much-coveted French citizenship. "I like that man," Sartre would say of Giscard in an interview that was released only after his death, as he had wished. "Once he did me a favor for which I am still very grateful."[12] "Sartre wrote to me," Giscard d'Estaing tells us, "to ask me a favor. He told me that his sight was getting worse every day, and that he could no longer read or write; he needed that young man to finish his work. Not the easiest case to plead, believe me: he was a former militant extremist. On the other hand, I was determined to do anything I could for Sartre. There were two reasons for this: first because he was assuming full responsibility for the young man, who, he maintained, was going to adjust to his new status, but mostly because he had told me he needed him to finish his work. I took care of this problem as discreetly as possible, and I think Sartre was grateful to me for it. Of course, we were far from sharing the same convictions or the same beliefs, but I have always had the greatest respect for the French tradition that he represented."[13]

"*A*T FIRST, our relationship was very difficult," Benny Lévy remembers. "So difficult that I often felt like quitting. I would arrive, ring the bell, and at times, he wouldn't even hear me. He'd be there, alone, dozing in his armchair, and, through the door, I could hear the music of France Musique coming from the radio that Simone de Beauvoir had left on for him, so that he wouldn't feel too lonely or too bored. It was a constant struggle against death. At times, I had the impression I was there to fend off sleep, lack of interest, or, more simply, torpor. . . . Yes, at first, what I was really involved in was a sort of resuscitation."[14] Pierre Victor entered and found himself in a large room: To his right there was a sofa and a series of bookshelves; to his left a large desk; across from him, at the opposite end of the room, a large bay window overlooked the tower, and, with his back to the window, so as not to be bothered by the light, sat Sartre, in his large armchair. "It was very hard, and strenuous for Sartre to learn to depend on others," Lévy goes on. "If, at the beginning, I often thought of quitting, it was because I doubted he would ever succeed. And yet, despite all these difficulties, I persevered because, deep down, I was convinced that this struggle against death was his only way of feeling alive." Then things started falling into place according to a schedule that included readings, discussions, and the preparation of different projects, precisely what Sartre's intelligence needed to regain some of its vitality. At first, the two philosophers worked on *Flaubert,* then on the French Revolution, then on the religious heresies and the gnosis, and finally on purely ontological questions. Victor read entire works to Sartre, and then they discussed them, violently, without any complacency, in a direct intellectual confrontation. "I like working with Victor," Sartre confessed to Robert Gallimard. "We have fun together. We really bawl each other out."[15]

Gradually, in the course of seven years, Victor's presence in Sartre's intellectual life, and then, naturally in his material, daily life, will become more and more relevant and indispensable. His comings and goings, in the shadow of the tower, will constantly intersect those of Beauvoir, Liliane, Michelle, and Arlette. "At first, between Simone de Beauvoir and myself there were only a few indications," Lévy remembers, "a sort of tacit agreement: I never told her how I was getting along, maybe she thought I was some sort of nurse, I don't know. Often she looked disarmed, troubled, overwhelmed by the situation. But, in the worst possible moments, the people who really loved Sartre concentrated all their efforts in hushing any possible conflict for the sake of life. That strong and yet unspoken agreement eventually led to the misunderstanding between Simone de Beauvoir and myself; she accepted our relationship without fully understanding what it meant." Thus, Sartre's friends find the cohesion of a team in their fight against death, but it is an artificial team consisting of people who hardly know each other, hardly speak to each other, and whose only common trait is their love for Sartre. Most of them will get to know each other only two or three years before Sartre's death, when he can no longer keep them separate, when he can no longer control their interactions and the various reactions these produce: attraction, sympathy, tacit hatred, overt dislike.

*L*OCKED UP in his *Flaubert,* Sartre had ceased to keep informed on the latest philosophical and paraphilosophical publications, or to participate in the ideological debates of his contemporaries. Victor reawakened his interest with his philosophical readings, his own ideas, and his interminable debates. And Sartre certainly appreciated those wild discussions that brought him up to date and kept him in touch with his own field of reference. His arguments with this young, eager, activist philosopher would often require an enormous investment of energy, but Sartre had always enjoyed questioning his own beliefs, plunging into often contradictory debates with people much younger than himself. At the time, Victor was barely twenty-eight: as a Maoist leader, he had often been criticized for his excessive self-assurance, his "verbal dogmatism," the radicalism of some of his views, and his paranoia vis-à-vis the police. There is no dearth of opinions concerning his character: from Pierre Goldmann's description—"a Talmudist astray in Maoism"[16]—via Roland Castro's pungent criticism—"the least humanist of all leftists, a monster of cynicism and mysticism"[17]—and François Châtelet's judgment—"a philosopher enthralled by the law"[18]—to the opinion of an ex-Maoist comrade—"a moralistic fool . . . capable of turning a whole audience around with his perfect speeches and crushing intelligence"[19]—or Maurice Clavel's formula—"a man from nowhere, and, maybe because of this, a redoubtable Sartrean."[20]

The relationship between Sartre and Victor was, to say the least, very particular—a mixture of crucial intellectual exchanges and less conscious emotional and symbolic ties. Victor would soon abandon history to bury himself in the study of the original text in its fullest sense: preferring silence to premature speech and delving into the only intellectual activity that he saw as noble—an exhaustive, pure, hard, internal analysis of the text. It would be impossible to under-stand Sartre's last years without examining all the aspects of the intellectual contest that took place between Sartre and Lévy in the shadow of the tower. Harshness, violence, reciprocal provocation, playful wrestling: was Sartre ever fully convinced by his adversary? Didn't he often let him have his way, as one would a rambunctious pup, trusting he would sooner or later be able to bring him to heel? Or should one trust Olivier Todd's, and others', perception of the relationship as involving the "corruption of an old man"? What did his "work with Sartre" really mean to Victor? Sartre was, at once, still Sartre and no longer Sartre. Sartre had insisted on a fraternal relationship, but what did the public at large think of this alleged parity between the monument of French culture and an unknown youth who treated him without any formality? Indeed, Victor was caught in an impossibly ambiguous role. He had almost complete power over Sartre: he was punctually at his door at eleven every morning, he stirred him out of his somnolence and torpor, he was paid to keep him alert and informed and to provide him with all the books that might interest him. He had to work for Sartre as well as with him, according to the myth of equality. In any case, their relationship was a bit false from the start. Sartre was aware of it and tried to explain it to Victor during one of the discussions they had for *Libération*, in 1977. "Either I am a doddering old fool you want to manipulate, or a great man from whom you expect to get food for your thoughts. There are two possibilities. But there is a third one, the best one: we could be equals."[21]

Their relationship involved more than just work: Sartre still re-lished the feeling of camaraderie he had shared with the militants of Proletarian Left. He would often accept Victor's invitations to dine with him in the suburbs, where he lived, eager to meet new people, young people, people who could still excite him with their subver-sive ideas. Sartre had introduced Victor to the pleasures of gas-tronomy, to rich dishes and good restaurants; now it was Victor's turn to introduce Sartre to his own gastronomic rituals, to the rowdy, disordered conviviality of a crowded table. And Sartre liked to play the role of the anonymous intruder in a group of young friends, he liked to be part of their jokes and complicities, as if these escapades had the power to regenerate him, if only by taking him away from his usual milieu: from his contemporaries, his friends at

Les Temps modernes, his past. Soon his famous formula "I think against myself" was going to turn into "I think against all Sartreans." In more than just one way, Sartre's relationship with Victor was his last betrayal of himself.

"What shocked me most—what shocked everybody most," Robert Gallimard remembers, "the first time I saw them together, was that Victor looked like a young boy, a young boy who felt absolutely free to address informally, with a "tu," somebody like Sartre, who had never, ever addressed anybody informally, not even Simone de Beauvoir. That really astonished me. And then Victor used to hold him in such high esteem, which, of course, pleased Sartre no end."[22] Despite the inevitable tensions and frictions, today all of Sartre's friends seem to agree in seeing the relationship between Sartre and Victor as an escapade. As if in Victor, Sartre had found the ideal friend with whom to indulge a number of illegitimate pleasures to which his other friends had no access. To his colleagues at *Les Temps modernes,* with their committees and their boring board meetings, he preferred the relentless and tiring but nonetheless amusing confrontations with Victor: at least, they excited him, stimulated him, forced him to react. "We, the veterans of *Les Temps modernes,*" Jean Pouillon admits, "reminded him of his past, we were 'obsolete,' no longer enough for him. Sartre always wanted to have projects, something, anything, that would propel him forward, and he really believed that Victor could give him that, the future he needed."[23] Within this context, it might well be that one of Victor's greatest assets was, paradoxically, his refusal either to perceive or give in to Sartre's physical weakness. "At times," Arlette tells us, "he would come up with a very crucial, complex question at the moment Sartre was about to give in to his fatigue; at other times, he would start reading to him very loudly, with extraordinary zest and passion, as if in a state of exaltation: it was quite scary." Was all this part of the confrontation between two different attitudes? To Sartre, who had always favored a playful approach to philosophical speculations, Victor often appeared rather puritanical. "Now and then," Arlette continues, "I would try to air out the room, bring in some tea, medicine, anything that might distract him a little from that intense intellectual pressure."[24] Simone de Beauvoir was aware of the youth and intellectual vigor that drew Sartre to Victor. "At that particular point, Sartre was seized by the desire to hold out, to survive himself, to go even further than he had in both revolution and subversion.

And since he could no longer do it by himself, he had to trust somebody else to help him do it. He couldn't see any longer, and he felt he had no future, neither personal nor political nor philosophical, so, he transferred all his dreams onto Victor, onto the militant intellectual he could no longer be. In Victor, he also found that atmosphere of camaraderie he liked so much; but later events proved he was wrong in trusting Victor so blindly."[25]

And, indeed, Sartre's relationship with Victor would soon upset the intellectual architecture on which his entire entourage had previously rested. His discussions with Beauvoir, the board meetings at *Les Temps modernes*, his exchanges with his old colleagues, everything seemed so old-hat next to Victor's eagerness, his ebullience, his relentless arguments. Everybody knew that Sartre's plan to "experiment with new forms of writing with another person" was more the delusion of an old man who refused to give up than a viable new approach. Besides, hadn't he always maintained that "meaning depended on style," that he could really think only *while writing*? Victor was probably the only one to really believe that his relationship with Sartre would result in a literary duet. And the fact that he believed it probably allowed Sartre to entertain the illusion of being still involved in an act of creation. His friends from *Les Temps modernes*, that is, the friends who had known him when he was thirty or forty, could easily detect the signs of deterioration that were now constantly marring their original image of Sartre. "It was very painful for me," Jean Pouillon tells us today, "when I was having lunch with him and Beauvoir at La Palette or at La Coupole, to see him spill half the contents of his fork onto his pants—it used to exasperate Beauvoir—and to realize that he had difficulty following a normal conversation: Beauvoir spoke fairly fast and I would try to keep up with her in my answers . . . now and then Sartre would also intervene to add something very pertinent, but it was always about a quarter of an hour later. One had to be alone with him to follow his rhythm. We should have done what Victor did. . . . Bost, Lanzmann, and myself could have done it had we wanted to, but we had our own work and not enough time to take care of both."[26]

Of course, unlike the others, Victor had never known the early Sartre. The man he met was already old, already tired. Free of all nostalgia, Victor could reassure him that he was still Sartre. He had the feeling he was in front of an oeuvre rather than a man. "By then," Arlette remembers, "he knew Sartre's works better than Sartre himself. And he had a prodigious memory: when Sartre could not remember certain things he had written, Victor was there to fill in the gaps."[27]

502

Everybody in "the family" was aware that Sartre had a foolish dream of sharing an intellectual future with Victor, a dream that Victor helped foster. This dream was keeping him alive, though nobody believed that the interaction between the two philosophers would ever produce anything whatsoever. On the other hand, how could they express their misgivings to this proud, blind writer who, with a big grin on his face, would repeatedly assure them that he'd publish a new book before the end of the year? How could they deprive him of this last joy, however absurd it might be? "They were basically mismatched," Simone de Beauvoir notes today. "Sartre was often distressed by the way their conversations kept going no-where." " 'Today, we have again gone full circle,' he would often tell me," Arlette remembers. "Victor was extraordinarily vain," Pouillon adds. "Once, during a board meeting at *Les Temps modernes,* he assumed the tone of a district attorney and demanded that we all, except himself of course, examine our past and write a self-criticism of our previous works. Sartre would never have tolerated anything of the sort." Arlette was also aware of certain discrepancies in their common intellectual project: "There was never a full intellectual confrontation . . . though, at times, they did quarrel." These discrep-ancies between Sartre and Victor were only increased when the latter began to discover Judaism, of which Sartre knew very little. Still, if their relationship had obvious limitations, it had also the merit of existing, of occupying Sartre and of entertaining him. "Victor certainly helped him defend himself, particularly against his women, who, without his new pupil's presence, would certainly have gotten the best of him," another intimate notes. "Victor helped him live," Simone de Beauvoir adds. "He did for Sartre what none of us could have done," Pouillon admits. "Given the situation, I can even under-stand how Victor might have tried to conquer Sartre: when we love someone—and Victor certainly admired Sartre—and we are sure of possessing the truth, what could be more natural than wanting to share it with the beloved? No, I will never go as far as accusing Victor of being Machiavellian." Others insist on a different aspect of the relationship: according to them, Victor protected Sartre against Beauvoir, who had become increasingly possessive toward him and often annoyed him.

Inevitably, Victor's increasingly absorbing presence in Sartre's life eventually assumed the traits of a real rupture, or, rather, a conflict that opposed the past to the future, *Les Temps modernes* to post-Maoism, the Sartre of the forties, fifties, and sixties to the Sartre of the seventies and the eighties. In short, it became a perfect reflection of what was happening within Sartre, according to the usual pattern of his life, always aiming at renewal, the unexpected, the new start. But it was also an illustration of "A Defeat," the unpublished novel Sartre had written when he was twenty: the confrontation between Frédéric and Richard, conceived in 1925, would find its final incarnation fifty years later in the relationship between Sartre and Victor. "Their talks," Sartre had written then, "always transcended dialectic aridity." "Let's be fair," Simone de Beauvoir continues her retrospective analysis, "Sartre no longer enjoyed going to *Les Temps modernes.* It bored him. He found the editorial board too routine-minded. He needed something else. He no longer felt like talking to a bunch of old Sartreans who had nothing new to tell him. Yes, to tell the truth, he was more drawn to what was new, young, and rejuvenating."[28] Jean Pouillon expresses all the impotance and lucidity he felt at Sartre's last treason with this powerful metaphor: "That was the real problem: Victor was like a prosthesis to Sartre. There was no way we could replace it: all we could do was complain about the nature of such a prosthesis."[29] And yet, though inevitable, the conflict between the new Sartre-with-prosthesis and his old friends at *Les Temps modernes* would burst open only in 1978, that is, five years after Victor's entrance into Sartre's daily life, five years when they had ample time to tackle a variety of projects, before everything fell to pieces.

O NE OF the projects they undertook together involved a new TV station, Antenne 2. In April 1974, France had learned of the death of its president, Georges Pompidou. Following the presidential elections, he was replaced by a very different type of man, who would eventually develop cordial relations with Sartre, de Gaulle's minister of finance, Valéry Giscard d'Estaing. Shortly after the election, the ORTF (Office de la radiodiffusion et télévision française) was split in two, and a second TV channel was announced for January 1975. Its president was Marcel Jullian, from the Midi, a former publisher known for his broad-mindedness. Open to all sorts of propositions, he immediately embarked on any number of projects, trusting in his eclecticism, his flair, and his total absence of television experience. "Long live freedom!" read the cable he had received from Maurice Clavel the day of his nomination. Clavel also pushed him to undertake a "Sartre project." The negotiations involving Sartre's and Clavel's respective teams would continue from November 1974 to September 1975. Jullian had initially approached Sartre in the hope, to use his own words, "of pulling him away from his own milieu, his prejudices against television and its henchmen, his obsessions."[30] Jullian had approached Sartre in the height of idealistic fervor, and in total contempt of certain glaring realities, such as the political limitations of his position as a state employee, the absence of any financial agreement with Sartre himself, and Sartre's advanced age. Jullian had gone to Sartre as a prematurely retired historical monument that he would free and resuscitate, but found himself instead, in front of a shrunken old man surrounded by a team he (Jullian) failed to appreciate.[31] These factors were soon going to turn into obstacles that would considerably narrow the scope of the project from the very start. But, despite these handicaps, the project interested Sartre and, for nearly nine months, kept him busy and alert.

"My occupation as a writer is completely destroyed," he told Michel Contat in 1975. "However, I can still speak. That is why, if television manages to find the money, my next work will be a series of broadcasts in which I will try to talk about the seventy-five years of this century. I am working on this with Simone de Beauvoir, Pierre Victor, and Philippe Gavi, who have their own ideas and who will do the editing, which I am incapable of handling myself. I might speak to them while they take notes, for example, or we might have a discussion, after which they will put the project together."[32] Later, he would also say that he considered those broadcasts as "part of his oeuvre." It was an interesting project that should have consisted of ten 90-minute broadcasts, each bearing on the French twentieth century as experienced by "a French intellectual, the child of intellectuals, born in 1905." This, in fact, was Sartre's alternative to Jullian's proposal, a series focusing on "The Intellectuals and the Masses." As time went by, however, Sartre's team narrowed the project down to "The Meaning of Revolt in the Twentieth Century," and then subdivided it into a number of different components such as the intellectual's revolt, the workers' revolt, and the feminist revolt. Nearly eighty scholars and historians were enrolled for the project by Victor, Gavi, André Glucksmann, Jacques Rancière, and Simone de Beauvoir. "We immediately put in a considerable amount of work," Daniel Lindenberg, responsible for preparing a study on

Nizan, remembers, "sure as we were that the project would be carried through."[33]

A thirty-page treatment was written and a director was found— François Truffaut, who, however, refused the offer. Roger Louis was then chosen. For some time, things seemed to be moving forward, despite the tensions, arguments, and conflicts among the teams involved. If in these post-Maoist years the aggressiveness of worker power had somewhat abated when it came to sectarian or ideological issues, it was still quite virulent whenever it came to more concrete forms of oppression, such as the recent Lip affair. Simone de Beauvoir's feminists, too, were demanding certain prerogatives they saw as imperative. In short, everybody tried to draw some personal advantage out of this providential project, which, among other things, allowed them to exploit a government medium that had always cut them off. In the shuffle, Sartre was often forgotten, sometimes mistreated, and, now and then, even attacked by these intellectuals resentful of the power of the media. Though he could not do without his team, since he needed somebody who would write for him, Sartre gave everybody the impression of being quite autonomous, of knowing where he was going, and of being perfectly aware of the limits within which he would let others manipulate him. And yet, some maintain that, when the entire project fell to pieces, in September 1975, Sartre gave it up immediately, as if relieved to be rid of an adventure that forced him into too many conflicts, whereas some of his colleagues would have preferred to reach a compromise with Jullian, even to their disadvantage.

More interesting than the prolonged negotiations that led to his abortive adventure are the motives that turned it into another missed rendezvous—the first one being the similarly aborted series "La Tribune des *Temps modernes*"—between Sartre and the national broadcasting media, motives that concern Sartre's continuously troubled relationship with the government or, more accurately, the statesmen of his country. Sartre's anti-Gaullist sprees and de Gaulle's occasional pro-Sartrean displays of consideration are generally better known than Giscard's civil and courteous relationship with the writer—"I remained in favor of the project to the end," he confides —or the obvious and hostile misgivings of Jacques Chirac, Giscard's prime minister. Indeed, behind all the more or less official hassles that opposed Sartre's team to Jullian's, was the conflict that separated these two most powerful political figures of the country in their respective attitudes toward intellectuals. De Gaulle had declared that

Voltaire could not be imprisoned, Giscard had sent Sartre a note conveying his deep regrets at the news of the writer's blindness and, later, had expressed his support for Jullian's project, but Chirac was from the very start openly against the Sartre project. There are traditions and there are traditions: a French intellectual of the highest order has to be handled with delicacy; too liberal or too conservative an attitude can only evoke certain legendary precedents, the conflicts that pitted Voltaire, Rousseau, Hugo, and Zola against the state; and one must always consider the charismatic, symbolic, and mythological aura of the intellectual in French history.

Was it a case of censorship? The negotiations broke down over one of Jullian's demands: a pilot broadcast to test public reaction. Sartre replied that he was no longer of an age to take exams. According to the writer Jean-Didier Wolfromm, who directed Jullian's team, the project had fallen through before that, when the administrative committee of French television decided to flunk the promotional trailer because of an ad in *Libération*. In short, if Sartre had initially accepted Jullian's proposition on condition of being given carte blanche, later, at the press conference that announced his definitive abandonment of the project, he explained: "I realized that the promise that I would be free to do what I pleased was preposterous. . . . I want it understood that it is I who am quitting. I've always been against television, I thought I could change, but I was wrong. This is my final good-bye: I will never work for television, not in France or anywhere else."[34]

*I*N BETWEEN the crises of hypertension, during the rare moments of lucidity occupied by intellectual projects or taped interviews, Sartre was kept abreast of world events—such as the Portuguese revolution and the repression of dissidents in Czechoslovakia—by his network of friends, his "family." It was a rather artificial form of semi-activity, but few outsiders were aware of this. Thus people kept turning to him for signatures, financial support, petitions, declarations. Some reacted with irony at the frequent appearance of Sartre's name haphazardly joined to those of Basque nationalists, Spanish prisoners sentenced to death, captive French soldiers, hunger strikers, Polish workers, Moroccan, Nigerian, Argentinian, Italian, Iranian prisoners. Besides these written endorsements, he also made a few physical appearances, on the arm of either Arlette, Michelle, or Beauvoir, at demonstrations in favor of Armenian refugees or Soviet dissidents. He also took several trips with overt political intentions: Portugal, Germany, Italy, the Middle East.

In February 1973, in an interview with the German weekly *Der Spiegel,* Sartre had declared: "I am very much interested in the Baader-Meinhof group. I believe it is a real revolutionary group, but I have the feeling it has started a little too soon." Klaus Croissant, Andreas Baader's lawyer, had read this declaration and contacted the philosopher: to protest against the conditions of German prisons, his client had begun a hunger strike, such as had already claimed the life of another prisoner. Sartre wrote the German government asking permission to visit Baader in his cell. After several refusals he finally obtained the right to enter the Stammheim prison, near Stuttgart, and spend some twenty-five minutes with Baader. He arrived from Paris on December 4, 1974 accompanied by Pierre Victor and Jean-Marcel Bouguereau, of *Libération,* and was led to Baader by Croissant and Daniel Cohn-Bendit, who acted as interpreter during the press conference that followed the visit. "Baader is confined to a small white cell," he declared in front of some hundred and fifty journalists, "where the only sounds he can hear are the footsteps of the guards three times a day. Daylight filters through a thick grid, an electric lamp remains lit all day long. . . . Conditions of life in the prison are intolerable. According to the convention on human rights, the prisoner is a man with all the qualities of a free man, but it seems as if the West German government uses different standards for political prisoners."[35] He convinced Heinrich Böll to join him in an appeal for an international commission for the protection of political prisoners. But his interview with Baader did not go very well. "I thought I'd find a friend in you but instead you are just another judge," the former militant member of the Red Army Faction had said, upset at Sartre's doubts about the political methods of the group. "Terrorism can be justified in Latin America," Sartre had declared, "but it is not politically valid in Western European countries. Judge von Drenkmann's murder can be explained, but politically it is unacceptable."[36] "The trip did not turn out as expected," Benny Lévy bitterly notes. "Today I regret it." The German ministers incriminated by Sartre's declarations availed themselves of the press to inveigh against Sartre's statements, which they deemed to be false and against his "tactless" intervention. More than a waste of time, the trip was a waste of Sartre's name, his power, and his health.

Unlike the trip to Frankfurt, those to Athens were fairly successful. There he met again an old flame, Hélène. Victor was with him, more as a cover than anything else. "I have never understood a thing about Sartre's relationships with women," he tells us, "but then he never understood anything about mine either." During one of these trips, Sartre agreed to deliver a lecture at the University of Athens. "This was the first time," Victor goes on, "that I had a direct experience of what he meant to people abroad. His entrance into the auditorium was extremely moving. As soon as he appeared, people started applauding, and they went on, slowly, for a very long time. It was a big thank you."[37]

His trip to Portugal, on the other hand, was meant as an expression of support: the revolution of the red carnations had been going on since Easter 1974, reawakening flames of sympathy, enthusiasm, and revolutionary romanticism among the extreme left in Europe. Sartre arrived in Lisbon with Beauvoir and Pierre Victor and spent the second week of April 1975 traveling through the country. Meant as homage and an expression of sympathy, like his earlier trips to Cuba, Brazil, and elsewhere, this trip also had an information-gathering function. In Portugal, he met workers, peasants, women, soldiers, and intellectuals. For him it was a duty. The fall of the Salazar-Caetano dictatorship marked the end of forty-eight years of a backward social and political regime, the oldest, most corrupt last bastion of fascism. The revolution of the red carnations, with its songs, its gaiety, and the unexpected support of the army, became a celebration for the movements of the European left. Sartre, tired but happy, followed the entire celebration, and then, back in Paris, he told *Libération* about it. "It might be possible to constitute another power," he explained, "worker power. Not in the form of a party, but in the form of cooperatives. In self-managed factories, the understanding among elements of the people constitutes a form of action that could not be undertaken by the Parliament or the army: that would be enough in itself to create a new authority." After tackling self-management, he returned to culture, and, more specifically, to "cultural dynamization": "All the writers I met were wondering about the possibility of a popular literature, a collective work, a means to animate villages: how could one establish a rapport with peasants? Maybe by reawakening in them an interest in their own peasant culture."[38] Were Sartre's readers disappointed with this "return from Portugal"? Did they find it too superficial, too predictable? Did they find Sartre tamer than usual, and much less enterprising? And yet journalists kept asking him for his opinions on such and such an event, such and such a question. In November 1979, Catherine Clément interviewed him about "the left, hope, and despair," for *Le Matin-Magazine*. In January 1980, Ivan Levaï invited him to participate in his radio program "Expliquez-vous," on Europe I: "We are moving back to the Cold War," Sartre explained. "We are in a very critical situation." He thus voiced his opposition to the internal exile of the dissident physicist Andrei Sakharov, and launched an appeal for the boycott of the Olympic Games, which, that year, were to be held in Moscow. Thus, in the name of human rights, he uncompromisingly attacked the Soviet regime, while at the same time affirming, "This, of course, does not mean that I am endorsing American imperialism."[39] His answers were concise and clear, but rather weak.

Sartre never fully disappeared from the political scene, but his presence started, gradually and almost naturally, fading away. His voice remained in our ears, but it also grew feebler, as did his anger. As for his physical strength, that was also slowly flagging. Each of his public appearances left those who loved him feeling uneasy, dismayed, and angry. Where was the Sartre they knew? Was he still somewhere inside that wobbly, puffy, blind little man? One day, a mad poet who kept bugging him for money, had stabbed him through the crack of the door and had wounded his left hand. And so when he appeared in his usual Montparnasse restaurants, clinging to the arm of some woman, he looked even frailer and older than usual with his bandaged left hand. Such scenes were fairly familiar to the clients of La Coupole or La Closerie des Lilas, who could thus follow the progress of Sartre's blindness, his heaviness, his trembling, his weakness, his premature senility. And they would look at each other in silence and consternation, seldom daring to express their dismay in an emotional whisper, "Is that Sartre?" Others, instead, were angry at him for having thus deteriorated: Sartre belonged to them, they could not accept his decay, his degradation. It is hard to see a myth fade. And there were others who loved him even more for it, such as Françoise Sagan, who always managed to prove her affection. On June 21, 1979, his last birthday, she sent him a wonderful letter, a "love letter to Sartre," that was then published in *Matin de Paris;* and, in her 1984 book, *Avec mon meilleur souvenir,* she spoke of the meals and laughter they had once shared.

Sartre's last two public appearances were memorable. On June 26, 1979, he was part of the delegation of intellectuals that went to the Elysée to ask the president of the republic to lend more substantial support to the boat people fleeing Vietnam and Cambodia. After the visit, he walked down the steps of the presidential palace helped by André Glucksmann, on one side, and, on the other, Raymond Aron. The two men were the same age, but Aron, in suit and tie, was still in great shape whereas Sartre, in his polo shirt and leather jacket, looked, by comparison, worse off than ever. The distress everybody felt at that sight was only increased when, in order to be recognized by Sartre, Aron had to whisper in his ear: "Mon petit camarade." Three months later, on September 26, Sartre was driven to the Père-Lachaise Cemetery for the burial of Pierre Goldmann, an editor at *Les Temps modernes* who had been murdered a few days earlier. Sartre and Beauvoir followed the public ceremony at some distance away from the crowd, but, as always, whenever they were needed, they were there.

A T THE beginning of 1978, a violent argument opposed Simone de Beauvoir to Pierre Victor. In the course of his readings, Victor had discovered the works of Emmanuel Levinas—one of the earliest harbingers of phenomenology in France—then he had gotten interested in the Cabala, and through this, had decided to push his research yet further and learn Hebrew—a rather uncommon itinerary for a nonbelieving Jew who had absolutely no religious vocation or background, from a family that observed Jewish holidays only occasionally and always critically. Victor shares his new interests with Sartre. "What next? Maybe he'll decide to become a rabbi!" Sartre, somewhat critical of Victor's frequently extreme passions, had joked with Arlette. Victor planned a short trip to Israel, which took place only a few months after Egyptian President Anwar el-Sadat's visit. Sartre accompanied him, along with Arlette, and received Israelis who wanted to talk to him in his hotel room overlooking the Jaffa Gate. Victor wanted to revive the Sadat spirit of détente among Israelis and Arabs, according to Arlette Elkaïm.[40] So, Sartre met some Israeli intellectuals, and some Palestinian intellectuals, for a series of discussions that, according to Arlette, always remained "very superficial." But Sartre was happy; and he was delighted when, in a restaurant in Jericho, he was approached by an enthusiastic young woman, who said, "Good morning Monsieur Sartre. Thank you for existing!" As part of the trip, Victor had taped a discussion between himself and Sartre on the Arab-Israeli conflict— a text that was meant to serve as a guideline for the trip, and, instead, turned into the cause of a serious conflict of its own.

"*I* DON'T mind being considered a 'universal consciousness,' " Sartre said during the discussion. "But I am not a universal consciousness. I am a particular consciousness."

Victor: "Since you are neither Solomon nor a universal consciousness, from what place do you speak?"

Sartre: "I have the subjective idea that the place where I am, France, is in the end the most appropriate place to play a role. Paris can be seen as a source of suggestions, a starting point."

Victor: "Then one goes back to the universal consciousness: Paris is the eighteenth century, Paris is the French Revolution."

Sartre: "Yes, as you know, I have always remained faithful to the French Revolution. I say 'Paris' because I must say something, but deep down things are very simple: I like to play the role of the third in a direct confrontation."

Victor had sent the text to Jean Daniel, the editor-in-chief of the *Nouvel Observateur,* for publication. "At first, I reacted as a journalist," Jean Daniel remembers. "I told myself: 'Sartre is eminently publishable.' But the text was bad, poorly written, and the ideas it expressed were rather odd, not exactly what one would have expected from Sartre."[41] Jacques-Laurent Bost, who was then also working at the weekly, saw the text and immediately alerted Beauvoir. "Bost called us from *L'Observateur,* " she tells us. "Indeed, the piece was worthless: they had spent only four days in Israel, not nearly enough time to formulate a clear idea of the situation. Sartre would never have done anything like that on his own. The text was really much too weak: Victor, who could not write, had taken advantage of Sartre's name to try to get it published. I told Sartre what we thought of the piece, and he told me: 'Then drop it, I don't really care about it.' "[42] Opinions concerning Sartre's reaction to the affair differ. Jean Pouillon remembers: "Sartre was furious. The whole affair displeased him: he did not want us to be right against Victor. He had agreed to do the piece and was very unhappy with our veto. But I still believe that, even though our interference hurt him somewhat, we were right in acting the way we did."[43] Suddenly, the rift between past and present was assuming a more serious aspect; Sartre, who did not like to displease his friends, found himself torn between the Sartre of the past—Beauvoir and *Les Temps modernes*— and the Sartre of the present—Victor and Arlette. He had listened to Beauvoir's objections and had not disagreed with them, but—and this is quite significant—he hadn't told Victor anything about them. Victor heard it all directly from Beauvoir at a *Temps modernes* meeting.

"When I spoke to Victor he flew into a rage. Never had he been so insulted. . . . At a *Temps modernes* conference that met at my apartment without Sartre, there was a violent quarrel between Victor, Pouillon, and Horst on the subject of the article. Pouillon and Horst thought it execrable. Victor insulted them, declaring later that we were all corpses, and he never took part in the meetings again."[44] Significantly, Sartre was absent during both the first and second confrontations between his past and his present. "Sartre did not feel at ease about that text," Benny Lévy admits today. "And I can easily understand why. It was not his initiative; he knew that certain passages could easily annoy the Israelis. . . . That bothered him; so he washed his hands of the whole matter."[45] Still, a precedent had been set: from that moment on, the two clans, stiffening in their respective attitudes, would avoid and mistrust one another. Tense since 1973, the rope had finally broken over a rather inane incident, but no reconciliation was any longer possible. Before, Sartre, Beauvoir, and Victor had often traveled and attended various functions together. From this moment on, however, Sartre will be either in the company of Beauvoir or Victor; never again with both at the same time. "Up until then," Beauvoir will later write, "Sartre's real friends had always been mine too. Victor was the only exception. I did not doubt his affection for Sartre nor Sartre's for him."[46]

These were the conditions under which the colloquium of March 1979, "Peace Today," took place. Organized by *Les Temps modernes* —and held together by Victor—it brought together a number of Israeli and Palestinian intellectuals, including Ely Ben Gal, Avisha Margalit, Iehoshua Harkabi, and Steinsaltz, on the Israeli side, and Ibrahim Dakkak, Ma'hamad Watad, Nafez Nazzal, Charaf, and Edward Said, on the Palestinian side. "It was a dismal afternoon," Said remembers. "It rained cats and dogs. We had lunch in the Alsatian brasserie at the Carrefour de l'Odéon. Sartre seemed unable to understand any foreign language, whether German or English, and even when we spoke French, he was quite absent. The following day, we met in Michel Foucault's apartment: he was perfectly willing to have us there but didn't want to participate in our discussions. The next day I made it very clear to all that I would also refuse to play a part in the colloquium unless Sartre spoke. I had come to Paris to hear Sartre's point of view on the matter and had absolutely no intention of fighting with the Israelis as if I were a circus animal or a gladiator, for the pleasure of a few Parisian intellectuals. Finally Sartre spoke. His speech was a series of platitudes: ritualistic, emo-

tionless formulas that gave us all—Palestinians and Israelis alike—
the sad impression that we were perceived as subhumans. Later, I
approached him directly, and knelt down by him so that he could
hear me better. He told me once again how much he respected Sadat,
and that was that. This colloquium left a very bad taste in my
mouth," Said concludes. "It was a disaster, and I think everybody
thought the same thing."[47]

513

*A*ND YET Sartre could not stop talking about his next book, the one
he was preparing with Victor, and whose title would be *Power
and Freedom*. "This book," he would explain, "will be the summa of
my political and moral theories. I would like to finish it by the end
of my life."[48] They had talked for hours and hours, and a friend of
Victor's had transcribed all the tapes: eight hundred pages that Arlette read back to Sartre during a summer at Junas. "This won't do,"
he would often complain to Arlette. Which meant that he and Victor
would have to rediscuss matters and that Arlette would have some
twenty more pages to read to Sartre, line by line, to correct according to his comments, and then reread once more for his approval. "It
was important that we be ahead of all political changes," Lévy explains today, "and, at the moment, the political circumstance of a
new right was becoming very threatening. So, we removed from our
reflections that whole part in which metaphysics could have been
expressed in a political language. Our discussions should have been
published in the fall of 1980, followed by the foundations of our
reflections, mostly hinging on Sartre's revision of the concept of
"being for others." As our work progressed we would each jokingly
wonder, 'How are *they* going to react?' insisting on a 'they' at once
terribly elusive and unavoidable. In any case, we were determined
to avoid the tantrums of 1978; we thought they might be shocked, but
we were far from envisaging the sort of violence that ensued."[49] All
those who had been irked by the last confrontation had hardened
their positions while waiting for the next one. Essentially, Sartre's
colleagues at *Les Temps modernes* believed that Sartre was rapidly
losing control and that they had to prevent him from drifting away
for good. As for Victor, profoundly hurt by the realization that his
emotional and intellectual investment in Sartre could be chalked off
by people with whom Sartre had not spoken for years, he had
decided that he would never let them get the best of him again.

This time, he took the text to Jean Daniel himself. "I took it home with me," Jean Daniel remembers, "because Pierre Nora was going to come over for dinner. Together, we read it very carefully: it was disturbing, it revealed a completely new twist in Sartre's position, but, even though it contained a few drastic changes on fundamental issues, it was very strongly written. . . . My telephone kept ringing all night long: Lanzmann for Simone de Beauvoir, Bost, Pouillon; they all begged me not to publish it. I did not know what to do. The next day, at the paper, I showed the text to Horst, who responded with a completely different opinion. 'They are all very excited,' he told me. 'They are all defending the Temple. I should probably do the same thing, but this time I am not going to. This text does not bother me in the least.' So, I decided to call Sartre himself, in Horst's presence, but I did not have the time to do it. Sartre called me himself. His voice was loud and clear, and he spoke with extreme authority. 'I believe you are quite troubled,' he said. 'My friends must have besieged you. Never mind them. I, Sartre, ask you to publish that manuscript, and to publish it in its entirety. If, however, you'd rather not do it, I'll publish it elsewhere; but I would be very grateful to you if you did it. I know my friends have gotten in touch with you, but their reasons for doing so are totally wrong: the itinerary of my thought eludes them all, including Simone de Beauvoir.' Seldom had Sartre been as clear, as precise, as much in control of both his thought and his language. Besides, when I called him back to tell him about a minor mistake, and asked him whether he had the text handy, he answered: 'I have it right here in my head.' And, indeed, he knew it by heart. 'I am counting on you,' he also told me. 'There are a few other projects I would like to discuss with you, including something on violence. I would like to work on something like that, if I have the time.' "[50]

This time, Simone de Beauvoir and Victor did not confront each other directly: anyway, they were no longer seeing each other. Instead, the confrontation took place between Beauvoir and Sartre himself, in his apartment on the Boulevard Edgar-Quinet, when he first showed her the entire manuscript. For the first time in their lives, they were in total disagreement. "Sartre was never really angry," according to Arlette. "He was very solid and never lost his cool. But this time, after the scene with Beauvoir, he was quite ruffled. He had never spoken to me about any trouble with Beauvoir, but, after this crisis, he told me he did not understand her. Apparently, while reading the text, she had gotten very angry, started crying, and finally threw the manuscript across the room. Sartre tried to talk to her and explain things, but she refused to listen."[51]

Apparently, Sartre was very upset by this sudden change in his relationship with Beauvoir. Nor is it sure that they ever fully made up in the two months that separated this scene from the end of his life. "I've just had lunch with those two austere muses," he would tell Arlette whenever he got back from lunching with Beauvoir and a close friend of hers, Sylvie Le Bon. "They did not speak to me once."[52] "I would like to come with you two to Belle-Ile for Easter," he told Sylvie on the other hand, "and forget about that whole thing once and for all."[53]

He had gone against Beauvoir's wishes, he was well aware of it, and, in fact, he had deliberately and obstinately taken his stance against his past, the guardians of the Temple, the Sartrean tribunal. "Sartre persisted in his position," Simone de Beauvoir lucidly assesses of the situation, "because we were all against him. He persisted out of weakness. He had to shield himself behind some false strength and, since he knew he was weak and broken, he had to flaunt it as much as possible. On the other hand, since he was no longer himself, he was doing all this on Victor's instigation. What Sartre never realized, and particularly not in those last discussions, is that Victor had pushed him to go against himself, to betray himself. No, he was completely blind to that, to Victor's Vischinski side. So, since he was unable to judge things with an open mind, and could not trust himself, he stiffened: he had staked a lot on Victor, and he refused to see that he had been wrong. He thought I refused to follow his lead, he thought I failed to understand him. He thought that I wanted to manipulate him, with the others at *Les Temps modernes,* whereas, in fact, he was being manipulated by Victor and by Arlette —to whom Victor had shrewdly gotten close after the crisis of 1978. He was terribly torn by all this, he did not want to face the truth. . . . Sartre refused to entrust anyone else with his future, but he no longer had any eyes, no longer had any future. . . . he already knew he did not have much time left."[54]

Sartre's clear, determined assertion of his will over Jean Daniel leaves us with the strong image of an old gentleman who continues to fight against imprisonment, censorship, stagnation. "Come on, Robert," he had told Robert Gallimard after all these crises, "you're not going to be like everybody else, you're not going to give me a piece of your mind, too! Do you realize how ridiculous it is to condemn me in the name of all worthy Sartreans! You'll see, when the book comes out, they'll change their minds."[55] This is how Arlette analyzes that whole sequence of events: "It was not their criticism that bothered him," she says, "as much as the appropriation, on the part of the *Temps modernes* group, of the Sartrean Truth. 'They're treating me like a dead man who has the gall to appear in public,' he told me. His work with Victor was dismantling all that the others had built, it was even putting Simone de Beauvoir's latest book, *All Said and Done*— a general assessment of their lives—into question, and was definitely challenging the *Temps modernes* group, whom, by now, he saw as mere guardians."[56] She still deplores the fact that not a single member of the editorial board bothered to go and see Sartre in person, to discuss the manuscript directly with him, and to explain to him what their actual objections were. It might have helped him understand. " 'Go talk to him?' Jean Pouillon answered me. 'And what for? Besides, I haven't even read that manuscript. What would be the point of talking to Sartre about it. We would just quarrel. . . . Either I'd fail to convince him, which might mean we would never see each other again; or I'd manage to convince him, but at what cost? What would I do then? I'd have to come and see him every morning, I'd become his nurse.' "[57]

*N*OBODY EMERGED untainted from this painful situation. Not his old friends, the guardians of the Sartrean Truth. Not his new friends, who may well have pushed him too far and, with his own consent, thrown his reputation into question. Already predictable in 1973, this final rupture ended up poisoning Sartre's last years. Torn between these two strong systems, he behaved as had always been his wont: he withdrew into himself, refusing to hear or to reconcile the irreconcilable. Despite his failing health, Sartre was not about to stop living, working, changing.

Aside from his closest friends, who painfully endured this last conflict, nobody else was aware of these tensions. In the middle of this stifling, clannish atmosphere, on March 20, Sartre was suddenly taken to the Broussais hospital for a pulmonary edema. While all this was going on in the wings, the *Le Nouvel Observateur* published the controversial interviews between Sartre and Benny Lévy, the real name Pierre Victor decided to use once and for all. Six years had gone by since the publication of the last volume of *Situations,* seven since the third volume of *The Family Idiot,* and five since *We Are Right to Revolt.* For three consecutive weeks, the readers of *Le Nouvel Observateur* were going to be surprised by the discussions between Sartre and Lévy titled "L'Espoir maintenant" (Hope

Now). Quite a discovery, not just because of the content of the discussions, but also because of their completely new form, a form Sartre had never before adopted. And, in fact, these were not just three more interviews like the ones with Catherine Chaîne about women or with Michel Contat, "Self-Portrait at Seventy." Benny Lévy was not respectfully addressing Sartre in order to obtain information or some explanation concerning his philosophical works. These were bits and pieces of conversations drawn out of the last few years of their collaboration, quite as informal as their relationship had been. The use of the informal "tu" was a must within the groups of May 1968 and their offspring, a ritual that distinguished those who belonged from those who did not. Sartre had soon "belonged," but this form of camaraderie, which showed a Sartre on equal footing with a thirty-year-old unknown, who had never written or published a thing and who claimed parity with France's foremost intellectual, had quite an impact on French readers. Sartre's remarks only increased the discomfort. Since *The Family Idiot,* Sartre had practically disappeared from the literary scene and had only occasionally re-emerged on the political scene. Few people knew anything about his life since 1973. And suddenly, there he was again, in a totally unexpected role, which left everybody flabbergasted.

"*F*OR SOME time now," Benny Lévy started the discussion, "you have been wondering about hope and despair, themes you have hardly broached in your writings."

Sartre: "Certainly not in the same way. I have always thought everybody needs hope to live . . ."

Lévy: "In *Being and Nothingness* . . . you may not have spoken of hope, but you did speak of despair."

Sartre: "Yes, I spoke of despair, but, as I have often pointed out, I don't see it as the opposite of hope. . . . I have never felt despair, nor have I ever, even remotely, seen despair as a quality I could possibly possess. . . . Thus, it was, in effect, Kierkegaard who greatly influenced me on that."

Lévy: "Odd, since you don't really like Kierkegaard."

Sartre: "True, which does not, however, mean he did not influence me. His words seemed to be very real to others, and I wanted to account for them in my philosophy. It was in fashion."

This was the general tenor of the discussions. Lévy relentlessly prodding Sartre with his philosophical questions, evidence of his profound knowledge of the Sartrean oeuvre; Sartre replying in a completely new way, with flat rhetoric, sluggish thought, weak arguments.

These discussions were Sartre's last public text concerning his final years. His death, however, was followed by innumerable explanations as each actor in the final drama added his or her bit of evidence to what was already becoming a public file. Simone de Beauvoir's *Adieux: A Farewell to Sartre*, published by Gallimard eighteen months after Sartre's death, was a scrupulous, clinical account, indeed, almost a journal, of Sartre's last decade. Confronted with this book, which read like an exorcism, readers reacted the way they always had toward this mythical couple: with utter respect or radical rejection. Oddly enough, nobody seemed to notice how intensely Beauvoirian it was; how, from both a thematic and a stylistic standpoint, it logically followed her earlier works, such as *A Very Easy Death, The Coming of Age,* and *All Said and Done.* "This is the first of my books," Beauvoir wrote, "—the only one no doubt—that you will not have read before it is printed. It is wholly and entirely devoted to you; and you are not affected by it. . . . When I say *you,* it is only a pretense, a rhetorical device. No one hears it. I am speaking to no one. In reality it is Sartre's friends that I am talking to."[58] With *Adieux,* the conflicts within the Sartrean family became quite public, and Arlette, directly implicated, answered a number of tendentious articles in an open letter to Simone de Beauvoir, which was published in *Libération.* "I appear in your memoirs for the first time," she wrote, "in the role of Bécassine, within the context of those famous discussions. This would not bother me nearly as much if your caricature of some of us were not also a betrayal of Sartre himself. I can no longer keep silent, this time you have gone much too far. . . . When Sartre and I were alone together, I tried as well as I could to be the eyes he had lost. . . . Nothing prevented you from sitting down with him, papers in hand, and giving him a detailed account of all your objections. He was, to say the least, quite surprised at your failure to do so."[59] A few months after this public dialogue, when Sartre's first unpublished works—*The War Diaries* and *Cahiers pour une morale*— were published during Easter 1982, a few journalists suddenly got very much interested in Sartre's legal executor, Arlette, his adopted daughter, and asked her for some interviews; they were all intrigued by this unknown character in Sartre's life, who, from now on, would be playing a crucial role in the management of his oeuvre.

Then, in the fall of 1984, Benny Lévy published an odd little book, *Le Nom de l'homme: Dialogue avec Sartre* (The Name of the Man: A Dialogue with Sartre). Contrary to everybody's expectations, Lévy eschewed all polemics in favor of a truly philosophical text, entirely devoted to a strong dense study of Sartre's work, almost a Judaic reading, absolutely subjective and personal, of all of Sartre's texts, in which he again displayed a remarkable knowledge of the entire oeuvre: easily shuttling between *Saint Genet* and the *Critique, Flaubert* and *Baudelaire, Anti-Semite and Jew,* and so on, he wove his own, personal interpretation through the Sartrean labyrinth. Thus, the history of a blind writer who insisted on living and thinking against himself and everybody else was gradually pieced together, like a serialized novel, over the course of several years.

W HILE THE French public was discovering a new Sartre in the discussions with Benny Lévy published in *Le Nouvel Observateur,* Sartre was in the intensive care unit of the Broussais hospital. His most intimate friends kept filing by his bedside. One doctor pleased him tremendously by saying he had read the latest issues of *Le Nouvel Observateur* with great interest. At the beginning of April, Benny Lévy had agreed to go to Jerusalem and Cairo for the Milan newspaper *Il Corriere della sera.* "I was in Cairo, my birthplace, when I learned that Sartre had been hospitalized and that it was the end. I immediately left Cairo and went to see him in the hospital. He was in the intensive care unit, strapped to various IVs, perfectly immobile. As soon as he saw me, he raised his head: 'Ah, Victor, we'll get back to work soon, don't worry.' He wanted to tell me about all the things we would be doing together as soon as he was out of there, he wanted to know about the reactions of foreign journalists and publishers to our discussions; some of them had already contacted us to get the rights to turn them into a small book."[60] Thus, in this schedule of visits, rigorously controlled by both Beauvoir and Arlette, each of the members of the "family" could see the dying philosopher, who was still talking about what he would be doing the rest of his life. One day, thanking Pouillon for the glass of water he was handing him, he said, "Next time, whisky at my place."[61] Sartre died at nine p.m., on April 15, 1980, in the Broussais hospital. Arlette was by his bedside. An hour later, the Agence France-Presse announced the news to the world.

"JEAN-PAUL Sartre Is Dead," read the *Libération* headlines. The first page of the paper was devoted entirely to him, with a large photo of the philosopher—at the beginning of the seventies—sitting on a bench in the Palais de Justice, his hands on his knees, and in the best of spirits as he is waiting to take the stand at yet another trial. "Sartre, this huge personality," Serge July wrote, "occupied his century the way Voltaire and Hugo occupied theirs . . . during the last forty years, he was everywhere, in all the writings, in every battle." "Sartre is dead," *Le Matin* announced, accompanying the page it had devoted to the event with a strange photo of a bespectacled Sartre, writing or reading in the middle of a great white light. "With him dies one of the few truly free men of our age," the commentary read, "one of the few honest men of this troubled, impotent age." "Jean-Paul Sartre's Death," *Le Figaro* printed on its first page, while, inside the paper, Jean d'Ormesson greeted the "last master of French thought." "His relationship with the Communist Party was not an easy one," Georges Marchais laconically noted in *L'Humanité*, while saluting "one of the greatest minds of our times." "Jean-Paul Sartre's Death," *Le Monde* echoed on its front page, and devoted eight full pages to "the passionate history of a committed intellectual." Every paper, whether national or regional, and every weekly, whether of the right or the left, devoted several pages of biography and photos to the event. Just a few days later, all the weeklies started publishing the personal accounts by various prestigious names. *L'Express, Le Nouvel Observateur, Le Point, Les Nouvelles littéraires* devoted both their covers and several pages to Sartre: more space than they had ever given to a literary story.

Testimonies from every conceivable source, excerpts from his published and unpublished works, lists of all the key dates—or what were presumed to be—in his life, his trips, his publications, all this was collated in a sort of immense family album that retraced the most crucial stages of our century. At bottom, this extraordinary buildup meant only one thing: the acknowledgement of a debt and the inability to quite pay it off. This frenzy of information often resorted to statistics, catalogues, simple enumerations: thus, Sartre was the author of some fifty works amounting to more or less fifteen thousand pages. These, in turn, could be subdivided into so many novels, so many short stories, so many articles, philosophical essays, etc., etc. Hence, *Libération* and *Le Matin* decided to prepare a special issue devoted entirely to Sartre: a real magazine of some thirty pages, a souvenir. For its cover, *Libération* chose a backlit photo of the philosopher walking along a Lithuanian beach, sometime in the fifties. *Le Matin* preferred the family-album style: the black-and-sepia photo of the young boy with long, golden curls analyzed by Sartre in *The Words*. Both magazines sold over a hundred thousand copies. On Friday evening, the eve of Sartre's burial, Bernard Pivot decided to cancel the planned program of "Apostrophes" and devoted the entire broadcast to a "Sartre Special," which included an odd confrontation between Benny Lévy and Raymond Aron.

The verbal inflation of the French press was immediately followed by that of its foreign counterpart: front page with photos in the case of both the *New York Times* and the *Washington Post*. "Despite his rupture with the PCF in 1956," the latter noted, "Sartre remained a communist." *Izvestia* devoted only five lines to the announcement of the death and the note that Sartre "had been a famous writer, philosopher, and polemicist." From Rome, the president of Italy, the socialist Sandro Pertini, sent a cable to Simone de Beauvoir in which he saluted "one of the most influential and original voices of the French consciousness [that had ever spoken out] for the highest human values of freedom and justice." The Italian press followed suit. "Our Friend, Our Master," was the title of Rossana Rossanda's article, which then concluded, "He lived and died running, generously, clearing some obstacles, falling, jumping back up, constantly putting everything into question. A splendid life." In Brazil, Jorge Amado told his audience that "the most important and most influential figure since the last war," had just died. In Athens, Melina Mercouri and Jules Dassin noted the loss of one of the greatest "activists of freedom." In London, Sir Alfred Ayer expressed his dismay at the "great loss" that had befallen "French culture." "A giant has just died," noted Professor Takeshi Ebisaka, a translator of Sartre's work, from Tokyo: "He has embodied the twentieth century, not just with his work, but also with his own attitude toward life." Even the Vatican, via *L'Osservatore Romano*, conveyed its somewhat reticent condolences for "the departure of one of the most prominent and controversial figures of the European intelligentsia." The president of Venezuela insisted on paying his official homage to Sartre at UNESCO.

All over the world, journalists kept hounding all sorts of personalities for a declaration, a statement, an opinion, a word: "I feel the loss of Jean-Paul Sartre," the president of the French Republic had declared, "as that of one of the greatest lights of our times. Jean-Paul Sartre always refused honors. I don't want the homage of the president of the republic to contradict this personal choice." Thus, the Elysée did not issue any official statement after the usual Wednesday meeting of the Council of Ministers. But the president, always respectful of Sartre's wishes, got in touch with the "family" and inquired as to Sartre's choice of burial, proposed an official funeral, delivered directives to facilitate its progress through the city, and had his private secretary, Jacques Wahl, represent him at the service. Then he informed Sartre's closest friends that he would personally go to the hospital to salute the writer's mortal remains. "At the hospital, the director was waiting for me," President Giscard d'Estaing remembers. "Then, I turned left and saw two coffins, one of them Sartre's. I was there for an hour. Nobody else showed up. Outside, there was a great commotion, everybody was talking about the funeral that was supposed to take place two days later, but there I was, alone, next to Sartre's coffin, in an anonymous hospital room. Leaving, I told myself that Sartre would probably have appreciated the starkness of my homage."[62]

"For Sartre," declared Daniel Cohn-Bendit to the Agence France-Presse, "the question was not so much to bring men together as to bring ideas together. He should not be remembered as the symbol of a leader he never wanted to be, but as that of a man who had always desired freedom. I believe many people share this desire." The immigrant workers' paper, *Sans frontières*, published a beautiful editorial by Saïd Bouziri: "Sartre went to Barbès to try and break the silence, to make sure that the immigrants would not be turned into scapegoats for everything, and, particularly, to keep fear away from their hearts. . . . Sartre was trying to establish a dialogue with the third world, as represented here. . . . His death is an immense loss." The only discordant notes in this chorus of praise came from a few Arab countries: "It is my opinion," the Palestinian political scientist Nafez Nazzal declared, "that his allegiance to Israel overrode all other concerns." Then things got more and more confused. Even *Bariona* was resuscitated to prove that, in his heart of hearts, Sartre was a crypto-Christian.

S ARTRE WAS dead, and life went on. All those who had loved him felt totally helpless in front of the avalanche of homages that kept pouring onto him. . . . a whirlwind in which all traces were confused, all chronology violated. He was, at once, a blond baby smiling in front of a boat at Thiviers, a Resistance fighter in Gide's garden, an existentialist guru in Saint-Germain-des-Prés, an anti-ambassador in Cuba, a graduating Normalien, with Aron, in 1925, an old man, with Aron, in 1979, a teacher frolicking with his students, a playwright rehearsing with his actors. He was shown smoking cigarettes, cigars, pipes; sitting in theaters and law courts, by prison doors and at political meetings; walking around a Chinese lake and along a Lithuanian beach; standing on a barrel; talking with Moravia, Godard, Khrushchev, François Périer, Nasser, Foucault, Nizan, Castro, Beauvoir, Genet, Cau, Michelle, Arlette.

The night of the wake, around his coffin, the veterans of *Les Temps modernes* had chatted, remembered, smoked, and drunk till five in the morning when one of the nurses had to insist they leave. "I won't say we had a great time," Jean Pouillon tells us, "but it was all right. We went out to get some whisky and then came back."[63] Bost, Pouillon, and Lanzmann were in charge of the funeral. Together, they went to the Montparnasse Cemetery to talk to the director and ask him a favor. Sartre hadn't anticipated anything. He wanted to be cremated, but, most of all, he did not want to end up in the spot that had been reserved for him next to his stepfather, in the Père-Lachaise Cemetery. The director of the Montparnasse Cemetery received Sartre's three friends with great civility: Sartre could, at first, be placed in a temporary grave, to the left of the gate, then he would be moved to a final resting place, in the first alley, to the right of the gate. "You'll see, it's very peaceful and not too far from Baudelaire. If I remember correctly, Sartre wrote a book on Baudelaire, didn't he?" He shook their hands, one by one, and then, approaching Pouillon, he added, with great pride, "I knew he would come to us."[64] Once this matter was settled, they decided the itinerary of the funeral: it would start from the hospital at two P.M., then file through the fourteenth arrondissement, past all Sartre's haunts, and enter the cemetery through the gate on the Boulevard Edgar-Quinet.

*T*HEY ARRIVED en masse at the Montparnasse Cemetery, with their children on their shoulders, so they would remember. An unexpectedly huge and variegated crowd. Scrambling, screams, fights. A man fell into the open grave onto the coffin. It was a Saturday afternoon, and more than fifty thousand people had come. Under a leaden gray sky, "Sartre's people" followed his coffin along a Sartrean itinerary extending nearly two miles, in spontaneous disorder.

It was even said that as the cortege passed La Coupole, some of its waiters came outside to bow. It was all modest and noble, sober and out of control. Sartre was going away, provoking by his departure one of the most unusual demonstrations of intellectual power in the late twentieth century. The lonely little man, isolated, anarchist, the childless father entered that day the realm of legend. Thrust, despite himself, up to the official pinnacle. Beggar forced to drag in his wake all the children of the century, to wear reluctantly the raiment of a star. The only writer to refuse the Nobel received on that day his tribute of homage and glory. No more craziness, no more defense. Falling, sliding, tumbling down infinitely into the vulgar pit of fame. In New York, on the day of Sartre's funeral, the French consul organized a service that included the showing of the film *Sartre by Himself*. Among the people in the audience was a small woman, with olive skin and hair tied in a tight bun. She was alone, anonymous. It was Dolorès.

*M*ILLIONS OF words of tribute to salute his departure, thousands of press dispatches in every tongue crisscrossing the globe, analyses, syntheses, photographs, quotations, from the masses of archives, words, papers, discussions. And yet a huge void: no funeral ode such as he had so often himself made for his comrades, Camus, Merleau, Nizan, Gide, Togliatti, Fanon. . . . No one to speak, at once lyrically and universally, as he had done when he saluted, with such panache, the life of his departed friends. Last flourish of the Untouchable? Perpetually elusive, active to the point of vertigo, Sartre might well have managed, to the day of his death, to avoid all such traps in weathered bronze and marble. "Death? I don't think about it," he had said two years before. "It has no place in my life, it will always be outside. One day, my life will end, but I don't want it to be burdened with death. I want," insisted the philosopher, "that my death never enter my life, nor define it, that I be always a call to life."

NOTES
BIBLIOGRAPHY
INDEX

NOTES

I. Toward Genius 1905–1939

SPOTLIGHT ON JEAN-BAPTISTE

1. This letter and the rest of Jean-Baptiste Sartre's letters quoted in this work are part of the Sartre family's private archives. They were found by Michèle Schmitt-Joannou, during her research in the French Southwest.
2. Archives of the Ecole Polytechnique.
3. Interview with Mme Raynaud, April 23, 1984.
4. All data concerning Jean-Baptiste Sartre's years in the navy are part of his personal files.
5. The navy historical archives, unpublished correspondence between the navy headquarters in the Far East and France, 1898–99,
6. Private family archives.

THE SORROWS OF ANNE-MARIE

1. Catalogue of the Albert Schweitzer exhibition at the Bibliothèque Nationale and the Strasbourg University library, 1975.
2. All the letters quoted in this chapter are also part of the Sartre family's private archives discovered in Périgueux.

THE PRIVATE BESTIARY OF A CHILD-KING

1. *The Words*, trans. Bernard Frechtman (New York: Vintage Books, 1981), p. 17.
2. *Ibid.*, p. 24.
3. *Ibid.*, p. 178.
4. *Ibid.*, p. 11.
5. *Ibid.*, p. 54.
6. *Ibid.*, p. 34.
7. *Ibid.*, pp. 105–6.
8. *L'Histoire d'Alsace racontée aux petits enfants* by Uncle Hansi and *Le Grand Livre de l'oncle Hansi* (Paris: Herscher, reissued in 1983).
9. Sartre-Schweitzer family archives.
10. From "Matériaux autobiographiques," unpublished manuscript prepared by Sartre for a television program (Jullian project, 1975). Daniel Lindenberg's archives.
11. *The Words*, p. 63.

12. All information concerning Nick Carter and the other reading of young Sartre was provided by Jean-Paul Mougin, of the review *A Suivre,* and by Pierre Pascal.

13. *The Words,* p. 133.

14. *Ibid.,* p. 217.

15. *Ibid.,* p. 219.

SCENES FROM LA ROCHELLE

1. "Jesus the Owl, Small-Town Schoolteacher," in *Selected Prose: The Writings of Jean-Paul Sartre,* trans. Richard McCleary (Evanston, Ill.: Northwestern University Press, 1974), p. 12.

2. Interview with Gérassi, quoted in Sartre, *Oeuvres romanesques* (Paris: Pléiade, Gallimard, 1981).

3. Conversation with Raymond de Magondeaux, as recorded by Michelle Schmitt, April 1983.

4. Interview with Guy Toublanc, February 14, 1984.

5. Interview with Gaston Blanchard, February 20, 1984.

6. Simone de Beauvoir, *Adieux: A Farewell to Sartre,* trans. Patrick O'Brian (New York: Pantheon Books, 1984), p. 292.

7. From "Matériaux autobiographiques."

8. Fernand Braudel and Ernest Labrousse, *Histoire économique et sociale de la France,* vol. 4, bk. 1, 1880–1914 (Paris: Presses Universitaires Françaises, 1979).

9. Interview with Sartre, by Catherine Chaîne, *Le Nouvel Observateur,* January–February 1977.

10. *Adieux,* p. 144.

11. From "Matériaux autobiographiques."

12. Letter dated September 1921.

A THOUSAND SOCRATES

1. Jean-Paul Sartre, preface to *Aden Arabie,* by Paul Nizan, trans. Joan Pinkham (New York: Monthly Review Press, 1968). Also reprinted in *Situations,* trans. Benito Eisler (New York: Braziller, 1965), p. 126. Hereafter cited as *Situations* (New York).

2. Sartre-Lannes family archives, Périgueux.

3. Interviews with Georges Canguilhem, June 8, 1982 and March 24, 1983.

4. Thesis by J.-F. Sirinelli, about the *khâgneux* and Normaliens of those years.

5. Unpublished text, Michel Rybalka's archives.

6. Paul Nizan, *La Conspiration* (Paris: Gallimard, 1938).

7. Published in *Les Ecrits de Sartre,* ed. Michel Contat and Michel Rybalka (Paris: Gallimard, 1970).

8. Unpublished text, partly published in *Le Magazine littéraire*, special issue on Sartre, 1970.

9. "Matériaux autobiographiques," p. 11.

10. Interviews with René Frédet, March 23, and June 29, 1983.

11. Paul Arthur Schilpp, "Interview with Sartre," *The Philosophy of Jean-Paul Sartre* (La Salle, Ill.: Open Court, 1982), pp. 5–51.

12. Henriette Nizan's archives.

13. French National Archives.

14. Allusion to the lines in Virgil's *Aeneid:* "Timeo Danaos et dona ferentes" (Beware of Greeks bringing gifts).

15. Allusion to Victor Hugo's collection of poems *Chansons des rues et des bois.*

16. All the information concerning the student revues is drawn from a conversation with Georges Canguilhem.

17. Jean Bruhat, *Il n'est jamais trop tard* (Paris: Albin Michel, 1982); and interviews with Jean Bruhat, October 9, 1978 and April 14, 1980.

18. Interviews with Jean Baillou, June 9, 1982, and with Emile Delavenay, May 16, 1983. Also, testimony of René Frédet and Georges Lefranc.

19. *Lettres au Castor et à quelques autres*, vol. 1 (Paris: Gallimard, 1983), p. 35.

20. Interview with Armand Bérard, April 16, 1983.

21. Interview with Jean Baillou, June 9, 1982.

22. Raymond Aron, *Le Spectateur engagé* and *Mémoires* (Paris: Julliard, 1981 and 1983).

23. Henriette Nizan's archives.

24. *Aden Arabie*, p. 60.

25. Interview with Georges Lefranc, May 26, 1982.

26. Conversations with Raymond Aron, April 30, 1980 and March 9, 1983.

27. Archives of the Ecole Normale Supérieure.

28. *The War Diaries*, trans. Quintin Hoare (New York: Pantheon Books, 1985), pp. 85–6.

29. *Les Nouvelles littéraires,* November 1926.

30. I have drawn all the information concerning Sartre's personality during his years at the Ecole Normale and in preparation for it from my correspondence and conversations with René Aillet, letters of September 24, October 11, and November 1, 1982; Marcel Bouisset letter of April 7, 1983; Maurice Deixonne, letter of April 27, 1983; Etienne Fuzellier, conversations, 1983; Henri Guillemin, letter of June 7, 1982; Vladimir Jankélévitch, letter of July 2, 1982; Olivier Lacombe, conversation of March 21, 1983; Robert Lucot, letter of April 3, 1983; André Monchoux, letter of March 23, 1983; Marcel Paquot, letter of March 23, 1983; Louis Robert, letter of March 25, 1983; Edouard Selzer, conversation of June 1, 1983; Pierre Vilar, conversation of June 2, 1982; Robert-Léon Wagner, conversation of April 28, 1980.

31. Arlette Elkaïm-Sartre's archives.

32. Conversation with Jeanne Virmouneix, recorded by Michèle Schmitt, April 1984.
33. Interview with Sartre, "Sartre et les femmes," by Catherine Chaîne, *Le Nouvel Observateur*, February 1977.
34. *Lettres au Castor*, p. 15.
35. *Ibid.*, p. 33.
36. *Ibid.*
37. *Ibid.*, p. 29.
38. "Une Défaite" pp. 81–2.
39. Conversation with Jean Baillou, June 9, 1982.
40. "Une Défaite," p. 36.
41. Chaîne, interview with Sartre.
42. *Ibid.*
43. Conversations with Maurice de Gandillac, April 22, 1980, May 10, 1982, and February 27, 1985.
44. Simone de Beauvoir, *Memoirs of a Dutiful Daughter*, trans. James Kirkup (Cleveland and New York: World Publishing Company, 1959), p. 355.
45. *Ibid.*, pp. 355–6.
46. *Ibid.*, p. 364.
47. *The War Diaries*, p. 75.
48. *Lettres au Castor*, pp. 42–4.
49. Alice Schwarzer, *After the Second Sex: Conversations with Simone de Beauvoir*, trans. Marianne Howarth (New York: Pantheon Books, 1984), p. 110.

JUST ONE SOCRATES

1. Prize Day speech (partly unpublished), archives of the Le Havre high school (in *Selected Prose*, pp. 53–9) and conversation with Claude Chartrel (archives curator), May 27 and 28, 1983.
2. *Lettres au Castor*, p. 46.
3. Sartre, *Oeuvres romanesques*, p. 1736.
4. Conversations with Jean Giustiniani, May 28 and 29, 1983.
5. According to Robert Marchandeau, in *Bulletin des anciens élèves du lycée François-Ier*, no. 75, special issue on Sartre, as reported by André Vogel, May 27, 1983.
6. According to Pierre Guitard, in *ibid.*
7. Conversation with Pierre Brument, May 27, 1983.
9. Conversation with Jacques-Laurent Bost, November 25, 1982.
10. According to Georges Le Sidaner, *Bulletin des anciens élèves*.
11. Sartre file, Archives of the Ministry of Education.
12. *Adieux*, p. 259.
13. All information concerning Sartre's stay in Le Havre from my conversations with Francis Bobée, May 29, 1982; Claire Bost, July 18, 1982; Jacques

Levavasseur, November 14, 1982. To the various reports drawn from *Bulletin des anciens élèves du lycée François-1er,* I would also like to add the names of Roger Fleury, Albert Palle, and Daniel Palmer.

14. Simone de Beauvoir, *The Prime of Life,* trans. Peter Green (Cleveland and New York: World Publishing Company, 1962), pp. 21–2.

15. *The War Diaries,* pp. 271–3

16. *Lettres au Castor,* p. 9.

17. Quoted in Sartre, *Oeuvres romanesques,* p. xliv.

18. *Nausea,* trans. Lloyd Alexander, (New York: New Directions, 1964), p. 6.

19. *Ibid.,* p. 26; *Oeuvres romanesques,* p. 1739; *Nausea,* pp. 63–4; *Oeuvres romanesques,* p. 1739.

20. *Memoirs of a Dutiful Daughter,* p. 361.

21. *Oeuvres romanesques,* p. 1728

22. *Ibid.,* p. 1755.

23. Jean-Toussaint Desanti, *Introduction à la phénoménologie* (Paris: Gallimard, 1976), p. 32.

24. *The War Diaries,* pp. 85–6.

25. Desanti, *Introduction,* p. 148.

26. *The War Diaries,* p. 184.

27. *La Transcendance de l'Ego* (Paris: Vrin, 1966), p. 18. Translated as *The Transcendence of the Ego* by Forrest Williams and Robert Kirkpatrick (New York: Farrar, Straus, and Giroux, n.d.), p. 93.

28. *Ibid.,* p. 31.

29. *Ibid.,* p. 105.

30. *Ibid.,* p. 106.

31. François H. Lapointe, *Jean-Paul Sartre and His Critics: An International Bibliography (1938–1980),* Philosophy Documentation Center, Bowling Green State University, Ohio, 1981, p. 329.

32. *The War Diaries,* p. 184.

33. Sartre–Paulhan unpublished correspondence, Jean Paulhan's archives.

34. *The War Diaries,* p. 184.

35. Unpublished texts of the Le Havre lectures reported by Simone de Beauvoir, Simone de Beauvoir's archives.

36. Conversations with Maurice de Gandillac, May 10, 1982 and February 27, 1985.

37. According to Jean-François Sirinelli, who met Susini in November 1980.

38. J.-B. Duroselle, *Politique étrangère de la France: La Décadence 1932–1939* (Paris: Le Seuil, 1979), pp. 57–61.

39. Pierre Mac Orlan, *Le Mystère de la malle no. 1* (Paris: Christian Bourgois, 1984), pp. 185–6.

40. *Ibid.,* pp. 162–3.

41. Conversation with Raymond Aron, March 9, 1983.

42. Conversation with Henri Brunschwig, March 18, 1983.

43. Details of Sartre's life in Berlin drawn from my correspondence with Henri Jourdan, letters of March 6 and 9, 1983.

44. *The War Diaries*, pp. 281–2.

45. *Ibid.*, p. 285.

46. *Ibid.*, p. 62.

47. *Ibid.*, p. 183.

48. Anecdote related to J.-F. Sirinelli by Eugène Susini.

49. Raymonde Vincent, *Le Temps d'apprendre à vivre* (Paris: Julliard, 1982), pp. 261–2.

DARK MOOD, MADNESS, OTHER JOURNEYS…

1. *The War Diaries*, p. 111.

2. *The Psychology of Imagination* (New York: Washington Square Press, 1966), pp. 202–3.

3. *The Prime of Life*, p. 169.

4. Conversation with Simone de Beauvoir, March 27, 1983.

5. *The Prime of Life*, p. 204.

6. *The War Diaries*, p. 4.

7. *Ibid.*, p. 78.

8. *Ibid.*

9. *The Prime of Life*, p. 205.

10. *Ibid.*, p. 194.

11. *Ibid.*

12. *Ibid.*, p. 193.

13. *Lettres au Castor*, p. 109.

14. *The Age of Reason*, trans. Eric Sutton (New York: Vintage Books, 1973), p. 73.

15. *The War Diaries*, p. 282.

16. Quoted in Sartre, *Oeuvres romanesques*, p. 1689.

17. *Lettres au Castor*, p. 79.

18. Censored passage from *Nausea*, *Oeuvres romanesques*, pp. 1736–7.

19. Quoted in Marcel Jean, *Autobiographie du surréalisme* (Paris: Le Seuil, 1978), p. 335. Breton's article is titled "Du Temps que les surréalistes avaient raison," and it is signed by twenty-six surrealists and their sympathizers, among them Dali, Eluard, Ernst, Magritte, Péret, Man Ray, Tanguy.

20. Conversation with Colette Audry, December 9, 1982.

21. Paul Nizan, *The Trojan Horse* (New York: Fertig, reprint ed. 1975), pp. 58–60.

22. *Ibid.*, p. 196.

23. *The Prime of Life*, p. 190.

24. *Lettres au Castor*, p. 113.

INTERLUDE: TWO YEARS OF HAPPINESS

1. Conversation with Robert Gallimard, November 18, 1982.
2. *Lettres au Castor*, p. 114.
3. *Ibid.*
4. *Ibid.*, p. 115.
5. Conversation with Jacques-Laurent Bost, November 25, 1982.
6. Correspondence between J.-P. Sartre and the Gallimards, quoted in *Oeuvres romanesques*, pp. 1691–4.
7. *Ibid.*
8. *Ibid.*
9. See *Débat*, no. 29, March 1984.
10. *Oeuvres romanesques*, pp. 1693–4.
11. Correspondence, Pléiade, p. 1694.
12. Conversation with Raoul Lévy, January 27, 1983.
13. Conversations with Gérard Blanchet, January 6 and July 26, 1983.
14. Conversation with Bernard Pingaud, February 3, 1983; as for *Le Trait d'union*, see Pinguad's article in *Le Matin*, April 15, 1981.
15. Conversation with Jacques Ghinsberg, December 21, 1982.
16. Alfred Tomatis, *L'Oreille et la vie* (Paris: Laffont, 1977), pp. 37–9.
17. Archives of the Ministry of Education, Sartre file.
18. Information concerning Sartre's years at the Lycée Pasteur drawn from my conversation with Jean Pouillon (who worked with Sartre after his *agrégation* in philosophy), August 17, 1982. Further information was supplied by Mlle Martin, secretary to the assistant headmaster from 1937 to 1942, during her conversation with Marie Nimier, October 12, 1982.
19. Letter dated July 27, 1937.
20. *Cahiers de la Petite Dame*, vol. 3, 1938–1945 (Paris: Gallimard, 1976).
21. See *Oeuvres romanesques*, pp. 1701–11.
22. *Ibid.*, pp. 1810–1917.
23. *Lettres au Castor*, p. 217.
24. *Ibid.*, p. 210.
25. *The Wall*, trans. Lloyd Alexander (New York: New Directions, 1948), pp. 142–3.
26. *Ibid.*, p. 144.
27. Paulhan unpublished correspondence, Jean Paulhan's archives, letter dated July 1937.
28. *Ibid.*, July 21, 1937.
29. *Ibid.*, August 13, 1938.
30. *Ibid.*, September 13, 1938.
31. Sartre-Paulhan unpublished correspondence, Jean Paulhan's archives, 1938.
32. *Ibid.*, Casablanca, summer 1938.
33. Letter dated 1939.

34. Sartre's articles on, respectively, Dos Passos, Mauriac, and Faulkner, *Nouvelle Revue Française* (*NRF*), February 1938, August 1938, February 1939.
35. *L'Action française,* April 13, 1939.
36. *Gringoire,* March 16, 1939. For more on the extreme right in the thirties, see J.-F. Sirinelli, "Action française, main basse sur le Quartier Latin," in *L'Histoire,* no. 51, December 1982.
37. *Ce Soir,* May 16, 1938.
38. *NRF,* November 1938.
39. See Claude-Jean Philippe, *Le Roman du cinéma* (Paris: Fayard, 1984).
40. From *Qu'est-ce que la littérature?* (Paris: Gallimard, 1947), translated by Bernard Frechtman as *What Is Literature?* (New York: Harper and Row, 1965).
41. *Lettres au Castor,* pp. 214–15.
42. *Ibid.,* p. 233.
43. *Ibid.,* p. 188.
44. *Ibid.,* p. 268.
45. *Ibid.,* p. 271.
46. *Marianne,* November 23 and December 7, 1938.

II. The Metamorphosis of War 1939–1945

A WAR À LA KAFKA

1. *Situations X* (Paris: Gallimard, 1976), p. 179.
2. Letter to Jean Paulhan, September 23, 1939.
3. *Adieux,* pp. 356 and 387–8.
4. French National Archives, "Prison Camps" file.
5. Letter to Jean Paulhan, December 13, 1939.
6. Letter to Adrienne Monnier, February 23, 1940, quoted in *Oeuvres romanesques,* p. 1911, and in the Introduction to *The War Diaries,* p. viii.
7. *The War Diaries,* pp. 43–4.
8. *Ibid.,* pp. 154–6, and 157.
9. "La Mort dans l'âme," variant, *Oeuvres romanesques,* p. 2055.
10. *Adieux,* p. 263.
11. Letter to Simone de Beauvoir, January 12, 1940, quoted in *Oeuvres romanesques,* p. 1903
12. French National Archives, "Prison Camps" file.
13. *Ibid.*
14. *Adieux,* p. 282.
15. Letter to Simone de Beauvoir, April 13, 1940, quoted in *Oeuvres romanesques,* p. 1906.
16. French National Archives, "Prison Camps" file.
17. *Ibid.*

18. *Ibid.*

19. Letter to Simone de Beauvoir, October 22, 1939, quoted in *Oeuvres romanesques*, p. 1895.

20. Letter to Jean Paulhan, December 13, 1939.

21. Letter to Simone de Beauvoir, October 26, 1939, quoted in *Oeuvres romanesques*.

22. *Ibid.*, January 6, 1940.

23. *Ibid.*

24. *The War Diaries*, p. 244.

25. *Ibid.*, pp. 72 and 73.

26. Unpublished war diaries, April 23, 1940.

27. *Ibid.*

28. *Ibid.*, January 9, 1940.

29. *Ibid.*

30. *Ibid.*, January 15, 1940.

31. *Ibid.*

32. *Ibid.*, December 3, 1940.

33. *Ibid.*, October 26, 1939.

34. *Ibid.*, January 6, 1940.

35. Quoted in *Oeuvres romanesques*, p. 1860.

36. Letter to Simone de Beauvoir, October 23, 1939.

37. *Ibid.*, April 15, 1940.

38. *Ibid.*, May 4, 1940.

39. *Ibid.*, January 25, 1940.

40. *Ibid.*

41. *Ibid.*, May 1, 1940.

42. *Ibid.*, November 27, 1939.

43. *Ibid.*, January 12, 1940.

44. *Ibid.*, January 11, 1940.

45. *Ibid.*, March 23, 1940.

46. French National Archives, "Prison Camps" file.

47. *The Prime of Life*, pp. 331 and 333.

48. *Lettres au Castor*, p. 391.

49. Claude Vervin, "Lectures de prisonniers," interview with Sartre, *Les Lettres françaises*, December 2, 1944, p. 3.

50. *Lettres au Castor*, pp. 291 and 658.

51. *Ibid.*, p. 307.

52. "La Mort dans l'âme," pages from the diary published in the journal *Messages, exercice du silence* (Brussels, 1942), and quoted in *Les Ecrits de Sartre*, pp. 638–49.

53. *Ibid.*

54. *Ibid.*

55. *Ibid.*

56. *Adieux*, p. 388.

57. *Troubled Sleep,* trans. Gerard Hopkins (New York: Vintage Books, 1973), p. 42.
58. *Ibid.,* p. 243.
59. *Adieux,* p. 389.
60. *Ibid.*
61. French National Archives, "Prison Camps" file.

A LOFTY CAPTIVITY

1. Vervin, "Lectures de prisonniers."
2. Jean-Paul Sartre, "Journal de Mathieu," an unpublished notebook, *Les Temps modernes,* September 1982.
3. *Ibid.,* p. 450.
4. Conversation with John Gérassi, 1973, quoted in *Oeuvres romanesques,* p. lxi.
5. *Les Temps modernes,* September 1982, p. 460.
6. "La Mort dans l'âme," variant, *Oeuvres romanesques,* p. 1580.
7. In *Jean-Paul Sartre, un film,* p. 67, and *Oeuvres romanesques,* p. 2147.
8. Conversation with John Gérassi, quoted in *Oeuvres romanesques,* p. lxi.
9. *Les Temps modernes,* September 1982.
10. *Ibid.,* p. 457.
11. *Ibid.*
12. *Ibid.,* pp. 451–2.
13. *Ibid.*
14. Marius Perrin, *Avec Sartre au Stalag XII D* (Paris: Delarge, 1980), pp. 128–9.
15. *Les Temps modernes,* September 1982, p. 472.
16. *Adieux,* p. 264.
17. *Ibid.*
18. Conversation with Jacques-Laurent Bost, November 25, 1982.
19. *Adieux,* pp. 410–11.
20. Perrin, *Avec Sartre,* pp. 107–8.
21. *Ibid.,* pp. 453–8.
22. *Ibid.,* p. 463.
23. *Ibid.,* pp. 65–6.
24. *Ibid.*
25. *Sartre on Theater,* ed. Michel Contat and Michel Rybalka, trans. Frank Jellinek (New York: Pantheon Books, 1976), p. 39.
26. Perrin, *Avec Sartre,* pp. 93 ff.
27. *Selected Prose,* pp. 75–7; bracketed sentence translated for the present book.
28. *Adieux,* p. 183.
29. *Sartre on Theater,* p. 185.
30. *Adieux,* p. 183.
31. *Les Temps modernes,* September 1982, pp. 474–5.
32. Perrin, *Avec Sartre,* pp. 127–8.

33. *Les Temps modernes,* September 1982, p. 466.
34. Perrin, *Avec Sartre,* p. 149.
35. *Les Temps modernes,* September 1982.
36. Vervin, "Lectures de prisonniers."
37. *Adieux.*

"SOCIALISM AND FREEDOM"

1. *Situations* (New York), p. 178.
2. Ernst Jünger, *Premier Journal parisien, 1941–1943* (Paris: Christian Bourgois, 1980), p. 15.
3. About French literature under the Occupation, see Gérard Loiseaux, *La Littérature de la défaite et de la collaboration* (Paris: Sorbonne, 1984).
4. *Adieux,* p. 390.
5. *The Prime of Life,* p. 381.
6. Conversation with Jean-Daniel Jurgensen, October 25, 1982.
7. J.-B. Pontalis, excerpts from a work in progress kindly made available by the author; and conversations with J.-B. Pontalis, May 11 and 18, 1983.
8. Conversations with Raoul Lévy, January 21 and 27, 1983.
9. Dominique Desanti, "Le Sartre que je connais," in *Jeune Afrique,* November 8, 1964.
10. Conversation with Dominique and Jean-Toussaint Desanti, July 7, 1982.
11. Conversation with Georges Chazelas, September 20, 1982.
12. Conversation with Jean Pouillon, August 17, 1982.
13. Conversation with Georges Chazelas.
14. Desanti, in *Jeune Afrique.*
15. Cf. Stéphane Courtois, *Le P.C.F. dans la guerre* (Paris: Ramsay, 1980).
16. Conversation with the Desantis.
17. Conversation with Georges Chazelas.
18. Louis François, general inspector of national education, report of 1947, French National Archives, 72 AJ 49.
19. Conversation with Simone Debout, July 21, 1982.
20. Conversations with Raoul Lévy, January 21 and 27, 1983.
21. Conversation with Simone Debout.
22. Conversations with Raoul Lévy.
23. Conversation with Jean-Toussaint Desanti.
24. Conversations with Raoul Lévy.
25. Conversation with Jean-Toussaint Desanti.
26. *The Prime of Life,* pp. 289–90.
27. *Ibid.*
28. Conversation with Mme Pierre Kaan, September 23, 1982.
29. *Ibid.*
30. Conversation with Jean Rabaut, August 23, 1982.
31. *The Prime of Life,* p. 392.
32. *Ibid.*

33. Gisèle Freund, *Le Monde et ma caméra* (Paris: Denoël, 1970), p. 94.

34. Letter to Jean Paulhan from Jean-Paul Sartre, unpublished correspondence, Jacqueline Paulhan's archives. Undated letter probably sent around August 26, 1939.

35. André Gide, *Journal 1939–1942* (Paris: Gallimard, 1946), p. 123.

36. *Ibid.*, September 15, 1941, pp. 158–9.

37. *The Prime of Life*, p. 393.

38. André Gide, *Correspondance avec Roger Martin du Gard, 1913–1951* (Paris: Gallimard, 1968), p. 237.

39. *The Prime of Life*, p. 393.

40. Jean Lacouture, *André Malraux* (Paris: Le Seuil, 1973), p. 276.

41. Conversation with Colette Audry, December 9, 1982.

42. *Adieux*, p. 363.

43. *The Prime of Life*, p. 396.

44. Conversation with Simone Debout.

45. Conversation with Jean Pouillon.

46. *Situations*, p. 231.

47. Conversation with Raoul Lévy.

48. Conversation with the Desantis.

49. Conversation with Georges Chazelas.

50. Conversation with Raoul Lévy.

51. Conversation with Jacques Debû-Bridel, October 8, 1982. In fact he would have liked to mention S. Jollivet by name.

52. *Ibid.*

53. Conversation with Jean Pouillon.

54. *The Prime of Life*, p. 384.

55. *Selected Prose*, pp. 138–9.

56. Jacques-Toussaint Desanti, *Un Destin philosophique* (Paris: Grasset, 1982), p. 149.

IMPASSE

1. *The Prime of Life*, p. 419.

2. *Ibid.*, p. 399.

3. *Ibid.*, p. 401.

4. *Situations III* (Paris: Gallimard, 1949), p. 11.

5. *Ibid.*, pp. 18–22.

6. *Sartre on Theater*, p. 188.

7. *The Prime of Life*, p. 385.

8. *Les Lettres françaises* clandestines, no. 12.

9. *Comoedia*, June 19, 1943, p. 1.

10. *La Gerbe*, June 17, 1943.

11. *Sartre on Theater*, p. 188.

12. *Ibid.*, pp. 190–1.

13. Unpublished letter, Paulhan archives.

14. All information concerning the French theater under the Occupation drawn from my conversations with Christian Casadesus, May 10 and October 14, 1982.
15. *The Prime of Life*, p. 412.
16. *Lettres au Castor*, vol. 1.
17. *The War Diaries*, p. 182.
18. *Being and Nothingness*, trans. Hazel Barnes (New York: Washington Square Press, 1966), p. 675.
19. *Ibid.*, p. 671.
20. *Ibid.*, p. 672.
21. *Ibid.*, p. 41.
22. André Gorz, *Le Traître* (Paris: Le Seuil, 1958), p. 243.
23. *Les Nouvelles littéraires*, October 29, 1964.
24. "Les pieds dans le plat," in *Le Nouvel Observateur*, April 21, 1980.
25. *Situations I* (Paris: Gallimard, 1947), p. 109.
26. *Alger républicain*, October 20, 1938.
27. *Situations I*, p. 133.
28. *Selected Prose*, pp. 152–3.

"A WRITER WHO RESISTED,
NOT A RESISTANCE FIGHTER WHO WROTE..."

1. From an unpublished Sartre interview with John Gérassi in 1973, quoted in *Oeuvres romanesques*, p. lxiii.
2. *Lettres au Castor*, p. 827, summer 1943.
3. From unpublished notebooks of Sartre.
4. *Lettres au Castor*, p. 831–2.
5. *The Prime of Life*, pp. 436 ff.
6. Claude Morgan, *Les Don Quichotte et les autres* (Paris: Guy Roblot, 1979), p. 140.
7. Conversation with Jean Lescure, September 21, 1982.
8. Jacques Debû-Bridel, *La Résistance intellectuelle en France* (Paris: Julliard, 1970), p. 95.
9. *Les Lettres françaises* clandestines, no. 6, April 1943.
10. *Ibid.*, no. 15, April 1944.
11. Jean Kanapa, *Comme is la lutte entière*, p. 256.
12. Conversation with Jean Bruller-Vercors, September 22, 1982.
13. Archives of the Ministry of Education.
14. Conversation with Mme Pierre Kaan, September 23, 1982.
15. Conversation with Pierre Piganiol, December 14, 1983.
16. Oudard file, French National Archives.
17. Cf. *Les Ecrits de Sartre*, pp. 110–1. Georges Michel's hypotheses seem quite pertinent. But it would be impossible, as Contat and Rybalka point out, to consider this text in 1941 as part of the experience of "Socialism and Freedom": all the members of the group—Debout, Desanti, Chazelas—have

confirmed my doubts. On the other hand—and the historical elements within the text itself are evidence of this—there are ample reasons for placing this text in 1943, during Sartre's meetings with Pierre Kaan.

18. Unpublished text, French National Archives.

19. *The Prime of Life*, p. 439.

20. *Ibid.*, pp. 442, 452, and 444.

21. *Ibid.*, p. 445.

22. Conversation with Simone de Beauvoir, March 22, 1983.

23. Conversation with Jean Balladur, November 16, 1982.

24. Jean Balladur's notes, personal archives.

25. Conversation with Jean Balladur.

26. Conversation with Jean Chouleur, February 22, 1983.

27. Cf. Sartre's own opinion in *Sartre on Theater*, p. 78: "Alain used to say that a teacher should not engage the emotions of his pupils."

28. Conversation with Robert Misrahi, October 7, 1982.

29. Archives of the Ministry of Education, Sartre file.

SPIRITUAL LEADER FOR THOUSANDS OF YOUNG PEOPLE

1. *The Prime of Life*, p. 455.

2. According to Simone de Beauvoir; see *ibid.*, p. 449.

3. *Lettres au Castor*, p. 834.

4. *The Prime of Life*, p. 418.

5. *Ibid.*, p. 457.

6. *Lettres au Castor*, p. 319.

7. Unpublished letter, Paulhan's archives.

8. *Situations I*, pp. 229–30.

9. According to Simone de Beauvoir; see *The Prime of Life*, pp. 449–52.

10. *Ibid.*, p. 454.

11. *Lettres au Castor*, p. 835.

12. *Combat*, April 15, 1947.

13. Private archives of the Le Havre lycée.

14. Unpublished screenplay, IDHEC archives, kindly made available by Marianne de Fleury.

15. Cf. Nino Frank, *Petit Cinéma sentimental*, pp. 167–74.

16. *Ibid.*, and conversation with Nino Frank, February 25, 1983.

17. *Les Lettres françaises* clandestines, April 15, 1944, p. 4.

18. *Lettres au Castor*, p. 835.

19. *Sartre on Theater*, p. 199.

20. *Combat*, February 9, 1945.

21. *No Exit*, trans. Stuart Gilbert (New York: Vintage Books, 1955), pp. 47, 36.

22. *Sartre on Theater*, p. 199.

23. According to Sartre himself, see *Situations IX* (Paris: Gallimard, 1972), p. 10.

24. Alain Laubreaux, in *Je suis partout*, June 4, 1944.
25. Quoted by Pierre-Marie Dioudonnat in *L'Argent nazi à la conquête de la presse française, 1940–1944* (Paris: Jean Picollec, 1981), p. 262.
26. *Germinal*, June 30, 1944.
27. *Horizon*, July 1945.
28. Unpublished letter to Marcel Jouhandeau, Paulhan archives.
29. *Journal des années noires* (Paris: Gallimard, 1947), p. 475, May 30, 1944.
30. Conversation with Guillaume Hanoteau, October 14, 1982.
31. For the text of both report and discussion see *Sartre on Theater*, pp. 6–29.
32. *The Prime of Life*, pp. 460–1.
33. *Ibid.*, p. 467.
34. Uncollected series of seven articles that appeared in *Combat*. August 29, 1944, pp. 1 and 2: "Colère d'une ville."
35. *Les Yeux ouverts dons Paris insurgé* (Paris: Julliard, 1944), p. 13.
36. *Combat*, August 29, 1944: "Colère d'une ville."
37. *Ibid.*, September 1, 1944: "Espoirs et angoisses de l'insurrection."
38. *Ibid.*, September 2, 1944: "La Délivrance est à nos portes."
39. *Ibid.*, September 4, 1944: "Un Jour de victoire parmi les balles."
40. *Les Lettres françaises*, no. 20, September 9, 1944.
41. *France libre*, November 1945.
42. *République française*, November 1945.
43. *Les Temps modernes*, no. 1, October 1945.
44. *Clarté*, no. 9, August 29, 1954. *Selected Prose*, pp. 161–4.
45. Janet Flanner, *Paris Journal 1944–1965* (New York: Harcourt Brace Jovanovich, 1977), p. 3.
46. Claude Morgan, *Les Don Quichotte*, p. 154.
47. Conversation with Guillaume Hanoteau, October 4, 1982.
48. Conversation with Jean Lescure, September 21, 1982.
49. Conversation with Jacques Debû-Bridel, October 8, 1982.
50. *Ibid.*
51. *The Prime of Life*, p. 445.
52. Conversation with Vercors, September 27, 1982.
53. Paulhan archives, unpublished letter dated December 10, 1944.
54. *Ibid.*, dated October 1, 1944.
55. See complete text in *Selected Prose*, pp. 155–60.
56. See Michel Butor's statements in the special issue of *Obliques*: "Sartre et les Arts," 1981, pp. 67–9.
57. "Signification de Sartre," in *Messages*, 1943, pp. 413–24.
58. Paulhan archives, unpublished letters dated 1944 (no months).

FROM BUFFALO BILL TO FDR: THE FIRST TRIP TO AMERICA

1. Unpublished notes, Simone de Beauvoir's archives.
2. *The Prime of Life*, p. 114.

3. William Faulkner, *Flags in the Dust* (New York: Vintage Books, 1974), p. 96.

4. *Situations I,* p. 9.

5. *Ibid.,* p. 68.

6. *Situations III,* pp. 122–3.

7. *Adieux,* p. 236.

8. *Situations I,* pp. 113–15.

9. Conversation with Henriette Nizan, February 23, 1982.

10. While Sartre's first article was making waves in France, the American press was up in arms about General William Donovan's imminent creation of the CIA; "American Gestapo" was how Senator Homer Capehart described it in February 1945. For further information about the American political situation at the time of Sartre's trip see Anthony Cave Brown's *The Last Hero: Wild Bill Donovan* (New York: Times Books, 1982).

11. J.-B. Duroselle, *L'Abîme* (Paris: Imprimerie Nationale, 1982).

12. *New York Times,* January 25, 1945.

13. *Ibid.,* January 13, 1945; and *Pour la victoire,* February 3, 1945.

14. *New York Times,* February 1, 1945.

15. *Le Figaro,* January 25, 1945.

16. *France-Amérique,* February 11, 1945.

17. *Ibid.,* February 4, 1945.

18. *Ibid.*

19. Conversation with Denis de Rougemont, July 11, 1983.

20. See complete text in *Vogue,* July 1945; and "New Writing in France," in *Oeuvres romanesques,* pp. 1917–21.

21. Conversation with Denis de Rougemont.

22. Stéphane Pizella, *Les Nuits du bout du monde* (Paris: André Bonne, 1953).

23. *Situations III,* p. 78.

24. *Ibid.,* pp. 120–1.

25. Claude Lévi-Strauss, *Le Regard éloigné* (Paris: Plon, 1983), pp. 348, 350, 358.

26. Pizella, *Les Nuits,* pp. 177–9.

27. "Un Français à New York," in *Combat,* February 2, 1945.

28. *Situations III,* pp. 116–17.

29. "Nick's Bar, New York City," *Selected Prose,* pp. 182–4.

30. Conversation with Dolorès, May 4, 1983.

31. This reconstruction was made possible thanks to articles and photos from Paule Neuvéglise's archives, and documents from archives of the FBI, the Department of State, and the Department of the Air Force.

32. *Le Figaro,* March 11 and 12, 1945.

33. *Combat,* March 8 and 9, 1945.

34. *Ibid.,* July 12, 14, and 30, 1945.

35. Conversation with Vladimir Pozner, November 3, 1982.

36. *Combat,* April 5, 1945.
37. *Ibid.,* June 7, 1945.
38. "Ce que j'ai appris du problème noir," in *Le Figaro,* June 16, 1945.
39. *Situations III,* pp. 99–100.
40. See Addison Gayle, *Richard Wright: Ordeal of a Native Son* (New York: Doubleday, 1980), pp. 162 and 171.
41. Anecdote related by Pizella, *Les Nuits,* p. 156.
42. Material obtained from the FBI.
43. *Adieux,* p. 227.

III. *The Sartre Years 1945–1956*

PARIS: THE ERA OF EXISTENTIALISM

1. Conversation with Marc Beigbeder, July 12, 1984.
2. *Lettres au Castor,* May 1, 1940, vol. 2, p. 201.
3. *The Prime of Life,* p. 410.
4. *Oeuvres romanesques,* p. 1911.
5. *Le Monde,* April 1947.
6. *Combat,* September 8, 1945.
7. *Terre des hommes,* November 3, 1945.
8. *Le Figaro,* November 3, 1945.
9. *Terre des hommes,* November 3, 1945.
10. Conversation with Maurice Nadeau, July 11, 1984.
11. *Petite histoire de l'existentialisme* (Paris: Club Maintenant, 1946), pp. 84–6.
12. *Pour ou contre l'existentialisme* (Paris: Atlas, 1948).
13. *Samedi soir,* November 3, 1945.
14. *Ibid.*
15. *Ibid.*
16. Quoted by Georgette Elgey, *La République des illusions* (Paris: Fayard, 1965), p. 509.
17. *Samedi soir,* November 17, 1945.
18. *Ibid.,* February 23, 1946.
19. *Ibid.,* December 21, 1946.
20. *Ibid.,* November 24, 1945.
21. *Ibid.,* December 15, 1945.
22. *Ibid.,* April 24, 1946.
23. Quoted in *Oeuvres romanesques,* p. 1927.
24. *Le Crapouillot,* no. 32, pp. 60 and 61.
25. *Les Nouvelles littéraires,* November 15, 1945.
26. Interview in *Paru,* December 1945.
27. *Le Monde,* December 11 and 15, 1945.
28. Christine Cronan, *Petit Catéchisme de l'existentialisme pour les profanes* (Paris: Dumoulin, 1948).

29. Quoted in Guillaume Hanoteau's *L'Age d'or de Saint-Germain-des-Prés*, (Paris: Denoël), 1965, p. 119.

544

30. *Combat*, September 8, 1945.
31. *Terre des hommes*, November 3, 1945.

NEW YORK

1. *Time*, January 28, 1946.
2. *Lettres au Castor*, p. 325.
3. *Ibid.*
4. *Cahiers pour une morale* (Paris: Gallimard, 1983), app. I, pp. 573–8.
5. *Lettres au Castor*, p. 330.
6. *New York Post*, April 9, 1946.
7. Conversation with Dolorès, New York, May 1983.
8. *Lettres au Castor*, p. 335.
9. *Life*, June 17, 1946.
10. Conversation with Henri Peyre, May 18, 1982; and letter from Henri Peyre, May 14, 1982.
11. Victor Brombert, *The Intellectual Hero* (New York: Viking Press, 1960).
12. *Atlantic Monthly*, August 1946, translated into French in *Les Ecrits de Sartre*, pp. 150–1.
13. *Yale French Studies*, Spring–Summer 1948.
14. Letter from Harry Levin, March 26, 1982.
15. *The New Yorker*, March 16, 1946.
16. *Salmagundi*, no. 56, spring 1982.
17. *Partisan Review Press*, 1947.
18. Conversation with William Barrett, May 25, 1982.
19. Conversation with Irving Howe, New York, May 20, 1982.
20. Conversation with William Phillips, May 15, 1983.
21. *Salmagundi*, no. 56, spring 1982.
22. Conversation with Norbert Guterman, New York, May 17, 1982.
23. Herbert Marcuse, "Existentialism: Remarks on J.-P. Sartre's *L'Etre et le Néant*," in *Philosophy and Phenomenological Research*, vol. 8 (March 1948), pp. 309–36, republished in *Studies in Critical Philosophy* (Boston: Beacon Press, 1973).
24. Conversation with Erving Goffman, Philadelphia, March 11, 1982.
25. In *Force of Circumstance*, trans. Richard Howard (New York: Putnam 1964), Simone de Beauvoir says she and Sartre met C. Wright Mills during one of their trips.
26. Conversation with Arthur Miller, New York, May 19, 1982.
27. *Situations III*, p. 132.
28. *Lettres au Castor*, pp. 333–5.
29. *Force of Circumstance*, p. 69.
30. *Lettres au Castor*, pp. 334–5.
31. See Henriette Nizan's account in *Les Nouvelles Littéraires*, April 1983.

IN THE ENGINE ROOM

1. In *Dimanche matin*, p. 210, and in *Les Enfants naturels*, 122.
2. Conversation with Jean Cau, June 20, 1984.
3. See Juliette Gréco, *Jujube* (New York: Stock, 1983).
4. Conversation with Louis Nagel, July 11, 1984.
5. *Life/Situations: Essays Written and Spoken*, trans. Paul Auster and Lydia Davis (New York: Pantheon Books, 1977), pp. 68, 69, and 70.
6. See *Oeuvres romanesques*, p. lxix.
7. *Anti-Semite and Jew*, trans. George T. Becker (New York: Schocken Books, 1948), p. 153.
8. *Ibid.*, pp. 19, 22, 25, 27, 37, 46, 49.
9. In a letter to Arnold Mandel published eight years later in *La Revue juive*, Geneva, June–July 1947, pp. 212–13.
10. *Cahiers pour une morale.*
11. *The War Diaries*, p. 251.
12. In "Entretien avec Madeleine Chapsal," *Les Ecrivains en personne* (Paris: Julliard, 1960), pp. 203–33. Reprinted in Sartre, *Between Existentialism and Marxism*, trans. John Mathews (New York: Pantheon Books, 1974), p. 13.
13. *The Family Idiot*, trans. Carol Cosman (Chicago: University of Chicago Press, 1981), p. ix.
14. Conversation with François Périer, May 28, 1982.
15. *Le Figaro*, April 25, 1949.
16. *Lettres au Castor*, p. 337.
17. *Cahiers pour une morale*, p. 13.

HARD TIMES WITH GROUP POLITICS

1. "La Nationalisation de la littérature," November 1945; "Matérialisme et révolution," June and July 1946; "Qu'est-ce que la littérature?" in six installments from February to July 1947; and, finally, in June 1948, "Ecrire pour son époque," which will be immediately translated into German, English, and Italian as, respectively, "Der Schriftsteller und seine Zeit," "We Write for Our Own Time," and "Scrivere per il proprio tempo."
2. *What Is Literature?*, p. 177.
3. *Les Lettres françaises*, December 28, 1945, p. 89.
4. *L'Existentialisme n'est pas un humanisme* (Paris: Editions Nagel, 1947), p. 61.
5. *Les Temps modernes*, July 1946, pp. 31–2.
6. *Le Figaro littéraire*, May 29, 1947.
7. *L'Humanité*, April 4, 1947.
8. *Situations* (New York), p. 244.
9. *What Is Literature?*, p. 204.
10. *Combat*, October 18, 1947.

11. Unpublished text, Institut National de l'Audiovisuel (INA).

12. Conversation with Raymond Aron, March 9, 1983.

13. *La Force des choses* (Paris: Gallimard, 1963), vol. 1, p. 194.

14. *L'Ordre de Paris,* October 22, 1947.

15. *Ibid.*

16. *Ibid.,* October 24, 1947.

17. *Carrefour,* October 29, 1949.

18. *Ibid.*

19. *Combat,* October 22, 1947.

20. *Entretiens sur la politique* (Paris: Gallimard, 1949), p. 22.

21. Conversations with Gilles Martinet, Rome, August 30 and September 1, 1984.

22. *Franc-tireur,* March 11, 1948.

23. *L'Humanité,* December 11, 1948: "Pour service rendu."

24. *Bataille socialiste,* March 19, 1948.

25. *La Gauche-*RDR, no. 1.

26. *Le Monde,* February 28, 1948.

27. *Le Figaro,* January 20, 1948.

28. *La Gauche-*RDR, no. 3, June 16–30, 1948.

29. *Ibid.,* p. 3.

30. *La Gauche-*RDR, no. 3.

31. *Entretiens sur la politique,* pp. 37, 40, and 51.

32. *Franc-tireur,* December 14, 1948.

33. Conversation with David Rousset, September 8, 1982.

34. *La Gauche-*RDR, November 1948.

35. Conversation with David Rousset.

36. *On a raison de se révolter* (Paris: Gallimard, 1974), p. 29.

37. *Ibid.*

38. *Franc-tireur,* June 30, 1948.

39. *On a raison de se révolter,* p. 30.

40. *Bulletin intérieur* RDR, May 1949.

41. *Ibid.,* June 1949.

42. *Le Monde,* October 27, 1949.

43. *Situations* (New York), "Merleau-Ponty."

44. Conversation with Paul Fraisse, November 1, 1982.

45. February 1949, p. 3.

46. *Peuple du monde,* June 18, 1949.

47. *Politique étrangère,* June 1949.

48. Conversation with David Rousset. This analysis would not have been possible without the help of Jean-René Chauvin's archives.

THE IMPASSE REVISITED

1. *La Force des choses,* p. 217.

2. *International Herald Tribune,* March 17, 1984.

3. Conversation with Bernard Pingaud, February 3, 1983.
4. Roger Nimier, *Correspondance avec Chardonne* (Paris: Gallimard, 1984), p. 95.
5. Roger Nimier, *Journée de lectures* (Paris: Gallimard, 1965), p. 251.
6. Pp. 18–19.
7. *Le Dernier des Mohicans* (Paris: Fasquelle, 1956), p. 10.
8. *Esprit*, 50th anniversary special number, January 1983, p. 74: "Les Belles années, de la guerre d'Indochine à Mai '68."
9. See complete text in *Les Ecrits de Sartre*, p. 146.
10. Jean Cocteau, *Journal: Le Passé défini* (Paris: Gallimard, 1984), pp. 314, 317–8.
11. In *Glas* (Paris: Denoël-Gonthier, 1980).
12. (New York: Vintage Books, 1968), p. xvi.
13. *Le Passé défini*, p. 282: July 21–23, 1952; pp. 302, 311.
14. Cited in *ibid.*, p. 324.
15. Claudel's *Journal*, Pléiade, vol. 2 (Paris: Gallimard, 1962); letter dated as follows: Brangues, August 18, 1952.
16. Article published in *La Littérature et le Mal* (Paris: Gallimard, 1957).
17. Cited by Cocteau, *Le Passé défini*, p. 391.
18. *Ibid.*, p. 322.
19. See *Les Ecrits de Sartre*, pp. 231–40; and *L'Avant-scène théâtrale*, special issue on Sartre, no. 402–3, 1968.
20. *Force of Circumstance*, p. 240.
21. *Paris-Presse-l'Intransigeant*, Saturday, June 9, 1951, p. 7.
22. *Force of Circumstance*, p. 242.
23. *La Force des choses*, vol. 1, p. 143.
24. Conversation with Gilles Martinet.
25. Conversations with Alberto Moravia, Rome, August 30 and 31, 1984.
26. Unpublished manuscript, "La Reine Albemarle," private archives.
27. *Ibid.*
28. Unpublished manuscript, "La Reine Albemarle," Sartre file at the Bibliothèque Nationale.
29. *Situations IV*, p. 442; first published in *France-Observateur*, July 24, 1952.
30. Conversations with Paul Tabet, the cultural attaché of the French Embassy in Rome.
31. Mary Welsh Hemingway, *How It Was* (New York: Knopf, 1951), pp. 280 and 281.
32. *Adieux*, p. 305.
33. *Situations*, pp. 64 and 67.
34. *Les Temps modernes*, January 1950.
35. *Situations* (New York), p. 266.
36. *Ibid.*, p. 270.
37. *Ibid.*, pp. 266–7.
38. In *Action*, January 24, 1952.

39. *L'Affaire Henri Martin* (Paris: Gallimard, 1953), pp. 57–8.
40. *Ibid.*, pp. 156–7.
41. Cited by Jean Orieux, *Voltaire* (Paris: Collection Champs, Flammarion, 1977), part 2, p. 192.

PIGEONS AND TANKS

1. *Paris-Presse-l'Intransigeant,* June 13, 1951, p. 7.
2. Dominique Desanti, *Les Staliniens* (Paris: Marabout, 1975), p. 303.
3. *Situations* (New York), pp. 287–8.
4. *La Force des choses,* vol. 2, p. 281.
5. *L'Express,* November 9, 1956; and "Le Fantôme de Staline," *Les Temps modernes,* November 1956, reprinted in *Situations VII* (Paris: Gallimard, 1965).
6. "Les Communistes et la paix," reprinted in *Situations VI* (Paris: Gallimard, 1964), p. 80.
7. *Ibid.*, p. 86.
8. *Situations* (New York), p. 288.
9. "Les Communistes et la paix," p. 134.
10. *Ibid.*
11. *Force of Circumstance,* p. 111.
12. Cf. Albert Camus, *Essais* (Paris: Pléiade, 1965), p. 772).
13. "Réponse à Albert Camus," *Les Temps modernes,* no. 82, August 1952, reprinted in *Situations* (New York), p. 71.
14. *Life/Situations,* pp. 63–4.
15. Cited by Jean-Pierre Rioux, *La France de la IVe République,* collection Points-Histoire (Paris: Le Seuil, 1980), p. 11.
16. *Libération,* October 16, 1952, and *Ce Soir,* October 17, 1952.
17. Desanti, *Les Staliniens,* p. 353.
18. *Ce Soir,* October 17, 1952.
19. Desanti, *Les Staliniens,* p. 357.
20. Conversation with Jean-Pierre Delilez, May 1982.
21. Conversations with Gilles Martinet, Rome, August 30 and September 1, 1984.
22. *Les Lettres françaises,* January 1–8, 1953.
23. Cited by Dominique Desanti, *Les Staliniens,* p. 358.
24. *Force of Circumstance,* p. 228.
25. Conversations with Gilles Martinet.
26. *Le Monde,* January 1, 1953.
27. Congrès des Peuples pour la paix, December 1952.
28. *Le Monde,* September 25, 1954.
29. See *Les Ecrits de Sartre,* pp. 704–5.
30. *Ibid.*
31. FBI Archives.
32. *Défense de la paix,* June 1953.
33. *France-Observateur,* March 19, 1943.

34. Etiemble correspondence, letter no. 154.
35. March 6, 1953.
36. Maurice Merleau-Ponty, *Sens et non-sens* (Paris: Nagel, 1978), p. 73.   *549*
37. "Merleau-Ponty vivant," first unpublished version.
38. Maurice Merleau-Ponty, *Adventures of the Dialectic*, trans. Joseph Bien (Evanston, Ill.: Northwestern University Press, 1973), p. 201.
39. *Combat*, Saturday, October 31, and Sunday, November 1, 1953.
40. Catalogue of the Albert Schweitzer exhibition at the Bibliothèque Nationale and the University of Strasbourg, 1975.
41. *Force of Circumstance*, p. 304.
42. See Annie Cohen-Solal and Henriette Nizan, *Paul Nizan, communiste impossible* (Paris: Grasset, 1980).
43. *Libération*, July 15, 1954, p. 3.
44. *Ibid.*
45. *Ibid.*, July 17–18, 1954, p. 3.
46. *Ibid.*, July 19, 1954, p. 3.
47. *Ibid.*, July 20, 1954, p. 3.
48. *Ibid.*
49. *Ibid.*
50. Jacques-Francis Rolland, *Un dimanche inoubliable près des casernes* (Paris: Grasset, 1984), p. 279.
51. *Paris-Presse-l'Intransigeant*, June 7, 1951.
52. *Situations X*, p. 220.
53. *Cahiers libres pour la jeunesse*, no. 1, February 15, 1960, conversation recorded by Jacques-Alain Miller and Raphaël Sorin.
54. *Combat*, June 7, 1955.
55. *Libération*, June 7, 1955.
56. *Le Monde*, June 1, 1955.
57. *Arts*, June 15–21, 1955.
58. *Discours sur l'imposture* (Paris, 1978).
59. *Théatre populaire*, no. 14, "Nekrassov juge de sa critique."
60. *France-Soir*, February 24, 1978.
61. June 8, 1955, p. 2. All information concerning Nekrassov drawn from Georges Werler's archives, and conversation with Georges Werler, February 1 and 22, 1983, and conversation with Maurice Delarue (director of the play in 1978, at the TEP), February 22, 1983.
62. *Kean*, p. 87, in the text published by the National Drama Center at Reims, Théâtre-Revue 17, program, 1983.
63. Unpublished manuscript available for consultation at the Bibliothèque Nationale in Paris, Mme Mauricette Berne, curator.
64. See above, pp. 46–63.
65. *Sartre by Himself*, a film directed by Alexandre Astruc and Michel Contat, screenplay trans. Richard Seaver (New York: Urizen, 1978), pp. 87–8.

66. *On a raison de se révolter*, p. 41.
67. In an interview with Jacqueline Piatier, *Le Monde*, April 18, 1964.
68. *L'Express*, November 9, 1956.
69. *The Words*, p. 253.

IV. A Man Waking Up 1956–1980

YOU'RE TERRIFIC

1. *Situations V* (Paris: Gallimard, 1964), p. 62. For a history of the article, see also Contat and Rybalka, *Les Ecrits de Sartre*, pp. 309–10.
2. *Situations I*, p. 58.
3. *Les Ecrits de Sartre*, pp. 309–10. The original text had been commissioned by *Le Monde*, which, however, deemed the final product much too violent for publication. Later, *Les Temps modernes* will publish a tamer version of the same piece.
4. *Situations V*, p. 60–5.
5. *Ibid.*, p. 60.
6. *Ibid.*, p. 68.
7. *Ibid.*, p. 59.
8. *Ibid.*, p. 66.
9. *Ibid.*, p. 67.
10. Edgar Morin, *Autocritique* (Paris: Le Seuil, 1959).
11. *Force of Circumstance*, p. 205.
12. Cf. above, p. 401.
13. See *Les Ecrits de Sartre*, p. 288.
14. Conversations with Dionys Mascolo, October 18, 24, and 26, 1984.
15. *Situations V*, p. 26.
16. *Ibid.*, p. 27.
17. *Ibid.*, p. 30.
18. *Ibid.*, p. 32.
19. *Ibid.*, p. 34.
20. *Ibid.*, pp. 38–9.
21. *Ibid.*, pp. 47–8.
22. See Pierre Viansson-Ponté, *Histoire de la république gaullienne* (Paris: Fayard, 1971).
23. *Ibid.*, p. 30.
24. *Situations V*, p. 98.
25. *Ibid.*, p. 100.
26. *Ibid.*, p. 128.
27. *Ibid.*, p. 137.
28. *Ibid.*, p. 144.
29. See Pierre Viansson-Ponté, *Histoire de la république gaullienne*, p. 128.
30. Conversation with Jean Pouillon, October 16 and 25, 1984.

31. *Adieux,* p. 328.
32. *Ibid.,* p. 319.
33. Madeleine Chapsal, *Les Ecrivains en personne* (Paris: Julliard, 1960), p. 9.   *551*
34. *Ibid.,* p. 10.
35. Conversation with Claude Faux, August 16, 1982.
36. *Situations* (New York), pp. 3–60.
37. Chapsal, *Les Ecrivains en personne,* pp. 22–3.
38. *L'Arc,* no. 30, p. 83.
39. *L'Express,* September 10, 1959.
40. *The Condemned of Altona,* trans. Sylvia and George Leeson, (New York: Knopf, 1961), pp. 132–3.
41. Conversation with Arlette Elkaïm-Sartre, November 11, 1984.
42. *The Condemned of Altona,* 177–8.
43. *L'Arc,* no. 30, 1966.
44. *Ibid.,* no. 30, 1960.
45. Conversation with Michelle Vian, June 10, 1982.
46. *Le Scénario Freud* (Paris: Gallimard, 1984), p. 49.
47. John Huston, *An Open Book* (New York: Knopf, 1980), pp. 294–6.
48. *Ibid.,* p. 294.
49. *Ibid.,* p. 296.
50. *Lettres au Castor,* vol. 2, p. 357.
51. Huston, *An Open Book,* p. 295.
52. *Lettres au Castor,* p. 358.
53. *Ibid.,* p. 360.
54. Huston, *An Open Book,* p. 296.
55. *Lettres au Castor,* p. 261.
56. Huston, *An Open Book,* p. 296.
57. *Ibid.*
58. *Lettres au Castor,* pp. 361 and 358.
59. Conversation with Robert Gallimard, November 18, 1982.
60. *Critique of Dialectical Reason,* trans. Alan Sheridan-Smith (London: Verso, 1976), p. 818.
61. Conversation with Jean Pouillon, October 25, 1984.
62. *Ibid.*
63. Chapsal, *Les Ecrivains,* p. 13.
64. Francis Jeanson, *Sartre dans sa vie* (Paris: Le Seuil, 1974), p. 214.
65. Conversation with Marceline Loridan, October 18, 1984.
66. Jeanson, *Sartre dans sa vie,* p. 214.
67. *Les Ecrits de Sartre,* pp. 723–9.
68. *Ibid.*

THE ANTI-AMBASSADOR

1. *Situations V,* p. 15.
2. *Ibid.,* p. 20.

3. *Ibid.*, p. 17.
4. *Force of Circumstance*, p. 331.
5. Unpublished text from the broadcast "Voici la Chine," produced by Claude Roy and Albert Riera, aired on March 24, 1956, INA Archives.
6. "La Chine que j'ai vue," *France-Observateur*, December 1 and 8, 1955.
7. *Ibid.*
8. In *Quotidien des ouvriers,* cited by *Libération,* May 6, 1983.
9. "Figures de Sartre," *Magazine littéraire,* September 1981, pp. 21–2.
10. "Fidel Castro parle," texts gathered by Jacques Grignon-Dumoulin, *Cahiers libres,* François Maspero.
11. *Obliques,* pp. 293–7.
12. *Ibid.*
13. *Le Nouvel Observateur,* March 24, 1960.
14. Sartre to Simone de Beauvoir, in *Force of Circumstance,* p. 491.
15. Unpublished, Sartre file at the Bibliothéque Nationale, partly reprinted in the articles of July 14 and 15, 1960.
16. "Ouragan sur le sucre," *France-Soir,* July 10 and 11, 1960.
17. Private archives.
18. FBI Archives.
19. According to Simone de Beauvoir, *Force of Circumstance,* pp. 509–69.
20. Jean Lacouture, *André Malraux,* p. 366.
21. *Adieux,* p. 368.
22. Agence France-Presse (AFP) dispatch, *Le Monde,* September 1, 1960.
23. Personal archives.
24. *Force of Circumstance,* p. 539.
25. *Tout compte fait* (Paris: Gallimard, 1972), p. 324.
26. Conversation with Bertrand Dufourcq, former French cultural counselor to Moscow, October 15, 1984.
27. Lena Zonina died in Moscow on February 2, 1985, at sixty-two; she had just published her first book, *Thinkers of Our Time: Reflections on French Writers of the 1960s and 1970s.*
28. The book was titled *Faux savants ou faux lièvres.* The preface was republished in *Situations VI,* pp. 23–68.
29. Conversation with Bertrand Dufourcq, former French cultural counselor to Tokyo and Sartre's host during the writer's trip, October 15, 1984.
30. See "Le Combat pour la liberté," by Takeshi Ebisaka, *Le Magazine littéraire,* September 1981, pp. 19–20.
31. Conversation with Yehoshua Rash, September 18, 1982.
32. Conversation with Menahem Brinker, July 27, 1982.
33. Gabriel Cohen, *Le Matin,* April 27, 1980.
34. These recordings were made available to me thanks to the joint efforts of Dani Karavan, Amalia and Fiska Furstenberg, and Arieh and Rachel Aharoni. Nathan Shaham kindly provided me with information concerning the impression Sartre made on leftist writers in Israel.

UNTOUCHABLE

1. Hamon and Rotman, *Les Porteurs de valises* (Paris: Albin Michel, 1979),
p. 73.
2. *Tracts surréalistes*, vol. 2, gathered by Maurice Nadeau, p. 391.
3. Conversation with Dionys Mascolo, October 18, 24, and 26, 1984.
4. Dionys Mascolo's personal archives.
5. Conversation with Roland Dumas, October 15, 1984.
6. *Ibid.*
7. *Le Procès du réseau Jeanson* (Paris: Maspéro), pp. 104–5.
8. *Ibid.*, p. 12.
9. *Le Monde,* September 25–26, 1960.
10. Conversation with Paule Thévenin, October 23, 1984.
11. *l'Aurore,* September 25–26, 1960.
12. *Le Figaro,* September 21, 1960.
13. *L'Express,* September 20, 1960.
14. *La Croix,* September 24, 1960.
15. *Le Monde,* September 24, 1960.
16. *Ibid.,* September 22, 1960.
17. *Le Droit à l'insoumission,* Dossier des 121, p. 32.
18. *Ibid.,* p. 34.
19. *Ibid.,* p. 32.
20. *Ibid.,* p. 33.
21. *La Croix,* October 4, 1960.
22. *Le Figaro,* October 7, 1960.
23. *L'Aurore,* October 7, 1960.
24. *Réforme,* October 1, 1960.
25. Conversation with Roland Dumas.
26. *Paris-Jour,* October 2, 1960.
27. *Le Dossier des 121,* p. 58.
28. Conversations with Jean Pouillon, October 16 and 25, 1984.
29. Conversation with Claude Faux, August 16, 1982.
30. Conversations with Jean Pouillon.
31. *Ibid.*
32. Conversation with Roland Dumas.
33. *Adieux,* pp. 368–9.
34. *Le Monde, Combat,* and *Le Figaro,* December 2, 1960.
35. Conversation with Dionys Mascolo.
36. Conversation with Claude Lanzmann, May 9, 1983.
37. *Situations III,* pp. 299 ff.
38. *Ibid.*
39. *El-Moudjahid,* December 1, 15, and 30, 1957, quoted in *Pour la révolution africaine* (Paris: Maspéro, 1964), p. 85.
40. *Force of Circumstance,* p. 592.

41. Maspéro archives, unpublished letter.
42. *Situations V*, p. 173.
43. *Ibid.*
44. *Ibid*, p. 186.
45. *Ibid.*, p. 175.
46. *Ibid.*, p. 185.
47. See Yves Lacoste, "Du tiers-mondisme à l'anti-tiers-mondisme," in *L'Autre Journal*, May 1985.
48. *Situations*, pp. 109–10.
49. *Ibid*, pp. 121–2.
50. *Ibid.*, p. 124.
51. *Ibid.*, p. 53.
52. *Le Magazine littéraire*, 1971, special issue on Nizan.
53. *Situations* (New York), p. 173.
54. *Ibid.*, p. 227.
55. *Ibid.*, pp. 296–7.
56. *Ibid.*, p. 326.
57. Interviewed on October 15, 1984.
58. Conversation with Robert Gallimard, February 22, 1985.
59. *Combat*, January 30, 1964.
60. *Le Monde*, June 2, 1955.
61. *Ibid.*, April 18, 1964.
62. Conversation with J.-B. Pontalis, April 29, 1985.
63. *Le Figaro*, October 23, 1964.
64. *Le Monde*, October 25–26, 1964.
65. *Rivarol*, October 29, 1964.
66. *Nouveaux Blocs-Notes*, pp. 431–3.
67. Nobel Academy archives, Stockholm, courtesy of Carl-Gustav Bjurström.
68. Conversation with Carl-Gustav Bjurström, May 21, 1985.
69. *L'Express*, October 27–November 1, 1964, p. 71.
70. Conversation with Louis Audibert, May 21, 1985.
71. *L'Arc*, October 1966.
72. *Cahiers de philosophie*, February 1966.
73. Conversation with Régis Debray, May 27, 1985.
74. Conversation with Georges Canguilhem, June 8, 1982.
75. In June 1985, an American director, John Strasberg, and members of the Actors Studio staged a few performances of *The Trojan Women* in Paris; this was the second production of the play.

BETWEEN FLAUBERT AND THE MAOISTS

1. *Paese Sera*, August 24, 1968.
2. AFP, *Le Monde*, December 3, 1968.
3. Interviewed on May 25, 1984.

4. "Vietnam: Imperialism and Genocide," report of Russell Tribunal, 1967. Text included in *Between Existentialism and Marxism*, pp. 82–3.

5. *Au coeur du Viêt-nam*, 96 photos by Pic (Paris: Maspéro, 1968).

6. *Le Nouvel Observateur*, April 26 and May 3, 1967.

7. For material on the sixties, see Maurice Achard and Anne-Marie Métailié, *Les Années soixante* (Paris: A.-M. Métailié, 1980).

8. *La Révolte étudiante: Les animateurs parlent* (Paris: Le Seuil, 1968), p. 70.

9. Conversation with Alain Geismar, February 12, 1985.

10. See *Les Ecrits de Sartre*, pp. 463–4.

11. *De Sartre à Foucault, vingt ans d'entretiens à l'Observateur* (Paris: Hachette, 1984).

12. *Le Nouvel Observateur*, June 19 and 26, 1968.

13. *Le Monde*, May 22, 1968.

14. Conversation with Raphaël Sorin, February 21, 1985.

15. Conversation with Jean-Marcel Bouguereau, August 26, 1984.

16. *Le Nouvel Observateur*, March 17, 1969.

17. *Ibid.*

18. Conversation with Alain Geismar.

19. *Life/Situations*, p. 43.

20. *Le Monde*, April 18, 1964.

21. *Life/Situations*, pp. 114–15.

22. *The Family Idiot*, vol. 1, trans. Carol Cosman (Chicago: University of Chicago Press, 1981), p. 5.

23. *The War Diaries*, pp. 102–3.

24. *Life/Situations*, p. 110.

25. *Situations IX*, p. 116.

26. *Ibid.*, p. 113.

27. *Ibid.*, pp. 118–19.

28. *Obliques*, 1975, p. 26.

29. *Situations IX*, pp. 113–14.

30. *Ibid.*, p. 114.

31. *Life/Situations*, p. 112.

32. *Situations IX*, p. 120.

33. *De Sartre à Foucault*, p. 31.

34. *Situations IX*, p. 118.

35. *Sartre, un film*, p. 130.

36. *Obliques*, 1975, p. 26.

37. See *Romans*, Pléiade, p. xcii.

38. Interviewed on May 18, 1983.

39. *Life/Situations*, p. 53.

40. Interviewed on February 12, 1985.

41. *La Cause du peuple*, May 1, 1970.

42. *On a raison de se révolter*, pp. 71–3.

43. *Ibid.*, p. 72.

44. *Ibid*, p. 73.

45. *Le Monde*, April 29, 1970.

46. Unpublished, INA Archives.

47. *L'Idiot international*, November 1970, pp. 8–9.

48. *L'Aurore*, October 22, 1970.

49. *Tout*, September 23, 1970, p. 8.

50. *J'accuse*, January 1971, pp. 17–9.

51. *La Cause du peuple*, January 5, 1972.

52. *Libération*, April 17, 1980.

53. *Ibid.*

54. *L'Idiot international*, September 1, 1970, "L'Ami du peuple," also in *Between Existentialism and Marxism*, p. 296.

55. *La Cause du peuple*, June 1972.

56. Unpublished interviews with F. M. Samuelson, October 23, 1978 and June 7, 1979.

57. *Life/Situations*, pp. 162 and 171.

58. *Le Nouvel Observateur*, June 19, 1968.

59. "Radioscopie," February 7, 1973.

60. *Tout*, February 1, 1971.

IN THE SHADOW OF THE TOWER

1. Arlette Elkaïm-Sartre's archives.

2. *Life/Situations*, pp. 4, 5, 6, 10.

3. *Adieux*, p. 64. I have recently learned from Maurice de Gandillac that the building at 29 Boulevard Edgar-Quinet was designed by Lecaisne, one of Sartre's classmates in *hypokhâgne* at the Lycée Louis-le-Grand, and was erected on the site of an old brothel. Conversation with Maurice de Gandillac, February 27, 1985.

4. *Le Monde*, July 28, 1977.

5. *Libération*, January 6, 1977.

6. Conversation with Benny Lévy, February 19, 1985.

7. *Adieux*, p. 111.

8. Conversation with Arlette Elkaïm-Sartre, March 5, 1985.

9. Conversation with Simone de Beauvoir, March 6, 1985.

10. *Life/Situations*, p. 77.

11. *Le Matin*, January 16, 1982.

12. Radio-Luxembourg.

13. Conversation with Valéry Giscard d'Estaing, May 6, 1985.

14. Conversation with Benny Lévy, February 25, 1985.

15. Conversation with Robert Gallimard, February 22, 1985.

16. Pierre Goldmann, *Souvenirs d'un obscur juif polonais né en France* (Paris: Le Seuil, 1975).

17. Roland Castro, *1989*, (Paris: B. Barrault, 1984).

18. Conversation with François Chatelêt, January 29, 1985.

19. *Libération*, December 24, 1984.

20. *Ibid.*
21. *Ibid.*, January 6, 1977.
22. Conversation with Robert Gallimard.
23. Conversation with Jean Pouillon, March 7, 1985.
24. Conversation with Arlette Elkaïm-Sartre.
25. Conversation with Simone de Beauvoir.
26. Conversation with Jean Pouillon.
27. Conversation with Arlette Elkaïm-Sartre.
28. Conversation with Simone de Beauvoir.
29. Conversation with Jean Pouillon.
30. *Délit de vagabondage* (Paris: Grasset, 1978), p. 299.
31. *Le Matin*, July 8, 1980, also interviewed on February 28, 1983.
32. *Life/Situations*, p. 4.
33. Conversation with Daniel Lindenberg, February 20, 1985.
34. *Le Monde*, December 27, 1975.
35. *Ibid.*, December 6, 1974.
36. *Ibid.*
37. Conversation with Benny Lévy.
38. *Libération*, April 22–26, 1975.
39. *Le Matin*, January 26, 1980.
40. Conversation with Arlette Elkaïm-Sartre.
41. Conversation with Jean Daniel, February 28, 1985.
42. Conversation with Simone de Beauvoir.
43. Conversation with Jean Pouillon.
44. *Adieux*, p. 110.
45. Conversation with Benny Lévy.
46. *Adieux*, p. 111.
47. Conversation with Edward Said, New York, May 17, 1982.
48. *Libération*, January 6, 1977.
49. Conversation with Benny Lévy.
50. Conversation with Jean Daniel.
51. Conversation with Arlette Elkaïm-Sartre.
52. *Ibid.*
53. Conversation with Simone de Beauvoir.
54. *Ibid.*
55. Conversation with Robert Gallimard.
56. Conversation with Arlette Elkaïm-Sartre.
57. Conversation with Jean Pouillon.
58. *Adieux*, preface.
59. *Libération*, December 3, 1981.
60. Conversation with Benny Lévy.
61. Conversation with Jean Pouillon.
62. Conversation with Valéry Giscard d'Estaing.
63. Conversation with Jean Pouillon.
64. *Ibid.*

BIBLIOGRAPHY

Sartre's Works

L'Imagination, Paris: Presses Universitaires Françaises, 1936. *Imagination: A Psychological Critique,* trans. Forrest Williams, Ann Arbor: University of Michigan Press, 1979.

La Transcendance de l'Ego, Paris: Vrin, 1937. *The Transcendence of the Ego,* trans. Forrest Williams and Robert Kirkpatrick, New York: Noonday Press, 1957.

La Nausée, Paris: Gallimard, 1938. *Nausea,* trans. Lloyd Alexander, New York: New Directions, 1964.

Le Mur, Paris: Gallimard, 1939. *The Wall,* trans. Lloyd Alexander, New York: New Directions, 1948.

Esquisse d'une théorie des émotions, Paris: Hermann, 1939.

L'Imaginaire, Paris: Gallimard, 1940. *The Psychology of Imagination,* New York: Philosophical Library, 1948. New York: Washington Square Press, 1966.

L'Etre et le Néant, Paris: Gallimard, 1943. *Being and Nothingness,* trans. Hazel Barnes, New York: Philosophical Library, 1956. New York: Washington Square Press, 1966.

Les Mouches, Paris: Gallimard, 1943. *The Flies,* in *No Exit and The Flies,* trans. Stuart Gilbert, New York: Knopf, 1948. In *No Exit and Three Other Plays,* New York: Vintage Books, 1955.

Huis Clos, Paris: Gallimard, 1944. *No Exit,* in *No Exit and The Flies,* trans. Stuart Gilbert, New York: Knopf, 1948. New York: Vintage Books, 1955.

Les Chemins de la liberté, vol. 1, *L'Age de raison,* Paris: Gallimard, 1945. *The Age of Reason,* trans. Eric Sutton, New York: Knopf, 1947. New York: Vintage Books, 1973.

Les Chemins de la liberté, vol. 2, *Le Sursis,* Paris: Gallimard, 1945. *The Reprieve,* New York: Knopf, 1947. New York: Vintage Books, 1973.

L'Existentialisme est un humanisme, Paris: Nagel, 1946. *Existentialism and Humanism,* London: Eyre Methuen, 1973.

Morts sans sépulture, Paris: Gallimard, 1946. *Morts sans sépulture,* in *Three Plays,* London: Hamilton, 1963. In *Men Without Shadows,* London: Penguin, 1962.

La Putain respectueuse, Paris: Gallimard, 1946. *The Respectful Prostitute,* in *Three Plays,* New York: Knopf, 1949. In *No Exit and Three Other Plays,* New York: Vintage Books, 1955.

Réflexions sur la question juive, Paris: Gallimard, 1946. *Anti-Semite and Jew*, trans. George T. Becker, New York: Schocken Books, 1948.

560

Baudelaire, Paris: Gallimard, 1946. *Baudelaire*, New York: New Directions, 1950.

Situations I, Paris: Gallimard, 1947.

Les Jeux sont faits, Paris: Nagel, 1947.

Les Mains sales, Paris: Gallimard, 1948. *Dirty Hands*, in *Three Plays*, New York: Knopf, 1949. New York: Vintage Books, 1955.

L'Engrenage, Paris: Nagel, 1948.

Situations II, Paris: Gallimard, 1948.

Les Chemins de la liberté, vol. 3, *La Mort dans l'âme*, Paris: Gallimard, 1949. *Troubled Sleep*, New York: Knopf, 1950. New York: Vintage Books, 1973.

Situations III, Paris: Gallimard, 1949.

Entretiens sur la politique, in collaboration with Gérard Rosenthal and David Rousset, Paris: Gallimard, 1949.

Le Diable et le Bon Dieu, Paris: Gallimard, 1951. *The Devil and the Good Lord and Two Other Plays*, New York: Knopf, 1960.

Saint Genet, comédien et martyr, Paris: Gallimard, 1952. *Saint Genet, Actor and Martyr*, trans. Bernard Frechtman, New York: Braziller, 1963; New York: Pantheon Books, 1983.

L'Affaire Henri Martin, Paris: Gallimard, 1953.

Kean, Paris: Gallimard, 1954. *The Devil and the Good Lord and Two Other Plays*, New York: Knopf, 1960.

Nékrassov, Paris: Gallimard, 1955. *The Devil and the Good Lord and Two Other Plays*, New York: Knopf, 1960.

Les Séquestrés d'Altona, Paris: Gallimard, 1959. *The Condemned of Altona*, trans. Sylvia and George Leeson, New York: Knopf, 1961.

Critique de la raison dialectique, preceded by *Questions de méthode*, Paris: Gallimard, 1960. *The Critique of Dialectical Reason*, trans. Alan Sheridan-Smith, London: Verso, 1976. *Search for a Method*, New York: Knopf, 1963; New York: Vintage Books, 1968.

Les Mots, Paris: Gallimard, 1963. *The Words*, trans. Bernard Frechtman, New York: Braziller, 1964. New York: Vintage Books, 1981.

Situations IV, Paris: Gallimard, 1964. *Situations*, trans. Benito Eisler, New York: Braziller, 1965.

Situations V, Paris: Gallimard, 1964.

Situations VI, Paris: Gallimard, 1964.

Les Troyennes, Paris: Gallimard, 1965. *Euripides' The Trojan Women*, trans. Ronald Duncan, New York: Knopf, 1967.

Situations VII, Paris: Gallimard, 1965.

L'Idiot de la famille, vols. 1 and 2, Paris: Gallimard, 1971. *The Family Idiot: Gustave Flaubert, 1821–1857*, vol. 1, trans. Carol Cosman, Chicago: University of Chicago Press, 1981.

Situations VIII, Paris: Gallimard, 1972. *Between Existentialism and Marxism,* trans. John Mathews, New York: Pantheon Books, 1974.

Situations IX, Paris: Gallimard, 1972. *Between Existentialism and Marxism,* trans. John Mathews, New York: Pantheon Books, 1974.

L'Idiot de la famille, vol. 3, Paris: Gallimard, 1972.

Un théâtre de situations, ed. Michel Contat and Michel Rybalka, Paris: Gallimard, 1972. *Sartre on Theater,* trans. Frank Jellinek, New York: Pantheon Books, 1976.

On a raison de se révolter, with Philippe Gavi and Pierre Victor, Paris: Gallimard, 1974.

Situations X, Paris: Gallimard, 1976. *Life/Situations,* trans. Paul Auster and Lydia Davis, New York: Pantheon Books, 1977.

Posthumous Works

Oeuvres romanesques, ed. Michel Contat and Michel Rybalka, Bibliothèque de la Pléiade, Paris: Gallimard, 1981.

Les Carnets de la drôle de guerre, Paris: Gallimard, 1983. *The War Diaries,* trans. Quintin Hoare, New York: Pantheon Books, 1985.

Cahiers pour une morale, Paris: Gallimard, 1983.

Lettres au Castor et à quelques autres, vols. 1 and 2, Paris: Gallimard, 1983.

Le Scénario Freud, with a preface by J.-B. Pontalis, Paris: Gallimard, Paris, 1984. *The Freud Scenario,* trans. Quintin Hoare, Chicago: University of Chicago Press, 1986.

Critique de la raison dialectique, vol. 2, Paris: Gallimard, 1985.

Special Issues of Journals Devoted to Sartre

L'Arc, no. 30, Paris, 1966.

L'Avant-Scène théâtrale, nos. 402–403, Paris, 1968.

Le Magazine littéraire, nos. 55–56, Paris, September 1977.

Le Magazine littéraire, nos. 103–104, Paris, September 1975.

Le Magazine littéraire, no. 176, Paris, September 1981.

Obliques, "Sartre," Paris, 1979.

Obliques, "Sartre et les arts," Paris, 1979.

Bibliographies

Contat, Michel, and Rybalka, Michel, eds., *Les Ecrits de Sartre,* Paris: Gallimard, 1970. *The Writings of Jean-Paul Sartre,* trans. Richard McLeary, Evanston, Ill.: Northwestern University Press, 1974.

Lapointe, François H., *Jean-Paul Sartre and His Critics: An International Bibliography, 1938–1975,* Philosophy Documentation Center, Bowling Green State University, Ohio, 1981.

Wilcocks, Robert, *Jean-Paul Sartre: A Bibliography of International Criticism,* Edmonton: University of Alberta Press, 1975.

General Bibliography

Aaron, Daniel, *Writers on the Left,* New York: Avon, 1961.

Achard, Maurice, and Métailié, Anne-Marie, *Les Années soixante,* Paris: A.-M. Métailié, 1980.

Agulhon, Maurice, *1848 ou l'Apprentissage de la République,* Paris: Le Seuil, 1973.

Aït, Ahmed Hocine, *Mémoires d'un combattant,* Paris: Sylvie Messinger, 1983.

Alleg, Henri, *La Question,* Paris: Minuit, 1961.

———, *Prisonniers de guerre,* Paris: Minuit, 1961.

Amouroux, Henri, *La Vie des Français sous l'occupation,* Paris: Fayard, 1961.

———, *La Grande Histoire des Français sous l'occupation,* 6 vols., Paris: Laffont, 1976.

Andeu, Pierre, and Grover, Frédéric, *Drieu La Rochelle,* Paris: Hachette, 1979.

Aron, Jean-Paul, *Les Modernes,* Paris: Gallimard, 1984.

Aaron, Raymond, *Essai sur les libertés,* Paris: Calmann-Lévy, 1965.

———, *Histoire et dialectique de la violence,* Paris: Gallimard, 1973.

———, *Les Marxistes imaginaires,* Paris: Gallimard, 1970.

———, *Mémoires,* Paris: Julliard, 1983.

———, *L'Opium des intellectuels,* Paris: Calmann-Lévy, 1955.

———, *D'une Sainte Famille à l'autre,* Paris: Gallimard, 1969.

———, *Le Spectateur engagé,* Paris: Julliard, 1981.

Aron, Robert, *Histoire de l'épuration,* Paris: Fayard, 1975.

Aronson, Ronald, *Jean-Paul Sartre: Philosophy in the World,* New York: Schocken Books, 1980.

Audry, Colette, *Sartre et la réalité humaine,* Paris: Seghers, 1966.

Azéma, Jean-Pierre, *De Munich à la Libération,* Paris: Le Seuil, 1979.

Barnes, Hazel E., *Humanistic Existentialism: The Literature of Possibility,* Lincoln: University of Nebraska Press, 1959.

———, *Sartre,* Philadelphia: Lippincott, 1973.

———, *Sartre and Flaubert,* Chicago: University of Chicago Press, 1982.

Barrett, William, *The Truants: Adventures Among the Intellectuals,* New York: Doubleday, 1982.

Beauvoir, Simone de, *La Cérémonie des adieux,* Paris: Gallimard, 1981.

Adieux: A Farewell to Sartre, trans. Patrick O'Brian, New York: Pantheon Books, 1984.

———, *La Force de l'Age,* vols. 1 and 2, Paris: Gallimard, 1960. *The Prime of Life,* trans. Peter Green, Cleveland and New York: World Publishing Company, 1962.

———, *La Force des choses,* vols. 1 and 2, Paris: Gallimard, 1963. *The Force of Circumstance,* trans. Richard Howard, New York: Putnam, 1964.

———, *L'Invitée,* Paris: Gallimard, 1943. *She Came to Stay,* Cleveland and New York: World Publishing Company, 1954.

———, *La Longue Marche,* Paris: Gallimard, 1957.

———, *Les Mandarins,* Paris: Gallimard, 1954. *The Mandarins,* Cleveland and New York: World Publishing Company, 1956.

———, *Les Mémoirs d'une jeune fille rangée,* Paris: Gallimard, 1958. *Memoirs of a Dutiful Daughter,* trans. James Kirkup, Cleveland and New York: World Publishing Company, 1959.

———, *Tout compte fait,* Paris: Gallimard, 1972. *All Said and Done,* New York: Putnam, 1974.

———, *La Vieillesse,* Paris: Gallimard, 1970. *The Coming of Age,* New York: Putnam, 1972.

——— (bibliography), *Les Ecrits de Simone de Beauvoir,* ed. Gontier Fernande and Francis Claude, Paris: Gallimard, 1979.

Beigbeder, Marc, *L'Homme Sartre,* Paris: Bordas, 1947.

Belvèze, commandant de, *Lettres 1824–1875,* Bourges, 1882.

Bosworth, Patricia, *Montgomery Clift: A Biography,* New York: Bantam Books, 1978.

Bourget, Pierre, *Paris 1940–1944,* Paris: Plon, 1979.

Boutang, Pierre, and Pingaud, Bernard, *Sartre est-il un possédé?* Paris: La Table Ronde, 1946.

Brassaï, *The Secret Paris of the Thirties,* New York: Pantheon Books, 1976.

Braudel, Fernand, and Labrousse, Ernest, *Histoire économique et sociale de la France,* vol. 4, bk. 1 (1880–1914), Paris: Presses Universitaires Françaises, 1979.

Brée, Germaine, *Camus and Sartre,* New York: Delta Books, 1972.

Briosi, Sandro, *Il Pensiero di Sartre,* Ravenna: Longo, 1978.

Brombert, Victor, *The Hero in Literature,* Greenwich, Conn.: Fawcett, 1969.

Buin, Yves, *Que peut la littérature?* Paris: U.G.E., 1965.

Buisson, Ferdinand, *La Foi laïque,* Paris: Hachette, 1912.

Burnier, Michel-Antoine, *Les Existentialistes et la politique,* Paris: Gallimard, 1966.

———, *Le Testament de Sartre,* Paris: Orban, 1983.

Busson, Jean-Pierre, "Les Officiers de la république," in *L'Histoire,* no. 36, July–August 1981.

Callot, Jean-Pierre, *Histoire de l'école polytechnique,* Paris: Charles Lavauzelle, 1982.

Campbell, Robert, *Jean-Paul Sartre, une littérature philosophique*, Paris: Editions Pierre Ardent, 1945.

564

Camus, Albert, *Essais*, Bibliothèque de la Pléiade, Paris: Gallimard, 1965. *Lyrical and Critical Essays*, New York: Knopf, 1968. *The Myth of Sisyphus and Other Essays*, New York: Knopf, 1955.

Carco, Francis, *Brumes*, Paris: Albin Michel, 1935.

Casarès, Maria, *Résidente privilégiée*, Paris: Fayard, 1980.

Castro, Roland, *1989*, Paris: B. Barrault, 1984.

Cau, Jean, *Croquis de mémoire*, Paris: Julliard, 1985.

Caute, David, *The Fellow Travelers: A Postscript to the Enlightenment*, New York: Macmillan, 1973.

———, *Communism and French Intellectuals*, New York: Macmillan, 1964.

Cave Brown, Anthony, *The Last Hero: Wild Bill Donovan*, New York: Times Books, 1982.

Caws, Peter, *Sartre*, London and Boston: Routledge and Kegan Paul, 1979.

Chapsal, Madeleine, *Les Ecrivains en personne*, Paris: Julliard, 1960. Also in *Between Existentialism and Marxism*, trans. John Mathews, New York: Pantheon Books, 1983.

La Charente-Maritime, collective work, Editions Bordessoules, 1981.

Claris, Gaston, *Notre Ecole polytechnique*, Paris: Imprimeries Réunies, 1895.

Claudel, Paul, *Oeuvres complètes*, Bibliothèque de la Pléiade, vol. 2, Paris: Gallimard, 1969.

Cocteau, Jean, *Journal: Le Passé défini*, Paris: Gallimard, 1969.

Au coeur du Viêt-nam, 96 photographs by Pic, Paris: Maspero, 1968.

Colombel, Jeannette, *Sartre ou le parti de vivre*, Paris: Grasset, 1981.

———, *Sartre, textes et débats*, Paris: Hachette, 1985.

Compagnon, Antoine, *La Troisième République des lettres*, Paris: Le Seuil, 1983.

Corti, José, *Souvenirs désordonnés*, Paris: José Corti, 1983.

Courtois, Stéphane, *Le P.C.F. dans la guerre*, Paris: Ramsay, 1980.

Craib, Ian, *Existentialism and Sociology: A Study of Jean-Paul Sartre*, Cambridge: Cambridge University Press, 1976.

Cronan, Christine, *Petit Catéchisme de l'existentialisme pour les profanes*, Paris: Dumoulin, 1948.

Cuming, Robert D., *Starting Point: An Introduction to the Dialectic of Existence*, Chicago: Chicago University Press, 1979.

Daniel, Jean, *L'Ere des ruptures*, Paris: Grasset, 1979.

———, *Le Temps qui reste*, Paris: Gallimard, 1984.

Danto, Arthur C., *Jean-Paul Sartre*, New York: Viking Press, 1975.

Debû-Bridel, Jacques, *La Résistence intellectuelle en France*, Paris: Julliard, 1970.

Delale, Alain, and Ragache, Giles, *La France de 68*, Paris: Le Seuil, 1978.

Derrida, Jacques, *Glas*, Paris: Denoél-Gonthier, 1980.

Desanti, Dominique, "Le Sartre que je connais," in *Jeune Afrique*, November 8, 1964.

———, *Les Staliniens*, Paris: Marabout, 1975.

Desanti, Jean-Toussaint, *Un destin philosophique*, Paris: Grasset, 1982.

———, *Introduction à la phénoménologie*, Paris: Gallimard, 1976.

Dioudonnat, Pierre-Marie, *L'Argent nazi à la conquéte de la presse française, 1940–1944*, Paris: Jean Picollec, 1981.

Droz, Bernard, and Lever, Evelyne, *Histoire de la guerre d'Algérie*, Paris: Le Seuil, 1982.

Duroselle, J.-B., *Politique étrangère de la France: La Décadence, 1932–1939*, Paris: Le Seuil, 1979.

———, *L'Abîme*, Paris: Imprimerie Nationale, 1982.

Elgey, Georgette, *La République des illusions*, Paris: Fayard, 1965.

Enard, Jean-Pierre, *Le Dernier Dimanche de Sartre*, Paris: Le Sagittaire, 1978.

Encrevé, André, *Protestants français au milieu du XIXe siècle, les réformés de 1848 à 1870*, thesis for the Doctorat d'Etat, University of Paris IV, 1983.

Fanon, Frantz, *L'An V de la révolution algérienne*, Paris: Maspero, 1959. *Studies in a Dying Colonialism*, New York: Monthly Review Press, 1965.

———, *Les Damnés de la terre*, Paris: Maspero, 1961. *The Wretched of the Earth*, trans. Constance Farrington, New York: Grove Press, 1966.

———, *Peau noire, masques blancs*, Paris: Le Seuil, 1952. *Black Skin, White Masks*, trans. Charles L. Markmann, New York: Grove Press, 1967.

———, *Pour la révolution africaine*, Paris: Maspero, 1964. *Toward the African Revolution*, trans. Haakon Chevalier, New York: Grove Press, 1968.

Fayolle, Gérard, *La Vie quotidienne en Périgord au temps de Jacquou le Croquant*, Paris: Hachette, 1977.

Feininger, Andreas, *The Face of New York*, New York: Crown Publishers, 1954.

Fejtö, François, *La Tragédie hongroise*, Paris: Pierre Horay, 1956.

Ferrières, Gabriel, *Jean Cavaillès*, Paris: Les Seuil, 1982.

"Fidel Castro parle . . ." texts collected by Jacques Grignon Dumoulin, *Cahiers libres*, Paris: Maspero, 1960.

Flanner, Janet, *Paris c'était hier*, Paris: Mazarine, 1981.

———, *Paris, Journal 1944–1965*, New York: Harcourt Brace Jovanovich, 1979.

———, *Uncollected Writings*, New York: Harcourt Brace Jovanovich, 1979.

Flouriet, Jean, *Cinq siècles d'enseignement secondaire à La Rochelle (1504–1972)*, Quartier latin, La Rochelle, 1973.

Fontaine, André, *Histoire de la guerre froide*, Paris: Le Seuil, 1967. *History of the Cold War*, trans. Renaud Bruce, New York: Pantheon Books, 1969.

Frank, Bernard, *Le Dernier des Mobicans,* Paris: Fasquelle, 1956.

———, *La Panoplie littéraire,* Paris: Julliard, 1958.

———, *Les Rats,* Paris: Flammarion, 1985.

Frank, Nino, *Petit cinéma sentimental,* Paris: La Nouvelle Edition, 1950.

Freund, Gisèle, *Mémoires de l'oeil,* Paris: Le Seuil, 1977.

———, *Le Monde et ma caméra,* Paris: Denoël, 1970.

Froment-Meurice, Marc, *Sartre et l'existentialisme,* Paris: Nathan, 1984.

Garaudy, Roger, *Une littérature de fossoyeurs: un faux prophète: Jean-Paul Sartre,* Paris: Editions sociales, 1948.

———, "Questions à Jean-Paul Sartre," *Clarté,* 1960.

Gayle, Addison, *Richard Wright: Ordeal of a Native Son,* Garden City, N.Y.: Doubleday, 1980.

Gendzier, Irene, *Frantz Fanon,* New York: Pantheon Books, 1973.

George, François, *Deux Etudes sur Sartre,* Paris: Christian: Bourgois, 1976.

Gide, André, *Correspondance avec Roger Martin du Gard, 1913–1951,* Paris: Gallimard, 1968. 2 vols.

———, *Journal 1939–1942,* Paris: Gallimard, 1946.

———, *Cahiers de la Petite Dame,* vol. 3 (1937–1945), Paris: Gallimard, 1976.

Glozer, Laszlo, *Wols photographe,* Paris: Centre Pompidou, 1978.

Goffin, Robert, *Jazz from the Congo to the Metropolitan,* New York: Doubleday, Doran, 1944.

Goffmann, Erving, *Asylums,* Garden City, N.Y.: Doubleday, 1961.

Goldmann, Pierre, *Souvenirs d'un juif polonais né en France,* Paris: Le Seuil, 1975.

Gontard, Maurice, *L'Oeuvre scolaire de la IIIe République: L'Enseignement primaire en France de 1878 à 1914,* Paris: Institut pédagogique national, 1965.

Gorz, André, *Adieu au prolétariat,* Paris: Le Seuil, 1980.

———, *Le Socialisme difficile,* Paris: Le Seuil, 1967.

———, *Le Traitre,* Paris: Le Seuil, 1958.

Granet, Marie, *Défense de la France,* Paris: Presses Universitaires Françaises, 1960.

Gréco, Juliette, *Jujube,* Paris: Stock, 1983.

Guéhenno, Jean, *Journal des années noires,* Paris: Gallimard, 1947.

Guérin, Daniel, *Quand l'Algérie s'insurgeait,* Paris: La Pensée sauvage, 1979.

Gunther, John, *Inside U.S.A.,* New York: Harper, 1947.

Hamon, Hervé, and Rotman, Patrick, *Les Porteurs de valises,* Paris: Albin Michel, 1979.

Hanoteau, Guillaume, *L'Age d'or de Saint German des Prés,* Paris: Denoël, 1965.

Heller, Gerhard, *Un Allemand à Paris,* Paris: Le Seuil, 1981.

Hervé, Pierre, *Lettre à Sartre et à quelques autres par la même occasion,* Paris: La Table ronde, 1956.

Houbard, Jacques, *Un père dénaturé,* Paris: Julliard, 1964.

Huszar, George B. de, *The Intellectuals*, Glencoe, Ill.: Free Press, 1960.

Isherwood, Christopher, *Goodbye to Berlin*, in *The Berlin Stories*, New York: New Directions, 1954.

Issacharoff, Michael, and Vilquin, Jean-Claude, *Sartre et la Mise en signe*, Paris: Klinksieck, 1980.

Jameson, Frederick R., *Sartre: The Origins of a Style*, New Haven, Conn.: Yale University Press, 1961.

———, *Marxism and Form*, Princeton, N.J.: Princeton University Press, 1971.

Janz, Curt-Paul, *Nietzsche*, Paris: Gallimard, 1984.

Jardin, André, and Tudesq, André-Jean, *La France des notables*, Paris: Le Seuil, 1973.

Jazz et Photographie, catalogue, ARC and Musée de l'Homme, Paris, 1984.

Jeanson, Francis, *Le Problème moral et la pensée de Sartre*, Paris: Le Seuil, 1947.

———, *Un quidam nommé Sartre*, Paris: Le Seuil, 1966.

———, *Sartre par lui-méme*, Paris: Le Seuil, 1955.

———, *Sartre dans sa vie*, Paris: Le Seuil, 1966.

Jullian, Marcel, *Délit de vagabondage*, Paris: Grasset, 1978.

Jünger, Ernst, *Premier Journal parisien, 1941–1943*, Paris: Christian Bourgois, 1980.

Kanapa, Jean, *Comme si la lutte entière*, Paris: Nagel, 1946.

Kern, Edith, *Existential Thought and Fictional Technique: Kierkegaard, Sartre, Beckett*, New Haven, Conn.: Yale University Press, 1970.

Lacouture, Jean, *André Malraux*, Paris: Le Seuil, 1973.

Laing, Ronald D., and Cooper, David G., *Reason and Violence: A Decade of Sartre's Philosophy, 1950–1960*, New York: Pantheon Books, 1983.

Laurent, Jacques, *Paul et Jean-Paul*, Paris: Grasset, 1951.

Lecarme, Jacques, *Les Critiques de notre temps et Sartre*, Paris: Garnier, 1973.

Legrand, Louis, *L'Influence du positivisme dans l'oeuvre de Jules Ferry: Les Origines de la laïcité*, Paris: Marcel Rivière, 1951.

Lejeune, Philippe, *Le Pacte autobiographique*, Paris: Le Seuil, 1975.

Le Roy, Eugène, *Jacquou le Croquant*, Paris: Gallimard, 1982.

Leroy, Jules, *Saint-Germain-des-Prés, capitale des lettres*, Paris: André Bonne, 1952.

Lévi-Strauss, Claude, *La Pensée sauvage*, Paris: Plon, 1983.

———, *Le Regard éloigné*, Paris: Plon, 1983.

Lévy, Benny, *Le Nom de l'homme, dialogue avec Sartre*, Paris: Verdier, 1984.

Loiseaux, Gérard, *La Littérature de la défaite et de la collaboration*, Paris: Publications de la Sorbonne, 1984.

Mac Orlan, Pierre, *Le Mystère de la malle n. 1*, Paris: Christian Bourgois, 1984.

Marcuse, Herbert, "Existentialism: Remarks on J.-P. Sartre's *L'Etre et le Néant*," in *Philosophy and Phenomenological Research*, vol. 8 (March 1948), pp. 309–36. Also included in *Studies in Critical Philosophy*, Boston: Beacon Press, 1973.

568

Maschino, Maurice, *L'Engagement*, Paris: Maspero, 1961.

Mauriac, François, *Nouveaux Blocs-Notes*, Paris: Flammarion, 1965.

Merleau-Ponty, Maurice, *Les Aventures de la dialectique*, Paris: Gallimard, 1955. *Adventures of the Dialectic*, Evanston, Ill.: Northwestern University Press, 1973.

———, *Sens et Non-Sens*, Paris: Nagel, 1948. *Sense and Nonsense*, Evanston, Ill.: Northwestern University Press, 1964.

———, *Signes*, Paris: Gallimard, 1948. *Signs*, Evanston, Ill.: Northwestern University Press, 1964.

———, *Le Visible et l'Invisible*, Paris: Gallimard, 1964. *The Visible and the Invisible*, Evanston, Ill.: Northwestern University Press, 1968.

Michel, Georges, *Mes années Sartre*, Paris: Hachette, 1981.

Morgan, Claude, *Les Don Quichotte et les autres*, Paris: Guy Roblot, 1979.

Morin, Edgar, *Autocritique*, Paris: Le Seuil, 1959.

Mounier, Emmanuel, *Oeuvres*, vols. 3 and 4, Paris: Le Seuil, 1962.

Murdoch, Iris, *Sartre*, London: Collins, 1953.

———, *Sartre, Romantic Rationalist*, New Haven, Conn.: Yale University Press, 1953.

Naville, Pierre, *L'Intellectuel communiste*, Paris: Rivière, 1956.

Nimier, Roger, *Correspondance avec Chardonne*, Paris: Gallimard, 1984.

———, *Journées de lecture*, Paris: Gallimard, 1965.

Nizan, Paul, *Aden Arabie*, Paris: Maspero, 1960. *Aden Arabia*, trans. Joan Pinkham, New York: Monthly Review Press, 1968.

———, *Le Cheval de Troie*, Paris: Grasset, 1935. *The Trojan Horse*, New York: Fertig, reprint ed. 1975.

———, *La Conspiration*, Paris: Gallimard, 1938.

Orieux, Jean, *Voltaire*, Paris: Flammarion, 1977.

Paxton, Robert, *Vichy France*, New York: Knopf, 1972.

Pécaut, Félix, *L'Éducation publique et la vie nationale*, Paris: Hachette, 1898.

Perrin, Marius, *Avec Sartre au Stalag XII D*, Paris: Delarge, 1980.

Petite Histoire de l'existentialisme, Paris: Club Maintenant, 1946.

Peyre, Henri, *Jean-Paul Sartre*, New York: Columbia University Press, 1968.

Philippe, Claude-Jean, *Le Roman du cinéma*, Paris: Fayard, 1984.

Pizella, Stéphane, *Les Nuits du bout du monde*, Paris: André Bonne, 1953.

Pommarède, Pierre, *La Séparation de l'Église et de l'État en Périgord*, Périgueux: Pierre Fanlac, 1976.

———, *Le Périgord oublié*, Périgueux: Pierre Fanlac, 1977.

Poster, Mark, *Existential Marxism in Post-War France: From Sartre to Althusser*, Princeton, N.J.: Princeton University Press, 1975.

Pour ou contre l'existentialisme, Paris: Atlas, 1948.

Prince, Gerald J., *Métaphysique et Technique dans l'oeluvre romanesque de Sartre*, Geneva: Droz, 1968.

Queneau, Raymond, *Pierrot mon ami*, Paris: Gallimard, 1938.

Rahv, Betty T., *From Sartre to the New Novel*, New York: Kennikat Press, 1974.

La Révolte étudiante: les animateurs parlent, Paris: Le Seuil, 1968.

Rebérioux, Madeleine, *La République radicale*, Paris: Le Seuil, 1975.

Ricateau, Maurice, *La Rochelle deux cents ans huguenote, 1500–1700*, La Rochelle: La Charente-Maritime, 1978.

Rioux, Jean-Pierre, *La France de la IVe République*, Paris: Le Seuil, 1980.

Rocal, Georges, *Croquants du Périgord*, Périgueux: Pierre Fanlac, 1970.

———, *Vieilles Coutumes du Périgord*, Périgueux: Pierre Fanlac, 1971.

Rolland, Jacques-Francis, *Un dimanche inoubliable près des casernes*, Paris: Grasset, 1984.

Rougemont, Denis de, *Journal d'une époque, 1926–1946*, Paris: Gallimard, 1968.

Roy, Claude, *Les Yeux ouverts dans Paris insurgé*, Paris: Julliard, 1944.

Saint-Exupéry, Antoine de, *Écrits de guerre*, Paris: Gallimard, 1982.

De Sartre à Foucault, vingt ans d'entretiens à L'Observateur, Paris: Hachette, 1984.

Schaff, Adam, *Marx oder Sartre?* Berlin: Deutscher Verlag, 1965.

Scheler, Lucien, *La Grande Espérance des poètes*, Paris: Temps actuels, 1982.

Schilpp, Paul-Arthur, *The Philosophy of Jean-Paul Sartre*, La Salle, Ill.: Open Court, 1982.

Seeberger, frères, *La France vue par . . .* , Paris: Belfond, 1979.

Sendick-Siégel, Liliane, *Sartre, images d'une vie*, Paris: Gallimard, 1978.

Servan-Schreiber, Jean-Jacques, *La Guerre d'Algérie, Paris-Match-Éditions n^0 1*, 1982.

Simone de Beauvoir aujourd'hui, interviews with Alice Schwarzer, Paris: Mercure de France, 1984. *After "The Second Sex": Conversations with Simone de Beauvoir*, trans. Marianne Howarth, New York: Pantheon Books, 1984.

Spiegelberg, Herbert, *The Phenomenological Movement*, The Hague: Nijhoff, 1960.

Sud, special issue on Faulkner, 1983.

Suhl, Benjamin, *Jean-Paul Sartre: The Philosopher as Literary Critic*, New York: Columbia University Press, 1970.

Suleiman-Rubin, Susan, *Le Roman à thèse*, Paris: Presses Universitaires Françaises, 1983.

Thody, Philip, *Jean-Paul Sartre: A Literary and Political Study*, London: Hamilton, 1960.

———, *Sartre: A Biographical Introduction*, London: Studio Vista, 1971.

Titzenthaker, Waldemar, *Berlin*, Verlag Berlin, 1968.

Todd, Olivier, *Un fils rebelle,* Paris: Grasset, 1981.

Tomatis, Alfred, *L'Oreille et la vie,* Paris: Laffont, 1977.

Tribunal Russell, le jugement final, Paris: Gallimard, 1968.

Troisfontaines, Roger, *Le Choix de Jean-Paul Sartre,* Paris: Aubier, 1945.

Truc, Gonzague, *De Jean-Paul Sartre à Louis Lavelle,* Paris: Tissot, 1946.

Vaïsse, Maurice, *Le Putsch d'Alger,* Brussels: Éditions Complexe, 1983.

Verdès-Leroux, Jeanine, *Au service du Parti: Le P.C.F., les Intellectuels et la culture, 1944–1956,* Paris: Fayard, 1983.

Verstraeten, Pierre, *Violence et éthique,* Paris: Gallimard, 1972.

Vian, Boris, *Chroniques de jazz,* Paris: La Jeune Parque, 1967.

————, *Chroniques du menteur,* Paris: Christian Bourgois, 1974.

————, *Manuel de Saint-Germains-des-Prés,* Paris: Chêne, 1974.

————, *Textes et chansons,* Paris: Julliard, 1966.

Viansson-Ponté, Pierre, *Histoire de la république gaullienne,* Paris: Fayard, 1971.

Vidal-Naquet, Pierre, *La Torture dans la république,* Paris: Minuit, 1972.

Vincent, Raymonde, *Le Temps d'apprendre à vivre,* Paris: Julliard, 1982.

Wahl, Jean, *Esquisse pour une histoire de l'existentialisme,* Paris: Éditions de l'Arche, 1949.

Warnock, Mary, *The Philosophy of Jean-Paul Sartre,* London: Hutchinson, 1965.

————, *Sartre: A Collection of Critical Essays,* Garden City, N.Y.: Doubleday, 1971.

Weber, Eugen, *La Fin des terroirs, modernisation de la France rurale 1870–1914,* Paris: Fayard/Editions Recherches, 1983. Original edition published by Stanford University Press, Stanford, Calif., in 1976, as *Peasants into Frenchmen.*

Wilkinson, James D., *The Intellectual Resistance in Europe,* Cambridge, Mass.: Harvard University Press, 1981.

Winock, Michel, *Histoire politique de la revue Esprit,* Paris: Le Seuil, 1975.

————, *La République se meurt,* Paris: Le Seuil, 1978.

Zevaco, Michel, *Fausta,* Paris: Fayard, 1941.

————, *Fausta vaincue,* Paris: Fayard, 1942.

————, *Les Pardaillan,* Paris: Fayard, 1941.

Documents

Albert Schweitzer exhibition catalogue, National Library of Strasbourg, 1975.

Bibliothèque Nationale exhibition catalogue, 1913.

Transcripts of the colloquium: *Les Protestants dans les débuts de la IIIe République, 1871–1885,* published by the Historical Society of French Protestantism, 1979.

BIBLIOGRAPHY

Unpublished correspondence between the Navy Headquarters in the Far
   East and France, 1898–1899. Historical archives of the Navy.

Journals

Action
L'Action française
Alger républicain
Arts
L'Aurore
Carrefour
La Cause du peuple
Ce Soir
Clarté
Combat
Comoedia
Congrès des peuples pour la paix
Le Crapouillot
Défense de la paix
Esprit
L'Express
Le Figaro
Le Figaro littéraire
France-Amérique
France Libre
France-Observateur
France-Soir
Franc-Tireur
La Gauche-R.D.R
La Gerbe
Germinal
Horizon
L'Humanité
L'Idiot international
International Herald Tribune
J'accuse
Je suis partout
Jeune Afrique

Les Lettres françaises
Les Lettres françaises clandestines
Libération
Life
Message
Le Monde
The New Yorker
New York Herald Tribune
New York Post
Les Nouvelles littéraires
Le Nouvel Observateur
L'Ordre de Paris
Paris-Journal
Paris-Presse-l'Intransigeant
Partisan Review
Partisans
Paru
Peuple du monde
Politics
Politique étrangère
Le Populaire de Paris
Pour la victoire
République française
La Revue juive de Genève
Salmagundi
Samedi soir
Les Temps modernes
Terre des hommes
Time
Tout
Vive la Révolution!
Vogue
Yale French Studies

572 *Archives*

Archives of the French Embassy in New York
Archives of the French Embassy in Rome
Archives of the Nobel Academy in Stockholm
Archives of Antenne 2 (a TV station)
Archives of the Bibliothèque Nationale
Archives of the Ecole Normale Supérieure, Rue d'Ulm, Paris.
Archives of the Ecole Polytechnique
Gallimard Archives
Maspero–La Découverte Archives
FBI Archives (U.S. Department of Justice, U.S. Department of State, U.S. Department of the Air Force)
Archives of the IDHEC (Institut des Hautes Etudes Cinématographiques)
Archives of the INA (Institut National de l'Audio-visuel)
Archives of the Lycée Condorcet, in Paris
Archives of the Le Havre lycée
Archives of the Lycée Henri-IV, in Paris
Archives of the La Rochelle lycée
Archives of the Lycée Pasteur, in Neuilly
Archives of the Navy (Defense Department), in Vincennes
Archives of the Department of Education
Archives of the Quai d'Orsay
French National Archives
Radio Luxemburg archives
Archives of the RTB (Radio-Télévision Belge)
Regional archives of the town of Périgueux

Private Archives

Jean Balladur
Simone de Beauvoir
Thierry Bodin
Georges Canguilhem
Jean-René Chauvin
Mme Roland Dorgelès
Arlette Elkaïm-Sartre
Jacques Ghinsberg

Daniel Lindenberg
Dionys Mascolo
Henriette Nizan
Jacqueline Paulhan
Michel Rybalka
Sartre-Lannes family
Sartre-Schweitzer family
Robert Villers

THESE ARE the photographs credits that appeared in the original French edition:

Photos A.F.P.: 36, 41; Robert Cohen–Agip: 32, 45, 49, 55; Bernand: 42: Jacques Boutineau Collection, Thiviers: 3; Brassaï: 25; Georges Canguilhem Collection: 19, 20; Annie Cohen-Solal: 2; Archives of the Ecole Polytechnique, Palaiseau, Photos H. Josse–Editions Gallimard: 5, 6, 7; Jacques Robert–Editions Gallimard: 51, 52; Gisèle Freund: 1, 40; Gisèle Freund Archives: 11; Brinon–Gamma: 34; Sas–Gamma: 50; Archives of the Israel Government Press Office: 47; Keystone: 38, 44; Yves Manciet: 30; Kibbutz Merhavia Archives: 48; Archives of the Navy (Defense Department), Vincennes, Photo H. Josse–Editions Gallimard: 8; Paris-Match/de Potier: 35; Special Collections, Photos Editions Gallimard: 4, 9, 10, 12, 13, 14, 15, 16, 17, 18, 21, 23, 24; Berretty–Rapho: 43; Doisneau–Rapho: 31; Niépce–Rapho: 53; Melloul–SYGMA: 54; Papillon–SYGMA: 27; William Leftwich–*Time Magazine:* 29; Photos U.P.I.-A.F.P.: 33, 46; Robert Villers Archives: 28; Lapi–Viollet: 26; C. Raimond-Dityvon Archives/Viva: 22; Photos X.-D.R.: 37, 39, 56, 57.

ABOUT THE AUTHOR

ANNIE COHEN-SOLAL was born in Algeria and has a Ph.D. in French literature from the Sorbonne. She has taught French literature, language, and culture in Berlin, Jerusalem, and Paris, and writes frequently about French intellectuals and politics for a variety of publications. Her first book, on Paul Nizan, was published in 1980 by Grasset.